BIRNBAUM'S 2018

Walt Disney World®

Expert Advice From the Inside Source

Wendy Lefkon EDITORIAL DIRECTOR

Jill Safro EDITOR

Jennie Hess CONTRIBUTING EDITOR

Clark Wakabayashi DESIGNER

Alexandra Mayes Birnbaum CONSULTING EDITOR

THE OFFICIAL GUIDE

Stephen Birnbaum FOUNDING EDITOR

EDITIONS

LOS ANGELES • NEW YORK

Contents

What's New?

To spotlight attractions, shows, restaurants, and events that are making (or have recently made) their debut, listings are marked with the stamp shown below. Look for it throughout the book. Here are some of the highlights:

For Steve, who merely made all this possible.

ISBN 978-1-4847-7378-9
FAC-038091-17216

Printed in the United States of America

Other 2018 Birnbaum's Official Disney Guides:

Disneyland
Walt Disney World for Kids

The Official Disney Fan Club

D23.com

SUSTAINABLE FORESTRY INITIATIVE Certified Sourcing
www.sfiprogram.org
SFI-00993
Logo Applies to Text Stock Only

A Word from the Editor

For some of us, our first Walt Disney World experience dates back to 1971, the year this new "Disneyland in Florida" made its debut. At that time, the Magic Kingdom was the only theme park to explore. Nonetheless, for those who came, it was love at first sight, and we've returned again and again. Fast-forward four-plus decades and Disney World boasts four theme parks, two water parks, dozens of hotels, hundreds of restaurants, and a whole lot more.

Editor Jill Safro consults with Mickey and Minnie, the ultimate Disney insiders.

Never before has there been so much incentive to visit (and revisit) the memory-making capital of the world. The Magic Kingdom wows guests with its mix of classic and contemporary shows and attractions, from Peter Pan's Flight to The Muppets Present . . . Great Moments in American History, plus a stirring new fireworks spectacular: Happily Ever After. Animal Kingdom's new land, Pandora—the World of Avatar, is home to Flight of Passage, a thriller that lets guests fly on the back of mountain banshee. The park also boasts evening safaris and a radiant nighttime spectacular, Rivers of Light. While Imagineers put the finishing touches on Toy Story Land at Disney's Hollywood Studios, guests may enjoy a spin through Toy Story Mania!, harness the Force at Star Wars–themed shows, and take a topsy-turvy ride at Rock 'n' Roller Coaster. At Epcot, *Frozen* fans are fired up for Norway's Frozen Ever After attraction, while Soarin' Around the World continues to send giddy guests to happy heights. And the dynamic Disney Springs is bursting with dining, shopping, and entertainment opportunities. Of course, that's just the tip of the iceberg, as so much of Walt Disney World has grown and evolved since our last edition. We are privileged and proud to provide readers with our extensively researched, insider look at some of the most cherished attractions, resorts, and eateries on Earth.

When Steve Birnbaum launched this guide in 1981, he made it clear what was expected of anyone who worked on it. The book would be meticulously revised each year, leaving no attraction untested, no snack or meal untasted, no hotel untried. First-hand experiences like these, accumulated over the years, make this book the most authoritative guide to the World. Our expertise, however, is not achieved by being escorted through back doors of attractions (although we would enjoy that). Instead, we wait in lines with everyone else, always hoping to have a Disney experience like that of any other guest. This year, in addition to investigating all of the nooks and crannies of Walt's vast World, we bonded with fellow park-goers while navigating the ambitious Fastpass+ attraction reservation system. And we'll continue to keep a close eye on it and other additions to the Walt Disney World vacation-planning universe—homework we're happy to do for readers like you.

After more than 45 fun-filled years, the World has vastly expanded—and so has our knowledge of the most popular vacation destination on the planet. On some occasions we've encountered sweltering weather and swelling crowds—times when even the happiest of travelers can turn into Grumpy for a moment or two. Had we known then what we know now, we could have spared ourselves some trying experiences. In one case, a staffer waited more than an hour to take a tour at the Studios. Standing in line with a notebook, she was asked by another guest if there was a quiz at the end. When she explained what she was doing, he expressed surprise to learn that she was waiting with the masses. But that's always been our strategy. We believe the best way to gather useful advice for a Walt Disney World guest is to be one. Over and over again!

Take Our Advice

We've done our best to keep you from making any tactical mistakes. We realize that even the most meticulous vacation planner needs detailed, accurate, and objective information to prepare a successful itinerary. To achieve that goal, we encourage the sharing of insight and information from Walt Disney World staffers—however the decision of whether or not to include such information is entirely up to the discretion of this book's editor.

To that end, we have packaged handy bits of advice in the form of sample itineraries and "hot tips" throughout the book. This advice comes directly from the copious notes we've taken during our thousands of days spent in Walt Disney World. We've also used our "Birnbaum's Best" stamp of approval wherever we deemed it appropriate, highlighting our favorite attractions and restaurants—the crowd-pleasers we believe stand head, shoulders, and ears above the rest.

You, the reader, benefit from the combination of our many years of experience that, together with our access to current insider information, makes this guide unique. We like to think it's indispensable, but we'll let you be the judge of that a few hundred pages from now.

Credit Where Credit Is Due

Enormous thanks to the teams of dedicated, detail-conscious Walt Disney World cast members from Guest Communications, the Disney Reservation Center, Food & Beverage, Merchandise, Resort Operations, Sports & Recreation, Attractions Operations, Disney Cruise Line, Disney Vacation Club, Marketing, and Disney Parks Synergy.

Kudos to Michelle Olveira for her skilled fact-checking and to Tracey Randinelli for her meticulous proofreading. Thanks also to copy editor extraordinaire Diane Hodges and to Jerry Gonzalez, Marybeth Tregarthen, Monica Vasquez, Jennifer Eastwood, Jessica Ward, Kinden Sevorwell, and Devon Munroe for their editorial support and production panache.

Heartfelt thanks to our photography team: Mike Carroll, Stacey Cook, Ana Rivera, and Lori Loftis—and, of course, Mickey Mouse and Minnie Mouse.

Hats off to those for whom doing Walt Disney World research is truly a labor of love. The "volunteer" class of 2018 includes the Safro family (Irene, Joy, Hayden Fullerton, and Delaney Irene), the Henning family (Amy, Chris, Avery, Elle, and Reid), the Lagano family (Judy, Chris, Jessica, Max, and Kyle), Linda Verdon, Margaret Verdon, Trace Schielzo, Denise Kiernan, Joe D'Agnese, Heather Pommerencke, Bob Cook, and Christina Fontana.

Of course, no list of acknowledgments would be complete without mentioning our founding editor, Steve Birnbaum, whose spirit, wisdom, and humor still infuse these pages, as well as Alexandra Mayes Birnbaum, who continues to be a guiding light—to say nothing of being a careful reader of every word.

The Last Word

Finally, it's important to remember that every worthwhile travel guide is a living enterprise; the book you hold in your hands is our best effort at explaining how to enjoy Walt Disney World at this moment, but its text is in no way etched in stone. Disney is constantly changing and growing, and in each annual edition we refine and expand our material to serve your needs even better. For this year's edition, though, this must be the final word.

Have a great visit!

— Jill Safro, Editor

DON'T FORGET TO WRITE!

No contribution is of greater value to us in preparing the next edition of this book than your comments on what we have written and on your own experiences at Walt Disney World. Please share your insights with us by writing to:

Jill Safro, Editor
Birnbaum's Walt Disney World 2018
Disney Editions
125 West End Ave., 3rd Fl.
New York, NY 10023

Getting Ready to Go

The key to a fabulous vacation at Walt Disney World is advance planning. This remarkably varied complex is too vast and diverse to allow a spontaneous visit to be undertaken with much success—especially when you consider the rapid rate at which the World has expanded and the introduction of Fastpass+, a system that allows guests to reserve attraction times up to 60 days in advance. It does not mean that even the most casual visitors can't have some significant fun, but they are bound to have regrets about things they missed because of time pressures or a simple lack of information. The purpose of this guide is to eliminate potential frustration while getting the biggest bang for your vacation buck.

What follows, then, is meant to provide a sensible scheme for planning a satisfying visit to Walt Disney World, one that will offer the most fun and the least amount of disappointment. But how do you know which of the countless activities will be the most enjoyable for you and your family? Do your homework. The best strategy is to make sure you have a clear idea of all that is available long before you arrive in the Orlando area. Note that details are subject to change.

When to Go

When talk finally turns to the best time to make a trip to Walt Disney World, Christmas and Easter are often mentioned, as well as the traditional summer vacation period—especially if there are children in the family. But there is also good reason to avoid these periods, namely the tremendous crowds they attract. And when Disney World is crowded, it can be very crowded, indeed. On the busiest days, visitors may wait in line more than two hours to experience the most popular attractions. That's at least twice as long as during less busy times of the year. Weekends, in general, are quite popular with locals. Sunday night through Wednesday is typically quieter.

Considering seasonal hours, weather, crowd patterns, and Disney resort rates, optimal times to visit Disney are usually mid-January through early February, late April through late May, and September through December (except Martin Luther King Day weekend, and Thanksgiving and Christmas weeks).

Note that during some of the less crowded times of the year—particularly during the winter—some attractions are closed for renovations. In addition, water parks are often closed for refurbishment during cooler months. Call 407-824-4321, or check *www.disneyworld.com* for a current schedule, updated each season.

Mid-November through December is a festive time of year the world over, and Disney World is no exception. The theme parks are decorated to the nines for the holiday season. Epcot holds stirring Christmas concerts, and the Magic Kingdom drapes Cinderella Castle in thousands of sparkling lights. Many other special events are held during this period, including Mickey's Very Merry Christmas Party in the Magic Kingdom (a separate admission ticket is required). The party brings a dusting of "snow"

to Main Street from about 7 P.M. to midnight for several days between mid-November and the first three weeks of December. It also features holiday shows around the park, including Mickey's Once Upon a Christmastime Parade, plus a unique holiday fireworks show. Select performances from Mickey's Very Merry Christmas Party are also staged in the park during regular hours on the days leading up to, including, and following Christmas. Note that this event often sells out way ahead of time. Get tickets in advance by calling 407-W-DISNEY (934-7639). Advance purchase prices start at about $90 (same-day purchases are higher). It's usually easier to snag tickets for dates earlier in the season.

Epcot celebrates with Holidays Around the World, including the nightly Candlelight Processional, complete with a mass choir, 50-piece orchestra, and a reading of the story of Christmas by a celebrity narrator. Dinner packages are available for some World Showcase restaurants. (We recommend the dinner package: It guarantees seating for dinner as well as preferred seating at the Candlelight Processional. Without a package, you should arrive at least two hours before showtime or risk being shut out of your preferred performance.) Disney's Hollywood Studios presents Jingle Bell BAM! on select evenings throughout the season. The show comes to life on and above the Chinese Theatre with colorful projections, special effects, fireworks, and festive holiday tunes.

Disney Springs gets into the spirit of the season with Christmas trees, twinkling lights, and jolly entertainment—including visits by Saint Nick. There are holiday decorations at each Walt Disney World hotel, too, including a Victorian Christmas at the Grand Floridian, a seaside party at the Yacht and Beach Club, and a Cajun holiday at Port Orleans Riverside.

For reservations, call 407-W-DISNEY (934-7639), a travel agent, or the Walt Disney Travel Company at 407-828-8101. Visit *www.disneyworld.com*, or call 407-939-7630 for additional information. Special-event tickets are sold separately.

HOT TIP!

The period of time between the week after Thanksgiving weekend and the week before Christmas is one of the less crowded and most festive times of the year.

Crowd Patterns

Day-to-Day Trends

Weekends tend to be among the most crowded days at Walt Disney World theme parks, followed by Mondays, Thursdays and Fridays. Morning through early afternoon is a bustling time for the theme parks and their popular "E-ticket" attractions. Days that offer Extra Magic Hours tend to be more crowded at their respective theme parks (see page 22). When the weather's steamy, the water parks tend to pack them in—so be sure to get an early start if you're headed to Blizzard Beach or Typhoon Lagoon.

When the time comes to plot an itinerary, it's helpful to know about crowd patterns beyond the four theme parks as well. As a rule, Disney Springs (formerly known as Downtown Disney) and Disney's water parks host their largest throngs on weekends. Of course, in these circles, a bigger crowd could possibly mean a better time. Golfers should note that weekend tee times are typically in the highest demand, while Monday and Tuesday tee times tend to be the easiest to come by.

Seasonal Shifts

The chart below indicates the density of crowds in the theme parks throughout the year. Though it's tough to generalize about a property as big and ever-changing as Walt Disney World—special events (such as the Disney Marathon and Epcot's Food & Wine Festival) and package deals can swell park attendance during a period typically marked by smaller crowds—the chart highlights historic trends.

Least Crowded means that there will be lines; however most shows and attractions can be visited with a bit less waiting than during busier times of the year.

Average Attendance refers to times when there are lots of people around, but lines are relatively manageable.

Most Crowded reflects times when lines at popular attractions can mean a wait of as much as two to three hours (or more). As a rule, when school is out, the crowds are most definitely in at Walt Disney World.

Least Crowded

- 2nd week of January through 1st week of February (excluding WDW Marathon Week and Martin Luther King Day Weekend)

- Week before Labor Day until the start of Epcot's Food & Wine Festival

- Week after Thanksgiving until the weekend at the start of Christmas week

Average Attendance

- 1st week of January (excluding New Year's Day, which is "most crowded")

- 2nd week of February until Presidents' week

- End of February through 2nd week of March

- Last week of April through May

- Period after Epcot's Food & Wine Festival ends until the weekend before Thanksgiving

Most Crowded

- All major holidays

- Presidents' week

- WDW Marathon Week

- 3rd week of March through 3rd week of April

- Easter week

- June through the 3rd week of August

- Epcot Food & Wine Festival

- Thanksgiving week

- Christmas through New Year's Day

- Any time school's out

Holidays & Special Events

Special events are staged at Walt Disney World throughout the year, not only to mark holidays but also to celebrate other interests. The dates and details below are subject to change without notice; call 407-824-4321 to confirm, or check out *www.disneyworld.com* for up-to-the-minute information about specific events.

JANUARY

Walt Disney World Marathon Weekend
(January 3–7, 2018): Some 20,000 entrants run through parks and other areas of the World during this 26.2-mile race (January 7). Characters and cast members are on hand for inspiration. Similar hoopla surrounds the half marathon (January 6). The 2-day Goofy Race and a Half Challenge (January 6 and 7) covers 4 theme parks and 39.3 miles. There is a 10K run (January 5) and a 5K family run on January 4. (It's okay to walk the 5K, but you must maintain a 16-minute mile.) Runners may take the "Dopey Challenge"—all of the aforementioned events within the pacing requirements—and earn a Dopey Challenge finisher medal. Packages are available. Call 407-939-4786 for package details or to book. For marathon weekend event information and schedules, call 407-938-3398, or visit *www.rundisney.com* for details. Tickets for this event generally go on sale in the April prior to the January races—and sell out within hours. Note that hotel rooms are in high demand for this event. Reserve yours as early as possible. For details on other Walt Disney World running events, visit *www.rundisney.com*.

Epcot International Festival of the Arts
(January 12–February 19): Epcot itself is a celebration of culture, cuisine, art, and entertainment. This festival takes those elements to the next level in a special salute to the creative arts. Expect curated art exhibits, jazzy musical performances, food kiosks featuring fanciful, artistic nibbles, workshops, lectures, and more. For the schedule and details about the Epcot International Festival of the Arts, visit *www.disneyworld.com/art*.

MARCH-JUNE

Atlanta Braves Spring Training (Late February–March): The Atlanta Braves have called Walt Disney World their spring training home for 20 seasons—and 2018 may be the last. For updates and a schedule of the games to be played at the ESPN Wide World of Sports Complex, visit *www.espnwwos.com/atlantabraves*.

Saint Patrick's Day (March 17): Everyone is Irish on Saint Patrick's Day—especially at Raglan Road's Mighty St. Patrick's Festival at Disney Springs. The family-friendly festivities include music, dancing, dining, and more. The festivities may start as early as March 16 and run through the 19th. (Of course, every day is a celebration of the Emerald Isle at Raglan Road, the Landing neighborhood's Irish pub.) Epcot's United Kingdom pavilion marks the day with Irish dining, dancing, and green beer.

Easter (April 1, 2018): Most of the Disney parks stay open late during the two weeks straddling Easter Sunday. The Easter Bunny greets guests in the Magic Kingdom. Epcot hosts an "Egg-stravaganza" hunt—cost is about $5 for a map with stickers (find all the eggs and win a prize). And many of the Disney World resorts offer special Easter-themed fun. Catholic and Protestant services may be offered at the Contemporary resort. Call 407-W-DISNEY for specifics. This is an extremely busy time to visit.

Epcot International Flower & Garden Festival (Early March–Memorial Day): Epcot is blooming with elaborate gardens (including

more than 30 million fragrant blossoms) and topiary displays, behind-the-scenes tours, gardening workshops, concerts, and guest speakers. Learn from the experts how to create a gorgeous garden. Pick up a Garden Passport and get it stamped as you explore the Outdoor Kitchens throughout the day. Passports are free and may be found at the Festival Center and at Outdoor Kitchen stations, and many shopping locations. Each Outdoor Kitchen has its own unique stamp.

Another popular element of the Flower and Garden Festival is the Garden Rocks concert series, presented at the America Gardens Theatre by the American Adventure pavilion. Past performers have included The Village People, Taylor Dayne, Little River Band, and Herman's Hermits starring Peter Noone. All shows are included with Epcot admission. Some seats may be reserved via Fastpass+ (see page 25)—the rest are available on a first-come, first-served basis.

Mother's Day (May 13): Celebrate Mom by treating her to a special Mother's Day buffet. Several WDW restaurants, such as Animal Kingdom Lodge's Boma—Flavors of Africa, Chef Mickey's and The Wave at the Contemporary, Ale & Compass Restaurant at Yacht Club, and the Swan's Garden Grove (dinner), have been known to offer Mother's Day meals. For details on the 2018 options, call 407-WDW-DINE (939-3463). Note that Walt Disney World resorts are very busy on Mother's Day weekend—book early.

Sounds Like Summer Concert Series (June–July): An Epcot tradition, tribute bands have guests dancing to the likes of the Bee Gees, Bon Jovi, the Eagles, U2, and more. Nightly shows are presented at the America Gardens Theatre at the American Adventure Pavilion. There are several shows each night, weather permitting. Seats are available on a first-come, first-served basis and are included with park admission.

JULY

Fourth of July Celebration: Double-size fireworks presentations over the Magic Kingdom, Epcot, and Disney's Hollywood Studios make for a very colorful night. Ben Franklin, Betsy Ross, and Disney characters greet guests at Epcot's American Adventure pavilion throughout the day. That pavilion's America Gardens Theatre hosts a patriotic show featuring an expanded cast of the Voices of Liberty. The evening's presentation of IllumiNations (Epcot's nightly lagoon show) may feature a patriotic finale. This is an exceptionally busy time to visit Walt Disney World—possibly the busiest.

SEPTEMBER-NOVEMBER

Night of Joy (September): Two nights of celebration highlight contemporary Christian music presented live at ESPN World of Sports Complex. For dates and tickets, call 407-827-7200. This popular event attracts a bit of a rowdy crowd (of mostly teens and young adults).

Epcot International Food & Wine Festival (early September–mid-November): Epcot's World Showcase celebrates the flavors of many different countries (even those not usually represented around the lagoon) through tastings (about $2 to $8 per sample), demos from top

A Tisket, A Tasket …

… a "Welcome to Walt Disney World Basket." The Disney Florist can deliver this and a striking array of themed surprises to any room on Disney property (and many that aren't). There's no occasion they can't rise to—from a birthday to Earth Day, from engagements to golden wedding anniversaries. A call to the Disney Florist (the only one serving Walt Disney World) can yield custom-tailored bouquets, baskets, and even Christmas trees. (They also have a division dedicated exclusively to Walt Disney World engagements.)

Not satisfied with a simple delivery to a resort room? The Florist folks encourage creativity. Got a favorite Disney character? Into the basket he or she goes! One package known as "Create a Fairy Tale" (complete with slipper and tiara) can actually be delivered to guests enjoying a romantic carriage ride.

For more information or to place an order, call 407-939-4438 (daily from 8 A.M. to 6 P.M.), or visit *www.disneyflorist.com*.

GETTING READY TO GO

chefs, and wine and cooking seminars. It's an exceptionally satisfying way in which to wander World Showcase. It's also insanely popular, so expect lots of company—especially in the evening. For details or to make a reservation for a special event (which you should do as far in advance as possible), visit *www.epcotfoodfestival.com*.

Halloween (late August–November 1, 2018): The festivities vary a bit from year to year. What follows is a sampling of what to expect:

Fort Wilderness Resort and Campground usually hosts a pumpkin-carving contest and a kids' costume contest, followed by a screening of a spooky movie. It also offers Halloween-themed wagon rides with storytelling and various surprises along the way.

The Magic Kingdom will play host to its Halloween spectacular, **Mickey's Not-So-Scary Halloween Party**, September through October. The special-ticket activities include a kids' costume parade, dancing, appearances by Disney villains (including a new Castle Forecourt show called **Hocus Pocus Villain Spelltacular**), trick-or-treating, and fireworks. This is an extremely popular Magic Kingdom event. Purchase tickets as far in advance as possible. And don't forget to wear a costume. (For costume guidelines, visit *www.disneyworld.com*.) Note that guests with tickets to the Halloween Party may be able to enter the park at 4 P.M. (Ask when you buy your ticket.) As a spooky bonus, **Mickey's Boo-to-You Halloween Parade** makes its way through the Kingdom during the Halloween party. Advance purchase prices start at about $75 (same-day purchases are higher). For additional details, call 407-827-7200.

Thanksgiving (November 24): All WDW restaurants are open on Turkey Day, many of them offering Thanksgiving specialties. For details, call 407-WDW-DINE (939-3463).

AdvoCare Classic (November 24–27): This early-season college basketball tournament features 8 NCAA teams and 12 games. Each team competes in one game a day and advances through a bracket-tournament format. Book your hotel early if you want to stay at a WDW resort for this popular weekend. For details, visit *www.http://espnevents.com*.

NOVEMBER–DECEMBER

Disney's Magical Holidays: Decorations and festivities abound in WDW's parks and resorts. The Magic Kingdom park hosts **Mickey's Very Merry Christmas Party** on select nights from early November through the first three weeks of December, complete with snow flurries on Main Street and complimentary hot cocoa. Entertainment for the special-ticket party includes **Mickey's Once Upon a Christmastime Parade** and a special edition of the fireworks show; select performances are staged during regular hours just before Christmas. (Guests with tickets to the Christmas Party may be able to enter the Magic Kingdom as early as 4 P.M.) Magic Kingdom may offer a holiday version of the Jungle Cruise, aka the Jingle Cruise. Finally, Queen Elsa lights the Castle on a nightly basis (with the help of Anna and Olaf). Details may change in 2018.

Epcot's **Holidays Around the World** (late November–late December) features the Christmas Candlelight Processional, including a choral concert, plus a celebrity narrator who reads the story of Christmas. The event is included with park admission, but seating is limited and it is exceptionally popular. Arrive at least 90 minutes before showtime, or book a dinner package (which combines dinner at a World Showcase eatery with guaranteed Processional seating). For more information, call 407-939-3463.

Disney Springs gets into the holiday spirit with a cheery mix of twinkling lights, seasonal music, a towering tree, and visits from the North Pole's most famous resident. Past years have brought carolers, stilt-walkers, and a lively holiday dance party.

New Year's Eve Celebration (December 31): There are extra-large fireworks displays over the Magic Kingdom, Epcot, and Disney's Hollywood Studios (though there are no fireworks at all at Animal Kingdom—imagine the stampede!). These parks stay open until approximately 1 A.M. Many of the resort restaurants, as well as the nightspots at Disney Springs, also welcome the new year Disney style.

Keeping WDW Hours

Since operating hours fluctuate quite a bit, call 407-824-4321, or visit *www.disneyworld.com* for current schedules.

THEME PARKS: Disney theme park hours vary seasonally. In May, September, October, parts of November and December, and all of January, the Magic Kingdom is usually open from 9 A.M. to 8 P.M.; Epcot is typically open from 9 A.M. to 9 P.M. (some Future World attractions may close at 7 P.M.), later during peak seasons; Disney's Hollywood Studios is open from 9 A.M. until about an hour after sunset; and Animal Kingdom is usually open from 9 A.M. till about 8 P.M. (or later). The parks take turns offering Extra Magic Hours throughout the week. That is, on any given day, one park may allow Disney resort guests to enter an hour early or stay in the park for two hours after it closes to the public. Participating Walt Disney World resorts have schedules at the front desk. (Note that while Extra Magic Hours are—by far—the best time to visit for guests craving shorter lines, some attractions do not operate during E.M.H.)

The Magic Kingdom keeps later hours through summer and other busy periods, including Christmas and Easter weeks. The parks may be open until 1 A.M. on New Year's Eve. Disney's Hollywood Studios often stays open until 10 or 11 P.M. in the summer, too.

DISNEY SPRINGS—MARKETPLACE, LANDING, AND TOWN CENTER: Shops are generally open from about 10 A.M. until 11 P.M. Sunday through Thursday; 11:30 P.M. on Friday and Saturday. Restaurant hours vary, with most venues open until 11 P.M. or midnight.

DISNEY SPRINGS, WEST SIDE: At the AMC cineplex, movies begin as early as 10 A.M. Restaurants are open from about 11:30 A.M. to midnight. Shops are open from about 10:30 A.M. to 11 P.M. (midnight on Friday and Saturday).

WATER PARKS: Water parks are open from about 10 A.M. to 5 P.M., but extend hours during summer months. Cabanas should be reserved in advance (see Hot Tips on page 221 and 223).

WDW PARK TRANSPORTATION: Bus, boat, and monorail transportation service begin one hour prior to park opening time and continue until about one hour after the parks close. Boats and monorails do not operate for Extra Magic Hours. For specifics, check at Guest Relations.

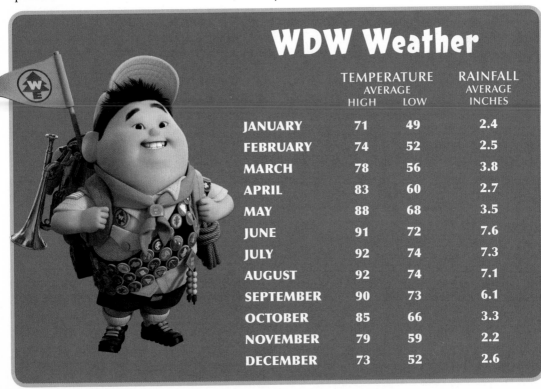

WDW Weather

	TEMPERATURE AVERAGE		RAINFALL AVERAGE
	HIGH	LOW	INCHES
JANUARY	71	49	2.4
FEBRUARY	74	52	2.5
MARCH	78	56	3.8
APRIL	83	60	2.7
MAY	88	68	3.5
JUNE	91	72	7.6
JULY	92	74	7.3
AUGUST	92	74	7.1
SEPTEMBER	90	73	6.1
OCTOBER	85	66	3.3
NOVEMBER	79	59	2.2
DECEMBER	73	52	2.6

How to Get There

By Car

While most visitors to the Orlando area fly in, many prefer to drive. If you opt for a road trip, figure on logging no more than 350 to 400 miles a day—a distance that won't wear you down so much that you can't enjoy your trip.

If you plan to navigate with GPS, note Walt Disney World's address in the Hot Tip at the top of page 15. Contact state tourist boards to inquire about free maps, too (yes, they still make

maps!); for a Florida map and guide, call 888-735-2872, or pick up a copy of *Rand McNally Road Atlas* or the *AAA North American Road Atlas*; both are sold in bookstores.

From Orlando International Airport

By car: During rush hour, take the airport's South Exit to the Central Florida Greeneway (Route 417) to Route 536, which leads to Walt Disney World. The tolls run about $4.

For the shortest route, take the North Exit to Route 528, going west toward Tampa. Pick up I-4 west, and go to a WDW exit. Tolls are about $4. The route is usually heavily trafficked, but manageable during non-rush periods of the day. It's busiest on weekday mornings and evenings and any time when a theme park is scheduled to open or close.

By Disney's Magical Express: This tailor-made, complimentary transportation program is available to guests staying at select Disney resorts. For more information, turn to page 16.

By car service: Reliable towncar service is available from Noris Limousines. Friendly drivers take guests directly to their resort. The company offers a special round-trip rate for Birnbaum readers—mention this book and expect to pay about $125 for up to four passengers for a towncar, or about $225 for a limo for up to 8 passengers. Reservations are required and cancellations must be made at least 48 hours ahead. Call 407-240-4533, or visit *www.norislimousines.com*. Prices may increase if there is a significant jump in prices at the pump.

Florida Towncar also offers direct service to Disney area resorts. And they offer our readers a special rate, too. Simply mention the Birnbaum Guide when you book your ride and expect a round-trip rate (*to and from Orlando International Airport only*) of about $125 for up to five passengers (that's $15 off). Call 407-277-5466 (from Florida) or 800-525-7246 (from out of state) up to 24 hours ahead, or visit *www.floridatowncar.com*. Online reservations should be made at least 24 hours ahead of pickup time.

By shuttle: At Orlando International Airport, Mears Motor Shuttle offers vans and buses 24 hours a day. It serves the Swan and Dolphin, Hotel Plaza Boulevard properties, and other non-Disney area hotels. Shuttles make multiple stops; a trip can take an hour or more. On the return trip, Mears requires guests be picked up at least 3 to 4 hours prior to flight times. Reservations should be made 24 hours ahead. There is often a long wait at the airport (even with a reservation), and employee attitudes fluctuate wildly. This is not our preferred mode of transit.

The shuttle cost to most hotels is $23 one way, $37 round-trip per adult; $18 one way, $28 round-trip per child ages 4 through 11; free for children under 4. Fares to International Drive properties are a little lower. There may be a very long wait to get on a shuttle at the airport, and service is not direct. Call 407-423-5566 for information, or visit *www.mearstransportation.com*.

By taxi: Metered cabs usually cost between $60 and $70 each way, depending on the destination—and the integrity of the driver (prices listed at the Orlando International Airport taxi stand are estimates). Some taxis can accommodate up to 9 people (for the price of one). Bell Services can call for a cab at any WDW resort. Note that many drivers do not have SunPass, so it'll cost you at least 45 cents a minute while waiting to pay each toll. What's more, many drivers do not know the area streets (or pretend not to)—resulting in bigger fares than necessary. Until cabs offer a flat rate to and from the airport, we are sticking with Magical Express or car services.

Note that gratuities are not included in transfer rates. It is customary to tip for good service.

Reputable automobile clubs offer help with breakdowns; towing; insurance that covers personal injury, accidents, arrest, bail bond, and lawyers' fees for defense of contested traffic cases; and travel-planning services, including free maps and route mapping. Services vary from one club to the next, and membership fees range widely, from about $50 to $120 a year.

By Air

When it comes to airfares, there is no real trick to unearthing the most economical ones: Simply shop around. Call a travel agent, browse the Internet, and keep these tips in mind:

- Take advantage of advance-purchase fares (lower rates that apply if a ticket is bought up to several weeks prior to departure).

- Fly when most people don't: For vacation destinations, that usually means leaving the ground on Tuesday or Wednesday.

Resources for Road Trippers

There are a variety of reputable national automobile associations to choose from. Among the leading clubs:

- **Allstate Motor Club Customer Service Center**
  P.O. Box 660021
  Dallas, TX 75266
  800-998-8697
  www.allstatemotorclub.com

- **American Automobile Association** (AAA)
  1000 AAA Dr. #28
  Heathrow, FL 32746
  407-444-7000 or 800-564-6222
  www.aaa.com

- **Auto Club of America**
  P.O. Box 21443
  Oklahoma City, OK 73156
  800-411-2007
  www.autoclubofamerica.com

- **Ford Customer Relationship Center**
  P.O. Box 6248
  Dearborn, MI 48126
  800-392-3673; *www.ford.com*

- **Geico**
  800-207-7847
  www.geico.com

- **Signature's Nationwide Auto Club**
  Attention: Customer Service
  P.O. Box 968008
  Schaumburg, IL 60196
  800-323-2002
  www.autoclub.com

Travelers may also check with state tourist boards for free maps. Other map sources are the *AAA North American Road Atlas* and the *Rand McNally Road Atlas*; they are sold in many bookstores.

- Keep in mind that the lowest airfares usually carry a penalty if you have to revise or cancel your ticket, and that most discounted tickets are nonrefundable.

- When you call to make a reservation, ask about any fare restrictions, including an obligatory Saturday night stay-over.

- Visit airline websites. They may e-mail details about discounted fares. Most offer a small discount for purchasing tickets online.

By Train

Amtrak serves the Orlando, Florida, area twice daily to and from New York City, with stops made along the way. The trip takes approximately 22 hours and costs from about $288 to $630 round-trip, coach. (Book early for lower fares; discounts are often available, so be sure to ask. Passengers over the age of 18 must present valid government-issued photo ID upon request.) If you're staying at Walt Disney World, plan to take a cab or shuttle to the area hotels. Rental cars are also available. They are not on-site, but are easily reached by shuttle.

For reservations and additional train information, call 800-USA-RAIL (872-7245), visit the Amtrak website at *www.amtrak.com*, or contact a travel agent.

By Bus

Greyhound provides frequent direct service to Orlando and Kissimmee (the latter is closer to Walt Disney World). From either destination, you can take a taxi to your hotel, but first check if your hotel offers shuttle service. For more information, contact Greyhound at 800-231-2222, or visit *www.greyhound.com*.

Disney's Magical Express Service

Disney's Magical Express service is for guests booked at a Walt Disney World–owned-and-operated resort and arriving at Orlando International Airport. Meant as a money-saver as well as a convenience, the service lets guests check luggage at their airport of origin, bypass baggage claim, and board a bus to their WDW resort. The luggage, which guests affix with special tags before leaving home, is usually delivered to the resort room within several hours of arrival. (Note that bags are delivered to rooms for flights landing between 5 A.M. and 10 P.M. If your flight arrives after 10 P.M., you'll need to take your bags with you to the Magical Express bus.) On the final day of a trip, prior to boarding the bus to the airport, guests who fly domestically with participating airlines (at press time, that included Alaska, American, Delta, jetBlue, Southwest, and United) check their luggage at their resort and receive a boarding pass for their airline. (Airline luggage fees apply.) Once at the airport, guests can skip the airline check-in counter and proceed to security. If you'd prefer to schlep your own bags, you can still hitch a free ride on the bus (provided that you are headed to a Disney resort). Here are some specifics:

• Magical Express service is booked when you book your resort and must be done at least 10 days prior to arrival. (Have flight information handy when you make the call.) Be sure to confirm.

• Reservations may be made via *www.disneyworld.com*, 407-W-DISNEY, or a travel agent.

• Tip the driver as you would had you paid for the trip: $1–$2 per bag is appropriate.

• Special luggage tags will be sent to the party that makes the reservation. These tags must be put on all bags that will be checked at the airport.

• Upon landing at Orlando International Airport (MCO), skip baggage claim (only if you tagged your bags) and go to the Disney Welcome Center, located in the Main Terminal Building on the B side, Level 1. Don't forget to have your transfer vouchers, MagicBands (see page 24), and a photo ID handy.

• On the return trip, expect to be picked up at least three hours before your scheduled flight departure time. Consider that when you make your air arrangements.

• If a member(s) of your party uses a wheelchair or scooter, tell the reservationist when booking your trip on Disney's Magical Express. Confirm reservations before you leave home.

• Guests flying on "non-participating" airlines are entitled to the free shuttle service, too.

The good news? It is super convenient, and it is a real money-saver. In fact, a family of four can shave at least $130 off their total vacation cost by taking the Magical Express as opposed to other forms of transportation. And it is beyond liberating to leave the lugging of the luggage to someone else. It's also handy to bypass check-in at the airport on the return trip. The downside? Well, to call any service "magical" is to elevate expectations. It's not really express, either—as most buses make multiple stops at Disney resorts. So if time is of the essence, it might not be the best choice. Same goes for the transportation of luggage. While the service truly eases the burden of many a family, it may take one to three hours to arrive at your resort room (occasionally, a bit more). So if you'll need anything right away—swimsuits, pajamas, medication, snacks, etc.—be sure to pack it in a day bag, carry it onto the plane, and transport it to the resort yourself. We could do without the video that's played throughout the journey, but the bus is comfy and the price is right.

Planning Ahead
Logistics

Organizing a trip properly takes time, but most travelers find the increased enjoyment well worth the effort. The fact is, planning can be a pleasant sort of "armchair" exercise, and kids will enjoy their visit to Disney all the more if they, too, are involved in the process. Take it from us, the more information you can gather, the better.

To assist in that effort, we immodestly recommend *Birnbaum's Walt Disney World For Kids*, a colorful look at the World, written for readers ages 7 through 14. For those planning to pair a Disney cruise with a Walt Disney World visit, cruise information beginning on page 309 is a good place to start.

HOT TIP!

So you're using the Birnbaum Guide to plan your trip to Walt Disney World. What are you going to do next? Go to *www.disneyworld.com*! There you can get WDW news and park hours, purchase tickets, make dining reservations, and more.

Information Sources

For additional information about Walt Disney World, call 407-W-DISNEY (407-934-7639), or visit *www.disneyworld.com*. Specifics such as park hours, ticket prices, refurbishment schedules, and directions are available through an automated system 24 hours a day. For information by mail, write to: Walt Disney World, P.O. Box 10000, Lake Buena Vista, FL 32830-1000.

Internet and smartphone users can tap into updates about happenings in the World, get information on trip planning, reserve a room, order tickets, book dining reservations, and get park hours and special-events listings by visiting *www.disneyworld.com*, *mydisneyexperience.com*, or the My Disney Experience mobile app. Disney Cruise Line vacation packages may be booked at *www.disneycruise.com*.

For info and discounts on (non-Disney) area attractions, restaurants, and hotels, contact the Official Visitor Information Center, 8723 International Drive, Suite 101, Orlando, FL 32819 (it's a satellite office of the Orlando Convention & Visitors Bureau); 407-363-5872, or 800-972-3304; *www.visitorlando.com*.

For details about other Central Florida attractions, contact Visit Florida; 888-735-2872 (to request a complimentary visitors guide and map) or 850-488-5607; *www.visitflorida.com*.

On-site Resources: Those staying at a WDW resort should consider their lobby concierge desk a primary resource. Resort guests also receive information via their room's TV. Fort Wilderness campers are advised to stop at the Pioneer Hall Info and Ticket Window, call extension 2788, or touch 11 on a phone near any restroom. Tablet and smartphone users can access *mydisneyexperience.com* or use the free app.

What to Pack

While there's no formal dress code at Walt Disney World, neat, casual clothing is the rule, with few exceptions. Most notably, jackets are required for men at Victoria & Albert's restaurant in the Grand Floridian resort. Generally speaking, T-shirts and shorts are fine during the day. For evening, slacks, jeans, or Bermuda-length shorts are appropriate. Bathing suits are a must, along with the appropriate attire for any sport you want to pursue.

Light sweaters are necessary even in summer—to wear indoors when air-conditioning gets chilly. From November through March, warmer clothing is a must for evening. Pack for weather extremes so you'll be comfy should it become unseasonably warm or cool. Bring sunscreen and don't forget the bug spray. (Leave selfie sticks at home—they are not allowed in Disney parks. Also forbidden: weapons of any kind, including toys.)

If possible, pack lightweight rain gear (a poncho is best). One of the most important items of all? Comfortable walking shoes (two pairs).

Guests at the resorts on Hotel Plaza Boulevard may access a tourist-information television station of their own. Some other area hotels also show a version of the programming, usually aiming to provide an overview of all Central Florida attractions.

For Day Visitors: When purchasing one-day admission to a given theme park, guests receive a complimentary guidemap and entertainment Times Guide for that park. Ticket holders may receive all four park guides upon request. Extra guidemaps are available at City Hall (in the Magic Kingdom) and at Guest Relations (in Epcot, Disney's Hollywood Studios, and Animal Kingdom), as well as in many shops and restaurants throughout the park.

Package Pointers

The sheer number and diversity of packages offering vacations in Central Florida are enough to bewilder even the savviest traveler. Still, such plans are worth exploring. Most offer the convenience of a vacation that's completely organized in advance, and one that will generally cost less than the sum of the same transportation, accommodations, and admission elements purchased separately. In addition, since most package providers purchase blocks of Disney resort rooms, they are an excellent source for securing a room on Walt Disney World property when the hotel of your choice is booked.

Southwest Vacations (800-243-8372), American Airlines Vacations (800-321-2121), *www.expedia.com*, *www.travelocity.com*, and the Walt Disney Travel Company (407-939-6244 or *www.disneyworld.com*) all offer packages that feature Walt Disney World on-site hotels, as well as choice off-property accommodations. Many packages include the added attraction of low-cost air transportation.

Vacations and other travel packages include certain perks and discounts. For possibilities, check the travel section of your local newspaper or consult a travel agent.

Walt Disney Travel Company offers four vacation plans: Magic Your Way base package, Magic Your Way Plus Dining package, Magic Your Way Plus Quick Service Dining package, and Magic Your Way Plus Deluxe Dining package. (Visit *www.disneyworld.com/dvd* to order a complimentary vacation-planning DVD.) Walt Disney Travel Company packages may include extras such as miniature golf vouchers and savings on participating recreation, dining, and shopping locations throughout WDW.

Travel agents may design packages around a specific type of vacation: say, a golf getaway, honeymoon, or family reunion. They may include extra elements such as unlimited tee times or a carriage ride. Still others are tied to an annual event, such as the Walt Disney World Marathon (see Holidays & Special Events on page 10). Air transportation, rental car, travel insurance, or airport transfers can be added to most packages.

The value of a package depends on your needs. Before considering options, use this book to help determine which of the accommodations, activities, and attractions most appeal to you. There's real value in some package elements, such as airport transfers. Several packages also include meals with the Disney characters, tennis lessons, golf greens fees, spa treatments, boat rentals, and the like.

Never choose a package that includes elements you don't want or won't have time to enjoy. While extras such as welcoming snacks may sound appealing, their cash value is negligible. Also beware of any packages that tout certain services as selling points that are actually available to every Disney guest.

Finally, we highly recommend insuring your trip when purchasing a package, as cancellation fees can be steep and emergencies do happen. Insurance ensures peace of mind (and wallet).

> ## HOT TIP!
> When purchasing a Walt Disney World package, pay attention to the type of WDW ticket that's included—and make sure you are able to customize the ticket to meet your needs. See page 21.

"Magic Your Way" Packages

"Magic Your Way" is the name of the game when it comes to Disney World vacation planning. The phrase, meant to reflect each individual's freedom to customize a vacation, covers quite the gamut of options. Most of all, it covers four vacation packages: Magic Your Way, Magic Your Way Plus Dining, Magic Your Way Plus Quick Service Dining, and Magic Your Way Plus Deluxe Dining. They can be booked through the Walt Disney Travel Company (407-939-7675), travel agents, and *www.disneyworld.com*.

The packages have some elements in common. They're all intended to be flexible and include a Disney resort stay and a theme park ticket of some kind. They come with "magical extras" such as discounts at select Walt Disney World dining, recreational, and shopping locations, as well as admission to one of WDW's mini golf courses and ESPN Wide World of Sports Complex. They must be paid for in full. Packages must be canceled at least 31 days before the trip to avoid a penalty. (For cancellations made 31 days or more prior to arrival, amounts paid minus fees assessed by third-party suppliers will be refunded.) Everyone staying in a room must have the same package and ticket options. Finally, they come with the following perks (also offered to guests with room-only reservations):

- Extra Magic Hours benefit: Walt Disney World resort guests may enjoy exclusive access to theme parks on select mornings and evenings. (For details, see page 22.)

- Disney's Magical Express service: complimentary transportation to and from the Orlando International Airport, plus complimentary baggage collection and delivery to your resort room. (See page 16 for details.)
- Complimentary use of the Walt Disney World transportation system (buses, boats, and the ever-popular monorail).

Magic Your Way Package: This package includes a stay at any Walt Disney World–owned-and-operated resort paired with a theme park ticket. The big decisions to be made here are (1) which Disney resort to reserve, and (2) the number of days and add-ons (if any) you want on your park ticket. (For additional information about Walt Disney World theme park ticket structures and pricing, turn to pages 21–24 of this chapter.)

Enchanting Extras

Walt Disney World offers an ever-changing slate of adventures, tours, and seasonal events, collectively known as the "Enchanting Extras Collection." The most widely offered experiences are detailed on the pages of this book. Seasonal offerings, aka "Limited Time Events," and new adventures join the lineup throughout the year. For more information or to make reservations for Disney's Enchanting Extras Collection, call 407-WDW-PLAY (939-7529), or visit *https://disneyworld.disney.go.com/events-tours/enchanting-extras-collection/.*

HOT TIP!

All multi-day theme park tickets expire 14 days after the first day is used. The "No Expiration" option was discontinued in February 2015. Tickets purchased prior to then will be honored at the parks.

Magic Your Way Plus Dining Package: Take the above description of the Magic Your Way package, throw in a Disney Dining Plan, and you've got a vacation plan with the chance to pre-pay for meals and choose from more than 100 different eateries. This package includes one quick-service meal, two snacks, plus one meal at a table-service restaurant per person, per night of your vacation. (For more on the Dining Plan, see the sidebar at right.) The package also includes a Magic Your Way base ticket and a Rapid Fill refillable mug for each member of your party participating in the package (see page 270).

Magic Your Way Plus Quick Service Dining Package: This plan includes two quick-service meals and two snacks per day, per guest and all meals are of the quick-service variety. It includes a Rapid Fill refillable mug for each member of the party participating in this package (see page 270).

Magic Your Way Plus Deluxe Dining Package: Similar to the two aforementioned packages, but this plan comes with three meals a day, all of which can be cashed in at any eatery that is a Dining Plan participant (regardless of whether it is quick service or table service).

VIP Tour? Sure!

You may have seen them in the theme parks—those cheery folks in the plaid vests. They are VIP guides, leading guests on customized trips through Walt Disney World.

The point is to minimize the hassle factor, while maximizing the overall magic component. Though participating in a VIP tour won't necessarily let you cut the line, it may yield some special seating for stage shows and parades. One tour guide can host up to 10 guests at a cost of about $175–$315 per hour. There is a 6-hour minimum per trip. Parties larger than 10 will require a second guide. Make your needs known when you book the tour. Cancellations must be made at least 48 hours in advance to avoid a fee. Call 407-560-4033 for additional VIP tour information or to make a reservation.

Disney Dining Plan

The Disney Dining Plan lets guests pre-pay for meals before they arrive at Walt Disney World. While convenient for some, it's not necessarily a money-saver. For Dining Plan options, visit *disneyworld.com*. Consider how much your party can consume before selecting a plan, as some include much more sustenance than others. Here's a summary of the standard (non-deluxe) table-service plan (details are subject to change):

Each day of the 2018 plan—which costs about $77 a day for adults and $27 for kids (ages 3 to 9) and is offered as part of the Magic Your Way Plus Dining package—includes:
• One table-service meal, including entrée, dessert (lunch or dinner), and one drink.
• One quick-service meal, including entrée, dessert, and a beverage.
• Two snacks, such as ice cream, popcorn, or a medium soft drink at select quick-service spots or snack carts.
• The option of exchanging two table-service meals for one meal at a high-end "Signature" restaurant or a dinner show, such as the Hoop-Dee-Doo Musical Revue.

To sum up: Say your family of four purchases a five-night package. Together you're entitled to 20 quick-service meals, 20 table-service meals, and 40 snacks. And you are free to use them in any way you want. That is, if you want to skip a meal one day or have five meals in a single day, by all means go for it. (Remember there is a finite number of meals allotted.) Usage can be tracked at Guest Relations in the parks and WDW resorts. Just present a MagicBand (see page 24) or room key card. Taxes are included, gratuities are not. Be sure to tip your servers. Hold on to your receipts, as they show your remaining meal balance. Note that guests over the age of 21 may have the option of ordering an alcoholic beverage.

In addition to traditional table-service meals, certain "character dining" experiences are available to Dining Plan participants, as are some Disney Springs locations. A Quick-Service Only Dining Plan is offered, too. Kids ages 3 to 9 must order from the kids' menu where available.

To find out which restaurants are participating, turn to our *Good Meals, Great Times* chapter. For updates, call 407-939-3463, or go to *www.disneyworld.com*.

Dining Plans must be purchased at the same time a WDW resort stay is booked. *If you get a Dining Plan with table-service meals, you must make reservations for restaurants.* Do so as far ahead as possible—180 days.

All About Theme Park Tickets

Buying a park ticket can be very simple. Do you plan on visiting one park on one day? Just pick up a One-Day Base Ticket. Perhaps you are a frequent visitor and expect to pass through theme park gates dozens of times over the next year. In that case, an Annual Pass is what you're looking for. Now, if your park-going plans lie somewhere in between (and most do), you will have to be a little more strategic.

When it comes to selecting the perfect type of admission ticket, it pays to do some homework. Study the options, evaluate your priorities, and make no hasty decisions. For starters, there are several major factors to consider: (1) total number of days you would like to visit theme parks, (2) to park-hop or not to park-hop, and (3) whether you want to pre-pay (and save some time) for "extras" such as admission to the water parks, the Memory Maker photo package, etc. The following information was correct at press time and is meant to help you make wise choices. Keep in

HOT TIP!

Note that, with the exception of Annual Passes, *all tickets expire within 14 days of first use.* Be sure to keep track of the date activated and remaining days. For help, visit a park Guest Relations or ticket window or a resort concierge counter.

mind that ticket prices are likely to rise in 2018—they always do. For updates, call 407-824-4321, or visit *www.disneyworld.com*.

Magic Your Way Tickets

Base Tickets: Available for 1 to 10 days. Valid for admission to one park per day—the Magic Kingdom (one-day Magic Kingdom base tickets are priced higher than the other parks), Epcot, Disney's Hollywood Studios, or Disney's Animal Kingdom. (The base ticket does not allow for park-hopping.) Unused days expire 14 days after the ticket is activated, which is the first day a park is visited. (For "peak" pricing, see page 26.) It's called a base ticket because, with the exception of Annual Passes, all tickets begin as such. Guests may customize tickets to fit their vacation needs. **Note that you can't use a second day's admission to enter a second park on the same day you visited another park—even with days remaining on a multi-day ticket. To do so, you must add the Park Hopper Option to the ticket.**

DID YOU KNOW?

The phrase "E-ticket ride" is American slang for "the ultimate in thrills." It comes from the early days of Disney parks, back when tickets were used for each attraction. E-tickets were reserved for the most elaborate and exciting rides of all.

Park Hopper Option: This option lets guests visit more than one theme park on a single day. The privilege extends through the length of the ticket. It costs about $40 to add it to a one-day Magic Kingdom base ticket and about $50 to add to a one-day base ticket for all other parks; about $55 for two- and three-day tickets to all parks; and about $69 for all other base tickets (regardless of the number of days on the ticket). We recommend checking operating hours for your planned visit. Hopping is a worthwhile option only if the parks are open late.

HOT TIP!

Want to maximize your theme-park-ticket dollar? Determine how many days you plan to visit the theme parks during your visit and get a multi-day pass for the exact number. It will save on your per-day price— and you won't waste any days. Should you run out of days, you can upgrade your ticket within 14 days of first use.

Park Hopper Plus Option: This add-on covers entry to Blizzard Beach and Typhoon Lagoon water parks, Disney's sports complex, miniature golf, or a round of golf at Disney's Oak Trail golf course. For about $64, you will get between two and ten visits to these spots. The number of visits depends on the number of days on your base ticket—the more days, the more visits.

Expiration: Unused days on multi-day base tickets expire 14 days after the first day is used. The No Expire option was discontinued in February 2015; tickets purchased prior to then will be honored at the parks, provided they have the No Expire option. Tickets bought before 2005 are valid, too—they pre-date the No Expire option.

Theme Park Platinum Annual Pass: This pass offers admission to the four theme parks for a year with no block-out dates. It can be used in more than one park on the same day (also known as park-hopping), and includes use of Disney transportation, as well as free parking at the theme parks, and a year's worth of PhotoPass downloads. Annual passes can be purchased at the entrance to any of the theme parks (they can be renewed there or by mail). A valid, government-issued photo ID must be presented for purchase by adults and may be required for future use of the pass. Passes are non-transferable. At press time, the cost was about $649 for adults and kids over age 3.

Annual Pass-bearers qualify for many Disney World discounts and benefits, such as reduced rates at select Disney resorts at certain times of year. A newsletter called the *Mickey Monitor* keeps passholders up to date regarding discount offers. The pass expires one year after it is first used. A discounted renewal rate applies if the pass is renewed before expiration. (The old pass must be presented in order to receive the discounted renewal rate.) A pass may be renewed by mail, online, or at any Disney theme park.

Platinum Plus Annual Pass: This pass has all the Theme Park Annual Pass offers and more— namely, admission to both water parks, ESPN Wide World of Sports complex (non-premium events only), a year's worth of PhotoPass downloads, plus a round of golf at the Oak Trail golf course. Platinum Plus Annual Passholders are eligible for the same discounts and benefits as Theme Park Annual Passholders. Platinum Plus

Extra Magic Hours

How'd you like to visit a Disney theme park before it opens to the public? Or stick around for hours after it's officially closed for the day—at no extra cost? Well, if you're a guest staying at a Walt Disney World–owned-and-operated resort, the Swan, Dolphin, or Shades of Green (a WDW resort for members of the military), you can. It is one of the major perks that comes with staying on Disney property.

Here's how it works: One park opens its doors an hour early or stays open two hours late on any given day. Basically, the park becomes something of a members-only private playground for Walt Disney World resort guests. So, provided that you have a WDW resort ID and valid admission media, you're in! No secret password necessary. Keep in mind that you will need park-hopping privileges if you plan to visit a park other than the one offering extra hours on any given day. If you don't plan to park-hop, you must visit the theme park offering Extra Magic Hours on that particular day. When a park opens early in the morning, guests are admitted starting one hour prior to the official opening time. Transportation to the park starts about 30 minutes before that. Be sure to have your MagicBand or WDW resort ID handy. Flash it and you'll be allowed to visit some (but not all) attractions and mingle with Disney characters.

In our opinion, Extra Magic Hours is the single-most valuable perk available to Walt Disney World Resort hotel guests.

Details about Extra Magic Hours are subject to change. Visit www.disneyworld.com for updates and the schedule for your planned visit.

Annual Passes can be purchased at the entrance to any of the four theme parks (they can be renewed there or by mail). A photo ID must be presented for purchase by adults and may be required for future use. Passes are non-transferable and they expire one year after first use. The cost is about $829 for adults and kids (over age 3).

Premier Annual Pass: This pass provides admission to all Disney theme parks and water parks in the U.S.A. (including Disneyland Park and Disney California Adventure) for one year. It also includes a year's worth of PhotoPass downloads, admission to the ESPN Wide World of Sports complex (non-premium events only) and the Oak Trail golf course. Unlimited park-hopping and parking are included, as are the same discounts offered with Disney's other annual passes (select merchandise, food, and resort discounts).

The Premier Pass costs about $1,439, plus tax. Guests already bearing a WDW or Disneyland Resort Annual Pass may upgrade to the Premier Pass at any time. For details, call 407-824-4321, or visit *www.disneyparks.com/Premier*.

> ## HOT TIP!
> If your child "outgrows" his or her park ticket (by turning 10), you can upgrade the ticket at any of the theme parks.

Deciding Factors

Choosing the Right Ticket: Before you make a decision, it helps to map out your vacation. Remember, all tickets start as Base Tickets. They are a bare-bones, admission-to-one-theme-park-at-a-time deal. That's perfect for many folks—especially those planning a relatively short stay. Still, the first step for every potential guest is to decide just how many days they plan to spend in the theme parks. Keep in mind that as days are added, the average price per day goes down. Unused days expire 14 days after the ticket is activated. Once the length of stay is determined, it's time to customize the ticket. (If the total number of days is undetermined, err on the side of caution—unused days can't be refunded, but you can add extra days up to 14 days after the ticket is first used.) Do you want to park-hop? Add about $69. Want to add the Park Hopper Plus Option? That's about $64.

If you are planning a longer visit, or two trips within a year, we recommend a multi-day Park Hopper or an Annual Pass. In addition to

unlimited admission to the parks, an Annual Pass entitles bearers to discounts on everything from dinner shows to room rates.

Note: Only one person per party needs to have an Annual Pass to net a discount on a WDW resort (when available). This option is great for travelers with flexible schedules, as the discounts do vary, and they are often announced shortly before going into effect.

Tickets with Unused Days: Prior to 2005, WDW tickets never expired. That is no longer the case. Any days remaining on a multi-day admission ticket now expire 14 days after the ticket is first activated (with the obvious exception of Annual Passes).

Attractions Outside the Theme Parks: Typhoon Lagoon and Blizzard Beach water park prices start at about $60 for one day and about $115 for an annual pass for adults; $54 for one day and about $115 for an annual pass for kids (ages 3 to 9). ESPN Wide World of Sports complex runs about $18 for adults, about $13 for kids (general admission). Prices are apt to rise in 2018.

My Disney Experience

"My Disney Experience" is the all-encompassing moniker attached to all vacation-planning tools managed via the My Disney Experience planning page or mobile app. It links cards and MagicBands (wristbands that are connected to various vacation features) and includes the Fastpass+ attraction reservation system (see page 25).

My Disney Experience: An app that can be downloaded for free and is compatible with most Android and Apple iOS smartphones and tablets, My Disney Experience is a tool for reserving tables at WDW restaurants and dinner shows; booking, revising, and keeping track of

> ## HOT TIP!
> To expedite your party's entrance experience, make sure each member is holding his or her own ticket or wearing their MagicBand before getting in line.

Fastpass+ assignments at theme park shows and attractions; viewing wait times; and more. For those guests without smartphones or tablets, *www.MyDisneyExperience.com* can be accessed by personal computer. It allows for the same advance planning. The service is free and requires guests to create an account (to which all members of the traveling party should be linked). Note that children under age 13 are not permitted to have live, individual accounts. Instead, parents create and manage a profile for each child (kids' profiles are attached to their parents'). There is a bit of a learning curve, so get started as soon as you can.

After linking a WDW resort reservation or vacation package and tickets to your account, guests may link MagicBands, make and monitor WDW dining reservations, book and track Fastpass+ times, and load the Memory Maker Photo Package (see page 27). It is important to link all accounts in your traveling party (parties larger than 10 should call 407-939-5277).

All guests may use this service, whether they stay on WDW property or not, provided they can access the website or utilize the app.

MagicBands: This accessory is something of a technological wonder—it can serve as a resort room key and be loaded with theme park and water park admission tickets. Guests can also use it to make purchases throughout Walt Disney World (provided the MagicBand is backed up with a credit card and a personal PIN code has been selected); use it for Disney's PhotoPass (see page 133), Fastpass+ (in conjunction with *MyDisneyExperience.com* or the associated app); and more. To use it to make a purchase in a shop or restaurant, just tap the not-so-hidden Mickey

HOT TIP!

Adults should always carry a government-issued photo ID. You'll need it should you have any issues with your MagicBand and to purchase alcohol while at WDW.

on the band to the Mickey head on the console. MagicBands are complimentary for guests at Disney–owned-and-operated resorts. The standard version comes in gray but may be customized in one of 8 different colors. (We recommend using different colors for each member of a party.) Bands customized 11 or more days ahead of arrival can be sent to your home. Bands customized within 6 to 10 days of your visit will be sent to your Disney–owned-and-operated resort. Bands ordered within 5 days cannot be customized and may be collected at your resort's front desk. Note that MagicBands cannot be shipped to all countries.

MagicBands are included with your Walt Disney World hotel reservation, but specialty versions may be purchased in the parks. Non-WDW-resort guests may also purchase MagicBands at any WDW theme park.

HOT TIP!

We recommend wearing the MagicBand on your dominant hand. That should make it easier to align it with Mickey heads when endeavoring to make a purchase or open a resort room door.

How Do You Book a Room? Let Us Count the Ways

You're ready to reserve a room at a resort on Walt Disney World property. How nice for you! But before you dial 407-W-DISNEY (934-7639) or a travel agent, know this: There are three different ways to book your WDW stay. It's best to know what you want in advance. It will save you time and spare confusion while on the phone. Here's the scoop:

• Room-Only Reservation—What you hear is what you get: a hotel room only. It requires an advance deposit and allows you to cancel up to 5 days prior to the start of the reservation (penalty-free). It comes with a 12-digit confirmation number.

• Walt Disney Travel Company Basic Plan—A package that includes room, luggage tags, and a round of mini-golf for the entire party. Must be paid in full 30 days before check-in and must be canceled at least 31 days prior to check-in to avoid a penalty. (The confirmation number has 8 digits.) We recommend adding trip insurance to the package (at an additional cost), just in case.

• Magic Your Way Base Package—Includes room and theme park tickets. It may be customized in many ways, such as adding the Disney Dining Plan, Water Park admission, and more (see page 21). Must be paid in full 30 days before check-in and must be canceled at least 31 days prior to check-in (any later and there will be hefty penalties). Once reserved, expect to get an 8-digit confirmation number.

Save Time in Line with Fastpass+

Walt Disney World's Fastpass+ is a service that was designed to allow guests to bypass the traditional standby line and enjoy a number of theme park shows and attractions with less of a wait. It's a virtual queue—one you join by visiting "My Disney Experience" via the Internet (with a computer, tablet, or smartphone). Once you've established an account, you can link your ticket (and those in your party) and access Fastpass+ to book times to visit attractions during a pending visit to the park.

To WDW veterans, the term Fastpass conjures happy memories of bypassing lines after securing assignments while visiting the parks. That concept is still the same, but the procedure has changed quite a bit. In fact, we wish they had called the new system something other than Fastpass+, because it really is a bold departure from the original. Think of Fastpass+ as an *advance reservation system*—one that is free to all guests bearing a valid park ticket.

Popular WDW attractions and shows (aka E-Ticket experiences) are often very crowded, with long waits and no guarantee you'll get in. By using Fastpass+, you can reserve a time to enjoy at least one popular ride (and several other attractions) during each day of your WDW visit. In most cases, you won't walk right in, but you will have an expedited wait time and guaranteed admission to some crowd-pleasers such as Toy Story Midway Mania!, Soarin' Around the World, Avatar Flight of Passage, and Peter Pan's Flight. Ideally, Fastpass+ aims to spread guests throughout the parks, making traditionally congested areas less so. For folks who prefer to do things on the fly or who find the new system a bit daunting or difficult to navigate, traditional standby lines will always be available. That said, tech-savvy, detail-minded guests may relax a bit, knowing each day of their vacation is pre-planned.

Begin by paying a visit to My Disney Experience via the Internet or mobile app. Set up an account and link it with your park ticket. Then, if it's within 30 days of your visit (60 if you are staying in a WDW–owned-and-operated resort or the Swan or Dolphin), you can start booking Fastpass+ assignments. When the one-hour Fastpass+ window kicks in, go to the attraction and touch your MagicBand or ticket card to the Fastpass+ redemption console, wait for the light, and head inside.

We recommend using Fastpass+ assignments for your must-sees. We've placed our Fastpass+ symbol (FP+) beside the listing for all shows and attractions that were included at press time. However, since experiences may be added or dropped, visit *www.mydisneyexperience.com* for updates. And remember, all WDW attractions continue to offer the option of standing in a traditional queue. Fastpass+ is just a bonus option for folks who like to plan ahead. By using it, we have gleaned the following (specifics may change, as the program was still in a fine-tuning phase as this book went to press):

- To make advance Fastpass+ reservations, you must have access to the Internet.
- It's possible to reserve a same-day Fastpass+ assignment via the mobile app and at a park kiosk—but getting convenient, same-day access to popular attractions is tough. Start early!
- Fastpass+ lets you experience at least 3 attractions or shows per day without waiting in the (usually) longer standby line. You may be able to get more same-day assignments via the app and at in-park kiosks once your first three have been used or the time has expired (pending availability).
- Although you are able to book up to 3 Fastpass+ assignments in one park in advance, you can make changes after you use your first Fastpass+ assignment of the day. Changes to original selections must apply to shows and attractions within the same park. To revise your selections, visit *mydisneyexperience.com*, use the My Disney Experience app, or go to an in-park kiosk.
- Fastpass+ allows for park-hopping after the first 3 Fastpass+ assignments have been used or the times have expired. After that you can make a selection for another park via the mobile app or at an in-park kiosk. Additional Fastpass+ assignments are available one at a time.
- Fastpass+ times are linked to your MagicBand (see page 24) or park ticket card and can be viewed, modified, or canceled via smartphone, tablet, computer, or in-park Fastpass+ kiosk. To use a Fastpass+ assignment, you'll need to touch a MagicBand or ticket card to a Fastpass+ reader device at the attraction.
- If you want to ride a major attraction twice, we recommend getting a Fastpass+ assignment and going to your attraction as soon as the park opens for your first ride. You can ride again when your Fastpass+ window kicks in.
- Fastpass+ assignments are non-transferable.
- Coordinating Fastpass+ assignments for large groups is possible, but it can be challenging.
- Write the assignment times on paper if you don't have a smartphone or in case your smartphone battery dies. You can check times at a park kiosk, but there is often a wait to do so.
- Select shows and character meet-and-greets may be included in the Fastpass+ system.
- All shows and attractions continue to offer traditional standby lines.
- Disney's Fastpass+ is an ever-evolving service. Details are subject to change.

PEAK TICKET PRICES†

		1-Day	2-Day	3-Day	4-Day	5-Day	6-Day	7-Day	8-Day	9-Day	10-Day
Base Ticket*	Ages 10 & UP	$119–$124	$199 ($99.50/day)	$289 ($96.33/day)	$350 ($87.50/day)	$370 ($74.00/day)	$390 ($65.00/day)	$410 ($58.57/day)	$420 ($52.50/day)	$430 ($42.78/day)	$440 ($44.00/day)
	Ages 3–9	$113–$118	$187 ($93.50/day)	$271 ($90.33/day)	$330 ($82.50/day)	$350 ($70.00/day)	$370 ($61.66/day)	$390 ($55.71/day)	$400 ($50.00/day)	$410 ($45.56/day)	$420 ($42.00/day)
ADD: Park Hopper**		$50–$55	$60	$60	$75	$75	$75	$75	$75	$75	$75
ADD: Park-Hopper Plus Option***		$65–$70 2 visits	$75 2 visits	$75 3 visits	$90 4 visits	$90 5 visits	$90 6 visits	$90 7 visits	$90 8 visits	$90 9 visits	$90 10 visits
ADD: Memory Maker****		$169/ $199	$169/ $199	$169/ $199	$189/ $199	$169/ $199	$169/ $199	$169/ $199	$169/ $199	$169/ $199	$169/ $199

† These are advance-purchase prices and do not include tax. Prices are lower during non-peak times of year. For specifics, visit *www.disneyworld.com.*

* Base Ticket admits guest to one theme park each day of use. Park choices are Magic Kingdom, Epcot, Disney's Hollywood Studios, and Disney's Animal Kingdom.

** Park Hopper Option entitles guest to visit more than one theme park on each day of use. Park choices are any combination of theme parks on each day of use.

*** Park-Hopper Plus option entitles guest to a specified number of visits to a choice of entertainment and recreation venues. Choices include Disney's Blizzard Beach water park, Disney's Typhoon Lagoon water park, and ESPN Wide World of Sports complex.

**** Guests who pre-pay for Disney's Memory Maker photo package pay the first price, those who make the purchase within 3 days of their WDW visit pay the second price. If you purchased Memory Maker at the advance purchase price, photos taken within 3 days of the date of purchase will not be included in Memory Maker and must be purchased separately. The Memory Maker Photo package is available to all guests. For details, see page 27.

The MagicBand is waterproof (but does not float), hypoallergenic, and can be adjusted to fit most wrists. If a MagicBand is lost, it can be disabled via the My Disney Experience app (and the website) or with the help of a cast member. MagicBands are non-transferable. No personal information is stored on the band—it only links to entitlements that were pre-purchased. Remember, you will need to use a PIN code to pay for things with your MagicBand.

Fastpass+: WDW's reservation system for most attractions, shows, and character meet-and-greets at its four theme parks is a free service, available to guests with valid theme park tickets. It may be accessed up to 30 days in advance via the My Disney Experience app or website. Guests with a reservation at a Disney–owned-and-operated resort may book Fastpass+ assignments up to 60 days prior to checking in. It's possible to make same-day Fastpass+ reservations, too—by using the aforementioned ways and by visiting a Fastpass+ kiosk in any of the WDW theme parks. Note that it is not possible to get Fastpass+ assignments at the attractions themselves. For details on Fastpass+, turn to page 25.

Memory Maker Photo Package: Memory Maker includes all photos taken in the parks, including those snapped on select attractions and character meal locations for your length of stay. You can review the photos at sites in the park, via the My Disney Experience app, or via the Internet (*https://mydisneyphotopass.disney.go.com/*). It is possible to customize photos with banners and Disney art, too. At press time, the same-day price was about $169; about $149 if pre-ordered.

(We think this is one of Walt Disney World's better values.) A one-day package is available for $59. Note that guests can still buy and customize photos via the traditional PhotoPass system (see page 133).

Purchasing Tickets

Admission tickets are sold at park entrances, WDW resorts, Four Seasons, the resorts on Hotel Plaza Boulevard, Orlando International Airport, the Transportation and Ticket Center (TTC), and Disney Springs Guest Relations. Cash, traveler's checks, American Express, Visa, MasterCard, Diner's Club, Discover, JCB Card, and Disney gift cards are accepted. (Disney Dollars are still accepted as payment for most Walt Disney World purchases, but they are no longer sold.) Not all tickets are available at each location, so call 407-934-7639 to confirm.

We recommend buying tickets in advance (it can save time when you arrive at the parks) from a travel agent, or in one of these ways:

Tickets by Phone: All tickets can be purchased by phone; call 407-W-DISNEY (934-7639). Allow 15 days for standard delivery; $15 for express delivery (allow 7 days); and $25 for international delivery (allow 12 days). There is no fee for pickup at a WDW Will Call window.

Tickets Online: Tickets can be bought through *www.disneyworld.com*. The fees for delivery are the same as those listed above.

Tickets at a Disney Store: Select multi-day theme park tickets are available for purchase at any local Disney Store.

Tickets by Mail (3- to 7-day Magic Your Way tickets only): Allow at least three to four weeks for processing, and include a return address. Send a money order (for amount due, plus $4 for handling), payable to Walt Disney World Company, to: Walt Disney World, Box 10140, Lake Buena Vista, FL 32830-0030. Attention: Ticket Mail Order.

Ticket Tag System

As a means of enforcing the non-transferability aspect of all Walt Disney World tickets, Disney has devised a system to trace each ticket to its rightful owner. The procedure is as follows: Touch your MagicBand or ticket to the shiny orb at any park entrance. While the machine is crunching the data encrypted on your MagicBand or ticket, gently press the tip of your forefinger onto the glowing gizmo perched beside the orb. Remove your finger and presto! Your MagicBand or ticket will link to your forefinger, giving you the green light to enter. All guests over age 3 have to do this every time they use the ticket. Remember to use the same finger every time you enter a park. (It's a good idea to wash your hands after this process.)

Money-Saving Tips

A Walt Disney World vacation can be an exceptionally expensive undertaking, but it is possible to keep costs down a bit. When budgeting for your trip, keep in mind that WDW prices are comparable to those in a big city. Here are a few tips to help you conserve cash.

Lodging

- When it comes to saving money on hotel accommodations, timing is truly the key. While off-season dates tend to vary depending on the hotel, value season for most Walt Disney World resorts generally means January through mid-February, late August through late September, and early November through late December. Weeknights are generally less expensive than weekend nights year-round.

- The Swan and Dolphin resorts often have rate specials when other WDW resorts have peak rates. Check *www.swandolphin.com*.

- Consider how much time you will actually spend at your hotel, and don't pay for a place with perks you won't have time to enjoy. Off-property hotels often allow kids to stay free in parents' rooms, but the cutoff age varies.

- When considering the cost-effectiveness of off-property lodging, factor in the time, money, and inconvenience of commuting to and from attractions.

- Realize, too, that the advantages of staying on-property (tops among them the Extra Magic Hours perk, Disney's Magical Express, and access to WDW's transportation system) also apply to those staying in the least expensive rooms in Disney's hotels. The most important addresses for budget-watching Disney fans, the All-Star and Pop Century resorts, offer the lowest rates on Disney property. Rooms at Caribbean Beach, Port Orleans French Quarter and Riverside, Disney's Art of Animation, and Coronado Springs are slightly higher priced. Also, note that the only difference between the least and most expensive rooms in a hotel is often the view. Consider how often you'll be looking out that window.

- The resorts on Hotel Plaza Boulevard, located next to Disney Springs, offer rooms starting at about $130 per night. (See page 106.)

Food

- Visit costlier establishments at lunchtime (if you so desire) rather than at dinner; entrées may cost a bit less at the midday meal.

- Club Level accommodations can absorb the cost of some meals, snacks, and cocktails—the more folks in the room, the better the value.

- Carry snacks and sandwich fixings and enjoy them picnic style wherever possible.

- Consider lodgings with kitchen facilities. The savings on food may be more than the extra accommodations expense. Note that small refrigerators are available in all guestrooms at Disney–owned-and-operated resorts (no charge).

- Staying on Disney property? We highly recommend purchasing a souvenir Rapid Fill mug. It's good for unlimited soft-drink refills (including coffee, tea, lemonade, soda pop, and more) at all WDW–owned-and-operated resorts (see page 270 for details).

- Pack kid-friendly snacks, such as fruit, cereal, or crackers. (Snack stands are plentiful, but not always handy or cost-efficient.)

- Don't plan on eating three big table-service meals a day. It gets expensive—and filling!

- Save money by having groceries delivered to your resort. Items such as bottled water, snacks, fruit, and breakfast bars can be enjoyed in the room or out of a backpack throughout the day. Our go-to for this type of service is *gardengrocer.com*. (This company is authorized to deliver to WDW, but is not affiliated with the Walt Disney Company.)

HOT TIP!

To save money on Walt Disney World golf, merchandise, food, behind-the-scenes tours and more, use the coupons at the back of this book!

Satisfying Substitutes

Fewer frills rarely mean less fun at Walt Disney World. Here are money-saving alternatives to two of Disney's higher-priced treats.

If you'd rather not spring for admission to Disney Springs West Side venues, consider taking a trip to the BoardWalk resort. Among other diversions, you will find Jellyrolls (a sing-along piano bar with a cover of about $12), Atlantic Dance Hall (a nightclub with no cover charge), and ESPN Club (a cover-free sports bar). A short walk will take you to the Swan hotel, home to the karaoke-friendly Kimonos Lounge.

If the Grand Floridian ($574–$1,072 a night) doesn't quite fit into your budget, consider staying in a Mansion room at Port Orleans Riverside ($199–$356 a night). Southern hospitality replaces Victorian splendor, and though the guestrooms aren't quite as spacious, the air of sophistication makes for a most satisfying stay. And for a sweet deal on a suite, consider the vibrant resort known as Disney's Art of Animation.

Discounts

- Theme Park Annual and Premium Annual Passholders receive so many discounts on meals, dinner shows, tours, room rates, and more that it may be worth purchasing an Annual Pass for longer visits or if you plan to take more than one trip within a year.

- WDW resorts that offer Annual Passholder discounts vary from month to month, and discounted rooms aren't always available for booking very far in advance. It's best to be flexible with travel dates. Annual Passholders may net deals on recreational opportunities, too. For details, call 407-W-DISNEY (939-7639). Passholders can save 20 percent at many WDW eateries by joining the Tables in Wonderland program (for a fee). For details, call 407-WDW-DINE (939-3463).

- Discounts on Disney World resort rates and theme park tickets are available to Florida residents, and seasonal promotions occur. Call 407-W-DISNEY (939-7639) for specifics.

- The Swan, as well as some off-property hotels, offers discounts to seniors and the Automobile Association of America (AAA) or AARP members as well. Some AAA branches provide discounts on park passes, as well as discounts on rooms, and more. Check with your local AAA branch for additional information.

HOT TIP!

Bring inexpensive, light rain gear from home. You'll need it—especially in the stormy months of summer.

HOT TIP!

It may be cheaper to get a family suite or spread out over two rooms in a "value" or "moderate" resort than to have everyone stay in one room at "deluxe" Disney digs.

- Web-based *travelocity.com* offers a variety of Disney vacation packages. Vacation Outlet sometimes offers packages at a reduced rate; visit *www.vacationoutlet.com*, or call 800-825-3633 for details.

- To request your free Orlando Magicard, visit *www.orlandoinfo.com/magicard*. Cardholders may net discounts at area hotels, restaurants, shops, and more.

- Disney Visa® Cardmembers who pay with their Disney Visa Card enjoy savings on merchandise, dining, and guided tours. Cardmembers can use the Disney Visa card wherever Visa is accepted. Details are subject to change. For specifics, visit *DisneyRewards.com* or *DisneyDebit.com*.

- Okay, so it's not exactly a discount, but we think that multi-day tickets are worth their weight in gold. The more days you purchase, the lower the cost is per day. (Just don't over-purchase days—unused days expire 14 days after a ticket is activated. Extra days can be added as needed.)

- Visit *disneyworld.disney.go.com/special-offers/* to see if any discounts apply for your WDW visit.

- For discounts on dozens of WDW restaurant, tours, recreational experiences, and more, see the coupons after page 352 of this book.

Making a Budget

A stay at Disney's kingdom need not cost a king's ransom (though it easily can). In fact, with a well-planned budget, money at Disney World can stretch relatively far.

Vacation expenses tend to fall into five major categories: (1) transportation (which may include any combination of costs for airfare, airport transfers, train tickets, car rental, gas, parking, and taxi service); (2) lodging; (3) theme park tickets; (4) meals; and (5) miscellaneous (recreational activities, cover charges, tips, souvenirs, postcards, forgotten items, and home expenses such as pet boarding, etc.).

When planning your budget, first consider what level of service suits your needs. Some people prefer to spend fewer days at Disney but stay at a deluxe hotel or dine at pricier restaurants, while others would rather make their money cover a longer vacation that includes a value-priced resort and less-expensive meals. The choice is up to you. Once you've established your spending priorities, determine your price limit. Then make sure you don't exceed it when approximating your expenses—without a ballpark figure to work around, it's easy to get carried away.

Sample Budget

The following is an example of a low- to moderately-priced budget designed for a family of four during "peak" season (two adults and two kids planning to stay at WDW for five nights and six days). Totals do not include transportation expenses or sales tax. Plan your budget accordingly.

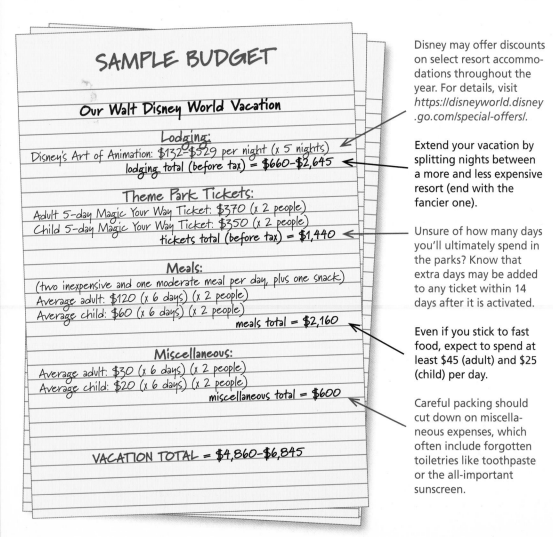

SAMPLE BUDGET

Our Walt Disney World Vacation

Lodging:
Disney's Art of Animation: $132-$529 per night (x 5 nights)
lodging total (before tax) = $660-$2,645

Theme Park Tickets:
Adult 5-day Magic Your Way Ticket: $370 (x 2 people)
Child 5-day Magic Your Way Ticket: $350 (x 2 people)
tickets total (before tax) = $1,440

Meals:
(two inexpensive and one moderate meal per day, plus one snack)
Average adult: $120 (x 6 days) (x 2 people)
Average child: $60 (x 6 days) (x 2 people)
meals total = $2,160

Miscellaneous:
Average adult: $30 (x 6 days) (x 2 people)
Average child: $20 (x 6 days) (x 2 people)
miscellaneous total = $600

VACATION TOTAL = $4,860-$6,845

Disney may offer discounts on select resort accommodations throughout the year. For details, visit *https://disneyworld.disney.go.com/special-offers/*.

Extend your vacation by splitting nights between a more and less expensive resort (end with the fancier one).

Unsure of how many days you'll ultimately spend in the parks? Know that extra days may be added to any ticket within 14 days after it is activated.

Even if you stick to fast food, expect to spend at least $45 (adult) and $25 (child) per day.

Careful packing should cut down on miscellaneous expenses, which often include forgotten toiletries like toothpaste or the all-important sunscreen.

Planning Your Itinerary

A TIMELINE

First Things First

- Make hotel and transportation arrangements as far ahead as possible. Note that many WDW hotels fill up more than six months ahead. Call 407-W-DISNEY (934-7639) to book a room; your confirmation should arrive within two weeks. Log it and other pertinent information in a notebook for future reference.

- Check park hours for your planned visit. (Hours are available up to 7 months ahead; call 407-824-4321, or visit *www.disneyworld.com*.) Closing times will be particularly helpful when making evening plans. Create a day-by-day schedule, deciding which area of WDW to visit on each day of your trip.

6 Months

- Choose dining spots from those listed in the *Good Meals, Great Times* chapter. Call 407-WDW-DINE (939-3463), visit *www.disneyworld.com/dine*, or use the My Disney Experience website or free mobile app to make restaurant reservations. Guests with a confirmed reservation at a WDW–owned-and-operated resort may call 180 days before scheduled check-in date and book dining reservations for up to 10 days of their planned stay. Guests with a reservation of 4 nights or more may book additional days of dining reservations at this time.

- Popular meals such as those at Cinderella's Royal Table, Le Cellier, and Be Our Guest Restaurant (dinner) should be booked 180 days ahead. Call 407-WDW-DINE (939-3463) and have a credit card handy.

- Dinner-show reservations may be secured up to 180 days in advance. Visit *www.mydisneyexperience.com*, or call 407-WDW-DINE (939-3463) for reservations.

- Unless you have a package that includes park admission, it's time to order tickets. Refer to pages 21–24 for details, and call 407-824-432. You may save money by purchasing select tickets in advance.

- Specialty cruises (see page 231) may be booked by calling 407-WDW-PLAY (939-7529).

- If you will be staying at a Walt Disney World resort or a resort on Hotel Plaza Blvd., you may book a tee time on one of WDW's golf courses now (see pages 236–237 for details). Golf lessons may also be reserved now. Call 407-WDW-GOLF (939-4653) for reservations. Those not staying on WDW property may make reservations 60 days ahead.

- Fishing excursions (see page 239) may be booked by calling 407-WDW-BASS (939–2277).

- Tennis lessons may be reserved by calling 321-228-1146. Turn to page 237 for information.

- Parasailing and waterskiing excursions (for details, see pages 238–239) may be booked by calling 407-WDW-PLAY (939-7529) or 407-939-0754 or by visiting *www.sammyduvall.com*.

- Trail-ride reservations may be made up to 180 days in advance. Call 407-WDW-PLAY (939-7529).

- If you'd like to add a behind-the-scenes tour to your vacation, now is the time to make a reservation.

3 Months

- Double-check park hours for your stay, as they may have changed. Take note of Extra Magic Hours (extended park hours for guests registered at a Walt Disney World–owned-and-operated resort).

60 Days

- If you have valid park tickets linked to a reservation at a participating WDW resort, you may book Fastpass+ selections for your entire stay starting 60 days ahead of the day you intend to check in (at a WDW–owned-and-operated resort), via the My Disney Experience website or app.

- Are you booked at a WDW–owned-and-operated resort? If so, check in online! (See page 66.)

30 Days

- If you have valid park tickets but aren't staying in a WDW resort, you may book Fastpass+ up to 30 days ahead.

11 Days

- If you haven't already customized your MagicBand color, today is the last day to do it and have it shipped to your home. If customized between 10 and 6 days before arrival, your band will be sent to your WDW resort. (All others may be picked up at your WDW–owned-and-operated resort. Non-customized bands are usually gray.)

1 Week

- Reconfirm all reservations. Finalize your schedule, including all confirmation numbers and Fastpass+ times.

Step-By-Step

Many visitors have a deep desire to cover each and every inch of Walt Disney World in the span of a few short days. While we hesitate to discourage these most ambitious of travelers, we feel the need to enlighten them: Walt Disney World is a staggeringly large place. In fact, it's nearly as big as San Francisco and jam-packed with about as many diversions as you might expect from a city that size. You could spend two full weeks on Walt Disney World property and still not have time to do it all. The theme parks alone require every bit of four days just to see the major attractions.

What's the best strategy for organizing a Walt Disney World visit? Make a list of the parks, attractions, and activities you most want to see and use it to create an itinerary. Don't forget to allow time for swimming, boating, or relaxing on a lakeside swing.

Assuming you've narrowed your "must-do" list to the barely manageable, we recommend a stay of at least four to five days. This allows for a visit to each of the theme parks and some time to enjoy many of the recreational activities at your resort, not to mention relaxing a bit. You are on vacation, after all. Longer stays can include water parks, Disney Springs, a dinner show, and more. When planning your days (which you should do before leaving home), be sure to take into account theme park hours and seasonal temperatures in Central Florida.

The following sample schedules assume that you eat breakfast at your resort (unless otherwise stated) and arrive up to 20 minutes before the official opening time. These schedules, though tirelessly tested and proven successful by Birnbaum's editors, are not carved in stone. Use them as a guide, tailoring the itineraries to suit your family's individual tastes. And use them in conjunction with complimentary theme park Times Guides (available at park entrances).

Note that we have not included specific instructions with regard to Fastpass+ in our sample itineraries. It's not because we don't use the service. In fact, we highly recommend using Fastpass+, even if working it into a daily schedule is an inexact science. Without it, there's always the risk of a long line or missing out on a "must-see." By all means, take advantage of the Fastpass+ opportunity every chance you get—especially first thing in the morning for the ultra-popular attractions. Not only might it make you feel like a VIP, but it will free up time in your schedule for things you otherwise might not have gotten to. (If you didn't pre-book Fastpass+, head to an in-park kiosk to see what's available.)

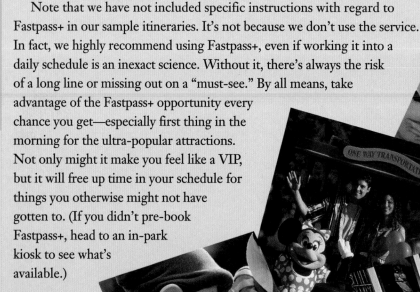

ONE-DAY SCHEDULE

❤ Begin the day with a brisk stroll down Main Street, U.S.A. —it opens earlier than the rest of the park. You can use the extra time to shop, relax, or have a light breakfast before watching Let the Magic Begin—the Magic Kingdom's "welcome to the park" show presented at Cinderella Castle. If you haven't pre-booked Fastpass+ assignments, do so via your smartphone or tablet or stop at an in-park kiosk. Check a park map for kiosk locations. Then head to Splash Mountain and Big Thunder Mountain Railroad. Finish up Adventureland with Pirates of the Caribbean, Jungle Cruise, The Magic Carpets of Aladdin, or Walt Disney's Enchanted Tiki Room.

❤ Make your way over to Frontierland to see The Muppets Present . . . Great Moments in American History in Liberty Square.

❤ Consider lunching at Columbia Harbour House or Pecos Bill's.

❤ If time allows, squeeze in The Haunted Mansion before the Festival of Fantasy parade. Watch the parade and move on to Fantasyland.

❤ See as much of Fantasyland as possible, including Dumbo, It's a Small World, Peter Pan's Flight, Seven Dwarfs Mine Train, and Under the Sea—Journey of The Little Mermaid.

❤ If the timing's right, head to the front of the Castle for a live stage show, or take a relaxing ride on Tomorrowland's PeopleMover.

❤ Haven't seen Tom Sawyer Island, the Haunted Mansion, or the Country Bear Jamboree? Go for it!

❤ Visit Space Mountain, Buzz Lightyear's Space Ranger Spin, Monsters, Inc. Laugh Floor, and the Tomorrowland Speedway.

❤ If there's an evening parade scheduled, watch it from Frontierland or Main Street, U.S.A.

❤ View the Happily Ever After fireworks from the middle of Main Street, U.S.A.

❤ If there's time, revisit a favorite attraction (guests are usually admitted right up until closing time).

Continued on page 34

ONE-DAY SCHEDULE

Continued from page 33

MAGIC KINDGOM MUSTS:

Here's a list of the attractions that put the magic in the Magic Kingdom. Note that these are all Fastpass+ attractions:

- Splash Mountain
- Big Thunder Mountain Railroad
- The Haunted Mansion
- Pirates of the Caribbean
- Peter Pan's Flight
- It's a Small World
- Space Mountain
- Buzz Lightyear's Space Ranger Spin
- The Many Adventures of Winnie the Pooh
- Seven Dwarfs Mine Train
- Under the Sea—Journey of The Little Mermaid
- Happily Ever After (fireworks)

More FASTPASS+ ATTRACTIONS:

- *Ariel's Grotto*
- *The Barnstormer*
- *Dumbo the Flying Elephant*
- *Enchanted Tales with Belle*
- *Jungle Cruise*
- *Mad Tea Party*
- *The Magic Carpets of Aladdin*
- *Mickey's PhilharMagic*
- *Monsters, Inc. Laugh Floor*
- *Princess Fairytale Hall*
- *Tomorrowland Speedway*
- *Town Square Theater*

LINE BUSTERS:
Even when the park is packed, there are some attractions with shorter or faster-moving lines. Among them are Tomorrowland Transit Authority PeopleMover, Walt Disney World Railroad, The Enchanted Tiki Room, Carousel of Progress, Country Bear Jamboree, Mickey's PhilharMagic, It's a Small World, and Tom Sawyer Island.

IF YOU HAVE YOUNG CHILDREN:

- Head directly to Fantasyland (walk right through the Castle if you can) and visit It's a Small World, Peter Pan, The Many Adventures of Winnie the Pooh, Under the Sea—Journey of The Little Mermaid, and Dumbo. Cool off at Casey Jr. Splash 'N' Soak Station.

- Stop for a spin in a teacup or a ride on Prince Charming Carrousel on the way to Frontierland. Sing along with Big Al and the gang at the Country Bear Jamboree.

- Check the schedule for Mickey's Royal Friendship Faire, the Castle stage show.

- Line up for the afternoon parade about 30 minutes early. Or skip the parade, finish up Fantasyland, and take a magic carpet ride in Adventureland. If it's hot (and your tot has swim diapers), head to the tiki statues near Jungle Cruise. They spit cool water!

- Most little ones enjoy Tom Sawyer Island and the Walt Disney World Railroad, too.

ONE-DAY SCHEDULE

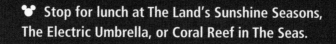

❤ If you haven't booked Fastpass+ assignments, you can do so via your smartphone or tablet and/or a park kiosk. Check a guidemap for locations. Then make a beeline for Future World's Soarin' Around the World and Test Track. Guests with no health issues and no susceptibility to motion sickness *whatsoever* should experience the out-of-this-world adventure known as the "highly intense" Mission: SPACE Orange Team. (Otherwise, ride Mission: SPACE Green Team—the gentler, non-spinning version.) Follow it up with The Seas with Nemo & Friends.

❤ World Showcase generally opens at 11 A.M., but Norway's Frozen Ever After attraction and Mexico's Gran Fiesta Tour boat ride welcome guests a bit earlier. Check a Times Guide and arrive as soon as possible. Try to book Fastpass+ for Frozen as far in advance as you can.

❤ Stop for lunch at The Land's Sunshine Seasons, The Electric Umbrella, or Coral Reef in The Seas.

❤ After exploring The Land, take time to screen the Disney & Pixar Short Film Festival in the Imagination pavilion. Afterward, visit ImageWorks, a small, high-tech playground. Kids love it—almost as much as they do the enthralling "leap frog" fountains just outside the pavilion.

❤ If you're up for some pin trading (or shopping), stop by Pin Central in Innoventions Plaza. (Workers displaying pins are always willing to swap Disney pins.)

❤ Check out Spaceship Earth before heading to Innoventions. If the Colortopia exhibit is open for business, pay it a visit.

❤ Make your way back to World Showcase by early evening and start your world tour at Canada. Proceed counterclockwise around the lagoon. Don't miss the *Impressions de France* movie in the France pavilion. And take in as much live entertainment as you can—World Showcase has a lot to offer!

❤ After dinner, scope out a spot to watch IllumiNations, the park's nighttime spectacular. (There are excellent viewing locations all around World Showcase Lagoon.) Return to your viewing spot about 30 to 40 minutes before the show.

TIMING TIP: If you have a World Showcase restaurant reservation, allow 30 to 40 minutes to get there from the front gate. Taking a FriendShip water taxi can save some time, but it isn't much faster than brisk walking.

Continued on page 36

Continued from page 35

EPCOT ESSENTIALS:

There is a lot to see and do at Disney's discovery park. Don't leave without investigating these outstanding attractions:

- Soarin' Around the World
- Frozen Ever After
- Test Track
- Spaceship Earth
- Turtle Talk with Crush
- Disney & Pixar Short Film Festival
- Living with the Land
- IllumiNations—Reflections of Earth
- Disney & Pixar Short Film Festival
- The Seas with Nemo & Friends
- The American Adventure show
- Mission: SPACE ("non-spinning" version)

FASTPASS+ ATTRACTIONS*:

Group A:
Test Track
Living with the Land
Soarin' Around the World
IllumiNations
Frozen Ever After
(in Norway)

Group B:
Mission: SPACE
Spaceship Earth
Turtle Talk
Epcot Character Spot
Journey Into Imagination
The Seas with Nemo & Friends
Disney & Pixar Short Film Festival

LINE BUSTERS:

Tired of long lines? Go to Disney & Pixar Short Film Festival in Imagination!, the movies in France, Canada, and China (*O Canada!*, *Impressions de France*, and *Reflections of China*), or The American Adventure. The Spaceship Earth line thins out in the afternoon, as do the lines for the attraction inside The Seas with Nemo & Friends and Gran Fiesta Tour starring the Three Caballeros in the Mexico pavilion.

IF YOU HAVE YOUNG CHILDREN:

- Begin the day by visiting the Epcot Character Spot and exploring The Seas with Nemo & Friends. Then head over to Imagination! to ride Journey Into Imagination with Figment and experience the ImageWorks interactive playground.

- At World Showcase, head to Norway's new Frozen Ever After attraction. Afterward, hit Mexico's boat ride: Gran Fiesta Tour Starring the Three Caballeros.

- Visit the Kidcot Fun Stop in each country. Don't miss the koi pond in Japan and Germany's tiny village.

- If the weather is warm, let little ones splash in the interactive fountain on the pathway joining Future World with World Showcase or the spray zone in front of Test Track.

* At press time, guests could reserve a Fastpass+ time for 1 attraction from Group A and 2 from Group B. That may change in 2018. Visit *www.MyDisneyExperience.com* for updates.

ONE-DAY SCHEDULE

❤ Some attractions open later in the morning; consult a park Times Guide for exact times. Also, many shows here run on a schedule (e.g., For the First Time in Forever—A Frozen Sing-Along Celebration, and Beauty and the Beast—Live on Stage). Use a tablet or smartphone or stop at a park kiosk to get Fastpass+ assignments if you haven't booked them in advance. *Note that seismic changes are in store for this park— some attractions may not be operating during your visit. All details are subject to change.*

❤ Toy Story Midway Mania! is wildly popular. Arrive as early as possible and pre-book a Fastpass+ assignment if you can.

❤ Daredevils should begin the day with Rock 'n' Roller Coaster, followed by some eye-opening drops at The Twilight Zone™ Tower of Terror.

❤ Peruse a park Times Guide. Select a time to take in For the First Time in Forever—A Frozen Sing-Along Celebration. Arrive early, just in case.

❤ If Beauty and the Beast is playing soon, grab a seat. Otherwise, plan to come back later and go to Voyage of The Little Mermaid (if it is operating during your visit).

❤ Pause for lunch at 50's Prime Time Cafe or Sci-Fi Dine-In Theater (with an advance reservation), ABC Commissary, Sunset Ranch Market, or Backlot Express.

❤ See Muppet★Vision 3-D, followed by Star Tours—The Adventures Continue, and the Indiana Jones Epic Stunt Spectacular. Take tots to see Disney Junior—Live on Stage.

❤ If you missed Beauty and the Beast—Live on Stage, go now, and if you haven't hit it yet, be sure to experience Tower of Terror.

❤ If Fantasmic! is being presented, you want to get a spot in line at least 50 minutes before showtime. Note that if you choose to skip Fantasmic!, plan to exit the park before the last performance breaks. If you do stay for the show, know that you can meander through select shops while the throngs exit.

❤ Is Star Wars: A Galactic Spectacular happening tonight? Make a point of catching this stellar fireworks show.

Continued on page 38

Disney's Hollywood Studios

ONE-DAY SCHEDULE

Continued from page 37

Continued from page 37

STUDIO STANDOUTS*:

If you're short on time, be sure to catch as many of the following four-star attractions at Disney's Hollywood Studios as possible. Note that they are all included in Fastpass+:

Group A:
Toy Story Midway Mania!
Rock 'n' Roller Coaster—Starring Aerosmith
Beauty and the Beast—Live on Stage
Fantasmic!

Group B:
The Twilight Zone™ Tower of Terror
Muppet★Vision 3-D
Star Tours—The Adventures Continue

More FASTPASS+ ATTRACTIONS*:

In addition to those listed on the left, these attractions are classified by Disney as Group B:

Disney Junior—Live on Stage!

Indiana Jones Epic Stunt Spectacular

Voyage of The Little Mermaid

For the First Time in Forever: A Frozen Sing-Along Celebration

LINE BUSTERS:
When lines abound at Disney's Hollywood Studios, we suggest the following: Indiana Jones Epic Stunt Spectacular (the theater fits about 2,000 guests at a time); Muppet★Vision 3-D; For the First Time in Forever: A Frozen Sing-Along Celebration (this theater also has a high capacity); and Star Wars Launch Bay.

IF YOU HAVE YOUNG CHILDREN:

• Begin with Toy Story Midway Mania! if your child is old enough to wear 3-D glasses, followed by the Voyage of The Little Mermaid attraction (but warn kids about moments of darkness and a thunderstorm) and Muppet★Vision 3-D. (If kids won't wear 3-D glasses, bypass the Muppets and head directly to Disney Junior—Live on Stage.)

• Have lunch at Sunset Ranch Market, then watch the parade (if it is offered). See Beauty and the Beast—Live on Stage. Skip Fantasmic!—it tends to terrify tots.

• Catch up with Disney characters at Animation Courtyard and on Pixar Place.

* At press time, guests could reserve a Fastpass+ time for 1 attraction from Group A and 2 from Group B. That may change in 2018. Visit *www.MyDisneyExperience.com* for updates.

ONE-DAY SCHEDULE

❤ Guests who arrive at park opening may enjoy a good-morning greeting from Disney characters. Many shows here run on a schedule, so check for times throughout the day. If you want to experience Flight of Passage or Expedition Everest without a big wait, book Fastpass+ or arrive as early as you can. Check the schedules for Festival of the Lion King, Flights of Wonder, and Finding Nemo—The Musical. Note that if you haven't booked Fastpass+ assignments, you can make same-day arrangements with your smartphone or tablet and/or at a Fastpass+ kiosk in the park (pending availability).

❤ As you enter the park, pass through the Oasis and head toward Pandora— World of Avatar. Daredevils should make a beeline for Flight of Passage. Follow that up with a calming cruise known as Na'vi River Journey.

❤ In Asia, tackle Expedition Everest, ride Kali River Rapids, then visit the tigers at the Maharajah Jungle Trek and see the Flights of Wonder bird show at the Caravan Stage.

❤ Plan to arrive at The Festival of the Lion King theater at least 45 minutes prior to your preferred showtime. If possible, mingle with Mickey and Minnie (at the Adventurers Outpost) before seeing Festival of the Lion King.

❤ Stop at Yak & Yeti, Harambe Market, Flame Tree Barbecue or Nomad lounge (inside Tiffins) for lunch. Then board the Wildlife Express train to Rafiki's Planet Watch. Bond with Disney characters, catch the Song of the Rainforest, and visit the Affection Section petting farm.

❤ After experiencing Africa's Kilimanjaro Safaris, take a relaxing hike on the animal-laden Gorilla Falls Exploration Trail.

❤ Make your way to DinoLand, stopping to take in It's Tough to be a Bug! along the way. After riding Dinosaur, catch Finding Nemo—The Musical (arrive early). Take young children to the Boneyard before leaving the area.

❤ Revisit favorite attractions. Keep in mind that Kilimanjaro Safaris now operates day and night—it's definitely worth checking out after the sun sets.

❤ If you haven't booked Fastpass+ for The Rivers of Light, Animal Kingdom's nighttime extravaganza, get in line at least an hour before showtime.

❤ When the sun sets, watch the Tree of Life "awaken" and cap off the day with the park's new nighttime spectacle: Rivers of Light.

Continued on page 40

Disney's Animal Kingdom

ONE-DAY SCHEDULE

Continued from page 39

ANIMAL KINGDOM ACES:

An abbreviated visit to Disney's Animal Kingdom is enough to make anybody growl. The following attractions should help soothe the savage beast, er, guest:

- Avatar Flight of Passage
- Dinosaur
- Kali River Rapids
- Kilimanjaro Safaris
- Gorilla Falls Exploration Trail
- Expedition Everest
- Finding Nemo—The Musical
- Maharajah Jungle Trek
- Flights of Wonder
- Festival of the Lion King
- It's Tough to be a Bug!
- Winged Enounters

FASTPASS+ ATTRACTIONS:

Dinosaur
Expedition Everest
Festival of the Lion King
Finding Nemo—The Musical
It's Tough to be a Bug!
Kali River Rapids
Primeval Whirl
Kilimanjaro Safaris
Rivers of Light
Avatar Flight of Passage
Na'vi River Journey

LINE BUSTERS: When herds of guests mob Disney's Animal Kingdom attractions, there are a few places to escape the stampede: The Oasis, Gorilla Falls Exploration Trail, Maharajah Jungle Trek, Discovery Island Trails, The Boneyard playground, and Rafiki's Planet Watch. (You have to take the Wildlife Express train to reach Rafiki's Planet Watch.)

IF YOU HAVE YOUNG CHILDREN:

- Explore the Oasis on your way into the park. As you cross the bridge to Discovery Island, stop at the Wilderness Explorer Headquarters and get started collecting badges. Then go to the Adventurers Outpost to meet Mickey and Minnie.

- Stop by the Tree of Life to notice all of the animal carvings in its trunk. (Note that the show inside the tree, It's Tough to be a Bug!, is very intense and may frighten young children.)

- Eat lunch at Pizzafari or head to DinoLand's Restaurantosaurus. Be sure to see The Boneyard playground, Flights of Wonder, and Triceratop Spin (in Chester and Hester's Dino-Rama).

- In Asia, go to the Maharajah Jungle Trek. Ride Africa's bumpy Kilimanjaro Safaris. See the Gorilla Falls Exploration Trail. Then take the Wildlife Express train to Rafiki's Planet Watch.

- End the day by viewing Rivers of Light. If you don't have a Fastpass+ assignment, arrive as early as possible.

HALF-DAY SCHEDULE

Morning/afternoon at the Magic Kingdom*

🐭 Arrive early—Main Street, U.S.A., opens before the rest of the park. Use extra park time to shop, nosh, and catch the park's welcoming show: Let the Magic Begin. Where to go next? It's a big decision. Know that the area you postpone may have long lines by the time you get there. We like to start in Adventureland.

🐭 Visit Pirates of the Caribbean, then head over to Splash Mountain (if you don't mind getting a little soggy) and Big Thunder Mountain Railroad.

🐭 Visit The Haunted Mansion, and then (if you plan on staying through the afternoon) grab a spot for the afternoon parade, Festival of Fantasy.

🐭 Watch the Festival of Fantasy parade (and wave hello to Anna and Elsa!) in Frontierland. Or skip the parade and go to Peter Pan's Flight, Winnie the Pooh, It's a Small World, Under the Sea—Journey of The Little Mermaid, and the Seven Dwarfs Mine Train.

🐭 Head to Tomorrowland to experience Space Mountain. Follow it up with Buzz Lightyear's Space Ranger Spin. Take youngsters for a relaxing trip on the PeopleMover (but warn them that there will be moments of total darkness).

Afternoon/evening at the Magic Kingdom*

🐭 Check a Times Guide and choose a time to take in Mickey's Royal Friendship Faire stage show (at Cinderella Castle). And don't miss the Festival of Fantasy parade. (Warn little ones about the parade's fire-breathing dragon.)

🐭 Explore Town Square Theater. If the wait to meet Mickey Mouse is more than 45 minutes, consider coming back in the evening—or get a Fastpass+ assignment.

🐭 Start in Adventureland. Ride the Jungle Cruise and Pirates of the Caribbean.

🐭 Head to Frontierland. Do Splash Mountain and Big Thunder Mountain Railroad. Then see the Country Bears or Tom Sawyer Island (the latter closes at dusk).

🐭 Hit the best of Fantasyland, including It's a Small World, Seven Dwarfs Mine Train, Peter Pan, Journey of The Little Mermaid, The Many Adventures of Winnie the Pooh, and the Mad Tea Party.

🐭 Join the afternoon street party known as Move It, Shake It, Dance & Play It! if it is offered (on Main Street, near Cinderella Castle).

🐭 Pop in at The Haunted Mansion and see The Muppets Present ... Great Moments in American History before dinner.

🐭 Now it's time for Tomorrowland. Go to Space Mountain or Buzz Lightyear's Space Ranger Spin.

🐭 Catch Once Upon a Time—a festive light show that is projected onto Cinderella Castle. And don't miss the Happily Ever After fireworks (presented rain or shine)!

* For details on where to meet Disney characters, see page 137.

Half Day with Young Children

Start at Town Square Theater. Meet Mickey inside. If it's close to parade time, grab a spot on the curb. After exploring Fantasyland (do not miss It's a Small World), consider the Country Bear Jamboree. Watch Mickey's Royal Friendship Faire at Cinderella Castle. Soar on a magic carpet in Adventureland, then head to Tomorrowland for Tomorrowland Speedway and Buzz Lightyear's Space Ranger Spin. Cap off the day with the Once Upon a Time castle projection show (best viewed from the Castle forecourt).

Magic Kingdom

HALF-DAY SCHEDULE

EPCOT

Morning/afternoon at Epcot

❦ Head directly to Norway's popular Frozen Ever After attraction, followed by Test Track and Soarin' Around the World (this requires a bit of legwork, but it is worth hitting the park's biggies as early as you can). If you're up for the "intense" Mission: SPACE, go for it. (We prefer the "less intense," non-spinning version of the attraction.)

❦ Visit The Seas with Nemo & Friends and Imagination! paviions before moving on to World Showcase—most of it opens at 11 A.M. Save Spaceship Earth for later, when the line dies down a bit. When hunger calls, stop for lunch. See the countries that interest you most, making sure to see Norway's Frozen Ever After (if you haven't already!), the show inside The American Adventure, and Mexico's boat ride: Gran Fiesta Tour Starring the Three Caballeros.

Afternoon/evening at Epcot

❦ If you don't have restaurant reservations and would like to try for dinner at a table-service restaurant, stop by Guest Relations to make them. If not, consider dining at the nearby BoardWalk resort (it's a short stroll or FriendShip ride away). Dining reservations may also be made by using the My Disney Experience mobile app. Note that reservations are recommended.

❦ See as much of Future World as possible before heading to World Showcase. (Both sections of the park generally stay open until about 9 P.M., but some Future World attractions close at 7 P.M.)

❦ Spend the evening touring World Showcase. Keep an eye on the clock so you can secure a good spot around the lagoon to watch the evening's presentation of IllumiNations—Reflections of Earth.

❦ Avoid the crush of exiting crowds by browsing the wares in the Mouse Gear shop in Future World or relaxing by the Fountain of Nations.

Half Day with Young Children

Begin with a visit to Frozen Ever After or the Epcot Character Spot, followed by The Seas with Nemo & Friends (take a ride in a clam-mobile, see Turtle Talk with Crush, and romp in Bruce's Shark World). Follow it up with a visit to Spaceship Earth. If your child is old enough to wear 3-D glasses, take in at least the first film in Imagination's Disney & Pixar Short Film Festival. It's a blast! Visit the Kidcot Fun Stops throughout the park and stop by the miniature village in Germany. If there's time, take in Journey Into Imagination with Figment and ImageWorks in the Imagination pavilion (if they are operating during your visit to the park).

WHERE TO MEET THE CHARACTERS*

Epcot Character Spot (Mickey, Minnie, Goofy); **Across from Epcot Character spot** (Baymax, Joy, Sadness); **Legacy Plaza West, near Spaceship Earth** (Daisy Duck); **Mexico** (Donald Duck); **Norway** (Anna and Elsa, in the Royal Sommerhus); **Germany** (Snow White); **France** (Belle and Aurora); **United Kingdom** (Mary Poppins, Alice in Wonderland); **China** (Mulan); **Morocco** (Jasmine and Aladdin); **Showcase Plaza** (Pluto).

Characters subject to change

HALF-DAY SCHEDULE

Morning/afternoon at Disney's Hollywood Studios

❤ Kick-start the day with a visit to Toy Story Midway Mania!, followed by For the First Time in Forever—A Frozen Sing-Along Celebration, and trips to Rock 'n' Roller Coaster and Tower of Terror (just don't do the thrill rides on a full stomach). From there, move on to Muppet★Vision 3-D and Star Tours—The Adventures Continue. Check a Times Guide and try to catch Captain Phasma's First Order March, featuring Star Wars Stormtroopers.

❤ See Beauty and the Beast—Live on Stage and the Indiana Jones Epic Stunt Spectacular, then explore Star Wars Launch Bay.

❤ For a quick bite, stop at The Backlot Express or Sunset Ranch Market.

❤ If time permits, go to Voyage of the Little Mermaid and/or revisit a favorite attraction.

Afternoon/Evening at Disney's Hollywood Studios

❤ Begin with Tower of Terror, Rock 'n' Roller Coaster, Beauty and the Beast—Live on Stage, and For the First Time in Forever—A Frozen Sing-Along Celebration.

❤ See Voyage of The Little Mermaid; Star Tours; Muppet★Vision 3-D; Toy Story Midway Mania!; and the Indiana Jones Epic Stunt Spectacular.

❤ Explore Star Wars Launch Bay before grabbing a spot in line for Fantasmic! Or skip Fantasmic! and revisit favorite attractions or shops. Watch Disney Movie Magic (if it is presented). And don't miss Star Wars: A Galactic Spectacular—a truly impressive fireworks show. (Try to watch from a spot in front of the Chinese Theatre, on Hollywood Boulevard.)

Half Day with Young Children

Start with For the First Time in Forever, followed by Disney Junior—Live on Stage, Voyage of The Little Mermaid, and Beauty and the Beast—Live on Stage. Youngsters ages 4 to 12 can harness the Force at the Jedi Training Academy. If the weather is warm, take tots to play in the spray from the giant bottle near Pixar Place. Skip Fantasmic!— it's just too intense (and a bit long) for most tykes.

WHERE TO MEET THE CHARACTERS*

Hollywood Boulevard at park opening time (characters vary); **Animation Courtyard** (Pluto plus Disney Junior friends such as Sofia the First and Jake from *Jake and the Never Land Pirates*); **Commissary Lane** (Minnie, Mickey, Goofy, Chip, and Dale); **Pixar Place** (Woody, Buzz, and Green Army Men); **Hollywood Blvd.** (Donald Duck); **Star Wars Launch Bay** (Chewbacca, BB-8, Kylo Ren, and Jawas); **Celebrity Spotlight** near Commissary Lane (Olaf).

Characters subject to change

HALF-DAY SCHEDULE

Morning/afternoon at Disney's Animal Kingdom

🐾 Go directly to Pandora—World of Avatar to ride Flight of Passage. Then head to Asia to ride the thrilling Expedition Everest and the soaking Kali River Rapids, and hike the Maharajah Jungle Trek.

🐾 Experience Flights of Wonder bird show on the way to Kilimanjaro Safaris and the Gorilla Falls Exploration Trail.

🐾 Check a Times Guide to see when the Festival of the Lion King show is playing today. Plan to arrive up to 45 minutes before showtime.

🐾 Finish up with Na'vi River Cruise, Finding Nemo—The Musical; Dinosaur; and It's Tough to be a Bug!—though the last two are intense for tots. Take little ones to The Boneyard playground instead.

Disney's Animal Kingdom After Lunch

🐾 Check a Times Guide for Festival of the Lion King schedule. Arrive up to 45 minutes before showtime. Then visit Mickey and Minnie at the Adventurers Outpost on Discovery Island. Be sure to soar on a mountain banshee on Flight of Passage in Pandora—The World of Avatar.

🐾 Head to the Kilimanjaro Safaris ride. Then do the Gorilla Falls Exploration Trail and take the train to Rafiki's Planet Watch.

🐾 Ride Expedition Everest and Kali River Rapids, and experience the Maharajah Jungle Trek. Try to catch Flights of Wonder, too (the first performance takes place in the late morning).

🐾 Wander the Discovery Island Trails and see It's Tough to be a Bug!

🐾 Before dinner, dodge dastardly dinos on Dinosaur.

🐾 Watch the Tree of Life awaken and line up for the evening's presentation of The Rivers of Light (arrive at least an hour early). Or take the time to revisit favorite attractions.

Half Day with Young Children

Scope out animal life in The Oasis before stopping at the Wilderness Explorer Headquarters on the bridge to Discovery Island. Then go to the Adventurers Outpost to meet Mickey and Minnie, followed by a visit to DinoLand U.S.A. Explore The Boneyard and ride TriceraTop Spin. If time allows, take the train to Rafiki's Planet Watch, where kids can bond with live animals (mostly goats). The Flights of Wonder bird show captivates guests of all ages. And the Na'vi River Cruise (in Pandora—The World of Avatar) is pleasant for most ages.

WHERE TO MEET THE CHARACTERS*

Park Entrance at park opening (characters vary); **Cretaceous Trail** (Donald Duck); **Discovery Island** (Tarzan and Flik); **Discovery Island Character Landing** (Daisy Duck and Pocahontas); **Adventurers Outpost on Discovery Island** (Mickey and Minnie); **Rafiki's Planet Watch** (Rafiki, Chip 'n' Dale); **Upcountry Landing** between Asia and Africa (Baloo and Louie); **DinoLand Service Station** (Pluto and Goofy); **It's Tough to be a Bug!** entrance (Russell and Dug).

*Characters subject to change

Making the Most of Longer Visits

Longer stays allow the chance to sample some of the World's myriad offerings. Spend another day in the one park you most enjoyed. Lounge by the pool, go biking, or play tennis or golf. Go shopping at Disney Springs. Cool off at one of Disney's innovative water parks. Have lunch at a WDW resort, and try a special dinner at Victoria & Albert's in the Grand Floridian or at Flying Fish at the BoardWalk resort. Sample the restaurants at Disney Springs or spend the evening at the BoardWalk. Take golf, tennis, or surf lessons. Go fishing or horseback riding. Visit a relaxing day spa. See a movie. Participate in a behind-the-scenes program. Play a round or two of miniature golf. Catch a game at the ESPN Wide World of Sports complex. Or just sit back, chill, and enjoy your resort. For even more ideas, see our *Sports*; *Everything Else in the World*; and *Good Meals, Great Times* chapters.

How to Save a Rainy Day

Florida rain showers come and go with such regularity that you could set your watch by them, especially during summer months. They're usually brief, though torrential. Of course, there are times when gray clouds linger longer. Here are some ways to make the most of a soggy day:

- See a movie (or two!) on one of AMC Theatres' many screens at Disney Springs.

- Head for an arcade—most Walt Disney World resorts have one. Games are appropriate for guests of all ages. (The arcades at Art of Animation and Contemporary are larger than most.)

- Don your rain gear and go to Epcot. The pavilions in Future World house a bounty of sheltered diversions. Ponchos are sold throughout WDW for about $9 each. (Keep in mind that crowds at all of the parks tend to dwindle a bit during inclement weather—as do the lines for popular attractions.)

- Swap your shoes for alley-friendly footwear and pound some pins at Splitsville—a bodacious bowling zone located at Disney Springs West Side. They serve food and drinks, too. (See page 217 for details.)

- Consider taking in an indoor event at the ESPN Wide World of Sports complex. For information, call 407-939-1500.

Customized Travel Tips:
Traveling with Children

Tell kids that a Walt Disney World vacation is in the works and the response is apt to be overwhelming! Our guide *Birnbaum's Walt Disney World For Kids 2018*, written for children ages 7 and up, can be a useful resource for getting them involved in the planning from the outset. Filled with information about the World from a kid's perspective, it can be used as a reference before and during the trip, a place to collect character autographs, and a post-trip souvenir.

Walt Disney World ranks among the easier spots on Earth for families with children. Keep in mind, however, that kids under 14 must be accompanied by a guest age 14 or older to enter the theme parks; kids under 10 must be accompanied by an adult at the water parks. Note that kids under age 7 must be accompanied by a person age 14 or older in order to board theme park attractions.

Child Care: In-room child-care service can be summoned to all Disney-owned resorts. The service is available 24/7, though it is not run by Disney. For pricing and to make a reservation with Kid's Nite Out, visit *www.kidsniteout.com*, call 407-828-0920 or 800-696-8105, or inquire at your resort's lobby concierge. Another company, Super Sitters, offers this child-care service as well. In addition to resort babysitting, they can accompany a party during theme park visits. This allows parents to take older kids on attractions while the sitter keeps an eye on the younger ones. To reach them, call 407-382-2558, or visit *www.super-sitters.com*.

Children's Activity Centers: The Polynesian Village, Animal Kingdom Lodge, Wilderness Lodge, Yacht and Beach Club, and Dolphin resorts each have an on-site children's activity center. The cheery centers accept (potty-trained) kids ages 3 through 12. For details and availability, phone 407-939-3463 for all but the Dolphin. "Camp Dolphin" operates daily from 5 P.M. to midnight and accepts children ages 4 through 12. Camp Dolphin costs $12 per hour, per child.

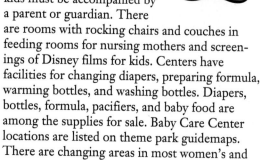

For information, call 407-934-4000.

Baby Care Centers: Located in all theme parks, these centers are for parents with young children. They are not meant as day care. All kids must be accompanied by a parent or guardian. There are rooms with rocking chairs and couches in feeding rooms for nursing mothers and screenings of Disney films for kids. Centers have facilities for changing diapers, preparing formula, warming bottles, and washing bottles. Diapers, bottles, formula, pacifiers, and baby food are among the supplies for sale. Baby Care Center locations are listed on theme park guidemaps. There are changing areas in most women's and in many men's restrooms.

Lost Children: Disney employees (also known as "cast members") will know what to do if a child starts to call for his or her parents. If your child wanders off, tell the nearest cast member and stop at the Baby Care Center or City Hall in the Magic Kingdom; at Guest Relations or the Baby Care Center in Epcot; at Guest Relations in Disney's Hollywood Studios; or at Guest Relations in Animal Kingdom. A computerized system allows for a detailed description of the child and his or her status, helping to reunite families quickly. It helps if your child has your mobile phone number, too. In emergencies, an all-points bulletin can be put out among cast members. The Guest Relations staff at each Disney park can help, too.

Parental Perk

Families with babies or small children should know about the "rider switch" policy (aka "baby swap") at the theme parks. At attractions with age or height restrictions, a parent who waits nearby with a young child while the other parent rides the attraction can go right on soon after the first parent comes off. Be sure to ask the attendant at the attraction's entrance. They'll tell you how to proceed.

Prepare youngsters for the possibility of an accidental separation. Direct him or her to contact the nearest park worker (someone wearing a costume and a name tag) and ask for help.

Refrigerators: For parents of young children, an in-room fridge is not a mere luxury, it's a necessity. Accommodations at all Walt Disney World–owned-and-operated resorts come equipped with a small fridge, free of charge. Many Disney Vacation Club Villas accommodations are equipped with full-size refrigerators.

Baby Food: Many parents choose to ship a box of food and baby supplies to their resort before they leave home. It is possible to purchase jars of baby food at most Disney resorts, but the selection is small. For a wider variety of foodstuffs to choose from, make a trip to the Winn-Dixie at 11957 South Apopka-Vineland Road. For addresses for a GPS, inquire at your resort's front desk.

Winn-Dixie and Publix, as well as nearby convenience stores, are also within a reasonable driving distance. Be sure to hire an authorized cab for the trip. Your resort staff can make the arrangements and give you an estimate of the cost. Another option is to order groceries from *gardengrocer.com*. They are authorized to deliver to most Disney-area hotels and stock a wide variety of items, including many organic, gluten-free, and kosher selections.

If you have a milk (or other food) need after hours, know that these Disney resorts have 24-hour snack bars: Grand Floridian, Polynesian Village, Dolphin, and Buena Vista Palace.

Bed rails: If you'd like bed rails for a child, it's best to request them in advance. Call 407-934-7639 and ask that they be added to your WDW resort reservation. Bed rails may be used on standard size beds, but not smaller pull-down beds. Inquire when you book your room.

Cribs: Some Walt Disney World resort rooms come with a small, portable playpen-like crib. Look for it in the closet. If it's not there, call to have one sent to your room. They're free, but somewhat flimsy. If you'd like something bigger or sturdier, consider renting a crib from Orlando Crib Rental. To do so, call 407-433-7770, or visit *www.orlandocribrental.com*.

Diapers: Each Disney resort has at least one shop in which to pick up diapers. If you're brand loyal, pack your own. (Consider shipping diapers

---

HOT TIP!

Small children may become a bit anxious when dropped off at one of Disney's child activity centers. If that's the case, plan to stick around until the trepidation passes. And prepare your child ahead of time. Let him or her know they'll be playing with other kids—coloring, playing games, watching movies, and the like. Reassure kids that you'll be nearby, and tell them what time you'll be coming back. That way, little minds can relax and have fun.

Tips for Tots

Walt Disney World is as toddler-friendly as it gets. Here are a few pointers to make it even more so:

PHOTO BY MIKE CARROLL

• Familiarize your child with Disney characters before your trip. That way they'll be more likely to enjoy meeting them and less likely to be frightened by them.

• Disney resort rooms are designed with little ones in mind, but we recommend packing baby-proofing items such as outlet plugs and doorknob covers or locks.

• Fireworks can scare little ones silly—and the booms can hurt sensitive ears. Pack noise-cancelling headphones to avoid discomfort. If your tot is spooked by loud noises, be prepared to make a hasty exit once the booms begin.

• Be sure to bring snacks when you head out for the day. It's tough to find toddler-friendly nibbles once you leave your resort.

• You will be asked to collapse your stroller before boarding a WDW resort bus or boat—but not on the monorail.

• Don't forget sunscreen that's sensitive to toddler skin. Pack a hat for an infant.

• Pack a small but treasured toy from home and keep it with you at all times.

• Don't underestimate the play value of a good splash. Take time to relax and enjoy the invaluable amenity that is the Walt Disney World resort pool. Of course, swim diapers are a must.

• Remember that your child may enter the parks for free until his or her third birthday.

• Pack a thermometer and your baby-friendly analgesic of choice—just in case.

Tips for Teens

When it comes to teenagers at Disney World, *The Little Mermaid*'s Ariel has plenty of company. Of course, be they of the fish or human variety, teenage guests have special needs all their own. Here are some tips from our WDW teen experts:

- Bring your own music source. It's perfect for the trip to Walt Disney World and for sitting poolside at your resort. But don't wear your earphones for your whole trip.

- Have some of your own money on hand. If it's your hard-earned cash, you probably won't spend it as quickly as you would Mom and Dad's!

- Pack a hat. Why? It's much easier to throw a hat on than waste time doing your hair.

- Try to get along with your brothers and sisters—even if it isn't always easy. Don't bug them to do the things you want to do all the time. Try to do things they want to do, too.

- One of the coolest things for teens to do is an Extra Magic Hours evening at one of the theme parks. They let you stay in a park after hours and ride many of the best rides with shorter waits! Another good thing to do at night is to go shopping, especially at Disney Springs.

- Attention, parents! Try to include your teens in planning the trip. If they get a say during planning, they'll be much happier when they arrive at Disney World. Also, don't make them get up every morning at 6 A.M. Try to give them a day or two to wake up late and lounge around the pool or a water park.

to your resort so you don't have to pack them.) Be sure to throw extra swim diapers into your bag each morning. You never know when you'll run into an interactive fountain on Disney property. They're necessary for pool use, too.

Resort Fun: Most WDW resorts have an arcade, while many have little playgrounds as well as kid-friendly pools (complete with pool parties), plus nightly campfires and screenings of Disney films. For details on special children's activities at Disney resorts, turn to page 230.

Strollers: Available for $15 for one day and $13 per day of a multi-day rental at stroller rental areas at each of the theme parks. (Strollers are not available for rent at the water parks.) Double strollers cost $31 for one day and $27 per day of a multi-day rental. Note that

HOT TIP!

If you have a baby, you'll need a stroller during your Walt Disney World visit. Although they may be rented at the theme parks, consider bringing one from home. It'll save you money and the hassle of getting one each time you visit a park. Plus, there's the convenience of using it all over WDW property. (Disney rents strollers at the parks and Disney Springs, but they are made of uncomfortable hard plastic and can't leave the place from which they are rented.)

When we do choose to rent a stroller, we call Magic Strollers (866-866-6177). For details, turn to page 67.

theme-park strollers are made of hard plastic and are not ideal for babies.

Strollers are not permitted inside attractions (they can be parked near each attraction entrance) and cannot be removed from the park in which they are rented. If a stroller disappears while you're in an attraction, a replacement may be obtained with a receipt. Guests have to pay only once a day for a stroller. If you rent one in the morning and plan to spend the afternoon at another park, just present your receipt for a replacement there.

If you'll need a stroller for several days, consider purchasing the Length of Stay rental ticket. It'll save you two dollars off the daily price, and it should cut down on time spent in the rental line. Simply buy the ticket on your first visit to a theme park and put your receipt in a safe place—that's what you'll need to show to get a stroller on the remaining days of your stay.

Disney Springs Marketplace and West Side rent single strollers for about $15 a day, plus a $100 refundable deposit (there are no doubles available here). You may also bring your own stroller into the parks.

Note: You will be asked to remove the child and fold your stroller before boarding Disney World buses and boats. There's no folding necessary when boarding the monorail.

Traveling Without Children

Walt Disney World has become an extremely popular destination for adults without children, appealing to singles, couples, and empty nesters alike. Disney has responded to the demand with an entertainment and dining selection for grown-ups without kids in tow.

Couples

There is a place for lovebirds at Walt Disney World. Actually, there are many spots in Walt's World perfectly suited to those with romantic intentions (provided, of course, that privacy is not a prerequisite!).

• Grown-ups love to roam the parks unencumbered by little ones and strollers. The Magic Kingdom's carousel-and-castle combo invokes the enchantment in true fairy-tale tradition. Epcot's World Showcase has the aura of a whirlwind tour (and the inspiration for a future trip?), with countries as exotic and far-reaching as Japan and Morocco. Disney's Hollywood Studios recaptures an era of starry-eyed elegance. And what could be more enjoyable than sharing a safari through Africa at Disney's Animal Kingdom?

  By day, there is romance in the theme parks for couples who are already inclined to hold hands; by night, the parks sparkle with an intensity that inspires sudden mushiness in those who never considered themselves the type, and that's before the fireworks.

• As Disney's themed resorts go about transporting guests to various times and places, they make quite a few passes through settings straight out of everyone's fantasy escape textbook—from the Victorian charms of the Grand Floridian to the exotic island getaway that is the Polynesian Village resort. You won't find a more inspirational backdrop than that at the rustic Wilderness Lodge, marked by geysers, waterfalls, steamy hot springs, and a grand stone fireplace. At the nostalgic

The Most Romantic Places in the World

WDW RESORTS

• Animal Kingdom Lodge
• Contemporary
• Grand Floridian
• Polynesian Village
• Port Orleans Riverside
• Wilderness Lodge
• Yacht and Beach Club

WDW RESTAURANTS

• Artist Point
• Cinderella's Royal Table
• Cítricos
• Jiko—The Cooking Place
• Le Cellier Steakhouse
• Monsieur Paul
• Narcoossee's
• Paddlefish
• Sanaa
• Victoria & Albert's
• Yachtsman Steakhouse

WDW LOUNGES

• Belle Vue Lounge at BoardWalk
• The Boathouse (dock seating) at Disney Springs
• Cítricos Lounge at Grand Floridian
• Il Mulino New York Trattoria Lounge at the Swan hotel
• The Lounge at The Wave . . . of American Flavors at Contemporary resort
• Nomad at Disney's Animal Kingdom
• Rooftop lounge at Disney Springs' Paddlefish

WDW THEME PARK SPOTS

• All of Epcot's World Showcase
• Happily Ever After fireworks presentation at the Magic Kingdom

BoardWalk resort, surrey bikes are available for romantic rides along the waterfront. And a peaceful stroll around Crescent Lake is a lovely way to cap off the day.

- The myriad of recreational activities that couples may enjoy at Walt Disney World includes tennis, golf, water-skiing, sailing, carriage rides, couples treatments at one of four on-property spas, and more.

Older Travelers

Disney World can sometimes be challenging for older travelers. And the heat, particularly in summer, can be hard to take. But with the proper planning and precautions, it's just as delightful for older visitors as for kids.

- Make special requests when you reserve your room. For example, if you need a wheelchair accessible room or grab bars in the bath—ask for them, and confirm requests before arrival.

- For slower times, visit the parks Monday through Wednesday. (Thursdays through Sundays tend to attract lots of locals.)

- The Florida sun tends to be brutal year-round. Always wear sunscreen (don't forget your hands) and a hat.

- Try to eat early or late to avoid the mealtime crowds. In the Magic Kingdom, select restaurants such as Tony's Town Square Restaurant and Columbia Harbour House. Or take the monorail to the peaceful Polynesian Village, Contemporary, or Grand Floridian resorts, where pleasant dining options abound (check ahead to find out which restaurants serve lunch). In Epcot, the Coral Reef restaurant and La Hacienda are pleasant spots. At Disney's Hollywood Studios, the Hollywood

Brown Derby offers a relaxing meal, as does Mama Melrose's Ristorante Italiano.

- If you need to refrigerate medicine, know that small refrigerators are included with the room rate at all Walt Disney

World–owned-and-operated resorts. Refrigerators can be provided at most other resorts for a small fee. Park First Aid Stations will store medicine, too.

- Don't underestimate distances at Epcot or Animal Kingdom; you may need to walk more than three miles in a day. Wear comfortable shoes and remember to take breaks.

- Pace yourself. It's smart to head back to your hotel for a swim or a nap in the afternoon and then return to the parks later on. The hotels connected by monorail are particularly convenient for this.

- Many Orlando-area hotels and attractions offer discounts to seniors and AARP members. Contact the Official Visitor Information Center (407-363-5872) for details.

- Be sure to pack extra doses of any medication—in case of travel delays or other reasons for an extended visit. Pack contact info for your doctors and copies of all prescriptions, too. It pays to be prepared.

Vacation Insurance

No one books a vacation expecting to cancel it at the last minute—yet sometimes life intervenes and it's simply unavoidable. So it may be worth working travel insurance into your vacation budget (we do). It may include coverage for trip cancellation and interruption, travel delay, loss of baggage, medical expenses, and more. Be sure to ask about travel insurance when you reserve your trip.

HOT TIP!

Even the fittest of seniors may want to avoid some of Walt Disney World's more physically challenging attractions. Do heed all warning signs at attraction entrances to thrill rides and consider steering clear of high-activity-level experiences such as the Magic Kingdom's Swiss Family Treehouse (seemingly endless stairs!), the Maharajah Jungle Trek, and Gorilla Falls Exploration Trail at Animal Kingdom (lots of walking and few places to rest).

Solo Travelers

Those who travel alone (be it for business or just for fun) can have as memorable a time here as they would anywhere else.

• Solo travelers with extra time should consider taking a behind-the-scenes tour.

• Many of the finer restaurants now have counters at which to eat—perfect for chatting with other diners.

• Sometimes, being a solo traveler can mean shorter wait times at attractions. Test Track is among those with "single rider" lines.

• Other opportunities for unencumbered travelers include parasailing and waterskiing (at the Contemporary), horseback riding (at Fort Wilderness), taking a spin in a motor boat, enjoying bass fishing (407-WDW-BASS; 939-2277) or surfing lessons (407-939-7873), and watching a game (at ESPN Wide World of Sports). Call 407-939-7529.

• Disney Springs's lounges and restaurants can prove to be fertile meeting places. The BoardWalk is another lively destination. Sports fans find its ESPN Club most inviting. And suds fans appreciate the home-brewed libations at Big River Grille & Brewing Works. Sushi lovers fit right in at the California Grill sushi bar (in the lounge section of the eatery).

• The lounges at most Walt Disney World resort hotels are relaxed and welcoming. The same convivial atmosphere prevails at the Tune-In Lounge in the 50's Prime Time Cafe at Disney's Hollywood Studios and at the Rose & Crown Pub (in the United Kingdom pavilion at Epcot's World Showcase).

Important WDW Telephone Numbers

Behind-the-Scenes Tours:
407-WDW-TOUR (939-8687)

Central Reservations:
407-W-DISNEY (934-7639)

Dining Reservations:
407-WDW-DINE (939-3463)

Dr. P. Phillips Hospital:
407-351-8500

Disney Floral & Gifts: 407-WDW-GIFT
(407-939-4438)

Emergency: 911

ESPN Wide World of Sports Complex:
407-939-1500

Florida Hospital Celebration Health:
407-303-4000

Golf Reservations:
407-WDW-GOLF (939-4653)

Recreation:
407-WDW-PLAY (939-7529)

Theme Park Lost and Found:
407-824-4245

Walt Disney Travel Company:
407-828-8101

Walt Disney World Information:
407-824-4321

Weather: 407-824-4104

Tips for International Travelers

GETTING READY TO GO

Visitors from outside the U.S. need not feel like strangers in a strange land when they arrive at Walt Disney World—even if they speak a language other than English. Information is readily available in many different languages. These tips may also be helpful:

- Free park maps can be found in Spanish, French, German, Portuguese, and Japanese at the entrance to all Disney parks, as well as at Guest Relations.

- Free translation services are available at all four theme parks and include a specially designed translation device called Ears to the World, Disney's Show Translator. The units are lightweight headsets that use wireless technology to provide synchronized narration at several popular theme park attractions. They are available in French, German, Japanese, Portuguese, and Spanish. There is no charge to use the service, but a $25 refundable deposit is required to borrow one.

- Several Disney resorts offer services for their international guests. Ask about them when you inquire about reservations.

- When making your reservations through 407-WDW-DINE or WDW-PLAY, ask to speak with a foreign-language host or hostess.

- Most WDW restaurants offer menus in various languages. Some have picture menus.

- Foreign currency exchange is available at Guest Relations in each of the theme parks. Traveler's checks may be purchased at the SunTrust bank in nearby Celebration, Florida.

- Disney's MagicBands can act as a charge card (as well as a room key). Purchases made at Walt Disney World will be billed to a credit card that is linked to the band.

- Many Disney employees are fluent in more than one language. Languages spoken are noted on employee name tags.

- Guests traveling long distances and through time zones should conserve their energy. It might be wise to relax by the pool on the day of arrival, instead of trying to fit in a full day at a theme park—it's never beneficial to start a vacation exhausted!

- Phone cards good for international calls can be purchased at several Disney World shops and in many resorts. Inquire at Guest Relations. Resist the urge to direct dial calls from resort rooms (see below).

Telephone Dos and Don'ts

It's a common practice for hotels to assess a surcharge for phone calls, and Disney is no exception. To avoid whopping bills, use your mobile phone, and keep these tips in mind for the hotel phone:

- A direct-dialed, long-distance call will set you back the cost of the call at the AT&T operator-assisted day rate, plus a 65 percent surcharge. The rate applies to both domestic and international long-distance. Applicable taxes are included.

- Prepaid phone cards are available for purchase in most WDW resort lobbies.

- There is no extra fee for guests making credit card, prepaid phone card, or any type of operator-assisted calls from a resort-room telephone.

- There is no charge to call an 800 number from a WDW resort room.

- Landline directory assistance 411 phone calls cost $1.99 each; a 555-1212 call costs $1.40.

- There's no charge to call from room to room within a resort—but there may be a charge to call one Disney resort from another.

- Cell-phone users, check with your carriers to avoid tallying up "roaming" charges. And switch your mobile phone from roaming to Wi-Fi whenever possible.

- All Walt Disney World–owned-and-operated resorts support mobile computing via laptop and tablet. Wi-Fi service is free.

Travelers with Disabilities

Disney tends to get high marks from travelers with disabilities because of attention paid to special needs. Here is an overview:

GETTING AROUND: Special parking is available for guests at the theme parks; ask for directions at the Auto Plaza upon entering. From the Transportation and Ticket Center (TTC), the Magic Kingdom is accessible by ferry or by monorail. All monorail stations are accessible to wheelchairs. The ramps are lengthy and a bit steep, but manageable.

Wheelchairs: Guests may bring their own wheelchairs. They also have the option of renting them at a theme park, BoardWalk resort, or from a local vendor. Wheelchairs may be rented in theme parks for $12 per day ($10 per day with a Length of Stay rental). In the Magic Kingdom, they are available at the Stroller and Wheelchair Rental. Epcot's rental areas are at the main entrance and at the International Gateway entrance. Oscar's Super Service rents wheelchairs at the Studios. At Animal Kingdom, wheelchairs may be rented at Garden Gate Gifts Stroller Rental area.

If you plan to visit the parks for several days, consider getting a multi-day wheelchair rental. Called a Length of Stay ticket, it comes at a $2-per-day discount. Pay for the entire stay when you first visit a theme park. Simply show your receipt the next time you visit a rental location.

The water parks have a small number of wheelchairs on hand. There's no charge, but the supply is limited. Guests must leave a valid ID as deposit. Disney Springs Marketplace Strollers & Wheelchairs rents wheelchairs for $12 a day, plus a $100 refundable deposit. Electric Conveyance Vehicles (ECVs) are available there for $50 per day with a $100 deposit. Wheelchairs at ESPN Wide World of Sports run $12 per day with a $100 refundable deposit. Walt Disney World Resorts with zero-depth-entry pools may have a small number of wheelchairs available to assist guests entering the pools.

Electric Conveyance Vehicles (ECVs) are available for rent in every theme park. They cost $50 for a day, plus a $20 refundable deposit. They usually sell out early. A word of advice: Practice makes perfect. So before you head into a thicket of park guests, take it for a test drive—and please do not exceed the speed of an average pedestrian.

> **HOT TIP!**
>
> For more information on the various services available to WDW guests with disabilities, call 407-824-4321, or visit *https://disneyworld.disney.go.com/faq/ guests-with-disabilities/attraction-access/*.

Equipment rented at a park cannot leave that park. If you will need to use it for the whole trip, consider calling a company that rents standard and electric wheelchairs, as well as scooters. Keep in mind that you will have to transport the wheelchair or scooter from your resort to your daily destinations. (Monorails and buses are equipped to accommodate, but some boats are not.) Two companies from which to rent are ScootAround (888-441-7575) and Walker Mobility (888-726-6837). Pickup and delivery (often for free or with a small surcharge) are available at all hotels in the WDW area (not just those on Disney property). In our opinion, guests are often better off renting from a local vendor or bringing their own equipment. The quality is generally better, and you don't have to worry about availability. The Walt Disney Company is not affiliated with, nor does it endorse, these companies.

Buena Vista Scooters has an on-property presence at Disney's BoardWalk resort. They have a few first-come, first-served ECVs. The cost is about $30 a day. It's possible to reserve in advance; visit *www.buenavistascooters.com*, or call 866-484-4797. These scooters have a two-day minimum rental period. The company provides free pickup and delivery to all Walt Disney World area resorts.

There are designated areas for guests using wheelchairs to view the fireworks at Epcot and to view the parades in each of the theme parks. Check a park guidemap for locations.

> **HOT TIP!**
>
> The theme park disability parking areas can be quite a distance from the wheelchair rental areas. If you require assistance, seek out a courtesy wheelchair to get you to the park's front entrance. The courtesy chairs are easily identified by their blue flags.

Accessibility: It's relatively easy to get around the parks by wheelchair. Most attractions are accessible to guests who can be lifted from chairs with assistance from a member of their party, and some can accommodate guests who must remain in wheelchairs. Consult each park's *Guide for Guests with Disabilities* (for a free set, write to Walt Disney World Guest Correspondence, P.O. Box 10000, Lake Buena Vista, FL 32830) for details about access, or check with the ride host or hostess. At the water parks, life jackets are available for travelers with disabilities.

All WDW hotels have accommodations equipped for guests with disabilities, including roll-in showers. Other features—which vary, depending on the resort—include wheelchair-accessible bathrooms, bed accessories, strobe-light smoke detectors, in-room Text Typewriters (TTYs), and more. The following resorts have zero-depth-entry pools: Art of Animation, Animal Kingdom Lodge, Caribbean Beach, the Contemporary's Bay Lake Tower, Grand Floridian, Polynesian Village, and Saratoga Springs. For help finding a hotel that fits your requirements, ask for the Special Reservations Department when you call Central Reservations (Voice: 407-939-7807; TTY: 407-939-7670).

RESOURCES: Visual Disabilities: Guests can get a handheld device that verbally describes each park as well as many attractions. Each requires a $25 refundable deposit. Portable tactile maps may be borrowed from Guest Relations in each theme park (with a refundable deposit). Braille guides, Braille menus at most restaurants, and Braille maps are also available.

Hearing Disabilities: Pay phones with Text Typewriters (TTYs) are available throughout Disney World; call 407-824-4321 or 407-827-5141. Sign language is offered at some shows. Call at least two weeks ahead for arrangements.

Assistive-listening devices that amplify attraction audio are available at City Hall in the Magic Kingdom and at Guest Relations in Epcot, Animal Kingdom, and Disney's Hollywood Studios. A $25 refundable deposit is required. Sites with assistive-listening systems are listed on park guidemaps.

Attraction Access

Most park attractions are accessible to guests who are able to get out of their wheelchairs (with or without assistance). And a growing number have queues that can be navigated in a wheelchair. When that's the case, guests are urged to do so. If a wheelchair cannot be accommodated in the queue area, ask an attendant to direct you to an auxiliary entrance. Such entrances are intended for guests using wheelchairs or with service animals. For specifics on this policy, guests should visit a Guest Relations location.

Captioning systems, including reflective and handheld devices, are available at theme park Guest Relations windows. The former project show dialogue onto panels; the latter provide captioning on personal devices at certain attractions. A $25 deposit is required.

Note: Trained service animals are permitted in all Disney parks.

Booking the Trip: These organizations specialize in assisting disabled travelers:
• The Society for Accessible Travel & Hospitality (2175 Hudson St., Fort Lee, NJ 07024; 212-447-7284; *www.sath.org*)
• Accessible Journeys (35 W. Sellers Ave., Ridley Park, PA 19078; 610-521-0339 or 800-846-4537; *www.accessiblejourneys.com*)
• Flying Wheels Travel (143 W. Bridge St., Owatonna, MN 55060; 507-451-5005 or 877-451-5006; *www.flyingwheelstravel.com*)

Vehicles: Both Wheelchair Getaways (*www.wheelchairgetaways.com*; 800-642-2042) and Mobility Works (*www.mobilityworks.com*; 877-275-4907) rent wheelchair-accessible vans and offer pickup and delivery for most Walt Disney World–area hotels.

GETTING READY TO GO

WDW Weddings & Honeymoons

Believe it or not, Walt Disney World is one of the most popular honeymoon destinations in the United States. Why the appeal? The resorts offer romantic stretches of white-sand beaches for evening strolls, fine restaurants, and a host of activities to rival almost any other destination. Add to that the fantasy of the Magic Kingdom, the wonder of Epcot, the glamour of Disney's Hollywood Studios, and the majesty of Animal Kingdom—plus Disney Springs and BoardWalk nightlife, water parks, and the nearby Disney Cruise Line—and it's not hard to see why Disney is tops with newlyweds.

After years of fending for themselves, folks looking to honeymoon here now have help at hand. A variety of packages cater specifically to newly married couples. For information, call toll-free: 877-566-0969.

The folks at Walt Disney World have also received oodles of requests from couples who wanted to actually get married at one of the theme parks. They responded by creating a program known as Disney's Fairy Tale Weddings. Today, couples can tie the knot in ceremonies at some theme parks.

The Yacht and Beach Club, BoardWalk, Polynesian Village, and Wilderness Lodge resorts also host their share of weddings. The newly refurbished Wedding Pavilion, on the grounds of the Grand Floridian Resort and Spa, offers a Victorian-style indoor setting with a prime view of Cinderella Castle and the Seven Seas Lagoon. The pavilion, which overflows with romantic ambiance, has seating for approximately 250 guests. Couples can fill their wedding albums with photos taken at Picture Point, under a trellis of climbing white roses, with the faraway castle in the background.

Weddings range from elegant affairs, without a hint of Disneyana, to ceremonies in which the bride arrives in Cinderella's horse-drawn Crystal Coach and Mickey and Minnie Mouse are among the guests at the reception.

At Franck's Bridal Studio, Disney specialists work with couples to customize each wedding. Among the services offered are cakes, photography, flower arranging, and musical entertainment. Franck's specialists can help secure accommodations, rehearsal dinners, bachelor and bachelorette parties, and more. FYI: Franck's was named for the character portrayed by Martin Short in Disney's *Father of the Bride*.

Honeymoon Registry

Launched, appropriately, on Valentine's Day, the gift registry lets happy couples plan their honeymoon. Gifts include theme park tickets, resort accommodations, spa treatments, and more. For more information or to sign up for the free Disney Honeymoon Registry, visit *www.disneyhoneymoonregistry.com*, or call 877-699-5884 during regular business hours.

For details about planning a Walt Disney World wedding and honeymoon packages, call 321-939-4610, or visit *www.disneyweddings.com*.

PHOTO BY JILL SAFRO

My Disney Experience

The folks at Disney have unveiled My Disney Experience—"a whole new way to plan and share your Walt Disney World vacation." All potential guests are invited to visit *MyDisneyExperience.com* or download the free app. After setting up a profile, guests can ostensibly use the site to book most elements of a Disney vacation, including hotel, restaurant reservations, and even Fastpass+ assignments for select theme park attractions. For details, see pages 23–27.

Fingertip Reference Guide

BARBERS AND SALONS

One of the most amusing places to get a haircut is the Magic Kingdom's old-fashioned Harmony Barber Shop. It's located beside the Car Barn in the Town Square section of Main Street. Cost is about $19 for adults and $18 for kids. Colored hair gel is $5 (kids love it). Treat tots to a very special "my first haircut" experience for $25. Hours are 9 A.M. to 5 P.M. daily. WDW resort guests may make reservations by calling 407-939-7529. Walk-ins are accommodated on a first-come, first-served basis.

Haircuts, coloring, manicures, and other services are available at Ship Shape at the Yacht and Beach Club (407-934-3260), Ivy Trellis at the Grand Floridian (407-824-3000, ext. 2581), Mandara Spa at the Dolphin (407-934-4772), the Kay Casperson Spa at Hilton Orlando Buena Vista Palace (407-827-3200), and the Casa de Belleza at Coronado Springs (407-939-7727).

BUSINESS SERVICES

Disney provides a range of services for those who simply must mix business with pleasure. Copiers, fax machines (also found at Guest Relations in the theme parks), and FedEx materials may be available at the lobby concierge or Business Center at many Walt Disney World resorts.

In addition, the Contemporary, Grand Floridian, Animal Kingdom Lodge, Yacht and Beach Club, Swan, Dolphin, and Coronado Springs resorts provide computers, printers, and Internet access for a fee. A video-conferencing center is located near Disney Springs. For more information, call 407-827-2000.

CAMERA NEEDS

Disney's PhotoPass photographers will happily snap shots of you with their camera (for details about PhotoPass, see page 133) or with your camera or mobile phone. Note that selfie sticks are not allowed in WDW parks.

Flash photography is not permitted inside any Disney attraction. Note that when capturing moments with Disney characters as video, refrain from using camera lights. (The lights are too bright for the characters' sensitive eyes.)

Camera Supplies: If you need a battery or a memory card, head to the Magic Kingdom's Town Square Theater; the Camera Center near Spaceship Earth or World Traveler at International Gateway in Epcot; The Darkroom on Hollywood Boulevard in Disney's Hollywood Studios; or Garden Gate Gifts in Disney's Animal Kingdom. One-time-use cameras are available at many shops throughout the World.

CAR CARE

There are three Speedway gas stations with convenience stores at WDW, all open 24/7. One is on Buena Vista Drive across from Disney Springs; another is on Floridian Way near Magic Kingdom Auto Plaza. The third, near BoardWalk resort on Buena Vista Drive, also has a car wash.

Breakdowns happen, but they don't spell disaster. All Disney roads are patrolled by police and security officers who can call for help. If you need a tow or other services, call the WDW Car Care Center (407-824-0976). The service is available to all WDW resort guests. Located in the Magic Kingdom Auto Plaza, the Car Care Center offers full mechanical services and free towing on-property, Monday through Friday, 7 A.M. to 7 P.M.; Saturdays 7 A.M. to 4 P.M.; Sundays 8 A.M. to 3 P.M. After hours, call 407-827-4777. For off-property car care, guests can rely on Riker's Roadside Services (407-855-7776) for vehicle towing, Riker's Automotive & Tire (407-238-9800) for repairs, or AAA (if you're a member).

DRINKING LAWS

In Florida, the legal drinking age is 21. Minors are permitted to accompany their parents to WDW lounges and bars, but might not be allowed to sit at the bar. In the Magic Kingdom, liquor is served at table service restaurants (lunch and dinner) and Be Our Guest Restaurant (dinner only). Alcohol is available throughout the other theme parks and Disney Springs.

Spirits are sold in at least one shop at most Disney resorts. Liquor may be purchased from room service at the Animal Kingdom Lodge, Contemporary, Grand Floridian, Polynesian Village, Yacht and Beach Club, BoardWalk, Swan, and Dolphin resorts; beer and wine are usually available for delivery at other resorts.

LOCKERS

Lockers can be found in the following theme park locations: to the right, just inside the Magic Kingdom entrance; beside Spaceship Earth (to the right, as you enter) in Epcot; near Oscar's

Super Service at the Studios; and just inside the entrance (to the left) at Animal Kingdom. Lockers are also available at the Transportation and Ticket Center (TTC).

Items too big to fit can be checked with the locker attendant at the Magic Kingdom, at Package Pickup in Epcot, and at Guest Relations at Disney's Hollywood Studios and Animal Kingdom. Cost is about $7 per day for small lockers and $9 for large ones (plus a $5 refundable deposit). Items may not be stored overnight. Lockers are cleaned out after the park closes.

Note: Be sure to save your rental receipt; it can be used again that day to secure a locker in any of the four theme parks.

LOST & FOUND

The extensive indexing system maintained by Walt Disney World's Lost and Found department is impressive, especially when a prized possession goes missing, whether it's false teeth or a camera. (Both have been lost in the past; the dentures were never claimed.)

If you lose (or find) something, report it at any one of these Lost and Found locations: the Transportation and Ticket Center (TTC), City Hall in the Magic Kingdom, the Guest Relations lobby near Spaceship Earth at Epcot, at Guest Relations in Disney's Hollywood Studios, Guest Relations near the Animal Kingdom park entrance, or the lobby concierge at any Walt Disney World resort. At Fort Wilderness, dial 7-2726 from a comfort station telephone; from outside the campground, phone 407-824-2726.

Items lost in a theme park may be claimed on the day of the loss at the park's Lost and Found, and thereafter at the Transportation and Ticket Center (TTC) Lost and Found station. To report lost items after your visit, call 407-824-4245. Hats, strollers, sunglasses, and Walt Disney World merchandise purchases are kept for one month; everything else is kept three months.

HOT TIP!

Nobody starts the day expecting to lose something. But trust us, it pays to plan ahead. Put your name and contact number on your valuables, especially cameras. Disney does a good job of tracking lost items, but it's a whole lot easier to pick a labeled camera out of the heap of lookalikes than it is to find your "little silver" one. (Yes, it happened to us!)

We highly recommend attaching contact information to all camera equipment. It makes it a whole lot easier for the folks at Lost and Found to pick your camera out of the giant, silver haystack!

MAIL

Postage stamps are sold at all WDW resorts; World of Disney at Disney Springs; at the Newsstand shop in the Magic Kingdom; at shops near the lockers in Epcot, Disney's Hollywood Studios, and Animal Kingdom.

The old-fashioned mailboxes in the theme parks are not official United States Post Office mailboxes, but postcards and letters (with postage) can be mailed from them. Postmarks read "Lake Buena Vista," not "Walt Disney World." Note: Don't mail anything time-sensitive —it takes much longer for mail to reach its destination when sent from here.

Mail may be addressed to guests in care of their hotel. The address for all WDW resorts is Walt Disney World, P.O. Box 10000, Lake Buena Vista, FL 32830.

MEDICAL MATTERS

Travelers with chronic health issues should carry copies of all prescriptions and get names of local doctors from hometown physicians. Disney is equipped to deal with minor medical issues. In the Magic Kingdom, next to the Crystal Palace restaurant, there is a First Aid Center staffed by a registered nurse; there is another such facility at Epcot in the Odyssey Center complex. At Disney's Hollywood Studios, the First Aid Center is inside the Guest Relations building at the main entrance. Animal Kingdom's First Aid Center is located on Discovery Island near the back side of Creature Comforts. **In the case of a medical emergency, call 911 and alert a cast member**. Paramedics will arrive as promptly as possible.

Walt Disney World resort guests and theme park day guests staying at other area hotels have access to services providing medical care. Centra Care Walk-In Urgent Care (*www.centracare.org*), owned and operated by Florida Hospital, has 20 area locations, most near pharmacies and with X-ray facilities. Guests in need of additional care will be transported to the hospital if necessary.

The main facility is at 12500 South Apopka Vineland Road (407-934-2273; close to Disney Springs and Hotel Plaza Boulevard) and is open 8 A.M. to midnight weekdays and 8 A.M. to 8 P.M. weekends. The Centra Care Walk-In facility at 8014 Conroy-Windermere Road (407-291-8975; near the resorts at Universal Studios Orlando) is open 8 A.M. to 8 P.M. weekdays and 8 A.M. to 5 P.M. on weekends. One location in Kissimmee is at 8201 W. Irlo Bronson Highway (407-465-0846). It's open 8 A.M. to 8 P.M. weekdays and 8 A.M. to 5 P.M. weekends. There is also a 24-hour in-room physician service (407-238-2000).

Round-trip courtesy transportation is provided from most area hotels to Centra Care clinics, and there is a no-tipping policy. Waits in clinics can be lengthy, but drivers can call ahead to learn which has the shortest wait. The most common maladies reported by Disney guests? Sunburn, blisters, fevers, earaches, and injuries from falls. For emergencies, alert a cast member and dial 911.

For Diabetics: All Disney parks and resorts can provide refrigeration services for insulin. WDW–owned-and-operated resort accommodations have refrigerators, and small refrigerators may be rented at most other resorts for a small fee. The fee may be waived for folks who need the fridge to store medicine, but a doctor's note may be required.

Prescriptions: Turner Drugs (407-828-8125) delivers medications to many area resorts, including those on Disney property.

MONEY

Cash, traveler's checks, American Express, MasterCard, Visa, Discover Card, Diner's Club, JCB Card, Disney Dollars, and Disney gift cards are accepted as payment for most WDW charges.

Guests staying at a WDW–owned-and-operated resort enjoy a purchasing perk: Provide a major credit card at check-in and a MagicBand or hotel ID may be used to cover most expenses incurred at Disney World. No need to carry a wallet! (They may be used to make purchases until midnight after you check out.) Day guests may buy Magic-Bands (about $13 each) and use them to make purchases, too. Just go to a My Disney Experience Service Center in any theme park and ask to link your valid MagicBand with a major credit card.

ATMs: Automated teller machines are scattered throughout WDW. Theme park locations include Magic Kingdom (near the locker rental, in City Hall on Main Street, U.S.A., in Frontierland near the Shootin' Arcade, and in the Space Mountain shop in Tomorrowland); Epcot (near the main entrance, on the path between Future World and World Showcase, at the American Adventure, and at International Gateway); Disney's Hollywood Studios (at the entrance and near Keystone Clothiers); and Animal Kingdom (near the entrance and by Chester & Hester's); plus the Transportation & Ticket Center (TTC) near the Magic Kingdom. Most resorts have ATMs; the Fort Wilderness ATM is at Pioneer Hall. There are three at Disney Springs: next to Tren-D in the Marketplace, and near the West Side's House of Blues and Starbucks. Most bank cards and credit cards are accepted; fees range from $2 to $3 (free for Chase customers).

Note: It's always a good idea to notify your bank that you'll be using your debit (or credit) card while on vacation. That should keep fraud protection software from freezing your account when you use it outside your home banking zone.

Banking: SunTrust, in Celebration, FL (about 4 miles from Disney Springs), offers a variety of services. Guests can get cash advances up to $5,000 on MasterCard, Discover, and Visa credit cards; receive incoming wire transfers up to $3,000 (for a $50 fee); and cash, replace, or purchase American Express traveler's checks. Fees may apply. This branch is open from 9 A.M. to 4 P.M. Monday through Thursday, 9 A.M. until 6 P.M. Fridays, and 9 A.M. to 12 P.M. on Saturdays; drive-through is open Monday through Friday from 8 A.M. to 6 P.M. It's located on Celebration Water Tower Place, 74 Blake Blvd., Celebration, FL; 407-964-3333.

Disney Dollars: While Disney stopped selling Disney Dollars in May 2016, Mickey's money may still be used for purchases at most Walt Disney World shops, eateries, and resorts.

Traveler's Checks: Even the most careful vacationer occasionally loses a wallet. Traveler's checks can take the sting out of that loss. Look for promotions by banks at home in the months preceding a vacation to see if one of the major brands—American Express, MasterCard, Visa, Citibank, and Bank of America—is available free. Stash the receipt bearing the check numbers in a place separate from the checks themselves, along with a piece of identification such as a duplicate driver's license or a spare credit card to speed the refund process should your checks get lost.

To purchase, cash, or replace American Express traveler's checks, guests may go to the SunTrust bank in Celebration, Florida. (If you do not have a record of the check numbers, first contact the place where you purchased the traveler's checks. Then, an American Express referral number is required; call 800-221-7282.)

Foreign Currency Exchange: Up to $50 per person in foreign currency may be exchanged daily at Guest Relations in the theme parks, and up to $500 at the Concierge desk at Disney resorts.

PETS

No pets (other than trained service animals) are allowed in the theme parks, Disney Springs, or the resorts, except at certain Fort Wilderness campsites. Of course, that's no reason to leave Fifi or Fido at home—especially when you can treat them to a pampered getaway at the new Best Friends Pet Resort, a sprawling luxury facility (don't call it a kennel!) complete with cat condos, doggy suites, and special accommodations for "pocket pets," including birds and hamsters. Cats or dogs from shared households may share quarters, but cats and dogs are not permitted to cohabitate.

The facility, which is now the only place to board animals at Walt Disney World, provides a full range of hospitality services, including day care (boarding in suites), grooming services, and doggy day camp (group sessions where pups play games and frolic with other dogs under the supervision of a trained animal counselor).

Best Friends Pet Resort is located at 2510 Bonnet Creek Parkway, across from Disney's Port Orleans resort. Its services are available to everyone, but guests staying at Walt Disney World resorts net discounts. Indoor boarding (which includes two walks) costs $39 per day for Walt Disney World resort guests; indoor/outdoor boarding (with one walk) runs $44 a day; vacation villas (one walk, play group, flat-screen TV, and a turndown biscuit) cost $66, and VIP luxury suites (two walks, two play groups, flat-screen TV, webcam, and bedtime story) cost $81 a day (and, with a 3-day minimum, they throw in a "Go Home Fresh" grooming service).

To prevent separation anxiety, guests are encouraged to visit their pets during regular operating hours. Though hours vary, Best Friends is usually open from about one hour before the earliest theme park opening to about one hour after the latest park closing. The center is not open to the public 24 hours, but it is staffed around the clock (a handy service for guests experiencing travel delays or other emergencies). There are several certified veterinary technicians on staff, and all associates are trained in animal first aid. For directions, details on services, further information, or to make reservations, visit *www.bestfriendspetcare.com/waltdisneyworldresort/*, or call 407-209-3126.

Be sure to bring along your pet's certificate of vaccinations, since Florida law requires proof of immunization for animals involved in biting incidents. Elderly pets must be in good health with bladder and bowel control, and be mobile. Pack your pet's favorite blanket or toy, too. And *never* leave your pet in the car—it is extremely dangerous, and it's against the law.

Outside Walt Disney World: A few hotels in the Orlando area, including the Rosen Inn at Pointe Orlando, let pets stay with guests (there is a $15 pet fee, plus tax, per night; 407-996-8585). Call Visit Orlando (407-363-5872) for more pet-friendly hotels.

RELIGIOUS SERVICES

Though religious services are occasionally offered on Disney property, regular services are available at local houses of worship.

Protestant: Sundays at 8 A.M., 9:30 A.M., and 11 A.M. at the Community Presbyterian Church, 511 Celebration Ave., Celebration, FL; 407-566-1633; *www.commpres.org*.

Muslim: Prayer takes place five times a day at the Islamic Center of Orlando, 11543 Ruby Lake Rd.; 407-238-2700; *www.icorlando.org*.

Catholic: The closest Catholic church is Mary, Queen of the Universe Shrine, 2½ miles southeast of Lake Buena Vista, at 8300 Vineland Ave. This church seats 2,000 people. For mass times, visit *www.maryqueenoftheuniverse.org*, or call 407-239-6600.

Jewish: Reform services are held at the Congregation of Reform Judaism (928 Malone Dr., Orlando; 407-645-0444; *www.crjorlando.org*), near Winter Park, about 20 miles from WDW. Conservative services are held at Temple Ohalei Rivka, aka the Southwest Orlando Jewish Congregation (11200 South Apopka Vineland Rd.; 407-239-5444; *www.sojc.com*), about two miles from Disney Springs.

SHOPPING FOR NECESSITIES

At least one shop in every WDW resort stocks a small selection of toiletries. In addition, over-the-counter health aids, plus many other useful items, can be purchased at the Emporium in the Magic Kingdom; they're kept behind the counter, so ask for what you want.

Aspirin, sunscreen, and sundries are also available at the Mickey's Star Traders shop in Tomorrowland. In Epcot, a small selection of sundries is sold in at least one shop in World

Showcase and one shop in Future World. At Disney's Hollywood Studios, stop by the Crossroads of the World souvenir stand. At Animal Kingdom, you can pick up the bare necessities at Island Mercantile.

Local supermarkets include Winn-Dixie (11957 South Apopka-Vineland Road) and Publix (4870 South Apopka-Vineland Road). WDW Speedway stations have convenience stores offering some groceries, snacks, drinks, and sundries. It's also convenient (and cost-efficient) to have groceries delivered directly to the hotel (all WDW resort rooms have a mini fridge in which to store perishables). Our source for grocery delivery is *www.gardengrocer.com*. Note that the aforementioned companies are not affiliated with or endorsed by the Walt Disney Company.

SMOKING

Disney's strict nonsmoking policy became even stricter with the adoption of the Florida Clean Air Act. Smoking (including e-cigarettes/vaping) is prohibited in all indoor and outdoor spaces, unless specifically designated as "smoking areas." All eateries are smoke-free, as are clubs and lounges. Tobacco products are not sold in the theme parks. Guests older than age 18 may purchase tobacco products at some Disney resorts and Disney Springs venues (with government-issued photo ID). Remember, this is a statewide tobacco smoking policy, so if you venture off Disney property, the same rules apply. If you have questions about the smoking policy at Walt Disney World, ask a cast member. Marijuana is prohibited in all Disney parks.

TELEPHONE CALLS

Every time a local call is placed from a Central Florida landline, callers must dial the area code and seven-digit number. The rule applies to calls made within the same area code as well as for those that connect with other area codes. For local calls, it is not necessary to dial 1 before the ten-digit number.

Lost Adults

Occasionally, traveling companions get separated in the crush of the crowds, or someone may fail to show up at a meeting spot. When this happens, it's good to know that messages can be left for phone-free or battery-free fellow travelers at Guest Relations in any of the theme parks.

HOT TIP!

The point is to escape the real world, so turn off that mobile phone—or at least stick to texting. That way the magic—for you and those around you—will be uninterrupted. If you have to make a call, do so by the nearest public phone station. And *PLEASE* do not use a phone while experiencing any Walt Disney World attraction. That's just plain rude.

Local calls made from pay phones cost about 50 cents each. Rates charged by non-Disney resorts can vary quite a bit (for all calls). Ask about rates and fees before making calls beyond your resort. See page 52 for more phone tips.

TIPPING

Tips are no less valued at Disney resorts than at any other hotel—$1 to $2 per bag is appropriate for lugging luggage; $2 to $3 per person, per night for housekeeping services (include a note to avoid confusion). Gratuities of 15 to 20 percent (excluding tax) are customary at full-service restaurants. (If service is exceptional or otherwise, adjust accordingly.) Gratuity is included in the room-service bill at WDW resorts and some off-property hotels. Meals that are prepaid with the Disney Dining Plan (except for dinner shows and Cinderella's Royal Table) *do not include gratuity*—please tip your servers.

Give cab drivers at least a 15 percent tip for good service. Baggage handlers at the train station and airport expect about $1 to $2 per bag. The same goes for Magical Express drivers. The ride is free, but it's customary to tip when bags are handled. (See page 16 for details about Disney's Magical Express service to and from Orlando International Airport.)

WEATHER

Call Walt Disney World Weather Information (407-824-4104), or check The Weather Channel website (*www.weather.com*).

WILDLIFE

Florida is home to a vast array of fauna, including alligators, armadillos, snakes, owls, manatees, and more. Never feed wild animals. Doing so alters their natural behavior and is often against the law.

Transportation & Accommodations

The popularity of Walt Disney World has made the region around Orlando one of the world's major tourism and commercial centers, and transportation sources—from a state-of-the-art airport to an efficient network of highways— bring visitors to the area by the millions.

There's no doubt that getting to and around the Walt Disney World region can be confusing. The only more perplexing dilemma may be choosing the best accommodations for your group from the huge assortment of resort hotels and motels.

The accommodations owned and operated by Disney itself range from futuristic towers to cabins buried deep in piney woods. In between are resorts that evoke striking images of Africa, the South Pacific, historic Florida, the Pacific Northwest, the Caribbean, New England, early Atlantic City, New Orleans, the Southwest, Mexico, and the sports, movie, and music worlds, plus a sprawling, well-maintained campground. And that list doesn't include the many villas or the studios and one-, two-, and three-bedroom "homes" that can be "purchased" through a special vacation-ownership system (aka Disney Vacation Club). What follows should help travelers sort out the broad range of lodging options within the borders of Walt Disney World. Regardless of where you plan to stay, we offer this important piece of advice: Book your room as far in advance as possible. You won't regret it.

Getting Oriented

The Central Florida city of Orlando is the municipality with which Walt Disney World is most closely associated. Disney World, however, is located in a far smaller community called Lake Buena Vista, 15 miles from Orlando's business center. All Walt Disney World hotels and restaurants are located in Lake Buena Vista.

HOT TIP!

Parking lots are cleverly labeled throughout Walt Disney World. Yet many drivers still misplace their vehicles. Avoid being dopey: Always snap a photo or jot down your parking location!

ORLANDO-AREA HIGHWAYS: The most important Orlando traffic artery is I-4, which runs diagonally through the area from southwest to northeast, cutting through the southern half of Walt Disney World. It then angles on toward Orlando and Winter Park, ending near Daytona Beach at I-95, which runs north and south along the Atlantic coast.

All the city's other important highways intersect I-4, and each has a name as well as a number. From south to north, they include U.S. 192 (aka Irlo Bronson Memorial Highway), which takes an east-west course that crosses the Walt Disney World entrance road and leads into downtown Kissimmee on the east; S.R. 528, aka the Beachline Expressway (formerly the Beeline), which shoots eastward from I-4; S.R. 435 (aka Kirkman Road), which runs north and south and intersects International Drive, where many motels catering to WDW visitors are located; U.S. 17-92-441 (aka Orange Blossom Trail), which runs north and south, paralleling Kirkman Road on the east; and S.R. 50 (aka Colonial Drive), which runs east and west. S.R. 429 (aka the Western Expressway) leads to a WDW entrance near Coronado Springs resort (exit 8).

WALT DISNEY WORLD EXITS: The 40-square-mile tract that is Walt Disney World is roughly rectangular. I-4 runs through its southern half from southwest to northeast. Major Walt Disney World destinations can be reached by taking the I-4 exits suggested in the paragraphs that follow; off the highway, clear signage makes it easy for visitors to get anywhere in the World.

DID YOU KNOW?

When it comes to fashion, Walt Disney World is the biggest clotheshorse of them all. There are more than 2.5 million garments in its corporate costume closet, making it the largest working wardrobe in the world.

This road is congested more often than not. Keep in mind that construction work and special events will often require rerouting of traffic patterns on I-4:

- **Exit 64A**, marked "192/Magic Kingdom," leads to the Magic Kingdom, Disney's Hollywood Studios, Fort Wilderness, and Palm and Magnolia golf courses, as well as the Grand, Floridian, Polynesian Village, Contemporary, and Wilderness Lodge resorts.

- **Exit 65** leads to the ESPN Wide World of Sports complex; Disney's Animal Kingdom; Blizzard Beach; Art of Animation; Coronado Springs; All-Star Music, Sports, and Movies; Pop Century; and Disney's Animal Kingdom Lodge. It is also a good alternate route to Disney's Hollywood Studios park.

- **Exit 67**, marked "Epcot/Disney Springs," leads to Epcot, Typhoon Lagoon, Disney Springs, Lake Buena Vista golf course, Disney's Saratoga Springs Resort & Spa, the BoardWalk, Caribbean Beach, Swan, Dolphin, Yacht and Beach Club, Port Orleans Riverside and French Quarter, and Old Key West resorts.

- **Exit 68**, marked "S.R. 535/Lake Buena Vista," is the best route to the resorts on Hotel Plaza Boulevard and the Crossroads of Lake Buena Vista shopping center. It can serve as an alternate route to Epcot.

HOT TIP!

The cost to valet park a vehicle at any Walt Disney World–owned-and-operated resort is $25 per day (not including gratuity). Depending on the resort, there may be a charge for self-parking, too.

TRANSPORTATION & ACCOMMODATIONS

WDW Transportation

Walt Disney World transportation is extensive, with boats, buses, and the monorail all doing their part to shuttle guests around.

One of the system's hubs is called the Transportation and Ticket Center (TTC), located near the Magic Kingdom. Monorail, bus, and ferry service connect the TTC to points throughout the World. Day visitors must park here before taking a monorail or ferry to the Magic Kingdom. (Most Disney resort guests can bypass the TTC via direct buses.)

The monorail runs along a circular route near the Magic Kingdom, making stops at the TTC, Polynesian Village, Grand Floridian, Magic Kingdom, and Contemporary. A separate extension of the monorail system connects the TTC to Epcot. Bus service is the cornerstone of the WDW transportation system. It is efficient, if a bit confusing. With occasional exceptions, buses arrive every 20 to 25 minutes, from one hour before park opening until about an hour after closing; bus stops are clearly marked. Travel times vary, depending on the route.

Although Disney resort guests are provided with complimentary transportation to all sites on-property, that transportation is not always direct. Build in extra time for travel, especially if you have restaurant reservations or a Fastpass+ assignment. Also, know that traveling between resorts usually requires at least one transfer. Disney's Express Bus theme park transportation is available for a fee (see page 64 for details).

From several WDW locales, water taxis usher guests to the Magic Kingdom, Epcot, Disney's Hollywood Studios, Disney Springs, or between resorts. Boats depart every 20 to 25 minutes.

Should You Rent a Car?

If you plan to spend all of your time on Walt Disney World turf, you can probably spare yourself the expense. Towncar, taxi, and shuttle service from the airport to all area hotels is available around the clock. Within the World, an exhaustive network of transportation brings guests from point to point (if not always immediately or directly). Most area hotels offer their own bus service to and from Disney theme parks (inquire in advance about schedules and costs, if any). Note that strollers must be collapsed before boarding Disney bus and water taxi transportation.

For those planning to resort-hop within Walt Disney World or any attractions outside Walt's world, taxis and services such as Uber and Lyft can often do the trick. A rental car is an option, too. It is easy (but pricey) to rent a car at the airport: National (800-227-7368), Alamo (800-327-9633), Avis (800-331-1212), Budget (800-527-0700), or Dollar (800-800-4000)—but note that the rates are much higher than at other locations due to hefty airport fees. For day (or multi-day) trips, consider Alamo or National at the Disney Car Care Center (407-824-3470; free shuttle service is available) or one of the rental agencies that have desks at the resorts on Hotel Plaza Boulevard, or simply inquire about car rental at the front desk of your resort. It is also possible (and convenient) to rent a car from National or Alamo at the Walt Disney World Dolphin resort. Keep in mind that area traffic can be brutal—always allow extra time to reach your destination, especially if you have a reservation.

EXPRESS BUS TRANSPORTATION: Guests bearing annual passes and tickets with the "park hopper" option may purchase an Express Transportation ticket and travel between Disney theme parks via fast, scheduled bus service. Buses, which drop guests inside the park gates, offer unlimited transfers between theme parks. (This service does not include WDW water parks.) Single-day tickets cost about $19 per person and Multi-day tickets (good for 7 consecutive days) run about $29. Purchase tickets at any theme park ticket window or Guest Relations location, all WDW hotel concierge locations, Swan and Dolphin ticket desks, Disney Springs' ticket window, and kiosks at in-park check-in locations. Guests check in near the exit of Buzz Lightyear's Space Ranger Spin at Magic Kingdom, on the east side of Spaceship Earth at Epcot, in the courtyard in front of Rock 'n' Roller Coaster at Disney's Hollywood Studios, and near the Dawa Bar entrance in Animal Kingdom.

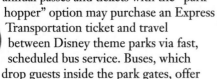

TAXI AND CAR SERVICE: Authorized taxis (run by Mears) are available for about $3 for the first mile, $2.40 per extra mile. Payment may be made with a credit card or cash. Ride-sharing services Uber and Lyft may transport guests at WDW, too. For assistance with taxis, go to your resort's bell services desk or download the Mears mobile app.

THE MONORAIL: The Walt Disney World monorail system is usually an easy (and to many, downright exciting) way to travel. There are two main loops, which converge at the Transportation and Ticket Center (TTC) stop. One loop connects the TTC with the Magic Kingdom (and the Polynesian Village, Grand Floridian, and Contemporary resorts). The other loop links Epcot with the TTC. Monorails run from about 7 A.M. until about one hour after park closing. Strollers don't have to be collapsed to ride.

    Timing Tip: It can take 5 to 10 minutes to get from stop to stop on the Magic Kingdom's resort monorail loop, making for a grand circle total of about 20 to 30 minutes. The monorail

may not run during Extra Magic Hours. Guests may pick up a Times Guide at a WDW resort front desk—it lists the monorail schedule.

Transportation Tips

- If you are staying at a Disney resort, you'll find travel info in a booklet in your room.

- Most buses are equipped with wheelchair lifts. Such buses have a blue emblem on the windshield and rear door.

- When using the WDW transportation system to get from your resort to a theme park, or from one park to another, allow an extra 45 minutes to get to your destination. Express Bus Transportation usually shaves time off park-to-park commutes.

- The interval between the arrivals of most Disney buses is about 20 to 25 minutes.

- Be forewarned: It takes a long time to travel by bus from resort to resort. Plan on a trip of up to 90 minutes and at least one transfer (at a park or at Disney Springs).

- Monorails usually run until one hour after the Magic Kingdom closing time (and they don't always run during Extra Magic Hours).

- Note that there is no direct transportation between Disney's BoardWalk and most other resorts. You must first travel to Disney Springs or a park and transfer to the appropriate bus (or take a cab).

- Try to avoid vacating a theme park just as it closes. Instead, plan to linger a bit in a shopping area, or grab a seat and watch the crowds crawl toward their respective buses, boats, cars, and monorails.

- If all seats are filled, guests will be asked to stand during transport on a bus or monorail (often at park opening and closing times).

- Keep in mind that the most obvious mode of transportation may not be the quickest. For example, it is often faster to walk to the Magic Kingdom from the Contemporary resort than it is to take the monorail.

- It's possible to rent a car from any Disney resort. For details, inquire at the lobby concierge desk, or contact the front desk.

- Walt Disney World resort guests who arrive with a car receive a complimentary parking permit upon check-in. The permit, good for the length of your stay, allows you to park at all parks and most other places on WDW property for free. Details are subject to change.

DID YOU KNOW?

The Walt Disney World monorail system—a 14.7-mile highway in the sky—has carried more than a billion passengers since 1971.

WDW Accommodations

With hundreds of resorts in the Orlando area to choose from, it's definitely a challenge to select a hotel. Here's our advice.

Weigh the Options: First decide whether to stay on or off Disney property. Many opt for a Disney resort because the conveniences and perks offered to resort guests are appealing (see page 66). Given that, there are still two major factors that tend to lure guests off property: vacation budget and itinerary.

Travelers on a tight budget may find off-property options that are quite reasonable. However, Disney offers rooms as low as about $97–$229 per night (depending on hotel and season), so choose off-property digs only if the price difference is substantial. WDW room rates are based on double occupancy. Additional adult guests will result in an increase in the rate. There is no charge for kids age 17 or younger.

Guests who will spend only part of their trip exploring Disney may also prefer an off-property hotel—one that's closer to the other attractions on their itinerary.

There's also the issue of what one considers deluxe. Disney–owned-and-operated "deluxe" resorts do tend to provide more amenities and services than their "moderate" and "value" counterparts, but do not always rival comparably priced accommodations in the real world.

Deciding Factors: Once the on- or off-property decision has been made, it's time to look at hotels. The big differences among on-property accommodations are in the size of the rooms and bathrooms, level of service, dining options, transportation options, recreational facilities, landscaping, location, and, of course, cost.

Consider how much time you'll spend in the room, whether you'd like to return to the hotel during the day, and if you'll have time to use all the amenities that are included. Parties with five or more members have an additional concern: how best to accommodate their group. It may be less expensive to reserve adjoining, value-priced rooms or a family suite (at All-Star Music or Art of Animation) instead of one luxe room or villa.

Ask the Right Questions: Once a hotel that meets all basic criteria is selected, it's best to do one last round of research, so there will be no surprises at check-in.

For example, ask about any possible hidden costs, like fees for shuttle service to and from Walt Disney World or taxes that may not be included in the quoted price. Though most off-property hotels offer transportation to Disney, the frequency and number of buses vary. Find out the exact schedule and the number of stops made. Ask where the bus picks up and drops off, too. Try to avoid those that stop in busy parking lots.

Some hotels advertise a misleading proximity to Disney. While a hotel may be a short distance from the border, the commute to the parks may be considerable. Get specifics. (Distance from your favorite park is also a factor to consider when staying on-property.)

Last but not least, do not underestimate the value of Extra Magic Hours—a complimentary perk offered exclusively to guests staying at all Disney–owned-and-operated resorts, plus the Swan and Dolphin (see page 22 for details).

Reserve a Room: Found the perfect hotel for your vacation needs? Book it before someone else does, and don't forget to ask about any special discounts, seasonal promotions, and cancellation policies.

A Room with a View

There's a lot to be said for throwing back the curtains and gazing at a breathtaking view, provided you have the time to appreciate it and your view is within your price range. The following is a breakdown of "views" you may select from at WDW resorts. It will help you choose the best category for your budget.

Although the categories vary, depending on the resort type, the "standard" is always the lowest rate available:

Value Resorts
Standard or Preferred = Location specific. The view can be parking lot, pool, garden, or anything else

Moderate Resorts
Standard View = Parking lot or landscaping
Water View = Pool, marina, lake, river

Deluxe Resorts
Standard View = Parking lot
Garden View = Landscaping
Water View = Pool, lake, or other water
Lagoon View = Seven Seas Lagoon
Savanna View = Animal pastures (at Animal Kingdom Lodge only)
Theme Park View = Magic Kingdom

Walt Disney World Resorts

Walt Disney World hotels fall into two categories: Disney–owned-and-operated and non-Disney–owned resorts. Of all the WDW properties, the Swan and Dolphin, Four Seasons, and the resorts on Hotel Plaza Boulevard don't belong to Disney. Services and benefits in these resorts are slightly modified (see pages 89, 104, and 106).

On-Property Perks: Walt Disney World resorts offer guaranteed admission (with ticket) to the parks in most instances (though there are times when a park hits capacity and no further admissions are allowed); use of the WDW transportation system; the convenience of charging most purchases to the hotel bill; free package delivery to resorts from most WDW shops; and the Extra Magic Hours benefit, which allows extra time in a select park on select days. Guests who stay at a Disney–owned-and-operated resort and arrive via air at Orlando International Airport are entitled to Disney's Magical Express service (see page 16). They also have a 60-day advance window for booking Fastpass+ experiences and attractions (non-resort guests have a 30-day window).

Room Amenities: Disney rooms come with a small safe, shampoo, phone with voice mail, a flat-screen TV, and free Wi-Fi. There is a hair dryer, iron (with board), small (unstocked) refrigerator (in all Disney–owned-and-operated resorts regardless of their category), and a coffeemaker (with coffee, sugar, and sweetened nondairy creamer) in many rooms. Laundry facilities, dry cleaning, and room service are offered in most resorts (for a fee).

Resort Primer

Payment Methods: Hotel bills and deposits may be paid by credit card, gift cards, traveler's checks, money order, cash, Disney Dollars, or personal check. Checks must bear the guest's name and address, be drawn on a U.S. bank, and be accompanied by proper ID (a valid driver's license or government-issued passport will do the trick).

Room Deposit Requirements: When booked through Central Reservations, a deposit equal to one night's lodging (or campsite rental) is required within 14 days of the time that a reservation is made. Reservations are automatically canceled if deposits are not received by the 14-day deadline. (Reservations booked less than 30 days prior to arrival will receive special instructions for deposits.) Reservations booked through the Walt

Online Check-in

Are you planning a stay at a Disney–owned-and-operated resort? If so, you can take advantage of Disney's online check-in service. Meant to streamline the actual check-in experience, the virtual service is available 60 days in advance of and up through arrival day.

Online check-in expedites the arrival experience by getting the pesky paperwork out of the way prior to arrival. Before you log on, know that you'll be asked to provide the following: the credit card that will be used for room charges, mobile number, address, arrival and departure times, the names of all guests, and room requests (but know that special requests are subject to availability).

With all that info already in the system, guests just need to show up at the resort and present a valid government-issued photo ID. In return, they get a welcome packet including MagicBands (if they didn't have them shipped home) and WDW info. There should be clear signs indicating the spot for packet pickup.

How does one check in via the Internet? Simply visit *www.disneyworld.com* and click on the checking-in section under My Disney Experience. Checking in online does not mean you can check in early. (Unless, of course, there is a room available—a happy surprise that has been known to happen.)

Disney World Travel Company are subject to a substantial cancellation fee. Ask about the cancellation policy when you book your room.

When booking by phone, guests may pay the deposit with a major credit card. Those who wish to use another payment method may do so by mailing it with the payment stub that comes with the reservation confirmation. Call to confirm that your payment was received.

Cancellation Policy: With the exception of Magic Your Way packages, deposits for resort stays will be fully refunded if the reservation is canceled at least five days before the scheduled arrival. Magic Your Way packages must be canceled at least 31 days ahead.

Additional Charges: If you need a crib that is sturdier than the provided Pack 'n' Play, you'll have to rent one from an outside company. For a recommendation, see page 47.

Check-in and Check-out: The relatively early check-out time (11 A.M. at all Walt Disney World–owned-and-operated lodgings) and the late check-in times (1 P.M. at the campsites, 3 P.M. in most hotels, 4 P.M. at Disney Vacation Club accommodations) often come as bit of a surprise. Guests who arrive before check-in time can pre-register, store luggage at Bell Services (without a fee), and head to the parks or relax by the pool.

Walt Disney World MagicBands: Issued upon check-in at Disney resorts (if not pre-ordered; see page 24), the bands (which double as room keys) entitle guests to use of all WDW

Magic Strollers

Brought to you by the folks behind Owner's Locker (above, right), this stroller-rental program is truly magical to the parenting populace. For starters, the strollers are all from the popular Baby Jogger City Mini and Summit series; they're delivered directly to  any Walt Disney World resort (and many other area hotels) by 7 A.M. on the day guests check in (when the reservation is made at least 24 hours in advance— otherwise delivery is by 10 A.M.) and picked up before 4 P.M. on the day guests head home; and the convenience of using the strollers anywhere and everywhere is a major plus.

Magic Strollers pricing is based on reservation length. For a price quote, simply visit www.magicstrollers.com and plug in your rental dates. We highly recommend getting the insurance, too. For a flat $25, it covers you for any damage or theft that may occur during the entire time you have the stroller. For details or to make a reservation, call 866-866-6177, or visit www.magicstrollers.com. To save $5 off a stroller rental, use the coupon at the back of this book!

Stash Your Stuff

If you count yourself among the merry multitudes who travel to Walt Disney World at least once a year, a system called "Owner's Locker" was devised with you in mind. Simply put, it lets you stash your vacation gear in a private purple locker in the WDW area and have it delivered to you each time you visit the Mouse. That means you'll have less to check at the airport (the locker is great for storing liquids and "must-check" items) and lighten your load overall. Say good-bye to lugging items such as sunscreen, baby supplies, rain gear, cooking items, non-perishable snacks, first aid supplies, toys, DVDs, rainy-day activities, and more.

It's called Owner's Locker because customers are given an industrial-strength, secure storage bin when they join the program (extra lockers may be purchased). After a one-time $75 membership fee—*waived for Birnbaum readers with a valid coupon**—expect to pay $105 a year ($10.50 per month) for the Moderate Plan (including one round-trip visit a year; $27.50 for each additional visit), or about $190 a year ($19 per month) for the Deluxe Plan, which allows for unlimited visits at no additional charge.

How does it work? As soon as you plan a WDW trip, schedule a round-trip delivery via www.ownerslocker.com. Your locker will make its way from a climate-controlled storage facility to your resort before check-in time. Call the Bell Services desk and expect the purple chest to arrive in minutes (don't forget to tip accordingly). Owner's Locker service is available at all Disney resorts and many other area hotels (though the business is not owned or operated by the Walt Disney Company). For details or to join, call 800-431-6588, or visit www.ownerslocker.com.

*The coupon at the end of this book will net you a $75 savings on the initial membership fee. You're welcome!

transportation (through the last day of your stay) and charge privileges (if linked to a credit card) to cover most purchases at Walt Disney World. You will be asked to program a personal pin code at check-in. Should you make a purchase on Walt Disney property, you will use that pin code to activate your MagicBand.

Note: Charges that are incurred on a Magic-Band or hotel ID after check-out will be reflected in a revised bill, which may be requested at the resort's front desk or e-mailed upon request. Swan and Dolphin guests may use their resort IDs to charge meals inside the two hotels only.

PHOTO BY AMY HENNING

TRANSPORTATION & ACCOMMODATIONS

Walt Disney World Resort Finder

	Name & Location	Setting/ Theme	Favored By	Romantic Hideaways
	Animal Kingdom Lodge* Animal Kingdom Area (page 99)	African wildlife preserve	Animal lovers—nearly every room affords a view of wandering wildlife Art aficionados—authentic African artwork abounds Disney Vacation Club members	Private balconies by moonlight Sunset lounge overlooking the savanna
	BoardWalk Inn* Epcot Area (page 91)	Turn-of-the-20th-century Atlantic City	Night owls—the entertainment options are numerous and right in the backyard Epcot lovers, who will appreciate the short commute Disney Vacation Club members	Moonlight strolls along the boardwalk A special fireworks cruise
	Contemporary* Magic Kingdom Area (page 76)	Retro-futuristic exterior, thoroughly modern interior	Families—the monorail whisks through it, and the Magic Kingdom is a short walk away Professionals, who can take advantage of the hotel's many business services Disney Vacation Club members	The rooftop lookout (available only to California Grill patrons), which helps make up for the resort's otherwise less-than-romantic atmosphere
	Grand Floridian Resort & Spa* Magic Kingdom Area (page 80)	Victorian seaside resort	Honeymooners—who will love spending much of their vacation basking in the resort's unebbing romantic atmosphere Magic Kingdom and monorail fans Disney Vacation Club members	Manicured rose gardens Honeymoon suites The Grand Lobby for a cocktail while an orchestra performs on the balcony
	Polynesian Village* Magic Kingdom Area (page 78)	South Pacific	Romantics—fireworks views and lush, tropical setting may make you swoon Vacationers looking for a hotel with a real resort feel Magic Kingdom and monorail fans Disney Vacation Club members	Beach swings for two Strolls on the beach
	Swan & Dolphin Epcot Area (page 89)	Beachfront whimsy	Guests who want many of the Disney perks but not necessarily the Disney hotel Bargain hunters—when WDW resorts are "peak," these resorts may offer discounts	A peaceful area beside the grotto pool waterfall
	Wilderness Lodge* Magic Kingdom Area (page 82)	America's grandest national parks	Sweethearts—love is always in the air at this resort Winter visitors—the warm, cozy atmosphere is even more inviting when the many fireplaces are roaring Disney Vacation Club members	Steamy, bubbling "hot springs" whirlpools The cozy alcoves hidden on each floor of the main building
	Yacht & Beach Club* Epcot Area (page 86)	Martha's Vineyard and Nantucket Island	Ambitious guests—those who plan to see and do everything Disney has to offer will like the central location Everyone—deluxe atmosphere and amenities appeal to all Disney Vacation Club members	The Yacht Club's peaceful gazebo Secluded whirlpools The beach—perfect for strolling hand in hand

Kids Adore	Dining Tip	Resort Category & Amenities	
The kopje, a rocky outcropping from which to spy on critters Story time beside the lobby fireplace Rustic bunk beds (on request) Animal-watching Lobby activities	Sample the exotic eats and atmosphere of Boma while savoring the sights of the savanna.		
The Keister Coaster, a 200-foot waterslide at the main pool The live entertainment on the boardwalk at night Board games in Belle Vue Lounge (available for use throughout the day)	Snack on Ample Hills Creamery's fabulous, freshly made ice cream while strolling along the boards. ❤️		
The "party" held every 45 minutes at Chef Mickey's fabulously fun character meals Watching the monorail whoosh through the resort Boat rides from the marina	Reserve California Grill for a time that's likely to coincide with the Magic Kingdom's fireworks show—or eat early and come back for the show with your receipt in hand. The view is amazing. ❤️	Full-service restaurants, fast-food spots, room service Luggage service Valet parking Swimming pools	**DELUXE**
Nightly marshmallow roasts and alfresco Disney films Having dinner with Cinderella and her friends at 1900 Park Fare Zero-depth-entry pool and a Mad Hatter–themed splash zone	Have a spot of traditional afternoon tea, accompanied by a scone, at the Garden View Lounge. ❤️	Beach access ‡ On-site recreation, such as boat rentals ‡	
The hula lessons offered in the Great Ceremonial Hall (on select days) The slide- and waterfall-endowed lava pool, plus a cool splash zone	The sushi served at Kona Cafe is second to none. Order it (and other menu items) to go and have a poolside picnic. (Place your order with a waiter near the counter seats at Kona Island.) ❤️	On-site kids' activities Most rooms sleep five guests	
The swan-shaped pedal boats The giant swan and dolphin statues perched atop their respective resorts A grotto pool complete with waterfall and winding waterslide	The Swan's Kimonos Lounge serves sushi with a side of karaoke. ❤️	Monorail, bus, or boat transport to all parks Movies Under the Stars (outdoor screenings of classic Disney films)	
Totem poles, an erupting geyser, and countless Hidden Mickeys—there's even a free tour to help guests find them	Sample Artist Point's signature dishes such as cedar plank Chinook salmon and aged buffalo strip loin, and housemade desserts: warm berry cobbler or warm doughnuts. Savor morning coffee from a fireside rocking chair.	‡ Except Disney's Animal Kingdom Lodge	
Stormalong Bay—the sand-bottomed, three-acre pool, with a waterslide and a neat shipwreck to play on	Cape May Cafe's bountiful nighttime clambake has many a surf-and-turf fan lining up for more. ❤️		

Name & Location	Setting/ Theme	Favored By	Romantic Hideaways
Old Key West Disney Springs area (page 97)	Key West	Guests looking for a homey, village atmosphere Disney Vacation Club members Those who appreciate roomy rooms	Private whirlpool tubs— they come with all accommodations but the studios
Saratoga Springs Resort & Spa Disney Springs area (page 96)	Historic Saratoga Springs, New York	Peace seekers—the atmosphere is meant to soothe Disney Vacation Club members Space seekers. The accommodations are generally more spacious than at other resorts.	Pretty gardens and meandering pathways Private whirlpool tubs— they come with all accommodations but the studios
Caribbean Beach Epcot area (page 85)	Tropical islands	Families—the colorful design, themed pool, and beach setting make this hotel ideal for families Pirate fans! The main pool and 384 rooms have a buccaneer theme.	Aruba beach—the hotel's longest, most secluded strip of sand
Coronado Springs Animal Kingdom area (page 101)	Mexico and Southwest USA	Conventioneers—which means more business services (and a health club), higher food prices, and slightly less family entertainment than at the other moderate resorts at WDW	The waterfront in the peaceful Casitas area The gazebo-style boat-rental dock at twilight
Port Orleans French Quarter & Riverside Disney Springs area (pages 94–96)	New Orleans French Quarter and Antebellum South, respectively	Lovebirds on a budget—the Riverside decor is like many of Disney's deluxe hotels, as is the romance factor, but the price is considerably less The French Quarter, which provides a peaceful, urban alternative	Any room in Magnolia Bend's stately mansions The peaceful gardens scattered about the Riverside quarters
All-Star Movies, Music, & Sports Animal Kingdom area (page 98)	Larger-than-life fun	Penny savers of all ages—these resorts offer fun, colorful theming, plus all the WDW perks, at a much lower price than at most other Disney resorts Space cravers—who adore the family suites at All-Star Music	All-Star Music's Jazz and Broadway areas (note that Music tends to attract more couples without kids than the other two themes)
Art of Animation ESPN Wide World of Sports area (page 103)	Classic and colorful Disney animation	Extended families and families with babies—it's great to have the extra sleeping area that comes with the family suites	The Drop Off pool bar is a sweet spot for a (quasi) quiet evening interlude
Pop Century ESPN Wide World of Sports area (page 102)	American pop culture	Budget watchers and nostalgia buffs—this sprawling resort celebrates pop history with bright colors and big icons Young athletes and their families— ESPN Wide World of Sports is located nearby	Sipping specialty cocktails poolside
Fort Wilderness Cabins and Campground** Magic Kingdom area (page 83)	Rustic woods	Seasoned RV enthusiasts—Disney's hookups are considered top-notch Families—who appreciate the modern amenities of the cabins, which fit six and fall into Disney's "moderate" category	Horse-drawn carriage rides The Fort Wilderness beach—perfect for viewing the Electrical Water Pageant on Bay Lake

❤ These resorts host character meals. † Known as "Disney Deluxe Villa Resorts" on *www.disneyworld.com*. Animal Kingdom Lodge, Beach

Kids Adore	Dining Tip	Resort Category & Amenities	
Crafts and games offered at Community Hall One super pool slide and poolside activities The pool's sand castle slide	Olivia's pleases all palates with a nice mix of pastas and fresh fish. The conch chowder is a yummy way to start a meal.	Kitchens or kitchenettes, restaurants, pizza delivery Luggage service Swimming pools and on-site recreation such as bike rentals Front-door parking Villas sleep 4–12	DELUXE VILLA RESORTS (DVC)+
The kids-only water-spray area near the pool Kid-oriented activities offered at Community Hall	Turf Club is a low-key, local dining room. Disney Springs's tempting array of eateries is just across the lake—and conveniently accessed by a walking path or water taxi.	Bus or boat transport to all parks Washers and dryers Boat to Disney Springs Movies under the Stars (outdoor screenings of Disney films)	
The fortress pool and Caribbean Cay Island The coconut postcards sold at the Calypso shop (real coconuts!) Pirate-themed rooms. Arrrr!	Try a kids' meal—it's served in a sand bucket with a shovel.	Restaurant, food court, limited room service Luggage service Swimming pools with slides	MODERATE
The Dig Site—which encompasses the resort's playground and main pool with its Mayan temple waterslide	To start the day in a pleasant way, consider breakfast at Las Ventanas. It's a bit quieter than the Pepper Market, and the sourdough French toast comes with pure maple syrup.	On-site recreation, such as bikes or boat rentals Movies under the Stars (outdoor screenings of Disney films) Rooms sleep four to five guests	
The pool, fishing hole, and play area at the Riverside's Ol' Man Island. And the "Royal Guest Rooms" rock! The French Quarter's Doubloon Lagoon—a sea-serpent-themed family pool	Sample the fresh beignets from the food court. You'll think you're in the Big Easy.	Bus transport to all parks	
Awe-inspiring, super-size icons— the movie and sports themes score the highest points Extra-large arcades Organized pool games and on-site activities for kids and families	Pick up a pizza at the pickup window in the food court and have a pizza party by the pool.	Food court, pizza delivery Luggage service	VALUE
The Righteous Reef soft-surface squirt zone Super-size icons from *Finding Nemo*, *Cars*, *The Lion King*, and *The Little Mermaid*	Dine in one of the loveliest food courts Disney has to offer: Landscape of Flavors. Indulge in made-to-order smoothies, hand-scooped gelato, and Mongolian barbecue.	Swimming pools Movies under the Stars (outdoor screenings of Disney films) Bus transport to all parks	
The state-of-the-art arcade Wildly oversize cell phones, yo-yos, bowling pins, and more The interactive water fountain near the playground	There are daily dance parties in the food court! At 8 A.M. each morning, the whole place does "The Twist," and at 6 P.M. guests may join cast members as everyone does "The Hustle."		
Pony rides, wagon rides, a blacksmith's shop, and campfire marshmallow roasts with Chip and Dale	Join the nightly campfire circle and roast marshmallows with Disney's famous chipmunk duo. Trail's End Restaurant offers hearty fare at a reasonable price.	Recipient of perfect ratings from *Trailer Life* and *Woodall's* magazines Bus transport to all parks Water transportation to Magic Kingdom	FT. WILDERNESS

Club, BoardWalk, Contemporary, Polynesian, and Wilderness Lodge also have DVC accommodations. **Wilderness Cabins are "moderate."

Rates* at WDW Properties

	Value	Regular	Peak
DELUXE‡			
Animal Kingdom Lodge			
Rooms (sleep 4 to 5)**	$336 – $636	$426 – $665	$436 – $768
Rooms–Club Level (5)	$558 – $684	$622 – $724	$701 – $806
BoardWalk Inn			
Rooms (5)	$429 – $680	$494 – $684	$555 – $767
Rooms–Club Level (5 to 6)	$624 – $936	$703 – $1,018	$797 – $1,165
Contemporary			
Rooms–Garden Building (5)	$400 – $647	$424 – $670	$458 – $703
Rooms–Tower (5)	$568 – $752	$602 – $745	$664 – $826
Rooms–Club Level (4)	$719 – $997	$745 – $1,087	$875 – $1,109
Grand Floridian Resort & Spa			
Rooms (5)	$574 – $844	$584 – $898	$684 – $1,072
Rooms–Club Level (5)	$688 – $1,214	$762 – $1,317	$917 – $1,528
Villas (4–12)	$559 – $3,224	$584– $2,992	$732 – $3,319
Polynesian Village			
Rooms (5)	$475 – $812	$520 – $869	$609 – $1,028
Rooms–Club Level (5)	$651 – $974	$717 – $1,090	$814 – $1,275
Swan & Dolphin (Rates were accurate at press time but are likely to change. Call 800-227-1500 for updates.)			
Rooms–Standard View (4)	starting at $169	starting at $189	starting at $209
Rooms–Upgraded View (4)	starting at $199	starting at $219	starting at $239
Suites (5 to 10)	starting at $369	starting at $389	starting at $409
Wilderness Lodge			
Rooms (4)	$325 – $698	$386 – $713	$464 – $819
Rooms–Club Level (4)	$543 – $847	$601 – $951	$713 – $1,097
Yacht & Beach Club			
Rooms (5)	$392 – $604	$484 – $661	$531 – $718
Rooms–Club Level (5)	$580 – $1,067	$683 – $1,018	$755 – $1,205

* Rates for certain days (including Friday and Saturday) may be higher than others. Call 407-934-7639 for details.

** Room Capacity: Numbers in parentheses reflect maximum occupancy based on existing beds. Playpen-like cribs can be requested for free in most resorts. Rates include up to two adults. There is an additional charge for each extra adult in a room. **Details are subject to change in 2018.**

Rates* at WDW Properties

	Value	Regular	Peak*
DISNEY VACATION CLUB			
Animal Kingdom Villas			
Studios (4)	$326 – $613	$364 – $689	$451 – $755
Villas (4–12)	$537 – $2,221	$549 – $2,521	$722 – $2,637
Bay Lake Tower (at the Contemporary resort)			
Studios (4)	$478 – $714	$538 – $740	$663 – $836
Villas (4–12)	$700 – $2,446	$750 – $2,950	$910 – $3,034
Beach Club Villas			
Studios (4)	$441 – $511	$471 – $543	$573
Villas (4–8)	$598 – $961	$638 – $1,278	$809 – $1,438
BoardWalk Villas			
Studios (5)	$441 – $511	$471 – $543	$573
Villas (4–12)	$598 – $2,453	$638 – $2,619	$809 – $2,659
Old Key West			
Studios (4)	$345 – $379	$388 – $427	$451 – $455
Bungalows (4–12)	$468 – $1,509	$513 – $1,752	$607 – $1,836
Polynesian Villas & Bungalows			
Studios (4)	$493 – $743	$533 – $828	$626 – $864
Bungalows (4–12)	$2,382 – $3,230	$2,560 – $2,807	$3,149 – 3,302
Saratoga Springs Resort & Spa			
Studios (4)	$341 – $433	$384 – $483	$441 – $515
Villas (4–12)	$463 – $1,711	$509– $1,931	$600 – $2,081
Wilderness Lodge Villas & Cabins			
Studios (4)	$409 – $473	$437 – $531	$564 – $595
Villas (4–8)	$577 – $2,649	$602 – $2,458	$815 – $2,727
Cabins (4–8)	$1,909 – $2,517	$2,026 – $2,335	$2,591

CALL 407-934-7639 FOR RESERVATIONS

‡ For information about suites, call 407-934-7639.

Note: The prices provided here were correct at press time, but rates are apt to rise. Charge is for one day, single or double occupancy. Details and prices are subject to change.

(continued on next page)

Rates* at WDW Properties

	Value	Regular	Peak*
MODERATE			
Caribbean Beach			
Rooms (4/5)**	$166 – $264	$199 – $323	$211 – $315
Coronado Springs‡			
Rooms (4)	$179 – $314	$208 – $343	$227 – $359
Port Orleans French Quarter and Riverside			
Rooms (4/5)	$199 – $296	$230 – $344	$250 – $356
Fort Wilderness Cabins			
Cabins (6)	$324 – $417	$376 – $439	$428 – $476
VALUE			
All-Star Movies, All-Star Music‡, and All-Star Sports			
Rooms (4)	$97 – $160	$121 – $186	$146 – $204
Family Suites (6)	$237 – $297	$291 – $354	$329 – $401
Art of Animation			
Rooms (4)	$132 – $174	$169 – $208	$182 – $229
Family Suites (6)	$315 – $398	$384 – $464	$415 – $529
Pop Century			
Rooms (4)	$112 – $177	$137 – $204	$159 – $227
FORT WILDERNESS CAMPGROUND			
Fort Wilderness Campsites			
Sites with partial hookup (10)	$53 – $73	$81 – $105	$128
Sites with full hookup (10)	$80 – $97	$105 – $132	$152
Preferred/Premium sites (10)	$91 – $119	$125 – $158	$168 – $175

CALL 407-934-7639 FOR RESERVATIONS

* Rates for certain days (including Friday and Saturday) may be higher than others. Call 407-934-7639 for details.

** Room Capacity: Numbers in parentheses reflect maximum occupancy based on existing beds. A trundle bed (for one) can be rented at some properties for $15 a day. Playpen-like cribs can be requested for free in most resorts. Rates include up to two adults. There is an additional charge for each extra adult in a room.

‡ For information about suites, call 407-934-7639.

Note: The prices provided here were correct at press time, but rates are likely to rise. Charge is for one day, single or double occupancy. Certain holidays and special events (such as WDW Marathon weekend) bring higher resort rates. Call 407-934-7639 for specifics. **Details are subject to change in 2018.**

2018 Seasonal Dates

When it comes to Walt Disney World resort rates, the calendar is a key factor. Traditionally, prices are higher during peak times of year (holidays, summer, school vacations, etc.) and lower during times surrounding holidays and when school is in session. Many resorts offer lower rates on most weeknights year-round. What follows is a sampling of dates for Disney–owned-and-operated resorts for 2018. For details or to make a reservation, call 407-934-7639, or visit *www.disneyworld.com*.

VALUE RATES APPLY: January 2–February 10 for Value and Moderate resorts; August 12–September 22 for Fort Wilderness Campsites; January 2–February 14 for Fort Wilderness Cabins; January 2–February 10, and August 24–September 20 for Deluxe and Disney Vacation Club resorts.

REGULAR RATES APPLY: February 11–February 14, February 25–March 8, April 8–May 27, August 12–August 25, September 16–October 27, and December 9–December 13 for Value and Moderate resorts; April 8–August 11 for Fort Wilderness Campsites; February 25–March 8, April 8–May 27, September 9–October 13, and December 9–December 13 for Fort Wilderness Cabins; September 21–October 13 for Deluxe resorts; February 11–February 14, February 25–March 8, April 15–July 5, September 21–October 13, November 2–November 8, and December 9–December 13 for Disney Vacation Club resorts.

HOT TIP!

For rates at the Four Seasons resort at Walt Disney World, call 800-267-3046 or visit *www.fourseasons.com/orlando/*. For the Walt Disney World Swan and Dolphin, visit *www.swandolphin.com*.

HOT TIP!

On weekends and when peak rates are in effect at Walt Disney World–owned-and-operated resort hotels, rates at Swan and Dolphin are often much lower. Conversely, Swan and Dolphin tend to have their highest rates on business days and during traditional convention times of year.

PEAK RATES APPLY: February 15–February 24, March 9–April 7, and December 14–December 20 for Value and Moderate resorts and Fort Wilderness Cabins; March 9–April 7 for Fort Wilderness Campsites; February 15–February 24 and March 9–April 14 for Deluxe resorts; February 15–February 24, March 9–April 14, and December 14–December 20 for Disney Vacation Club resorts.

Category Conundrum

Value vs. Moderate vs. Deluxe—which resort category is best for you? Categories reflect the price of a room, the style of the accommodation, and the level of service.

- Deluxe properties (the most expensive) are defined by their larger, practically appointed rooms, several restaurants, and such amenities as extended room service hours. This category generally includes Disney Vacation Club properties.

- Moderate properties (in the middle range, price-wise) feature comfortably sized rooms, full-service restaurants and food courts, and bellhop luggage service.

- Fort Wilderness Camping covers campsites, but not Wilderness Cabins (which fall into the Moderate resort category).

- Value properties (the least expensive category) offer fewer frills and smaller quarters. Meals are offered at food courts. Recreation and transportation options are limited.

Magic Kingdom Area

Contemporary & Bay Lake Tower

Watching the monorail trains disappear into the Contemporary's 15-story A-frame tower never fails to impress. The sleek trains look like long spaceships docking as they glide inside the resort.

Passengers, for their part, are impressed by the cavernous lobby, with its tiers of balconies and, at its center, the soaring 90-foot-high, floor-to-ceiling tile mural depicting scenes from the Southwest. (Look carefully and you may spot the five-legged goat.)

This imposing structure has 656 rooms in its main tower and garden building, plus those in Bay Lake Tower—occupied exclusively by members of the Disney Vacation Club. There are shops, snack bars, restaurants, lounges, a marina, beach, health club, and more. The pool area incorporates two whirlpools and a waterslide. The convention center offers business services. One of the resort's most notable features is its 15th-floor observation deck. From here, guests dining at the resort's California Grill can enjoy a bird's-eye view of the Magic Kingdom. Another huge bonus: a walking path to the Magic Kingdom (it's a 5- to 10-minute stroll away).

A club-level package is available for guests who stay in the hotel's 14th-floor suites. Amenities include express check-in and check-out, complimentary (light) continental breakfast, evening refreshments, and nightly turndown service. The 12th floor also provides guests with special club-level privileges. To contact the Contemporary, call 407-824-1000.

ROOMS: Boasting a sleek and contemporary design, the standard rooms here are evenly apportioned among the main tower and garden building. All rooms located in the tower have private balconies and (magnificent) views of Bay Lake or the Magic Kingdom. Want to wake up with a view of Cinderella Castle? Request an odd-numbered, park-facing room in the Tower. Most Contemporary rooms can accommodate five guests (plus a child under 3). Typical units have a daybed and two queen-size beds; some rooms have a king-size bed and a daybed. And every room has a flat-screen TV.

Business-minded folks rejoice over the desk space and high-speed Internet connection (free

PHOTO BY JILL SAFRO

of charge). While the ceiling fans have gone away, room temperature may be set as low as 65 degrees. A heads-up: The bathrooms here, though elegant in design, are far from user-friendly. There's not much shelf or counter space, the flat sinks tend to stay wet, the floor can be slippery, and the sliding doors don't lock.

Connecting rooms may be requested, though not guaranteed. Suites, consisting of a living room and one or two bedrooms, can accommodate 4 to 12 people. Weekday newspapers may be picked up in the lobby (free of charge). Other amenities include hair dryers and coffeemakers.

The monorail may be heard from lower rooms in the main tower. For maximum quiet, request a park view on a higher floor or stay in the garden wing. Of course, all rooms get serenaded by the nightly fireworks at the nearby Magic Kingdom park.

The 15-story Bay Lake Tower, a Disney Vacation Club property that sits next to the Contemporary and is connected by a covered walkway, mimics the colors and strong horizontal lines of its neighbor. The tower's crescent shape hugs a lakeside pool.

Studios sleep up to four and offer a kitchenette, queen-size bed, and double sleeper sofa. Sleeping up to five, the one-bedroom villas have full kitchens, two bathrooms, a king-size bed in the master bedroom and queen sleeper sofa, and a sleeper chair in the living room. Two-bedroom villas sleep up to nine, and the two-story grand villas sleep up to 12. All configurations feature a flat-screen TV and free Wi-Fi.

WHERE TO EAT: In addition to the many restaurants and snack spots, 24-hour room service provides a wide range of offerings.

California Grill: On the 15th floor. The specialty is California fare—flatbreads, grilled meats, seafood, and market vegetables. An added treat: the spectacular view of the Magic Kingdom fireworks for dining guests.

Chef Mickey's: Mickey and his pals host daily buffets at this fourth-floor institution. Breakfast and brunch feature Mickey waffles as well as traditional items. Dinner offers carved meats, daily specials, and a variety of entrées, plus a sundae and dessert bar.

Contempo Cafe: A quick-service spot with freshly prepared fare (there's a grab-and-go selection, too), this snack bar is on the fourth floor, next to Chef Mickey's.

The Wave . . . of American Flavors: A splendid spot on the first floor, this eatery offers healthy, creative, locally sourced fare all day.

WHERE TO DRINK: The Contemporary resort is home to several of the World's most inviting lounges.

California Grill Lounge: On the resort's 15th floor, adjoining the California Grill. Picture windows provide a dramatic backdrop for sipping California wines and other drinks and nibbling on appetizers. Seating is limited.

Contemporary Grounds: This lobby coffee bar serves cappuccino, espresso, latte, and other gourmet coffees, plus pastries and snacks.

Outer Rim: On the fourth-floor concourse, overlooking Bay Lake, the Outer Rim serves beer, wine, cocktails, and specialty drinks.

Sand Bar and Cove Bar: These poolside spots offer drinks and light snacks.

The Wave . . . of American Flavors Lounge: Inside The Wave restaurant, this bar features wine flights, locally crafted beer, specialty drinks, cocktails, and The Wave's full menu. It's a great destination if you find yourself caught without a dinner reservation.

WHAT TO DO: Volleyball nets may be set up on the beach. Waterskiing, wakeboarding, parasailing, and fishing excursions may be arranged (see *Sports* for details).

Arcade: Game Station, a spacious arcade, can be found on the resort's fourth floor.

Bass Fishing: See page 239.

Boating: Sea Raycer motorboats, Boston Whaler Montauks, and other boats may be rented at the resort's marina.

Health Club: The Olympiad Fitness Center has strength machines, bicycles, sauna, treadmills, lockers, and massage (by appointment). Equipment use is free to Contemporary guests.

Parasailing: Supervised excursions are offered at the marina. Cost is about $95 per person, or $170 for two to ride tandem. Reservations are necessary; call 407-939-0754.

Shopping: The fourth-floor concourse is home to several shops. Fantasia sells plush animals, games, accessories, clothing for kids, and more. Fantasia Market proffers newspapers, magazines, books, snacks, soft drinks, and liquor. Bay View Gifts (BVG) carries character merchandise and apparel for all ages, items with the Contemporary resort logo, jewelry, home decor items, kitchenware, baked goods, and candy.

Swimming: In addition to a round, lakeside pool, the free-form pool features a 17-foot-high curving slide, interactive squirt zone for little ones, and a whirlpool or two. Life jackets may be borrowed at no cost. Cabanas can be rented at Bay Lake pool. Call 407-W-DISNEY for pricing and to make reservations.

Tennis: Two tennis courts are available to guests of the Contemporary resort and Bay Lake Tower. No charge.

Watercraft Excursions: Guided excursions on personal Jet Ski-like watercraft are offered for $80 per half hour or $135 per hour. Call 407-939-0754.

Waterskiing, Wakeboarding, Tubing: Ski boats with instructors may be rented for $85 per half hour or $165 per hour at the marina. Call 407-939-0754 for reservations and pricing.

TRANSPORTATION: The Contemporary resort is connected to the Transportation and Ticket Center (TTC) and the Magic Kingdom by monorail. From the TTC, Epcot can be reached by transferring to another monorail. Buses take guests to Disney's Hollywood Studios, Animal Kingdom, Blizzard Beach, Typhoon Lagoon, and Disney Springs. Watercraft travel from the marina to Magic Kingdom, Fort Wilderness, and Wilderness Lodge. Guests may walk to the Magic Kingdom (it takes about 5 to 10 minutes).

PHOTO BY JILL SAFRO

Polynesian Village

The Polynesian Village resort is as close an approximation of the real thing as Walt Disney World's designers could create. The vegetation is lush, and the architecture summons the tropics. The mood is set by a completely renovated lobby that features bright, open areas and sweeping vistas of the Seven Seas Lagoon. The structure in which it is housed, the Great Ceremonial House, is the central building in the Polynesian Village. The front desk, shops, and most of the restaurants are located here. Flanking the Ceremonial House on either side are 11 two- and three-story village longhouses named for various Pacific islands. The Bora Bora Bungalows on the Seven Seas Lagoon are part of the Disney Vacation Club accommodations at the resort. The monorail stops at this hotel, making it a convenient place to stay; in fact, it's just a short ride to the Magic Kingdom.

Club-level service offers such amenities as express check-in; continental breakfast; cookies and soft drinks every afternoon; cocktails, hors d'oeuvres, and desserts in the evening; and a lounge with a prime view of the Seven Seas Lagoon and Cinderella Castle (not to mention the nightly fireworks display). Club-level rooms and suites are located in the Tonga and Hawaii buildings. The telephone number for the Polynesian Village is 407-824-2000.

DID YOU KNOW?

The white sand on the beaches near the Polynesian and Grand Floridian resorts and along the Seven Seas Lagoon actually came from the bottom of Bay Lake, located behind the Contemporary resort.

ROOMS: Many of the recently refurbished rooms have balconies, and most have a view of the gardens, Seven Seas Lagoon, or one of the resort's swimming pools. Many rooms have two queen-size beds and a daybed, and can accommodate five guests (plus a child under age 3). Adjoining rooms may be requested (but are not guaranteed). The Polynesian's suites—located in the Tonga building—can accommodate four to nine guests. Some have a king-size bed in the bedroom and one queen-size bed in the parlor. Amenities include a flat-screen TV, free Wi-Fi, coffeemaker (with coffee), hair dryer, and a small refrigerator. This is one of a few WDW resorts to offer snacks and soft drinks via vending machines. Details are subject to change.

WHERE TO EAT: Room service is available between 7 A.M. and midnight. There's also an interesting selection of eateries at which to dine:

Capt. Cook's: On the lobby level of the Great Ceremonial House. This is a good spot for light fare 24 hours a day. In addition to packaged salads and sandwiches, there are items such as pastries and fresh fruit, plus a made-to-order section, too. This is the place to head when you wish to fill your resort mug. (For a one-time purchase fee, you're entitled to unlimited soft-drink refills at all Rapid Fill locations for the length of your stay.)

Kona Cafe: On the second floor of the Great Ceremonial House. This family restaurant serves lunch and dinner with an Asian flair (including sumptuous sushi), while the breakfast menu is filled with traditional American selections.

Kona Island: This spot serves as coffee bar by day, featuring fresh-brewed Kona coffee (including many specialty drinks), plus pastries, fruit, and bagels. In the evening, this casual corner morphs into an extension of the Kona Cafe dining room (featuring excellent sushi and other items). Grab a seat and place your order with a member of the Kona Cafe waitstaff.

Oasis Grill: Set beside the Oasis pool and available exclusively to Polynesian resort guests, the Grill serves up items such as cheeseburgers, fish tacos, chicken avocado wraps, and more.

'Ohana: On the second floor of the Great Ceremonial House, 'Ohana serves family-style dinners roasted in a fire pit. Disney characters host a breakfast each morning.

Pineapple Lanai: The Polynesian Village is a happy place for fans of that chilly, tropical treat known as the Dole Whip (frozen pineapple dessert). It is served (plain, with vanilla soft-serve, or as a float) at this kiosk near the Lava pool.

PHOTO BY JILL SAFRO

WHERE TO DRINK: As might be expected, both the drink offerings and the settings in which they are served are as tropical as they come. Guests may sip a drink at the following:

Barefoot Bar: Adjacent to the Lava Pool, this watering hole is open seasonally.

Oasis Bar: An alfresco lounge, Oasis offers beer, wine, sangria, specialty cocktails (we dig the Frosty Pineapple), and drinks sans alcohol. The Oasis Bar is available exclusively to Polynesian resort guests.

Tambu Lounge: There's a tropical air about this lounge near 'Ohana. There's a full bar, but we go straight for the creamy, frozen piña coladas (available with or without alcohol).

Trader Sam's Grog Grotto: The spirited first-floor lounge is next to Captain Cook's snack bar. Sam's is a welcome addition to the Disney bar scene, offering tropical drinks and small plates in a richly themed locale. There is indoor and outdoor seating, with the patio tables much easier to snag than bar stools. FYI: Trader Sam is the "head salesman" in the Magic Kingdom's Jungle Cruise attraction.

WHAT TO DO: A wide range of activities is available at the Polynesian, including a jogging path. Fishing excursions can also be arranged.

Bass Fishing: See page 239 or call 407-WDW-BASS (939-2277).

Boating: Sea Raycer boats, Boston Whaler Montauks, and pontoon boats may be rented at the marina. Specialty cruises are available.

Shopping: BouTiki is the place for resort-wear, souvenirs, and more. Moana Mercantile sells Disney souvenirs, toys, magazines, and fashions. It's also stocked with food, spirits, soft drinks, snacks, and other fixings for an impromptu room party.

Lilo's Playhouse: The supervised activity program for (potty-trained) kids ages 3 through 12 is offered between 4:30 P.M. and midnight. The cost is about $55 (plus tax) per evening. Reservations are recommended; call 407-939-3463. Walk-ins are accepted on a first-come, first-served basis.

Swimming: There are two pools here: the Oasis, an unguarded, zero-depth-entry pool near the Samoa, Niue, Hawaii, Tokelau, and Rarotonga buildings; and the larger free-form Lava pool, near the marina. The latter is complete with slide and zero-depth-entry. There is also the Kiki Tiki Splash area (an aquatic playground for little ones), a hot tub with views of Cinderella Castle, and an expanded poolside deck. A limited number of wheelchairs are available to borrow for use in the pool. The beaches are strictly for sunbathing, sand-castle-building, afternoon snoozing, and fireworks viewing (no swimming allowed).

HOT TIP!

As signs posted along the beaches indicate, swimming and wading are not permitted in any of Walt Disney World's lakes. The rule is meant to protect guests from unguarded water and from exposure to naturally occurring bacteria and dangerous wildlife, such as alligators and snakes, common to Florida lakes.

TRANSPORTATION: The Polynesian Village is on the monorail line to the Magic Kingdom and the Transportation and Ticket Center (TTC). It's also possible to get to the TTC via walkway (it takes 5 to 10 minutes). From the TTC, Epcot can be reached by transferring to another monorail. Buses take guests to Disney's Hollywood Studios, Animal Kingdom, Epcot, Blizzard Beach, Typhoon Lagoon, and Disney Springs. Watercraft travel from the marina to Magic Kingdom.

Grand Floridian Resort and Villas

At the turn of the 20th century, Standard Oil magnate Henry M. Flagler saw the realization of his dream: The railroad he had built to "civilize" Florida had spawned along its right-of-way an empire of grand hotels, lavish estates, prominent families, and opulent lifestyles. High society blossomed in winter, as the likes of John D. Rockefeller and Teddy Roosevelt checked into the Royal Poinciana in Palm Beach, enjoying the sea breezes from the oceanside suites.

Unfortunately, the hotel was lost to a fire, and Florida's golden era faded with the Depression. But nearly a century after Flagler first made Florida a fashionable resort destination, Walt Disney World opened a grand hotel—an 867-room Victorian structure with gabled roofs and carved moldings—on 40 acres of Seven Seas Lagoon shorefront, between the Magic Kingdom and the Polynesian Village.

Like its late-19th-century predecessors, the Grand Floridian resort boasts abundant verandahs, ceiling fans, intricate latticework and balustrades, turrets, towers, and red-shingle roofs. And yet, it offers all the advantages of modern living, including monorail service. With five restaurants, multiple lounges, five shops, an arcade, convention center, two pools, a kids' splash zone, a marina, and full-service health club and spa, the Grand Floridian is not only a grand hotel but also a complete resort.

The main building houses the Grand Lobby, a palatial space soaring five stories to a ceiling of stained-glass domes and glittering chandeliers. Palms and an aviary decorate the sitting area; an open-cage elevator carries guests to the shops and restaurants on the second floor. The turn-of-the-20th-century theme is everywhere,

PHOTO BY JILL SAFRO

DID YOU KNOW?

Movie buffs may find the Grand Floridian strangely familiar. Its design is based, in part, on that of the Hotel Del Coronado in California. Scenes from the classic film *Some Like It Hot* were shot there.

from the employees' costumes to the shop displays, restaurants, room decor, and music played by the lobby band. The phone number for the Grand Floridian resort is 407-824-3000.

ROOMS: The rooms are filled with charm, decorated as they might have been a century ago—with printed wall coverings, marble-topped sinks, ceiling fans, and Victorian woodwork. Modern amenities include hair dryer, bathrobes, mini fridge, TV, nightly turndown service, coffeemaker, weekday newspaper (available in the lobby), and free Wi-Fi Internet service.

The main building houses club-level rooms and suites; lodge buildings, each four and five stories high, contain standard rooms, slightly smaller "attic" chambers, and suites. Villas, located in a building near the Beach pool, are available to rent when not occupied by Disney Vacation Club members.

Most rooms measure more than 400 square feet and include two queen-size beds, plus a daybed, to accommodate up to five people. Many rooms have a terrace. Suites include a parlor, plus one, two, or three bedrooms; there are queen-size beds in the bedrooms. Most of the 15 Deluxe King Rooms, located on the second, third, fourth, and fifth floors, enjoy wonderful views.

On the third floor, the club-level desks offer such services as reservations and information. The fourth floor features a quiet seating area where continental breakfast and evening refreshments are served. Club-level service is also available in the Sugarloaf building.

WHERE TO EAT: Most restaurants and lounges are located on the first two floors of the main building. Room service is available 24/7.

Cítricos: The largest of the hotel's restaurant serves market-fresh cuisine from southern Europe. It's open for dinner only. All menu items are available in the lounge, too.

Gasparilla Island Grill: This 24-hour snack bar offers fresh-made selections such as sandwiches, salads, and flatbreads.

Grand Floridian Cafe: Its peaches-and-cream color scheme and verandah-like feel make this a good place for a simple sit-down meal. All meals are served.

Narcoossee's: This sophisticated restaurant and bar has a romantic shoreline location. The seasonal menu includes items such as sustainable seafood paired with award-winning wines. Guests may sip cocktails on the verandah.

1900 Park Fare: A buffet restaurant decorated with carousel horses, plants, and Big Bertha, the carnival organ. Characters host breakfast and dinner daily. This character experience is an excellent alternative to Cinderella's Royal Table in the Magic Kingdom and much easier to reserve.

Victoria & Albert's: The eatery is named after the former queen and prince consort of England. It serves a prix-fixe menu of 7 to 10 courses (to guests ages 10 and up). Jackets are required for men, and reservations are a must.

WHERE TO DRINK: Guests will find the refined lounges here to be lovely escapes. Cítricos and Narcoossee's both have bars, complete with a full menu for dining. Drinks (bought in Mizner's Lounge) may also be enjoyed in the majestic lobby.

Cítricos: Proof that good things come in small packages (eight bar stools and four tables), this lounge has an extensive wine list, specialty coffees, and full menu.

Garden View Tea Room: This pretty spot offers a view of the hotel's lush, landscaped garden and pool area. Afternoon tea is served (as are finger sandwiches and small desserts).

Mizner's Lounge: Named after the eccentric, wildly prolific architect who defined much of the flavor of Florida's Palm Beach County, this bar is on the second floor.

Narcoossee's: Located in the heart of the restaurant, this lounge offers an extensive wine list and craft beer selection, plus a full bar and menu.

Pool Bars: These bars (known as Courtyard and Beaches) both feature a variety of beverages, while Beaches also serves lunch and dinner.

WHAT TO DO: The Grand Floridian offers many of the recreational facilities of a beach resort. Fishing excursions can be arranged (refer to the *Sports* chapter for details).

Arcade: Arcadia Games is adjacent to the Gasparilla Island Grill (near the marina).

Bass Fishing: See page 239.

Boating: Boston Whaler Montauks, pontoon boats, and Sea Raycer speedboats are available for rent (by the hour or half hour) at Captain's Shipyard Marina. The *Grand 1* yacht (including a captain and first mate) can be rented for about $700 an hour and accommodates up to 18 guests.

Campfire: Resort guests are invited to gather round the campfire (on select nights) and roast marshmallows under the stars. (Guests may bring their own marshmallows or purchase s'mores kits for about $5.) Afterward, everyone is treated to a screening of a Disney film.

Golf: The resort is conveniently close to Disney's Magnolia, Palm, and Oak Trail golf courses. Call 407-WDW-GOLF (939-4653), or visit *www.disneyworldgolf.com* for information or to reserve tee times.

Health Club: The full-service exercise facility, adjacent to the Senses spa, is outfitted with fitness equipment. (Oddly enough, there is no restroom. Health Club patrons may use the facilities at the nearby restroom at the pool.)

Salon: The Ivy Trellis salon offers a full line of hair-care services.

Shopping: On the first floor of the main building is Summer Lace, specializing in women's resort-wear and swimwear, and Sandy Cove, for gifts, sundries, and home decor. One level up is the cheerful M. Mouse Mercantile character shop, Basin for bath supplies, and Commander Porter's, a men's shop.

Spa: The spa at Disney's Grand Floridian resort is a pampering palace called Senses—A Disney Spa. In addition to treatments offered at its sister spa at the Saratoga Springs resort (see page 229), this spot also offers many soothing packages.

Treatment hours are usually 8 A.M. to 8 P.M. daily. Prices start at about $135 for a 50-minute massage and about $150 for a facial. To book an appointment, call 407-WDW-SPAS (939-7727). For info, visit *http://disneyworld.com/spas/*.

Swimming: There are two large pools for guests to cool off in. Both pools have zero-depth-entry, and the Beach Pool also has waterfalls and a 181-foot slide. There's an *Alice in Wonderland* splash zone for kids up to 48 inches tall (and their guardians). Kids get absolutely giddy when the Mad Hatter's gigantic hat tips over, dumping massive amounts of water onto bathers below.

TRANSPORTATION: The Grand Floridian is connected to the Transportation and Ticket Center (TTC) and Magic Kingdom by monorail. From the TTC, Epcot can be reached by transferring to another monorail. Buses take guests to Disney's Hollywood Studios, Animal Kingdom, Blizzard Beach, Typhoon Lagoon, and Disney Springs. Watercraft travel from the marina to Magic Kingdom.

Wilderness Lodge, Villas, & Cabins

This resort artfully recalls the spirit of the early American West and the feeling of the National Park Service lodges built during the early 1900s. These grand structures architecturally unified the elements of the unspoiled wilderness parks, kept harmony with nature, and incorporated the culture of Native Americans. The Wilderness Lodge artfully recaptures this rustic charm.

The resort is located between the Contemporary resort and Fort Wilderness on Bay Lake. The majestic lobby is an eight-story, log-structured building. Massive bundled log columns support a series of trusses, while two Pacific Northwest totem poles soar 55 feet into the air. Four levels of corridors surround the lobby, providing access to guestrooms, sitting nooks, and terraces. The monorail does not stop here. Club-level service is available on the top floor of the Lodge. There are villas, here, too: Boulder Ridge Villas and Copper Creek Villas and & Cabins (Copper Creek is the newest addition to the Disney Vacation Club family). The telephone number for the Wilderness Lodge is 407-824-3200.

ROOMS: Most of the Lodge's 725 guestrooms have two queen-size beds and a balcony. Some have a queen-size bed and bunk beds. Bathrooms have separate vanity areas with double sinks. The wallpaper has a Native American–motif border, and the colorful bedspreads and plaid curtains add to the decor. Images of wildlife complete the theme. Rooms include an iron (with board), a hair dryer, coffeemaker (with coffee), mini fridge, free Wi-Fi, flat-screen TV, and weekday newspaper (available in the hall or the lobby).

The 126 Boulder Ridge villas are housed in a five-story building adjoining The Lodge. This tribute to turn-of-the-20th-century design is also one of the two Disney Vacation Club properties at this resort. The style of the villas building was inspired by the grandeur of Rocky Mountain geyser country. At Copper Creek, guests may choose from studios, 1-, 2-, and 3-bedroom villas, and lakeside cabins.

Each studio has a queen-size bed, a double sleeper sofa, and a pull-down twin-size bunk bed, plus a kitchenette with microwave, coffeemaker, and mini refrigerator. Villas sleep 4 to 12 guests and have dining areas, kitchens, laundry facilities, master baths with bubble-jet tubs, and DVD players. They include a king-size bed in the master bedroom, a living room with a queen sleeper sofa, and either two queen-size beds or a queen-size bed and a double sleeper sofa in the extra bedrooms.

Each of the 26 waterfront Cascade Cabins feature two bedrooms (and sleep up to 8), two bathrooms, large dining and living room spaces, floor-to-ceiling windows, exposed wooden beams, and an interior-exterior stone-hearth fireplace.

Villas and cabins are available to all guests when not occupied by Disney Vacation Club members.

WHERE TO EAT: The Northwest theme is carried out with flair in the hotel's eateries. Room service runs from 6:30 A.M. to 11 A.M. and 4 P.M. to midnight.

Artist Point: Decorated with art representing painters who first chronicled the Northwest landscape, this fine-dining spot features game, steak, salmon, and other seafood, as well as wines from the Pacific Northwest.

Geyser Point Bar & Grill: With its cedar beams and natural stone, this rustic, waterside spot invites guests to pair small plates with beverages from the Pacific Northwest.

Roaring Fork: Fast food and light snacks are available at this snack bar. This is also the site of the resort's "refillable mug" station. (For details, refer to page 270.) Roaring Fork hours are generally about 6 A.M. until midnight.

Whispering Canyon Cafe: A boisterous, family-style restaurant with all-day dining.

WHERE TO DRINK: Two spots are available for a relaxing break.

Geyser Point Bar & Grill: Geyser Point is a waterside retreat with a full bar featuring a vast array of beer, wine, cocktails, and soft drinks.

Territory Lounge: This lounge honors the survey parties who led the move westward. In addition to specialty drinks, microbrewed beer and snacks are served.

WHAT TO DO: The resort offers many recreational activities. Teton Boat & Bike Rental is in the Colonel's Cabin by the lake. Fishing excursions may be arranged (refer to the *Sports* chapter for details).

Arcade: The Buttons and Bells Arcade has about 30 different games to enjoy.

Bass Fishing: See page 239.

Biking: Bikes may be rented for scenic rides around the resort. A three-quarter-mile path leads to Fort Wilderness.

Boating: A variety of watercraft may be rented for trips around Bay Lake and the Seven Seas Lagoon.

Carolwood Pacific Room: A fireplace and railroad memorabilia add atmosphere to this relaxing room, equipped with comfy seating, tables, and games. It is located in the Wilderness Lodge Villas building.

Children's Program: The Cub's Den is a supervised dining and entertainment club for (potty-trained) kids ages 3 through 12. Activities, including Disney movies and Western-themed arts and crafts, keep kids entertained from 4:30 P.M. to midnight. The cost is $55 per evening, per child. Dinner and a snack are included. Call 407-939-3463 for reservations. Walk-ins are available on a first-come, first-served basis.

Health Club: The only thing rustic about the Sturdy Branches health club is the structure it's housed in. Open 24 hours, it features modern equipment, a sauna, and more. Massage and facial services are available. To make an appointment, call 407-939-7727.

Shopping: Wilderness Lodge Mercantile stocks necessities and sundries, as well as a line of clothing with the Wilderness Lodge logo and Disney character merchandise. There is a small selection of grocery items, too. The mercantile is usually open until about 11 P.M. There's also a pin-trading cart in the lobby.

Swimming: The zero-depth-entry Boulder Ridge Cove pool looks as if it were carved from the rockscape. A beach, a kiddie pool, two whirlpool tubs, and a geyser complete the design. Fire Rock Geyser erupts on the hour from early morning until 10 P.M. Kids dig the splash zone.

TRANSPORTATION: Boats go to the Magic Kingdom, Contemporary, and Fort Wilderness. Buses go to Magic Kingdom, Epcot, Disney's Hollywood Studios, Animal Kingdom, Blizzard Beach, Typhoon Lagoon, and Disney Springs. (The Fort Wilderness bus does not stop here.)

Fort Wilderness Resort & Campground

The very existence of this canal-crossed expanse—with more than 750 acres of cypress and pine—always surprises visitors who come to Walt Disney World expecting to find nothing more than theme parks.

Tucked among the campsites are hundreds of Wilderness Cabins for rent, complete with housekeeping service. The cost is comparable to that of some of the more expensive rooms at Disney resorts, but each sleeps up to 6 guests and

PHOTO BY JILL SAFRO

offers about 500 square feet of space. The phone number for the Fort Wilderness resort and campground is 407-824-2900.

CAMPSITES: Fort Wilderness has 843 traditional sites. They feature electricity hookups (30/50-amp), water, sanitary disposal, free Wi-Fi, and cable television. Partial-hookup campsites supply electricity and water hookups only. All campsites feature a paved driveway pad, picnic table, and charcoal grill. Most loops have at least one air-conditioned comfort station complete with restrooms, private showers, ice machine, phones, free Wi-Fi, and a laundry room. A site allows for occupancy by up to ten. Each site has room for one car plus the camping vehicle. Other cars may be parked in the main lot at Fort Wilderness.

The various campground areas are designated by numbers. The 100–500 loops are closest to the beach, the Settlement Trading Post, and Pioneer Hall. The 1500–2000 loops are farthest away from the beach and many other Fort Wilderness activities, but they are quieter and more private. Premium campsites are big-rig friendly and are wider and deeper to accommodate large vehicles. Pets are welcome at certain campsites for a nightly charge of $5. They can frolic at Waggin' Tails Dog Park, the "off leash" pet play area.

WILDERNESS CABINS: These woodland dwellings offer a rustic escape (with all the comforts of home, plus housekeeping). Falling into WDW's "moderate" resort category, the interiors of the six-person, log cabin-like buildings are decorated with wilderness accents. Each one is shaded by a pine canopy. Cabins include air-conditioning, full kitchen, free Wi-Fi, two TVs, full bath, hair dryer, iron, a deck, picnic table, and charcoal grill. DVD players are available upon request.

Note: No extra camping equipment allowed; all guests must be accommodated in a cabin.

WHERE TO EAT: There is a bona fide restaurant here, but many folks opt to cook their own meals. A small selection of supplies is sold at the Meadow Trading Post and the Settlement Trading Post. Ask about nearby grocery stores when you check in, or use *www.gardengrocer.com*.

P&J's Southern Takeout: Aka Trail's End To Go, this venue serves hearty fare for breakfast, lunch, and dinner. Place your order at the counter on the far left of the Trail's End eatery. You can chow down at nearby (unshaded) tables or take the grub to go.

Trail's End: This log-walled spot in Pioneer Hall serves home-style fare three times a day. Spirits are available. The breakfast buffet delivers a hefty bang for the buck.

WHERE TO DRINK: Cocktails are served at Crockett's Tavern in Pioneer Hall.

FAMILY ENTERTAINMENT AFTER DARK: The Hoop-Dee-Doo Musical Revue is quite popular and offered year-round. Another crowd-pleasing dinner show, Mickey's Backyard Barbecue, is offered seasonally. For reservations, call 407-939-3463. There's a free nightly campfire/sing-along near the Meadow Trading Post.

WHAT TO DO: There's plenty of free activities to choose from, including two pools (the Meadow Swimmin' pool has an aquatic play zone for tots and a slide), tennis courts, and campfire sing-alongs with Chip and Dale. For a fee, guests can enjoy wagon, pony, and carriage rides, fishing trips, archery, boats, bikes, and more. For details, see *Everything Else in the World* and *Sports*.

TRANSPORTATION: Buses circulating at 15- to 30-minute intervals provide transportation within the campground, while buses and boats connect Fort Wilderness to the rest of the World. The Magic Kingdom, Contemporary, and Wilderness Lodge are best reached via watercraft that depart from the marina. Buses to Wilderness Lodge depart from the Settlement stop only. Buses to Epcot, Animal Kingdom, Disney's Hollywood Studios, Blizzard Beach, Typhoon Lagoon, and Disney Springs leave from the Outpost stop.

Electric golf carts and bikes may be rented outside the Reception Outpost as an alternative means of getting around within the campground. Call 407-824-2742 for golf cart reservations. Available to Fort Wilderness guests only, golf carts cost about $59 per day, $378 per week. To drive a golf cart, guests must have a valid license and be at least 18 years old.

Epcot Area

Caribbean Beach

This vibrant hotel—which is set on 200 acres southeast of Epcot and near Disney's Hollywood Studios—is in the midst of a massive refurbishment. When the pixie dust settles (after 2018), expect a bounty of new dining, shopping, and recreational opportunities.

The resort is composed of brightly colored "villages" surrounding a 45-acre lake called Barefoot Bay. Each village is identified with a Caribbean island: Trinidad, Aruba, Jamaica, Martinique, Barbados (the latter two are unavailable for the time being). The resort currently features pastel walls, white railings, and vividly colored metal roofs. There are 2,109 rooms in all, making Caribbean Beach one of the largest hotels in the United States.

The villages consist of a cluster of two-story buildings, a guest laundry, and a lakefront stretch of white-sand beach. Guests check in at the Custom House, a reception building that projects the feeling of a tropical resort. Decor, furnishings, and staff costumes all reflect the Caribbean theme. (Old Port Royale—a complex located near the center of the property—is in the process of being re-imagined as Centertown: a lively waterfront dining, shopping, and relaxing enclave.) Stone walls, pirates' cannons, and tropical birds and flowers add to the atmosphere.

The lakeside recreation area includes a pool with waterfalls and a slide; the main beach; the Barefoot Bay Bike Works, where bicycles may be rented; and a 1.2-mile promenade around the lake that's perfect for biking, walking, or jogging. Kids love it here. The telephone number for the Caribbean Beach resort is 407-934-3400.

ROOMS: Rooms are located in two-story buildings in each island village. A typical 340-square-foot room has two queen beds, and most sleep up to four. Some rooms can sleep up to five (with a fold-down bunk-size bed). The rooms here are a bit larger than standard rooms at Disney's other moderate resorts. Rooms are decorated in tones softer than the colors found on the exterior. Many have a super-kid-friendly pirate motif. Each room has a small fridge, coffeemaker (with coffee), and free Wi-Fi. A note for the budget-conscious: All rooms here are identical in terms of size and comfort, and the only difference between the most and least expensive is the view. To minimize time spent walking, request a room nearest the lobby or bus stop when you check in.

WHERE TO EAT: While Caribbean Beach resort undergoes an extensive refurbishment, its traditional dining destinations (Old Port Royale food court, Shutters restaurant at Old Port Royale, Calypso Trading Post, and Banana Cabana pool bar) will be replaced by new options. Here are some dining choices for guests to enjoy in 2018:

Centertown: A bountiful "all-you-care-to-eat" buffet is offered for lunch and dinner. Expect family-friendly selections at both meals. Soft drinks and cocktails are served.

In-room Dining: Guests may have pizza, sandwiches, and pasta delivered to their room from 4 P.M. until midnight. To order, press Pizza Delivery on the in-room phone. Beer and wine are also sold. (Please have a government-issued

photo ID handy to prove you're at least 21 years old.) Note that an 18-percent gratuity and a $3 delivery charge applies to in-room orders.

Island Markets: There are three grab-and-go locations where guests can pick up prepared food for breakfast, lunch, and dinner. You'll find them near the Martinique pool and in the Aruba and Jamaica regions of the resort.

WHERE TO DRINK: While the resort is being refurbished, the best spot to pick up a cocktail or soft drink is at the Centertown dining location.

WHAT TO DO: There are many recreational opportunities here. The promenade around the lake is ideal for walking, biking, or a jog.

Arcade: Goombay Games at Old Port Royale offers a selection of amusements.

Biking: Bikes may be rented at Barefoot Bay Bike Works. Rides may take guests around the resort's scenic 45-acre Lago Dorado.

Fishing: Guided fishing excursions are offered on Barefoot Bay. Call 407-WDW-BASS (939-2277) for updates.

Playground: A playground is located on the Caribbean Cay Island.

Shopping: Calypso Straw Market carries swimwear and items featuring the resort's logo.

PHOTO BY MIKE CARROLL

Swimming: Each village has its own pool, and the main pool—which has a Caribbean-themed setting, conjuring up images of high-seas pirate adventures—has 2 slides, 2 whirlpool spas, and a splash zone for kids under 48 inches tall. Youngsters simply adore it.

TRANSPORTATION: Buses go to the Magic Kingdom, Epcot, Disney's Hollywood Studios, Animal Kingdom, and Blizzard Beach. Other bus routes lead to Disney Springs and Typhoon Lagoon. Getting around within the resort is done via buses bearing an "Internal Resort Shuttle" sign.

Yacht & Beach Club and Beach Club Villas

The New England seaside exists at Walt Disney World in the form of the Yacht and Beach Club, and the Beach Club Villas. Situated beside Epcot, the resorts, designed by noted architect Robert A. M. Stern, are set around a 25-acre lake. The adjacent properties share most facilities—including a convention center offering business services—and transportation options.

The Yacht Club's design evokes images of the New England seashore hotels of the 1880s. Guests enter the five-story beige clapboard building along a wooden-planked bridge. Hardwood floors and brass enhance the nautical theme. A lighthouse on the pier serves as a beacon to welcome guests back to the hotel from WDW attractions. To reach the Yacht Club by telephone, call 407-934-7000.

Distance from the ocean is irrelevant over at the sand-and-surf-focused Beach Club resort. A walkway leads past a croquet court to beachside cabanas on the white-sand shore. Guests are met by hosts and hostesses dressed in colorful beach resort costumes of the 1870s. The phone number for the Beach Club resort is 407-934-8000.

ROOMS: Yacht Club rooms are decorated in a nautical motif. The Beach Club's rooms are also amply sized and, naturally, reflect a beach motif. In each room, the furniture is white, and (at the Yacht Club) the headboard design on the one king-size bed or two queen-size beds incorporates small ships' wheels. Some rooms have daybeds. Most of the suites have a king-size bed as well as two sleeper sofas and a fold-down, single bunk. In the bathrooms, there is a separate vanity with double sinks. Each room has a ceiling fan, iron (with board), hair dryer, weekday newspaper (pick up a free copy in the lobby), free Wi-Fi, mini fridge, coffeemaker (with coffee, sugar, and nondairy creamer), and a small safe. Club-level rooms (with exclusive access to a room with a concierge, snacks, and drinks) are available.

A five-story building beside the Beach Club is home to 177 two-bedroom equivalents. The villas are available to Disney Vacation Club members. (They are available to all guests when not occupied by Vacation Club members.) Each studio has a queen-size bed, a double sleeper sofa, and a fold-down bunk-size bed, plus a kitchenette with a microwave, coffeemaker, and mini fridge, as well as a flat-screen TV and DVD player. Larger villas sleep four to eight, and all have a dining area, kitchen, laundry room, and a master bath with whirlpool tub. They include a king-size bed in the master bedroom, living room with queen sleeper sofa, and either two queen-size beds or a queen-size bed and a double sleeper sofa.

WHERE TO EAT: The themes of yachting and the sea play a role in the eateries found at their respective resorts. Room service is available 24/7.

Beach Club Marketplace: Stop here for hot and cold breakfast items such as scrambled eggs, croissants, and pastries, as well as soup, salads, sandwiches, and snack selections. Rapid Fill mugs may be purchased and filled here, too.

Beaches and Cream Soda Shop: An old-fashioned spot with massive appeal, this classic soda fountain doles out frosty shakes, malts, and varied ice cream sundaes. Burgers and sandwiches are served as well. The shop is located between the Yacht and Beach Club resorts.

Cape May Cafe: An indoor clambake is held here at the Beach Club each night. The varied and bountiful buffet features several types of clams and mussels, plus beef ribs and chicken. A character breakfast is presented daily.

Ale & Compass Restaurant: The newly refurbished eatery serves breakfast, lunch, and dinner. It is located at Yacht Club, just off the lobby (near the Ale & Compass Lounge).

Hurricane Hanna's Waterside Bar & Grill: Sandwiches, salads, burgers, and other snacks are served here. A full bar is also located here, and poolside beverage service is available. If you purchase a refillable resort mug, this is a spot to top it off during your stay.

Market at Ale & Compass: A sleek addition to the Yacht Club, Market offers freshly prepared selections for breakfast, lunch, and dinner. Breakfast items include spinach and feta pastries; ham, egg, and

cheese rolls; and sticky buns. Lunch and dinner feature paninis (grilled chicken or Italian), vegetarian sandwiches, and more. There is a grab-and-go area and many snack items to choose from. Rapid Fill mugs may be purchased and filled here.

Yachtsman Steakhouse: Select cuts of aged beef are the specialty of the house. Fresh seafood and poultry are also offered.

WHERE TO DRINK: The lounges in both resorts offer a variety of specialty drinks in relaxing seaside settings.

Ale & Compass Lounge: This Yacht Club lobby lounge, featuring specialty cocktails and wine, provides a nice respite after a long day. (The bartender arrives at about 5 P.M.)

Crew's Cup: The place to try beer shipped in from the world's seaports before dining at Yachtsman Steakhouse next door.

Martha's Vineyard: This quiet lounge at the Beach Club offers selections from American and international vineyards, served by the glass or bottle, as well as a full bar and appetizers.

WHAT TO DO: There is enough to do here to fill an entire vacation. A sand volleyball court may be found near the Beach Club. Equipment is available at no cost at the Ship Shape health club. Bikes and boats may be rented.

HOT TIP!

Portable playpen-like cribs that accommodate one child under age 3 are available at all Disney resorts. Ask about them when you call to reserve your room. They're free. (If you'd like a more substantial sleeping apparatus for your toddler, refer to page 47 of the *Getting Ready to Go* chapter.)

The Fantasia Gardens Miniature Golf complex is close by, and guided fishing excursions may be arranged (see *Sports*). And last but not least, the BoardWalk entertainment district is a short walk around the lake.

Arcade: Lafferty Place Arcade has about 60 video games and pinball machines.

Boating: Pontoons, Boston Whaler Montauks, Sea Raycers, and other boats are available for rent at the Bayside Marina.

Children's Program: The Sandcastle Club, for potty-trained kids ages 3 through 12, is open 4:30 P.M. to midnight. Cost is $55 per evening, per child (including dinner and a snack). Reservations are recommended; call 407-939-3463. Walk-ins are accepted on a first-come, first-served basis. The Club has programming to entertain and educate little ones—with surprise visits from Disney pals.

Health Club: The Ship Shape health club has strength and cardio machines and is open 24/7 to resort guests age 14 and older. (Request an "after hours" key card during operating hours.) Massage and facial services are available. For an appointment, call 407-939-7727.

Salon: The Ship Shape salon sits between Yacht and Beach Club, poolside. It offers a full line of hair care services; call 407-939-7727.

Shopping: At the Yacht Club, Market at Ale & Compass is an all-purpose shop stocked with character merchandise and sundries. At the Beach Club, the Beach Club Marketplace has a similar selection of goods.

Swimming: Between the marina and the beach is the centerpiece of the dual resort—Stormalong Bay, a three-acre pool that's like a mini water park. There is a lagoon expressly for relaxed bathing, and another with currents, jets, and sand-bottomed areas. Several whirlpools are scattered throughout the area. Adjacent to the main pool is a shipwreck, where guests can enjoy a waterslide. There is one unguarded pool and whirlpool at the far end of each hotel. There is also an unguarded pool by the Beach Club Villas. Guests may sunbathe on the beach, though swimming is not permitted.

Tennis: There is one lighted tennis court on the Yacht Club side of the property. Rental equipment is available at the Bayside Marina.

TRANSPORTATION: Guests travel to Epcot and Disney's Hollywood Studios via FriendShip water taxis or walkways. Buses go to the Magic Kingdom, Animal Kingdom, Disney Springs, Typhoon Lagoon, and Blizzard Beach.

Meetings & Conventions

Convention centers at Walt Disney World range in size from 20,000 to 200,000 square feet. The Dolphin's center, featuring an exhibit hall and an executive boardroom, is the largest; the Swan provides additional space. The Contemporary has three ballrooms and a spacious pre-function area with lots of natural light. The convention center at the Yacht and Beach Club is reminiscent of a grand turn-of-the-century New England town-meeting hall. The Grand Floridian Resort and Spa has a lavish center with silk brocade walls. The BoardWalk offers a smaller conference area with a lakeside gazebo for outdoor events. And Coronado Springs, the first moderately priced Disney resort to offer convention facilities, boasts one of the largest hotel ballrooms in the U.S.

Among the unique services available to Disney conventioneers is the use of Disney characters and performers for events. Special events can even be held in the parks. Resort business centers have clerical staffs and computers, in addition to faxing and photocopying equipment. (These services are available to all resort guests.)

Those interested in scheduling a convention should call 321-939-7221. Organizers are advised to book their events six months in advance, especially for large groups.

Swan & Dolphin

These sister resorts, situated near the shores of Crescent Lake, can easily be distinguished by the 47-foot swan and 56-foot dolphin statues that top them. The waterfalls, rows of palm trees, and beachfront location all reflect the tropical Florida landscape that was their inspiration. Both hotels were designed by noted architect Michael Graves as examples of "entertainment architecture." The turquoise waves on the colored facade of the Swan's 12-story main building and two 7-story wings are clearly evidence of this design, as is the Dolphin's exterior mural, which features a banana-leaf pattern. The soaring 27-story triangular tower at the center of the Dolphin is flanked by four 9-story guestroom wings.

The resorts share extensive convention facilities, many recreational options, and a host of restaurants. The Swan and Dolphin are operated by Westin and Sheraton, respectively, but are treated as Walt Disney World resorts; guests here enjoy most WDW resort benefits, most notably access to Extra Magic Hours and a 60-day advance window for Fastpass+ selections. One notable difference: Guests cannot use their room keys to charge purchases on WDW property, with the exception of within the Swan and Dolphin resorts themselves. The direct line for the Swan and Dolphin is 407-934-3000. Reservations for either resort may be made by calling 888-227-1500, visiting *www.swandolphin.com*, or through Facebook at *www.facebook.com/swananddolphin*.

ROOMS: All rooms have gotten a fresh look, reflecting the hotels' water-themed architecture. Amenities include weekday newspaper delivery, safes, mini fridge, irons and boards, two dual-line telephones, and high-speed, wireless Internet access. Rooms equipped for guests with disabilities are available. Valet parking is $28 per day (plus tax); self-parking is $20 a day.

There are 758 rooms and 55 suites at the Swan, each with one king-size or two queen-size "Westin Heavenly Beds." At the Dolphin, the 1,509 rooms and 114 suites feature two double beds or one king-size heavenly bed. Swan rooms also include a separate vanity and dressing area.

WHERE TO EAT: In addition to many restaurant choices, 24-hour room service provides an extensive all-day dining menu. (The room service here is considered among the best at Walt Disney World.)

Cabana Bar & Beach Club: This full-service poolside spot near the Dolphin serves burgers, grilled chicken sandwiches, flatbreads, and more. The full bar serves specialty drinks.

The Fountain: Homemade ice cream is the specialty at this Dolphin eatery. Huge sundaes, shakes, malts, and burgers are also offered.

Fresh: Designed to resemble a cheerful marketplace, this Dolphin spot serves breakfast and lunch only. The menu features "healthy, sustainable, and organic" fare.

Garden Grove Cafe: This Swan eatery, which features a park-like atmosphere, serves three meals daily. A buffet breakfast with Disney characters is held on Saturdays and Sundays, while a character dinner takes place nightly.

Il Mulino New York Trattoria: The highly acclaimed Italian restaurant is located on the first floor of the Swan. The setting, which is reminiscent of an old-world trattoria, is relaxed yet vibrant. Features such as *Piatti per il Tavolo* (family-style dining) and wood-fired pizzas complement Il Mulino New York's family-friendly Walt Disney World locale.

Picabu: A cafeteria with a bit of flair. The 24-hour convenience store here sells snacks and sundries. It has Starbucks coffee, too.

HOT TIP!

The Swan and Dolphin resorts run seasonal promotions throughout the year. For information, call 888-828-8850, or visit *www.swandolphin.com*.

Shula's: An upscale celebration of two American favorites: steak and pro football. It's a bit pricey, but the steaks are superb and the side orders are big enough to share. There is a children's menu (chicken, cheeseburgers, etc.). The (enforced) dress code is business casual.

Splash Terrace: A poolside cafe near the Swan serving specialty sandwiches, pizza, and snacks. A full-service bar is also located here.

Todd English's bluezoo: This eatery features coastal cuisine, beef, and chicken dishes with international and domestic influences.

WHERE TO DRINK: It's easy to find a nice cocktail spot in this neck of the woods.

Java Bar: This spot at the Swan offers a quick bite for early birds on the go. Enjoy specialty coffees, light breakfast items, and fresh pastries until 6:30 P.M. most days.

Kimonos: The Asian decor makes this Swan lounge an inviting place for sake, sushi, and other Japanese selections. Karaoke is a house specialty. This place is generally hopping a bit later than most other Walt Disney World resort lounges.

Lobby Lounge: A cozy Dolphin area featuring wine and specialty drinks.

Shula's Steak House Lounge: Settle into a comfy chair and sip a drink in this lounge adjacent to Shula's dining room.

WHAT TO DO: The Swan and Dolphin share many recreation options. Volleyball nets and hammocks are set up on the beach. The Fantasia Gardens Miniature Golf complex and Board-Walk are nearby (the proximity to BoardWalk and Epcot is a big plus). Disney's Hollywood Studios is a FriendShip water taxi ride (or about a 20-minute walk) away.

Arcades: A room full of video games is located near Picabu at the Dolphin. Another game room can be found near the Splash cafe at the Swan.

Boating: Watercraft are available for rent on the beach between the Swan and Dolphin.

Children's Program: Camp Dolphin welcomes children (potty-trained) ages 4 through 12 and has supervised activities from 5 P.M. to midnight. Cost is about $12 per child, per hour.

Health Clubs: There is a fitness center near the pool area at the Dolphin. State-of-the-art equipment is available. There's also a smaller health club with basic exercise equipment near Splash Terrace at the Swan.

Playground: A sandy play area with swings and jungle gyms is located on the beach near the grotto pool.

Shopping: Disney Cabanas, located in the lobby of the Swan, features character merchandise and sundries. Four shops may be found at the Dolphin. Sugar3 allows chocolate lovers the chance to savor some tasty concoctions. Lamont's offers resort-wear for men and women. Daisy's Garden is the place to find character goods at the Dolphin. Galleria Sottil is the Dolphin's art gallery. Expect to find paintings, sculptures, and other assorted works of art. The Cabana Beach Hut, by the Dolphin pool, specializes in "pool-fun" essentials, while the 24-hour convenience store within Picabu sells grocery items and sundries.

Spa and Salon: The Mandara Spa features full-service body treatments, plus hairstyling, manicures, pedicures, and more.

Swimming: In addition to a shared kids' wading pool, there are two lap pools, and a themed grotto pool with slides between the Swan and Dolphin. Several whirlpools are scattered around the area.

Tennis: Four hard-surface tennis courts are located behind the pool area closest to the Swan resort. They are open 24 hours a day and are fully lighted. Racquet rentals and lessons may be coordinated at the resort's health club.

TRANSPORTATION: Guests travel to Epcot and Disney's Hollywood Studios via ferryboats or walkway. (It takes about 10 minutes to walk to Epcot's back entrance and about 20 minutes to reach Disney's Hollywood Studios on foot. Water taxis don't move much faster—and they make multiple stops—so allow plenty of time to reach either destination.) Buses go directly to the Magic Kingdom, Animal Kingdom, Disney Springs, Typhoon Lagoon, and Blizzard Beach.

BoardWalk Inn & Villas

The enchantment of a bygone era is recaptured at the BoardWalk. The resort combines a waterside entertainment complex with deluxe hotel accommodations and vacation villas. Dining, recreation, shopping, and entertainment venues line the boardwalk, and twinkling lights trim the buildings. The ambience continues throughout, with detailed architecture featuring colorful facades, flagged turrets, and striped awnings, all reminiscent of the turn of the 20th century. BoardWalk resort is adjacent to Epcot's International Gateway and connected to it via walkway. The phone number for BoardWalk is 407-939-5100.

ROOMS: Accommodations here evoke the charm of early Eastern-seaboard inns. Most have private balconies or patios. The BoardWalk Inn has 372 deluxe hotel rooms decorated with cherrywood furniture, boardwalk postcard-print curtains, and light green accents. Guestrooms at the inn sleep up to five, and feature two queen-size beds (or one king-size bed) and a child's daybed. Romantic two-story garden suites each have a private garden enclosed by a white picket fence. They sleep four, and have a living room on the first floor and a king-size bed in the unenclosed, bedroom loft. The inn also has club-level rooms and suites.

The 282 two-bedroom equivalents are collectively called BoardWalk Villas. These are Disney Vacation Club villas, available to everyone when not occupied by members. Each studio has a queen-size bed and double sleeper sofa, plus a kitchenette with microwave, coffeemaker, and small refrigerator. Larger (one-, two-, and three-bedroom) villas sleep 4 to 12 people, and feature dining areas, fully equipped kitchens, laundry facilities, master baths with whirlpool tubs, and flat-screen television with DVD player. They also include a king-size bed in the master bedroom, living room with a queen sleeper sofa, and a queen-size bed, plus a double sleeper sofa in any additional bedrooms.

Rooms at the BoardWalk Inn include weekday newspapers (available near the elevators and in the lobby). All rooms have an iron and board, hair dryer, and free Wi-Fi.

WHERE TO EAT: This resort has a wealth of dining and snacking options. A variety of vendors along the boardwalk tempt with hot dogs, crêpes on a stick, gourmet coffee, and more. For those looking to eat in, room service is available.

Ample Hills Creamery: Enjoy hand-crafted ice cream made with hormone-free milk from grass-fed cows and organic cane sugar at this ice cream shop next to the ESPN Club. If you can't commit to one (or two) of the day's flavors, fear not: a small sample will help a heap.

Big River Grille & Brewing Works: This working brewpub features a full menu, complemented by fresh specialty ales. Guests may observe the brewmaster through floor-to-ceiling glass walls.

BoardWalk Bakery: A popular stop that offers baked goods, sandwiches, soups, and salads. This is also the place to refill a Rapid Fill resort mug.

Resort Roundup

What's the best place to stay at Walt Disney World? It's a tough question—and one that Birnbaum editors are asked all the time. The answer? Well, it depends. Do you have a favorite park? What's your price range? Will a clown's tongue that doubles as a pool slide make your day? All factors to consider. That said, here are our favorites in each of Disney's price categories:

BIRNBAUM'S ★BEST★ DELUXE

Yacht Club: In addition to a picturesque setting, this resort is all about location. For starters, you can walk to Epcot (and the Studios if you're feeling ambitious). Of course, you can always take a water taxi. You're a stone's throw from the excitement of the bustling BoardWalk entertainment district, but get to enjoy the relative peace of life on the quieter side of Crescent Lake. Excellent dining options abound. And the Stormalong Bay pool area is tops. We enjoy the Beach Club, too, but Yacht Club is a bit quieter and there are more rooms with full balconies.
Honorable mentions: Contemporary and Polynesian Village

BIRNBAUM'S ★BEST★ MODERATE

Port Orleans Riverside: One need not be a Southern aristocrat to live like one. Many of the guest buildings at this resort, formerly known as Dixie Landings, were designed to look like historic mansions. Even the food court has a certain Southern ambience. There's a table-service restaurant and a cozy lounge (which may offer entertainment). Kids enjoy dropping their hooks in the fishing hole (strictly catch-and-release) and splashing in the free-form pool on Ol' Man Island. Pretty gardens and a relatively reasonable price add to the appeal.
Honorable mention: Coronado Springs

BIRNBAUM'S ★BEST★ VALUE

Art of Animation: This colorful "value" property has some of the boldest and brightest theming around and a top-notch food court—but what sets it apart is the stunning Big Blue Pool and the adjacent splash zone. The family suites are a true value—we're particularly fond of the *Cars*-themed accommodations, but all areas get a thumbs-up.
Honorable mention: Pop Century

BoardWalk Pizza Window: This walk-up window sells pizza by the slice and the pie. It's open for lunch and dinner.

BoardWalk Carts: Stands along the boardwalk offer snacks such as corn dogs, pretzels, hot dogs, and frozen margaritas.

ESPN Club: A serious sports bar for serious sports fans, ESPN provides sports video entertainment and all-day dining. Get there early if a big game (or game day) is scheduled.

Flying Fish: The Fish features a show kitchen, and its upscale menu emphasizes expertly prepared seafood, steak, and fresh seasonal items.

Trattoria al Forno: An Italian eatery, Trattoria features old-world favorites for the whole family. Breakfast is a character affair.

WHERE TO DRINK: Guests have a multitude of options right in their backyard.

AbracadaBAR: This enchanting enclave proffers potent potables and alcohol-free elixirs in an escapist environment.

Atlantic Dance Hall: This waterfront club is an elegantly designed dance spot. You must be at least 21 to enter. There's usually no charge, but there are exceptions for special events.

Belle Vue Lounge: Listen to old-time tunes on antique radios and play board games in this cocktail lounge near the lobby. The room is open all day, but the bartender doesn't arrive until 5 P.M.

Jellyrolls: Dueling pianos provide entertainment in a casual warehouse atmosphere. The cover charge is about $12 nightly. You must be at least 21 to enter Jellyrolls and able to prove it. Note that this place cranks the A.C. year-round.

Leaping Horse Libations: The carousel-themed pool bar at Luna Park serves a variety of cocktails, as well as sandwiches and snacks.

WHAT TO DO: The three-quarter-mile pathway encircling Crescent Lake provides a ready venue for walkers and joggers. Guests may rent boats from Yacht and Beach Club's Bayside Marina. The Fantasia Gardens Miniature Golf complex is nearby. At the resort itself, Ferris W. Eahlers Community Hall lends and rents equipment for many recreational pursuits, including croquet, pool, table tennis, badminton—even books and DVDs. Fishing excursions can be arranged.

Arcade: Side Show Games Arcade has a selection of video games.

Biking: Ferris W. Eahlers Community Hall offers bicycles for rental. A (strenuous) trip around Crescent Lake on a pedal-powered surrey bike (a canopied quadracycle) is also offered for a fee.

Health Club: Muscles & Bustles health club has steam rooms, modern exercise machines and circuit-training equipment. The health club is open 24 hours a day for BoardWalk guests.

Midway Games: This area on the Board-Walk's WildWood Landing features games of luck and skill similar to those found along traditional boardwalks. There is a charge to play.

Shopping: Dundy's Sundries in the lobby is the source for basic necessities. Character Carnival on the boardwalk has children's apparel as well as character merchandise. Screen Door General Store stocks some groceries, dry goods, snacks, and beverages. Thimbles & Threads, also on the boardwalk, carries apparel for men and women. Wyland Galleries features marine and environmental art.

Swimming: The BoardWalk's swimming area, Luna Park, has a pool with a 200-foot slide, "Keister Coaster," patterned after a wooden roller coaster. (The slide, shown at right, is a clown's tongue. Most kids get a big kick out of it.) A family of elephants is found posed through-out the area; their trunks act as a shower for adults on the pool deck or children in the wading pool. The resort has two unguarded pools. There are three whirlpools, one in each pool area.

Tennis: There are two tennis courts (with lights). Rent equipment at Community Hall.

TRANSPORTATION: Guests may travel to Epcot and Disney's Hollywood Studios via ferryboats or walkways. (It takes about 10 minutes to walk to International Gateway, aka

Epcot's back door. The stroll to Disney's Hollywood Studios takes about 20 minutes.) Buses transport guests to the Magic Kingdom, Animal Kingdom, Typhoon Lagoon, Blizzard Beach, and Disney Springs.

Disney Vacation Club

Disney Vacation Club grants members the convenience of flexible vacations from year to year, with the ability to choose when and where to visit, how long to stay, and the type of accommodations. It starts with the purchase of a real estate interest in a Disney Vacation Club property. For a one-time purchase price and annual dues, members can enjoy vacation stays at Aulani Resort & Spa (in Oahu, Hawaii); Bay Lake Tower at Contemporary resort, Animal Kingdom Villas, The Villas at Disney's Grand Floridian Resort & Spa, Old Key West Resort, Beach Club Villas, BoardWalk Villas, the Boulder Ridge Villas and Copper Creek Villas & Cascade Cabins at Disney's Wilderness Lodge (note that the "Boulder Ridge Villas" and the "Copper Creek Villas & Cascade Cabins" are separate DVC properties), Saratoga Springs Resort & Spa, and the Polynesian Villas & Bungalows at WDW; Disney's Vero Beach Resort in Florida; Disney's Hilton Head Island Resort in South Carolina; and the Villas at Disney's Grand Californian Resort & Spa in Anaheim, California; plus access to additional destinations around the globe. Through Member Getaways, members may also elect to stay at their choice of more than 500 resorts worldwide, including most Disney resorts and the Disney Cruise Line.

Disney's Vero Beach Resort is a two-hour drive from Walt Disney World. It has villa-type accommodations comparable to those at Disney's Old Key West Resort—with lush surroundings, the beach, and local sights. The proximity makes it easy to tack a beach vacation onto a WDW visit.

Disney Vacation Club information centers may be found at each of the Walt Disney World hotels and theme parks. For more information, call 800-800-9100, or visit *www.disneyvacationclub.com*.

PHOTO BY JILL SAFRO

Port Orleans French Quarter

This 1,008-room resort invites comparisons to the historic French Quarter of New Orleans.

Starting at the entrance gate, with its wrought-iron portal and overgrown landscape, the appeal of the Delta City surrounds arriving guests. The entry drive leads to the heart of the "city," which is Port Orleans Square. The central building was based on a turn-of-the-20th-century mint. The Mint houses check-in facilities, a shop, food court, and an arcade. It has a vaulted ceiling, and the check-in desks are designed as bank-teller windows. The musical notes in the mural are the notes to "When the Saints Go Marching In." To reach Port Orleans French Quarter, call 407-934-5000.

ROOMS: The guestrooms are located in seven 3-story buildings (with elevators). Each room has two queen beds; some king-size beds are available. The rooms are a bit smaller than the standard rooms at the more expensive Disney hotels, but they are comfortable for a family of four. (Rooms with a small bunk can fit 5, provided that the fifth person is kid-sized.) Buildings are brightly colored and have wrought-iron railings of varying designs. Connecting rooms may be requested but can't be guaranteed. The least expensive rooms overlook gardens or parking areas, and the most expensive rooms offer water views. All guestrooms have a coffeemaker (with coffee), mini fridge, and Wi-Fi.

WHERE TO EAT: A counter-service food court has several dining options. Disney Springs, and its plethora of eateries, is accessible by boat or bus.

Sassagoula Floatworks & Food Factory: A variety of specialty foods is available in this food court, including gumbo, chicken with red beans and rice, freshly made beignets, and other traditional Creole dishes. Burgers, pizza, ice cream, and baked goods are also on the menu.

WHERE TO DRINK: A pool bar operates seasonally, and guests on a quest for a cocktail may head to Port Orleans Riverside—it's a short bus ride away. Of course, there's always Disney Springs or any theme park other than the Magic Kingdom. (Epcot has quite a few sipping spots.)

WHAT TO DO: A themed pool is the highlight of the recreational opportunities here.

Arcade: South Quarter Games is located at Port Orleans Square. The arcade has a selection of state-of-the art, interactive games.

Biking: Bicycles and surrey bikes are available for rent at Port Orleans Riverside.

Carriage Rides: Refer to page 226 for details on carriage rides.

Fishing: Two-hour guided fishing excursions are available (see *Sports*).

Shopping: Jackson Square Gifts & Desires, located at Port Orleans Square, features Disney character merchandise, clothing bearing the Port Orleans resort logo, and sundries.

Swimming: Doubloon Lagoon is a pool built around a bright blue sea serpent. The waterslide is actually the mythical creature's tongue—kids love it. There is a whirlpool, too. Port Orleans French Quarter guests are also invited to swim in the pool at Ol' Man Island at Port Orleans Riverside.

TRANSPORTATION: Buses go to the Magic Kingdom, Epcot, Disney's Hollywood Studios, Animal Kingdom, Typhoon Lagoon, Blizzard Beach, and Disney Springs. Small water taxis transport guests to Disney Springs, too.

Port Orleans Riverside

Here, the city feel of the French Quarter gives way to the rural South. The resort is divided into "parishes." Closest to the "city," guestrooms are found in Mansion homes; farther upriver are the Bayou guestrooms, with a more rustic feel. The phone number for the Port Orleans Riverside resort is 407-934-6000.

ROOMS: The 2,047 Mansion and Bayou rooms are of the same size, and each has two queen beds (some king-size beds are available); nearly 400 of the Bayou rooms have a bunk-size bed (recommended for kids under age 9) as well. The Magnolia Bend Mansion rooms are situated in elegant manor homes with stately columns and grand staircases. The Bayou rooms are in rustic, weathered-wood buildings that are tucked among flora native to the area. Although all buildings have two to three floors, only the Magnolia Bend Mansions have elevators.

The Bayou rooms surround Ol' Man Island, a 3½-acre recreational area with a pool, playground, and fishing hole. Decorative touches include wood and tin armoires and pedestal sinks with brass fittings. The closet space is not enclosed. The rooms are a bit small, but they can accommodate four guests. Rooms have a coffeemaker (with coffee), fridge, and Wi-Fi (no charge).

More than 500 Riverside rooms invite guests to live like royalty. These "Royal Guest Rooms" feature special touches inspired by Disney's animated classics (all featuring royalty of some sort), ornately decorated beds with fiber-optic special effects, custom bed coverings and drapes, artwork featuring Princess Tiana and other regals, and more. If you want the royal treatment while residing at Port Orleans Riverside, make your wishes known when you book the room. Note that the rates for these rooms run higher than for standard rooms.

WHERE TO EAT: In addition to a restaurant and food court, the hotel offers limited pizza delivery from 4 P.M. until midnight.

Boatwright's Dining Hall: This 200-seat table-service eatery, next to Riverside Mill, serves Cajun specialties and American fare for dinner. Reservations are recommended.

Riverside Mill: This food court resembles an old-fashioned cotton mill with a working waterwheel that powers the cotton press inside. The five counter-service stands offer all sorts of choices. The basic selections are available for breakfast. **Pizza 'n' Pasta** has pasta dishes, pizza, and bread sticks; **Grill Shop** offers fried fish, chicken nuggets, and burgers; **Carving Station** serves freshly sliced turkey; **Specialty Shop** offers soup and sandwiches; and the **Bakery** serves pastries, ice cream, yogurt parfait, and more. If you buy a resort refillable mug, the Riverside Mill is where you fill it.

WHERE TO DRINK: Two lounges possess an enticing degree of charm.

Muddy Rivers: The poolside bar serves beer, wine, cocktails, and soft drinks. Seasonal.

River Roost: Situated in a room designed as a cotton exchange, this lounge features specialty drinks and light hors d'oeuvres.

WHAT TO DO: Many of the resort activities are offered at Ol' Man Island, a recreation center featuring a pool, whirlpool, wading pool, interactive fountains, and a playground.

Arcade: The Medicine Show Arcade features a small selection of games.

Biking: Bicycles for all ages can be rented.

Carriage Rides: Horse-drawn carriages take guests for 25-minute rides throughout the resort grounds. Carriages hold up to 4 adults or 2 adults and 3 small kids. Each trip departs from the marina. Call 407-939-7529 for reservations.

Fishing: Two-hour guided fishing excursions are available (see *Sports*). It is also possible to drop a line at the Fishin' Hole on Ol' Man Island. Catch-and-release only.

Playground: An elaborate play area is located on Ol' Man Island next to the pool.

Shopping: Fulton's General Store in the Riverside building stocks Disney character merchandise, clothing, and sundries.

Swimming: In addition to the main pool and kiddie pool at Ol' Man Island, there are five unguarded pools at the resort. Guests may also swim in the French Quarter pool.

PHOTO BY JILL SAFRO

TRANSPORTATION: Buses go from Port Orleans Riverside to Magic Kingdom, Epcot, Disney's Hollywood Studios, Animal Kingdom, Typhoon Lagoon, Blizzard Beach, and Disney Springs. Water taxis also ferry guests to and from Disney Springs. Guests may walk to Disney Springs, too.

Disney's Saratoga Springs Resort & Spa

Just across the lake from the happy hustle and bustle of Disney Springs (reachable by bus, boat, or convenient walkway), this Disney Vacation Club resort is a calm complement to its nearest neighbor. Disney's Saratoga Springs Resort & Spa aspires to recapture the heyday of upstate New York country retreats of the late 1800s. The resort covers 65 acres. Some accommodations are nearly a mile from the main building. To contact Saratoga Springs, call 407-827-1100.

ROOMS: There are studios and villas with one, two, and three bedrooms. A studio consists of a room with a queen-size bed and a double sleeper sofa, bathroom, kitchenette, microwave, and coffeemaker. All units have a porch or a balcony, access to complimentary laundry facilities, and Wi-Fi (no charge).

One-bedroom villas have a king-size bed in the master suite and a queen-size sleeper sofa in the living room. The one bathroom has a whirlpool tub. The full kitchen has a fridge, stove, microwave, toaster, coffeemaker, dinnerware, and dishwasher. Each unit has a washer and dryer.

Two-bedroom villas have an additional bath and bedroom, with either one queen-size bed and a double sleeper sofa or two queen-size beds. The three-bedroom Grand Villa has similar features as the two-bedroom models, but is about twice the size and has four bathrooms.

The resort's Treehouse Villas, elevated on pedestals and designed to blend into the woodsy environment, offer serene views of the surrounding treetops. Each "cabin-casual" villa has a full kitchen, flat-panel TVs, three bedrooms, and two bathrooms, and sleeps up to nine.

WHERE TO EAT: There are two eateries here and dozens across the lake. Several barbecue areas are available to resort guests. Note that the only room service is pizza delivery.

The Artist's Palette: Supposedly set in a converted artist's loft, this spot offers all meals. Among the simple selections are salads, sandwiches, flatbreads, and baked goods.

Turf Club Bar & Grill: Dinner is served in this spot with a horse-racing motif.

Groceries: In-room grocery delivery is available from Artist's Palette. If you've got a car, ask for directions to a grocery store.

WHERE TO DRINK: In addition to local bars, guests imbibe at nearby Disney Springs.

Backstretch Bar: A poolside watering hole.

On the Rocks: A pool bar serving the usual battery of cocktails.

Turf Club Bar & Grill: This spot serves a variety of drinks, plus it has a pool table.

WHAT TO DO: Besides enjoying spa treatments, guests may rent bikes, play basketball, swim, walk, swat tennis balls, and more.

Arcade: Expect to find the usual bells and whistles at "Win, Place, or Show."

Biking: Bicycles may be rented from Horsin' Around Rentals.

Golf: The resort is adjacent to the Lake Buena Vista golf course.

Health Club: This spot features strength and cardio machines and a selection of weight-lifting equipment.

Playground: There is a small kids' play area near an unguarded pool. (Be sure to supervise youngsters at all times.)

Shopping: The Artist's Palette stocks a variety of souvenirs and sundries.

Spa: Senses, the award-winning spa, offers massage therapy, manicures, facials, aromatherapy, and more. Call 407-939-7727 for an appointment.

Swimming: High Rock Spring cascades down rugged rock work and feeds into a free-form, heated zero-depth-entry pool. The splash zone has a waterslide, two whirlpools, and a play area for kids. There are four unguarded pools, too.

Tennis: Two clay courts are at the ready.

TRANSPORTATION: Buses go from Saratoga Springs to all theme and water parks. Boats ferry guests to Disney Springs (it's about 10 to 25 minutes on foot). The internal bus makes 7 stops throughout the resort. Buses arrive every 20 minutes.

Disney's Old Key West Resort

Escape to the spirit of the Florida Keys. Disney's Old Key West Resort is the original Disney Vacation Club property, but villas not occupied by members are available for nightly rental. It has the laid-back feel of a resort community and all the amenities that go with resort life. The homey accommodations have lots of space and the convenience of kitchen facilities, making the resort nice for longer stays. The telephone number for Old Key West is 407-827-7700.

VILLAS: A studio consists of a large room with two queen-size beds, a table and chairs, a small fridge, free Wi-Fi, microwave, and sink. Bathrooms are spacious. Each of the one-bedroom villas has a king-size bed in the master bedroom and a queen-size sleeper sofa and a sleeper chair in the living room; the master bath has a whirlpool tub, sink, and shower.

The two-bedroom villa features a king-size bed in the master bedroom, two queen-size beds in the second bedroom, living room with queen-size sleeper sofa and TV with DVD player, free Wi-Fi, dining room, and a kitchen with a fridge, dishwasher, toaster, and coffeemaker, plus plates, flatware, cooking utensils, and more.

The master bathroom is divided into two rooms with an extra-large whirlpool tub and a sink in one and an oversize shower, sink and vanity, and toilet in the other. There's a porch or balcony off the living room and bedroom, and ceiling fans in each room. The configuration of the two-story, three-bedroom Grand Villas is similar to that of the two-bedroom models, but adds a third bedroom with two double beds.

As for capacity, studios sleep 4 and one-bedroom villas sleep 5 people; two-bedroom villas sleep 9 guests, and the two-story, three-bedroom villas accommodate 12.

WHERE TO EAT: In addition to the restaurant, there are grills and picnic tables. Select food and pizza delivery is available from 4 P.M. to midnight.

Good's Food to Go: The perfect place to pick up ham and cheese on Texas toast, bread pudding, and breakfast platters in the morning. Burgers, salads, sandwiches, and snacks are offered later in the day.

Olivia's Cafe: This full-service restaurant serves Key West favorites, plus more traditional items, for breakfast, lunch, and dinner. Menus change seasonally.

WHERE TO DRINK: The watering holes at Old Key West are as laid-back as they come.

Gurgling Suitcase: This tiny bar serves specialty drinks, wine, beer, and soft drinks.

Turtle Shack: This poolside spot serves pizza, salads, sandwiches, and light snacks. Open seasonally.

WHAT TO DO: At Conch Flats Community Hall, table tennis, board games, a large-screen TV, DVD rentals, and planned activities are offered. There are basketball, shuffleboard, and volleyball courts, and equipment is available at Hank's Rent 'N Return.

Arcade: The Electric Eel Game Room is in the Hospitality House; the Flying Fish Game Room is by the Turtle Shack snack bar.

Biking: Bikes and surrey bikes may be rented from Hank's.

Health Club: The Fitness Center offers a nice variety of exercise equipment.

Playground: There are three kids' play areas located throughout the resort.

Shopping: Conch Flats General Store has groceries, books, sundries, and more.

Swimming: The main, guarded pool is located behind the Hospitality House. It features a 125-foot waterslide inside what appears to be a giant sand castle. There is a whirlpool, a kiddie pool, and a sandy play area nearby. The resort has three unguarded, "quiet" pools.

Tennis: There are two lighted courts by the main pool, plus a third on Old Turtle Pond Road.

TRANSPORTATION: Buses go to the theme parks, water parks, and Disney Springs. Water taxis also make the trip between the resort and Disney Springs.

Animal Kingdom Area

All-Star Movies, Music, & Sports

The All-Star resorts are among the most brightly and boldly themed at Walt Disney World. Each resort has 1,500 to 1,920 rooms housed in ten buildings devoted to five Disney movies, types of music, and sports.

The All-Star Movies resort celebrates five classic Disney films: *Toy Story*, *The Mighty Ducks*, *Fantasia*, *101 Dalmatians*, and *The Love Bug*. Buildings are adorned with such icons as 40-foot Dalmatians and wildly oversize versions of Buzz Lightyear and Woody.

At the All-Star Music resort, Broadway, country, jazz, rock, and calypso are the themes. A walk-through, neon-lit jukebox; a three-story pair of cowboy boots; and a Broadway theater marquee are among the giant icons.

Sports fans will find themselves in a world of baseball, football, tennis, surfing, or basketball at the All-Star Sports resort. Brightly colored, larger-than-life football helmets, surfboards, tennis balls, basketball hoops, and baseball bats adorn the buildings.

As value resorts, the All-Star properties offer few frills, but the service and whimsical atmosphere are pure Disney.

Guests check in at Cinema Hall for All-Star Movies, Melody Hall for All-Star Music, or Stadium Hall for All-Star Sports. To reach All-Star Movies, call 407-939-7000; to phone All-Star Music, call 407-939-6000; to contact All-Star Sports, call 407-939-5000.

ROOMS: The guestrooms, measuring 260 square feet, are rather small compared with those at Port Orleans, which are 314 square feet. Each

guestroom has two double beds, a vanity area with a sink, a bathroom, free Wi-Fi, a small dresser, and a small table with chairs.

All-Star Music has 215 Family Suites. Each one sleeps up to six and has two bathrooms, a "master" bedroom with its own TV, Wi-Fi (free of charge), and a kitchenette with counter space, mini fridge, sink, microwave, and coffeemaker.

WHERE TO EAT: There are three food courts—World Premiere in Cinema Hall, Intermission in Melody Hall, and End Zone in Stadium Hall. Each features a bakery, convenience store, grab-and-go items, and stations geared to pizza, pasta, salads, and burgers. Each food court has a seating areas with a beverage bar. The All-Star resorts deliver pizza and salads to rooms from about 5 P.M. to 1 A.M.

WHERE TO DRINK: There are no traditional lounges at the All-Star resorts; however, the convivial Silver Screen Spirits, Singing Spirits, and Grandstand Spirits pool bars serve drinks throughout the day and evening.

WHAT TO DO: Guests may swim in any of the All-Star resort pools. Guests may rent boating equipment at any WDW resort marina.

Arcades: Each of the All-Star resorts has its own arcade.

Playground: A playground is located in each hotel's courtyard area.

Shopping: Maestro Mickey's in Melody Hall, Sport Goofy's Gifts and Sundries in Stadium Hall, and Donald's Double Feature in Cinema Hall all have magazines, books, character merchandise, and sundries.

Swimming: Each hotel has two pools and one kiddie pool. The main pool at All-Star Movies has a *Fantasia* theme (look for Sorcerer Mickey). The smaller Duck Pond Pool is based on *The Mighty Ducks*. At the All-Star Music resort, the Calypso Pool is in the form of a giant guitar, while the Piano Pool bears a striking resemblance to a grand piano. At All-Star Sports, Surfboard Bay has an ocean motif. The smaller Grand Slam Pool pays tribute to our national pastime.

TRANSPORTATION: Buses make pickups at All-Star's Cinema Hall, Melody Hall, and Stadium Hall for trips to each of the theme parks, water parks, and Disney Springs. Each resort has its own bus stop.

A word about All-Star resort transportation: The bus service at these "value" resorts tends to be slightly more efficient than at other locations. The combination of fewer stops and connections is a bonus for guests staying here.

Disney's Animal Kingdom Lodge & Villas

At first glance, Disney's Animal Kingdom Lodge evokes images of a sleepy, little thatched-roof game lodge in the wilds of southern Africa. Upon closer examination, however, it's clear that the only things sleepy or little about this place are the small creatures that live in its shadow. Those animals, along with their more sizable cousins, inhabit acres of meticulously re-created African savanna that practically surround the resort. Birds and all manner of hoofed animals, including giraffes, zebras, and Thomson's gazelles, call the wildlife reserve home. With the freedom to wander within a dozen or so yards of the lodge itself, these critters allow guests to go on safari without leaving their balconies.

The resort is located about one mile from Disney's Animal Kingdom park (which is accessible by bus). The lobby is a huge, high-ceilinged room, richly appointed with colorful African artwork and artifacts. The biggest draw here is the four-story observation window overlooking the savanna. It's one of many portals through which to gaze upon wildlife.

Like the African game lodges on which it is based, Disney's Animal Kingdom Lodge was constructed using a semicircular design. From

overhead, it looks a bit like a horseshoe. This allows for maximum animal-viewing potential. Indeed, many of the resort's guestrooms have direct views of the savanna areas. Be sure to specify your viewing preference when you book a room. The telephone number for Disney's Animal Kingdom Lodge is 407-938-3000.

ROOMS: The 970 rooms, which are noticeably smaller than those at other deluxe Disney resorts, feature dark-wood furniture, sand-colored walls, and earth-tone carpets. Deluxe rooms are a tad more spacious than their standard counterparts. Most rooms have two queen beds (some king beds are available) and sleep up to four people; bunk beds are available in some rooms. All rooms have balconies. Suites include a parlor, plus one or two bedrooms; there are king-size or queen-size beds in the bedrooms. Bathrooms have a separate vanity area with double sink. Rooms have an iron

PHOTO BY MIKE CARROLL

PHOTO BY MIKE CARROLL

(with board), hair dryer, free Wi-Fi, and small fridge. Free weekday newspapers may be picked up near the elevators. Club-level service is available.

The Villas are located in Jambo House and in the Kidani Village, an area that features thatched-roof, hewn-timber homes. Also included in this village are a pool, fitness center, shop, table-service restaurant, and more. As with all DVC resorts, the homes are available to guests when not being used by members. For information on this member of the Disney Vacation Club family, call 800-800-9100, or visit *www.disneyvacationclub.com*.

WHERE TO EAT: In addition to its restaurants, the hotel offers round-the-clock room service.

Boma—Flavors of Africa: Boma is modeled after a bustling African marketplace. The restaurant boasts many types of cuisine in what chefs describe as a "global fusion" style. Served buffet style, the cuisine is a lovely mix of French, Malaysian, Indian, Chinese, and English.

Jiko—The Cooking Place: The colors of sunset are the backdrop for this reliable restaurant. Wines are from South Africa.

The Mara: A high-quality quick-service spot, The Mara offers above-average made-to-order flatbreads, African stew, chicken pita, and salads, plus kid-pleasers as burgers and chicken nuggets.

Sanaa: This Kidani Village star features African- and Indian-inspired cuisine.

WHERE TO DRINK: The lounges here are rustic and inviting. Some even offer the opportunity to sip cocktails while observing wildlife.

HOT TIP!

Balloons are not permitted at Disney's Animal Kingdom Lodge—it's a safety issue for the animals. You can check yours at the Bell Services desk, free of charge.

Cape Town Lounge and Wine Bar: Located inside Jiko—The Cooking Place, this spot features wines from South Africa.

Maji and Uzima Springs: These poolside bars serve specialty and traditional drinks.

Sanaa: A 24-seat lounge located within the restaurant of the same name.

Victoria Falls: Set alongside a soothing waterfall, this mezzanine-level lounge features coffee, tea, domestic and South African wines, and assorted cocktails.

WHAT TO DO: Spying on African wildlife is the main event in these parts. However, if you can manage to pry yourself away from those hoofed exhibitionists for a bit, there are plenty of other diversions available—including tennis, basketball, shuffleboard, and a barbecue pavilion. Note that guests are welcome to partake in activities offered at other Disney resort hotels.

Arcades: Pumbaa's Fun & Games and Safari So Good are both stocked with the latest games.

Children's Program: The Simba's Clubhouse play area, for (potty-trained) kids ages 3 through 12, is open in the evenings, starting at 4 P.M. It costs $15 per hour, per child (with a 2-hour minimum). Reservations are required; call 407-939-3463. Kids can learn about the resort's wildlife through nature-themed activities.

Health Club: The Zahanati Massage and (24-hour) Fitness Center has exercise equipment, sauna, and spa services, including massage, facial, and nail services. To make an appointment, call 407-939-7727. Kidani Village's Survival of the Fittest also offers exercise equipment.

Playground: The Hakuna Matata playground is located near the Uzima pool.

Shopping: Zawadi Marketplace stocks Africa-themed gifts, Disney-character merchandise, clothing with the Animal Kingdom Lodge logo, and sundries. Johari Treasures tempts shoppers at Kidani Village.

Swimming: The resort's main pool, Uzima, is meant to resemble a watering hole. More impressive than the size of the zero-depth-entry pool, however, is the view from the pool deck. There is a kids' pool and two whirlpools nearby. Kidani Village is home to another pool (Samawati Springs) and to Uwanja Camp, a watery playground.

Tennis: There are two clay courts available to all Animal Kingdom Lodge guests.

TRANSPORTATION: Buses go to the Magic Kingdom (a 25- to 30-minute ride), Epcot, Disney's Hollywood Studios, Animal Kingdom, Typhoon Lagoon, Blizzard Beach, and Disney Springs.

Coronado Springs

This resort reveals its Southwestern U.S.–Mexican theme in such elements as a tiled and stucco lobby with a fountain and a pyramid with water tumbling down from it that appears to have created the Mayan ruin–themed pool. The 1,912 rooms are found in three guest areas that stretch around Lago Dorado, a 22-acre lake. (It can take five minutes or more to walk to the farthest rooms. Many guests opt to use the bus that makes a loop around the resort.) The food court and restaurant are near the lobby. A convention center offers access to business services. The phone number for Coronado Springs is 407-939-1000.

Note: A 15-story tower, complete with rooftop restaurant, is being erected at Coronado Springs. Construction should be complete by 2019, when the tower will start hosting guests.

ROOMS: Standard rooms are smaller than those at Disney's deluxe hotels, but adequate for up to four; each has two queen beds (some king-size beds are available). In-room amenities include a coffee-maker, refrigerator, hair dryer, and free Wi-Fi. In the Casitas area, where most suites are located, terra-cotta guest buildings occupy a citylike landscape. In the pueblo-style Ranchos, scattered along a dry streambed, rooms have a rustic feel. Cabanas, located along the rocky palm-lined beach, reflect the casual feel of their namesake.

WHERE TO EAT: In addition to two full-service restaurants and food court, limited room service is available for breakfast and dinner.

Cafe Rix: A quick-service eatery, Rix has offerings for breakfast, lunch, and dinner.

Las Ventanas: This quiet, table-service destination serves three meals a day.

Maya Grill: Open for dinner, Maya offers seafood, steak, and authentic Mexican dishes.

Pepper Market: High ceilings make this nontraditional food court feel like an open-air market. The fare includes tacos, empanadas, pizza, pasta, and omelets made to order.

WHERE TO DRINK: There are three places to wet your whistle at Coronado Springs.

Laguna Bar: A lagoonside lounge outside the lobby, this spot serves drinks daily.

Rix Lounge: This lounge provides cocktails and appetizers, and is in the main building.

Siestas Cantina: In the Dig Site area, this pool bar lets swimmers and archaeologists enjoy drinks and light fare (three meals a day).

WHAT TO DO: There is an array of water sports in which to participate, as well as volleyball and a short nature trail.

Arcade: Iguana Arcade is in the Dig Site area.

Biking: Bikes and surrey bikes may be rented at La Marina.

Fishing: Two-hour, guided fishing excursions are offered on the 22-acre Lago Dorado. Call 407-WDW-BASS. Fishing excursions are offered seasonally.

Health Club & Salon: La Vida fitness center offers strength and cardio equipment 24/7, plus spa services (by day). The salon provides a full line of hair care services (including a "Perfectly Prepared Princess" package), beard and mustache trim, manicures, pedicures, facials, and more. Hours are generally from 9 A.M. until 7 P.M. daily. To make an appointment, call 407-939-3965.

Playground: The Explorer's Playground, part of the Dig Site area, includes a sandbox, complete with Mayan carvings waiting to be excavated.

Salon: Casa de Belleza Salon is located next to La Vida Health Club. It's a full-service facility.

Shopping: Panchito's Gifts & Sundries is where to find souvenir items with a Southwestern flavor, Disney merchandise, and necessities.

Swimming: The main pool is in the Dig Site area. It surrounds a Mayan pyramid and features a towering 123-foot waterslide. There is a whirlpool and a kiddie pool. Each guestroom area features an unguarded pool.

TRANSPORTATION: Buses go to the Magic Kingdom, Epcot, Disney's Hollywood Studios, Animal Kingdom, Typhoon Lagoon, Blizzard Beach, and Disney Springs.

ESPN Wide World of Sports Area

Pop Century

What do you get when you mix decades of American pop culture with a Disney resort? Pop Century! Like the All-Star resorts, Pop Century is a vivid celebration of Americana. The 2,880-room resort represents the second half of the twentieth century. The resort's larger-than-life "time capsules" commemorate the toys, fads, dance crazes, and catchphrases that swept the nation from the 1950s through the 1990s. It's groovy . . . you dig?

As a WDW value resort, the Pop Century property offers few frills, but the service is good, the atmosphere's colorful, and the transportation is efficient. There's even a peaceful lake to stroll around on temperate days. (It's shared by Pop's next-door neighbor, Disney's Art of Animation resort.) Guests check in at Classic Hall, which also features a food and merchandise location, arcade, and guest services desk. To contact Disney's Pop Century resort, call 407-938-4000.

ROOMS: The guestrooms measure 260 square feet (a bit smaller than Port Orleans' rooms, which are 314 square feet). Each room has two double beds, a vanity area with a sink, a bathroom, a small dresser, a table with chairs, a fridge, and free Wi-Fi.

WHERE TO EAT: The food court features a bakery and a convenience market, plus several stands geared to pizza, pasta, and burgers. The Pop Century resort delivers pizza to guestrooms from about 4 P.M. to midnight.

WHERE TO DRINK: Petals is a bar located near the Hippy Dippy pool.

WHAT TO DO: Guests may swim in any of the Pop Century resort pools and enjoy a 1.4-mile walk or run around Hourglass Lake.

Arcade: Revisit classic video games or discover some new ones at Fast Forward arcade.

Playground: There is one soft-surface playground.

Shopping: The Everything Pop shop has a selection of books, character merchandise, sundries, and snacks.

Swimming: The hotel has three pools (in the shapes of a bowling pin, computer, and a flower), plus a kiddie pool.

TRANSPORTATION: Buses stop at Classic Hall for trips to each of the four theme parks, Blizzard Beach and Typhoon Lagoon water parks, and Disney Springs.

PHOTO BY JILL SAFRO

Art of Animation

The Walt Disney World resort landscape has gotten a serious burst of color thanks to this exceptionally vivid celebration of Disney animation. A "value" resort, Disney's Art of Animation made its debut in 2012.

Pop Century's next-door neighbor (the resorts share access to Hourglass Lake and the nearly 1.4-mile jogging path that surrounds it), Art of Animation boasts colossal figures from classic animated films. It also has three themed pools, playgrounds, festive courtyards, an arcade, and a splash zone featuring everyone's favorite clownfish, Nemo. The resort also offers free Wi-Fi, laundry, and dry cleaning (fees apply for the last two services).

ROOMS: The 864 standard rooms, which are housed in *The Little Mermaid*–themed buildings, sleep up to 4 and come with the usual amenities afforded to Walt Disney World's "value" resorts (see page 75 for details). Each measures 277 square feet and has two double beds, a vanity area with a sink, a bathroom, a small dresser, a table with chairs, and free Wi-Fi. The 1,120 festive family suites, which are themed to *Cars*, *Finding Nemo*, and *The Lion King*, feature 3 separate sleeping areas, accommodate up to 6

guests, and come with 2 flat-screen TVs, a queen-size bed, double-size pull-down bed, and sleeper sofa. Each 565-square-foot suite has a living room, 2 bathrooms, and a kitchenette (with a small refrigerator, microwave, and coffeemaker).

WHERE TO EAT: The brilliantly hued Landscape of Flavors food court features four unique cooking stations serving international favorites, Mongolian barbecue, burgers, pizza, pasta, sandwiches, fresh smoothies, and hand-scooped gelato. It's open for breakfast, lunch, and dinner. There is a grab-and-go selection, too. In-room pizza delivery is also an option.

WHERE TO DRINK: The Drop Off is a full-service bar located near the Big Blue Pool.

WHAT TO DO: Guests may swim in any of the Art of Animation resort pools, walk or jog around Hourglass Lake, and more.

Arcade: Pixel Play Arcade is in Animation Hall, across from Landscape of Flavors.

Jogging and Walking: The resort is encircled by a trail that's almost 1.4 miles long.

PHOTO BY JILL SAFRO

Playground: The Righteous Reef playground can be found in the middle of the Finding Nemo courtyard.

Shopping: The Ink and Paint Shop has a selection of books, character merchandise, Art of Animation resort–themed souvenirs, sundries, and snacks.

Swimming: The hotel has three pools: Flippin' Fins, Cozy Cone, and The Big Blue Pool, plus a *Finding Nemo*–themed splash zone known as The Schoolyard Sprayground.

TRANSPORTATION: Buses stop at Animation Hall for trips to each of Walt Disney World's four theme parks, Blizzard Beach and Typhoon Lagoon water parks, and Disney Springs.

PHOTO BY JILL SAFRO

Resort on Dream Tree Blvd.

Four Seasons Orlando

Walt Disney World welcomed a Four Seasons resort into its happy hotel fold in 2014. The 443-room luxury property boasts more than 26 lakeside acres of elegant design, as well as a multitude of recreational diversions and high convenience for Disney guests. Spanish Revival architecture reflects Florida's Golden Age mansions and is surrounded by a vibrant array of 72,000 plants and nearly 1,000 palm trees. Check-in begins at 4 P.M. daily. Check-out time is 12 P.M. There is a 24-hour business center, plus ample meeting space suitable for conferences and social functions. Four Seasons Orlando resort is an AAA Five-Diamond award winner. For additional information or to make reservations for the hotel, call 800-267-3046, or visit *www.fourseasons.com/orlando.*

ROOMS: All rooms have furnished balconies, one king or two double beds, twice-daily housekeeping service, newspaper delivery, 24-hour room service, and high-speed Internet and Wi-Fi. Rooms also come with a safe, coffeemaker (with coffee), DVD player, iPod docking station, flat-screen TV, and minibar. There are terry-cloth bathrobes to use throughout your stay (kids' robes are available upon request). Accommodations feature luxurious marble bathrooms with double sinks and soaking tub, hair dryer, lighted makeup mirrors, and a TV in the mirror (yes, *in* the mirror!). Hypoallergenic bedding is available upon request. Cribs may be requested (no charge), as can high chairs, bottles, and toddler toys. Babysitting services may be arranged for an hourly fee (reservations must be made at least 24 hours in advance).

The resort has many rooms that are accessible for guests with disabilities. Make your needs known when you book the room. Four Seasons is a nonsmoking resort.

Room categories include (distant) Park View, Lake View, Golden Oak View, and Four Seasons Rooms. Park View rooms offer a distant view of the Magic Kingdom and Happily Ever After, the park's nightly fireworks presentation. Lake View rooms have views of a lake, golf course, or pool area. Golden Oak rooms offer "residential views" of privately owned homes, while Four Seasons rooms have limited views.

Suites have king beds, two bathrooms, and living area with queen sleeper sofa. To book a room, call 800-267-3046. For suites (including the 9-bedroom Royal Suite or Presidential Suite), call 407-313-6734.

The lobby's Disney Planning Center assists with the purchase of park tickets, making Disney dining reservations, reserving special events, and more. When it comes to Walt Disney World privileges, the resort fits somewhere between Swan and Dolphin and the resorts on Hotel Plaza Boulevard. Among the perks:

• Complimentary transportation to Disney World destinations is provided by a Four Seasons luxury motor coach. (There are on-site vehicles available for rent, too.)

• Guests may use the theme parks Package Express delivery service. Merchandise can be delivered directly to the resort from any WDW theme park and many shops (no charge).

• Fastpass+ selections may be booked starting 30 days before arrival. (Refer to page 25 for details on this system that allows guests to book advance reservation times for theme park shows and attractions.)

• Disney characters visit the resort's Ravello restaurant for the "Good Morning Breakfast" on Thursdays and Saturdays year-round (and on Tuesdays during school breaks and major holidays). Expect the likes of Goofy and his pals.

WHERE TO EAT: There are four full-service eateries and a coffee bar, plus 24-hour in-room dining. Reservations are recommended for Capa and Ravello (call 407-313-6161).

Capa: This contemporary, Spanish-style steakhouse specializes in prime cuts, tapas (appetizer portions), and local seafood such as freshly shucked oysters. There is indoor and outdoor seating at this rooftop hot spot. Capa is open for dinner only, 6 P.M. to 10 P.M.

Lickety-Split: Located in the lobby, this is the perfect place for gourmet coffees and quick bites. Selections include breakfast pastries, grab-and-go items, gelato, and more. There is indoor and outdoor seating.

PB&G: Think pulled pork, smoked brisket, burgers, and creative salads at this Southern-style smokehouse and rotisserie, located poolside (all seating is alfresco). Open 11 A.M. to 6 P.M.

Plancha: A relaxed Cuban-American eatery, Plancha is located at the Tranquilo Golf Club. It offers salads, the classic Cubano sandwich, and chorizo burgers. The cocktail menu includes mojitos and Hemingway daiquiris. The hours are 10 A.M. till 6 P.M.

Ravello: Guests are invited to watch the action in this modern Italian eatery's open kitchen. In addition to regionally influenced specialties, Ravello serves fresh bread and pizza, and housemade pasta. Two private dining rooms are also available. Ravello is open for breakfast (6:30 A.M. to 11 A.M.) and dinner (5:30 P.M. to 10 P.M.). The dress code here is "smart casual."

WHERE TO DRINK: Guests may quench their thirst and enjoy creatively prepared nibbles at a duo of lovely lounges.

Lobby Bar: Drinks mix well with the appetizers, entrées, and desserts at this lounge.

Capa Bar: As you sip a beverage on the patio, you may also enjoy the Magic Kingdom's fireworks. Capa Bar is open from 5 P.M. to 11 P.M.

WHAT TO DO: There's no getting bored in these parts. The Explorer Island play province could be enjoyed for days on end. In addition to a swimmer's paradise, the amusing island boasts a rock-climbing wall, volleyball, basketball, pool, Ping-Pong, and more. Outdoor movies are presented on select nights.

Children's Program: The resort's complimentary "Kids for All Seasons" program is open to youngsters ages 4 to 12, daily from 10 A.M. until 6 P.M. Trained staffers supervise and entertain kids throughout the day. Little ones under ages 4 are welcome to participate if accompanied by a guardian.

Fun and Games: The Mansion on the resort's Explorer Island is a family-focused hangout with outdoor activities such as table tennis, bocce ball, and pool (the kind you play with a cue stick). The Hideout has video games, basketball hoops, and beach volleyball.

Golf: Golfers may argue that the resort's crowning glory is the secluded course at the Tranquilo Golf Club. The Tom Fazio–designed, 18-hole, 6,968-yard, par 71 course is a certified Audubon sanctuary with abundant opportunities to view local wildlife between swings. Amenities include a pro shop, instruction, driving range, putting green, club rental, and a restaurant (Plancha). The course is open to both guests of the hotel and daytime visitors (fees apply). To reserve tee times, call 407-313-7777.

Health Club: The 24-hour Fitness Centre has cardiovascular equipment, weights, and yoga, plus a steam room, sauna, and whirlpool spa. Certified trainers are on hand, too (for a fee).

Movies: The resort presents alfresco films on select nights at the Star Struck "dive-in" movie screen (near the pool on Explorer Island).

Spa: The Spa at Four Seasons evokes the peace and natural beauty of Florida's Everglades. The Zen zone features 18 treatment rooms, as well as two bungalows for private retreats. There are also outdoor lounges and a whirlpool. The Salon provides hairstyling, manicures, pedicures, and other services.

Swimming: The resort's swimming areas are part of an enormous playground known as Explorer Island: The Oasis, a lakeside adults-only pool; The Explorer Pool, a zero-depth-entry family pool; Splash Zone, a soft-surface interactive fountain area that sprays water up to 30 feet in the air; a 1,203-foot-long lazy river, complete with a waterfall and bubbling rapids; and two 242-foot waterslides.

Tennis: The resort sports three Har-Tru tennis courts for play and instruction (fees apply to both activities).

Weddings: From the rehearsal dinner to the ceremony, reception, and even the honeymoon, Four Seasons can accommodate the wishes for most fairy-tale occasions, from intimate to grand. Wedding specialists may be reached by calling 407-313-6745, or visiting *www.fourseasons.com/orlando/weddings*.

TRANSPORTATION: A complimentary bus goes to the Transportation and Ticket Center (TTC) every 30 minutes (from there, guests take a ferry or monorail to the Magic Kingdom); buses go to Epcot, Disney's Hollywood Studios, and Animal Kingdom once every hour. Airport and individual transfers throughout the Walt Disney World area are available for a fee.

Resorts near Disney Springs

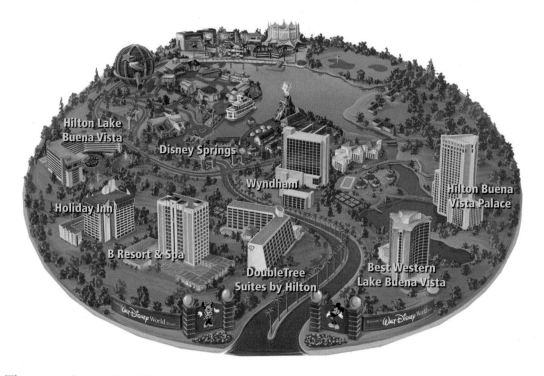

These seven hotels—Best Western Lake Buena Vista, DoubleTree Suites by Hilton, Wyndham, B Resort & Spa, Hilton Buena Vista Palace, Hilton Orlando Lake Buena Vista, and Holiday Inn—though inside WDW boundaries, are neither owned nor operated by Disney. However, a few have been here since the park opened in 1971 or soon thereafter (under different names), accommodating Mickey enthusiasts from the very beginning. The hotels are not Disney themed, though several have meals hosted by Disney characters and all have Disney shops. For details, visit *disneyspringshotels.com*.

Often referred to as Disney Springs Resort Area Hotels, they line the mile-long Hotel Plaza Boulevard. The Hilton, Buena Vista Palace, and Wyndham are across from the Disney Springs Marketplace, with its shops, restaurants, and nightlife. The other four properties are a 10- to 25-minute stroll away. The privileges of staying in one of these hotels include:

• Car rental desk on the premises (at select Hotel Plaza Boulevard resorts).

• Free bus service to the four theme parks, with limited service to Disney Springs, Typhoon Lagoon, and Blizzard Beach. The buses, which are not part of the Disney transportation network, make stops every 30 minutes, beginning one hour prior to park opening; be sure to allow extra time for bus travel. One bus serves the Hilton, DoubleTree, Holiday Inn, and B Resort & Spa; another serves the other hotels (it takes at least ten minutes to stop at all resorts on the loop). Note that buses load and unload in the middle of the parking lot at some of the parks.

• Pedestrian bridges connect Hotel Plaza Boulevard with Disney Springs Marketplace.

• Flexibility to book tickets for both on- and, in most cases, off-WDW-property attractions.

• Preferred access to Disney golf courses.

• A "Passport to Savings" coupon book with exclusive discounts and specials on dining, shopping, and entertainment.

• Reservations for Disney dinner shows and theme park restaurants.

Note that guests staying in the resorts on Hotel Plaza Boulevard do have to pay for parking at Disney parks and other Disney World attractions, and they cannot charge purchases made at Disney World shops and restaurants with a resort ID (though they can buy a MagicBand and link it to a major credit card).

To book a room at a Disney Springs Area Hotel Plaza Boulevard resort, call the resort itself or call Walt Disney World Central Reservations at 407-W-DISNEY (934-7639). Resorts on Hotel Plaza Boulevard are included in several Walt Disney Travel Company packages.

All of the hotels offer nonsmoking rooms and accommodations for travelers with disabilities. To get to the hotels from the airport, take Exit 68 off I-4.

BEST WESTERN LAKE BUENA VISTA RESORT:

This 18-story hotel is surrounded by pines and has an entry lined with oaks draped in Spanish moss. Each of the 325 spacious, smoke-free rooms and suites features either one king-size bed and a queen sofa bed or two queen-size beds, as well as floor-to-ceiling windows and furnished balcony. Rooms also come with free Wi-Fi, flat-screen TV, coffeemaker, refrigerator, safe, hair dryer, and iron with board. Baths have one sink and plenty of counter space.

Each of the four suites occupies a corner of the 18th floor and features a wet bar, two phones, two TVs, a refrigerator, microwave, whirlpool tub, and an impressive glassed-in porch with skylights and a ceiling fan. Rooms on the seventh floor and higher offer views of Disney Springs or the other resorts on Hotel Plaza Boulevard.

The hotel also has a fitness center, business center, game room, heated pool, small kiddie pool, sundry store, Disney gift shop, and guest laundry facilities (for a fee).

Trader's Island Grill is open for lunch and dinner. The Flamingo Cove offers poolside or inside seating and serves lunch, dinner, drinks, and snacks. For guests on the go, there's Market-place Café. It offers a variety of grab-and-go items, as well as Pizza Hut Express selections. For each paying adult, one child (age 10 or younger) eats for free. This perk is offered at all of the hotel's restaurants. Room service is also an option.

Rates for this hotel range from about $99 to $239 for rooms; about $299 to $399 for suites. Parking fees apply for both self- and valet parking. There is an additional daily resort fee. Best Western Lake Buena Vista Resort, 2000 Hotel Plaza Blvd., Lake Buena Vista, FL 32830; 407-828-2424 or 800-348-3765; *www.lakebuenavistaresorthotel.com*.

DOUBLETREE SUITES BY HILTON:

This 229-unit property has a stellar staff, homey atmosphere, and low-slung facade reminiscent of WDW's Contemporary hotel. Upon check-in, families receive a bag of chocolate chip cookies. The only all-suite hotel in the Disney Springs area, it has roomy (625 square feet) units, each with a living room and sleeper sofa, dressing area, and separate bedroom. The one-bedroom suites sleep up to six; there are five two-bedroom suites. Most of the bedrooms have two queen beds; a few king beds are available.

The decor features cheerful blues and greens offset by contrasting neutrals. Room amenities include two TVs, small refrigerator, coffeemaker, microwave, hair dryer, high-speed Internet (for a fee), small dining/work table, and safe.

Recreational facilities include a heated pool, splash pad for kids, and a whirlpool in a land-scaped area, plus a fitness room, two lighted tennis courts, jogging trail, and small play-ground. Evergreen, a full-service restaurant with a pool bar, offers a breakfast buffet, lunch, and dinner, as well as snacks and sandwiches throughout the day. Cocktails are available at

the lobby bar. A market/deli provides snacks and groceries. There is a Budget Rental Car desk by the lobby.

Rates range from about $99 to $399. Parking fees apply for self- and valet parking. DoubleTree Suites by Hilton Orlando, 2305 Hotel Plaza Blvd., Lake Buena Vista, FL 32830; 407-934-1000 or 800-222-8733; *www.doubletreeguestsuites.com.*

PHOTO BY JILL SAFRO

WYNDHAM: The Wyndham offers two distinct lodging opportunities: A 19-story tower with 232 rooms is known as Wyndham Lake Buena Vista, while the Wyndham Garden section features 394 rooms spread over two 5-story buildings. (Be sure to make your preference known when you make your reservation.) The resort sports a spiffy look, obvious upon stepping into the cheerful Bermuda-themed lobby. Most rooms have two double beds, though 77 king-bed rooms are available. There are 7 spacious suites. All accommodations include a refrigerator, coffeemaker, free Wi-Fi, TV, plush bedding, a safe, hair dryer, iron, and daily newspaper (upon request). Guests receive a discount at many shops and restaurants at nearby Disney Springs—safely accessible via pedestrian bridge.

Extensive recreational facilities include an exercise room, two lighted tennis courts, a sand volleyball court, and a basketball court. The impressive Oasis Aquatic Playground features a heated pool with zero-depth-entry, interactive features such as water cannons, and a hot tub. Kids-only activities are offered. There's a health club, arcade, and business center, too.

Lake View Restaurant (on the mezzanine level) serves breakfast and dinner. Breakfast is hosted by Disney characters on Tuesday, Thursday, and Saturday. Sundial is open 24 hours and has snacks and light fare. For cocktails, there's Horizons Bar (next to Lake View), the Eclipse lobby bar, and Oasis pool bar.

A lobby merchandise shop sells assorted sundries and Disney-themed souvenirs. Room rates range from about $119 to $159 year-round; suites range from $150 to $350. There is an additional (daily) resort fee for other amenities, as well as an $8-per-day parking fee. Wyndham, 1850 Hotel Plaza Blvd., Lake Buena Vista, FL 32830; 800-624-4109 (Wyndham Lake Buena Vista); 844-482-8444 for Wyndham Garden; *www.wyndhamlakebuenavista.com.*

HILTON LAKE BUENA VISTA: Aka Hilton Orlando Lake Buena Vista, this hotel gets high marks for its 23 well-groomed acres, laid-back ambience, pool area, and upscale shops. The 814 rooms, all of which have been extensively refurbished, are outfitted with two queen or one king bed (suites are available for larger parties), have minibars, voice mail, safes, and high-speed Internet access.

Among the resort's restaurants and lounges, Andiamo Italian Bistro, open daily from 5:30 P.M. until 11:30 P.M., offers American and Italian fare, while Benihana Steakhouse and Sushi serves Japanese favorites and entertainment (both eateries serve dinner only); Covington Mill serves breakfast and lunch (with Disney characters attending Sunday breakfast); Rum Largo Pool-side Bar and Cafe serves burgers, sandwiches, salads, and tropical drinks alfresco; Mainstreet Market, open 24 hours, is part deli, part country store (serving Starbucks coffee). For light meals,

PHOTO BY JILL SAFRO

snacks, or drinks, drop by John T's lounge. There is an Avis car rental on the premises. And Disney Springs is a 5- to 10-minute walk away, across a pedestrian footbridge.

Recreational facilities include a tropical whirlpool, two heated swimming pools, a kiddie pool, fitness room, and large game room. Rates range from $99 to $299; suites are $149 to $1,500. Parking charges apply for self-parking and valet. Hilton, 1751 Hotel Plaza Blvd., Lake Buena Vista, FL 32830; 407-827-4000 or 800-782-4414; *www.hiltonorlandoresort.com*.

Note: As of January 1, 2016, the Hilton no longer participates in Walt Disney World's Extra Magic Hours program.

HOLIDAY INN: This family-friendly hotel features 323 nonsmoking rooms that have either one king or two queen beds. Some are available with views of nearby Disney Springs. Guestrooms are decorated in earth tones and include a flat-screen TV with DirecTV, Keurig coffee-maker, microwave, mini fridge, safe, and hair dryer. Bathrooms have granite countertops and feature Bath & Body Works products. Free high-speed Wi-Fi is available in all guestrooms and restaurants, as well as in the lobby.

The Palm Breezes Restaurant, located in the atrium, serves three meals a day (kids through age 12 eat free). Palm Breezes has a grab-and-go section, a bar, and provides room service. There is a zero-depth-entry heated pool, a whirlpool, Disney store, and 24-hour fitness center. Parking

charges apply for self- and valet parking. There is an additional daily resort fee.

Room rates range from approximately $129–$272. Holiday Inn; 1805 Hotel Plaza Blvd., Lake Buena Vista, FL 32830; 407-828-8888 or 888-465-4329; *www.hiorlando.com*.

B RESORT & SPA: A glitzy addition to Hotel Plaza Boulevard, B pulls out all the modern stops in its 394 guestrooms and suites. Amenities include large HD flat-screen TVs, bunk beds, in-room safe, beverage cooler, and iPad/iPod docking stations. Select rooms have sleeper sofas and kitchenettes. Free wireless Internet service is available to all guests. Complimentary loaner iPads are available upon request.

Resort guests may enjoy the outdoor, heated infinity-edge saltwater pool with interactive water features, the 5,000-square-foot B Indulged full-service spa and wellness center, and the B Active fitness center. American Kitchen Bar & Grill, the resort's signature restaurant, features "farm to table dining" and presents a salad bar on the back of a 1950s cherry-red Ford pickup truck that sits in the middle of the restaurant. Stop by the Pick-Up—a casual one-stop shop and ice cream parlor just off the lobby—which serves quick breakfasts, snacks, and various sundries.

B Resort, 1905 Hotel Plaza Boulevard, Lake Buena Vista, FL 32830. For reservations or additional information, visit *www.bresortlbv.com*, or call 407-828-2828 or 888-662-4683.

HILTON BUENA VISTA PALACE: The tallest hotel in the Disney Springs area and the largest of the resorts based at Hotel Plaza Boulevard (it's actually near the intersection of Hotel Plaza Boulevard and Buena Vista Drive) is a cluster of towers set on 27 acres. The resort, which is also known as Hilton Orlando Buena Vista Palace, is quickly (and safely) connected to Disney Springs via pedestrian bridge.

Each of the 1,011 rooms has a ceiling fan, high-speed Internet access, two queen beds or one king, a coffeemaker, 32-inch flat-panel TV, and weekday newspaper in the lobby. Most rooms have a balcony or patio. In addition, there are 103 one- and two-bedroom suites and two-story penthouses with microwaves. Twin/queen sofa beds are in suites and rooms with king beds. All guestrooms have a small safe and refrigerator.

The hotel also provides daily room service (breakfast is served from 6 A.M. to 11 A.M. and dinner is offered from 4 P.M. to 11 P.M.), a Disney shop, and a guest laundry room. Dining spots include the lakeside Letterpress restaurant, which serves breakfast, lunch, and dinner. Disney characters are in attendance on Sunday mornings from 8:30 A.M. till 11:30 A.M. Citrus 28 Grab N Go, open from 6 A.M. to 11 A.M., features freshly prepared light meals and snack items, plus drinks (including Starbucks coffee); Sunnies Lobby Lounge offers appetizers, snacks, and cocktails until 1 A.M., and Shades Pool Bar & Restaurant serves burgers, fries, wraps, beverages, and more.

The resort's impressive new recreation zone features a zero-depth-entry pool with lazy river

PHOTO BY JILL SAFRO

Shades of Green

Shades of Green is a recreational retreat for active and retired military personnel and their families, members of the reserves and the National Guard, and U.S. Department of Defense employees. This 586-room resort is near the Grand Floridian but is not linked with the monorail system.

The resort features two tennis courts, two pools, a small health club, restaurant, bar and lounge, gift shop, arcade, laundry facilities, and free transportation around WDW.

Room rates are based on military or civilian grade. Select multi-day tickets are offered at a discount. The property's three golf courses—the Palm, the Magnolia, and Oak Trail—are open to all WDW guests (see *Sports* for details). All other activities are for hotel guests and their families only.

Disney's Magical Express motor coach service is not available to guests staying at this resort. The number for Shades of Green is 407-824-3400; *www.shadesofgreen.org*.

Float Lagoon, a pool designated for grown-ups, and poolside food and beverage service. Pool cabanas may be rented. There's a fitness center with Life Fitness Equipment and the luxurious Kay Casperson Lifestyle Spa and Boutique. For spa reservations, call 407-827-3200, or visit *http://www.buenavistapalace.com/spa-en.html*.

Rates for rooms are generally about $125 and up per night (no charge for kids under 18); suites, which sleep four to eight, are $149 and up. Rollaways cost $35 per night; cribs are free. There is an Alamo/National car rental desk here, too. Hilton Buena Vista Palace, 1900 Buena Vista Dr., Lake Buena Vista, FL 32830; *www.buenavistapalace.com*; 407-827-2727 or 866-397-6516.

HOT TIP!

The Hilton Buena Vista Palace is just a 5-minute walk from the Marketplace at Disney Springs. It is directly across the street, safely and easily accessed by an elevated pedestrian walkway.

Magic Kingdom

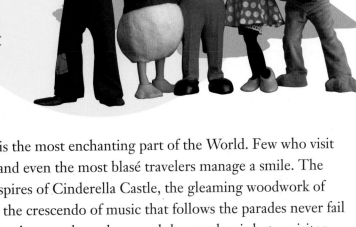

MAGIC KINGDOM

The Magic Kingdom is the most enchanting part of the World. Few who visit it are disappointed, and even the most blasé travelers manage a smile. The sight of the soaring spires of Cinderella Castle, the gleaming woodwork of the Main Street shops, and the crescendo of music that follows the parades never fail to have an effect. Even when the crowds are large and the weather is hot, a visitor who has toured this wonderland dozens of times can still look around and think how satisfying this place is for the spirit.

What makes the Magic Kingdom timeless is its combination of the classic and the futuristic. Both childhood favorites and space-age concepts have a home here. Every "land" has a theme, carried through from the costumes worn by the hosts and hostesses and the food served in the restaurants to the merchandise sold in the shops, and even the design of the trash cans. Thousands of details contribute to the overall effect, and recognizing these touches makes any visit more enjoyable.

But the delight most guests experience upon first glimpse of the Magic Kingdom can disappear when disorientation sets in. There are so many bends to every pathway, so many sights and sounds clamoring for attention, it's too easy to wander aimlessly and miss the best the Magic Kingdom has to offer. So we earnestly suggest that you study this chapter before your visit.

MAGIC KINGDOM

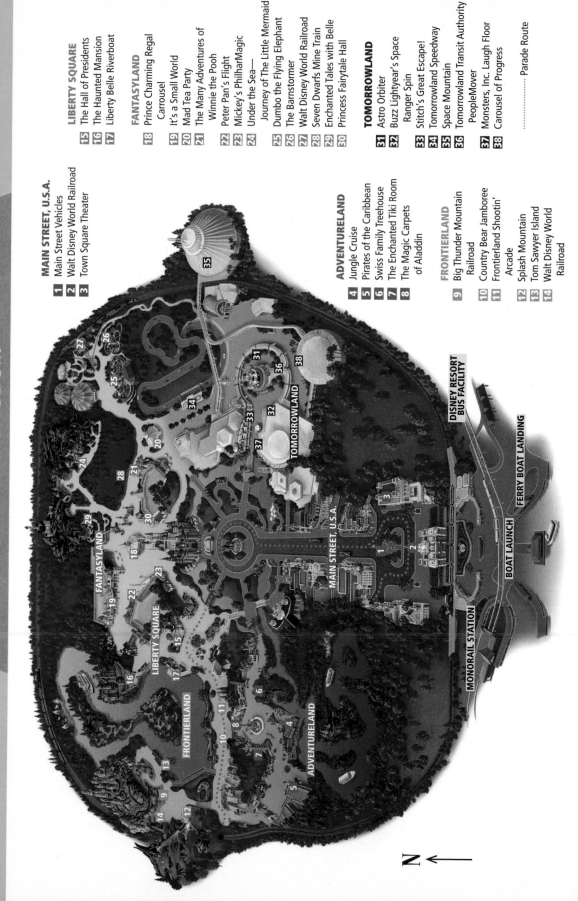

MAIN STREET, U.S.A.
1. Main Street Vehicles
2. Walt Disney World Railroad
3. Town Square Theater

LIBERTY SQUARE
15. The Hall of Presidents
16. The Haunted Mansion
17. Liberty Belle Riverboat

FANTASYLAND
18. Prince Charming Regal Carrousel
19. It's a Small World
20. Mad Tea Party
21. The Many Adventures of Winnie the Pooh
22. Peter Pan's Flight
23. Mickey's PhilharMagic
24. Under the Sea—Journey of The Little Mermaid
25. Dumbo the Flying Elephant
26. The Barnstormer
27. Walt Disney World Railroad
28. Seven Dwarfs Mine Train
29. Enchanted Tales with Belle
30. Princess Fairytale Hall

TOMORROWLAND
31. Astro Orbiter
32. Buzz Lightyear's Space Ranger Spin
33. Stitch's Great Escape!
34. Tomorrowland Speedway
35. Space Mountain
36. Tomorrowland Transit Authority PeopleMover
37. Monsters, Inc. Laugh Floor
38. Carousel of Progress
.... Parade Route

ADVENTURELAND
4. Jungle Cruise
5. Pirates of the Caribbean
6. Swiss Family Treehouse
7. The Enchanted Tiki Room
8. The Magic Carpets of Aladdin

FRONTIERLAND
9. Big Thunder Mountain Railroad
10. Country Bear Jamboree
11. Frontierland Shootin' Arcade
12. Splash Mountain
13. Tom Sawyer Island
14. Walt Disney World Railroad

Getting Oriented

When you visit Walt Disney World's original theme park, it's vital to know the lay of the "lands." The Magic Kingdom has six lands—Main Street, U.S.A.; Adventureland; Frontierland; Liberty Square; Fantasyland (including the Storybook Circus area); and Tomorrowland. Main Street begins at Town Square, located just inside the park gates, and runs directly to Cinderella Castle. The area in front of the castle is known as the Central Plaza or the Hub. Bridges over the waterways here serve as passages to each of the themed lands.

As you enter the Hub, the first bridge on your left goes to Adventureland; the next, to Liberty Square and Frontierland. On your right, the first bridge heads to Tomorrowland; the second, to Fantasyland. The end points of the pathways leading to the lands are linked by a street that is roughly circular, so that the layout of the Magic Kingdom resembles a wheel.

Guidemaps and Times Guides are available at the park entrance, at City Hall in Town Square, and at many shops. You'll find them to be valuable navigational and scheduling resources.

HOW TO GET THERE

Take Exit 64B off I-4. Continue about four miles to the Auto Plaza and park; walk or take a tram to the main entrance complex, known as the Transportation and Ticket Center (TTC). Choose a seven-minute ferry ride or a slightly shorter trip by monorail for the last leg of an anticipation-filled journey.

By WDW Transportation: From the Grand Floridian and Polynesian Village: monorail or boat. From the Contemporary: monorail or walkway. (It's roughly a 7- to 15-minute stroll, depending on the pace.) From Epcot: monorail to the Transportation and Ticket Center (TTC), then transfer to the Magic Kingdom monorail or ferry. From Disney's Hollywood Studios and Animal Kingdom: bus. From the resorts on Hotel Plaza Boulevard: bus to the TTC, then transfer to a ferry or monorail. From Fort Wilderness: boat or bus. From Wilderness Lodge: boat or bus. From Disney Springs: bus to any Walt Disney World resort and transfer to the Magic Kingdom bus (or monorail). From all other Walt Disney World resorts: buses.

PARKING

All-day car parking at the Magic Kingdom starts at $20 for day visitors (free to WDW resort guests with a valid resort ID, MagicBand, or an annual pass; trucks, trailers, and RVs cost more; preferred parking costs $40). Bear left after passing through the Auto Plaza; attendants will direct you into a lot. Several preferred lots are within walking distance of the TTC; all others are served by trams.

Note the section and aisle in which you park. (Even better: take a photo with your phone.) The parking ticket allows for re-entry to the parking area throughout the day.

HOURS

The Magic Kingdom is generally open from 9 A.M. to about 8 P.M. However, during busy seasons, it's open later. It's best to arrive up to an hour before opening time. Guests are allowed to wander Main Street, U.S.A., before the rest of the park opens for the day. It's possible to shop and grab breakfast before Let the Magic Begin—the Castle stage show that kicks off each day. If you prefer to avoid the morning crush, consider postponing your visit until 1 P.M. or later.

Note that on select days, the Magic Kingdom opens early or stays open late for WDW resort guests only (this is known as Extra Magic Hours). For details, visit *www.disneyworld.com*, or call 407-824-4321. The park tends to be more crowded on such days, so plan accordingly. We recommend booking Fastpass+ assignments in advance.

GETTING AROUND

Walt Disney World Railroad steam trains make a 20-minute loop of the park, stopping to pick up and drop off passengers at stations on Main Street, Frontierland, and Fantasyland. (It's an efficient way to travel when parades are being run or there's a lot of foot traffic.) Horseless carriages, a fire engine, and horse-drawn trolleys take turns offering one-way trips down Main Street (during non-peak hours).

Park Primer

BABY FACILITIES

The best place in the Magic Kingdom to take care of little ones' needs is the Baby Care Center. This cheery site, equipped with changing tables and facilities for nursing mothers, is next to the Crystal Palace restaurant. Disposable diapers are for sale at the Baby Care Center (if possible, bring your own—the packages are small and a tad pricey). All park restrooms are equipped with changing facilities.

CAMERA NEEDS

Box Office Gifts in the Town Square Theater has memory cards and batteries, disposable cameras, and more. Selfie sticks are not permitted in the park.

DISABILITY INFORMATION

Most Magic Kingdom shops and restaurants, and many attractions, are accessible to guests using wheelchairs. Additional services are available for guests with visual or hearing disabilities. The *Guide for Guests with Disabilities* provides an overview of all services available, including transportation, parking, and attraction access. You can pick one up at the park entrance or at City Hall. For more information, see the "Travelers with Disabilities" section of the *Getting Ready to Go* chapter.

FERRY VERSUS MONORAIL

For guests arriving by car or bus, it's necessary to decide whether to travel to the Magic Kingdom by ferry or monorail. The monorail usually makes the trip from the Transportation and Ticket Center (TTC) in about 6 minutes, while the ferry takes about 7. During busy seasons, the ferry will often get you there faster (long lines can form at the monorail, and most people don't make the short walk to the ferry landing). Guests who use wheelchairs should note that while the monorail platforms are accessible, the ramp

HOT TIP!

Certain attractions keep shorter hours than the Magic Kingdom itself (e.g., The Enchanted Tiki Room, The Country Bear Jamboree, and Tom Sawyer Island). To make sure you catch your favorites, check a Times Guide when you enter the park.

leading to the boarding area is a bit on the steep side, prompting many guests to opt for the ferry.

FIRST AID

A registered nurse tends to minor medical problems at the First Aid Center, located near the Crystal Palace restaurant. For medical emergencies, alert a cast member and call 911.

INFORMATION

City Hall, just inside the park entrance, serves as the Magic Kingdom's information headquarters. Guest Relations reps can answer questions and help with MagicBands. Guidemaps and Times Guides, updated weekly (including details about entertainment and character greeting times and locations), are also available here. Should you have problems with your ticket or a question about the number of unused days remaining on a ticket, City Hall is good place to go.

LOCKERS

Attended lockers are located just inside the park entrance, all the way to the right. Lockers are also available at the Transportation and Ticket Center (TTC). Cost is $8–$10 per day (plus a $5 refundable deposit) for unlimited use. If you "hop" to another park on the same day, you don't have to pay to get another locker. Simply present your receipt to the attendant and you're all set.

LOST & FOUND

On the day of your visit, report lost articles at City Hall or at the TTC. Recovered items can also be claimed at these locations. After your visit, call 407-824-4245.

LOST CHILDREN

Report lost children at City Hall or the Baby Care Center, and alert the nearest Disney employee to the problem.

MONEY MATTERS

The Magic Kingdom has five Automated Teller Machines (ATMs): near the locker rental site; in City Hall on Main Street, U.S.A.; near the Frontier Shootin' Arcade; near Pinocchio Village Haus; and in the shop next to Space Mountain. Most foreign currency can be exchanged at City Hall.

Credit cards (American Express, Visa, Master-Card, JCB, Discover Card, and Diner's Club) are accepted as payment for admission, merchandise, and at most dining locations. Traveler's checks and Disney gift cards are accepted most places, as are MagicBands and WDW resort ID cards (when backed up with a major credit card). Some food and souvenir carts accept cash only.

While no longer sold, Disney Dollars are still accepted for dining and purchases at most Walt Disney World locations and may be exchanged for U.S. currency. (Production of new Disney Dollars was discontinued in 2016.)

PACKAGE PICKUP

Individual shops can arrange for purchases to be transported to the Package Pickup at the Main Street Chamber of Commerce, next to City Hall, for pickup between noon and park closing time (at least three hours after purchase). Packages may be sent to most Disney resorts, too. The delivery service is free.

PARK RULES

To ensure a comfortable, safe, and enjoyable experience for all guests, visitors are asked to comply with all Park rules, signs, and instructions including:

- All bags are subject to inspection.
- Guests are subject to screening via wand and/or metal detector.
- Proper attire is required.
- Smoking is allowed in designated areas only.
- Selfie sticks are not permitted in Disney parks.
- Weapons (including toys) are prohibited.

For additional details and a complete listing of Disney Park Rules, visit Guest Relations or go to *www.disneyworld.com/ParkRules*.

SAME-DAY RE-ENTRY

Wear your MagicBand if you used it for admission or retain your ticket if you plan to return later the same day.

SECURITY CHECK

All guests entering Disney parks are subject to a thorough security check, including a metal detector screening. Backpacks, parcels, purses, etc., will be searched by security personnel before guests may pass through the entrance.

HOT TIP!

Will you need a stroller during your visit? Consider bringing one from home. It will save you money, and it can be used all over WDW. (Disney rentals may not be removed from the parks.) Chances are your baby buggy is more comfortable than the ones in the parks, too—they are made of hard plastic. If yours is too cumbersome for travel, consider buying an "umbrella" stroller or renting a user-friendly carriage from a company such as Magic Strollers (see page 67).

STROLLERS & WHEELCHAIRS

Wheelchair Rental, located just inside the entrance, all the way to the right, offers wheelchairs (some oversized) and Electric Conveyance Vehicles (ECVs). Strollers are available under the Main Street Train Station. The cost for strollers is $15 per day ($13 per day with a multi-day rental); double strollers cost $31 per day ($27 a day with a multi-day rental); wheelchairs are $12 per day, $10 with multi-day rental; $50 per day for ECVs, with a $20 refundable deposit. Quantities are limited. Hold on to your receipt; it can be used on the same day to get a replacement stroller or wheelchair at any of the theme parks. Multi-day rentals, called Length of Stay tickets, save you two dollars off the daily price. Keep your receipt handy.

To prevent your stroller from getting lost in a sea of stroller clones, consider personalizing it with an item such as a ribbon or a sign. Do not leave valuables in an unattended stroller.

Admission Prices

ONE-DAY BASE TICKET*
(Restricted to use only in the Magic Kingdom. Prices are presented in the following order: Value, Regular, and Peak. **Prices do not include tax and are likely to rise in 2018.**)

Adult...$107/$115/$124
Child**.......................................$101/$109/$118

* 1-Day tickets purchased in 2018 must be used by December 31, 2019

** 3 through 9 years of age; children under age 3 free

Main Street, U.S.A.

Marceline, Missouri, the tiny rural town that was his boyhood home.

Most of the structures along the thoroughfare are given over to shops, and each one is different. Some emporiums are big and bustling, others are relatively quiet and orderly; some are spacious

HOT TIP!

Attention, early birds: Guests (with tickets) are welcome to visit Main Street, U.S.A., before the posted Magic Kingdom opening time. You can spend 30 to 45 minutes moseying along the nostalgic thoroughfare, grabbing some breakfast (for dining details, refer to *Good Meals, Great Times*), and shopping for souvenirs (packages can be held at the park's Package Pickup location free of charge). As park opening time approaches, head to the Castle forecourt stage for a lively, character-laden show known as Let the Magic Begin.

and airy, others are cozy and dark. Inside and out, maintenance and housekeeping are superb.

White-suited sanitation workers patrol the street to pick up litter and quickly shovel up any evidence of the horses that pull the trolley cars from Town Square to the Hub. As in the rest of the Magic Kingdom, the pavement here is washed down every night with hoses. There's one crew of maintenance workers whose sole job is to change the little white lights around the roofs; another crew devotes itself to keeping the woodwork painted. As soon as these people have worked their way as far as the Hub, they start all over again at Town Square. The greenish, horse-shaped, cast-iron hitching posts are repainted 20 times a year on average—and totally scraped down each time.

The "attractions" along Main Street, U.S.A., are relatively minor compared to the really big deals such as Tomorrowland's Space Mountain, Frontierland's Splash Mountain, or The Haunted Mansion in Liberty Square. But each and every shop has its own quota of merchandise that is meant as much for show as for sale. It's almost as entertaining to watch the cooks stir up gooey batches of fudge or peanut brittle at the Main Street Confectionery as it is to actually savor a sample. The shop windows, particularly at the Emporium, are also worth a look.

Stepping onto Main Street, U.S.A., is like jumping through a time portal. Welcome to turn-of-the-twentieth-century America! Horse-drawn trolleys are the transportation of choice, peppy patriotic music underscores the bustle of merry, moving masses, and the tantalizing aroma of fresh-baked cookies perfumes the air.

A rose-colored retrospective? Maybe. But this is Disney's version of a small-town Main Street—and the charm of this nostalgic land is lost on no one. Anchored by an old-fashioned train station at one end and a fairy-tale castle at the other, Main Street, U.S.A., whisks you from reality to fantasy in a few short blocks.

All of the addresses here feature fresh coats of paint, curlicued gingerbread moldings, and pretty details. Add to that the baskets of hanging plants and gaslights, and Main Street, U.S.A., becomes a true showplace—both in the bright light of high noon and after nightfall, when the tiny lights edging all of the rooflines are flicked on.

The street represents an ideal American town. Although such a town never really existed, many claim to have served as the inspiration for it. Chances are Walt Disney got the idea from

Once you start to meander along Main Street, be sure to notice the names on the second-story windows. Above the Uptown Jewelers store (near the Confectionery) is that of Walt's nephew, Roy E. Disney. And you will see Walt's name above the ice-cream parlor. Other names are those of people closely connected with The Walt Disney Company.

WALT DISNEY WORLD RAILROAD:

The best introduction to the Magic Kingdom, the 1½-mile journey on this rail line is as much a must for the first-time visitor as it is for railroad buffs. It offers an excellent orientation as it passes by most of the park's major lands.

Walt Disney himself was a railroad aficionado. During the early years of television, viewers watched films of him circling his own

backyard in a one-eighth-scale train, the Lilly Belle (named for his wife). The 1928 steam engine is the same age as Mickey Mouse.

The Walt Disney World Railroad also has a Lilly Belle among its quartet of locomotives. The others are named Roy O. Disney, Walter E. Disney, and Roger E. Broggie (a Disney Imagineer who shared Walt Disney's enthusiasm for antique trains). All of them were built in the U.S. around the turn of the century and later taken to Mexico to haul freight and passengers in the Yucatán, where Disney scouts found them in 1969. The United Railways of Yucatán was using

PHOTO BY JILL SAFRO

them to carry sugarcane. Brought north once again, they were completely overhauled, and even the smallest of parts were reworked or replaced.

The train circles the park in about 20 minutes, making stops in Main Street, U.S.A., Frontierland, and Fantasyland. Trains arrive every 5 to 10 minutes. The line is usually shorter in Frontierland, but there's rarely a long wait at any station. The train is the best way to reach the exit when parades take over Main Street, U.S.A.

Note: The Walt Disney World Railroad does not run during fireworks presentations.

MAIN STREET VEHICLES: A number of these can be seen traveling up and down Main Street—horseless carriages and jitneys patterned after turn-of-the-century vehicles; a spiffy scarlet fire engine; and a troop of trolleys drawn by Belgians and Percherons, two strong breeds of horse that once pulled plows in Europe. These animals—weighing in at about a ton each and shod with plastic (easier on their hooves)—pull the trolley the length of Main Street about two dozen times during each of their working days. Between shifts, they can be seen resting inside Main Street's Car Barn. Feel free to stop by the entrance to say hello. At day's end, they go home to their barn at Fort Wilderness.

Note: Main Street Vehicles generally operate during daytime hours on off-peak days.

TOWN SQUARE THEATER: FP+ Themed as a Victorian-era theater, this is an ideal spot to meet and mingle with Mickey Mouse. Of course, this being a magic kingdom, Mickey has a few tricks up his sleeve. Yep, in addition to all his other skills, the Mouse is a master magician. Who knew? Note that this is strictly a "backstage" experience, as Mickey's magic show is still in the rehearsal stage. The wait here can be quite long—get a Fastpass+ if you can.

FP+ = Fastpass+ attraction (see page 25)

Adventureland

Adventureland seems to have even more atmosphere than the other lands. That may be due to its neat separation from the rest of the Magic Kingdom by the bridge over Main Street on one end and by a gallery-like structure (where it merges with Frontierland) on the other, or, possibly, it's because of the abundance of landscaping.

The centrally located attraction, The Magic Carpets of Aladdin, sets the tone for this corner of the Kingdom. Still surrounded by tropical splendor, the area has the look and feel of a bustling marketplace—the likes of which one might stumble upon in Agrabah. Shops here offer imports from around the globe.

As guests stroll away from Main Street, U.S.A., they just may hear the sound of beating drums, the squawks of parrots, and the regular boom of a cannon. Paces quicken. And the wonders that are soon to be encountered do not disappoint.

Calling All Pirates!

Captain Jack Sparrow needs your help. He knows there's treasure to be found and enemies to fight in Adventureland (yeah, that means you, Captain Barbossa!), but Jack can't do it alone. So he's recruiting Magic Kingdom guests to join his pirate posse.

The interactive quest, "A Pirate's Adventure—Treasure of the Seven Seas," begins at The Crow's Nest, near the Pirates of the Caribbean attraction. That's where potential pirates use a MagicBand or talisman (which activates magical effects throughout the land) and a mission map. There are five missions in all, some of which involve dodging blow darts and cannon fire. It's free to play (how's that for a little hidden treasure?!), and the maps and talisman are yours to keep. Arrrrr!

SWISS FAMILY TREEHOUSE: This is everybody's idea of the perfect treehouse, with its many levels and comforts—patchwork quilts, mahogany furniture, candles stuck in abalone shells, even running water in every room. Based on the wondrous banyan-tree home in Disney's 1960 rendition of the classic story *Swiss Family Robinson*, it rarely fails to intrigue. It's easy to understand why, when given the chance to leave the island (several adventures later), all but one member of the Robinson family chose to stay on. The only modern convenience the Robinsons could use? An elevator! Expect to burn off a few calories climbing up and down the stairs. Be sure to enjoy the view of the park from the tree-top.

The Spanish moss draping the branches is real; the tree—unofficially called *Disneyodendron eximus*, a genus that is translated roughly as "out-of-the-ordinary Disney tree"—was constructed by the props department. Some stats: Its concrete roots poke 42 feet into the ground, and about 300,000 lifelike polyethylene leaves "grow" on the tree's 1,400 individual branches.

JUNGLE CRUISE: FP+ Inspired in part by the 1955 documentary *The African Lion* and the classic film *The African Queen*, this ten-minute adventure is one of the crowning achievements of Magic Kingdom landscape artists for the way it takes guests through surroundings as diverse as a Southeast Asian jungle, the Nile Valley, and an Amazon rainforest. Along the way, passengers encounter zebras, giraffes, lions, headhunters, and more (all of the Audio-Animatronics variety); they also see elephants bathing and tour a temple—while listening to an amusing, though corny, spiel delivered by the skipper. (Bet you didn't know that Schweitzer Falls was named after the famous doctor Albert . . . Falls.)

This classic adventure, which is best enjoyed by daylight, is one of the park's slower-moving attractions. It's popular with guests of all ages.

WALT DISNEY'S ENCHANTED TIKI ROOM:

Welcome to a tropical (and blissfully air-conditioned) paradise! After a pre-show greeting courtesy of talented toucans known as Clyde and Claude, guests stroll into the legendary Tiki Room. Here, fine-feathered legends José, Michael, Pierre, and Fritz take center stage—as they did when the attraction first opened at Disneyland in 1963. Cherished for its historical significance (the Tiki Birds starred in the original Audio-Animatronics attraction), the show has evolved a bit over time.

The performance features the aforementioned friends, plus some 200 additional birds, flowers, and tiki statues singing up a tropical storm. Let's all sing like the birdies sing!

THE MAGIC CARPETS OF ALADDIN: FP+

Adventureland's high-flying attraction is conveniently situated in the Agrabah–themed center of the action. It features not one, but 16 carpets that soar through the air in a fashion similar to those airborne elephants over in Fantasyland. Each flying carpet accommodates four guests at a time. Depending on where you sit, you'll have control of the carpet's movement (vertical controls are in the front row; side-to-side are in the back row). Be prepared to dodge the occasional stream of liquid, courtesy of an expectorating camel.

BIRNBAUM'S ★ BEST ★ PIRATES OF THE CARIBBEAN: FP+

Quite simply, this is one of the very best of the Magic Kingdom's classic adventures. The beloved ten-minute cruise is a Disneyland original, added to Walt Disney World's Magic Kingdom (in slightly revised form) due to popular demand. Here, guests board a small boat and set sail for a series of scenes showing a pirate raid on a Caribbean island town, dodging cannon fire and weathering one small, though legitimate, watery dip along the way. There are singing donkeys, plastered pigs, and marauding miscreants; the observant may note a few familiar rapscallion residents. Beloved scallywag Captain Jack Sparrow has dropped anchor here, as has his nefarious nemesis, Captain Barbossa. And there's soon to be a new pirate in town! Following an extensive ride refurbishment in 2018, the famous redhead (and longtime resident of the attraction) is joining forces with the local marauders and hopes to help the townspeople "unload" their valuables at the Mercado Auction.

While it may not be the World's most politically correct attraction, the rendition of "Yo Ho, Yo Ho, a Pirate's Life for Me"—the catchy theme song—makes the somewhat unsavory scenario into something that comes across as good fun.

And, yes, this is the attraction that inspired the *Pirates of the Caribbean* movies—which, in turn, inspired the attraction.

Frontierland

With the Rivers of America lapping at its borders and Big Thunder Mountain rising up in the rear, this re-creation of the American Frontier encompasses the area from the Mississippi River to the Southwest, from the 1770s to the 1880s. In these parts, shops, restaurants, and attractions have unpainted barn siding or stone or clapboard walls, and there are several wooden sidewalks of the sort Marshal Matt Dillon used to stride along. The Walt Disney World Railroad makes a stop here.

FRONTIERLAND SHOOTIN' ARCADE:
This modest arcade is set in an 1850s town in the Southwest Territory. Positions overlook Boothill, a town complete with bank, jail, hotel, and cemetery.

Genuine Hawkins .54-caliber buffalo rifles have been refitted, and when the infrared beam strikes any of the targets, an interesting result is triggered. Struck tombstones rise, sink, spin, or change their epitaphs; hit a cloud and a ghost rider gallops across the sky; a bull's-eye on a grave digger's shovel causes a skull to pop out of the grave.

There is an additional charge to play here (usually about a buck—bring quarters).

COUNTRY BEAR JAMBOREE:
The Country Bears may never make it to the Grand Ole Opry, but they don't seem to mind. Disney's brood of banjo-strummin' bruins has been playing to packed houses in Grizzly Hall for more than a quarter century. Judging by all the toe tappin' and hand clappin' that accompany each performance, the show remains a countrified crowd-pleaser. As for the few folks who aren't charmed by the backwoods ballads and down-home humor, well, they just have to grin and bear it.

As guests are settling into their seats (all of which provide a decent view), Buff, Max, and Melvin are beginning to grumble. Despite their status as permanent fixtures in the theater, the mounted animal heads would rather not "hang around all day" waiting for the show to get going. The 11-minute revue opens with a rousing ditty by the Five Bear Rugs. The wheels set in motion, the remaining songs come fast and furious. Together, they capture the spirit of a genre that has a tendency to celebrate and lampoon itself simultaneously.

For example, Bunny, Bubbles, and Beulah bemoan "All the Guys That Turn Me On Turn Me Down"; Henry, the easygoing emcee who sports a coonskin cap (still attached to the 'coon), belts out "The Ballad of Davy Crockett"; and Big Al, the oversize tone-deaf fan favorite, woefully croons "Blood on the Saddle," much to the delight of the giggle-prone audience.

Timing Tip: This attraction typically opens at 11 A.M. each day, even when the rest of the park opens earlier in the morning.

TOM SAWYER ISLAND:
This patch of land in the middle of the Rivers of America has hills to scramble up; a working windmill, Harper's Mill, with an owl in the rafters and a perpetually creaky waterwheel; and a few pitch-black caves. To reach the island, guests take a raft across the river. (It's the only way to get there and back.)

Paths wind this way and that, and it's easy to get disoriented. Keep an eye out for mounted maps scattered about the island.

There are two bridges here—a suspension bridge and a barrel bridge, which floats atop some lashed-together wooden barrels. When one person bounces, everybody lurches—and all but the most chickenhearted laugh. Both of the bridges are easy to miss, so be sure to keep your eyes peeled.

PHOTO BY JILL SAFRO

Across the suspension bridge is Fort Langhorn. Poke around and you'll discover a twisting and slightly scary escape tunnel. Walk along the pathway on the banks of the Rivers of America and you'll find your way back to the bridges.

The whole island seems as rugged as backwoods Missouri and, probably as a result, it actually feels a lot more remote than it is—enough to be able to provide some welcome respite from the bustle.

One particularly pleasant way to relax here is at a waterside table. It's sometimes possible to buy a snack—and you are always welcome to bring your own. Restrooms are beside the main raft landing and inside Fort Langhorn.

Timing Tip: This attraction closes at dusk.

BIRNBAUM'S **★BEST★** **SPLASH MOUNTAIN:** FP+ On the day this attraction made its official 1992 Walt Disney World debut, everyone got soaked—thanks in part to a particularly potent Florida rain cloud. But the rain wasn't entirely responsible for the sea of soggy Magic Kingdom guests. The five-story drop into an aqueous briar patch was. And a steady stream of thrill-seekers has been taking the plunge ever since.

HOT TIP!

If you'd like to get soaked on Splash Mountain, sit on the right side of the log.

In this guaranteed smile inducer, guests enjoy a waterborne journey through brightly colored swamps and bayous, and down waterfalls, and are finally hurtled from the peak of the mountain to a briar-laced pond five stories below.

Splash Mountain is based on the animated sequences in Walt Disney's 1946 film *Song of the South*. The scenery entertains as the story line follows Br'er Rabbit as he tries to reach his "laughin' place." It's tough for a first-time rider to take in all the details, since the tension of waiting for the big drop is all-consuming.

It is a bit terrifying at the top, but once back on the ground, it seems most riders can't wait for another trip—even though they may get drenched. (Water-wary guests are sometimes seen wearing rain ponchos on this attraction. On the other hand, if you want to get soaked, try to sit up front or on the right; seats in the back receive a smaller splash.)

By the second or third time around, it's possible to relax a bit, enjoy the interior scenes, and take in the spectacular views of the Magic Kingdom from the top of the mountain. At this point, you may even manage to keep your eyes open for the duration of the final fall—or at least part of it.

Splash Mountain's designers not only borrowed characters and color-saturated settings from *Song of the South*, but also used quite a bit of the film's Academy Award–winning music in this attraction. As a matter of fact, the song in Splash Mountain's final scene, "Zip-a-Dee-Doo-Dah," has become something of a Disney anthem over the years.

Note: You must be at least 40 inches tall to ride Splash Mountain. The final drop may be too scary for some kids (and grown-ups!). There's a small play area for parents to tend to tykes while older kids ride. If you'd like to absorb as little precipitation as possible, sit on the left side of the log—though no seat is splash free.

PHOTO BY JILL SAFRO

BIRNBAUM'S BEST

BIG THUNDER MOUNTAIN RAILROAD: FP+ It's certainly not hard to spot Big Thunder, the lone red rock formation this side of the Mississippi. Even newcomers to the Magic Kingdom will be able to distinguish the landmark from its famed counterparts—Splash and Space mountains—because it's the only one that actually looks like a real mountain range. The designers took Utah's Monument Valley as inspiration, and the resemblance is actually quite remarkable.

According to Disney legend, the 2.5-acre mountain is chock-full of gold. Unfortunately for the residents of Tumbleweed, the local mining town, a flood has ruined any chance of uncovering the remaining gold. Before the prospectors find drier land, they are having one last party at the saloon to celebrate their riches. Even though in danger of washing away, they don't seem too worried—and guests who decide to take a trip on the Big Thunder Mountain Railroad have nothing to worry about either.

After passing through the new interactive queue area, guests are advised to "hang on to your hats and glasses 'cause this here's the wildest ride in the wilderness." Do heed the warning, but don't despair. The ride, though thrilling, is relatively tame, so relax and enjoy the sights. (Passengers seated nearest the caboose experience more turbulence than those seated closer to the front.)

A bleating billy goat atop a peak, a family of possums hanging overhead, and a dark cavern full of bats, not to mention chickens, donkeys, and washed-up miners, can be spotted along the way. Be sure to keep an eye out for the not-yet-sunken saloon—it's easy to miss the first time around.

A continuous string of curves and dips around Big Thunder's pinnacles and caverns is sure to please thrill-seekers of all ages, but the adrenaline surge is caused by more than just the speed of the trip. The added sound of a rickety track, a steam whistle that blows right before the train accelerates into a curve, and an unexpected earthquake all compound the passengers' anticipation, making this attraction one of the Magic Kingdom's most popular.

Note: You must be at least 40 inches tall and immune to motion sickness to experience the Big Thunder Mountain Railroad attraction.

Timing Tip: Plan to visit early in the morning, during a parade, or just before closing time. Of course, you can always plan ahead and get a Fastpass+. If you will be visiting during a parade, consider taking the Walt Disney World Railroad to the Frontierland station. The train circumvents much of the parade congestion.

PHOTO BY MIKE CARROLL

Sorcerers of the Magic Kingdom

Uh-oh—Disney villains are trying to take over the Magic Kingdom, and *you* can help defeat them. How? First, Merlin the magician will make you (and everyone with you) an apprentice sorcerer. Then you'll use magic spell cards to beat the bad guys and save the park.

The interactive game starts at the Firehouse on Main Street, U.S.A., or in Liberty Square (behind Ye Olde Christmas Shoppe). Simply present your valid park ticket or MagicBand and you'll receive a special key card, five magic spell cards, and a map. (The folks behind the counter can answer questions, too.) As you follow the clues, you will try to prevent villains from stealing Merlin's crystal ball and keep the Magic Kingdom safe.

There is no extra charge to play, and the magic spell cards are yours to keep. You may get a new set of cards each day you visit the park. Having trouble getting a complete set? Know that other guests are often eager to trade. Many guests—of all ages—enjoy collecting the cards as much as they do playing the game.

Liberty Square

The transition between Frontierland on one side and Fantasyland on the other is so smooth that it's hard to say just when you arrive at Liberty Square, yet ultimately, there's no mistaking the location. The small buildings are clapboard or brick and topped with weather vanes; the decorative moldings are Federal or Georgian in style; the glass is sometimes wavy; and there are flower boxes in shop windows. There's a bounty of shops, plus two of the park's most famous attractions—The Haunted Mansion and The Hall of Presidents—and the Liberty Tree Tavern, one of the few table-service restaurants in the Magic Kingdom park. There's a convincing replica of the Liberty Bell, too.

THE HALL OF PRESIDENTS: The Hall of Presidents attraction made its debut with the Magic Kingdom park way back in 1971. At press time, a newly refreshed version of the classic show was in the works for 2018. Previous incarnations of this multimedia celebration of U.S. leaders has covered the country's origins, the framing of the Constitution, and national triumphs and struggles from the Civil War (which lead Abraham Lincoln to deliver the Gettysburg Address) to the present day. Throughout, it has focused on the role of United States presidents in the shaping of American history and has applauded the ordinary people who have risen to the nation's highest office and led us through extraordinary circumstances.

All 45 U.S. presidents will be represented in the theater. The observant may note that there are only 44 Audio-Animatronics figures on the stage. No, Disney Imagineers did not misplace a president. Grover Cleveland served two non-consecutive terms, so he is the 22nd and 24th president of the United States. Donald Trump, number 45, will be added to the Hall by early 2018.

Displays in the pre-show area give guests a chance to gaze upon bits of Americana, such as painted eggs from a White House Easter egg hunt and dresses from former first ladies (exhibit items will change from time to time).

This attraction is being completely refurbished. Details were not available at press time, but the new show will continue to present its patriotic tribute to the leaders of the United States of America—as well as a special vantage point of the nation's history. All details are subject to change.

THE MUPPETS PRESENT . . . GREAT MOMENTS IN AMERICAN HISTORY:
Hear ye, hear ye! Greats moments in history (all American) are being reenacted in 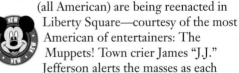 Liberty Square—courtesy of the most American of entertainers: The Muppets! Town crier James "J.J." Jefferson alerts the masses as each show is about to begin (check a Times Guide if you'd like to plan ahead) and he's joined by the likes of the super patriotic Sam Eagle, Kermit the Frog, Miss Piggy, The Great Gonzo, and other fuzzy patriots. Gather below the windows at and beside The Hall of Presidents attraction as Kermit and Company act out such historical moments as Paul Revere's ride, the ratification of the Declaration of Independence, and much more. This Muppet-y celebration of American life, liberty, and the pursuit of happiness is fun for all ages.

PHOTO BY JILL SAFRO

LIBERTY BELLE RIVERBOAT: Based in Liberty Square and built in dry dock at Walt Disney World, this is a genuine steamboat. Its boiler turns water into steam, which is then piped to the engine, which drives the paddle wheel that propels the boat. It is not the real article in one key respect, however: It moves through the nine-foot-deep Rivers of America on an underwater rail.

The pleasant ride, with narration by an actor playing Mark Twain, is a good way to beat the heat on steamy afternoons. En route, a variety of props creates a sort of Wild West effect: moose, deer, a burning cabin, and the like. The tour is completed within 17 minutes. Note that this attraction usually opens an hour or so after the park itself and shuts down before other park attractions do.

BIRNBAUM'S
★BEST★

THE HAUNTED MANSION: FP+ This eerie, eight-minute experience is among the Magic Kingdom's most enjoyable. However, guests who expect to be scared silly when they enter the big old house, modeled after those built in New York's Hudson River Valley in the eighteenth century, will be just a tad unfulfilled. This haunted house steers clear of anything too terrifying, and a good-spirited voice-over keeps the mood light. Still, some of the scenes, as well as the darkness, may be too much for some tykes.

Once you're inside the portrait hall, entered after passing through the front doors, it's amusing to speculate: Is the ceiling moving up, or is the floor dropping? It's also where you will

meet your "Ghost Host" and learn how he met his untimely demise.

The spooky journey through the mansion takes place in a Doom Buggy. The attraction is full of tricks and treats for the eyes; just when you think you've seen it all, there's something new: staircases to nowhere, bats' eyes on the wallpaper, a terrified cemetery watchman and his mangy mutt, and the image of a creepy lady in a floating crystal ball (aka Madame Leota).

One of the biggest jobs of the maintenance crews here is not cleaning up, but keeping things dirty. The mansion is littered with some 200 trunks, chairs, dress forms, harps, rugs, and assorted knickknacks and requires a lot of dust. Cobwebs are bought in liquid form and strung up by a secret process.

When waiting to enter, take time to enjoy the interactive queue area. And on the way out, take a moment to pay your respects at the pet cemetery. Mr. Toad, we hardly knew you. *Sniff, sniff.*

Fantasyland

Walt Disney called this a "timeless land of enchantment," and his successors termed it "the happiest land of all"—and it is, for many. It is also the home of a number of rides that are particularly well liked by children of all ages.

CINDERELLA CASTLE: Just as Mickey stands for all the merriment in Walt Disney World, this storybook castle represents the hopes and dreams of childhood—a time in life when anything is possible and dreams really do come true.

At a height of 189 feet (and sporting 27 turrets), Cinderella Castle is nearly twice the height of Disneyland's Sleeping Beauty Castle. For inspiration, Disney Imagineers looked to the palaces of author Charles Perrault's France, still showplaces of Europe. The design took the form of a romanticized composite of such courts as Fontainebleau, Versailles, and famed chateaux of the Loire Valley. Of course, they also turned to the original designs for the fairy-tale castle in Disney's 1950 classic, *Cinderella*.

Unlike real European castles, this one is made of steel and fiberglass; in lieu of dungeons, it has service tunnels. However, like many fabled castles, it is surrounded by a moat. And from any vantage point, Cinderella Castle looks as if it came straight from the land of make-believe.

Mosaic Murals: The elaborate murals beneath the castle's archway rank among the true wonders of the World. They tell the story of the little cinder girl and one of childhood's happiest happily-ever-afters, using a million bits of glass

PHOTO BY JILL SAFRO

in some 500 different colors, plus real silver and 14-karat gold.

Cinderella Wishing Well: This pleasant alcove, nestled along a path to Tomorrowland, is a nice spot from which to gaze at the castle. Any coins tossed into the water are donated to children's charities. Don't forget to make a wish as you part with your penny.

PRINCE CHARMING REGAL CARROUSEL: Not everything in the Magic Kingdom is a Disney version of the real article. This carrousel, discovered at the now-defunct Olympic Park in Maplewood, New Jersey, was built back in 1917 (technically making it the oldest attraction in the park). That was the end of the golden century of carrousel building, which began around 1825. During the Disney refurbishment, many of the original horses were replaced with horses made of fiberglass. No two of the 90 horses are exactly alike. Can you spot Cinderella's horse? Hint: It's the only one with a golden ribbon on its tail.

ARIEL'S GROTTO: **FP**+ The Little Mermaid spends most of each day greeting guests in her Fantasyland grotto. She loves to pose for photos and sign autographs. PhotoPass photographers will happily snap your photo with her, too.

FAIRYTALE GARDEN: This special spot is tucked beside Cinderella Castle. Several times a day, Merida (the heroine from *Brave*) stops by to visit with guests. Check a park Times Guide for appearance schedule. Character subject to change.

MICKEY'S PHILHARMAGIC: **FP**+ Mickey Mouse and a panoply of his pals (including Donald, Simba, and Ariel) strut their musical stuff in this 3-D production.

The show is an amalgam of music, effects, and animation. Of course, this being Fantasyland, the film is by no means ordinary. It's colorful, crisp, and to the delight of many a goggle-wearing guest, three-dimensional. The lively experience unfolds on a 150-foot-wide canvas. Special effects and surprises take place off-screen, too.

As with many attractions, there are moments of darkness. If you're unsure as to whether your child might find this (or any attraction) unsettling, express your concern to an attendant. They will help you make the right decision. Note that all guests must wear 3-D glasses to enjoy the show.

BIRNBAUM'S ★BEST★ PETER PAN'S FLIGHT: FP+

"Come on, everybody, here we go!" So says Peter Pan at the start of this nonstop flight to Never Land. The 3-minute adventure, which takes you soaring in a pirate ship, fancifully retells the story of Peter Pan—a boy with a knack for flying and an immunity to maturity. The effects in this classic Fantasyland attraction are simple, but enchanting.

The journey starts in the Darling family nursery—which siblings Wendy, Michael, and John quickly abandon to follow Peter Pan on a trip to his homeland. As in Disney's animated feature, one of the most beautiful scenes—and one that makes this attraction a treat for grown-ups as well as smaller folk—is the sight of nighttime London, dark blue and speckled with twinkling lights. Keep your eyes peeled for Big Ben and Tower Bridge.

By the time you spot your first mermaid, you're deep in the heart of Never Land. Alas, something is terribly wrong—Captain Hook and his buccaneer buddies have taken the Darling kids captive. It's all really a trap for Peter (Hook is still peeved at Pan for serving his hand to Tick Tock the crocodile). Does everyone live happily ever after? We'll never tell.

HOT TIP!

Many Fantasyland attractions are dark, and, in some cases, special effects may be too intense for tots and small children. However, they all tend to *love* It's a Small World. Nothing scary about that!

PRINCESS FAIRYTALE HALL: FP+ Practice your curtsey as you approach this hall—once inside you'll meet regals such as Cinderella, Elena of Avalor, Rapunzel, and Tiana. Characters vary. This royal residence occupies the space formerly occupied by the Snow White's Scary Adventures attraction. And the line here can be scary—get a Fastpass+ if you can.

IT'S A SMALL WORLD: FP+ *Hola! Guten Tag!* Hello! No matter what language you speak, what you look like, or where you live, you still have a lot in common with folks the world over (including an especially high tolerance for a singsong melody that repeatedly reminds us that it's a small world, after all). That's the message driving this ten-minute boat ride around the world.

Originally created for New York's 1964–65 World's Fair, the attraction is an oldie but goodie (and is quite popular with young children). The ride moves at slightly swifter than snail's pace, drifting past hundreds of colorfully costumed dolls from around the world—all of whom know all the words to the ride's infectious theme song (written by the Sherman Brothers).

A showcase of diversity, the attraction is a simple celebration of human similarities. It's also a relaxing alternative to many of the park's higher-tech, longer-line attractions.

DUMBO THE FLYING ELEPHANT: FP+ This is purely and simply a kiddie ride, though children of all ages have admitted to loving it.

A beloved symbol of Fantasyland, the ride moved to the Storybook Circus area and doubled in size—but rest assured, the Dumbo experience remains the same. Consider stopping here early in the morning, or during a parade, when the line—which is often prohibitively long—thins a bit. Inspired by the 1941 film classic *Dumbo*, the ride lasts a memorable two minutes.

Note: Guests in Dumbo's standby line receive a pager and are free to frolic in a covered play zone while they wait to ride. The lines for Dumbo tend to dwindle late in the day, especially when the park is open late.

THE BARNSTORMER: FP+ At this mini roller coaster attraction, guests of most sizes follow the same fluky flight path taken by the daredevil pilot known as the Great Goofini. Don't let the size fool you: This 1-minute ride proves that big thrills do indeed come in small packages. Although guests as young as 3 may ride, they must be at least 35 inches tall. It may be too turbulent for some.

CASEY JR. SPLASH 'N' SOAK STATION: The famous locomotive Casey Jr. invites Magic Kingdom guests to cool off in this colorful, interactive splash zone, conveniently located beside Fantasyland's train station. Be sure to dress tykes in swim diapers.

MAD TEA PARTY: FP+ The theme of this two-minute ride—in a group of oversize teacups that whirl and spin wildly—was inspired by a scene in the Disney Studios' 1951 movie production of *Alice in Wonderland*. During the sequence in question, the Mad Hatter hosts a tea party for his un-birthday.

Unlike many rides in Fantasyland, this is not just for younger kids; the 5-to-20-something crowd seems to like it best. Keep in mind that when the cups stop spinning, your head may continue to do so. Skip this ride if you suffer from motion sickness or if you've recently enjoyed a snack. Don't miss the woozy mouse that pops out of the teapot at the center of the platform—he ignored our advice.

BIRNBAUM'S BEST **THE MANY ADVENTURES OF WINNIE THE POOH:** FP+ Everyone's favorite honey-lovin' cub treats Magic Kingdom guests to continuous, wild and whimsical 3½-minute tours of his home turf—the Hundred Acre Wood.

The attraction features a most unlikely form of transportation: honey pots! They whisk (and bounce) guests through the pages of a giant storybook and into the Hundred Acre Wood,

where the weather's most blustery. The wind is really ruffling the feathers of one of the locals. Sight gags abound, from a bubble-blowing Heffalump (hey, this is Fantasyland) to a treacherous flood that threatens to sweep Tigger, Piglet, and the rest of the gang away. When Pooh saves the day, it's time to celebrate— and everyone is invited to the party.

Like other Fantasyland attractions, some parts of this one take place in the dark. Some children may find it a bit unsettling. That said, little ones dig Pooh's interactive queue area. While waiting to ride or for others to do so, youngsters can bang on giant vegetable "drums," play tug-of-war with a gopher, and scrawl their names in a flowing wall of honey.

UNDER THE SEA—JOURNEY OF THE LITTLE MERMAID: FP+ In the Magic Kingdom's first attraction to feature everyone's favorite Disney mermaid, guests are invited to board continuously moving clam-mobiles and embark on a jolly journey above and below sea level. Along the way, they join Ariel, Flounder, and all of their aquatic acquaintances, and enjoy major musical movements and pivotal plot points from the classic animated feature. It's fun for the whole family.

BIRNBAUM'S BEST **SEVEN DWARFS MINE TRAIN:** FP+ Heigh-ho, heigh-ho! A roller coaster is whimsically transporting guests on a musical journey through the workplace of the Seven Dwarfs—the mine where a million diamonds shine. The ride vehicles swing back and forth a bit as they zoom along the track, so folks with motion sickness or other health issues should sit this one out. Intensity-wise, the smooth, family-friendly attraction fits between the Barnstormer coaster and Big Thunder Mountain Railroad. The queue has a few interactive surprises, too. This 2½-minute attraction is extremely popular— get a Fastpass+ assignment if you can. Guests must be at least 38 inches tall to ride.

ENCHANTED TALES WITH BELLE: FP+ This clever mix of show and character meet-and-greet is one of those "you have to see it to believe it" experiences. Located in Maurice's exquisitely detailed cottage, the 30-minute experience includes lifelike Audio-Animatronics versions of Lumiere and Madame Wardrobe, plus an audience-participation performance by Belle in Beast's library. There are lots of parts to play— be sure to volunteer!

Tomorrowland

The original Tomorrowland attempted a serious look at the future. But as Disney planners discovered, it isn't easy to portray a future that persists in becoming the present. So the old Tomorrowland has given way to a friendlier, space-age town whose neighborhood atmosphere is more in keeping with the other lands in the Magic Kingdom. This is the future that never was, the fantasy world imagined by the science-fiction writers and moviemakers of the 1920s and '30s. It's a land of sky-piercing beacons and glistening metal, where shiny robots do the work, whisper-quiet cars glide along an elevated highway, and even time travel is possible.

Note: Tomorrowland attractions are described in the order in which they are encountered upon entering the land from the Hub and heading away from Cinderella Castle.

STITCH'S GREAT ESCAPE!: Like its predecessor, The ExtraTERRORestrial Alien Encounter, this attraction features the adventures of a renegade alien. In this case, however, said extraterrestrial is more of a menace than a threat—not so much scary as ill-mannered and mischievous.

The action begins with a short pre-show, followed by the crowd spilling into a circular theater-type room. All chairs face center, where there's a mysterious tube. (Sit up straight when the shoulder harness is lowered—this will enhance the effects and make for a slightly less restraining experience.)

What's the fuss about? Bad-boy Stitch, aka Experiment 626, is being moved to a prison processing center, and you have been recruited to keep an eye on him. Spoiler alert: The blue rascal escapes every time. While amusing to some, this attraction is starting to show its age, and the effects aren't quite as special as they used to be.

Note: Some kids will be frightened by dark moments and loud noises. Shoulder restraints may spook claustrophobes and/or cause discomfort to sensitive shoulders. You must be at least 40 inches tall to enter. This attraction may not be open during all of 2018. For updates, visit *www.disneyworld.com*.

BIRNBAUM'S ★BEST★ BUZZ LIGHTYEAR'S SPACE RANGER SPIN: FP+ The Evil Emperor Zurg is up to no good. As soon as he rounds up enough batteries to power his ultimate weapon of destruction—KERPLOOEY!—it's curtains for the toy universe as we know it. It's up to that Space Ranger extraordinaire Buzz Lightyear and his trusty Junior Space Rangers (that means you) to save the day.

So goes the story line of Tomorrowland's video-game-inspired spin through toyland. The adventure is experienced from a toy's point of view. Guests begin their 4½-minute tour of duty as Space Rangers at Star Command Action Center. This is where Buzz gives his team a briefing on the mission that lies ahead. Then it's off to the Launch Bay to board the ride vehicles. The ships feature dual laser cannons, glowing lights, and a piloting joystick.

Once Junior Space Rangers blast off, they find themselves surrounded by Zurg's robots, who are mercilessly ripping batteries from toys. As Rangers fire at targets, beams of light fill the

air. For every target hit, you will be rewarded with sound effects and points. The points, which are tallied automatically, are accumulated throughout the journey. Although the vehicles follow a rigid "flight" path (they're on a track), the joystick allows riders to maneuver the ships, arcing from side to side or spinning in circles while taking aim at their surroundings.

When the star cruiser arrives at Zurg's spaceship, it's showdown time. Will good prevail over evil? Or has time run out for the toy universe?

HOT TIP!

To up your score at Buzz Lightyear's Space Ranger Spin, keep the trigger depressed at all times. Also, be sure to aim for moving or distant targets—they provide some of the biggest point payoffs. The target on top of the volcano is worth 50,000 points, and the one beneath Emperor Zurg will net you a whopping 100,000 points every time you zap it!

And will you score enough points to be a Galactic Hero? Most people improve their scores with a little practice. Note that seats on the left side of the ride vehicle have better access to the high-point-yielding targets in the first room.

MONSTERS, INC. LAUGH FLOOR: FP+ That Mike Wazowski is one enterprising eyeball. It seems the fuzzy fellow from *Monsters, Inc.* has opened a comedy club. Why? Well, it turns out his hometown is experiencing a bit of an energy crisis. Mike's clever plan is to tap into a decidedly alternative (not to mention free) fuel source to provide power for Monstropolis . . . laughter. But where can he gather enough giggles to fuel an entire city?

In a 400-seat theater in Tomorrowland, that's where. To accomplish his goal, monster of ceremonies Mike has recruited a couple of cornball comedians. Their job is to make you laugh yourself silly. And they are not too proud to resort to slapstick while doing so. Guests are encouraged to text a joke while waiting in the queue. (Standard text messaging rates apply.)

TOMORROWLAND TRANSIT AUTHORITY PEOPLEMOVER: Boarded near Astro Orbiter, these trains (known to Disney purists as the WEDway) move at a speed of about seven miles per hour along almost a mile of track, beside or through most of the attractions in Tomorrowland. They are operated by a linear induction motor that has no moving parts, uses little power, and emits no pollution.

The peaceful, breezy excursion through Tomorrowland takes about ten minutes. There's rarely much of a wait to board. It's one of our favorites. However, moments of darkness (as the train passes through Space Mountain) may be a bit unsettling for some little ones. Warn them before you board.

ASTRO ORBITER: Here, passengers fly for two minutes in machine-age rockets designed to look more like oversize Buck Rogers toys than twenty-first-century space shuttles. Riders are surrounded by vibrantly colored, whirling planets as they get an astronaut's-eye view of Tomorrowland.

TOMORROWLAND SPEEDWAY: FP+ Little cars that burn up the tracks at this attraction provide quite a bit of the background noise in Tomorrowland. Kids especially enjoy the not-so-speedy, herky-jerky driving experience.

The vehicles have rack-and-pinion steering and disc brakes, but unlike most cars, they run along a track. Yet even expert drivers have trouble keeping them going in a straight line. (Don't panic when you notice the lack of a brake pedal—when you take your foot off the gas, the

car comes to a quick, if not screeching, halt.) The one-lap tour of Tomorrowland takes about five minutes.

Note: You must be at least 54 inches tall to drive the car by yourself. Guests must be at least 32 inches tall to ride shotgun. Babies younger than 12 months may not go on the ride.

BIRNBAUM'S ★BEST★ SPACE MOUNTAIN: FP+ This attraction, which blasted onto the Magic Kingdom scene in 1975 (and was completely refurbished in 2009), is a can't-miss crowd-pleaser for throngs of thrill-seekers. Rising to a height of more than 180 feet, this gleaming steel-and-concrete cone houses an attraction that most people call a roller coaster. The ride takes place in an outer-space-like darkness that gets inkier and scarier as the journey progresses. The rockets that roar through this blackness attain a maximum speed of just over 28 miles per hour—but somehow it feels a whole lot faster.

The Space Mountain experience is wild enough to send glasses, purses, wallets, and even an occasional set of false teeth plummeting to the bottom of the track, so be sure to find a safe place for your possessions before the ride starts. It's also turbulent enough to upset the stomachs of those so unwise as to ride it immediately after eating. (Those who change their minds at the last minute have access to a "chicken" exit.)

Note: Guests who are under 44 inches are not permitted to ride, and you must be in good health and free from heart conditions, motion sickness, back or neck problems, or other physical limitations to ride. Expectant mothers must skip the trip. Children under age 7 must be accompanied by a guest age 14 or older.

WALT DISNEY'S CAROUSEL OF PROGRESS: First seen at New York's 1964–65 World's Fair and moved here in 1975, this 20-minute experience showcases the evolution of the American family and how life changed— and ostensibly progressed—with the advent of electricity. The hook here is that as a scene ends, the audience moves to the next one—not unlike being on a carousel (hence the name of the attraction). This is a great place to escape the crowds and heat, not to mention take a much-needed load off weary feet.

Shopping

No one travels to the Magic Kingdom just to shop. But as many a visitor has learned, shopping is one of the most enjoyable pastimes here.

The Magic Kingdom's boutiques and stores stock much more than just Disneyana. Along with the more predictable items in Main Street shops, it's possible to find cookbooks and dishes, pirate hats and toy frontier rifles, 14-karat gold charms, and filigreed costume jewelry. In Adventureland, shops boast many items imported from the exotic regions the area represents. Throughout the park, stores generally have merchandise that complements the themes of the various lands.

HOT TIP!

Your WDW shopping spree doesn't have to end when your vacation does. Simply download the free Shop Disney Parks mobile app and shop away. To download, visit *www.DisneyWorld.com/shop*.

In some shops, you can watch people at work: a candy maker hand-dipping caramel apples in the Main Street Confectionery, a glassblower crafting wares in Main Street's Crystal Arts, etc.

We recommend shopping in the early afternoon, rather than at the end of the day, when the shops are more crowded. However, keep in mind that Main Street shops do stay open about a half hour after park closing, in case you need any last-minute gifts on the way out.

Main Street

THE ART OF DISNEY: Nestled inside the Main Street Cinema, the shop showcases Disney-inspired fine art and collectibles, books, Vinylmation, puzzles, and more. This spot also sells collector pins. And, yes, you can still watch Mickey cartoons here, too.

BOX OFFICE GIFTS: Inside Town Square Theater, this shop has camera supplies such as memory cards, batteries, and disposable cameras. It's also the place to view and pick up PhotoPass photos and purchase MagicBand paraphernalia.

THE CHAPEAU: This Town Square shop is the place to buy mouse ears and have them monogrammed, and to shop for straw hats, baseball caps, pins, and assorted other headgear.

CURTAIN CALL COLLECTIBLES: After visiting Mickey Mouse at the Town Square Theater, guests may shop for souvenir items featuring assorted Disney characters, including the Big Cheese himself.

CRYSTAL ARTS: Cut-glass bowls, vases, glasses, and plates glitter in the cases of this crystal-chandeliered emporium. They have a lovely selection of miniature Disney characters meticulously crafted from glass. An engraver or a glassblower is often at work. There's a fireplace, too. Stop here to watch craftspeople mold shields and carve metal—impressive!

Where to Eat in the Magic Kingdom

A complete listing of all Magic Kingdom eateries—full-service restaurants, fast-food emporiums, and snack shops—can be found in the *Good Meals, Great Times* chapter. See the Magic Kingdom section, beginning on page 244.

DISNEY CLOTHIERS: This shop offers clothing for young girls, including shirts and sleepwear, all of which incorporate Disney characters. Look for bags and accessories, too.

EMPORIUM: Framed by a two-story-high portico, the Magic Kingdom's largest gift shop stocks stuffed animals and toys, T-shirts, kitchen items, home decor, hats, and more.

The cash registers always seem to be busy, especially toward the end of the afternoon and before park closing. Nearby lockers make for convenient storage of purchases.

Don't forget to peer into the windows, which usually feature elaborate displays ranging from seasonal themes to character tableaux. Shop early (Main Street opens about an hour before the rest of the park), and remember to take advantage of package pickup or delivery to your Walt Disney World resort.

HARMONY BARBER SHOP: Situated next door to the Main Street Car Barn, the quaint, old-fashioned setting for this working shop (with occasional appearances by a harmonizing quartet) merits a peek even if you have no need for a trim. It's open from 9 A.M. to about 5 P.M. daily. This is a popular spot for a child's first haircut, but they serve grown-ups, too (haircuts and beard/mustache trims). Colored gel hair treatments are offered,

Let It Rain

The show doesn't stop just because of a storm. Instead, shops throughout the Magic Kingdom sell plastic Disney Parks–branded ponchos and umbrellas to outfit guests who find themselves in need. (If there is lightning in the area, some attractions will temporarily cease operation.)

too. For an appointment, call 407-WDW-PLAY (939-7529). Walk-ins are accepted, too (though there may be a wait).

MAIN STREET FASHION AND APPAREL: Character-related gifts and apparel are the hallmarks of this spot. The shop also stocks golf shirts, bags, hats, sweatshirts, and accessories. You'll find it next to Casey's Corner.

MAIN STREET CHAMBER OF COMMERCE: This is the place to go if you have any Magic Kingdom purchases "sent to the front of the park" (aka Package Pickup). Allow at least three hours for the package to get here. It's located near City Hall.

MAIN STREET CONFECTIONERY: Tasty chocolates are sold in this old-fashioned pink-and-white paradise. A delight at any time of day, but more so when the cooks in the shop's glass-walled kitchen dip apples in gooey caramel. Then the candy sends up clouds of aroma that you could swear were being fanned out onto the street. There is a selection of fresh-made fudge, along with jelly beans, marshmallow crispy treats, and dozens of other confections that will satisfy any sweet tooth.

NEWSSTAND: No newspapers are sold in the Magic Kingdom—even at its newsstand, which is near the park entrance. (It's to the left, just inside the entrance.) The stand sells character merchandise and souvenirs.

THE SHADOW BOX: Watching Rubio Artist Co. silhouette cutters snip black paper into the likenesses of children is one of Main Street's more fascinating diversions. The Shadow Box is at the corner of Main and Center streets.

UPTOWN JEWELERS: Designed to resemble a turn-of-the-twentieth-century collectibles shop, this spiffy store specializes in jewelry, watches, handbags, scarves, purses, wallets, shoes, phone cases, and other gift items. This location is also home to the Disney Parks/PANDORA Jewelry Collection. Other wares include cosmetics, tote bags, luggage, back-packs, and more.

WHEELCHAIR AND ECV RENTAL: Guests may rent strollers at a spot under the Main Street Train Station. Wheelchairs and a limited number of Electric Conveyance Vehicles (ECVs) are offered at a separate location, directly across

Disney's PhotoPass

As you wander the theme parks, Disney cast members will be happy to snap your picture—just ask! After mugging for the camera, you'll be asked to scan your MagicBand (see page 24) or a PhotoPass card. It'll link all such photos together for viewing on the Internet. You can ogle and e-mail the low-res images for free for up to 45 days after they are taken. High-quality prints of various sizes are for sale. To purchase or peruse photos, visit *mydisneyphotopass.com* or use a My Disney Experience account. Each park has a spot for photo viewing. Check a park guidemap for locations. Individual photo downloads start at about $16.95, while the unlimited Memory Maker Package runs about $169 if purchased in advance. (This is a bit of splurge, but a very convenient way to get quality shots of your whole party.) Say cheese!

from the Newsstand, just inside the park entrance. All rentals are offered on a first-come, first-served basis. (Hold on to your receipt—it'll get you a replacement stroller or wheelchair should yours disappear during the day or if you "hop" to another park.) Note that items rented here cannot be taken outside the Magic Kingdom.

Adventureland

AGRABAH BAZAAR: Stop here and find clothing and accessories covered with animal prints and images, toys and costumes with a safari theme, and items featuring The Orange Bird. The bazaar has a nice selection of musical instruments and tropical-wear, too.

BWANA BOB'S: Stop here for tropical-themed jewelry, bags, pins, and hats, plus sunglasses, disposable cameras, and more.

ISLAND SUPPLY: This small tropical shop features a large selection of sunglasses.

THE PIRATES LEAGUE: More than just a crew of plank-walkers, this group of savvy pirates transforms guests into one of their own—in exchange for booty, of course. Once you're swashbuckled up, they'll snap your photo in the

"secret" treasure room. Call 407-WDW-CREW (939-2739) for pricing or to make a reservation. The Pirates League is in the Plaza del Sol Caribe Bazaar, by the Pirates of the Caribbean.

PLAZA DEL SOL CARIBE BAZAAR: Ahoy there, mateys! A swashbuckler's delight, the joint adjoining the Pirates of the Caribbean sells stuff celebrating both the attraction and the feature films of the same name. It also stocks other pirate booty, including Jolly Roger flags, rings, dolls, pirate costumes, themed hats, and eye patches. If that's not enough treasure for you, check out the candy and snacks. The pièce de résistance for pirate fans? Pirate makeovers! (See the previous entry, The Pirates League.) This is one of our favorite shops.

ZANZIBAR TRADING COMPANY: Across from Adventureland's famed Egg Roll Wagon, this corner shop stocks jungle collectibles, including hand-crafted wood items imported from Kenya and letter openers. Also found here are straw and woven items, drums, and animal-print apparel.

Frontierland

BIG AL'S: Named for the most popular (and least talented) member of the Country Bears, this riverfront shop is known for its selection of headwear, including Davy Crockett caps.

BRIAR PATCH: Toys and cuddly character items, plus kids' apparel and hats for the whole family, are featured wares at this shop, located near the Splash Mountain exit. There's also a pair of rocking chairs for those who need to take a load off.

PHOTO BY JILL SAFRO

FRONTIER TRADING POST: This is the place to shop for collector pins and the associated accoutrements. Since it's got the largest selection of pins in the park, they might want to rename this the Pin Trading Post. F.T.P. also boasts a selection of Western-themed T-shirts, plus Woody- and Jessie-style hats.

PRAIRIE OUTPOST & SUPPLY: Stop by this turn-of-the-twentieth-century general store for candy (including a wall of jelly beans), coffee, cookies, jams, jellies, and kitchen accessories.

Liberty Square

LIBERTY SQUARE PORTRAIT GALLERY: In the midst of Liberty Square, guests may have their portraits drawn in this open-air studio.

MEMENTO MORI: Welcome, foolish mortals—to a spooky and spectacular shop dedicated to all things Haunted Mansion. Here you'll find everything from gargoyle candle holders and hourglasses to "Ghost Host" gear and hitch-hiking ghost figurines. It's also possible to have your portrait taken, Haunted Mansion style. Yep, for about twenty bucks, you can be transformed into a spirited version of your future, ghoulish self. So creepy, but so cool!

YE OLDE CHRISTMAS SHOPPE: A wide variety of festive Yuletide items, including decorative Disney-themed gifts and trinkets (many of which can be personalized) and ornaments, is available year-round. Look for items such as stockings, tree toppers, and more.

Fantasyland

BIBBIDI BOBBIDI BOUTIQUE: Housed inside Cinderella Castle, this shop offers young guests the opportunity to be transformed into princesses and knights. Magical makeovers are available from 8 A.M. to 7 P.M. Prices vary. Magic Kingdom admission is required to enter this location. (There is an additional Bibbidi Bobbidi Boutique shop at Disney Springs. While there is no admission fee, there is a charge for services at both locations.) For pricing information or to book a reservation, call 407-WDW-STYLE (939-7895). Photo packages are offered, too. Reservations are strongly recommended.

BIG TOP SOUVENIRS: Step inside the big tent for Disney-themed merchandise and snacks galore. It's in the Storybook Circus part of Fantasyland, just across from the Dumbo the Flying Elephant attraction.

BONJOUR VILLAGE GIFTS: Visit this charming boutique in Fantasyland for items inspired by Disney's *Beauty and the Beast*. Expect to find apparel, T-shirts, toys, royal dinnerware, Cogsworth clocks, glowing goblets, tapestries, castle artwork, and more. Also sold: jigsaw puzzles, Mrs. Potts tea sets for kids, and books (Belle would approve).

CASTLE COUTURE: Can't get enough Disney princess merchandise? Stop here for royal toys, costumes, dolls, and kids' "princess apparel," plus jewelry and accessories.

HUNDRED ACRE GOODS: Located at the exit of The Many Adventures of Winnie the Pooh, this shop has wares featuring the folks from the Hundred Acre Wood (among other places). Among the items the Pooh bear proffers are toys, hats, shirts, toddler clothing, and more.

SIR MICKEY'S: Expect to find all sorts of Disney character-themed clothing and souvenir items in this shop with a design based on *The Brave Little Tailor*, the cartoon in which Mickey defeats a giant to win the hand of Princess Minnie. (It was one of the most elaborate and expensive Mickey Mouse cartoons ever made.) Mouse ears may be monogrammed here, too.

Tomorrowland

MERCHANT OF VENUS: The place for anything and everything Stitch to Star Wars, including a build-your-own lightsaber station, plush toys, games, and Vinylmation collectibles. It is located across from Astro Orbiter.

MICKEY'S STAR TRADERS: This is one of the better places to go in the Magic Kingdom for Disney-themed items: plush toys, hats, shirts, candy, etc. Sunglasses and sun-care products are also available. The Tomorrowland Transit Authority passes through here, too. (To catch a glimpse of the T.T.A., look up!)

TOMORROWLAND LIGHT & POWER COMPANY: After zipping through space, stop here to peruse Space Mountain–themed shirts and merchandise, plus MagicBands with character themes and accessories for cell phones and tablet computers. It's possible to charge mobile phones here, too.

Entertainment

In this most magical corner of the World, a slate of live performances ranks among the more serendipitous discoveries. The Magic Kingdom's entertainment mix includes dazzling high-tech shows and old-fashioned numbers alike. To keep apprised of the offerings on any given day, pick up a current guidemap and Times Guide.

While details may change in 2018, what follows is a good indication of the park's entertainment repertoire. Visit *www.disneyworld.com* to confirm specifics and schedules.

CAPTAIN JACK SPARROW'S PIRATE TUTORIAL: So you wanna be a pirate? Captain Jack and his mate Mack are looking for new recruits near the Pirates of the Caribbean in Adventureland. They'd like to test your pirate skills (swordplay, menacing looks, etc.) and decide whether you're worthy of the Pirate's Oath and the title of honorary buccaneer.

CASEY'S CORNER PIANO: A peppy pianist tickles the ivories of a snow-white upright, just outside Casey's Corner on Main Street.

ONCE UPON A TIME: A 14-minute animated, musical celebration of Disney storytelling, this takes place on Cinderella Castle. Yes, *on* the castle. (The beloved WDW icon has evolved into a high-tech canvas for Disney artists without losing any of its charm.) The action starts with Chip (from *Beauty*

and the Beast) asking his mom to tell him a story. Mrs. Potts doesn't need to be asked twice—and starts to tell stories that begin with "Once upon a time..." And then a montage of memorable movie moments lights up the night. Chip and Magic Kingdom guests hear stories and songs from Disney classics including *Alice in Wonderland, Tangled, Cinderella, Peter Pan, Winnie the Pooh,* and more. How do all the stories end? Happily, of course! The front and sides of the Castle offer slightly different viewing experiences—so if you've already enjoyed it from one vantage point, you might want to try another. In addition to the regular show, Once Upon a Time may include seasonal updates. Check a park Times Guide for this nighttime show's performance schedule.

CITIZENS OF MAIN STREET: Performers clad in 19th-century costumes interact with guests throughout the day. They've even been known to burst into song from time to time. Keep an eye out for the Mayor, the Socialite, the Fire Chief, and the Suffragette crusading for women's right to vote.

DAPPER DANS: You just might encounter a barbershop quartet while strolling down Main Street. Conspicuously clad in straw hats and striped vests, the ever-so-jovial Dapper Dans tap-dance and let one-liners fly during their short, four-part-harmony performances.

BIRNBAUM'S ★BEST★ HAPPILY EVER AFTER: A dynamite, pyrotechnic/ digital projection extravaganza, Happily Ever After is presented most nights when the Magic Kingdom stays open after dark. This jubilant new nighttime spectacular takes place on and above Cinderella Castle. Showtimes vary—check a park Times Guide for specifics. Happily Ever After is ideally viewed from Main Street, U.S.A., but can be seen from many perspectives throughout the park. The 18-minute show is typically presented rain or shine, but may be canceled due to inclement weather.

FAIRYTALE GARDEN: Merida from *Brave* greets guests in this nook beside Cinderella Castle each day. Check a Times Guide for specifics. Character is subject to change.

FLAG RETREAT: At about 5 P.M. each day (check a current Times Guide), patriotic music fills the air as a color guard marches to Town Square, in Main Street, U.S.A., and takes down the American flag that flies from the flagpole.

BIRNBAUM'S ★BEST★ FESTIVAL OF FANTASY PARADE:

FP+ A musical celebration of Disney Animation, this parade wends its way down Main Street once a day. The festival focuses on Disney friends who frequent Fantasyland. Kids love to wave to favorite characters—especially Anna and Elsa. The elaborate floats (including the one at right) are quite impressive.

Festival of Fantasy highlights the classic tales of *Tangled*, *The Little Mermaid*, *Sleeping Beauty*, *Pinocchio*, *Brave*, *Dumbo*, and more.

HOEDOWN HAPPENING: Every now and then a happy hoedown happens in Frontierland. Disney pals such as Bre'r Bear, Bre'r Fox, and Bre'r Rabbit pop in, as do several of those muscially inclined Country Bears. An interactive display, this hoedown usually wraps up with the Hokey Pokey. Do join in! The seemingly spontaneous party isn't listed in the Times Guide—so you best ask a local cast member about the next possible performance.

BIRNBAUM'S ★BEST★ MICKEY'S ROYAL FRIENDSHIP FAIRE:

Mickey and his band of merrymakers are hosting a joyous festival in front of Cinderella Castle, and they are welcoming friends old and new—including you!

Goofy has invited folks from *The Princess and the Frog*; Donald's guests include friends he met at the Snuggly Duckling in the Land of the Enchanted Woods; and Daisy introduces her guests Rapunzel and Flynn Ryder. Mickey has a very special surprise for *Frozen* fans: He traveled all the way to The Land of Mystic Mountains to invite Olaf, Anna, and Elsa (who brings along a little of her trademark icy magic). Festivities include lively dancing, special effects, and memorable music—including an original song. The show is presented daily (but may be canceled due to inclement weather). Check a Times Guide for showtimes during your visit.

LET THE MAGIC BEGIN: The Magic Kingdom park kicks off each morning with a whimsical welcome ceremony. The 5-minute show begins as the Royal Majesty Maker invites guests to gather 'round the Castle forecourt. Mickey Mouse soon takes the stage to greet eager parkgoers. He's joined by Minnie, Pluto, Chip, Dale, princes, princesses, and one very special Fairy Godmother. With a wave of her wand and a "Bibbidi bobbidi boo!"— the Magic Kingdom's day has officially begun. Have fun!

MAIN STREET PHILHARMONIC: Clad in bright red and white, Disney World's merry marching band serenades guests with old-school marches, big-band standards, and classic Disney ditties. Each performance lasts about 20 minutes.

MAIN STREET TROLLEY SHOW: A dozen colorfully clad performers arrive via trolley and put on a cheery song and dance show "right down the middle of Main Street, U.S.A."

MOVE IT, SHAKE IT, DANCE & PLAY IT!: Whether you are celebrating a special occasion or just the fact that you are in the Magic Kingdom, this dance party is a treat. A spectacle of music and dance, the 35-minute jubilee invites guests to join in the fun as dancers and Disney characters take over the street by Cinderella Castle. There is often an early evening performance of this party.

THE MUPPETS PRESENT . . . GREAT MOMENTS IN AMERICAN HISTORY: The Muppets are coming, the Muppets are coming! In fact, they come to Liberty Square several times a day to reenact the drafting of the Declaration of Independence and Paul Revere's Ride. The fuzzy cast is as follows: Kermit the Frog, Miss Piggie, Gonzo, Fozzie Bear, and that superpatriotic bird: Sam Eagle. The show takes place in the windows above and next door to Hall of Presidents. Standing room only. (The action is easily viewed from most vantage points in the square.) Check a Times Guide for the schedule.

Holiday Happenings

It's a rare holiday that passes quietly in the Magic Kingdom. During certain holidays, such as Christmas, New Year's Eve, and the Fourth of July, the park breaks curfew, staying open extra late and stepping up its nighttime entertainment.

On these occasions, special performances of parades and the fireworks are often in store. Entertainment plans are subject to change, so it's wise to call 407-934-7639 for info and schedules.

EASTER: Easter is a delightful, if a bit crowded, time to visit the Magic Kingdom. Mr. and Mrs. Easter Bunny have been known to appear in the park to help guests celebrate the occasion.

FOURTH OF JULY: The busiest day of the summer—and with good reason: There's a double-size fireworks extravaganza that lights up the skies above Cinderella Castle and the Seven Seas Lagoon. It's a thrilling display.

HALLOWEEN: This most spooky of holidays is celebrated on select nights from September through October with a special-ticket event: Mickey's Not-So-Scary Halloween Party. The park closes a bit early on nights when the party takes place. (Guests bearing tickets to the party can stay in the park.) Expect characters in costume, creepy music and fog effects, and trick-or-treating throughout the park. It's a hoot! Mickey's Boo-to-You Halloween Parade takes place, as does a special edition of the fireworks show. Visit *www.disneyworld.com/halloween*, or call 407-824-4321 to order tickets to the party.

CHRISTMAS: A towering Christmas tree goes up on Main Street, and the Magic Kingdom is decked out as only Disney can do it. (Cinderella Castle is draped in 250,000 sparkling lights!)

On select nights in November and December, the park hosts a special-admission celebration known as Mickey's Very Merry Christmas Party. The festivities, complete with hot chocolate, cookies, and snow flurries on Main Street, include a running (or two) of Mickey's Once Upon a Christmastime Parade, holiday shows, and a special Happily Ever After fireworks show. Disney characters are on hand, too.

The Christmas party is a very popular (and enjoyable) event. Purchase tickets way ahead of time. And don't forget to wear red and green; *www.disneyworld.com/christmasparty*.

NEW YEAR'S EVE: It has always been true that on December 31 the throngs here are body to body. Expect a dazzling, supersize fireworks display and oodles of happy holiday decorations. There's plenty of nip in the air as the evening goes on, so dress accordingly.

Where to Find the Characters

Mickey and his pals make appearances throughout the day—but you can often find him at Town Square Exposition Hall. Tinker Bell greets guests there, too. Alice and her Wonderland friends may be found near the Mad Tea Party. Pooh and Tigger frequent Fantasyland. Disney regals such as Tiana and Elena greet guests in Princess Fairytale Hall. You'll find Goofy, Donald, Daisy, and Minnie at Pete's Silly Sideshow in Fantasyland. And various characters greet guests in Town Square at park opening time. Ariel greets folks in her Fantasyland grotto. Friends from *Mary Poppins* may appear in Liberty Square. And Anna and Elsa lead the Festival of Fantasy parade. Feel free to wave hello!

Check a Times Guide for updated information. Eateries such as Cinderella's Royal Table and the Crystal Palace offer opportunities to mingle with various characters, too. (See page 282.)

MAGIC KINGDOM

• Start at a Fastpass+ kiosk to book Fast-passes for as many attractions as possible (if you haven't reserved in advance).

• For the best fireworks view, stand on Main Street between Town Square and Casey's Corner. (If you stand too close to the castle, some of the show may be obstructed.)

• Low on battery power? Charge your phone in the back of the Space Mountain shop or rent power packs from a kiosk.

• If you're driving to the park, start out very early. Most people arrive between 9:30 A.M. and 11:30 A.M., and the roads and parking lots are jammed. Plan to be at the gates to the Magic Kingdom before they open, and then be at the end of Main Street when the rest of the park opens.

• Table-service restaurants are in high demand in this park. Book yours as early as possible. And don't forget to confirm.

• Eager to meet Mickey Mouse? Head for the Town Square Theater on Main Street (near the train station). He likes to greet guests there. Get a Fastpass+ if you can.

• You can get in line for an attraction right up until the minute the park closes.

• Avoid the mealtime rush hours by eating early or late: before 11:30 A.M. or after 2 P.M., and before 5 P.M. or after 8 P.M.

• At busy times, take in these less-packed attractions: The Country Bear Jamboree, The Enchanted Tiki Room, Walt Disney's Carousel of Progress, and the PeopleMover.

• The Main Street plaza gardens are a pleasant place for a picnic.

• Use a smartphone to check all attraction wait times via the My Disney Experience app (which may be downloaded for free).

• Break up your day. Consider heading back to your hotel (if it's not too far) for some swimming. Be sure to hold on to your admission pass, stroller and/or wheelchair receipt(s), and your parking stub so that you can re-enter the Magic Kingdom.

• If your party decides to split up, set a meeting place and time. Avoid meeting in front of Cinderella Castle, since this area can become quite congested.

• The best way to get to the park's exit during parades is to take the Walt Disney Railroad. Board the train in Frontierland or Fantasyland and take it all the way to Main Street, U.S.A.

• For a full-service meal, be sure to make reservations in advance by calling 407-WDW-DINE (939-3463).

• Park guests have the right to chicken out at any time while waiting in line. In other words, should you or a member of your party have second thoughts about soaring on Space Mountain, visiting with the grinning ghosts of the Haunted Mansion, or braving another attraction, simply inform an attendant and you'll be discreetly whisked out a special exit.

• If you have rented a stroller, return it just before the fireworks presentation. That way, after the show, you'll be able to make a beeline for your bed rather than stand in a line to return the stroller.

• Some merchandise found in shops at Walt Disney World may be purchased with the Shop Disney Parks app and through Guest Services. Call 877-560-6477 for info.

• Travel light. The fewer bags you have, the faster you'll pass through security.

• Allow extra time to get to the park entrance—area traffic and passing through security can cause delays—especially during peak times.

Hidden Mickeys

Disney Imagineers have hidden Mickey's image all over Walt Disney World. Some are easier to track down than others. Here are some of the most popular "Hidden Mickeys" at the Magic Kingdom. How many can you find? Check the box when you spot each one!

❤ **Pirates of the Caribbean:** As you enter the main building and jump on the standby line (the queue on the left), keep your eyes peeled for four large gun cabinets hanging on both sides of the wall (you'll pass a set of smaller ones on the right before reaching these). The locks on the cabinets form Hidden Mickeys. ■

❤ **Splash Mountain:** About halfway through the ride and in the room with jumping water, look quickly to your right and find a turtle floating on its back on a small geyser. Now look just above and behind the turtle for one of the most creative Hidden Mickeys in the park: It's a bobber attached to a fishing line. There is a more obvious one in the clouds beside the riverboat in the "Zip-a-dee-doo-dah" room, after the big splash. ■

❤ **Big Thunder Mountain Railroad:** At the very end of the ride and after the train slows, look to your right to find two sets of gear shifts laying on the ground. The second set forms a Hidden Mickey, although you may notice that the dimensions are not quite proportional (Mickey's "ears" are significantly smaller than his "head"). ■

❤ **The Haunted Mansion:** In the ghostly party scene, look at the bottom left corner of the banquet table for a Hidden Mickey made of two saucers and a plate. ■

❤ **Carousel of Progress:** In the Christmas scene, look to the far left for four nutcrackers lined up on top of the fireplace. The nutcracker farthest to the left is a Mickey nutcracker. Also in this scene, look for a Mickey plush toy in a box under the Christmas tree and a special pepper grinder on the kitchen counter (it's best seen from seats on the right side of the theater). ■

❤ **Buzz Lightyear's Space Ranger Spin:** Once you enter the interior queue, look for a poster on the right called "Planets of the Galactic Alliance"

and find the planet "Pollost Prime." One of the continents forms a Mickey profile. Keep your eyes open during the attraction's space video scene (about halfway through) and you'll see this same planet fly by on the right. ■

❤ **Under the Sea—Journey of The Little Mermaid:** When entering the scene where everyone's favorite crab sings "Under the Sea," you may spot several purple corals that form Mr. Mouse's head. (Hint: Two are on the floor and one is on a wall.) ■

❤ **It's a Small World:** Don't rush into the queue, because the wait time sign forms a Hidden Mickey if you tilt your head to the left. Once on the ride, pay close attention to the Africa room and search for purple leaves hanging from the ceiling that form several Hidden Mickeys. (Hint: They're by the giraffes.) ■

❤ **The Magic Carpets of Aladdin:** You'll feel like a pro once you find this small but very cool Hidden Mickey. First find the Agrabah Bazaar shop (across from the Magic Carpets of Aladdin exit) and find the pole with a thick blue stripe at the bottom. Take three steps toward the attraction and look down to find a charm in the cement with a Mickey in the center. ■

❤ **Tomorrowland Transit Authority People-Mover:** Toward the end of the ride, you will glide past a futuristic lady getting her hair done. That lady has a Hidden Mickey on her belt buckle! (Hint: She's on the right side of the ride vehicle's forward motion.) ■

❤ **Swiss Family Treehouse:** As you make the trek up (and down) the treehouse stairs, take a good look at the giant tree trunk. Cleverly camouflaged by moss and bark? A subtle-but-familiar silhouette. ■

Specifics may change during 2018.

Where in the World?

All of the photos on this page were taken at the Magic Kingdom. Do you know where? We challenge you to find all the spots where these images were shot and snap a photo for yourself as you discover each one. Happy hunting! (For locations, turn to page 352.)

Epcot

EPCOT

I magine a place with an entertainment inventory that includes both a rich sampling of world cultures and a fun, enlightening journey to the technological frontier. You now have an inkling of the eye-opening and mind-broadening potential of Epcot—a place that's evolved most imaginatively since the day it opened.

Walt Disney suggested the idea back in 1966: "Epcot will be an experimental prototype community of tomorrow that will take its cue from the new ideas and technologies that are emerging from the creative center of American industry." It would never be completed, he said, but would "always be introducing and testing and demonstrating new materials and systems." On October 1, 1982, Walt Disney's dream became a reality. Test Track puts guests on the thrilling inside track of the fast-paced world of automobile design. A re-imagined Soarin'—now known as Soarin' Around the World—delivers the breathtaking sensation of flight. And old favorites like Turtle Talk with Crush and Spaceship Earth continue to ignite the creative forces within us all. In keeping with the ever-evolving tradition, Epcot guests will be treated to major, park-wide enhancements for years to come.

The park consists of two areas of exploration: Future World and World Showcase. The former examines ideas in science, technology, and other topics in ways that make them downright irresistible. The latter celebrates the diversity of the world's peoples, portraying a stunning array of nations, with extraordinary devotion to detail.

Think of Epcot as Disney's playground for curious and thoughtful guests of all ages. The experiences it delivers—all of them wonders of the real world—continue to amaze, educate, inspire, and (of course) entertain.

EPCOT

JAPAN

MOROCCO

FRANCE

INTERNATIONAL GATEWAY

THE AMERICAN ADVENTURE

UNITED KINGDOM

ITALY

CANADA

GERMANY

IMAGINATION!

THE LAND

CHINA

SHOWCASE PLAZA

NORWAY

EPCOT CHARACTER SPOT

MEXICO

THE SEAS WITH NEMO & FRIENDS

TEST TRACK

INNOVENTIONS

MISSION: SPACE

SPACESHIP EARTH

To Buses

Entrance Plaza

WORLD SHOWCASE LAGOON

N

Getting Oriented

Triple the Magic Kingdom park and you have an idea of the size of Epcot. As for layout, the park is shaped something like a giant hourglass. The pavilions of Future World fill the northern bulb, while the international potpourri called World Showcase occupies the southern bulb. Future World is anchored on the north by the imposing silver "geosphere," dubbed Spaceship Earth.

As you pass through Epcot's main Entrance Plaza, Spaceship Earth looms straight ahead. Pathways curve around the 180-foot-tall geosphere, winding up at Innoventions Plaza. Here, you'll see signs for Innoventions and Epcot Character Spot, housed in buildings that cradle the plaza. Beyond this central area, there are two roughly symmetrical north-south avenues; these are dotted with the pavilions that form the outer perimeter of Future World. Mission: SPACE and Test Track flank Spaceship Earth on the east, while Imagination!, The Land, and The Seas with Nemo & Friends lie to the west.

In World Showcase, the international pavilions are arranged around the edge of sparkling World Showcase Lagoon, with The American Adventure directly south of Spaceship Earth on the lake's southernmost shore. A walkway from Future World leads to World Showcase Promenade, a 1.2-mile thoroughfare that wraps around the lagoon, winding past each World Showcase pavilion in the process.

HOW TO GET THERE

Take Exit 67 off I-4. Continue along to the Epcot Auto Plaza; if you park in a distant lot, take a tram to the park's main entrance.

By WDW Transportation: From the Grand Floridian, Contemporary, and Polynesian Village: hotel monorail to the Transportation and Ticket Center (TTC), then switch to the TTC-Epcot monorail. From Magic Kingdom: express monorail to the TTC, then switch to the TTC-Epcot monorail. From Disney Springs: bus to any resort, then transfer to an Epcot bus or boat. From Disney's Hollywood Studios, Disney's Animal Kingdom, all other Walt Disney World resorts, Four Seasons resort, and the resorts on Hotel Plaza Boulevard: buses.

Note: A second Epcot park entrance, called International Gateway, provides entry directly to World Showcase. It may be reached via walkways and the FriendShip water launches from Disney's Hollywood Studios, plus the Swan, Dolphin, Yacht and Beach Club, and BoardWalk resorts. The boat drops guests between the France and U.K. pavilions. It is possible to purchase theme park admission here, at Epcot's "back door."

PARKING

All-day car parking at Epcot starts at $20 for day visitors (free to WDW resort guests with a valid resort ID, MagicBand, or an annual pass; trucks, trailers, and RVs cost more; preferred parking costs $40). Attendants will direct you to one of several lots. Trams circulate regularly, providing transportation between the distant lots and the main entrance. Be sure to note the section and aisle in which you park. Parking tickets allow for re-entry here (and other Disney parks) throughout the day.

HOURS

Future World is usually open from about 9 A.M. to 9 P.M. (though some attractions may close at 7 P.M.). World Showcase hours are about 11 A.M. to 9 P.M. (though some attractions open earlier). During certain holiday periods and summer months, hours are extended. It's best to arrive a bit before the posted opening time. On select days, the park opens one hour early or stays open two hours late for Disney resort guests only. For schedules, call 407-824-4321, or visit *www.disneyworld.com*.

GETTING AROUND

Water taxis, called FriendShip launches, ferry guests across the World Showcase Lagoon. Docks are located near Mexico, Canada, Germany, and Morocco. (The only other way to traverse the vast area is on foot.) Boats typically close a few hours before the park does.

Admission Prices

ONE-DAY BASE TICKET*
(Restricted to use only in Epcot. Prices represent Walt Disney World's Value, Regular, and Peak rates; they do not include tax; and they are expected to rise in 2018.)

Adult ....$99/$107/$119
Child** ....$93/$101/$113

* 1-Day tickets purchased in 2018 must be used by December 31, 2019

** 3 through 9 years of age; children under age 3 free

Park Primer

BABY FACILITIES

There are changing tables and facilities for nursing mothers at the Baby Care Center, located between Test Track and the Mexico pavilion. Disposable diapers may be kept behind the counter at some Epcot shops; just ask.

CAMERA NEEDS

The Camera Center in Entrance Plaza and World Traveler at International Gateway stock memory cards, batteries, disposable cameras, and other accessories. Note that selfie sticks are not permitted in the park.

DISABILITY INFORMATION

Nearly all attractions, shops, and restaurants are accessible to guests using wheelchairs. Parking for guests with disabilities is available. Additional services are available for guests with visual and hearing disabilities. The complimentary *Guide for Guests with Disabilities* is available at the park entrances and at Guest Relations. It provides a detailed overview of all services. For more information, turn to the *Getting Ready to Go* chapter of this book.

FIRST AID

Minor medical problems can be handled at the First Aid Center, located between Test Track and the Mexico pavilion. Keep in mind that many guests could avoid a trip to First Aid simply by staying well hydrated. If you have an emergency, notify an employee and call 911.

INFORMATION

Guest Relations, which has one location to the right of the main entrance plaza and another next to Spaceship Earth, is equipped with guidemaps, Times Guides, and a helpful staff. Same goes for International Gateway (Epcot's back entrance).

LOCKERS

Lockers are found immediately west of Spaceship Earth. Cost is $8–$10, plus a $5 refundable deposit for unlimited use all day.

LOST & FOUND

Lost and Found is located at Guest Relations near Innoventions. To inquire about lost items after your visit, call 407-824-4245. If you find an item, give it to a cast member (aka employee).

LOST CHILDREN

Alert an employee and report lost children at Guest Relations or the Baby Care Center.

MONEY MATTERS

There are Automated Teller Machines (ATMs) at the main entrance, on the path between Future World and World Showcase, at International Gateway (near United Kingdom), and at The American Adventure. Some foreign currency may be exchanged at Guest Relations. Major credit cards (American Express, JCB, Discover, Diner's Club, Visa, and MasterCard), traveler's checks, Disney Dollars, and Disney gift cards are accepted throughout WDW. MagicBands and Walt Disney World resort IDs are accepted at most park locations (if backed up with a major credit card).

PACKAGE PICKUP

Epcot shops can arrange for most purchases to be transported (for free) to the Gift Stop in Entrance Plaza or International Gateway in World Showcase for later pickup.

SAME-DAY RE-ENTRY

Be sure to wear your MagicBand (if you used it for admission) or retain your ticket if you plan to return later the same day.

SECURITY CHECK

Guests entering Disney theme parks are subject to a thorough security check. All bags will be searched by security personnel before guests may enter the park. A metal detector screens park guests. Weapons (including toys) are prohibited. For details and a complete listing of Walt Disney World Park Rules, visit Guest Relations or go to *www.disneyworld.com/ParkRules*.

STROLLERS & WHEELCHAIRS

Strollers, wheelchairs, and Electric Conveyance Vehicles (ECVs) may be rented from venues at both park entrances. Wheelchairs are also available at the Gift Stop. Cost is $15 for single strollers, $31 for double strollers, and $12 for wheelchairs. A Length-of-Stay rental yields a $2-per-day discount. It's $50 a day for an ECV, plus a $20 refundable deposit. Quantities are limited. ECVs tend to sell out early. Keep your rental receipt; it can be used that same day to get a replacement at Epcot or another theme park.

Future World

HOT TIP!

If you've got small children in your party, be sure to visit Frozen Ever After at Norway in World Showcase, and The Seas with Nemo & Friends and the Imagination! pavilions in Epcot's Future World. And don't miss the Kidcot Fun Stop craft areas in World Showcase.

A mere listing of the basic themes covered by the pavilions at Future World—agriculture, communication, car design, the ocean, the land, energy, imagination, technology, and space—tends to sound a tad academic. But when these serious topics are presented with a special flair, they become part of an experience that ranks among Disney's most entertaining.

Some of these subjects are explored in the course of lively and unusual "adventures," involving a whole arsenal of motion pictures, special effects, and Audio-Animatronics figures so lifelike that it is hard to remain unmoved. The basic elements are also appealing in their own right, from the palm-tree-dotted Entrance Plaza to the dramatic fountain just past Spaceship Earth, the many-faceted "geosphere" that has become the universal symbol of Epcot.

The park is so vast that it's hard to know what to do first. Many guests stop at Spaceship Earth on their way into Future World. As a result, they end up spending more time waiting in line than they need to. A wise alternative is to save Spaceship Earth for later in the day (when the lines inevitably thin out), and head for Soarin', the "less intense, non-spinning" Mission: SPACE, The Seas with Nemo & Friends, and Test Track (if jarring motion isn't an issue for you) as soon as the park opens (the lines tend to stay long throughout the day). Take in Frozen Ever After and as many Future World attractions as time allows, making sure to experience Test Track, and save World Showcase for the evening

hours. This strategy works well for families. (Refer to page 35 for a detailed version of this plan of attack.)

Another alternative—one that requires quite a bit of extra walking, but can help skirt a long line or two—is to explore Future World until the rest of World Showcase opens at 11 A.M. Then, in the afternoon, when many guests have shifted over to World Showcase, return to Future World. And although long lines can be found during peak seasons at Soarin' Around the World, Mission: SPACE, Test Track, Spaceship Earth, The Seas with Nemo & Friends, the Epcot Character Spot, and Living with the Land throughout most of the late morning and afternoon, from late afternoon until park closing is usually less hectic. But don't forget to make it back to World Showcase in time to see the park's nighttime spectacular, IllumiNations—Reflections of Earth.

Left a Legacy?

Epcot has invited guests to "Leave a Legacy" near its front gate since its big Millennium Celebration. And? More than 550,000 have done so! They left their mark, in the form of a one-inch-square tile affixed on massive stone walls. While the program has officially come to a close, the cluster of monoliths continues to stand near the base of Spaceship Earth.

To find a tile, inquire at the Leave a Legacy locating station inside the Camera Center by Spaceship Earth. Details are subject to change.

SPACESHIP EARTH FP+

As it looms impressively just above the Earth, this great, faceted silver structure looks a little bit like a spaceship ready to blast off. It appears large from a distance, and it seems even more immense when viewed from directly underneath. It's no surprise that some visitors simply stop beneath it and gawk.

The show inside, which explores the continuing quest by human beings to create the future, remains one of Epcot's compelling—if slower moving—attractions. It's an intriguing, narrated journey through time. It also has an interactive element that's a real hoot.

A common misconception about Spaceship Earth is that it is a geodesic dome. Not so. It is a geosphere. A geodesic dome is only half a sphere, while Spaceship Earth is almost completely round. Affectionately known to many simply as "the Ball," Spaceship Earth is a sight to behold.

Noted science-fiction writer Ray Bradbury, together with consultants from the Smithsonian Institution, the Los Angeles area's prestigious Huntington Library, the University of Southern California, and (among others) the University of Chicago, collaborated with Disney in developing this memorable 14-minute journey. It begins in an inky-black time tunnel, complete with a musty smell that suggests the dust of ages, and continues through history from the days of Cro-Magnon man (30,000 or 40,000 years ago) to the future.

Every scene is executed in exquisite detail. The symbols on the wall of that Egyptian temple really are hieroglyphics, and the content of the letter being dictated by the pharaoh was excerpted from a missive actually received by an agent of a ruler of the period. Later on you'll catch a glimpse of a 1970s mainframe computer room and a garage scene depicting the creation of the personal computer.

All of these sights are enough to keep heads turning as the "time machines" wend their way upward. The most dazzling scene is saved for the ride's finale, when the audience is placed in outer space—with a prime view of our beautiful, blue planet, also known as Spaceship Earth. The journey winds down with a clever, custom look at your own future, courtesy of a touch screen in the ride vehicle. Details are subject to change.

HOT TIP!

Many of Walt Disney World's moving attractions—such as Spaceship Earth—can be slowed down to make the boarding process safer for guests with physical limitations and guests who can transfer from a wheelchair (with assistance from someone in their party). Ask a cast member as you and your party enter the attraction.

The post-show area—Project Tomorrow—features several interactive areas all emphasizing technology and its influence on daily life. Themes include medicine, power, and accident avoidance. Plan to spend up to an hour in this high-tech playground.

INNOVENTIONS

Innoventions celebrates the ingenuity and wonders of modern life. This zone has featured many interactive, hands-on exhibits. The lone exhibit today is a vibrant one that informs and inspires guests about the power of color: Colortopia. Three interactive areas really bring

HOT TIP!

The line for Spaceship Earth is usually quite long during the early morning hours and relatively short in the late afternoon and evening.

color to life. Kids (and kids at heart) love to paint the walls with electronic paintbrushes. Expect to spend about 30 minutes or so exploring this wonderful world of color.

One of Walt Disney's dreams for Epcot was for the exhibits to change periodically. And indeed they do. So keep in mind that the exhibit mentioned here may close in 2018, and new ones may be added.

HOT TIP!

Innoventions Plaza is home to Pin Central. This area, between Innoventions and the Epcot Character Spot, is the pin-trading headquarters for Epcot. (Of course, there are many other pin-trading locations throughout Walt Disney World.)

MOUSE GEAR: This enormous shop continues to offer a selection of Disney merchandise. Mouse Gear stocks character memorabilia, key chains, T-shirts, hats, candy (including a wall of jelly beans and various gummy treats), Magic-Bands and associated paraphernalia, mugs, photo albums, jewelry, towels, footwear, toys, and more—making this the best source for character merchandise in Epcot. There are also items related to the park itself, along with Disney-themed apparel and children's clothing. Mouse Gear stays open about a half hour longer than the park does.

THE ART OF DISNEY: This is Epcot's spot for a special assortment of Disney collectibles. The store showcases a wide variety of art inspired by Disney animation and theme parks. There is a collection of unique pieces by acclaimed artists, including prints, sculptures, figurines, and more.

THE SEAS WITH NEMO & FRIENDS

Welcome to one of the largest facilities ever dedicated to humanity's relationship with the ocean. It was designed by Disney Imagineers, in cooperation with oceanographic experts and scientists—and may get a name change in 2018.

Though it enjoys the distinction of being one of Future World's original pavilions, what used to be known as The Living Seas is as fresh as ever—thanks to a little clownfish called Nemo and some of his fishy friends.

Once inside, guests can find the animated critters' real-life counterparts, including clown-fish, blue tangs, sharks, and puffer fish.

The pavilion also features a Nemo-themed ride, an interactive encounter with an animated turtle, and an engaging post-show area. Little ones enjoy frolicking in Bruce's Shark World—a hands-on play area that celebrates the ocean's toothiest residents. From there, take a look at a simulated Caribbean coral reef environment. For the record, the crowning jewel of the pavilion is the simple-but-spectacular Turtle Talk with Crush.

SEA BASE ALPHA SHOP: All visitors to this pavilion filter though this shop on their way back out to Future World—and many stop to shop. In addition to many a Finding Nemo-themed item, this retail location celebrates other creatures of the sea—in the form of shirts, hats, plush toys, and more.

BIRNBAUM'S ★BEST **TURTLE TALK WITH CRUSH:** FP+ If ever there was an attraction that left guests smiling and asking, "How do they do that?!"—this is it.

PHOTO BY JILL SAFRO

The concept is simple enough—a 10-minute, animated show featuring the surfer-dude sea turtle from *Finding Nemo*. The amazing part? The cartoon critter interacts with the audience. In doing so, he imparts turtle-y wisdom, answers questions, and cracks more than a few jokes. You have to see it to believe it. To do that, you'll have

EPCOT

Under the Sea

Three behind-the-scenes tours offer guests a closer look at life in The Seas with Nemo & Friends underwater environs: DiveQuest gives certified scuba divers the opportunity to explore one of the world's largest aquariums. Epcot Seas Aqua Tour lets guests snorkel The Seas. And Dolphins in Depth offers guests the chance to learn about dolphin behavior as they closely observe researchers and trainers interacting with dolphins. Reservations for any tour can be made by calling 407-WDW-TOUR (939-8687). Save money by using the coupons at the end of this book. For details on all of these programs, turn to pages 232–234 of the *Everything Else in the World* chapter.

to wait your turn—it's extremely popular with guests of all ages. It's totally awesome, dude. Oh, and Dory has been known to pop in for a visit, too. Note that kids are encouraged to sit on the floor in front of the big screen. There are benches to accommodate the rest of Crush's guests.

THE SEAS WITH NEMO & FRIENDS ATTRACTION: FP+ Imagineered in the style of classic family attractions, this undersea adventure is fun for everyone. In it, guests climb aboard a clam-mobile and enter a colorful coral reef. It seems Nemo has wandered off again, and his teacher, Mr. Ray, needs help finding him. So keep your eyes peeled! There's a bit of suspense

involved—including moments of darkness and a stressful jellyfish encounter—but rest assured, it all ends happily.

CARIBBEAN CORAL REEF: The man-made reef exists in an enormous tank that holds about six million gallons of salt water and more than 60 species of sea life. Among the 2,000 or so inhabitants are turtles, angelfish, sharks, dolphins, and diamond rays. It's worth it to stop by as the park opens—that's usually when breakfast is served to the fish.

Guests sometimes get to see scuba divers testing and demonstrating diving gear and underwater monitoring equipment as they carry on training programs with dolphins.

THE LAND

Occupying six acres, this enormous skylighted pavilion examines the nature of one of everybody's favorite topics—food. It also gives guests a chance to soar above the clouds in a celebration

FP+ = **Fastpass+ attraction (see page 25)**

of flight. A film, *The Circle of Life*, uses characters from *The Lion King* to deliver an entertaining yet inspirational message about humanity and the environment. A boat ride explores farming in the past and future. Narration gives visitors the chance to learn about the experimental agricultural techniques practiced in the pavilion.

Timing Tip: The Land pavilion's Soarin' Around the World is an exceptionally popular attraction. So much so that Fastpass+ assignments may all be gone early. It's best to visit first thing in the morning or get a Fastpass+ far in advance!

HOT TIP!

Got a rumbly in your tumbly? Head for Sunshine Seasons in The Land pavilion. There's a variety of counter-service choices—apt to please even the pickiest of eaters.

LIVING WITH THE LAND: FP+ This pavilion's 13½-minute boat ride through meticulously re-created natural locales opens with a dramatic storm scene. Guests sail through tropical rainforests, prairie grain fields, and a family farm. As the boat passes through each realistic setting, recorded narration offers commentary on humanity's ongoing struggle to cultivate and live in harmony with the land. Note the details that make each setting so convincing, such as sand blowing over the desert and light flickering from the television in the farmhouse window.

In the next segment, guests enter a plant research laboratory and solarium. Here, our planet's major food crops are being grown in research projects, along with rare new crops that may someday help meet Earth's ever-growing dietary needs.

Also of interest are the experiments being conducted to explore the practice of farming fish, and a desert farm area, where plants get nutrients through a drip irrigation system that delivers just the right amount of water—important in a dry climate.

As unreal as they appear, all the plants on view in the experimental greenhouses are living. In contrast, those in the biomes (the ecological communities viewed from the boat ride) were made in Disney studios out of lightweight plastic that simulates the cellulose found in real trees. The trunks and branches were molded from live specimens; the sycamore in the farmhouse's front yard, for example, duplicates one that stands outside a Burbank, California, car wash. Thousands of polyethylene leaves were snapped on.

Note that all of the greenhouse flora is quite real—please resist the urge to touch plants or the sand in which they live. Details are subject to change in 2018.

Club Cool

Future World's Club Cool is a great place to beat the heat. Located near the Fountain View coffee shop, it is Coca-Cola's complimentary International Tasting Station. Here, you can sample eight different soft drinks from around the world, some tastier than others.

After you've quenched your thirst, courtesy of the Coca-Cola Company, you may have a desire to do some shopping. Not coincidentally, there's plenty of Coke merchandise to choose from (at this point, you will have to open your wallet or wave that MagicBand if you'd like a souvenir).

At press time, Club Cool was open for business during Future World's regular operating hours. Details may change in 2018.

EPCOT

BIRNBAUM'S ★BEST★ SOARIN' AROUND THE

WORLD: FP+ Up, up, and away! On this high-flying Epcot ride (it's one of the most popular attractions at Walt Disney World), you will be suspended in a hang-glider-type vehicle up to 45 feet in the air, above a giant IMAX projection dome, and treated to an aerial tour of awe-inspiring landscapes and treasured landmarks. Soarin'

Character Connection

Where do Disney characters hang out when they aren't marching in parades or dancing in shows? The Epcot Character Spot! FP+ This brilliantly hued, Zip-a-Dee-Doo-Dah zone is the place to go to meet Disney faves such as Mickey Mouse, Minnie Mouse, and Goofy. The gang visits here throughout the day, but it's best to arrive early in the morning—as the line gets downright beastly in the afternoon. The entrance to the Character Spot is next to Fountain View. Check a park Times Guide for the character appearance schedule during your visit to Epcot. Get a Fastpass+ assignment if you can. Just across the way from the Epcot Character spot, there's another opportunity to meet Disney favorites. Stop here to mingle with Baymax from *Big Hero 6* and *Inside Out*'s Joy and Sadness (note that this spot does not offer Fastpass+). Details are subject to change.

Mad About the Mouse?

Can't get enough of all things Disney? Then D23 is the place to be. It's the official community for Disney superfans. To join, you'll need nothing more than a computer or smartphone and an unebbing enthusiasm for the House that Walt built. Upgrade to Gold Membership ($80 annual dues) to net access to special events, an official membership card and certificate, a subscription to the D23 magazine, a collectible gift (plus the chance to purchase exclusive merchandise), and more. For additional details or to join the club, visit *www.d23.com*. FYI: Walt Disney founded what would become the Disney Studios in 1923. Hence, the name D23.

has been delighting park guests with its wraparound glory since 2005—but these days, instead of hovering over one state (California), visitors are treated to a much broader tour.

Soarin' Around the World showcases some of the world's most glorious sights: The Great Wall of China, the plains of Africa, the oceans of Fiji, the Grand Canyon, Egyptian pyramids, and much more. With the wind in your hair and your legs dangling in the breeze, the hang glider feels so real that you may even be tempted to pull up your feet for fear of tapping the rooftops and landscapes below.

The flight takes about 6 minutes and employs synchronized wind currents, scent machines, and a (new) musical score set to a film that wraps 180 degrees around you. The re-imagined version of this attraction touched down in 2017. It features an all-new digital screen and projection system and is a hit with all ages—get a Fastpass+ assignment if you can.

Note: You must be 40 inches tall and free of back problems, heart conditions, motion sickness, and other physical limitations to ride. It's calmer

HOT TIP!

Epcot is much bigger than it seems, so allow lots of time to get from place to place. (It can take more than a half hour to walk from Spaceship Earth to The American Adventure in World Showcase.) Keep this in mind if you have restaurant reservations or hope to snag a nice IllumiNations viewing location on the World Showcase promenade.

than traditional "thrill" rides, but the sensation of flight is quite realistic. If you're afraid of heights, sit this one out. Remember to place loose items in the pouch under your seat or on the floor in front of you—and be sure to collect them at the end of the flight.

THE CIRCLE OF LIFE: This 20-minute film uses animation and live action to illustrate some of the dangers to our environment, as well as potential solutions. Presented as a fable featuring *The Lion King*'s Simba, Timon, and Pumbaa, the film takes an optimistic approach to a serious subject. It is shown in the Harvest Theater, just inside the entrance to The Land. Soon after the film begins, Simba's startled by the exuberant shout of "Timber!" and is drenched by the splash of a fallen tree in the water. The culprits are none other than his friends Timon and Pumbaa, who are clearing the savanna for the development of the Hakuna Matata Lakeside Village. Young Simba seizes the opportunity to tell them a tale about creatures who sometimes forget that everything on Earth is connected in the circle of life: humans.

Simba demonstrates to Timon and Pumbaa the consequences of progress, as his lessons are driven home by visual evidence of humans' mistreatment of the air, water, and land. (Timon: "And everybody was *okay* with this?") The effect is a mix of entertainment and a message about responsibility.

Note: The Circle of Life may not be shown in all of 2018. Check *www.disneyworld.com* or the My Disney Experience app or website for updates.

IMAGINATION!

The oddly shaped pyramids that house the Imagination! pavilion are quite a striking sight to behold. They certainly set the stage for the atypical experiences inside. One of the attractions is Journey Into Imagination with Figment, a slow-moving tour of the Imagination Institute. Also located here is the Disney & Pixar Short Film Festival.

Another pavilion highlight is the pair of quirky fountains outside—the Jellyfish Fountains, which spurt streams of water that spread out at the top, looking for an instant like their namesake sea creature, and the Leap Frog Fountains, which send out smooth streams of water that arc from one garden plot to another in the most astonishing fashion. Kids just can't get enough of them.

BIRNBAUM'S ★BEST★ DISNEY & PIXAR SHORT FILM FESTIVAL: FP+ Head to the Magic Eye Theater to enter the imaginative worlds of three animated shorts. Though films are subject to change, the one that is expected to play throughout 2018 is *Get a Horse*. It stars everyone's favorite mouse as he, Minnie, and their friends Horace Horsecollar and Clarabelle Cow delight in a manic, musical wagon ride. It combines with two other films to make for a most merry movie experience. The shorts are presented in 3-D (pick up your glasses on the way into the theater) and features entertaining "4-D" effects.

This unexpectedly delightful attraction has appeal for guests of all ages, provided they are

old enough to wear 3-D glasses. For updates on the films set to be screened during your stay, visit *www.disneyworld.com.*

JOURNEY INTO IMAGINATION WITH FIGMENT: FP+

Figment, the tiny purple dragon with the orange wings and yellow eyes, is on hand to guide guests on an imaginative quest. The intended goal? To figure out, once and for all, the best way to capture your imagination.

The journey takes place inside the Imagination Institute, where guests are invited to tour the institute's various labs, such as the Sight Lab, the Sound Lab, and Smell Lab. All in all, it's a very tame experience, save for the occasional blast of air or flashing lights.

Nostalgia buffs, take note: The classic song "One Little Spark," which made its debut with the original incarnation of this ride, underscores the show once more. Note that this attraction may not be open in all of 2018.

IMAGEWORKS LABS: It's a rare tot-aged ImageWorks visitor who doesn't experience at least some of the emotion felt by the little one who cried when her parents tried to tear her away. There used to be much more to explore, but it's still worth a look-see.

TEST TRACK FP+

BIRNBAUM'S ★BEST Fasten your safety belt! This high-octane pavilion puts guests through the creative and frenetic motions of automobile design and testing. The experience starts with guests designing a vehicle in the attraction's high-tech pre-show area. What is important to you in a car: efficiency, power, responsiveness, or capability? Use a touch screen to design your car with your priorities in mind, then take your virtual "SimCar" over to the Sim Track and give her a test drive. (Yes, they easily could have dubbed this attraction Sim Track—a Test Track by any other name would be just as cool.)

The 4-minute ride is similar to the original version of Test Track—there's lots of zigging

and zagging on the front end followed by a dramatic near-miss with a big noisy truck. Along the way, you'll learn how well your car did in each of the categories featured in the design stage. Finally, a long straightaway feeds into a series of banked turns and another straight shot that sends vehicles rocketing around the pavilion at top speed (up to 65 mph!). The computer-controlled, six-seater vehicles are equipped with video and audio, but no steering wheels or brake

HOT TIP!

If you don't mind splitting up your party, head for the "single rider" line at Test Track. It generally moves faster than the standby line.

pedals. After all is said and done, guests may create a 15-second commercial for their new car and send the video to a friend via e-mail.

Note: Kids under 7 must be accompanied by a guest over age 14; guests under 40 inches cannot ride; passengers must be free of back problems, heart conditions, motion sickness, and other physical limitations. Pregnant women are advised to sit this one out.

MISSION: SPACE FP+

Think you've got "the right stuff"? Well, this is your chance to prove it. Epcot's out-of-this-world attraction has a bold mission—to give you a chance to feel the excitement and extreme intensity of space travel without ever leaving the planet.

There are actually two ways to travel to Mars at this attraction: the "highly intense" way (aka Orange Team) and the "less intense" experience (Green Team). The original Mission: SPACE attraction provides a galaxy of thrills for many brave and sturdy theme park guests. The adventure begins with a white-knuckle blast-off of a spacecraft (which has snug seating for four) on an important mission to Mars. The sustained G-force during the launch is intended to be most realistic. Once en route, expect a rather strange, spectacular sensation. It's not quite weightlessness, but according to astronauts who've felt the real thing, it's pretty darn close. (So much so that it also tends to duplicate the not-so-spectacular sensation of space sickness. In fact, Mission: SPACE has the dubious distinction of being the first attraction in theme park history to be equipped with motion-sickness bags.)

Throughout the journey, you're expected to work with your fellow crew members (assuming the roles of navigator, captain, engineer, and pilot) to accomplish the mission. For the "highly intense" version, we recommend ignoring this call to duty and keeping your eyes glued directly to the screen. This will allow you to sit back and enjoy the ride and decidedly downsize the dizziness factor.

The original attraction can wreak havoc on the equilibrium. To cut the chances of losing your lunch, keep your eyes open at all times and fixed on the screen in front of you. You may be tempted to tilt your head or shut your eyes. Don't. (We promise you will arrive on Mars whether you fulfill your astronaut duty or not.)

Bottom line? Most guests who don't get queasy on the "highly intense" Orange Team version tend to rave about Mission: SPACE. For us, well, we admit we prefer the ride's gentler version—aka the Green Team. It's intended for those who would rather not spin. The experience is a bit different on "Mission: SPACE-lite," but it gives everyone a chance to ride without getting queasy. The effects may be toned down, but they are quite extraordinary. We completely enjoy the "less intense," non-spinning mission to Mars.

Note: All guests must be at least 44 inches tall and free of back and heart problems, motion sickness, and other physical limitations. Pregnant women must skip the trip, as should anyone with claustrophobic tendencies. In fact, if you have any health issues whatsoever, sit this out. And don't eat before riding!

EPCOT

PHOTO BY JILL SAFRO

Backstage Adventures

Epcot offers an intriguing and inspiring lineup of "backstage" opportunities. Experiences range from a walking "world tour" to an up-close encounter with majestic creatures of the sea. Tours and prices are subject to change in 2018; for information or to make reservations, call 407-WDW-TOUR (939-8687).

BEHIND THE SEEDS (Daily; every hour between 10:30 A.M. and 4:30 P.M.): An opportunity for guests of all ages to get a closer look at the greenhouses and fish farm that are part of The Land pavilion at Epcot. During the tour, guests will have close encounters with insects and plants. A guide shares knowledge of hydroponics growing systems and crops from around the globe. Expect to be on your feet for the full hour of this experience. Cost is $25 per adult, $20 per child (ages 3–9). This tour is best enjoyed by sturdy adults and older kids. Reservations may be made in advance or at the tour desk on the lower level of The Land (near the entrance to the Soarin' Around the World attraction). Theme park admission is required, but not included.

DIVEQUEST (Tuesday–Saturday; 4:30 and 5:30 P.M.): The highlight of the 2½-hour program is a 40-minute underwater adventure—complete with sharks, turtles, rays, and other fish—in The Seas with Nemo & Friends aquarium. Participants must show proof of current scuba certification. Cost is about $180 per person. Guests ages 10 through 12 must dive with a parent or guardian. Gear is provided. Epcot admission is not required or included.

DOLPHINS IN DEPTH (Tuesday–Saturday; 9:45 A.M.): This 3-hour Epcot program (about 30 minutes takes place in the water) teaches guests about dolphin behavior as they interact with the social sea creatures and observe researchers and trainers working with them. Cost is about $199 per person. The minimum age is 13. Guests ages 13 to 17 must be accompanied by a paying adult. Park admission is not required or included. Wet suits are provided; wear your own swimsuit.

EPCOT SEAS AQUA TOUR (Tuesday–Saturday; 12:30 P.M.): A 2½-hour program (about 30 minutes of which is in the water) that lets guests learn about and interact with ocean life in The Seas with Nemo & Friends pavilion. First, guests watch a video about sea creatures, then they join them in their habitat using a Supplied-Air Snorkel system. Cost is about $145. Gear is included, as are light refreshments, a souvenir gift, and a group photo. Guests must wear swimsuits. The tour is open to guests age 8 and up. Park admission is not required or included.

THE UNDISCOVERED FUTURE WORLD (Daily; 8:30 A.M.): Walt Disney dreamed about making the world a better place. In this 4-hour tour, guests are taken back to the creation of Epcot and learn about Walt's lofty ambitions and his legacy.

Guests walk to Future World pavilions and learn how each area celebrates humanity's accomplishments and challenges. The goal is to share the vision behind the park.

Cost is about $69 per person. Guests must be at least 16 years old to take this walking program. Park admission is required but is not included.

WORLD SHOWCASE: DESTINATIONS DISCOVERED (daily; 8:15 A.M.): A 4½- to 5-hour walking tour of World Showcase, DestiNations Discovered covers the culture, architecture, and design details of several of the park's international pavilions. Lunch is included at the Rose & Crown dining room in the U.K. pavilion. Cost is about $109 per person. Theme park admission is required, but not included. For pricing, schedules, and additional details call 407-939-8687, or visit *www.disneyworld.com*.

EPCOT

World Showcase

Noble sentiments about humanity and the fellowship of nations, which have motivated so many World's Fairs in the past, also inhabit World Showcase. But make no mistake about it: This area of Epcot is unlike any previous international exposition.

The group of pavilions that encircles World Showcase Lagoon (a body of water that is the size of several football fields, with a perimeter of about 1.2 miles) demonstrates Disney conceptions about participating countries in remarkably realistic, consistently entertaining styles. You won't find the real Germany here—rather, the country's essence, much as a traveler returning from a visit might remember what he or she saw.

Shops, restaurants, and attractions are housed in a group of structures that is an artful pastiche of all the elements that give that nation's countryside and towns their distinctive flavor. Although occasional liberties have been taken when scale and proportion required them, careful research governed the design of every nook and cranny.

Equally impressive is the cuisine. With no fewer than 14 upscale eateries to choose from, it's no wonder some guests here do nothing but nosh. (That is especially true during Epcot's popular International Food & Wine Festival, a time when dozens more nations contribute to an already fortified international menu. See page 11 for additional information.)

In the shops, many of the wares represent the country in whose pavilion they are sold. Craftspeople are occasionally on hand to demonstrate their arts. Thanks to special cultural-exchange programs and recruiting efforts, many World Showcase staffers hail from the countries the pavilions represent.

A diverse lineup of entertainment ensures that all visitors experience more than a little culture, foreign or otherwise. The entertainment is as authentic as the Disney casting directors can make it, with native performers commonly featured and new festivities always in the works.

Pavilions are described in the order in which they are encountered while moving counterclockwise

HOT TIP!

Most World Showcase pavilions open at about 11 A.M. However, guests may use the International Gateway entrance as much as a half hour prior to Future World's official opening time.

Phineas and Ferb: Agent P's World Showcase Adventure

Calling all secret agent wannabes! How would you like to help Perry the Platypus save the world from the evil Dr. Heinz Doofenshmirtz? Here's your chance. The interactive game is based on the Disney Channel show *Phineas and Ferb*. Of course, one need not be familiar with the show to get a kick out of the Epcot version. Once you borrow a F.O.N.E. (Field Operative Notification Equipment) or have a smartphone programmed at a special kiosk (near Italy, Norway, or the United Kingdom), you are ready to start the scavenger hunt.

If you and your team follow instructions and find the clues, you will complete your mission: to save the world! There's no extra charge to play, but guests do have to return the F.O.N.E.'s after they declare "mission accomplished."

around the World Showcase Lagoon after crossing the bridge from Future World. All entertainment offerings are subject to change.

CANADA

Celebrating the many beauties of the U.S.A.'s neighbor to the north, the area devoted to the Western Hemisphere's largest nation is complete with its own mountain, waterfall, rushing stream, rocky canyon, mine, and splendid garden massed

with flowers. There's even a totem pole, a trading post, and an elaborate, mansard-roofed hotel similar to ones built by Canadian railroad companies as they pushed west around the turn of the twentieth century. All this is imaginatively arranged somewhat like a split-level house, with the section representing French Canada on top, and another devoted to the mountains alongside it and below. From a distance, the Hôtel du Canada, the main building here, looks like little more than a bump on the landscape—as does Epcot's single Canadian Rocky Mountain. But up close, they both seem to tower as high as the genuine article.

The gardens were inspired by the Butchart Gardens, on Vancouver Island, British Columbia, a famous park created on the site of a limestone quarry. The hotel is modeled, in part, after Ottawa's Victorian-style Château Laurier. Musical entertainment takes place at the Mill Stage, a theater on the World Showcase Promenade (on the United Kingdom side of the pavilion).

O CANADA!: Step into the Circle-Vision 360 film, *O Canada!*, and find yourself surrounded by the breathtaking sights and sounds of this northern nation. Of course, you won't be alone—Canadian actor Martin Short stars as your guide, taking guests through prairies, plains, snowfields, rivers, rocky mountainsides, and beyond. Humor and hockey are included. The motion picture provides a you-are-there feeling that makes all of this spectacular scenery still more memorable. Know that you'll have to stand for the show, as there are no seats in this theater.

NORTHWEST MERCANTILE: Found to the left upon entering the pavilion's plaza, this spot features NHL T-shirts (Canadian teams, of course), plush toys (moose, owls, otters, etc.), and maple-flavored snacks, tiny totem poles, dream catchers, pajamas, plus other Canada-themed collectibles. Skeins of rope, tin scoops, lanterns, and antique ice skates hanging from the long beams overhead set the mood, together with the structure itself.

PHOTO BY JILL SAFRO

UNITED KINGDOM

In the space of only a few hundred feet, visitors to this pavilion stroll from an elegant London square to the edge of a canal in the rural country-side—via a bustling urban English street framed by buildings that constitute a veritable rhapsody of historic architectural styles. But one scene leads to the next so smoothly that nothing ever seems amiss. Here again, note the attention to detail: the half-timbered High Street structure that leans a bit, and the hand-painted "smoke" stains that make the chimneys look as if they have been there for centuries. When a thatched roof is required, it's right where it should be—though the roof may be made of plastic broom bristles because fire regulations prohibit the real thing. Off to the side is a pair of scarlet phone booths identical to those that used to be found around the U.K. And there are eight architectural styles characteristic of the streetscapes, from English Tudor to Georgian and Victorian.

There is no major attraction in this pavilion; instead, it features half a dozen shops and a pub that serves a selection of beers and ales that would be the toast of any "local" in London itself. The Rose & Crown serves snacks, too. There's lots of entertainment, including an acoustical group called Quickstep. Every Wednesday through Sunday, the four-member band can be heard playing songs that draw from Scottish, English, and Irish traditions. In the pub, a lively pianist has been known to play late into the evening. A band known as British Revolution plays classic rock favorites in the garden courtyard. They're a true crowd-pleaser. (Entertainment at this pavilion is subject to change during 2018.)

THE CROWN & CREST: This shop looks like a backdrop for a child's fantasy of the days of King Arthur, with its high rafters decked out with bright banners, a fireplace (and crossed swords above), and wrought-iron chandelier. Souvenirs featuring the Union Jack flag are the stock-in-trade at this emporium adjoining the Sportsman's Shoppe. Name histories and family crests are also available, as are swords, shields, and knights in shining armor. There's also a line of Guinness Stout merchandise (think glasses, shirts, bottle openers, etc.).

HOT TIP!

A nice place to watch IllumiNations is from the patio at the Rose & Crown Pub in the United Kingdom pavilion. Try to snag a lagoonside table—whether within the pub's boundaries or in the self-serve sitting area nearby—at least 30 minutes before the show is set to begin.

SPORTSMAN'S SHOPPE: Head here for clothing and accessories centered on uniquely British locales and sports. You can expect to find a large selection of football (soccer) team gear. Don't miss the tartan map on the wall opposite The Crown & Crest; it identifies plaids from Glen Burn and Gordon to Langtree and St. Lawrence. There's a nice selection of shirts and souvenirs featuring the Rose & Crown Pub (the U.K. pavilion's watering hole), too. Outside, the shop resembles a stone manor built during the last half of the sixteenth century.

PHOTO BY JILL SAFRO

THE TEA CADDY: Fitted out with heavy wooden beams and a broad fireplace to resemble the Stratford-upon-Avon cottage of William Shakespeare's wife, Anne Hathaway, this shop stocks English teas, both loose and in bags, in a wide variety of flavors. Other items include teapots, china, biscuits, and assorted candies.

THE TOY SOLDIER: There's a nice selection of rock-'n'-roll-themed items here, highlighting well-known British bands, as well as merchandise featuring the gang from the Hundred Acre

Wood: Pooh, Piglet, Eeyore, and Tigger, too. TV fans will appreciate the selection of items featuring favorite British programs such as *Dr. Who*, *Monty Python*, etc.

THE QUEEN'S TABLE: This shop (opposite the Sportsman's Shoppe) is one of the loveliest in all of Epcot. That is particularly true of the store's elegant Adams Room, embellished with elaborate moldings and a crystal chandelier. The setting is a lovely background for the handbags, jewelry, soaps, and other fragrant items that are available.

Don't neglect to inspect small, serene Britannia Square outside the shop farthest from the promenade. But for its small size and the Florida climate, it feels like London itself.

INTERNATIONAL GATEWAY

Informally known as Epcot's back door, the International Gateway is between the United Kingdom and France pavilions. There's a ticket window just outside the gate. (Yes, it's possible to enter and exit the park here.) Note that all guests are subject to a thorough security screening. All bags are searched here and all guests must pass through a metal detector before they may enter the park. A screening wand may be used, too. In addition to restrooms and an ATM, International Gateway is also home to:

FRIENDSHIP LANDING: Disney's water taxis, known as FriendShip boats, ferry guests to the Yacht and Beach Club, BoardWalk, and the Swan and Dolphin resorts, and finally to Disney's Hollywood Studios (the last stop before the boat returns to the resorts and back to Epcot). The dock is located just outside the International

Where to Eat in Epcot

A complete listing of all Epcot eateries—full-service restaurants, fast-food emporiums, and snack shops—can be found in the *Good Meals, Great Times* chapter. See the Epcot section, beginning on page 251.

Gateway entrance. It's possible to walk to all of the aforementioned destinations, too. (It takes about 30 minutes to reach the Studios on foot.)

STROLLER AND WHEELCHAIR RENTAL:
Strollers and wheelchairs may be rented here. Hold on to your rental receipt; it can be used on the same day in all WDW theme parks, should you leave and return later on. It's possible to get a replacement stroller here. Note that ECVs are only available at the park's front entrance.

WORLD TRAVELER: Candy, cookies, soft drinks, books, kitchen items, disposable cameras, backpacks, strollers (for purchase), and a package pickup depot are located at this spot near the United Kingdom pavilion. Disney fashions, home items, character merchandise, and Epcot souvenirs are also for sale here.

FRANCE

The buildings here have mansard roofs and casement windows so Gallic in appearance that you may expect to see a Bohemian poet looking down from above. A canal-like offshoot of the lagoon seems like the Seine itself; the footbridge that spans it recalls the old Pont des Arts. There's a kiosk like those that punctuate the streets of Paris and a bakery whose heavenly rich aromas announce its presence long before it's visible.

Shops sell perfumes and other items. Their roofs are of real copper or slate, and the cabinetry is finely crafted. Galerie des Halles—the iron-and-glass-ceilinged market that Paris once counted as one of its most beloved institutions—lives again. But perhaps most special of all are the people. Hosts and hostesses who hail from Paris and the French provinces answer questions in French-accented English. Keep an eye out for Serveur Amusant, the comedic waiter who does one heck of a balancing act.

An interesting background note: The main entrance to the pavilion recalls the architecture of Paris, most of which was built during the Belle Epoque ("beautiful age"), the last decades of the nineteenth century.

Don't miss the garden on the opposite side of this pavilion. It is one of the most peaceful spots in World Showcase.

BIRNBAUM'S ★BEST★ IMPRESSIONS DE FRANCE: Shown in the Palais du Cinéma, a little theater that's not unlike the one at Fontainebleau, this enchanting 18-minute film takes viewers on a trip through France.

The film shows off a beautiful tree-dotted estate, fields and vineyards at harvest time, a flower market and a pastry shop, a glacier, and a harbor full of squawking gulls. Viewers visit the Eiffel Tower; Versailles and its gilt Hall of Mirrors (just outside Paris); Mont Saint Michel; the French Alps; and Cannes, the star-studded resort city on the Mediterranean coast. All this is even more appealing thanks to a superb soundtrack, consisting almost entirely of the music of French classical composers.

The exceptionally wide screen adds yet another dimension. This is not a Circle-Vision 360 film like the movies shown at China and Canada. The France film used only five cameras, and it is shown on five large projection surfaces—200 degrees around. It's a beautiful film, one of the park's best. We recommend stopping for a French pastry break after the show.

PLUME ET PALETTE: One of the loveliest shops in World Showcase, this Art Nouveau–inspired location is home to the Givenchy Shop—the only location in the world that carries the complete line of Givenchy fragrances, skin care products, and cosmetics.

LA SIGNATURE: Another beautiful spot, this boutique features a nice selection of Guerlain cosmetics and fragrances.

L'ESPRIT DE LA PROVENCE: This little shop stocks a selection of textiles, ceramics, and kitchen accessories from the Provence region of Southern France. They offer loose chocolates and children's books, too.

LES HALLES BOUTIQUE DE CADEUX:
Everything from Eiffel Tower statuettes to Impressionist-style prints is offered at this location near the exit of the cinema. Mugs, tote bags, T-shirts, berets, flags, and picture frames are

among the offerings available. The area is based on Paris's now-demolished Les Halles, the city's old fruit and vegetable market. This space is also the location of the ever-popular bakeshop known as Les Halles Boulangerie & Patisserie.

LES VINS DE FRANCE: Selections in this wine shop range from the inexpensive to the pricey, from *vin ordinaire* going for several dollars to upward of $99 for a rare vintage. Wine tastings are held here to sample the offerings (for a price). Other wares include wine glasses with a World Showcase theme, books about wine, bottle openers and toppers, aprons, candy, kitchenware, and soaps. There's a big barrel of ice cold beer, too. Dig in for a sudsy treat.

HOT TIP!

Don't try to fit all of the World Showcase movies into one day, especially if you are traveling with kids.

MOROCCO

Nine tons of tile were handmade, hand cut, and shipped from Morocco to Epcot to create this World Showcase pavilion. To capture the unique quality of this North African nation's architecture, Moroccan artisans came to Epcot to practice the mosaic art that has been a part of their homeland for thousands of years.

Koutoubia Minaret, a meticulously detailed replica of the famous prayer tower in Marrakesh, stands guard at the entrance. A courtyard with a fountain at the center leads to the medina (Old City). Between the traditional alleyways and the more modern sections are the pointed arches and swirling patterns of the Bab Boujeloud gate, a replica of the one that stands in the city of Fez. An ancient working waterwheel irrigates the gardens, and the motifs repeated throughout the buildings include carved plaster and wood, tile, and brass. Live entertainment may be presented at the Morocco Pavilion, on World Showcase Promenade. Check a Times Guide for specifics.

THE BRASS BAZAAR: Interspersed among the decorative brass plates in this store are ceramic pitchers, planters, pots, ornate bottles of rosewater, serving sets, colorful maps, wooden collectibles, books, framed prints, baskets, tiles, couscous, hummus, and tabbouleh mixes, lamps, spices, and other Moroccan selections.

THE ART OF HENNA: In the market for a temporary henna body decoration? Look no farther than this cozy corner of the Morocco pavilion. Henna "tattoos" are available—for a fee—in various sizes and designs between 1 P.M. and 9 P.M. daily (hours may vary).

CASABLANCA CARPETS: In addition to handmade carpets, this store features an intriguing and eclectic selection of merchandise. Look for lamps, fez hats, jewelry, books, and more.

MARKETPLACE IN THE MEDINA: Hand-woven baskets, sheepskin wallets and bags, assorted straw hats, drums, sandals, postcards, scarves, jewelry, clothing, and small carpets are among the available wares.

SOUK AL MAGREB: This waterside enclave located on the World Showcase promenade spills over with hand-crafted keepsakes. Look for Moroccan lamps, baskets, and leather goods. One can also find rosewater and coffee products.

TANGIER TRADERS: This is the place to shop if you're in the market for a fez, woven belts, leather sandals and purses, and other traditional Moroccan clothing and accessories.

JAPAN

Serenity rules in Japan. Except, of course, when the pavilion resounds with traditional music performed by a drum-playing duo or group.

The landscaping, designed in accordance with traditional symbolic and aesthetic values, contributes to the pavilion's peaceful mood. Rocks, which in Japan represent the enduring nature of the Earth, were brought from North Carolina and Georgia (since boulders are scarce in the Sunshine State). Water, symbolizing the sea (which the Japanese consider a life source), is abundant; the Japan pavilion garden has a stream and pools inhabited by koi (fish). Evergreen trees, which in Japan are symbols of eternal life, are here in force.

Disney horticulturists created this very Japanese landscape using few plants native to that country because the climate there is so

different from that of Florida. Among the few trees here native to Japan are the sago, near the courtyard entrance to the Katsura Grill; the two Japanese maple trees, identifiable by their small leaves, not far away (near the first stairway from the promenade on the left side of the courtyard as you face it); and the prickly monkey-puzzle trees, near the walkway to the promenade, on The American Adventure side of the pagoda. Needle-sharp thorns make the latter the only species of tree that monkeys cannot climb.

The pagoda was modeled after an eighth-century structure located in the Horyuji Temple, in Nara, Japan. The striking torii gate on the shore of World Showcase Lagoon derives from the design of the one at the Itsukushima shrine in Hiroshima Bay.

BIJUTSU-KAN GALLERY: Housing an ever-changing cultural display, this small museum has offered, among other exhibitions, the Kitahara Collection of Tin Toys, featuring toys produced between 1880 and 1970. Most recently, the exhibit "Kawaii—Japan's Cute Culture" was featured here.

MITSUKOSHI MERCHANDISE STORE: There are kimonos, T-shirts bearing Japanese characters, fine jewelry, and a selection of bowls and vases meant for flower arranging for sale at this spacious store set up by Mitsukoshi—a four-centuries-old retail firm.

DID YOU KNOW?

The five stories of the Japanese pagoda symbolize earth, water, fire, wind, and sky.

The shop features a wall of sake selections (and a small sake bar), plus chopsticks, bonsai, jewelry, china, paper fans, and origami products. There is also a bounty of snacks, candies, and teas. You can even get an oyster and discover a pearl! The pleasant atmosphere and variety of merchandise make this establishment a most rewarding experience for both the casual browser and the serious shopper. The building's design was inspired by the Gosho Imperial Palace, which was constructed in Kyoto in 794 A.D.

THE AMERICAN ADVENTURE

BIRNBAUM'S
★BEST★ When it came to creating The American Adventure, the center-piece of World Showcase, Disney Imagineers were given relatively free rein. So the 110,000 bricks of the imposing Colonial-style structure that houses a stirring show, fast-food restaurant, and shop are the real thing—patiently crafted by hand from soft Georgia clay.

The show inside stands out because of its wonderfully evocative settings, its detailed sets, and the 35 superb Audio-Animatronics players, some of the most lifelike ever created by the Disney organization. A stellar a cappella vocal group called Voices of Liberty periodically serenades guests in the building's foyer. By all means, catch a performance.

THE AMERICAN ADVENTURE SHOW:
One of the most ambitious Epcot attractions, this 26-minute presentation celebrates the American spirit from the nation's birth. Beginning with the arrival of the pilgrims at Plymouth Rock and their harsh first winter on the western shore of the Atlantic, the Audio-Animatronics narrators—a lifelike Ben Franklin and a thoroughly convincing Mark Twain—recall key people and events in American history: the Boston Tea Party, George Washington and the grueling winter at Valley Forge, the influential abolitionist Frederick Douglass, the celebrated nineteenth-century Nez Perce chief Joseph, and many more. The Philadelphia Centennial Exposition is remembered, along with women's rights campaigner Susan B. Anthony, telephone inventor Alexander Graham Bell, and the steel giant and philanthropist Andrew Carnegie. Naturalist John Muir converses onstage with Teddy Roosevelt. Charles Lindbergh, Rosie the Riveter, Jackie Robinson, and Walt Disney are represented. So are John Wayne, Lucille Ball, Margaret Mead, John F. Kennedy, Martin Luther King Jr., and Billie Jean King.

The idea is to recall episodes in history, both negative and positive, that contributed to the growth of the spirit of America, by engendering "a new burst of creativity" (in the designers' words) "or a better understanding of ourselves as partners in the American experience."

For information about how each of the many featured historical figures spoke during his or her lifetime, researchers contacted historians and cultural institutions—the Philadelphia Historical Commission, the State Historical Society of Missouri, the Department of the Navy's Ships Historical Branch, and others. When recordings were not available, educated guesses were made: Alexander Graham Bell's voice was created on the basis of contemporary comments about his voice's clarity, expressiveness, and crisp articulation, combined with the fact that his father taught elocution. A highlight of the show is the majestic music played by the Philadelphia Symphony Orchestra.

Seats toward the front of the house afford the best view (and sound). If you have some extra time before the show, be sure to read the inspirational quotes that line the walls—Jane Addams, Charles Lindbergh, Herman Melville, and Ayn Rand are among the prominent Americans who are quoted.

AMERICAN HERITAGE GALLERY:
Inside the pavilion (on the right side of the grand lobby), the addition of this art gallery brought Epcot's grand total to six. Its current exhibition is from the The Kinsey Collection. The exhibit features more than 40 pieces of art, artifacts, books, and sculptures that, together, tell an inspirational story of African-American history.

HERITAGE MANOR GIFTS: Visit this shop to find Americana in all of its red-white-and-blue glory. Gifts include T-shirts, tote bags, pillows, tri-corner hats, flags, and books about U.S. history. "Made in America" merchandise includes wine, moonshine, candy, beer biscuits, soaps, candles, and items celebrating U.S. cities.

THE AMERICA GARDENS THEATRE:
An ever-changing slate of live entertainment is presented throughout the year in this lakeside amphitheater in front of The American Adventure pavilion. American Music Machine, a popular a cappella group, performs contemporary music throughout the day. Concert series such as Eat to the Beat and Sounds Like Summer take place on this stage, too—as does the popular Candlelight Processional, which is offered up during the holiday season (see page 12).

Showtimes are posted at the theatre and in the park Times Guide. For details, visit *www.disneyworld.com*.

ITALY

The arches and cutout motifs that adorn the World Showcase reproduction of the Doge's Palace in Venice are just the more obvious examples of the attention to detail lavished on the individual structures in this relatively small pavilion. The angel perched atop the scaled-down campanile was sculpted on the model of the original, right down to the curls on the back of its head. It was then covered with real gold leaf, despite the fact that it was destined to be set almost 100 feet in the air.

The other statues in the complex, including the sea god Neptune presiding over the fountain in the rear of the piazza, are similarly exact. And the pavilion even has an island like Venice's own, its seawall appropriately stained with age, plus moorings that look like barber poles, with several distinctively Venetian gondolas tied to them. St. Mark the Evangelist is also remembered, together with the lion that is the saint's companion and Venice's guardian. These can be seen atop the two massive columns that flank the small arched footbridge that connects the island to the mainland. The only deviation from Venetian reality is the alteration of the site of the Doge's Palace in reference to the real St. Mark's Square.

The quaint pavilion is equally interesting from a horticultural point of view. The island boasts kumquat trees, citrus plants typical of the Mediterranean, and a couple of olive trees that can be seen on the sidewalls of a shop. Originally located in a Sacramento, California, grove, the olive trees arrived in Florida via flatbed truck a bit slimmer than when they started out. (Arizona border inspectors decreed that the trees be trimmed to the ten-foot width required by state law; therefore, the ancient olives were shorn en route. The hardy trees survived, leaving only their scars to remind visitors of the ordeal; the darker bark is what remains of the original, while the lighter areas are new growth.) The tall, narrow trees that stand like dark columns are Italian cypresses, which are common in their native country.

LA BOTTEGA ITALIANA: This shop on the edge of the piazza features a selection of red and white Italian wines. (If it's early in the day, take advantage of Epcot's Package Express service and have bottles sent to the park exit—so you don't have to carry them all day.) Items such as cappuccino makers, wine glasses, olive oil, spices, chocolate, cookies, espresso, cookbooks, and decorative bottle toppers are also on hand. It's also possible to purchase an ice cold Italian beer.

IL BEL CRISTALLO: There is an abundance of Italian fragrances, shirts, and accessories, plus purses, wallets, and bags, inside this shop (just off the promenade on the Germany side of the piazza). Other featured wares include scarves, ties, fragrances, and jewelry. This shop also boasts a large assortment of exquisite, hand-crafted Venetian masks (which range in price from about $30 to $500).

GERMANY

There are no villages in Germany quite like this one. Inspired by various towns in the Rhine region, Bavaria, and the German north, it boasts structures reminiscent of those found in urban enclaves as diverse as Frankfurt, Freiburg, and Rothenburg. There are stair-stepped rooflines and towers, balconies and arcaded walkways, and so much overall charm that the scene seems to come straight out of a fairy tale. The beer hall to the rear is almost as lively as those at Munich's famed Oktoberfest, especially late in the evening. The shops, which offer a range of merchandise from wine and sweets to ceramics and cuckoo clocks, toys, and books (and even art), are so tempting that it's difficult to leave the area empty-handed.

The elements that constitute the Germany pavilion are described here as they would be encountered while walking counterclockwise around the cobblestone-paved central plaza. (The plaza is known as the St. Georgsplatz, after the statue at its center.) St. George, the patron saint of soldiers, is depicted with a dragon that legend says he slew during a pilgrimage to the Middle East.

Try to time your World Showcase peregrinations to take you to the Germany pavilion on the hour, when the handsome, specially designed glockenspiel at the plaza's rear can be heard chiming in a melody composed specifically for the pavilion.

DAS KAUFHAUS: This two-story structure, whose exterior is patterned after a merchants' hall known as the Kaufhaus (located in the German town of Freiburg im Breisgau), stocks athletic apparel and footwear.

DER TEDDYBAR: Located adjacent to the Volkskunst clock shop, this is a toy store with a bit of flair. It's home to one of Walt Disney World's best selections of toys, including an assortment of stuffed keepsakes. Duffy the Disney Bear is among the plush items sold here. They also stock bears of the gummy variety.

KARAMELL-KÜCHE: This caramel display kitchen tempts with housemade sweet treats made from buttery caramel. Many items are made fresh in the on-stage kitchen. Favorites include fresh strawberries hand-dipped in chocolate and drizzled with gooey caramel, caramel-filled chocolate chip cookies, crunchy apples enveloped in caramel, chocolate or vanilla

cupcakes topped with rich vanilla icing with a dab of caramel on top, packaged Werther's candies, and much more. Don't come here on an empty stomach—you could go bankrupt!

KUNSTARBEIT IN KRISTALL: This shop to the left of the Biergarten features Austrian and crystal jewelry (including tiaras), beer mugs, wine glasses in traditional German tints of green and amber, and crystal decanters. Glassware may be etched on the spot.

STEIN HAUS: The "house" is really a tiny shop that celebrates *bier*, featuring steins, mugs, shirts, and collectibles.

VOLKSKUNST: Small and appealing, this establishment is filled with a burgher's bounty of German timepieces, plus a smattering of other items made by hand in the rural corners of the nation. As for cuckoo clocks, some are small and unobtrusive, while others are so immense that they'd look appropriate only in some cathedral-ceilinged hunting lodge. This is also one place to pick up a traditional German beer stein, wine accessories, bells, books, crafts, and music.

WEINKELLER: Germany's wine shop, situated between the cookie shop and the crystal shop toward the rear of St. Georgsplatz, offers about 50 varieties of German wine. Wine tastings are held here daily (for a fee). The selection includes vintages meant for everyday consumption, plus a few fine estate wines. These are white (with a few exceptions), because white wine constitutes the bulk of Germany's vinicultural output. (Only 20 percent of German wine bottlings are red.) The setting itself is quite attractive—low-ceilinged and cozy.

DIE WEIHNACHTS ECKE: A shop like this can set a visitor's mind to thoughts of Christmas—even on the steamiest dog days of summer. Ornaments, decorations, and gifts manufactured by various German companies line the shelves.

One item of note is the pickle ornament. Pickle ornaments are considered a special Christmas tree decoration by many families in Germany. Historically, it is always the last ornament hung on the tree, with a parent hiding it among the other ornaments. Kids gleefully search for it—and the one who finds it gets a special little present from St. Nicholas, left for the most observant child. Can you find the pickle ornament on each tree in the shop? It's not easy!

CHINA

Dominated by the Disney equivalent of Beijing's Temple of Heaven and announced by a pair of banners that proclaim good wishes to passersby (the Chinese characters translate to: "May good fortune follow you on your path through life" and "May virtue be your neighbor"), this pavilion conveys a level of serenity that offers an appealing contrast to the hearty merriment of the bordering Germany and the gaiety of nearby Mexico. Part of this quiet environment is the by-product of the soothing, traditional Chinese music. The gardens also make a major contribution. They are full of rosebushes native to China, and there is a century-old mulberry tree (to the left of the main walkway into the pavilion), with a pomegranate tree and a wiggly-looking Florida native known as a water oak nearby.

The number of stones in the floor of the pavilion's main structure is not random; the center stone is surrounded by nine stones

PHOTO BY JILL SAFRO

because nine is considered a lucky number in China. Around the edge of the outer room rise 12 columns—because 12 is the number of months in the year and the number of years in a full cycle of the Chinese calendar. Be sure to stand on the round stone in the center: Every whisper is amplified.

A spacious emporium is devoted to Chinese wares, and two restaurants add to the overall atmosphere. However, all this is secondary to the motion picture shown inside the Temple of Heaven—a Circle-Vision 360 film that is one of the most diverting World Showcase attractions. Keep in mind that this is a standing-room-only viewing experience.

REFLECTIONS OF CHINA: This cinematic presentation shows the beauties of a land that few Epcot visitors have seen firsthand—and does it so vividly that it's possible to see the film twice and still not fully absorb all the wonderful sights.

The film replaced *Wonders of China*, the Circle-Vision 360 movie that played at Epcot's China pavilion since 1982. Just as with the original, filmmakers used nine cameras to capture cultural and scenic images that wrap completely around viewers. The majestic tour includes some rural stops, plus visits to cities such as Hong Kong, Macau, Beijing, and Shanghai.

The film includes footage of many landmarks, such as the 2,400-year-old Great Wall and Tiananmen Square, as well as some newer cultural developments. Overall, it showcases the majesty of this ancient country and highlights some of the more dramatic changes that have taken place over the past 20 or so years. Note that the theater has no seats.

Village Traders

Located between the Germany and China pavilions, this open-air shop sports a selection of hand-crafted gift items from Africa, India, Spain, and Australia. Browse through such souvenirs as wind chimes, handbags, hats, and, of course, T-shirts.

HOUSE OF WHISPERING WILLOWS:
When exiting, pass by the House of Whispering Willows, an exhibit of ancient Chinese art and artifacts. Changed periodically, it invariably includes fine pieces from well-known collections.

HOUSE OF GOOD FORTUNE: This vast emporium, located off the narrow, charming Street of Good Fortune, offers a huge assortment of merchandise—lanterns, hats, wine, beer, fine jewelry, silk robes, shoes (including a variety of sandals and flip-flops), prints, porcelain items, tea sets, candles, neckties, Buddah statues, chess sets, reading glasses, and much more. Kids adore the huge variety of panda-themed plush toys. Handheld fans may be personalized on the spot.

NORWAY

Set between Mexico and China is Norway, a pavilion added to the World Showcase mix in 1988. Built in conjunction with Norwegian companies, the pavilion celebrates the rich history, folklore, and culture of one of the Western world's oldest countries.

The cobblestone town square is an architectural showcase of the styles of such Norwegian towns as Bergen, Alesund, and Oslo. There's also a Norwegian castle fashioned after Akershus, a 14th-century fortress still standing in Oslo's harbor; the castle here houses the Akershus restaurant. Few can resist walking into the bakery for a taste of its treats. In a show of modernity, a statue of Norway's legendary marathoner Grete Waitz stands behind the bakery. Shops stock handicrafts and folk items: hand-knit woolens, wood carvings, and glass and metal artwork.

Frozen fans can also visit Arendelle, in the popular attraction Frozen Ever After. And for those guests who would like to meet Anna and Elsa of *Frozen* fame—great news: They're here!

ROYAL SOMMERHUS—MEET ANNA & ELSA: Attention, *Frozen* fans! Princess Anna and Queen Elsa greet guests throughout the day in this pavilion's Royal Sommerhus. Fastpass+ is not available for this meet-and-greet, but the wait time posted is usually quite accurate. FYI: Arendelle, the fictional kingdom in which the ladies live, is said to be in Norway.

FROZEN EVER AFTER: FP + Be prepared to let it go as you're swept off to Arendelle in this enchanting new boat ride. The adventure celebrates the story from the film *Frozen* and the characters that have become near and dear to just

about everybody's heart: Anna, Elsa, Olaf, Kristoff, and Sven—plus the Snowgies from the *Frozen Fever* animated short. The attraction, which replaced Maelstrom, immerses guests in favorite moments and music from the film. This happy addition to World Showcase can have daunting waits—we highly recommend reserving a Fastpass+ assignment well in advance. Otherwise, head here as soon as the park opens for the day.

THE PUFFIN'S ROOST: Here you should find a nice variety of Norwegian gifts. Sweaters, activewear, high-quality winter wear, Viking helmets, trolls, toys, fragrances, fine jewelry, and candy are among the wares for sale at the Roost. The back room is stocked with all things *Frozen*. Want to pose for a photo with a giant troll? You've come to the right place!

STAVE CHURCH GALLERY: Inside the wooden stave church, there is a small exhibit that explores Norwegian culture. It's interesting (and sad) to note that only about 30 stave churches remain in Norway today.

PHOTO BY JILL SAFRO

PHOTO BY MIKE CARROLL

MEXICO

The tangle of tropical vegetation surrounding the great pyramid that encloses this pavilion and the Mexican restaurant at the lagoon's edge on the promenade provides only the barest suggestion of the charming area inside.

Dominated by a re-creation of a quaint plaza at dusk, the pyramid's interior is rimmed by balconied, tile-roofed, colonial-style structures. Crowding a fountain area is a quartet of stands selling Mexican handicrafts, and to the left is a shop stocked with other handsome wares. A visit by a Mariachi Cobre band keeps things lively—as does the tequila bar. To the rear, the San Angel Inn serves authentic fare. Behind it, a waterborne attraction features a whirlwind Mexican tour.

Take a look at the cultural exhibit inside the pyramid entrance on the way in. Note that the building was inspired by Meso-American structures dating from the third century A.D.

GRAN FIESTA TOUR STARRING THE THREE CABALLEROS: Big news: The Three Caballeros (that would be Donald Duck, Panchito, and José Carioca) are reuniting for a big show in Mexico City! Unfortunately, the ever mischievous Donald has gone missing in Mexico—and guests join Panchito and José in the quest to find him. In doing so, you will be treated to a whirlwind (slow-moving) boat tour of the country. The cheery montage of film, props, and Audio-Animatronics figures is reminiscent of It's a Small World, though on a smaller scale.

Trivia buffs should note that the Audio-Animatronics versions of the Three Caballeros that appear in the finale made their original Disney World debut in 1971. They were a part of the Magic Kingdom's original Mickey Mouse Revue in the Fantasyland Theatre—and remained there until 1980 (when the show left WDW for Tokyo Disneyland). This attraction usually opens at 9 A.M. Details are subject to change.

LA PRINCESSA DE CRISTAL: Presented by Arribas Brothers and located next to the entrance to the Gran Fiesta Tour Starring the Three Caballeros attraction, this alcove offers crystal tiaras, character figurines, rings, bracelets, necklaces, and glass slippers. If you're lucky, you'll get to watch glass blown by an in-house artisan.

PLAZA DE LOS AMIGOS: Brightly colored artwork, sombreros, malachite, baskets, decorative parrots, mariachi music (available on CD), musical instruments, and pottery make this mercado (market) at the plaza's center as bright and almost as lively as one in Mexico itself. Brilliantly hued papier-mâché piñatas figure strongly in the scenery here. Authentic pre-Columbian figures are on display. Also available for purchase are spices, hot sauce, salsa, liquors, cocktail accessories, and candy.

EL RANCHITO DEL NORTE: Located on the lagoon side of World Showcase Promenade, this spot features gifts and souvenirs.

LA TIENDA ENCANTATA: Visit this store inside the pyramid and you'll discover fine jewelry, bags, scarves, accessories, and assorted women's fashions.

PHOTO BY JILL SAFRO

SHOWCASE PLAZA

DISNEY TRADERS: Merchandise combining the charm of classic Disney characters and Epcot themes is the primary stock-in-trade. Sundries are also sold.

PORT OF ENTRY: A shop carrying fashions for the whole family, accessories, plush dolls, and toys. It has food and wine-related items, too.

Entertainment

Epcot presents an intriguing array of live performances each day, making it very important to consult a park Times Guide when you arrive. For updates, call 407-824-4321.

AMERICA GARDENS THEATRE: The lagoonside venue at The American Adventure pavilion hosts an ever-changing program of live entertainment, such as the popular Garden Rocks concert series presented during the annual Flower and Garden Festival.

ILLUMINATIONS—REFLECTIONS OF EARTH: FP+ This nighttime spectacular presents the entire history of our planet in 13 minutes—from its creation to the present and a look toward the future. A dazzling mix of lasers, fireworks, fountains, and music, this show is a highlight of any Epcot visit.

The extravaganza, visible from anywhere on the World Showcase promenade, takes place nightly at closing time. There are excellent viewing locations all around the World Showcase Lagoon. Note that additional viewing areas have been added to the stretch between the Germany and China pavilions. Details are subject to change.

KIDCOT FUN STOPS: There is an activity area in each of the countries of World Showcase. These spots invite kids to play games and make colorful cut-outs of Duffy the Disney Bear.

WORLD SHOWCASE PERFORMERS: It's all but impossible to complete a circuit of World Showcase without catching performances while en route. Keep an eye on the schedule and be sure to take in entertainment at each pavilion, often performed by natives of the country represented. Among the possibilities: worldly acrobats, a Mexican mariachi band, an American a cappella group, Moroccan belly dancers, Japanese drummers, and more.

Holiday Happenings

During certain holidays, such as Easter week, the Fourth of July, Thanksgiving, Christmas week, and New Year's Eve, Epcot usually offers extended hours and presents additional entertainment to celebrate the respective occasion. Call 407-824-4321, or visit *www.disneyworld.com*, for schedules and details.

CHRISTMAS: Epcot is exceptionally festive throughout the holiday season. The park celebrates Christmas with a gigantic tree and its popular candlelight choral processional.

The Candlelight Processional, a stirring presentation of traditional holiday songs, features a reading of the Christmas story by a celebrity narrator. This is a very popular event—and one of our favorites. See page 12 of the *Getting Ready to Go* chapter for details.

HOT TIPS!

- Use a smartphone or stop at a Fastpass+ kiosk to book Fastpasses for as many attractions as possible (if you haven't reserved in advance).

- On your way into the park, pick up a free guidemap and a Times Guide. Consult the entertainment schedule first thing.

- Lines throughout Epcot are longest at midday and shortest in the early evening.

- During peak seasons, preferred reservation times at Epcot's table-service restaurants book quickly—make reservations as far in advance as possible. However, some tables may be available on a first-come, first-served basis (with a bit of a wait). Arrive a few minutes ahead of your reservation time.

- Most World Showcase restaurants seat guests until park closing. To make advance plans, call 407-WDW-DINE (939-3463).

- Kids can get autograph books or World Showcase passports (sold for about $10 inside the park) stamped in each of the 11 countries represented in the park. It's a nice added layer to an Epcot "world tour."

- Interactive fountain areas at Epcot provide guests of all ages with an opportunity to cool off. Be sure to pack swimsuits (and waterproof diapers) for little ones who'll undoubtedly spend time splashing in the water.

- If you plan to play at ImageWorks, the interactive play area inside Imagination, take along the e-mail address of a friend. It may come in handy.

- Allow plenty of time to explore the hands-on exhibits at Innoventions and the post-shows at Spaceship Earth and Mission: SPACE.

- Epcot is a good park to "hop" to from another park (provided your ticket has the hopper option). It's usually open until 9 P.M. or later.

- FriendShip water taxis are unlikely to transport you across World Showcase Lagoon any faster than a brisk walk, but they are a peaceful, foot-friendly way to make the half-mile-plus journey.

Where to Find the Characters

Epcot Character Spot is a good place to meet Disney characters, including Mickey, Minnie, and Goofy (near Fountain View coffee in Future World). Baymax, Joy, and Sadness greet guests just across from Epcot Character Spot. Characters such as Mickey, Chip, and Dale host meals at the Garden Grill in The Land pavilion. Princesses invite you to join them for a meal at Norway's Akershus Royal Banquet Hall. Anna and Elsa meet folks in Norway, too. Snow White mingles at the Germany pavilion. Donald Duck greet guests in Mexico. Belle visits France. Mulan appears in China, while Daisy and others have been known to stop by Future World's Legacy Plaza West. Check a Times Guide for schedules and greeting locations.

Hidden Mickeys

These are some of the most popular "Hidden Mickeys" at Epcot. How many can you find? Check the box when you spot each one!

❤ **Mission: SPACE:** When your ship lands on Mars, you may spy a Mickey on a rooftop to the right of the landing strip. (It's made of satellite dishes.) ■

After you exit the ride and enter the gift shop, look up in the center of the room to find a side profile of Mickey painted on the ceiling. ■

❤ **Mexico:** Toward the end of the Gran Fiesta Tour boat ride, you'll see a barge on your left. On that barge is a Hidden Mickey made of strategically arranged bongo drums. ■

❤ **Living with the Land:** As you walk through the queue, try to find the three bubbles on the large mural that come together to form a Hidden Mickey. (Hint: It's near the middle of the mural.) ■

About halfway through the ride, you may notice a water hose coiled into the shape of Mickey Mouse's noggin'. ■

❤ **The American Adventure pavilion:** Look for a painting of early American settlers crossing a river with covered wagons. One of the wagon-pulling oxen has a Mickey near its left front leg. ■

Another painting features workers constructing a building. Check out the tops of the beams behind the construction team. They form a classic Hidden Mickey! (The painting is on the first floor, on the right, and toward the back of the rotunda.) ■

❤ **France:** Check out the meticulously pruned bushes on the canal side of the France pavilion— one of them is shaped like a classic Mickey.

Be sure to eyeball the grates surrounding the trees near the entrance to Les Chefs de France. There are several H.M.s in the intricate grillwork. ■

While in France, pay close attention to the wedding party scene in the *Impressions de France* movie—there is a Hidden Mickey on a second-floor window! ■

❤ **Canada:** It's easy to find the totem poles in this pavilion—but it's a bit more challenging to find the Hidden Mickey on the left one. ■

❤ **The Seas with Nemo & Friends:** In Bruce's Shark World, look for two large posters—one titled "Did You Know?" and the other titled "Bruce's Shark World" (they are on opposite sides of the room). Each has an oyster in the lower right-hand corner that contains Mickey-shaped pearls. If you pay attention at the shark tank, you'll be rewarded with a Hidden Mickey sighting (or two). The Mouse's head appears on the bottom of the tank, shaped by strategically placed rocks. ■

❤ **Journey Into Imagination with Figment:** About halfway through the ride and as you move through Figment's house, look up in the bathroom. Figment's commode forms a Hidden Mickey with two red circles on the ground next to it. ■

❤ **Spaceship Earth:** In the Renaissance scene, look quickly to your left to find the first painter standing in front of a table (his back is to you). On the top left of the table, three white-paint circles form a Hidden Mickey. ■

Later in the ride, keep your eyes open for a Hidden "WDI" (the abbreviation for Walt Disney Imagineering) on the microphone of the radio broadcaster (on your left). ■

❤ **Germany:** Look up to spot three armor-wearing fellows festooning a facade to the right of the clock in St. Georgsplatz. The suit closest to the glockenspiel sports an H.M. ■

❤ **Japan:** Finding the koi pond here is easy—but can you find the Hidden Mickey in the pond? And no, it's not a Mickey fish! ■

Specifics may change during 2018.

Where in the World?

All of the photos on this page were taken at Epcot. Do you know where? We challenge you to find all the spots where these images were shot and snap a photo for yourself as you discover each one. Happy hunting!

(For locations, turn to page 352.)

EPCOT

Disney's Hollywood Studios

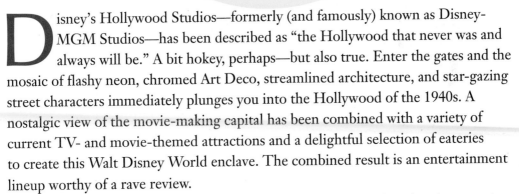

D isney's Hollywood Studios—formerly (and famously) known as Disney-
MGM Studios—has been described as "the Hollywood that never was and
always will be." A bit hokey, perhaps—but also true. Enter the gates and the
mosaic of flashy neon, chromed Art Deco, streamlined architecture, and star-gazing
street characters immediately plunges you into the Hollywood of the 1940s. A
nostalgic view of the movie-making capital has been combined with a variety of
current TV- and movie-themed attractions and a delightful selection of eateries
to create this Walt Disney World enclave. The combined result is an entertainment
lineup worthy of a rave review.

   Since opening in 1989, the park has continued to grow and evolve. At press time,
major changes were in the works. Imagineers are hard at work building Toy Story–
and Star Wars–themed lands. While they wait for these new play zones to be unveiled,
guests may enjoy some newer experiences right now—many of which celebrate the
awakening of the Force. Favorites include Star Tours—The Adventures Continue and
Star Wars: A Galactic Spectacular, a rousing fireworks extravaganza that thrills guests
of all ages. The park's current lineup of attractions boasts such classic crowd-pleasers
as the Twilight Zone™ Tower of Terror, the rollicking Rock 'n' Roller Coaster, and
an explosive struggle between good and evil in Fantasmic! Each adds a new dimension
to the Hollywood term "action."

A Beauty and the Beast—Live on Stage

B Fantasmic!

C The Twilight Zone™ Tower of Terror

D Rock 'n' Roller Coaster

E Animation Courtyard

F Disney Jr.—Live on Stage!

G Walt Disney—One Man's Dream

H Voyage of The Little Mermaid

I Star Wars Launch Bay

J Toy Story Midway Mania!

K Muppet★Vision 3-D

L Star Tours—The Adventures Continue

M Indiana Jones™ Epic Stunt Spectacular

N The Chinese Theatre

O For the First Time in Forever: A Frozen Sing-Along Celebration

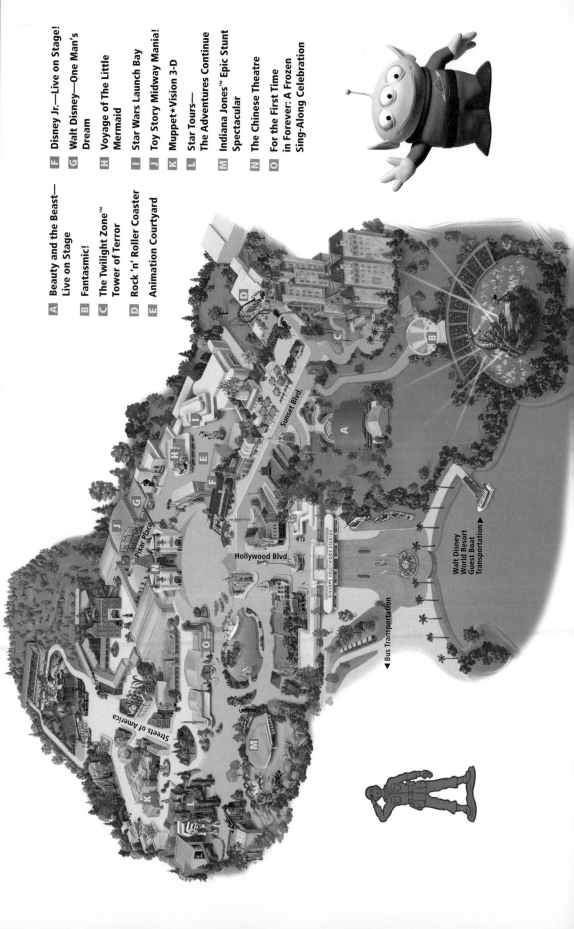

Sunset Blvd.

Pixar Place

Hollywood Blvd.

▲ Bus Transportation

Walt Disney World Resort Guest Boat Transportation ▲

Streets of America

Getting Oriented

The Disney's Hollywood Studios park has a layout with no distinctive shape or main thoroughfare. As such, the Studios can be a bit of a challenge to navigate. Study a guidemap as you enter.

The park entrance is at Hollywood Boulevard. This shop-lined avenue leads straight to Hollywood Plaza, address of the Studios' Chinese Theatre, a replica of Grauman's Theatre. Walking along Hollywood Boulevard toward the plaza, you will come to Hollywood Junction. Here, a wide, palm tree dotted street known as Sunset Boulevard branches off to the right.

Stroll down Sunset Boulevard and you'll come across The Hollywood Hills Amphitheater, home of Fantasmic! and Rock 'n' Roller Coaster. At the street's far end is The Hollywood Tower Hotel, home of The Twilight Zone™ Tower of Terror. The strip is also graced with shops, the Sunset Ranch Market, and the Theater of the Stars amphitheater, where Beauty and the Beast —Live on Stage is performed daily.

HOT TIP!

All information listed on these pages was accurate at press time, but details are apt to change. For updates on the shows and attractions at Disney's Hollywood Studios, visit *www.disneyworld.com.*

Stand in Hollywood Plaza, facing the Chinese Theatre, and you'll notice an archway just off to your right. This leads to Animation Courtyard, home to Disney Junior—Live on Stage and Star Wars Launch Bay. Pixar Place leads to Toy Story Midway Mania! If you turn left off Hollywood Boulevard, you're on course for such attractions as Indiana Jones Epic Stunt Spectacular and Star Tours—The Adventures Continue. Just beyond Star Tours there is another entertainment zone.

HOW TO GET THERE

Take Exit 64B off I-4. Continue about half a mile to reach the parking area. Take a tram to the park entrance.

By WDW Transportation: From the Swan, Dolphin, Yacht & Beach Club, and BoardWalk: boat, or walkway. From Fort Wilderness: bus from the Outpost stop. From Epcot: boat or bus. (Fitness-minded folks may hoof it from Epcot's International Gateway exit to the Studios. The walk takes about 20 to 30 minutes.) From Magic Kingdom, Animal Kingdom, all other Walt Disney World resorts and the resorts on Hotel Plaza Boulevard: bus only. From Disney Springs: bus to any Walt Disney World resort and transfer to a Studios bus or boat.

PARKING

All-day parking at the Studios starts at $20 for day visitors (free to WDW resort guests and annual passholders; $40 for premium lots). Trams circulate regularly, providing transportation from the parking area to the park entrance. Be sure to note the section and the aisle in which you park. The parking ticket you receive allows for re-entry to the parking area throughout the day.

HOURS

Disney's Hollywood Studios is usually open from about 9 A.M. until about one hour after sunset. During certain holiday periods and summer months, hours are extended. It's best to arrive about 20 minutes before the posted opening time—guests are often let in early. Depending on the season, some stage shows do not open until late in the morning.

Admission Prices

ONE-DAY BASE TICKET*
(Restricted to use in Disney's Hollywood Studios. Prices represent Walt Disney World's Value, Regular, and Peak rates; they do not include tax; and they are expected to rise in 2018.)

Adult ....$99/$107/$119
Child**..$93/$101/$113
* 1-Day tickets purchased in 2018 must be used by December 31, 2019
** 3 through 9 years of age; children under age 3 free

Park Primer

BABY FACILITIES

Changing tables and facilities for nursing mothers can be found at the Baby Care Center at Guest Relations near the park entrance.

CAMERA NEEDS

The Darkroom on Hollywood Boulevard stocks a variety of camera supplies, including memory cards, batteries, disposable cameras, and more. Note that selfie sticks are not permitted in the park.

DISABILITY INFORMATION

Most Walt Disney World attractions, restaurants, shops, and shows are accessible to guests using wheelchairs. Additional services are available for guests with visual or hearing disabilities. Stop by the park's Guest Relations window when you arrive. For a detailed overview of the services offered, including transportation, parking, attraction access, and more, pick up a free copy of the *Guide for Guests with Disabilities*. For more information, refer to the *Getting Ready to Go* chapter of this book.

FIRST AID

Minor medical problems can be handled at the First Aid Center, located next to Guest Relations at the park entrance. For medical emergencies, alert a cast member and call 911.

INFORMATION

Guest Relations, located just inside the park entrance, has free guidemaps, Times Guides, and an ever-resourceful staff. To make dining arrangements for certain Studios eateries, visit *www.disneyworld.com* or call 407-939-3463.

LOCKERS

Lockers, found by Oscar's Super Service, just inside the park entrance, cost $10 per day for large lockers, $8 a day for small ones (plus a $5 refundable deposit) for unlimited use all day. They may be rented from the Crossroads of the World kiosk, directly across from Oscar's classic pickup truck. Your receipt entitles you to a locker at any other WDW theme park on the same day (not including the deposit).

LOST CHILDREN

Report lost children at Guest Relations and alert a Disney employee to the problem.

LOST & FOUND

Located at Guest Relations, near the park entrance. To report lost items after your visit, call 407-824-4245.

MONEY MATTERS

There is an Automated Teller Machine (ATM) just outside the park entrance and by the Sunset Club Couture shop. In addition to U.S. currency, credit cards (American Express, Visa, JCB, MasterCard, and Diner's Club), traveler's checks, Disney gift cards, Disney Dollars, MagicBands, and WDW resort key cards are accepted at most park locations. (MagicBands and resort key cards must be backed up with a major credit card.)

PACKAGE PICKUP

Shops can arrange for purchases to be transported to Package Pickup, next to Oscar's Super Service (by the park entrance), where they can be picked up later in the day. Note that packages may take several hours to get to Package Pickup—plan accordingly. The service is free.

SAME-DAY RE-ENTRY

Be sure to wear your MagicBand (if you used it for admission) or retain your ticket if you plan to return later the same day.

SECURITY CHECK

Guests entering Disney theme parks are subject to a thorough security check. All bags will be searched by security personnel before guests may enter the park. A metal detector screens guests. Weapons (including toys) are prohibited. For details and a complete listing of Walt Disney World Park Rules, visit Guest Relations or go to *www.disneyworld.com/ParkRules*.

STROLLERS & WHEELCHAIRS

Strollers, wheelchairs, and Electric Conveyance Vehicles (ECVs) may be rented from Oscar's Super Service, inside the park entrance on the right. Cost for strollers is about $15; about $12 for wheelchairs. A double stroller costs $31. A Length of Stay rental ticket saves wheelchair and stroller renters $2 a day. Cost for ECVs is $50, plus a $20 refundable deposit. Keep the receipt—it can be used on the same day for a replacement at any WDW theme park. Quantities are limited (especially for ECVs).

The Main Attractions

Disney's Hollywood Studios has a brand of attractions altogether unique. Some offer guests behind-the-scenes looks at the creative and technical processes that generate television shows and movies. Others go so far as to allow guests to gain a bit of showbiz experience along with the insight. Still others present popular characters and stories in new forms—from stage shows to thrill rides.

Note: Large chunks of this park will be under construction throughout 2018 as Imagineers complete Toy Story Land and continue building a new land known as Star Wars: Galaxy's Edge. All details are subject to change as construction progresses. Visit *www.disneyworld.com* for updates.

The Twilight Zone™ Tower of Terror FP+

BIRNBAUM'S **★BEST★** The Hollywood Tower Hotel is the creepy home of a spectacular thrill ride. On the facade of the 199-foot-tall building hangs a sparking electric sign. As the legend goes, lightning struck the building on Halloween night in 1939. An entire guest wing disappeared, along with an elevator carrying five people.

The line for the ride runs through the lobby, where dusty furniture, cobwebs, and old newspapers add to the eerie atmosphere. As guests enter the library, they see a TV brought to life by a bolt of lightning. Rod Serling invites them to enter The Twilight Zone.

Guests are led toward the boiler room to enter the ride elevator. (This is your chance to change your mind about riding—ask an attendant to point you toward the "chicken exit.") Once you take a seat in the elevator, the doors close and the room begins its ascent. At the first stop, the doors open and guests peek down a corridor. Among the effects is a ghostly visit by the hotel guests who vanished. The doors close and you continue the trip skyward.

At the next stop, you enter another dimension, a combination of sights and sounds reminiscent of *The Twilight Zone* TV series. In fact, Disney Imagineers watched each of the 156 original *Twilight Zone* episodes at least twice for inspiration. This part of the ride is a somewhat disorienting experience, in part because the elevator moves horizontally.

What happens next depends upon the whim of Disney Imagineers, who have programmed the ride so that the drop sequence is chillingly random. At the top (about 157 feet up), passengers can look out at the Studios below. Once the doors shut, you plummet 13 stories. The drop lasts about two seconds, but it seems a whole lot longer.

Just when you think it's over, the elevator launches skyward, barely stopping before it plunges again. And again. As you exit, Rod Serling claims this is the kind of thing "they don't tell you about in any guidebook." It's been our privilege to prove him wrong.

From the time you are seated, the trip takes about five minutes. Note that you must be at least 40 inches tall to ride. It is not recommended for pregnant women, people with heart conditions, or with back or neck problems. Though thrilling (and scary), the drops are surprisingly smooth. Still, if you'd rather not experience the sensation of being a human yo-yo, sit this one out.

PHOTO BY JILL SAFRO

Rock 'n' Roller Coaster Starring Aerosmith FP+

BIRNBAUM'S BEST The fastest roller coaster in Walt Disney World history is guaranteed to rock your world. Rock 'n' Roller Coaster is ideally suited for those who consider the Tower of Terror just a little on the tame side.

The indoor attraction reaches a speed of nearly 60 miles per hour—in 2.8 seconds flat. Other twists include two loops and a corkscrew —marking the first time Disney has turned guests upside down on American soil.

The ride's premise is this: The rock band Aerosmith has cut their recording session short because they are late for a concert. As they rush out, they offer you a backstage pass to the show. The only thing standing between you and the big show is a classically chaotic Los Angeles freeway.

In an effort to get to the show on time, you will zip through the nighttime Los Angeles streets in a stretch limo. The ride vehicles (designed to resemble limousines) are equipped with a high-tech sound system (five speakers per seat make for a mega-decibel ride), and the remainder of the journey features rockin' synchronized sound— adding a dramatic dimension to the roller coaster experience most daredevils have come to expect.

You must be free of back, neck, and heart problems to experience this topsy-turvy tour. Expectant mothers should sit this one out. Guests must be at least 48 inches tall to ride. Details are subject to change in 2018.

Beauty and the Beast– Live on Stage FP+

BIRNBAUM'S BEST Here's the show that inspired the Broadway musical. Several times each day, Belle, Gaston, Mrs. Potts, and the rest of the cast of the Disney film *Beauty and the Beast* come to life at the 1,500-seat Theater of the Stars, near the Tower of Terror, on Sunset Boulevard.

The 30-minute show is as entertaining as they come. The staging is just right, and the music's simply addictive as it traces the classic tale—from Belle's dissatisfaction with her life in a small French town to the climactic battle between the staff of the Beast's castle and Gaston and the townspeople. Lumiere and friends perform the song "Be Our Guest" with a delightful display of dancing flatware. The show includes most of the songs from the classic film. Check a park Times Guide for the performance schedule. Latecomers can often find seats in the bleachers (in the back of the theater). Note that some scenes (especially when Gaston leads a brigade to "kill the beast") can be intense for some young children.

PHOTO BY JILL SAFRO

Voyage of The Little Mermaid FP+

One of Disney's Hollywood Studios' most popular attractions, this is a 17-minute live musical production, adapted from the Disney animated classic. The show is presented in a theater with an underwater feel. In it, many of the film's beloved animated characters, such as Flounder, Scuttle, and Sebastian, are brought to life by puppeteers. The show opens with a lively rendition of "Under the Sea," then animated clips from the movie are shown as performers join the puppets on stage.

Ariel is the star and performs songs from the film. Prince Eric makes an appearance, and an

enormous Ursula glides across the stage to steal Ariel's voice. Of course, as in the movie, the happy ending prevails. The story line is a little bit disjointed, hopping from scene to scene, and some of the signature songs are missing. However, most viewers are familiar with the film, so this choppiness doesn't detract much from the show.

There are a number of special effects, including cascading water, lasers, and a lightning storm that may be a bit frightening for very young children. Note that many of the effects are best enjoyed from the middle to the rear of the theater. All audience members get spritzed with water—don't wear silk!

Keep in mind that, although this is a Fastpass+ attraction, performances are still presented at scheduled times throughout the day. Current showtimes are listed in the Times Guide. Plan to arrive at least 15 to 30 minutes before the scheduled start time. This attraction may not be operating in all of 2018.

Disney Junior–
Live on Stage! FP+

Fans of Disney Junior shows should enjoy this live, audience-participation production. It features kid favorites such as *Mickey Mouse Clubhouse*, *Doc McStuffins*, *Sofia the First*, and *Jake and the Never Land Pirates* (all from popular Disney Junior TV shows). Familiar characters engage guests with stories, song, and dance as they visit each of the aforementioned Disney Junior realms. The fun culminates with a birthday party for

HOT TIP!

This park will have areas under construction for the foreseeable future, as Imagineers build Toy Story– and Star Wars–themed lands, and other new play zones. Until the dust settles, consider this a good park to "hop" to or from, using a multi-day ticket with park-hopping privileges.

Minnie Mouse. Very young guests tend to be the most enthusiastic members of the audience.

The performance space holds large crowds (of mostly tiny people) at a time. There are a few seats, but there's plenty of room to sprawl out on the carpeted floor. Details may change in 2018. Visit *www.disneyworld.com* for updates.

Toy Story
Midway Mania! FP+

BIRNBAUM'S ★BEST This engaging experience is an energetic, interactive toy box tour with a twist: Guests wear 3-D glasses as they take aim at animated targets with toy cannons. The adventure is about as high-tech as they come, yet rooted in classic midway games of skill. As points are scored, expect effusive encouragement from a cast of cheerleaders—*Toy Story*'s Woody, Buzz, Hamm, Rex, Trixie, and, of course, the Green Army Men.

HOT TIP!

Don't sweat the accuracy number in Toy Story Midway Mania!—it's meaningless. Fire as fast and furiously as possible. That way, you'll hit more targets in less time!

Fans of the Magic Kingdom's Buzz Lightyear's Space Ranger Spin will no doubt delight in this adventure, which takes the experience of the interactive attraction into a whole new dimension. As far as skill level goes, there's something for everyone at Toy Story Mania!—from beginners to seasoned gamers alike.

Note: This is a wildly popular attraction with guests of all ages. Get there as early in the morning as you can, and try to snag a Fastpass+ assignment as far in advance as possible. The herky-jerky motion of this ride (as the vehicles move from scene to scene) may be too much for folks with sensitive backs or other health issues.

FP+ = Fastpass+ attraction (see page 25) 179

Toy Story Land

To infinity and beyond! Disney's Hollywood Studios will transport park guests to the adventurous outdoors of Andy's backyard. The new 11-acre land (which was still under construction as this book went to press) is scaled to make people feel like they've been shrunk to the size of Woody, Buzz, and the gang. As the (toy) story goes, Andy designed this land with the use of building blocks, game board pieces, plastic buckets, and other playthings.

In addition to the wildly popular Toy Story Midway Mania! attraction, the land features a new family-friendly roller coaster known as **Slinky Dog Dash** (Andy built it with his Mega Coaster Play Set). Also in the yard: **Alien Swirling Saucers**—an attraction in which guests take a spin in a toy flying saucer and try to elude the legendary Claw. (If the thought of swirling makes you woozy, sit this one out.) The opening date for Toy Story Land was not set at press time, but it is expected to happen in 2018. For details on this playful new zone (including height requirements), visit *www.disneyworld.com*, or the My Disney Experience app or website.

Indiana Jones™ Epic Stunt Spectacular FP+

Earthquakes, fiery explosions, and other dramatic events give guests insight into the science of movie stunts and effects at this 2,000-seat amphitheater. Stunt people re-create scenes from Indiana Jones films and demonstrate the skills required to keep audiences on the edge of their seats. But the 30-minute show isn't all flying leaps. Guests also see how the elaborate stunts are pulled off—safely—while the crew and an assistant director explain what goes on both in front of and behind the camera.

In one segment, a dramatic scene from *Raiders of the Lost Ark* is staged. A 12-foot-tall rolling ball chases a Harrison Ford look-alike out of the temple. The flames are so intense that the audience can feel the heat. The crew then dismantles the set, revealing the remarkable lightness of movie props, as assistants roll the ball uphill for the next show.

In a scene at a busy "Cairo" street market, "extras" chosen from the audience play the scene in which Indy pulls a gun while others are fighting with swords. The explosive action continues and leads to a desert finale in which the hero and his sweetheart make a death-defying escape.

There are moments during this show when audience members might wonder if something has actually gone wrong. But by revealing tricks of the trade, the directors and stars show that what appears to be dangerous is actually a safe, controlled bit of movie magic.

The stunt show may not operate in all of 2018. For updates and additional information, visit *www.disneyworld.com*, or use the My Disney Experience mobile app or website.

Walt Disney: One Man's Dream

Follow Walt Disney from "Mickey Mouse to the Magic Kingdoms" in this multi-media exhibit next to the Voyage of The Little Mermaid attraction. Among the treasures included in this tribute to the man behind the mouse are Walt's second-grade school desk, the original Audio-Animatronics Abraham Lincoln from the 1964 New York World's Fair, *Mickey Mouse Club* props, Jungle Cruise and Spaceship Earth models, costumes from *Mary Poppins*, and more. A small movie theater screens sneak peeks at upcoming Disney films.

Note: This attraction may not be operating in 2018. For updates on its status during your trip to the park, visit *www.disneyworld.com*.

Disney Movie Magic

An homage to "a Hollywood that never was, and always will be," this new nightly show celebrates 80 years of (mostly) Disney cinema classics. Expect to see a myriad of memorable movies, from *Mary Poppins* to *Guardians of the Galaxy*.

The cutting-edge projection display fittingly uses the facade of the park's Chinese Theatre as its silver screen. (The structure is a full-scale replica of Grauman's Chinese Theatre, a landmark Hollywood movie palace.)

The 10-minute show is best viewed from Hollywood Boulevard, close to the Chinese Theatre. Get there early—and don't forget the popcorn! The show may not be presented in all of 2018. Details are subject to change.

Star Tours—The Adventures Continue FP+

BIRNBAUM'S ★BEST★ Inspired by George Lucas's blockbuster series of Star Wars films, this beloved attraction—which originally opened in 1989—is better than ever. A new Star Tours experience touched down in 2011, complete with a new story line. The 3-D experience offers guests the opportunity to ride on (modified) StarSpeeders, the exact same type of flight simulator used by military and commercial airlines to train pilots.

A galaxy of trouble awaits Jedi wannabes, but fear not—the Force will be with you. The best part? There are more than 50 different adventures, so multiple visits yield multiple surprises—and several of those surprises involve scenes from *Star Wars: The Force Awakens* and *Star Wars: The Last Jedi*.

This is a turbulent trip—seat belts are definitely required. Passengers must be free of back problems, heart conditions, motion sickness, and other physical limitations to ride. Guests under 40 inches tall and kids younger than 3 may not ride. Pregnant women must skip this one. To all who ride: Fasten your seat belt and may the Force be with you.

HOT TIP!

Beware of Stormtroopers! Captain Phasma leads a battery of the baddies from Star Wars Launch Bay to a stage by The Chinese Theatre several times a day. Check a park Times Guide for the schedule of Captain Phasma's First Order Stormtrooper March.

Star Wars Launch Bay

Guests don't have to wait for the Star Wars–themed land to be completed to get a fix of the Force—Star Wars Launch Bay offers an immersive atmosphere in which to experience both the Light and Dark sides. Housed in the space formerly occupied by Art of Animation, Launch Bay features props and movie memorabilia (some genuine, some replicas) celebrating Star Wars and the recently reawakened Force. In addition to Light and Dark galleries, guests may encounter characters such as Chewbacca, BB-8, and Kylo Ren. Details may change in 2018—check *www.disneyworld.com* for updates.

Jedi Training— Trials of the Temple

Jedi Padawans can learn to harness the Force and properly wield a lightsaber right here in Disney's Hollywood Studios. The 30-minute training program is offered several times a day. To participate, all potential participants (ages 4 to 12) should sign up at the Indiana Jones Adventurers Outpost (between Indiana Jones Epic Stunt Spectacular and the 50's Prime Time Cafe) as early as possible (during regular park hours). Kids who make the cut (determined on a first-come, first-served basis) receive a receipt complete with a time to return.

Arrive about 30 minutes before showtime to receive a loaner cloak. When the Jedi master arrives, kids receive lightsabers (strictly for the show) and start the training session. Instruct kids to pay close attention to the lesson—they'll need their new skill set to search for a hidden temple and face their fears, not to mention simulate a lightsaber battle against Darth Vader and other dark side representatives. Check a Times Guide for the schedule.

Muppet★Vision 3-D 🄵🄿+

BIRNBAUM'S ★BEST★ One of the most entertaining attractions at the Studios, this 3-D (though some describe it as 4-D) movie is quite remarkable. A funny 12-minute pre-show gives clues about what's to come. Once inside the theater, many will notice that it looks just like the one from Jim Henson's classic TV series *The Muppet Show*. Even the two curmudgeonly fellows, Statler and Waldorf, are sitting in the balcony, bantering with each other and offering their typically critical commentary on the show.

The production comes directly from Muppet Labs, presided over by Dr. Bunsen Honeydew—and his long-suffering assistant, Beaker—and introduces Waldo, the "Spirit of 3-D." Among the highlights is Miss Piggy's solo, which Bean Bunny turns into quite a fiasco. Sam Eagle's grand finale leads to trouble as a veritable war breaks out, culminating with a cannon blast to the screen, courtesy of everyone's favorite Swedish Chef.

Including the pre-show, expect to spend about 29 minutes with Kermit and company. Shows run continuously throughout the day. Note that guests must wear 3-D glasses to enjoy this show. If your child is too young to keep the glasses on, skip this Muppet encounter.

For the First Time in Forever: A Frozen Sing-Along Celebration 🄵🄿+

Have you ever heard of a song called "Let It Go"? Yep, we thought so. But have you ever had the privilege of singing it with Queen Elsa herself? Now's your chance! In fact, the whole *Frozen* gang is on hand for a spirited audience-participation sing-along.

Presented in the Hyperion Theater, the 30-minute show features a retelling of the *Frozen* story, courtesy of a duo of Arendelle storytellers. It includes clips from the beloved film (presented on a ginormous screen) and live appearances by Anna, Kristoff, and (eventually) Elsa. Guests of all ages are encouraged to sing along with a few *Frozen* ditties. Don't know all the words? Just follow the bouncing snowflake.

This celebration is very popular with *Frozen* fans of all ages—book a Fastpass+ selection if you can. You won't regret it. Oh and don't wear your finest attire—you will get snowed on!

Shopping

Hollywood Boulevard

CELEBRITY 5 & 10: Modeled after a 1940s Woolworth's, this large shop carries housewares such as pillows, towels, teapots, aprons, and Mickey ice-cube trays, plus items that can be personalized—including Mouse ears.

COVER STORY: A small area located just through The Darkroom, this is the place to pick up your picture if you've had it taken by any of the park photographers. Frames are offered, too.

CROSSROADS OF THE WORLD: In the middle of the entrance plaza, Mickey Mouse keeps watch from atop this Hollywood Boulevard landmark. The kiosk deals mostly in pins, but has souvenirs, sundries, hats, and sunglasses, plus park guidemaps and Times Guides. This is also the place to stop if you'd like to rent a locker.

THE DARKROOM: The Art Deco facade of this shop features a giant camera, so it's easy to find. Cameras (including the disposable kind) and photography accessories are sold here.

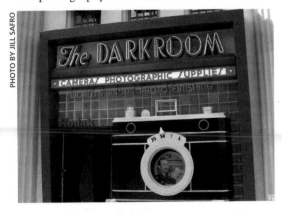

KEYSTONE CLOTHIERS: Disney–themed women's and men's fashions and accessories are Keystone Clothiers' specialties of the house.

MICKEY'S OF HOLLYWOOD: The place to find character shirts, hats, plush toys, watches, socks, bags, books, snack items, slippers, and sunglasses, plus items emblazoned with the park's logo. It has a penny-press machine, too.

MOVIELAND MEMORABILIA: This kiosk, located just to the left of the Studios' main entrance, stocks shoes, bags, stuffed toys, hats, sunglasses, key chains, and other souvenirs.

Movieland Memorabilia is accessible from both inside and outside the park entrance.

OSCAR'S SUPER SERVICE: In addition to renting strollers and wheelchairs, Oscar stocks diapers, strollers (to buy), snacks, sundries, soft drinks, and souvenirs.

Sunset Boulevard

LEGENDS OF HOLLYWOOD: Modeled after the Academy Theater, which was built in Inglewood, California, in 1939, this store offers items featuring Disney characters and films—with an emphasis on the gang from Star Wars.

MOUSE ABOUT TOWN: An excellent source for clothing featuring the Mouse. Expect hats, ties, shirts, jackets, pajamas, accessories, and more. There's a line of clothing with a golf theme, and another featuring ESPN.

ONCE UPON A TIME: This shop's exterior replicates the Carthay Circle Theatre in Hollywood, where *Snow White and the Seven Dwarfs* premiered in 1937. The cheery store specializes in children's apparel, plush toys, and souvenirs with Disney touches.

PLANET HOLLYWOOD SUPERSTORE: This shop sells items branded with the P.H. logo. Look for T-shirts, hats, mugs, bottle openers, rain gear, and more. The store also displays movie memorabilia (some of it is a tad unsettling for tykes). Details may change in 2018.

ROCK AROUND THE SHOP: Survive Rock 'n' Roller Coaster and earn the right to shop here. Look for music-related items, plus shirts, hats, and other rockin' memorabilia.

SUNSET CLUB COUTURE: A sophisticated selection of fashion accessories (watches, bracelets, purses, hats, etc.), plus family apparel with a Mickey or Minnie theme is sold here.

SUNSET RANCH PINS AND SOUVENIRS: This open-air shop carries Disney collector pins, plus plush character toys, souvenirs, memory cards, and assorted sundries.

SWEET SPELLS: This shop within the Beverly Sunset building has candy, cookies, and other ooey, gooey snack items. Candy apples can be sectioned for sharing—or not.

TOWER GIFTS: Inside the Hollywood Tower Hotel, near the Tower of Terror exit, this spot specializes in Hollywood Tower Hotel merchandise—shirts, towels, robes, front desk bells, glasses, bellhop hats, handbags, and Tower of Terror Jenga. They stock collector pins, too. The shop is a good place to wait for the rest of your party should you decide to skip the trip to The Twilight Zone via the Tower of Terror.

REEL VOGUE: Spin your big-screen dreams from reel to real in this elegant emporium of Tinseltown treasure: toys, gifts, games, snacks.

Beyond the Boulevards

LAUNCH BAY CARGO: Located inside the Star Wars Launch Bay, Cargo offers Star Wars–themed collectibles for fans of all ages. It features a nice variety of autographed memorabilia, replica costumes and props, plus books and toys, and more. Guests may customize mobile phone cases, too.

THE DISNEY STUDIO STORE: Expect to find T-shirts, hats, and accessories inspired by Disney films at this Animation Courtyard shop.

IN CHARACTER: In front of the Voyage of The Little Mermaid attraction, this costume shop has everything a child needs to dress like a Disney princess—plus dolls and plush toys.

INDIANA JONES ADVENTURE OUTPOST: Next to the Indiana Jones attraction, you'll discover adventure clothing, as well as memorabilia emblazoned with the Indy insignia.

IT'S A WONDERFUL SHOP: Spot the snowman out front and you've found this perpetual celebration of Christmas. Tree ornaments, stockings, and nutcrackers line the shelves all year long. Ho ho ho!

SPECIAL FX MAKE-UP: Wanna get your face painted like a cat, puppy, princess, superhero or something equally festive? Head here. Most paint jobs cost about $15.

STAGE 1 COMPANY STORE: Situated near the exit of Muppet★Vision 3-D, guests can find toys, shirts, and other merchandise with the likenesses of Kermit the Frog, Miss Piggy, Fozzie Bear, and other Muppet characters, as well as items featuring Mickey and his pals.

TATOOINE TRADERS: A shop near the Star Tours exit, Tatooine Traders has souvenirs themed to Star Wars, as well as the Star Tours attraction. This is also the place to "build your own lightsaber." Wanna brag about being selected as the Star Tours Rebel Spy? Pick up a T-shirt here!

Where to Eat in the Studios

A complete listing of eateries at the Studios—full-service restaurants, quick-service emporiums, and snack shops— can be found in the *Good Meals, Great Times* chapter. See the Disney's Hollywood Studios section, beginning on page 260.

Entertainment

In these parts, it's almost always showtime. The following list is a good indication of the Studios' stage presence. As always, we advise that you check a park Times Guide for schedules.

CITIZENS OF HOLLYWOOD: This troupe of enthusiastic performers infuses Hollywood Boulevard with old-time, Tinseltown ambience. Would-be starlets searching for their big break, fans seeking guests' autographs, and gossip columnists chasing leads entertain daily.

JEDI TRAINING: TRIALS OF THE TEMPLE: Star Wars fans and Jedi-wannabes can learn the ways of the Force right here in Walt Disney World. A Jedi Master is on hand to teach young Padawans how to harness the power of the Force and wield a lightsaber, as well as help them fend off a duo of Stormtroopers. Expect an appearance by a notorious villain who will attempt to turn them to the Dark Side. "Younglings" ages 4 through 12 may participate. For additional information, see page 182.

BIRNBAUM'S BEST **STAR WARS: A GALACTIC SPECTACULAR:** An aptly named extravaganza, this fireworks show is indeed spectacular. The Star Wars saga plays out in vibrant pyrotechnic bursts, colorful projections, and synchronized sound. It is presented during peak times of year—be sure to catch it if you can. The best vantage point is from Hollywood Boulevard, facing The Chinese Theatre—but the show can be enjoyed from practically anywhere in the park: just look up.

STAR WARS: A GALAXY FAR, FAR AWAY: A stage show presented in front of the Chinese Theatre, this intergalactic celebration features iconic moments from the Star Wars saga. Vignettes shine the spotlight on favorites such as Chewbacca, Rey, BB-8, Darth Vader, and others. There's not much to it, but audiences don't seem to mind. It seems Star Wars really is a *force* to be reckoned with! Check a park Times Guide for the performance schedule.

Trip the Light Fantasmic!

BIRNBAUM'S BEST FP+ Fantasmic!, a lavish musical production, plays on select nights at The Hollywood Hills Amphitheater on Sunset Boulevard. A dramatic mix of fireworks, fountains, lasers, and Disney characters, it invites guests to take a peek into the dream world of Mickey Mouse.

Though similar to its Disneyland counterpart, half of this 26-minute production is original. The action follows Mickey through a series of dreams. In the first dream, he appears at the base of a mountain, shoots fireworks from his fingertips, and conducts an orchestra of colorful fountains. (Guests seated up front get spritzed.) Soon, Mickey is plagued by nightmares as Disney villains take over his dreams. (This has been known to scare small children.) In the end, the Mouse and his pals prevail (of course!).

Seating begins about 90 minutes before showtime—though some guests line up even earlier. Check a Times Guide for the schedule. We recommend sitting toward the back—the view is good and it's easier to get out after the show. There is standing room, too. After the finale, plan to sit for a bit. It can take 20 minutes for the crowd to exit the theater.

Timing Tip: The show is presented on select nights. Check a Times Guide for the schedule during your visit. On nights when Fantasmic! is presented twice, see the later show. Afterward, as the masses exit the park, take some time to browse the shops that keep their doors open after hours.

HOT TIPS!

- Check *www.disneyworld.com* or the My Disney Experience app or website for showtimes, wait times, and updates about Toy Story Land (including when the new land is set to open).

- Unless you actually enjoy waiting in line, get Fastpass+ assignments whenever you can.

- Resist the urge to enjoy a snack just before riding The Twilight Zone Tower of Terror, Rock 'n' Roller Coaster, or Toy Story Midway Mania!

- Some attractions keep shorter hours than the park itself. Check a Times Guide when you arrive. It lists current hours and schedules.

- Wanna meet a snowman? This is the only WDW park in which Olaf meets and greets guests. Visit with him at Celebrity Spotlight.

- For a table-service meal, make a reservation before you arrive at the park for these eateries: 50's Prime Time Cafe, Mama Melrose's Ristorante Italiano, Hollywood Brown Derby, Sci-Fi Dine-In Theater, or Hollywood & Vine. For details, refer to the *Good Meals, Great Times* chapter of this book.

- Some shops on Hollywood Boulevard are open about about 30 minutes past park closing time.

- Walt Disney: One Man's Dream is an exhibit dedicated to the man who started it all. If it's open during your visit, be sure to pay it a visit.

- Your tot may love The Muppets, but if he or she won't wear the glasses necessary to enjoy Muppet★Vision 3-D, skip the attraction.

- There is a water taxi link between Disney's Hollywood Studios and Epcot. The boat docks to the left as you exit the Studios. You may also reach Epcot, as well as all other parks, by bus. Ambitious athletes may choose to walk. (It'll take you about 20 to 30 minutes to make the trip on foot, depending on your pace.)

- While Imagineers finish up Toy Story Land and continue building a Star Wars–themed land, this is a prime park to "hop" to or from.

- Go to Rock 'n' Roller Coaster, Tower of Terror, and Toy Story Midway Mania! very early in the day, before crowds build up. And book Fastpass+ assignments as far in advance as possible. You won't regret it.

- Fantasmic! is presented on most nights. Check a Times Guide to see when it will be offered during your visit. Know that the show may be canceled due to inclement weather.

- Many attractions and shows stop admitting guests prior to the park's closing time (and some don't open until a few hours after the park does). Check a Times Guide for schedules. Attractions that you may enter up until the last minute include The Twilight Zone™ Tower of Terror, Rock 'n' Roller Coaster Starring Aerosmith, Muppet★Vision 3-D, and Star Tours—The Adventures Continue.

- If you choose to skip Fantasmic!, plan to exit the park before the show ends. This way, you'll avoid the inevitable bottleneck at the exit. If you're watching the show, consider making your exit before the big finale.

Where to Find the Characters

You'll find Disney Junior characters—including Sofia the First, Doc McStuffins, and Jake, the Never Land Pirate—in Animation Courtyard. Woody and Buzz may be found at the Toy Story Camera Department on Pixar Place. Mickey Mouse mingles with park-goers in a festive spot dubbed "Mickey and Minnie starring in Red Carpet Dreams." Of course, Minnie appears at that location, too. Goofy, Chip, and Dale greet guests on Commissary Lane. Olaf may be found at the Celebratory Spotlight meet-and-greet location. Various Disney characters interact with diners at the Hollywood & Vine restaurant, too. (Disney Junior characters are on hand for breakfast and lunch; Minnie, Mickey, Goofy, Donald, and Daisy host dinner.)

Hidden Mickeys

These are some of the most popular "Hidden Mickeys" at Disney's Hollywood Studios. How many can you find? Check the box when you spot each one.

❤ **Front Entrance Gates:** This is an easy one. Simply look for Mr. Mouse in the grillwork of the gates at the entrance. ◼

❤ **Rock 'n' Roller Coaster:** In the pre-show room, look on the floor on the right side of the room just in front of the guitar stand to see some wire coiled into a Hidden Mickey. ◼

❤ **Star Tours—the Adventures Continue:** Keep an eye on the folks walking past the "window" in the second room you enter while waiting for the attraction. One of the droids sports mouse ears. ◼
   There's a Hidden Mickey in the shop at the ride's exit, too—on the front panel of a counter. ◼

❤ **Twilight Zone™ Tower of Terror:** Take a peek at the balcony in the lobby, and you may spot a row of Mickeys. ◼
   Then, as you watch the pre-show, pay close attention to the "disappearing guests." The little girl is clutching a plush Mickey Mouse. ◼

❤ **Mama Melrose's Ristorante Italiano:** As you enter, look for the Dalmatian in the waiting area. One of its spots is Mickey-shaped. ◼

❤ **Stage 1 Company Store:** Inside the store, locate a tall bureau with paint cans on the top (the shelves are covered with Disney hats for sale). On the desk area, you'll find a green Hidden Mickey. ◼

❤ **The Hollywood Brown Derby:** Look for two Hidden Mickeys in the cloud mural outside the restaurant. One is on the left side, above the red Stage 5 sign. ◼
   The other H.M. can be found on the far upper right-hand side. ◼

❤ **Cover Story:** There is a sign in the window of this Hollywood Boulevard shop that says "Melrose." Find it, then look below it for a pattern that creates many Hidden Mickeys in the store's structure. ◼

❤ **Tune-In Lounge:** There are several tables in the lounge area of 50's Prime Time Cafe. Take a look at the tabletops to see some Hidden Mickeys! ◼

❤ **Sid Cahuenga's One-of-a-Kind Antiques and Curios Shop:** Sid's is a Guest Information Center offering assistance with My Disney Experience and Fastpass+ questions and issues. On the porch of this former shop is a very special Dalmatian—it has a Hidden Mickey spot on its left hind leg. ◼

❤ **The Trolley Car Cafe:** Look for a number on the building's facade (near the top, facing Sunset Boulevard. It's not a traditional Hidden Mickey, but it is a significant date for the Mouse. ◼

❤ **Muppet★Vision 3-D:** Mickey first appears in a test pattern in the lobby. ◼
   Next you'll notice him in balloon form during the show's finale. ◼
   As you exit, you'll see a poster detailing Five Reasons to Return Your 3-D Glasses. Take a close look at the artwork beside number 2. It has a Hidden Mickey! ◼

❤ **Toy Story Midway Mania!:** Keep your eyes peeled for a sign that says "Circus Fun!"—the dot in the exclamation point is a pink Hidden Mickey. (The sign is on the wall as the ride vehicle rotates into position for the last game of the ride.) ◼

Specifics may change during 2018.

Where in the World?

All of the photos on this page were taken at Disney's Hollywood Studios. Do you know where? We challenge you to find all the spots where these images were shot and snap a photo for yourself as you discover each one. Happy hunting! (For locations, turn to page 352.)

DISNEY'S HOLLYWOOD STUDIOS

1

2

3

4

5

6

Disney's Animal Kingdom

With a mix of lush landscapes, thrilling attractions, and close encounters with exotic animals, this is clearly a theme park raised to a different level of excitement. Here, guests do more than just watch the action—they live it. They become paleontologists, explorers, and students of nature. And if, by doing so, they leave with nothing more than a big smile, Disney will have accomplished one of its major goals. But many guests come away with a little bit more: a renewed sense of respect for our planet and for the life-forms we share it with (not to mention a few boffo souvenirs).

The shows and attractions at Disney's Animal Kingdom are meant to engage, entertain, and inspire. They immerse guests in a tropical landscape and introduce them to creatures from the past and present—as well as a few that exist only in our collective imagination. As Animal Kingdom marks its 20th birthday (it opened on Earth Day in 1998), it offers more opportunities for adventure than ever before. To that end, the newest neighborhood on the block, Pandora—The World of Avatar, has been transporting guests to other-worldly heights since it opened in 2017.

The park, which is accredited by the Association of Zoos and Aquariums, is home to more than 2,000 animals representing 300 different species. Most of the creatures are of the animate variety, as opposed to the Audio-Animatronics kind. Despite that, you won't see many beasts behind bars here. Instead, you'll go on safari and see a menagerie of wild critters living in spacious habitats, with remarkably few separations visible to the naked eye.

The following pages will help you get the most out of your visit to Disney's Animal Kingdom. It is, after all, a jungle out there.

THE OASIS

ENTRANCE PLAZA

PANDORA—THE WORLD
OF AVATAR

DISCOVERY ISLAND

AFRICA

ASIA

DINOLAND U.S.A.

AFRICA

A Kilimanjaro Safaris

B Gorilla Falls
   Exploration Trail

C Wildlife Express
   to Rafiki's Planet Watch

D Rafiki's Planet Watch

E Festival of the Lion King

DISCOVERY ISLAND

F The Tree of Life

G Discovery Island Trail

H It's Tough to be a Bug!

ASIA

I Flights of Wonder

J Maharajah Jungle Trek

K Kali River Rapids

L Expedition Everest

DINOLAND U.S.A.

M Dinosaur

N The Boneyard playground

O Finding Nemo—The Musical

P Chester & Hester's Dino-Rama!

**PANDORA—THE WORLD
OF AVATAR**

Q Avatar Flight of Passage

R Na'vi River Journey

190

Getting Oriented

Though Disney's Animal Kingdom encompasses about five times the area of its Magic Kingdom counterpart, one need not be in training for the Olympics to tackle it. Most of the land is reserved for non-homo-sapien critters. By all estimates, pedestrians rack up about the same amount of mileage in one day here as they do in a day over at Epcot.

The park's layout is relatively simple: a series of sections, or "lands," connected to a central hub. In this case, the hub is Discovery Island, an island surrounded by a river and home to the Tree of Life, the park's icon. Discovery Island is connected by bridges and paths with all other lands: the Oasis, DinoLand U.S.A., Asia, Africa, and Pandora—The World of Avatar.

As you pass through A.K.'s entrance plaza, you approach the Oasis. Feel free to meander at a leisurely pace, absorbing the soothing ambience of a thick, elaborate jungle, or you can proceed more quickly and plan to revisit this relaxing region later on. Each of several pathways deposits you at the foot of a bridge leading to Discovery Island. As you emerge from the Oasis, you'll see the awe-inspiring Tree of Life, a 14-story Disney-made tree, looming ahead. The massive tree, which stands near the middle of the island, is surrounded by the Discovery Island Trail.

To the southeast lies DinoLand U.S.A., home of countless prehistoric animals, a fossil dig, a high-spirited stage show called Finding Nemo—The Musical, and an attraction that's sure to induce a mammoth adrenaline surge: Dinosaur. Behind Discovery Island and to the northwest is Africa, where guests may go on an African safari, explore a nature trail, and hop aboard the Wildlife Express train to Rafiki's Planet Watch, the park's research and education center. To the southwest is the park's newest land: Pandora—The World of Avatar. Its major draws are the thrilling Flight of Passage and the calm Na'vi River Journey. Asia lies northeast of Discovery Island. Here, guests come face-to-face with an angry Yeti (aka the Abominable Snowman) on the Expedition Everest coaster-style ride, encounter real tigers on the exotic Maharajah Jungle Trek, and take a daring journey through the rainforest on a raft at the splashy Kali River Rapids.

HOW TO GET THERE

Take Exit 65 off I-4. Then follow the signs to Disney's Animal Kingdom. Trams run between the parking lot and the main entrance.

By WDW Transportation: From all Walt Disney World resorts: buses. From Disney Springs: bus to any resort or the TTC, then transfer to an Animal Kingdom bus. From the Magic Kingdom: ferry or monorail to the TTC, then bus to Animal Kingdom. From Epcot, Disney's Hollywood Studios, and the resorts on Hotel Plaza Boulevard: buses.

PARKING

All-day parking at Animal Kingdom starts at $20 for day visitors (premium parking costs $40); it's free to guests staying in Walt Disney World–owned-and-operated resorts. Trams circulate lots regularly, providing transportation from the parking area to the park entrance. Be sure to note the section and aisle in which you park. The parking ticket allows for re-entry to the parking area throughout the day.

HOURS

Although hours are subject to change, the gates are generally open daily from about 9 A.M. until about 9 or 10 P.M. During the summer months and other periods, hours may change. It's best to arrive up to a half hour before the official opening time. For current park schedules, call 407-824-4321, or visit *www.disneyworld.com*.

Admission Prices

ONE-DAY BASE TICKET*
(Restricted to use only in Animal Kingdom. Prices represent Walt Disney World's Value, Regular, and Peak rates; they do not include tax; and they are likely to rise in 2018.)

Adult ....$99/$107/$119
Child**..$93/$101/$113
* 1-Day tickets purchased in 2018 must be used by December 31, 2019
** 3 through 9 years of age; children under age 3 free

Park Primer

BABY FACILITIES

Changing tables and facilities for nursing mothers can be found at the Baby Care Center on Discovery Island, near Creature Comforts. It's also possible to buy certain necessities, such as formula and diapers, at this facility.

CAMERA NEEDS

Basic supplies such as memory cards, batteries, and disposable cameras are sold at shops such as Garden Gate Gifts, Disney Outfitters, Duka La Filimu, Mombasa Marketplace, and Chester and Hester's Dinosaur Treasures. Note that selfie sticks are not permitted in the park.

DISABILITY INFORMATION

Nearly all of the Animal Kingdom attractions, shops, and restaurants are accessible to guests using wheelchairs. (Note that the park terrain is a bit bumpy.) Additional services are available for guests with visual or hearing disabilities. The *Guide for Guests with Disabilities* provides a detailed overview of the various services offered, including transportation, parking, and attraction access. (For more information, refer to the *Getting Ready to Go* chapter of this book.)

FIRST AID

Minor medical problems can be handled at the First Aid Center, located on Discovery Island on the northwest side of the Tree of Life, near the local Starbucks (aka Creature Comforts).

INFORMATION

Guest Relations, located just inside the park entrance, is equipped with guidemaps, Times Guides, and a helpful staff. Free guidemaps are also available in many shops.

LOCKERS

Lockers are located just inside the main entrance area, near Guest Relations. Cost is $10 for large lockers, $8 for small ones (plus a $5 refundable deposit), for unlimited use all day.

LOST & FOUND

Lost & Found is at Guest Relations, just inside the park entrance. To report lost items after your visit, call 407-824-4245. We recommend affixing contact information to valuables. That'll make them easier to track.

LOST CHILDREN

Report lost children at the Baby Care Center, on Discovery Island (by Creature Comforts), and alert a Disney employee to the matter.

MONEY MATTERS

There is an ATM at the park entrance and another in DinoLand. Currency exchange is done at Guest Relations. In addition to U.S. cash, credit cards (American Express, Diner's Club, Discover Card, JCB, MasterCard, and Visa), Disney gift cards, traveler's checks, and Disney resort IDs and MagicBands (backed up with a credit card) are accepted for admission and merchandise, and meals at most restaurants. Note that Disney Dollars, while no longer sold, are still accepted as cash at most WDW venues.

PACKAGE PICKUP

Shops can arrange for purchases to be sent to Garden Gate Gifts for later pickup or directly to a Walt Disney World resort (packages should be ready for pickup about three hours after purchase). The service is free.

SAME-DAY RE-ENTRY

Be sure to wear your MagicBand or retain your ticket if you plan to return later the same day.

SECURITY CHECK

Guests entering all Disney parks are subject to a thorough security check. All bags will be searched by security personnel before guests may enter the park. A metal detector screens guests. Weapons (including those of the toy variety) and selfie sticks are among the items that are prohibited. For details and a complete listing of Disney Park Rules, visit *www.disneyworld.com/ParkRules* or any WDW Guest Relations location.

STROLLERS & WHEELCHAIRS

Strollers, wheelchairs, and Electric Conveyance Vehicles (ECVs) may be rented at Garden Gate Gifts. The cost is $15 for strollers and $12 for wheelchairs (double strollers cost $31 a day). Length of Stay rentals yield a $2-per-day discount. It's $50 for ECVs, plus a $20 refundable deposit. Quantities are limited (and they run out early in the day). Keep your receipt; it may be used the same day to get a replacement here or at the other theme parks.

The Oasis

Traditionally, one has to travel across a long, sunbaked stretch of desert in order to experience the soothing atmosphere of a tropical oasis. With that in mind, think of the Animal Kingdom parking lot as a concrete version of the Sahara. Once you've trekked across it, your journey takes you through the park's front gate and entrance plaza. What's that up ahead? Could it be a towering African tree? Here in Central Florida? It must be a mirage.

But, no. Within seconds you arrive at the Oasis, a thriving tropical garden filled with waterfalls, running streams, and lush vegetation. The transition is by no means a subtle one. Guests are immediately enveloped in a world of nature. The peaceful setting is most idyllic.

Though not a full-fledged "land" per se, this small jungle simply oozes atmosphere. It is thick and elaborate, and comes complete with critters. (Some are more difficult to spot than others. When searching for the naturally camouflaged creatures, remember to look up occasionally.) As park visitors walk along the pathways, they may catch glimpses of different kinds of animals, from babirusas and iguanas to anteaters and birds. As in the rest of Disney's Animal Kingdom park, there is the illusion that guests are walking among the wildlife.

The Oasis is at once an exciting and calming experience. It sets the stage for what's to come. Guests have several options once they've entered the Oasis. They can continue on a northerly path, making tracks toward the Tree of Life and across a bridge to Discovery Island. They can proceed at a more snail-friendly pace, keeping a tally of the various life-forms that they spot. Or they can simply take time to stop and smell the flowers.

> "I have learned from the animal world. And what everyone will learn who studies it is a renewed sense of kinship with the Earth and all of its inhabitants."
>
> — **WALT DISNEY**

Timing Tip: Making a trip through the Oasis is the only way to get in (and out of) Animal Kingdom. Some paths can become congested during the hours closest to opening and closing times. To beat the crowds, use the path to the left when you enter the park early in the day.

Discovery Island

PHOTO BY JILL SAFRO

Once you've passed through the Oasis, you will come to a bridge spanning a peaceful river. The bridge leads to Discovery Island, an area at the center of Disney's Animal Kingdom and the hub from which all other realms of the park may be reached.

Discovery Island is defined by the brilliant colors, tropical surroundings, and equatorial architecture of Africa and the South Pacific. The facades of the buildings are all carved and painted based on the art of nations from around the world. Don't fail to notice all the bright, whimsical folk-art images representing various members of the animal kingdom.

This island is the shopping and dining center of Animal Kingdom. Many of the theme park's fast-food restaurants can be found here, including Pizzafari and Flame Tree Barbecue.

HOT TIP!

Take a minute to study a guidemap as you enter Animal Kingdom. It will give you a sense of the layout. The park Times Guide provides information about showtimes for Festival of the Lion King, Finding Nemo— The Musical, and other attractions.

By far the most striking element standing on Discovery Island is the Tree of Life. It is on the map, but chances are you'll have no trouble finding it. Rising from the middle of the island and as tall as a 14-story building, the Tree of Life is hard to miss.

The Tree of Life

The Tree of Life is the dramatic 145-foot icon of Disney's Animal Kingdom. The imposing tree, with its swaying limbs and gnarled trunk, looks an awful lot like the real thing—from a distance. Up close, it's apparent that this is a most unusual bit of greenery. Covered with more than 325 animal images, it is a swirling tapestry of carved figures, painstakingly assembled by a team of artisans. The tree, though inorganic, stands as a symbol of the connected nature of life on Earth. We think Joyce Kilmer would have approved.

DISCOVERY ISLAND TRAIL: The Walkway that wraps around the Tree of Life allows guests to get a close-up view of the trunk and even play a game of "spot the animals." (The spiraling animal images go all the way to the top of the tree. You'll need binoculars if you hope to see them all.) Scattered about the tree's base is a variety of animal habitats. Animals can be seen

HOT TIP!

Would you like to meet Mickey and Minnie before they head out on their next adventure? Make your way to the Adventurers Outpost on Discovery Island. The globe-trotting mice like to greet guests at their exploration headquarters.

in a very open, somewhat traditional park-like setting, with lush grass, trees, and other vegetation. Others to which you may be introduced for the very first time as you meander through the exhibits include ring-tailed lemurs (not quite monkeys' uncles, more like cousins).

BIRNBAUM'S BEST **WINGED ENCOUNTERS— THE KINGDOM TAKES FLIGHT:** This dramatic show features a flock of free-flying macaws. Because of their claws? No, because they're macaws! (Sorry, we couldn't resist a quote from the Enchanted Tiki Room.) Six types of this beautiful bird, some with wingspans of up to 60 inches, are

Wilderness Explorers

In the movie *Up*, Russell is a very dedicated— and decorated—Wilderness Explorer. He is on a constant quest to add to his merit badge collection. Now Animal Kingdom guests can be Wilderness Explorers, too. Start by heading to the W.E. Headquarters at the Oasis bridge. After taking the official pledge, guests receive field guides describing a variety of challenges. Complete a challenge and earn a badge! There are about 30 different badges to collect. There is no extra charge to become a Wilderness Explorer, and the badges are free. While targeted to the 7- to 10-year-old set, the challenges are fun for the whole family.

included. Expect them to swoop and soar above your head and Discovery Island. It is quite thrilling. Check a park Times Guide for showtimes. If you think you might be spooked by a close encounter with our fine-feathered friends, stand toward the back of the crowd.

THE TREE OF LIFE AWAKENS: The park icon "awakens" each night with a lively projection and music show that features stunning visuals, animal spirits, and enchanted fireflies that combine to reveal stories of wonder and showcase the magic of nature.

BIRNBAUM'S BEST **IT'S TOUGH TO BE A BUG!:** FP+ Inside the trunk of the Tree of Life is a 430-seat auditorium featuring an eight-minute, animated 3-D film augmented by some surprising "4-D" effects. The stars of the show are the world's most abundant inhabitants—insects. They creep, crawl, and demonstrate why, someday, they just might inherit the Earth. It's a bug's-eye view of the trials and tribulations of their multi-legged world.

As guests enter The Tree of Life Repertory Theater, the orchestra can be heard warming up amid the sounds of chirping crickets. When Flik, the emcee (from *A Bug's Life*), appears, he dubs audience members honorary bugs and instructs them to don their bug eyes (3-D glasses). Then the mild-mannered ant introduces some of his less-mild-mannered cronies, including a Chilean tarantula, dung beetles, and "the silent but deadly member of the bug world"— the stink bug. What follows is a manic, often humorous, revue.

Note: The combination of intense effects and frequent darkness tends to terrify tots and young kids. And anyone at all leery of spiders, roaches, and their ilk is advised to skip the performance, or risk being seriously bugged.

Africa

The largest section of Disney's Animal Kingdom, Africa, is bigger than the whole Magic Kingdom park. This 110-acre, truer-than-life replica of an African savanna is packed with pachyderms, giraffes, hippos, and other wild beasts. All guests enter Africa through Harambe, a village based on a modern East African coastal town. It is the dining and shopping center of Animal Kingdom's version of Africa.

The instant you walk across the bridge to Harambe, you are transported to Africa. Everything here is authentic, from the architecture to the landscaping to the merchandise in the marketplace. The result was achieved after Disney Imagineers made countless trips to the continent. After seven years of observing, filming, and photographing the real thing, they re-created it here in North America. It even feels a bit warmer here than it does at the other theme parks!

The animals that live here, however, are not re-creations. They are quite real, most varied, and extremely abundant. In fact, this chunk of land puts the animal in Animal Kingdom.

Kilimanjaro Safaris FP+

BIRNBAUM'S ★BEST★ The Kilimanjaro Safaris have something for everyone: lovely landscapes, majestic, free-roaming animals, and a thrilling adventure. It is everything you may expect from an actual trip to Africa, and (hopefully) more.

The 20-minute safari begins with a brief introduction from a guide who does double duty as your driver.

Once you climb aboard the ride vehicle, look at the plates above the seat in front of you. They will help you identify the animals you see. And have those cameras ready.

As the vehicle travels along dirt roads, you'll spot free-roaming wild animals: zebras, antelope, hippos, elephants, warthogs, rhinos, lions, and more. Some animals wander near your vehicle, and others cross its path. (Don't worry—only the harmless critters can approach. Others, such as lions and cheetahs, are unable to invade your safe, personal space.)

The majesty of the Serengeti may lull you into a state of serenity, but it's merely the calm before the storm. You'll soon be jostled and jolted as the vehicle crosses pothole-filled terrain, rickety bridges, and flooded dirt roads.

Good news, safari fans—evening safaris have become a reality. While the Kilimanjaro Safaris attraction is enjoyable at any time of day, it's nice to ride before *and* after the sun sets. Day or night, try to get a Fastpass+ assignment—the lines can be lengthy at this popular destination. It can be challenging to spot distant animals in low light, but the overall experience is pretty cool—and some animals are more active at night.

If you're prone to motion sickness, back trouble, or have other physical limitations, sit this one out. The ride is a rather bumpy one.

PHOTO BY JILL SAFRO

PHOTO BY JILL SAFRO

Festival of the Lion King FP+

BIRNBAUM'S *BEST* In addition to rustling up grubs in their corner of Disney's Animal Kingdom, the talented cast of *The Lion King* performs a 30-minute stage show in the Harambe Theater.

Presented in the round, this lavish musical revue is as bright and boisterous as they come. The dramatic opening features a parade of performers in colorful costumes. What follows is an intriguing, energetic interpretation of the film, including songs, dances, and acrobatics. With the exception of Timon, who plays himself, lead characters are portrayed by humans draped in bold African costumes.

Songs include Scar's nasty version of "Be Prepared," as well as "The Circle of Life," and a rousing rendition of "The Lion Sleeps Tonight."

Timing Tip: Although this theater accommodates nearly 1,400 guests at a time, plan to arrive at least 45 minutes before a performance time.

> **"How could this earth of ours, which is only a speck in the heavens, have so much variety of life, so many curious and exciting creatures?"**
>
> **— WALT DISNEY**

Gorilla Falls Exploration Trail

This self-guided walking trail winds past communities of gorillas and other rare African animals. Access it at the end of the Kilimanjaro Safaris or by the entrance in Harambe.

The first major stop on the trail (previously known as Pangani, which translates to "place of enchantment" in Swahili) is the Research Station.

Just outside are a free-flight aviary and an aquarium teeming with fish. Not far away is the hippo exhibit, which provides close-up views of hippopotamuses both in and out of water.

Farther along the trail there is a scenic overlook point, where you can get an unobstructed view of the African savanna. This is also known as the "Timon" exhibit, featuring a family of perky meerkats. Afterward, you may catch an up-close glimpse (through a glass wall) of a cavorting gorilla or two.

As you come to the end of the suspension bridge, you'll find yourself in a beautiful green valley. Congratulations! You've finally reached the gorilla area—an experience well worth the wait. (Note that you may have to wait a little bit longer for that first gorilla sighting. Our evolutionary cousins have been known to play hide-and-seek in the lush vegetation.)

Rafiki's Planet Watch

On the east side of the village of Harambe is the Harambe Train Station. That's where you board the Wildlife Express and experience a behind-the-scenes look at a Disney park while en route to Rafiki's Planet Watch.

As part of the 5½-minute, narrated trip, you'll glide past the buildings where animals sleep. All guests disembark at the Rafiki's Planet Watch station and cover the remaining distance on foot. (It's about a 5-minute walk—and you may encounter Disney characters and/or animal experts en route.) Note that you will have to reboard the Wildlife Express train to return to Harambe Village.

While Animal Kingdom's stories often carry a conservation theme, this part really brings the message home. This is the park's conservation headquarters and veterinary lab, as well as the research and education hub. Exhibits are geared to spark curiosity about wildlife and conservation efforts around the world. Here are a few highlights:

Habitat Habit!: An outdoor discovery trail that yields glimpses of cotton-top tamarins, and helpful hints on how to share our world with all members of the animal kingdom.

Affection Section: An animal encounter area with critters (mostly goats) to see and touch. Be sure to stop at the hand-washing station before leaving this area.

Conservation Station: The center of Disney's effort to promote wildlife conservation awareness. Be sure to take note of the huge animal murals—they are beautiful and chock-full of Hidden Mickeys. There may also be an opportunity to meet Doc McStuffins. You'll also find:

Animal Cams: Use these guest-operated video cameras to spy on gorillas, hippos, bats, and other critters throughout the park.

Rafiki's Planet Watch Video: This show provides information about endangered animals.

Song of the Rainforest: A thoroughly entertaining "3-D" audio show that surrounds guests with sounds of the rainforest.

Keep in mind that Rafiki's Planet Watch is an excellent place to meet Rafiki himself, as well as other Disney character friends.

DID YOU KNOW?

There are 27 million gallons of water flowing in Animal Kingdom's Discovery River. That's enough water to fill about 1,800 average-sized swimming pools!

HARAMBE WILDLIFE PARTI: Party animals, aka uninhibited theme park guests, are invited to dance and frolic with special entertainers and local street musicians and enjoy the rousing rhythms of live African music. It's also possible to sample some exotic food and drink (note that fees apply for beverages and snacks). Check a park Times Guide for the day's Harambe Wildlife Parti performance schedule.

Let There Be ... Night Light!

After the sun sets on the savannah, Animal Kingdom guests gather along the Discovery River for the park's new nighttime spectacular known as Rivers of Light **FP+**. The illuminating musical experience celebrates the magic of animals (including humans) and the natural world. It features a blend of lively performers, glowing lanterns that float in the air, and theatrical animal imagery.

The ceremony begins with the arrival of a pair of mystical hosts, two complimentary forces who come to the river bearing gifts of light. They set out from shore on lantern vessels, engaging in a dramatic dance of water and light to summon the animal spirits. With these storytellers as guides, the wonders of the show unfold, building to a dramatic finale, complete with bursts of light as animal images soar to the sky—signifying the ancient belief that when animals passed from one world to another, they danced in the sky and became beautiful rivers of light.

Timing Tip: The show is presented on most nights—and it is very popular. Do your best to secure a Fastpass+ assignment well in advance. If not, plan to arrive at least an hour before the show starts. Check a Times Guide for the schedule during your visit. Afterward, as the masses exit the park, take some time to browse the shops that may keep their doors open a bit after hours.

FP+ = Fastpass+ attraction (see page 25)

Pandora—
The World of Avatar

According to the blockbuster film *AVATAR*, Earthlings have a distant, idyllic destination to look forward to in the 22nd century: Pandora, a magnificent moon orbiting the planet Polyphemus about 4.4 light-years from Earth. Pandora, with its lush, bioluminescent rainforest environment, is home to floating mountains and incredible life-forms, including trees that stand a thousand feet tall and a myriad of infinitely diverse creatures—such as native people known as the Na'vi. These blue humanoids travel via flying mountain banshees and have a sophisticated culture based on a deep connection to each other and all life on Pandora. That connection is rendered possible via the majestic and sacred Tree of Souls.

If Pandora sounds like a place you'd like to visit, you're not alone—*AVATAR* was one of the biggest movie sensations of all time. The good news is humans don't have to wait until the 22nd century to visit the wondrous world of Pandora. Thanks to Disney Imagineering magic, it has come to Animal Kingdom. This land, aka the Valley of Mo'ara, opened in 2017. Note that one need not be familiar with the movie to appreciate a visit to Pandora—The World of Avatar.

Avatar Flight of Passage FP+

BIRNBAUM'S ★BEST★ The crown jewel of Animal Kingdom's newest neighborhood, Flight of Passage invites adventurers to take a scenic trip to Pandora on the back of a flying mountain banshee (aka ikran). The joyful 3-D journey takes place in a cutting-edge, simulator-like environment and offers much more than a thrill a minute. Guests are treated to a bird's-eye view of all the sights, sounds, and smells of the majestic moon that the Na'vi call home.

A high-flying "E-Ticket" attraction, Flight of Passage is a most realistic, immersive experience. It is not recommended for guests with motion sensitivity, heart conditions, fear of heights, claustrophobia, or any other such issues. This attraction is quite popular—book a Fastpass+ assignment if you can. Guests must be at least 44 inches tall to experience this ride.

HOT TIP!

The escapist land has many wonders to discover—some are best enjoyed by day, while others shine at night. If time allows, revisit the Valley of Mo'ara after the sun sets. You'll be glad you did.

Na'vi River Journey FP+

A musical voyage into Pandora's bioluminescent forest, this trip is calm and family-friendly (though some wee ones may be spooked by the large and somewhat daunting Na'vi shaman). The adventure begins as guests board canoes and venture down a mysterious, sacred river hidden within the rainforest. The grandeur of Pandora is revealed as canoes float past exotic glowing plants and an array of exotic creatures, including native humanoids known as Na'vi. The journey culminates in an encounter with a Na'vi shaman, who has a deep connection to the life force of Pandora and sends positive energy into the forest with her music.

Na'vi River Journey is generally appreciated by guests of all ages (though timid tykes who are spooked by darkness may find parts of this expedition a tad unsettling). This indoor attraction provides a nice opportunity to visit the Na'vi world while resting your feet and enjoying a refreshing dose of A.C.

DID YOU KNOW?

The common spirit of Pandora—where all life-forms are constantly connected to each other, the environment, and their host planet—is based on the concept of Gaia, proposed by chemist James Lovelock in 1970 and described in Isaac Asimov's novel *Foundation's Edge* in 1982.

Asia

PHOTO BY JILL SAFRO

HOT TIP!

Everyone and everything gets wet on Kali River Rapids. Items that simply must stay dry should be stored in a locker (across the pathway at the attraction's entrance) or with a non-riding member of your party.

On the far side of a Himalayan-style bridge, beyond an ancient temple, lies the tranquil village of Anandapur (Sanskrit for "place of delight"). The buildings' design was inspired by structures in Thailand, Indonesia, and other Asian countries known for their rich architectural history.

A product of Disney Imagineering, the village epitomizes the complex, enduring relationship between the animals and ecosystems of the Asian continent. The tiny village borders an elaborate re-creation of a Southeast Asian rainforest. As such, Disney's Asia is an ideal location for trekking through the lush jungle, shooting the rapids on a raging river, and gazing upon the multi-hued inhabitants of this treasured terrain.

Kali River Rapids FP+

Before guests board rafts at Kali (pronounced KAH-lee) River Rapids, a wise voice admonishes that "the river is like life itself, full of mysterious twists and turns." What the voice doesn't say is that this particular river is also full of splashing water and a blazing inferno. This may be business as usual for some daring souls, but for most of us, these elements make for one dramatic, drenching adventure.

All guests begin the journey in the offices of Kali River Rapids Expeditions, a river rafting company. A slide show offers a look at the sometimes unscrupulous business of logging—how it has ravaged the rainforest and deprived

animals of habitats. But, thanks to ecotourism (among other things), there is hope. Peaceful voyages give people a new appreciation and sense of responsibility for this endangered land.

A 12-seater raft whisks "ecotourists" up a watery ramp and through an arching tunnel of bamboo. It proceeds onward, through a hazy mist and past remnants of an ancient shrine. As the raft moves along curves of the river, guests enjoy views of undisturbed rainforest.

The tranquility is shattered by a startling sight. A huge chunk of forest has been gutted by loggers. On both sides of the river, the forest has vanished. As guests absorb the image, they are besieged by more disturbing sights and sounds. Straight ahead, the river is choked with a tangled arch of burning logs—and the raft is headed straight for it. Suddenly, the rainforest isn't the only thing endangered.

Kali River Rapids is an especially soggy experience. It is the rare guest who leaves the ride without a thorough soaking. Should you wish to repel as much precipitation as possible, pack a plastic poncho. Stash valuables in a nearby locker while you ride (no charge).

Note: This is a very bumpy adventure. In order to experience it, you must be at least 38 inches tall. It is not recommended for pregnant women, guests with heart conditions, people with back or neck problems, or anyone who hopes to stay dry.

Maharajah Jungle Trek

Welcome to the jungle! The Maharajah Jungle Trek is a self-guided walking tour of a tropical paradise, complete with roaming tigers and dense greenery. Throughout the expedition, trekkers encounter a deluge of flora and fauna typically found in the rainforests of Southeast Asia. Komodo dragons, fruit bats, and a conglomeration of colorful birds call this corner of Animal Kingdom home. Majestic Asian tigers can be spotted stalking ancient ruins, strategically separated from would-be prey. Deer and antelope graze and frolic nearby, blissfully oblivious of their fearsome neighbors' proximity.

Approximately midway through the thicket stands a rustic, tin-roofed assembly hall. Step inside to witness the breathtaking sight of giant fruit bats showing off their six-foot wingspans. As you look through the windows, thinking that the crystal clear glass was cleaned by a super-diligent window washer, think again. There is no

glass in some of the windows—and, therefore, nothing separating you from the giant creatures hanging about on the other side. What keeps the big bats from getting up close and personal with guests? They're a lot less interested in humans than humans are in them. (Can't say that we blame them.) Note that some viewing areas are adorned with wire or glass—for guests who are more comfortable with a bat buffer.

Flights of Wonder

A 1,000-seat, open-air theater, the Caravan Stage features performances by actors wearing nothing but feathers and the occasional crown. Members of more than 20 different bird species have starring roles in Flights of Wonder, a high-flying celebration of the winged wonders of the world. Hawks, owls, falcons, and even chickens have been known to awe spectators as they swoop, soar, and strut their stuff in each 20-minute performance. Some demonstrate how they hunt. Others display their grape-grabbing or money-grubbing talents. Check a park Times Guide for the schedule. This show has morphed quite a bit from its original incarnation. It's a hoot!

Expedition Everest FP+

BIRNBAUM'S BEST Walt Disney World's mountain range is a bit more intense these days, as the world's tallest mountain—Everest—has risen from the peaceful village of Serka Zong in Animal Kingdom's Asia. Like its sister peaks, Space, Splash, and Big Thunder, this E-ticket precipice promises to deliver "coaster thrills, spills, and chills." Does it deliver on that promise? Boy, does it ever.

The attraction features an old tea train chugging and churning as it climbs up and around snowcapped peaks. Suddenly, the track comes to an end in a gnarled mess of twisted metal. Lurching forward and backward, the train hurtles through caverns and icy canyons before depositing guests in the presence of the legendary Yeti (aka the Abominable Snowman)—who's not too happy that you've scaled the mountain he so fiercely protects.

Feeling up to the challenge of a dramatic, high-speed train ride? If you are free of heart, back, and neck problems, are not pregnant, have no fear of heights (or abominable snowpeople), and are at least 44 inches tall, go for it. As always, never eat right before experiencing a ride as topsy-turvy as this one.

HOT TIP!

Fastpass+ assignments for Expedition Everest tend to go quickly. Get yours as early as possible.

PHOTO BY JILL SAFRO

DinoLand U.S.A.

If the look and feel of DinoLand U.S.A. seems familiar, there's a reason: It was designed to capture the flavor of roadside America. It is a mixture of culture and kitsch—the likes of which you might stumble upon during a cross-country road trip. Here, you may ride a flying Triceratop, jump into gigantic footprints, and browse through a typically tacky roadside souvenir stand, where you can pick up some dinosaur mementos for the folks back home.

This corner of Animal Kingdom comes complete with its own dramatic entrance: a 50-foot skeleton of a brachiosaurus. As guests stroll beneath the bones, they find themselves smack in the middle of a paleontological dig. Here, guests of all ages (especially little ones) have the chance to play paleontologist as they dig through a fossil-packed pocket of dino discovery.

DID YOU KNOW?

Many of the benches in Disney's Animal Kingdom are made of recycled plastic milk jugs. It takes roughly 1,350 jugs to make a single bench.

The dinosaurs that dwell here, though often quite animated, are all of the inanimate variety. But do keep your eyes peeled for the prehistoric life-forms that actually live in this land—that is, for real creatures that exist in the here and now, but whose ancestors kept company with the likes of the carnotaurus and its cousins from the Cretaceous era.

The Boneyard

The Boneyard gives guests—especially the very young ones—an opportunity to dig for fossils in a discovery-oriented playground. They will excavate the ancient bones of a mammoth in this re-creation of a paleontological dig (think huge sandbox). They will also unearth clues that may help them solve the mystery of how and when the creature met its untimely demise.

For serious "boneheads" who just aren't satisfied with simple digging, there are plenty of other bone-related activities here. Youngsters can

bang out a primitive tune on a bony xylophone (it's located near the car; to make a sound, firmly press on a rib), zip down prehistoric slides, and work their way through a fossil-filled maze. While exploring, watch your step: If you happen to wander into a giant dinosaur foot-print, you might be greeted with a somewhat ominous roar.

While in DinoLand, be sure to check out the OldenGate Bridge. It's a gateway structure made from a dinosaur skeleton. The bridge links one end of The Boneyard with the other. This is a good place to take young children while other members of your party ride Dinosaur.

Chester & Hester's Dino-Rama!

A colorful land-within-a-land, Chester & Hester's is an area ideally suited for roadside carnival fans. Located just beyond The Bone-yard playground, this wild-and-woolly zone features old-fashioned midway games and two rides: Primeval Whirl and TriceraTop Spin.

PRIMEVAL WHIRL: FP+ A small roller coaster (with spinning cars) that seems to have been plucked from a traveling fair, this ride may have a familiar feel to it. By all means, give it a whirl—it's a truly wild ride. You must be at least 48 inches tall to spin. Skip it if you are pregnant or susceptible to motion sickness or think the jarring bumps will cause you discomfort.

PHOTO BY JILL SAFRO

TRICERATOP SPIN: The ride is apt to please fans of the Magic Kingdom's Dumbo the Flying Elephant and the Magic Carpets of Aladdin. Guests ride in one of the 16 flying dinos, each of which resembles an oversize tin toy. It's rather tame when compared to its Dinosaur attraction neighbor, but certainly worth checking out—especially for young dinosaur groupies.

FOSSIL FUN GAMES: Chester & Hester's Dino-Rama is home to several silly games of skill, including Whac-A-Packycephalosaur

Get Involved

When it comes to conservation efforts, the folks at the Walt Disney Company want you to do as they say—and as they do: The Disney Conservation Fund helps nonprofit groups protect and study endangered and threatened animals and habitats. The fund has supported projects from more than 330 non-profit organizations, protecting more than 400 different animal species. And guests who contribute money while making purchases at Animal Kingdom shops and restaurants help make a difference, too.

Of course, as a trip to Animal Kingdom makes clear, there are many ways to help our planet's wild inhabitants. Stop by Rafiki's Planet Watch during your visit. There, you can get information about conservation efforts in your neck of the woods. Don't leave your enthusiasm behind when you leave the park.

(smack mischievous dinos with a mallet), Mammoth Marathon (roll balls into holes to move your woolly mammoth in a race to the finish line), Bronto-Score (basketball toss), Comet Crasher (toss "comets" into moving cups), and Fossil Fueler (a gas-station-themed squirt game). Just like the midway games after which they are modeled, these games come with a fee. Game coupons may be purchased at the souvenir stand in the games area and at Chester & Hester's Dinosaur Treasures. Each game costs about $3 per person. Dino-themed prizes are awarded to winners.

If you'd rather stick to included-with-the-price-of-admission diversions, we highly recommend checking out the fun-house mirror for some simple, silly fun.

HOT TIP!

For a slightly less turbulent experience on the Dinosaur attraction, request an inside seat near the front of the ride vehicle.

Dinosaur FP+

BIRNBAUM'S ★BEST★ This dizzying adventure begins with guests being strapped into vehicles and catapulted back in time to complete a dangerous, albeit noble, mission: to rescue the last iguanodon—a 16-foot plant-eating dinosaur—and bring him back to the present. The iguanodon, which lived more than 65 million years ago (during the Cretaceous period), just might hold the answer to the mysterious disappearance of his dino brethren.

Throughout the frenetic quest to locate the elusive iguanodon, you cling to an out-of-control vehicle while dodging blazing meteors and a mix

of friendly and ferocious dinosaurs. Soon you encounter the carnotaurus—a fearsome, carnivorous dinosaur. The carnotaurus, which has horns like a bull and a face like a toad, is a remarkably unsightly specimen. In fact, all of the dinos move as though they were alive. Even their nostrils move as they "breathe."

This 3½-minute attraction offers more than a thrill a minute. You rocket through time, are practically pelted by meteors, and narrowly escape becoming a dino dinner as the carnotaurus suddenly turns the tables and chases you!

Guests reach the attraction through the Dino Institute, a museum-like building deep in the heart of DinoLand. Here, you'll be treated to a pre-show by Bill Nye the Science Guy (audio only) and see a dinosaur skeleton and an assortment of fossils and other artifacts.

This is an extremely rough (and dark) attraction. You must be at least 40 inches tall to experience it. It should be skipped by pregnant women, or people with heart conditions, back or neck problems, or any other physical limitations. Small kids will most definitely be frightened.

Finding Nemo— The Musical FP+

DinoLand is just about as far off Broadway as one could be. Yet this show's got the ingredients of a Broadway smash: beloved characters (e.g., Marlin, the overprotective clownfish dad; Nemo, his curious son; and Dory, the endearing royal blue tang with the short-term memory loss); original songs by a Tony-winning composer (Robert Lopez); and dancers, acrobats, and the theatrical puppetry of Michael Curry (who designed the richly detailed puppets seen in the Broadway version of Disney's *The Lion King*). You can catch this 40-minute performance at the enclosed and air-conditioned Theater in the Wild. Check a Times Guide for showtimes— and get there early.

This show has appeal for guests of all ages, but the 40-minute run time is a tad too long for some kids (especially the wee ones).

HOT TIP!

When the park is open late, Disney's Animal Kingdom is a great park to "hop" to. It's always a touch cooler in the evening, the animals are just as active (if not more so) as they are during the day, and the bioluminescent flora and other touches make Pandora—The World of Avatar shine.

Where to Find the Characters

You'll discover Mickey and Minnie at the Adventurers Outpost on Discovery Island (Fastpass+ is available). Pluto and Goofy mingle with guests in DinoLand, by the entrance to Chester & Hester's Dino-Rama. Donald can usually be found nearby, on the Cretaceous Trail. Russell has a clubhouse on Discovery Island, near It's Tough to be a Bug! Rafiki and Doc McStuffins hang out at Rafiki's Planet Watch. Baloo and King Louie greet folks at Asia's Upcountry Landing (near the Flights of Wonder bird show). Look for Tarzan and Pocahontas at Character Landing on Discovery Island. Characters such as Daisy, Goofy, and Mickey join Donald for meals at Tusker House in Harambe (near the Kilimanjaro Safaris). Reservations are required for all Tusker House meals.

Shopping

Entrance Area

GARDEN GATE GIFTS: Stop here for snacks, sundries, shirts, hats, plush toys, and camera supplies. ECVs may be rented. (Wheelchairs and strollers rentals are nearby.) This is also the park's package pickup and PhotoPass viewing location.

OUTPOST: A small shop located just outside the park's entrance, Outpost offers character merchandise, snacks, and souvenirs.

Pandora—The World of Avatar

WINDTRADERS: A nice shoppers retreat, Windtraders specializes in Na'vi cultural items (the Na'vi are the native inhabitants of Pandora), plus toys, science kits, and more. Would you like to adopt your own mountain banshee (aka ikran)? Head here.

Discovery Island

DISCOVERY TRADING COMPANY: This sprawling shop is themed as a shipping company that celebrates working animals—camels, elephants, and others. Here, you'll find character merchandise, clothing, candy, and Disney paraphernalia. The Trading Company stays open about a half hour after the park closes for the day. It's connected to the Riverside Depot, which also sells character-themed items.

ISLAND MERCANTILE: Nature-themed gifts and apparel are the stock-in-trade here. There's an abundance of clothing (for the whole family), plus various items with an animal theme and Disney souvenirs.

Africa

MOMBASA MARKETPLACE & ZIWANI TRADERS: An African marketplace and trading company, these connected shops feature animal toys, safari clothing, T-shirts, books, and Africa-themed gifts such as pottery, masks, and musical instruments. A woodcarver makes crafts onsite.

OUT OF THE WILD: Located just outside the exit of Rafiki's Planet Watch, this open-air shop stocks a variety of souvenirs.

ZURI'S SWEETS SHOP: Guests visiting Harambe Market will discover Zuri's, a treat lover's paradise. In addition to sweets with a *Lion King* theme, Zuri sells items such as wine, African-inspired dinnerware, African-spice popcorn and spice rubs, plus barbecue sauce from Animal Kingdom's Flame Tree Barbecue.

Asia

BHAKTAPUR MARKET: A small shop with a big Asian influence, Bhaktapur sells summer shoes, bags, robes, shirts, teapots and teas, toy dragons and plush animals, chopsticks, and items with a Yak & Yeti theme.

MANDALA GIFTS: A stone's throw from Royal Anandapur Tea Company, this cozy spot offers Asian-inspired clothing, scarves, and handbags, plus souvenirs with Disney's Animal Kingdom park logo.

SERKA ZONG BAZAAR: Located at the exit of Expedition Everest (it can be accessed from the outside for those who prefer to skip the ride), this bustling bazaar sells souvenirs with a Yeti theme, plus a slew of shirts, hats, purses, postcards, books, plush toys, pins, frames, etc., that celebrate the Expedition Everest attraction.

DinoLand U.S.A.

CHESTER & HESTER'S DINOSAUR TREASURES: Themed as an American roadside souvenir stand, this shop pays homage to all reptiles and prehistoric animals. There is a small selection of dino-themed merch, but Chester and Hester are more focused on Disney stuff. They sell snacks, too.

THE DINO INSTITUTE SHOP: It should come as no surprise that you'll find dino-themed items and other souvenirs here. It's also the spot to view (and buy) that photo of you looking terrified while riding Dinosaur.

Entertainment

HARAMBE WILDLIFE PARTI: A lively street festival, Harambe Wildlife Parti kicks off daily in the late afternoon. Exotic entertainment includes acts such as Muziki, a musical, stilt-walking shaman; the elegant, dancing Karubi Sisters; the interactive (and comical) skilled soccer antics of the Harambe Soccer Meerkats; and the colorfully costumed Harambe Village Acrobats. The Parti offers the excitement of an African village bursting with entertainment and surprises for all.

DISCOVERY ISLAND CARNIVALE: This exuberant dance party ends the day and welcomes the night with musicians, stilt walkers, and more. The nightly jubilee winds its way from one end of Discovery Island to the other, eventually arriving at the Discovery Island Stage. Check a park Times Guide for the schedule.

DI-VINE: So convincing is Di-Vine, that many a guest fail to notice she is actually a graceful entertainer and not, well, an actual vine.

HOT TIPS!

- Disney's Animal Kingdom sometimes extends its hours—it may operate well into the evening.

- Most of Animal Kingdom's attractions take place outdoors. Don't become overheated! Make a point of slipping into air-conditioned shops and restaurants from time to time to cool off.

- Narrow, winding paths, grooved pavement, and hilly terrain make this the most challenging Disney theme park in which to navigate a wheelchair or heavy stroller.

- Check the My Disney Experience mobile app or website to get an idea of attraction wait times.

- When the weather gets steamy, keep a reusable water bottle with you at all times.

- Rainforest Cafe generally keeps longer hours than the park does. (Buses run until one hour after park closing time.)

- The line for Kilimanjaro Safaris tends to dwindle a bit by midday. See it then (the experience is enjoyable at any time of day).

- Get a Fastpass+ for Avatar Flight of Passage as soon as you possibly can—they run out quickly. It is a wildly popular ride!

- Bumpy rides aren't for everyone—or for every camera. When it comes to thrill (or wet) rides, it's smart to stash your camera in a locker or with a non-riding member of your party.

- Island Mercantile on Discovery Island stays open a half hour after the park closes.

Where to Eat in Animal Kingdom

A complete listing of eateries at Disney's Animal Kingdom—table-service restaurants, fast-food spots, and snack stands—can be found in the *Good Meals, Great Times* chapter. See the Animal Kingdom section, beginning on page 264.

Hidden Mickeys

These are some of the most popular "Hidden Mickeys" at Animal Kingdom. How many can you find? Check the box when you spot each one!

❤ **Tree of Life:** A Hidden Mickey made of moss is on the front of the Tree of Life just to the right of the tiger and to the left of the buffalo. Although you may be able to spot it from several vantage points, the best place is right when you enter Discovery Island and before the path splits to Africa and DinoLand. ■

❤ **Kilimanjaro Safaris:** Pay close attention to the flamingo pond on your left just after you enter elephant country. The center island is shaped like a Hidden Mickey (sit toward the left side of the ride vehicle for the best view). ■

❤ **Maharajah Jungle Trek:** There are more than 10 Hidden Mickeys throughout this jungle trek, but we suggest hunting for these two to start: Inside the first archway near the tiger exhibit, pay attention to the mural on the left and look for three leaves that form a Hidden Mickey underneath the extended arm of a king. ■ Now walk to the second arch and look at the mural on the right to find a Hidden Mickey in the clouds. ■

❤ **Gorilla Falls Exploration Trail:** Okay, while not a Hidden Mickey, the Hidden Jafar found in this trail is well worth searching for. Just past the gorilla viewing area, you'll reach a suspension bridge. Look directly to your right and you'll see a huge 3-D head of Jafar carved out of the rock that's covered in moss. ■

❤ **Rafiki's Planet Watch:** Conservation Station is a Hidden Mickey paradise with more than 20 Mickeys in the entrance mural alone. Two favorites: Just inside the building on the right, find a possum with a Hidden Mickey in its eye. ■ Then look above it to find a butterfly with two Hidden Mickeys (one on each wing) ■. For good measure, here's a third: Find a frog just to the right of an alligator on the left wall, then find Mickey's smiling face under the frog's right eye. ■

❤ **Expedition Everest:** To find this Hidden Mickey, you'll need a Fastpass+ assignment for Expedition Everest. As you travel through the Fastpass+ queue, pay close attention to the Yeti Museum room. In the second display of expedition artifacts and supplies, look for a lantern on a shelf—three dents in the metal form a sideways Hidden Mickey. ■

❤ **It's Tough to be a Bug!:** This is one of the more challenging Hidden Mickeys to locate at Disney's Animal Kingdom, but cast members are happy to help you spot it if you need them to. After you enter the "underground" room with all the silly musical posters (but before entering the main theater), find the other entrance to the far side of the room. Now look at the far left wall. This well-concealed (but very cool) Hidden Mickey is hiding in the shadows. ■

❤ **DinoLand U.S.A.:** First, find the two large dinosaurs holding up a "Chester & Hester's Dino-Rama" sign near the TriceraTop Spin ride. Stand directly underneath the sign and close to the blue dinosaur. Look at the dino's wrist—there's a Hidden Mickey on it! ■ Then head to the dig site area of The Boneyard playground. Can you spot where two hard hats and a fan combine to form another H.M.? ■

❤ **Dinosaur:** Before you travel back in time, your ride vehicle passes a laboratory scene on the left (the vehicle actually stops here for a second to give you plenty of time to look). Search carefully to find a blue Hidden Mickey drawn on the lower left corner of a whiteboard. ■

❤ **Cretaceous Trail:** At the end of this short DinoLand trail sits a proud dino. We think he's proud of the Hidden Mickey on his back! ■

Specifics may change during 2018.

Where in the World?

All of the photos on this page were taken at Disney's Animal Kingdom. Do you know where? We challenge you to find all the spots where these images were shot and snap a photo for yourself as you discover each one. Happy hunting! (For locations, turn to page 352.)

1

2

3

4

5

6

Everything Else in the World

W hile the total turf of the World encompasses about 40 square miles, the theme parks cover a mere fraction of the property. Much of the remaining Walt Disney World terrain is crammed with irresistible activities of a variety and quality seldom found anywhere else.

There's superb golf and tennis, beaches for strolling and sunbathing, lakes for boating and fishing, canoes to rent and winding streams to paddle along, bicycles for hire, campfire sites, horseback riding, hot-air ballooning, nature trails, and picnic grounds. The recreation options continue with Typhoon Lagoon, a lushly land-scaped, state-of-the-art water park complete with surfing lagoon; and Blizzard Beach, a thrilling, watery wonderland that translates the hallmarks of a ski resort to the realm of swimming.

A lineup of lavish spas provides guests with ample opportunity to pamper themselves silly. Intriguing "backstage" programs invite the curious to slip behind the scenes and learn about the workings of Walt Disney World. Add to all that, Disney Springs—a dining, shopping, and entertainment district including a colorful assortment of shops, shows, and restaurants. The expansive play zone, formerly known as Downtown Disney, has a new neighborhood: Town Center. It seems this really is a World without end.

Disney Springs

Sprinkled across 120 acres are the shops, lounges, restaurants, and entertainment sites that collectively make up Disney Springs. This timeless place, previously known as Downtown Disney, consists of four neighborhoods interconnected by a flowing spring and vibrant lakefront: Marketplace, Town Center, The Landing, and West Side. The re-imagined enclave, which recently completed a major metamorphosis, is a definite hotspot. The spirited waterfront zone boasts more than 180 establishments—all there for your dining, shopping, and playing pleasure.

Guests staying at most Disney–owned-and-operated resorts can reach Disney Springs via bus. Water taxis ferry guests to and from Saratoga Springs, Port Orleans French Quarter, Port Orleans Riverside, and Old Key West. Safe, convenient pedestrian bridges connect the area with the resorts on Hotel Plaza Boulevard.

There is a $20 charge for valet parking. (It's available near the entrance to the Orange and Lemon parking garages from 10 A.M. till 2 A.M. and on the far end of the West Side, from 4 P.M. till 2 A.M.) Self-parking is free. For details, visit *www.disneysprings.com* or *www.disneyworld.com*, or call 407-934-7639.

Disney Springs Essentials

GUEST RELATIONS: Located at the Disney Springs Welcome Center in the area's Town Center, Guest Relations the place to go for information or help making dining reservations; for Lost and Found; to purchase tickets; and more. Stroller and wheelchair rentals are available at Sundries Rentals in Town Center, near the Orange parking garage. There are several ATMs scattered throughout the Disney Springs district. Details are subject to change.

HOW TO GET THERE: Disney Springs is accessible from exit 67 off I-4.

By WDW Transportation: From Old Key West, Port Orleans French Quarter and Riverside, and Saratoga Springs: boat or bus. From all other WDW resorts: bus. There is one-way bus service from Disney theme parks to Disney Springs after 4 P.M. The Marketplace is within walking distance of Saratoga Springs and some resorts on Hotel Plaza Boulevard. For more details, see *Transportation & Accommodations*.

By Ride-Sharing Service or Taxi: Guests may use Lyft and Uber to get to and from Disney Springs. Authorized cabs service the area, too. The cost of cabbing to most WDW resorts is usually $15 to $30 (plus gratuity). Ride-sharing rates may be lower—but surge-pricing is always a possibility. The Disney Springs address is 1486 Buena Vista Drive, Orlando, FL 32830.

WEST SIDE

THE LANDING

Marketplace

Located on the shores of Lake Buena Vista, the Marketplace is a relaxing setting for shopping, dining, and much more. The waterside district is sprinkled with gardens featuring whimsical topiaries. Little kids are fond of the Disney Springs carousel (see Marketplace Rides, page 213). While many guests opt to eat at a table-service restaurant, others grab a bite from the Earl of Sandwich and sit at outdoor tables. (Refer to *Good Meals, Great Times* for restaurant details.) Afterward, some gravitate toward Dockside Margaritas for live music and a nightcap.

Shopping

The descriptions that follow suggest the types of wares each store offers. Most shops in the Disney Springs Marketplace are typically open daily from about 10 A.M. to 11 or 11:30 P.M.

ARRIBAS BROS.: This shop sells hand-crafted items from Spanish artisans and designers. Large cut-glass bowls and vases are available, along with mugs, sculptures, and other wares, many of which can be personalized. Aspiring Cinderellas will appreciate the sparkly selection of tiaras and glass slippers. It is located between Basin and Marketplace Co-op.

THE ART OF DISNEY: Original Disney art, porcelain figures, ceramics, posters, and other collectibles are available at this engaging gallery.

BASIN: Products designed to clean you up and calm you down are the stock-in-trade at this soothing establishment. Candles, soaps, and bath crystals are some of the wares on hand. A sampling area allows shoppers to try before they buy. The bath bombs are the best!

TOWN CENTER

MARKETPLACE

BIBBIDI BOBBIDI BOUTIQUE: This country parlor-inspired location gives young guests (ages 3 through 12) the royal treatment with the help of Fairy Godmothers-in-Training. Kids can get their faces painted with glitter makeup, do their nails and hair, and even don tiaras. The boutique is open daily. Youngsters are transformed into princesses and princely royal knights. Reservations are encouraged; call 407-939-7895 for reservations and pricing (cheap it is not). Note that this shop is adjacent to Once Upon a Toy.

DESIGN-A-TEE: Aspiring fashion designer? Step into T-shirt central, visit one of 8 computer kiosks, and design away. First, select a size and color for the shirt (there are sample shirts to help you gauge size). Next, choose art from a set of categories such as Characters, Pirates, Princesses (which includes Princes), or Celebrations. Finally, personalize your creation with text of your own choosing. When you're finished, a ticket will be printed for you. Present it to the cashier to pay for your shirt and plan to come back in a half hour or so to pick it up. Peruse the wares in Disney's Days of Christmas while you wait.

PHOTO BY JILL SAFRO

DISNEY'S DAYS OF CHRISTMAS: Here is the best place to deck the halls Disney style— it's the largest Christmas shop on WDW property. In addition to character items, the shop boasts a large assortment of hand-crafted ornaments. Other items to look for: Mickey Mouse nutcrackers, Santa hats with mouse ears, stockings, cards, and books. Some ornaments can be personalized.

DISNEY'S PIN TRADERS: This shop boasts a tremendous assortment of collector pins and various pin-collecting accessories.

DISNEY'S WONDERFUL WORLD OF MEMORIES: Preserve the memories of your Walt Disney World adventure with the frames, photo albums and other merchandise from this shop across from Disney's Days of Christmas. Camera supplies (memory cards, batteries, straps, cases, and chargers) are available, too. There's a make-your-own Disney charm bracelet station and a wall of mouse ear hats just waiting to be personalized.

GOOFY'S CANDY COMPANY: One-stop shopping to satisfy sugary cravings, this shop has a sumptuous selection of chocolates, a dipping kitchen, and much more.

On warm days, we gravitate to the corner of this shop known as Goofy's Glaciers for a frozen slushie treat, available in flavors with goofy names such as Rootin' Tootin' Red, Orange You Happy, and Pucker Purple. They also serve coffee, cookies, pastries, and ice cream. Another temptation here: the create-your-own specialty apple station.

THE LEGO STORE: World of Disney's neighbor, this playful emporium is a showcase for larger-than-life LEGO models. It also invites guests to flaunt their creativity in an interactive outdoor play area. A computer hub lets guests design LEGO structures and play games. The store sells a vast selection of LEGO products.

PHOTO BY JILL SAFRO

LEFTY'S: Step up to southpaw central for scissors, can openers, writing implements, notebooks, and more—all made especially for the differently handed. The open-air stand also sells shirts and hats lauding left-handedness.

HOT TIP!

Fancy a trip in a floating car? Head to the Amphicar dock near The Boathouse restaurant (The Landing). The rare auto/boats drive into the lake—and guests are treated to a 20-minute guided tour of Disney Springs (for about $100).

LITTLE MISSMATCHED™: Mismatched sock syndrome has finally been solved: Nothing here matches. In addition to socks (which are sold in packs of three), the store sells colorful pajamas, pencil pouches, backpacks, and other miscellany.

MARKETPLACE FUN FINDS: Here's the place to find Disney merchandise at low prices. In fact, most items in the store are under $25. Hey, that *is* fun!

MICKEY'S PANTRY: Stop here for Disney-themed glasses, cookbooks, cooking utensils, and wine, plus spices, teas, and coffees. Many of the designs are subtle, others not so much: Mickey pasta, anyone? Note that the Spice & Tea Exchange is located inside Mickey's Pantry.

MARKETPLACE CO-OP: A cavernous retail zone, the Co-op is home to specialty shops: **Wonder-Ground Gallery** is a contemporary art space

Marketplace Rides

Disney Springs Marketplace has two kiddie rides for tykes to enjoy: a carousel and a tiny train. The cost for each is $3 per child ($5 to ride twice). Be sure to purchase a token before boarding (payment can be made with Visa, MasterCard, or cash). Parents can accompany children on the train (no charge, provided they ride in the same car; kids under 36 inches tall must be accompanied by a guest over age 14). The train can only accommodate two adults per trip and grown-ups may not ride in the engine car. For the carousel, kids under 42 inches tall must be accompanied by a guest age 14 or older (who rides for free). The rides are between The Earl of Sandwich and Marketplace Fun Finds.

showcasing unusual collections and emerging artists; **Cherry Tree Lane** appeals to "the sophisticated woman with a passion for scarves, shoes, bags, and jewelry"; **D-Tech on Demand** is a place to personalize and customize electronic accessories; **Centerpiece** showcases home products for folks who dig a dash of Disney in their furnishings, textiles, and everyday ware. **Twenty Eight & Main** specializes in apparel and accessories for distinguished gentlemen who happen to love Disney parks. **Disney Tag** features whimsically designed travel gear and accessories. The variety of merchandise at the Marketplace Co-op puts this area on top of many a Disney treasure-hunter's must-do list.

ONCE UPON A TOY: A sprawling toy box, this site has plush toys, action figures, a Mr. Potato Head play zone, and a Build Your Own Lightsaber station. Oodles of brand names are represented. Be sure to look up—there's a model train set suspended from the ceiling.

THE PEARL FACTORY: Pick an oyster, any oyster. Then pry it open (with assistance), and *voila*—a pearl! The cost is about $16 per oyster, and you are guaranteed a genuine pearl. The open-air shop proffers pearl earrings and necklaces, too.

SILHOUETTE PORTRAITS: A classic Disney "lasting memory," single silhouettes cost $12, doubles $22, triples $26, and quads $30 (plus tax). You will receive three copies. Black oval frames go for about $9 apiece. It takes the artist about a minute per silhouette—which is pretty amazing when you think about it.

THE SPICE & TEA EXCHANGE: Neatly nestled into a corner of Mickey's Pantry, this fragrant destination offers the opportunity to purchase gourmet spices, salts, peppers, sugars, teas, and more. It's a unique shopping experience thanks in part to a large selection of sample jars in which you are encouraged to stick your nose.

EVERYTHING ELSE IN THE WORLD

PHOTO BY JILL SAFRO

Where to Eat at Disney Springs

A complete listing of restaurants, bars, and snack spots can be found in the *Good Meals, Great Times* chapter. See the Disney Springs restaurant listings, beginning on page 266. Most of the restaurants here are open from about 11 A.M. until about 11 P.M. or later.

TREN-D: The Mouse is quite a trendsetter. Need proof? Swing by this boutique. It is bursting with quirky Disney merchandise, from loungewear to jeweled sunglasses and other trendy accessories.

WORLD OF DISNEY: A gigantic space stuffed with a huge selection of Disney merchandise, this is the place for one-stop shopping. Colorful rooms provide the backdrop for the array of goods. Characters are available on everything from watches to luggage. (If you're an Annual Passholder, you may receive a discount when you present it at the register. It depends on the type of pass, and the discount is subject to change.)

The Landing

Shopping

APEX BY SUNGLASS HUT: Specializing in sporty shades, this eyeglass emporium is located across the street from Paradiso 37.

THE ART OF SHAVING: A premium shave shop, Art of Shaving offers high-end men's grooming supplies—razors, brushes and shaving sets, and aromatherapy-based products—plus the Barber Spa: a place for guests to relax and get a shave and/or a haircut from a master barber.

THE BOATHOUSE BOATIQUE: Adjacent to The Boathouse restaurant, this shop features a bounty of nautically themed treasures. Among the wares here: clothing, jewelry, and games—plus engravable paddles and life rings.

CHAPEL HATS: Fashion-forward headwear for men and women is the stock-in-trade at this sleek spot. With shelving made of reclaimed wood, decorative tables made from old shipping container hatch doors, and Arts and Crafts–style mirrors, Chapel Hats has classic appeal.

ERIN MCKENNA'S BAKERY NYC: Folks with dietary restrictions (and those just looking for a sweet treat) will be in the pink at this bustling bakeshop. According to founder Erin McKenna, the place "focuses on the underserved people with gluten, dairy, egg, and soy sensitivities, the health-minded, and, most importantly, allergic kids who are often unable to indulge. The goal is to make eating vegan and gluten-free fun and delicious." Mission accomplished.

THE GANACHERY: A fresh take on an old apothecary, the star of this show is housemade ganache—Disney's own recipe for a luxurious mixture of melted chocolate and cream. The decadent treats aren't cheap, but many a chocolate fanatic finds them worthy of a splurge.

HAVAIANAS: Head here for vibrant flip-flops with a Brazilian flair. Some styles incorporate Disney characters, too.

SANUK: Retire those pinchy old shoes and replace them with cool and comfy footwear for the whole family at Sanuk. (If we could wear our Sanuks every day, we would.) FYI: *Sanuk* is the Thai word for fun.

West Side

AMC DISNEY SPRINGS 24: The most popular multi-screen movie theater complex in Florida is also one of the largest. The many screens show a wide selection of current movie releases. The seats are roomy and comfortable—and some of the theaters offer seat-side food and beverage service (see page 266 for details). For current movie schedules, visit *amctheatres.com*.

BONGOS CUBAN CAFE: Situated across from the AMC Theatres on the edge of Village Lake, Bongos echoes the style of clubs in Miami's South Beach. Created in part by Gloria Estefan, it features the flavors and rhythms of Cuba and other Latin American countries. The bold design is dramatic yet whimsical. Guests dine and, if the mood strikes, even dance amid the tropical decor (and one remarkably oversized pineapple, which houses a multi-level cocktail lounge). Live entertainment is often presented on Friday and Saturday nights.

HOUSE OF BLUES: A combination restaurant-music hall with standing room for 2,000, House of Blues was inspired by one of America's most celebrated musical traditions. There is a lively

dose of jazz and country, plus a little bit of R&B and some rock 'n' roll thrown into the music mix. The Southern-inspired cooking lures diners here—especially on Sunday mornings, when the chefs prepare an all-you-care-to-eat buffet feast, complemented by live gospel music. Tickets can be purchased in advance through Ticketmaster (call 407-839-3900, or visit *www.ticketmaster.com*) or the House of Blues box office (407-934-2583).

Coming Attraction

Basketball fans are drooling (or is that dribbling?) at the prospect of an interactive play zone masterminded by the folks at the National Basketball Association. Coming soon to Disney Springs, the NBA Experience is described as a "one-of-a-kind destination" featuring games and hands-on activities for the whole family. For details on this venue's opening date and pricing information visit *www.disneyworld.com*.

The House of Blues restaurant features a mélange of hearty cuisine, including jambalaya, slow-smoked pulled pork, shrimp with grits, and bread pudding.

JALEO: The flavors of Spain are coming to Disney Springs in 2018! Once the doors open at this new eatery, the menu will feature an extensive menu of tapas that celebrate the regional diversity of classic and contemporary Spanish cuisine. Think paella cooked over a wood fire and hand-carved Jamon Iberico de Bellota (premium ham). The multi-level eatery features a first-floor grab-and-go area with Spanish-style sandwiches. Reservations are recommended for the restaurant. For additional information, visit *www.disneyworld.com*, or use the My Disney Experience mobile app or website.

Shopping

CANDY CAULDRON: Stop here for some homemade sweets in an open candy kitchen. Among the biggest crowd-pleasers here are the made-to-order specialty apples—fresh, crunchy apples slathered in the candy coating of your choice. Yum! Kids love to peek through the windows and watch the candy makers at work.

CURL BY SAMMY DUVALL: You have to figure that anybody who spent not one but 17 years as a champion water-skier has to know quite a bit about trends in beachwear and water-sport equipment. See for yourself at this high-end surf shop. Among the wares you will find sunglasses, watches, jewelry, activewear, headphones, and shoes. The shop can be found next door to Splitsville. It's usually open from 10:30 A.M. until 11 P.M. Save 10 percent off your purchase with the coupon at the back of this book.

FIT2RUN—THE RUNNER'S SUPERSTORE: A super stop for guests on the run, this shop

HOT TIP!

Cirque du Soleil fans take note: The popular Disney Springs show, La Nouba, took its final bow in 2017—after about 9,500 performances. While it is unlikely that a new Cirque du Soleil show will be presented in 2018, we recommend checking *www.cirquedusoleil.com* and *www.disneyworld.com* for updates.

Up, Up, and Away!

You can float up to 400 feet above Disney Springs while beneath one behemoth of a balloon. Touted as the "world's largest tethered helium balloon," it carries up to 29 guests at a time in a gondola that measures 19 feet in diameter. Flights last 8 to 10 minutes. Guests board from a platform on the West Side (near Starbucks). Tickets are sold at a nearby window. The cost is about $20 (plus tax) for adults (age 10 and up) and $15 for kids ages 3 to 9. Babies fly free. Flights begin at 8:30 A.M. daily (weather-permitting) and operate on a first-come, first-served basis. It is operated by Aerophile—"The World Leader in Balloon Flight."

sells footwear, apparel, performance sunglasses, jogger strollers, and more. Need help selecting the perfect shoe for you? Take advantage of this shop's complimentary evaluation and high-tech video gait analysis. There's even an indoor track to test shoes before you purchase them. Ready, set, run! You'll find it next to Splitsville.

MARVEL SUPER HERO HEADQUARTERS: Calling all would-be agents of S.H.I.E.L.D.: You can gear up at this shop, plus snag Super-Hero-themed (Spider-Man, Captain America, etc.) costumes, shirts, action figures, hats, books, mugs, glassware, and other items—all featuring characters from the Marvel Universe. One item of note: Iron Man mouse ears.

ORLANDO HARLEY-DAVIDSON: No motorcycles for sale here (though any employee will happily tell you how to purchase one), but the custom Harleys on display are definitely ogle-worthy. Hog fans can browse Harley-Davidson T-shirts, sweatshirts, hats, and other collectibles. Save 15 percent off your purchase of $75 or more by using the coupon at the back of this book.

POP GALLERY: This gallery features artist-signed limited-edition sculptures and paintings, as well as high-end gift items.

SOMETHING SILVER: The AMC Theatres next-door neighbor, Something Silver is "an eclectic jewelry boutique." It sells fashionable jewelry (rings, earrings, bracelets, and charms) and a collection of timeless classics for men, women, and children.

SOSA FAMILY CIGAR COMPANY: For adults only, this shop specializes in premium cigars. Feel free to puff away here—the shop is a rare "authorized" smoking zone. In addition to the art of hand-rolling, Sosa features an authentic solid cedar humidor room to keep the wares as fresh as possible. Note that guests must be at least 18 years old with state-issued photo ID in order to smoke tobacco products in the state of Florida.

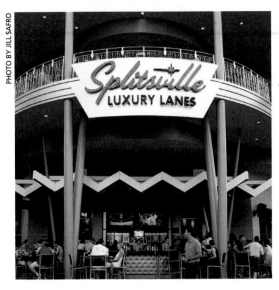

SPLITSVILLE LUXURY LANES™: Come for some casual bowling, stay for some fab food and live entertainment. This West Side venue features 30 bowling lanes, two high-end kitchens, a full bar, live music—and billiards to boot. Housed in what was once the Virgin Megastore, this massive 'ville (50,000 square feet) is fun for all ages. However, some areas are restricted to guests over the age of 21 (with legal ID to prove it). It's generally open until about 2 A.M. daily; the restricted "ages 21 and up" area is open on Fridays and Saturdays after 10:30 P.M. Shoppers can peruse merchandise at Memory Lanes, a shop tucked into a corner on the first floor of Splitsville. Look for items such as shirts, pants, hats, glasses, jewelry, and more. For details, visit *www.splitsvillelanes.com* and refer to page 268.

STARBUCKS: That ubiquitous mermaid icon can be spotted on the shore of Lake Buena Vista. Expect all of the Starbucks specialties—from fresh-brewed, free-trade cups of joe to sweet and chilly Frappuccinos. Breakfast sandwiches, fruit, and oatmeal are served. Baked treats include cupcakes, muffins, scones, and cake pops. Teas, smoothies, fruit, veggies, juice, milk, soda, and water are also offered. (There are several Disney Dining Plan snack options to choose from.)

HOT TIP!

For more info on Disney Springs' 185 dining, shopping, and entertainment venues, plus its activity and special event schedules, visit *www.disneysprings.com*.

STAR WARS GALACTIC OUTPOST: The Force is strong with this store. So is its pull on folks strolling the promenade at Disney Springs, West Side. It boasts an impressive bounty of toys, clothes, and accessories inspired by the epic space saga: hats, shirts, handbags, dresses (yes, we actually spotted a Darth Vader dress), costumes, pins, R2-D2 and C-3PO mouse ears, lightsaber key chains, and many more items featuring characters from the Star Wars films. There's a build-your-own lightsaber station, too.

SUNGLASS ICON: Looking for some super-cool shades? This snazzy shop is full of high-end brands to protect your peepers.

UNITED WORLD SOCCER: Fútbol fans, rejoice! Gather garb to support your favorite club and load up on gear to tackle the game yourself—right here at the well-stocked United World Soccer shop. Gather garb to support your favorite club and load up on gear to tackle the game yourself—right here at the well-stocked United World Soccer shop. The *goal* is to meet all your soccer needs. Score!

WETZEL'S PRETZELS (The Marketplace): Whether you prefer pretzels on the salty or sweet side, this kiosk has something to satisfy. Also served: hot dogs wrapped in a soft pretzel, lemonade, frozen lemonade, and ice cream (cones, cups, and sundaes). To save some money at Wetzel's Pretzels, use the coupon at the back of this book.

HOT TIP!

Disney Springs requires quite a bit of walking stamina. Expect to log a couple of miles per visit—especially if you plan to walk from the Marketplace to the West Side (and back again!). We recommend strollers for small children—and very comfortable shoes for all. And make use of the (free) Disney Springs water taxi service whenever possible. The small ferry boats make stops at docks in the Marketplace, The Landing, and West Side.

Town Center

The architectural design of Town Center's Town Square is "Spanish Revival," drawing from a rich history of explorers that landed in Florida centuries ago. It was ostensibly founded in the 1850s, on the banks of one of the Sunshine State's freshwater springs—where its original homestead still stands, having been restored and converted to a family restaurant (D-Luxe Burger). The commercial district of Town Center was designed in the Mediterranean revival style that was popular in Florida in the 1920s, whereas the Welcome Center area features the wooden American revival architecture that was prevalent in the 1930s. Overall, this sophisticated area has a focus on shopping, but also brings several inventive dining opportunities and other pleasant diversions. For more information on dining locations, refer to the *Good Meals, Great Times* chapter of this book.

Dining

AMORETTE'S PATISSERIE: Classic and contemporary cakes and pastries are the stars in this high-end pastry shop where guests can watch the chefs decorate signature cakes in the on-stage finishing kitchen. Amorette's lovingly packages sweet treats in old-fashioned hatboxes. Champagne, sparkling wine, hot chocolate ganache, and crepes are also served. FYI: Amorette means "little love" in French.

BLAZE FAST FIRE'D PIZZA: This eatery lets hungry guests "build their own artisanal pizzas." Custom-made pizzas are prepared in about three minutes—they don't call it "fast fire'd" for nothing. The 5,000-square-foot restaurant also serves freshly prepared salads and desserts.

D-LUXE BURGER: Come for the burgers, stay for the shakes at this Town Center quick-service location. D-Luxe Burger is a comfy spot for a casual bite. The creatively prepared burgers (most big enough to share) are served on fresh-baked buns. Pair yours with freshly cut fries (which come with a variety of dipping sauces) and (scrumptious) artisanal gelato shakes (with rotating flavors such as vanilla, chocolate, raspberry, strawberry, salted caramel, and s'mores). There is a kids' menu, too. Beer, wine, and soft drinks are served. D-Luxe Burger has ample indoor and outdoor seating (the latter overlooks the water, aka the springs).

CHEF ART SMITH'S HOMECOMIN': Created by Chef Art Smith, Homecomin' is a "farm to fork" restaurant, showcasing the flavorful bounty of the Sunshine State. The menu features Southern favorites such as Low Country shrimp and grits, deviled eggs, and Art's famous fried chicken. Desserts are made daily and delivered by a bakery in Florida's Hamilton County. Guests (over age 21) can quaff creative libations—including signature moonshine craft cocktails—from the adjacent Southern Shine bar.

SPRINKLES CUPCAKES: "The world's first cupcake bakery," as dubbed by Food Network, the Beverly Hills–based Sprinkles now serves said signature cakes, slow-churned ice cream, and cookies here at Town Center. The handy cupcake ATM dispenses treats 24/7.

FRONTERA COCINA: Six-time James Beard winner Chef Rick Bayless has brought his signature gourmet Mexican cuisine to Frontera Cocina. The eatery features Mexican specialties such as hand-crafted tortas, tacos, salads, and classic Mexican braised meat entrées, all prepared with locally sourced ingredients. Margaritas, cocktails and craft beers, wine, and soft drinks are served.

Retail Roundup

Disney Springs, Town Center may look retro-elegant, but the shopping opportunities here are markedly *au courant*. Treasure-seekers may peruse wares at these new retail locations:

ALEX AND ANI • American Threads • Anthropologie • Coca-Cola Store • Columbia Sportswear • D-Living • Edward Beiner • Everything But Water • francesca's • Free People • JOHNNY WAS • Johnston & Murphy • kate spade new york • Kiehl's • Kipling • LACOSTE • Levis • Lilly Pulitzer • L'Occitane En Provence • Lucky Brand • Luxury of Time by Diamonds International • M·A·C Cosmetics • Melissa Shoes • Na Hoku • Oakley • PANDORA • Sephora • Shore • Sperry • Stance • Sugarboo• Superdry • Tommy Bahama • TROPHY ROOM • UGG • Under Armour • UNIQLO • UNOde50 • Vera Bradley • Vince Camuto • Volcom • Zara

For additional information about these and other new Town Center shopping destinations, visit *disneysprings.com*.

BoardWalk

A stroll at Disney's BoardWalk is a journey back in time. Inspired by the Middle Atlantic seaside attractions of the early 1900s, BoardWalk recaptures the carefree atmosphere of that bygone era. The resort is surrounded by restaurants, clubs, and amusements similar to those enjoyed by beachgoers of yesteryear. It's bordered by a wood-planked walkway that hugs the shore of Crescent Lake. By day, BoardWalk is a peaceful place to soak up sun, enjoy lunch, or simply walk the boards. After dark, the place turns into a twinkling center of nighttime activity—some of it elegant, some of it downright raucous.

Midway games of the BoardWalk challenge onlookers to test their luck and skill at a collection of classic carnival games, while strolling performers enchant passersby of all ages with magic shows, balloon tricks, or other antics.

BoardWalk is open to everyone. Although there is no admission price, individual venues may charge a cover. There is a $25 charge for valet parking (even for guests staying at a Walt Disney World–owned-and-operated resort). Self-parking was free at press time, but subject to change. For dining details, refer to this book's *Good Meals, Great Times* chapter.

Clubs

ATLANTIC DANCE HALL: This is a lovely atmosphere in which to dance the night away. A deejay cranks up tunes, tempting guests to twist and shout on the spacious dance floor. Request your favorite music videos and bust a move while they play on the big screen.

In addition to traditional cocktails, the club serves specialty drinks. Sample one in the "big room" or on the waterfront balcony.

Guests must be 21 or older, with a legal photo ID, to enter. There was no cover charge at press time, but that could change. Hours are generally 9 P.M. until 2 A.M., Tuesday through Saturday.

This club is known for reinventing itself; specifics may be different during your visit.

ESPN CLUB: A casual sports bar/restaurant, ESPN aims to please sports enthusiasts of all kinds. It has a broadcast facility, table-service eatery, and a bar.

Nearly 100 TVs broadcast sports events, so guests always know the score. (Need to make a

pit stop at a crucial moment of the game? Don't sweat it . . . there are even TVs in the bathrooms.)

As you enter the club, you're at The Sidelines area. You can catch a game on a TV above the "penalty box" bar or sit at a nearby table. Beer, wine, and soft drinks are available, as is the usual (and some unusual) pub fare.

Sports Central, the main dining area, has a big screen showing—what else?—the big game. The kitchen is open until 11:30 P.M. for meals, midnight for appetizers and desserts.

While ESPN Club does accept weekday lunch reservations, it's primarily a first-come, first-served establishment. However, the Club may offer premium seating for select "Big Games." Call 407-566-5656 for reservations and/or additional information.

JELLYROLLS: You might want to warm up your vocal cords before crossing the threshold. They don't call it a sing-along bar for nothing: Guests are expected to sing, clap, and join in the fun at this warehouse home of dueling pianos. You'll hear everything from Gershwin to *Grease*. The piano players take requests, so plan ahead. Write the request—a cocktail napkin will do—and slip it onto the piano. (Although it's not required, we recommend slipping a tip along, too. It will increase the odds of you hearing the request and help the musicians pay their rent.)

Jellyrolls is open from 7 P.M. until 2 A.M. nightly. There is usually a $12 cover charge to enter. (Note that the cover charge may vary.) To get in, you must be at least 21 years old and willing to prove it. It's often quite chilly in this venue (year-round). Bring a sweater.

Water Parks
Typhoon Lagoon

PHOTO BY JILL SAFRO

This splashy playground was inspired by an imagined legend: A typhoon hit a resort village many years ago, and the storm—plus an ensuing earthquake and volcanic eruption—left the village in ruins. The locals, however, were resourceful and rebuilt their town as this "wateropolis."

The centerpiece of Typhoon Lagoon is a huge watershed mountain known as Mount Mayday. Perched atop its peak is the *Miss Tilly*, a marooned shrimp boat originally from Safen Sound, Florida. *Miss Tilly*'s smokestack erupts every half hour, shooting a 50-foot flume of water into the air.

The surf lagoon is huge: giant slides snake through caves, tamer ones offer twisting journeys, and tiny slides delight small kids. Guests under age 14 must be accompanied by someone over age 14.

SURF POOL: The main swimming area holds nearly three million gallons of water, making it one of the world's largest wave pools. The blue lagoon is surrounded by a white-sand beach, and its main attraction is the waves that come crashing to the shore every 90 seconds. Less adventurous swimmers can loll about in two relatively calm tide pools, Whitecap Cove and Blustery Bay.

HOT TIP!

Guests entering Typhoon Lagoon are subject to a thorough security check. All bags will be checked and a metal detector will be used. Weapons—including toys— are strictly prohibited.

CASTAWAY CREEK: The "creek" is a 2,100-foot circular river that winds through the park and offers a lazy, relaxing orientation to Typhoon Lagoon. Tubes are the best way to make the trip along the three-foot-deep waterway. Guests pass through a rainforest, where they are cooled by mists and spray; through caves and grottoes that provide welcome shade on hot summer days; and through an area where "broken" pipes from a water tower unleash refreshing showers. There are several exits along the way. It takes 20 to 35 minutes to ride around the whole park.

CRUSH 'N' GUSHER: This "water coaster" thrill ride is one of a kind. In it, daredevils are whisked along a series of flumes and tossed and turned as they weave through an abandoned tropical fruit factory. There are three spillways to choose from: Banana Blaster, Coconut Crusher, and Pineapple Plunger.

GANGPLANK FALLS, KEELHAUL FALLS, AND MAYDAY FALLS: These white-water rides offer guests a variety of slippery trips, two of them in inner tubes. All of the slides course through caves and waterfalls and past rock work, making the scenery an attraction in itself. Gangplank Falls gives families a chance to ride together in a three- to five-passenger craft.

HUMUNGA KOWABUNGA: These three speed slides, reported to have been carved into the landscape by the historic earthquake, will send guests zooming through caverns at speeds of 30 miles per hour. The 214-foot slides each offer a 51-foot drop, and the view from the top is a little scary. But it's over before you know it, and once-wary guests hurry back for another try. Guests must be at least 4 feet tall and free of back trouble, heart conditions, and other physical limitations to take the trip. Pregnant women are not permitted to ride.

KETCHAKIDDEE CREEK: Open only to those children 48 inches tall or under (and their adult guardians), this area has small rides for pint-size visitors. All children must be accompanied by an adult. There are slides, fountains, waterfalls, squirting sea life, a mini-rapids ride, an interactive tugboat, and a grotto with an inviting veil of water.

MISS ADVENTURE FALLS: A family-friendly raft ride near Crush 'n' Gusher, this attraction takes guests on a tour of treasures and artifacts left behind by Captain Mary Oceaneer, an adventurous treasure hunter who became stranded at Typhoon Lagoon after a big storm. Each watery voyage takes about 2 minutes. Kids under 10 must be accompanied by an adult.

STORM SLIDES: The Jib Jammer, Rudder Buster, and Stern Burner body slides send guests off at about 20 miles per hour down winding slides, in and out of rock formations and caves, and through waterfalls. It's a somewhat tamer ride than Humunga Kowabunga, but still offers a speedy descent. The slides run about 300 feet, and each offers a different view and experience.

SURFING: Surf clinics are offered on select mornings before the park opens. For information, call 407-WDW-SURF (939-7873).

Essentials

WHEN TO GO: Typhoon Lagoon gets very crowded early in the day. Hours vary seasonally, but the park is generally open from 10 A.M. to 5 P.M., with extended hours in the summer months. All of the pools are heated in the winter. Note that this park is usually closed for refurbishment during certain winter months. The park may also close due to bad weather. Selfie sticks are not permitted. Call 407-824-4321 for updates.

HOW TO GET THERE: Bus service begins from all resorts about one hour before Typhoon Lagoon opens for the day. The buses stop at the water park and then at the Disney Springs before 10 A.M. After 10 A.M., resort buses stop at Disney Springs and then Typhoon Lagoon. Buses stop running from the water park about one hour after it closes. Parking is free.

LOCKER ROOMS: Restrooms with showers and lockers are close to the entrance. Small lockers cost $10 to rent for the day, while large ones cost $15. Towels rent for $2 (it's okay to bring your own); life jackets and tubes are free.

FIRST AID: A first aid station capable of handling minor medical problems is located just to the left of Leaning Palms.

WHERE TO EAT: Typhoon Lagoon's two eateries offer similar fare and outdoor seating. Leaning Palms has burgers, pizza, salads, and snacks. Typhoon Tilly's (open seasonally) serves fish & chips, wraps, BBQ pork sandwiches, and ice cream. Let's Go Slurpin' has frozen drinks and spirits. Guests may bring their own food and drink to enjoy in designated picnic areas. Alcoholic beverages and glass containers may not be brought into the park. Coolers are allowed. All-Day Refillable Mugs, which may be purchased for about $11, come with a day's worth of soft drink refills.

BEACH SHOP: Singapore Sal's is set in a ramshackle building left a bit battered by the typhoon. Swimsuits, sunglasses, hats, towels, sunscreen, souvenirs, water shoes, and Typhoon Lagoon logo products are available.

Admission Prices

Prices do not include sales tax and are subject to change. **Note:** Admission is an option with a Magic Your Way ticket that includes a Park Hopper Plus add-on, and is also included with a Premium Annual Pass.

	ADULTS	CHILDREN*
One-Day Ticket	$62	$56
Annual Pass	$125	$125

* 3 through 9 years of age; kids under age 3 free. Tickets allow for park-hopping, provided both water parks are open on day of admission.

Blizzard Beach

A wintry, watery wonderland, Blizzard Beach is said to be the result of a freak storm that dropped a mountain of snow onto Walt Disney World, prompting the construction of Florida's first ski resort. When temperatures soared and the snow began to melt, designers prepared to close the resort. But when they spotted an animal sliding down the slopes, they realized that they had created an exciting water adventure park! The slalom and bobsled runs became downhill waterslides. The ski jump is one of the world's tallest (120 feet) and fastest (60 miles per hour) free-fall speed slides.

HOT TIP!

Guests entering Blizzard Beach are subject to a thorough security check. All bags will be checked and a metal detector will be used. Weapons—including toys—are strictly prohibited.

The centerpiece of Blizzard Beach is the snowcapped Mount Gushmore and its Summit Plummet. Most of the runs are on the slopes of this mountain, which tops out at 90 feet. At the summit, swimmers have a choice of speed slides, flumes, a white-water raft ride, and an inner-tube run. Most guests reach the top of Mount Gushmore via chairlift. The lift has a gondola for guests with disabilities. There are stairs, too. Kids under 14 must be accompanied by a guest over age 14. One-piece bathing suits are best.

CROSS COUNTRY CREEK: This meandering 3,000-foot waterway circles the entire park. A slow current keeps visitors moving merrily along. Inner tubes, which are free, are the most pleasant way to travel. The ride includes a trip through a bone-chilling ice cave, where guests are splashed with the "melting ice" from overhead.

HOT TIP!

Early birds get the lounge chairs around these parts. If you want to snag a chair at either of Disney's water parks, arrive as close to park opening as possible.

DOWNHILL DOUBLE DIPPER: Guests travel down these two parallel 230-foot-long racing slides at speeds of up to 25 miles per hour. The partially enclosed water runs feature ski-racing graphics, flags, and time clocks. You must be 48 inches tall to ride.

MELT-AWAY BAY: A one-acre pool at the base of Mount Gushmore, the "bay" has its own wave machine. There are no tsunamis here, however—just a pleasant, bobbing wave.

RUNOFF RAPIDS: On this inner-tube run, guests careen down three twisting, turning flumes in a single or double tube.

SKI PATROL TRAINING CAMP: An area designed for preteens, Frozen Pipe Springs looks like an old pipe and drops sliders into eight feet of water. The Thin Ice Training Course tests agility as kids try to walk along broken "icebergs." At the Ski Patrol Shelter, guests under 60 inches grab on to a T-bar for an airborne trip. At any point in the ride they can drop into the water below. Ski patrol participants also experience Cool Runners, where riders can count on hurtling and whirling over lots of moguls on twin inner-tube slides. No bunny slopes for these brave daredevils.

SLUSH GUSHER: This double-humped water-slide offers a brisk journey through a snow-banked mountain gully. Topping out at 90 feet, Slush Gusher is the tallest slide of its kind. You will find it on Mount Gushmore, next to Summit Plummet. Guests must be at least 48 inches tall to take the plunge.

SNOW STORMERS: A trio of flumes descends from the top of the mountain. Guests race down, (headfirst while lying on a mat) on a switchback course that includes ski-type slalom gates.

SUMMIT PLUMMET: This thrilling ride begins 120 feet in the air on a platform 30 feet above the top of Mount Gushmore. Brave souls

(who are at least 48 inches tall) travel about 60 miles per hour down a 350-foot slide.

TEAMBOAT SPRINGS: The longest family white-water raft ride in the world takes six-passenger rafts down a twisting, 1,400-foot series of rushing waterfalls.

HOT TIP!

Premium cabana-like spaces known as Polar Patios are available for rental. They include an attendant, beverages, towels, and more. Patios accommodate up to six guests and cost about $225–$340 per day. Premium umbrella spaces are available, too. For details or to make reservations, call 939-7529. Prices vary seasonally.

TIKE'S PEAK: A kid-size variation of Blizzard Beach, this attraction features mini versions of Mount Gushmore's slides and a snow-castle fountain play area. Adults must be accompanied by a child to enter this zone. Kids must be under 48 inches to enjoy most attractions in this area.

TOBOGGAN RACERS: An eight-lane water-slide sends guests racing over a number of dips. They lie on their stomachs on a mat and travel headfirst down the 250-foot route.

Essentials

WHEN TO GO: As a guest favorite, Blizzard Beach gets very crowded early in the day. Hours vary seasonally, but the park is generally open from 10 A.M. to 5 P.M., with extended hours in summer.

All pools are heated in winter. The park is often closed for refurbishment during certain winter months. Know that it may also close due to inclement weather. For schedules, call 407-WDW-PLAY (939-7529).

HOW TO GET THERE: Blizzard Beach may be served by the buses that go to and from Animal Kingdom park, Epcot, and/or Disney's Hollywood Studios. Parking is free.

LOCKER ROOMS: There are restrooms with showers near the main entrance. Other restrooms and dressing rooms are located around the park. Small lockers cost $10 for the day, while large lockers cost $15. Towels rent for $2 (outside towels are permitted), and life jackets and tubes may be used for free.

WHERE TO EAT: Burgers, hot dogs, pizza, salads, and drinks are sold at Lottawatta Lodge in the main village area. (Remote snack stands, Avalunch and The Warming Hut, are open seasonally.) Polar Pub offers soft drinks and spirits. Frosty the Joe Man Coffee Shack serves coffee drinks. Frostbite Freddy's sells BBQ brisket nachos, orange swirl cones, and more. There are picnic areas for those who pack their own food. Alcohol and glass containers may not be brought into the park. Coolers (smaller than 24 inches long, 18 inches high, and 15 inches wide) are allowed. All-Day Refillable Mugs (about $11 each) come with a day's worth of soft drink refills.

FIRST AID: Minor medical problems are handled at this station near the main entrance.

BEACH SHOP: The Beach Haus shop stocks bathing suits, T-shirts, shorts, sunglasses, hats, sunscreen, beach towels, and more.

Admission Prices

Prices do not include sales tax and are likely to rise in 2018. **Note:** Admission is an option with a Magic Your Way ticket that includes a Park Hopper Plus add-on, and is also included with a Premium Annual Pass.

	ADULTS	CHILDREN*
One-Day Ticket...............	$62	$56
Annual Pass....................	$125	$125

* 3 through 9 years of age; children under age 3 free. Tickets allow for water-park hopping, provided both water parks are operating on the day of admission.

Daredevil Disney

You've catapulted through the galaxy on Space Mountain, braved an encounter with an angry Yeti at Expedition Everest, and become something of a human yo-yo on the Tower of Terror. Now what? Believe it or not, there are plenty of thrills awaiting you outside the theme park gates. Some of them, such as the wedgie-inducing slides at the water parks, are well known. Others may be lower key, but they're definitely high octane. Here's a rundown of our favorite theme-park-alternative thrill rides.

BALLOONING: Going up! A huge, tethered, helium balloon (run by Aerophile–"The World Leader in Balloon Flight") lifts guests 400 feet high into the sky. Moored to a landing at Disney Springs West Side, the balloon can accommodate up to 29 guests at a time—treating all to sweeping panoramic views of Walt Disney World and beyond. It operates on a first-come, first-served basis Sunday through Thursday from 8:30 A.M. until 11 P.M. and from 10:30 A.M. until midnight on Friday and Saturday. Adults pay about $20 per flight, while kids (ages 3 through 9) pay about $15. Expect to be airborne for about 8 to 10 minutes. This attraction does not operate during windy or inclement weather.

MOTORBOATING: If you've been to Walt Disney World before, you've no doubt seen folks tooling about in zippy little motorboats. But have you ever actually given one a try? It's an experience we highly recommend.

For starters, the watercraft known as Sea Raycers are indeed speedy. And it's an experience everyone can enjoy—though guests need to be at least 12 years old and at least 5 feet tall to drive. Expect to pay about $32 for a half hour (for up to two passengers), $40 for 45 minutes, and $45 for one hour. (Prices do not include tax.) A signature from a parent or guardian is required for all drivers between the ages of 12 and 18. Be sure to wear a watch, as you're apt to lose track of time. For more info, turn to page 238.

PARASAILING: Even if you've never had the urge to be a human kite, consider giving this a whirl. After a simple liftoff from the back of a boat, you and your parachute gradually climb skyward. Before you know it, you're eye level with the roof of the Contemporary resort hotel.

A few peaceful minutes later, the hotel and the nearby Magic Kingdom appear to have shrunk considerably. It's not unlike the illusion of flying over London in Peter Pan's Flight. Only this flight's no illusion: You're really 450 to 600 feet above it all. And don't worry about the landing. It's generally as smooth as the trip itself. The attendants simply reel you in for a soft touchdown on the back of the boat.

For information on prices and reservations, turn to page 238.

PERSONAL WATERCRAFT EXCURSIONS: Strap on a life vest and hang on! Sammy Duvall Watersports Centre (located at the Contemporary resort marina) offers Jet Ski–like adventures on WDW's Bay Lake. All participants must be at least 16 years old. For details, see page 239.

SURFING: When the sun comes up, so does the surf at Disney's Typhoon Lagoon. On select days, guests can take part in a surf clinic taught by competitive surfers. Instructors control the height of the waves—and they give Mother Nature a run for her money.

If you've never hung ten before, know this: It ain't easy. But once you've managed to get up on a board, it's a blast. Lessons are offered before the park opens for the day.

For more information, call 407-939-7873.

WAKEBOARDING: Walt Disney World wakeboarding in a word? Intense! Hang on tight as you are pulled at high speeds and tear back and forth across Bay Lake. The high-octane adventure is open to all ages and skill levels. Inner tubes may be used, too. Sammy Duvall instructors offer private lessons to kids and beginners. Up to five friends or family members may ride in the boat for free (if space allows). For details, see page 239.

WATERSKIING: Florida weather being what it is (hot), waterskiing (as well as wakeboarding and tubing) never really goes out of season. It's a refreshing way to see the sights of Bay Lake—and a serious workout to boot. Sammy Duvall instructors are on hand to assist. Up to five friends or family members may ride in the boat for free (if space allows). For additional information, see page 239.

Fort Wilderness

In a part of the state where campgrounds tend to look like dried pastures—barren and very hot—the Fort Wilderness Resort and Campground, located almost due east of the Contemporary resort, is an anomaly—a forested, 750-acre wonder of tall slash pines, white-flowering bay trees, and ancient cypresses hung with Spanish moss. Native Americans from the Seminole tribe once hunted and fished here.

There are more than 800 campsites arranged in several campground loops (including sites that are big-rig ready). There are more than 300 Wilderness Cabins (which fall into Disney's "moderate" resort category) available for rent, completely furnished and fitted with all the comforts of home. For additional information, refer to the *Transportation & Accommodations* chapter of this book.

Scattered throughout the campground loops are sporting facilities, including two tennis courts and many small playgrounds, basketball, tetherball, and volleyball courts. Fort Wilderness has riding stables (with rather mellow horses), two swimming pools, a marina full of boats, a canoe livery, bikes and golf carts for rent, and a nature trail. Some facilities are available to Fort Wilderness guests only; some are open to all.

There's a pony farm (which offers rides to young guests for a fee) and a barn that's home to the horses that pull the Magic Kingdom's Main Street trolleys. The barn houses a small museum that celebrates horses and the cherished role they've played in Disney history.

Two stores—the Settlement Trading Post and the Meadow Trading Post—stock campers' necessities, a limited supply of groceries, and souvenirs. And then there's Pioneer Hall, the home of the Hoop-Dee-Doo Musical Revue dinner show (described in the *Good Meals, Great Times* chapter). This rustic structure (made of white pine shipped from Montana) also houses a popular (and reasonably priced) buffet restaurant and a small lounge area. Mickey's Backyard Barbecue is offered here during busy times of the year (when the weather's nice).

ARCHERY: It takes a steady hand to hit the bull's-eye at the Fort Wilderness Archery Experience. After a brief training session led by a skilled guide, participants (age 7 and up) get to shoot for that coveted bull's-eye. Cost is about $45. To book the Fort Wilderness Archery Experience, call 407-WDW-PLAY (939-7529).

SWIMMING: There are two pools for campers' use. The Meadows Pool complex has a twisting slide and water play area. Note that the pools are open to Fort Wilderness guests only. Swimming and wading are not allowed at the beach (due to a naturally occurring bacteria found in many Florida lakes, and the presence of native wildlife such as alligators and snakes).

BIKE RENTALS: Bicycles may be rented at the Bike Barn for trips along the paths of Fort Wilderness—or just for getting around. Bikes cost about $9 per hour or $18 per day. Helmets are included at no extra charge. Florida law mandates that all guests age 16 and under wear helmets when biking.

BLACKSMITH SHOP: The pleasant fellow who shoes the draft horses that pull trolleys in the Magic Kingdom park is on hand most mornings to answer questions and talk about his job; occasionally, guests may even watch him at work, fitting the big, friendly animals with the special polyurethane-covered, steel-cored horseshoes that are used to protect the animals' hooves. This shop is located at the Tri-Circle-D Ranch.

BOATING: Fort Wilderness is ribboned with tranquil canals that make for peaceful canoe trips of one to three hours. Canoe rentals are available at the Bike Barn for about $13 per hour. For a trip around Bay Lake, zippy little Sea Raycer motorboats, Boston Whaler Montauks, and pontoon boats are available for rent at the marina, at the north end of the campground. They may be used to cruise on Bay Lake and the adjacent Seven Seas Lagoon. (Refer to the *Sports* chapter for details.)

CAMPFIRE SING-ALONG: Held nightly (weather permitting) near the Meadow Trading Post at the center of the campground, this evening program features Disney movies, a sing-along, and a marshmallow roast. Chip and Dale often put in an appearance. It's open to WDW resort guests only. There is no charge to attend, but s'mores kits come with a small fee. You may roast your own marshmallows for free.

CARRIAGE RIDES: Guests may enjoy a relaxing carriage ride through the picturesque grounds of Fort Wilderness or Port Orleans Riverside resort. The rate for each 25-minute ride is $45.

Carriages can hold up to 4 adults, or 2 adults and up to 3 small kids. Reservations are a must. Rides are offered nightly. Call 407-WDW-PLAY (939-7529) for information or to make a reservation. Walk-up reservations are sometimes possible. (Ask the driver about buying tickets. If they're available, expect to pay with cash, Magic-Band, or Disney Resort ID. Credit cards are not accepted.) Rides may be canceled due to inclement weather. Cancellations must be made at least 24 hours ahead to avoid paying full price.

Guests are picked up in front of Crockett's Tavern at Pioneer Hall or by the marina at Port Orleans Riverside. Feel free to bring your own liquid refreshments.

ELECTRIC CART RENTALS: Available at Reception Outpost (about $60 per day) for sight-seeing or transportation. Renters must be at least 18 years old and have a valid driver's license. Reservations are necessary; call 407-824-2742 for reservations and information.

FISHING EXCURSIONS ON BAY LAKE: Walt Disney World's restrictive fishing policy means plenty of angling action—largemouth bass weighing two to eight pounds, mainly—for those who sign up for fishing excursions.

The price ranges from approximately $235 to $270 for up to five people for a two-hour excursion (one additional hour is about $100) and includes gear, a guide, and soft drinks; no license is required. The price varies based on time of day, with the early morning trips commanding the highest rate.

Know that all fishing is strictly catch-and-release. Call 407-WDW-BASS (939-2277) for exact times and to make reservations. To stretch your WDW fishing dollar, use the coupon at the back of this book.

FISHING IN THE CANALS: In addition to largemouth bass, catfish and panfish can be caught here as well. Those without their own fishing gear will find rods and reels for rent at the Bike Barn. No license is required. Fort Wilderness resort guests may toss their lines in right from the shore (canals only). All WDW fishing is strictly catch-and-release. For pricing and more info, visit *www.disneyworld.com*. Fort Wilderness is the only place on Walt Disney World property where canal fishing is allowed.

PLAYGROUNDS, VOLLEYBALL, TETHER-BALL, AND BASKETBALL COURTS: These are scattered throughout the camping loops. There is no charge to use the courts.

ELECTRICAL WATER PAGEANT: Originally presented for the dedication of the Polynesian Luau dinner show in 1971, this cavalcade of lights is presented nightly on the waters of Bay Lake and the Seven Seas Lagoon. The pageant consists of two strings of seven barges, each carrying a 25-foot-tall screen of lights featuring King Neptune and creatures of the sea. And it's all set to music. The show can be seen from the beach at Fort Wilderness, as well as from the Contemporary, Polynesian Village, and Grand Floridian resorts. (We've caught it while waiting for the monorail at the Magic Kingdom, too.) Ask for the schedule at your resort's lobby concierge desk. Details are subject to change.

PONY RIDES: This enclave behind Pioneer Hall is home to some friendly ponies. Pony rides, offered seasonally, are available between 10 A.M. and 5 P.M. for $8 (cash only). Riders must be at least 2 years old and under 48 inches tall. The weight limit is 80 pounds. Kids must be able to hold on by themselves. A parent or guardian leads the pony. The farm is a good place to visit before the Hoop-Dee-Doo Musical Revue.

TENNIS: Two tennis courts are available; play is on a first-come, first-served basis.

TRAIL RIDES: Guided horseback trips depart five times daily from the Trail Blaze Corral and take riders on a leisurely, meandering ride through the Florida wilderness, where it is not uncommon to see birds, deer, and even an occasional armadillo. Galloping is not part of the experience, so you don't need riding know-how to sign up. Cost is about $46 per person. Kids under age 9 are not allowed to ride. Parents must sign consent forms for kids under age 18. There is a weight limit of 250 pounds. Sturdy shoes with defined heels are recommended; open-toed shoes are not permitted. Reservations are necessary; call 407-WDW-PLAY (939-7529) up to 180 days in advance.

TRI-CIRCLE-D RANCH: This corner of Fort Wilderness is the place that the world champion Percherons and the draft horses that pull trolleys down Main Street in the Magic Kingdom call home. WDW guests are welcome to stop in and say hello. The Tri-Circle-D insignia above the barn door—two small circles atop a large one with the letter D inside—is the WDW brand. The barn is also the site of a museum that pays tribute to horses and their role in Disney history. The ranch is also home to the Dragon Calliope— the horse-drawn musical instrument that Walt Disney purchased for the Mickey Mouse Club Circus Parade at Disneyland Park in the 1950s. It's quite impressive.

WAGON RIDES: The wagon departs from Pioneer Hall at 6 P.M. and 8:30 P.M. and carries guests on a trip through wooded areas near Bay Lake. Each ride lasts about 25 minutes and concludes at Pioneer Hall. Purchase tickets from the wagon ride host: $8 for adults, $5 for kids ages 3 through 9. Children under age 12 must be accompanied by an adult. Reservations are not accepted, so get there early.

Group wagon rides are available by calling 407-824-2832 (at least 24 hours in advance). The price is about $300 per hour. Note that wagon rides may be canceled due to inclement weather.

WILDERNESS BACK TRAIL ADVENTURE: A 2-hour "off-road" Segway tour of Fort Wilderness, this experience costs about $95 per person. For details, refer to page 234 or call 407-WDW-TOUR (939-8687).

Essentials

HOW TO GET THERE: From outside the World, take Magic Kingdom Exit 64B off I-4 onto U.S. 192, go through the Magic Kingdom Auto Plaza, and, bearing to your right, follow the Fort Wilderness signs. This is the most expeditious way to go, even for Walt Disney World resort guests.

By WDW Transportation: Buses or boats. Buses can get you just about anywhere, but allow yourself plenty of time—the transportation system, while efficient, is time-consuming.

Boats are also available from Magic Kingdom marinas (about a 30-minute ride) and from the Contemporary and Wilderness Lodge resorts (about a 25-minute ride).

WHERE TO EAT: For a description of the Trail's End restaurant and its take-out service, refer to the *Good Meals, Great Times* chapter.

The Settlement Trading Post, located near the beach at the north end of the campground, and the Meadow Trading Post, near the center of Fort Wilderness, offer a small supply of food staples. For serious grocery shopping, head to a nearby supermarket or order from *www.gardengrocer.com*. Ask the lobby concierge for directions.

HOT TIP!

Festive, horse-drawn "sleigh rides" may be offered at Ft. Wilderness from Thanksgiving week through December. For details or reservations, call 407-WDW-PLAY.

WDW Spas

Spa Tips

- Reserve treatments far in advance and be sure to confirm all appointments.

- If you'll feel more comfortable with either a male or a female spa therapist, let your preference be known when you make your reservation. The spas will accommodate such requests whenever possible.

- Plan to arrive 30 minutes prior to your appointment. That'll give you time to change and relax. (Arriving late will reduce your treatment time.)

- Guests under age 18 must be accompanied by an adult to enjoy a spa treatment.

- If you're scheduled for a body treatment, leave clothes in a locker. Robes (and slippers) are provided.

- Leave valuables in your resort-room safe.

- Guests are required to keep cell phones and electronic devices turned off at all times.

- It's always smart to take a shower before a treatment—especially if you've been at the beach or running around theme parks.

- Drink plenty of water after your spa visit. It will counter any dehydrating effects you may experience as the result of a treatment.

- Build time into your schedule to enjoy post-treatment relaxation time at the spa. You'll want to hold on to that glow as long as possible! Bathing suits are required for whirlpools, steamrooms, and other areas.

- Most spas add a 20 percent gratuity with each spa service. Additional gratuities may be added at your discretion.

- Cancellations must be made more than 4 hours in advance to avoid paying full price.

For many guests, a day at the theme parks is an exciting test of physical endurance—complete with sprinting (say, from Dumbo to Splash Mountain before that Fastpass+ time expires), weight lifting (toting tired toddlers), and long-distance hiking (covering more than a mile to reach the American Adventure from Epcot's front gate—and back again!). Fortunately, there are many ways to rest and rejuvenate weary bones, throbbing feet, and noise-addled noggins. Chief among them is a visit to a soothing spa (aah). There are four such spots on Disney property, open to all WDW visitors.

SENSES, A SPA AT DISNEY'S GRAND FLORIDIAN RESORT: You don't need a magic wand to make your stress disappear—not if you can pay a visit to the Grand Floridian pampering palace, Senses. In addition to the treatments offered at its sister spa at the Saratoga Springs resort (see page 229), this spot offers a selection of packages. Among them: the 3-hour Me Time Magic (de-stress bath, massage, organic facial, and pedicure), Gentleman's Retreat (featuring a facial, custom massage, manicure, and pedicure), and the Spa for Two package (custom firm massage for two and pedicure for two).

Services include facials for women, men, and teens, including a Berry Bliss facial and a Tropical Coconut Cream facial; revitalizing aromatherapy baths, and an herbal body-toning wrap. Massage options include: Swedish, warm stones, warm bamboo, foot and leg, and one specially designed for expectant mothers. Manicures, pedicures, and other hand and foot treatments are also available. There are manicures for kids, too.

Treatment hours are usually 8 A.M. to 8 P.M. Friday through Sunday, 9 P.M. to 6 P.M. Monday through Thursday. Prices start at about $145 for a 50-minute massage and $140 for a facial, plus gratuity. For more information or to book an appointment at the Grand Floridian spa, call 407-WDW-SPAS (939-7727). For details, visit *https://disneyworld.disney.go.com/spas/*.

BIRNBAUM'S ★**BEST**★ **MANDARA SPA AT THE DOLPHIN:** As exotic as it is peaceful, Mandara is on the must-do list for all guests looking to swap their stress for a big, relaxed smile.

Mandara specializes in treatments meant to reflect the "beauty, spirit, and traditions of both Eastern and Western cultures." The spa menu showcases Balinese massage, a variation of Swedish massage. It incorporates stretching, "vigorous yet relaxing" movements, and elements of acupressure. Of course, that's just one of many services offered here—all of which emphasize physical wellness and spiritual well-being. Other treatments include the Mandara customized massage, Hot Stone Therapy massage, and the Mandara Deep Tissue Muscle massage. The Elemis Visible Brilliance Facial ($160) targets dark circles under the eyes while smoothing wrinkles. And the exotic Elemis Musclease Aroma Spa Ocean Wrap ($140, plus gratuity, for 50 minutes) envelopes the body in an aromatic seaweed mask to relieve stiff joints and muscular tension.

In addition to Balinese-inspired architecture, two interior gardens provide retreats before guests begin the spa ritual. The goal here is to provide a place for guests to rejuvenate their minds as well as those aching "I can't believe I covered four theme parks in two days!" muscles. For more information, call 800-227-1500 or 407-934-4772, or visit *www.swandolphin.com*.

SENSES, A SPA AT DISNEY'S SARATOGA SPRINGS RESORT: Just as Saratoga Springs in New York was developed around the healing mineral waters of the springs, this spa incorporates the healing powers of nature into its design and theming. Services include the ultimate facial to hydrate and revitalize skin (105 minutes) and a warm bamboo massage (75 minutes), the 4-hour Senses Signature package (massage, facial, and pedicure), and the "Berry Bliss Facial" (50 or 80 minutes). Also on tap: Swedish massage, warm-stone massage, and rejuvenation treatments focused on the hands and feet, plus body wraps and scrubs. Manicures, pedicures, and organic facials are options, too. Prince and princess pedicures are offered to kids ages 4 through 12 (when accompanied by an adult).

Located on the shore of Lake Buena Vista, the spa is near the Fitness Center at the Saratoga Springs resort. The hours are generally from 8 A.M. to 8 P.M. A 50-minute massage starts at about $145, with facials going for about $140 (plus gratuity). A variety of packages is available. For more information and to make reservations, call 407-WDW-SPAS (939-7727).

THE SPA AT HILTON BUENA VISTA PALACE: A plush, peaceful place, this spa is as well equipped as they come. High-tech chairs with whirlpool footbaths make getting a pedicure a special event. And a cool-mud Theme Park Leg Relief Wrap can put the spring back in the step of even the most labored of lower limbs. Landscaped, outdoor whirlpools, plus locker room saunas and steam rooms, are there to aid in the relaxation process.

Among the more than 75 soothing treatments from which to choose are aromatherapy and massage, including shiatsu, Swedish, deep-tissue, and reflexology. A variety of special facials (including one for sun-stressed skin), scrubs, and wraps are available. The spa also offers massages for kids, as well as Little Princess facials, manicures, and pedicures. A salon offers the usual lineup of services.

The Spa at the Buena Vista Palace hotel is across from the Disney Springs Marketplace, on Buena Vista Drive. Hours are usually 8 A.M. to 8 P.M. but vary seasonally. A 25-minute massage costs about $70, and facials are about $70. Full- and half-day packages are available, as are custom packages. For information, call 407-827-3200. Reservations are recommended and are accepted up to one year in advance. Details are subject to change.

Internet Access at WDW

We'll resist the urge to chastise you for insisting on checking your office e-mail while on vacation (since we're similarly obsessed) and instead happily report that all Walt Disney World resorts offer free in-room, wireless Internet access. Of course, you'll need to supply the hardware. Complimentary Wi-Fi (wireless fidelity) is offered at all Walt Disney World–owned-and-operated resorts, plus the four theme parks and Disney Springs. Naturally, your computer, tablet, or phone must be Wi-Fi ready. Note that in-room, wireless Internet service is also available at the Four Seasons and the Walt Disney World Swan and Dolphin resorts.

If you'd like to access a computer but didn't pack your own, ask your lobby concierge to direct you to the nearest resort business center. There you can e-mail, upload, download, and print to your heart's content. Fees vary—be sure to inquire before you start using business center services.

Just for Kids

Walt Disney World may appeal to the kid in all of us, but some activities are meant for the actual young—not just the young at heart. With the exception of the Princess Tea Party, the following programs are specifically for guests who can't remember life before smartphones. (Grown-ups can relax while their kids are entertained.) The programs are quite popular and accommodate a limited number of guests—so book early: 407-WDW-PLAY (939-7529). Note that the adventures listed are not offered every day. Reservations are required and are available up to 180 days in advance.

ALBATROSS TREASURE CRUISE: Thar be treasure in Crescent Lake! Kids are invited to follow clues and join in the hunt. The 2-hour quest takes young adventurers to several stops and includes a reading of "The Legend of the Albatross." The ship weighs anchor at the Yacht Club marina on select mornings at about 9:30 A.M. Cost per child is about $39. It's open to potty-trained guests ages 4–12. Participants should wear socks and sneakers.

PONY RIDES: Young cowpokes can ride aboard petite ponies at the Tri-Circle-D Ranch at the Fort Wilderness Resort and Campground. Guests must be at least 2 years of age, under 80 pounds, no taller than 48 inches, and able to hold on by themselves. Closed-toe shoes are a must. A guardian leads the pony. Rides are offered from 10 A.M. until about 4 P.M. daily. Cost is $8 per child; cash only. Reservations are not accepted.

ISLANDS OF THE CARIBBEAN PIRATE CRUISE: Young buccaneers board a battered pirate ship at Caribbean Beach resort and set sail with a seasoned scallywag at the helm. The captain tells tall tales and leads his crew through treacherous waters (okay, they're actually quite calm) on a hunt for treasure. The cost per child is about $39. It's open to potty-trained guests ages 4–12. Cruise participants must wear socks and sneakers.

PERFECTLY PRINCESS TEA PARTY: Young regals (and their grown-up guardians) are encouraged to dress like their favorite princess for this festive tea party, offered daily from 10:30 A.M. to noon (except Tuesdays and Thursdays) in the Garden View Tea Room at Walt Disney World's Grand Floridian resort. The tea party is hosted by Miss Rose Petal, a magical rose from Aurora's garden that has come to life to lead storytelling, sing-alongs, and a princess parade. Guests may take a break from sipping tea and eating cake to visit with Princess Aurora, aka Sleeping Beauty.

All guests between the ages of 3 and 9 get a My Disney Girl doll, dressed as Princess Aurora, plus accessories. The cost for one adult and child (ages 3–9) is $334, including gratuity (tax is extra). Each extra child is about $234 (plus tax), while an extra adult pays about $99 (plus tax). If you'd like a child under age 3 to receive the merchandise, they should be listed as a 3-year-old. Reservations are required and may be made up to 180 days ahead.

PIRATE ADVENTURE: Ahoy there, mateys! In this adventure, young pirates don bandannas and hit the high seas in search of treasure. The ship shoves off at the Grand Floridian marina on select mornings. From there, it visits exotic ports of call (other resort marinas), where guests collect valuable treasures and enjoy a light snack. It's available to potty-trained kids ages 4–12 on select mornings. Cost per child is about $39. Reservations are required and are available up to 180 days ahead. Note that participants should wear socks and sneakers.

WONDERLAND TEA PARTY: Fans of Alice and her Wonderland friends will have a blast at this party presented at 1900 Park Fare at Disney's Grand Floridian resort. During the event, kids decorate and eat cupcakes. They'll also be treated to a story and have tea with the characters. The cost is about $50 per child, ages 4–12 (potty-trained). The tea party is offered Monday through Friday at 2 P.M.

Specialty Cruises

At Walt Disney World, every evening ends with a bang—which comes in the form of pyrotechnic spectaculars. Two such presentations, the Magic Kingdom's Happily Ever After fireworks show and Epcot's IllumiNations: Reflections of Earth, are seen by scores of park-goers on a nightly basis. However, these displays are also enjoyed by a privileged few, far removed from the hubbub of theme park crowds yet close enough to marvel at the subtleties of each brilliant burst. These are the guests who chose to book a specialty cruise. This vintage vantage point is available to everyone, provided that the rates don't break the budget and that reservations are made in advance. Of course, there is the other extreme: a peaceful, moonlit cruise on the quiet waterways of the World. This option is also available to guests who book a specialty cruise.

Reservations are accepted up to 24 hours ahead; advance reservations, accepted up to 180 days ahead, are strongly recommended. While specifics may change, the following is an indication of what was available at press time.

THE GRAND I: This striking 52-foot Sea Ray Sedan Bridge yacht escorts up to 18 guests at a time. A 3-hour tour of the Seven Seas Lagoon and Bay Lake culminates with a front-row seat for the Magic Kingdom's fireworks whenever possible. (The vessel has an audio feed that allows guests to hear the show's soundtrack.)

The *Grand I* yacht departs from the Grand Floridian, but can stop at the Polynesian Village, Contemporary, Wilderness Lodge, or Fort Wilderness on request. It starts at about $700 (plus tax) per hour to rent, with the per-boatload fee covering up to 17 guests, plus a driver and a deckhand. Butler and private dining service are available (for an additional fee). This is the most luxurious watercraft experience at Walt Disney World. Call 407-824-2682 for more *Grand I* yacht pricing details or to make a reservation.

PONTOON BOATS: More practical than luxurious, Disney's fleet of pontoon boats still delivers a crowd-pleasing cruise experience. The boats, which accommodate up to 10, take guests on tours of the Seven Seas Lagoon and Bay Lake, near the Magic Kingdom, as well as Crescent Lake, near Epcot's World Showcase. Those in the Magic Kingdom area are treated to VIP viewing of the fireworks show (as well as the audio), while Epcot-area cruisers take in IllumiNations: Reflections of Earth when available. All pontoon boats offer the Happily Ever After soundtrack—a special treat.

Pontoon cruises last about one hour. Magic Kingdom fireworks excursions depart from the Grand Floridian, Polynesian Village, Contemporary, Wilderness Lodge, and Fort Wilderness marinas. IllumiNations cruises leave from the Yacht Club marina. The cost for cruises (which includes a driver) starts at about $299 to $349, plus tax, per boatload (higher for fireworks cruises). Call 407-WDW-PLAY (939-7529) for additional details or to make reservations.

Pirates & Pyrotechnics

Avast, ye hearties! There's a new pirate–themed adventure at Walt Disney Word: The Pirates & Pals Fireworks Voyage. In it, brave buccaneers board a pirate ship—conveniently moored at the Contemporary Resort marina—and set sail on Bay Lake and Seven Seas Lagoon. Before weighing anchor, participating pirates enjoy unlimited snacks and soft drinks on the dock. They can mingle with Captain Hook and Mr. Smee, who are all too eager to meet the recruits. After a pirate parade, guests board Captain Patch's ship and set sail. Patch will test your knowledge of Disney trivia, sing some sea shanties, and position your vessel in a perfect location to view the Magic Kingdom's fireworks show, Happily Ever After. Cost is about $121 per adult, $43 per child (age 3–9). For additional information or to make a reservation, call 407-939-7529.

Tours and Programs

Here's your chance to experience Walt Disney World from the inside out. Adult guests may be required to carry a photo ID when attending backstage programs. Tours and prices are subject to change in 2018; for information or to make reservations, call 407-WDW-TOUR (939-8687) between 8 A.M. and 8 P.M. (daily) and have your credit card handy. Photography is not permitted while in "backstage" areas of Walt Disney World. Prices quoted do not include tax. For details on The Power of the Park Side, a Star Wars–themed, 7-hour adventure at Disney's Hollywood Studios, refer to the Hot Tip on page 180 and visit *www.disneyworld.com*.

BACKSTAGE MAGIC (Monday through Friday; 9 A.M.): This is one of Disney World's best programs. Highlighting the nearly 8-hour exploration of the Magic Kingdom, Disney's Hollywood Studios, and Epcot may be an underground tour of the Magic Kingdom's Utilidors—Disney's tunnel system. Lunch is included, as are a few surprises. Cost is $275, plus tax. Park admission is not required or included. Guests must be at least 12 years old. This is one of the most popular WDW experiences—book early.

BACKSTAGE TALES (Daily; 7:30 A.M.): This Animal Kingdom tour offers a look at conservation, animal care, behavioral studies, and the Animal Nutrition Center and Veterinary Hospital. The cost is about $90, and theme park admission is required, but not included. Guests must be at least 12 years old to participate.

BEHIND THE SEEDS (Daily; every hour between 10:30 A.M. and 4:30 P.M.): An opportunity for guests of all ages to get a closer look at the greenhouses and fish farm that are part of The Land pavilion at Epcot.

During the tour, guests will have close encounters with insects and plants. A guide shares knowledge of hydroponics growing systems and crops from around the globe. Expect to be on your feet for the full hour of this experience. Cost is $25 per adult, $20 per child (ages 3–9). This tour is best enjoyed by sturdy adults and older kids. Reservations may be made in advance or at the tour desk on the lower level of The Land (near the entrance to the Soarin' Around the World attraction). Theme park admission is required.

CARING FOR GIANTS (Daily; groups depart between 10 A.M. and 4:30 P.M.): Guests of all ages are introduced to the majestic world of African elephants in this 60-minute backstage experience. The elephant experts share strategies for day-to-day care of the gentle giants, plus a host of fascinating facts. African cultural representatives are also on hand to share stories about Disney's conservation efforts in their homeland. All the while, guests observe Disney's elephant herd from a distance of just 80 to 100 feet. Cost is about $30 per person. Park admission is required, but not included.

DISNEY'S FAMILY MAGIC TOUR (Daily; 10 A.M.): Families and friends may join in this 2-hour "scavenger-hunt-style" quest to save the Magic Kingdom. Cost is $39 (it's available to everyone, but recommended for parties with kids between the ages of 4 and 12). Magic Kingdom admission is required but is not included.

DIVEQUEST (Tuesday–Saturday; 4:30 and 5:30 P.M.): The highlight of the 2½-hour program is a 40-minute underwater adventure—complete with sharks, turtles, rays, and other fish—in The Seas with Nemo & Friends aquarium. Participants must show proof of current scuba certification. Cost is about $180. Guests ages 10–12 must dive with a parent or guardian. Gear is provided. Epcot admission is not required or included.

DOLPHINS IN DEPTH (Tuesday–Saturday; 9:45 A.M.): This 3-hour Epcot program (about 30 minutes takes place in the water) teaches guests about dolphin behavior as they interact with the social sea creatures and observe researchers and trainers working with them. Cost is about $199 per person. The minimum age is 13. Guests ages 13 to 17 must be accompanied by a paying adult. Park admission is not required or included. Wet suits are provided; wear your own swimsuit.

EPCOT SEAS AQUA TOUR (Tuesday–Saturday; 12:30 P.M.): A 2½-hour program (about 30 minutes of which is in the water) that lets guests learn about and interact with ocean life in The Seas with Nemo & Friends pavilion. First, guests watch a video about sea creatures, then they join them in their habitat using a Supplied-Air Snorkel system. Cost is about $145. Gear is included, as are light refreshments, a souvenir gift, and a group photo. Guests must wear swimsuits. The tour is open to guests age 8 and up. Park admission is not required or included.

KEYS TO THE KINGDOM (Daily; 8:30, 9, and 9:30 A.M.): A 5-hour tour that offers an on-site orientation to the history and workings of Walt Disney World's original theme park, the Magic Kingdom. Guests visit an attraction (waiting in the regular attraction line) and take a peek at the Utilidors (the legendary tunnels underneath the park). Cost is about $99, plus theme park admission. Lunch is included. Guests must be at least 16 years old to participate in the tour.

PHOTO BY JILL SAFRO

THE MAGIC BEHIND OUR STEAM TRAINS (daily; 7:30 A.M.): A 3-hour tour that gives guests an inside look at the Walt Disney World Railroad. In addition to an exploration of Walt Disney's passion for steam trains, guests visit the backstage "roundhouse" where the steam trains are stored and join the opening crew as they prepare for the daily railroad operation in the Magic Kingdom. Guests must be at least 10 to take the tour. Cost is about $54 per person. Theme park admission is required but not included in the tour price.

SAVOR THE SAVANNA: EVENING SAFARI EXPERIENCE (Daily; 4:30, 5:30, and 6:30 P.M.): A private, guided journey, this experience is limited to 12 guests per excursion. The evening safari adventure begins with a journey deep in the heart of Harambe Wildlife Preserve. It offers secluded viewing areas of the savanna, plus a sampling of African-inspired, tapas-style nibbles and regional wines, beer, and soft drinks.

Cost is about $169 per person, plus tax. (The price includes food, drinks, and a keepsake.) Guests must be at least 8 years old to participate in this walking program. Park admission is required but is not included in the tour price.

THE UNDISCOVERED FUTURE WORLD (Daily; 8:30 A.M.): Walt Disney dreamed about making the world a better place. In this 4-hour tour, guests are taken back to the creation of Epcot and learn about Walt's lofty ambitions and his legacy.

Guests walk to Future World pavilions and learn how each area celebrates humanity's accomplishments and challenges. The goal is to share the vision behind the park.

Cost is about $69 per person. Guests must be at least 16 years old to participate in this walking program. Park admission is required but is not included. Details are subject to change.

WALT DISNEY: MARCELINE TO MAGIC KINGDOM (Daily; 8:15 A.M.): Explore how events in Walt Disney's life helped shape the Walt Disney World Resort and the attractions within it in this 2½- to 3-hour walking tour. As one of Walt's final visions, the Magic Kingdom shares many similarities with the story of his life. By using the park as a walking timeline, guests discover how Walt's life inspired him to create some of the most cherished stories and attractions the parks have to offer. Guests also get an insider look at several of those aforementioned attractions. Tours cost $49 per person (plus park

PHOTO BY MIKE CARROLL

Wild Africa Trek

A thrilling, 3-hour adventure, the Wild Africa Trek is not for the faint of heart or those with any trepidation about teetering high in the air on a rickety rope bridge.

The guided tour, which is offered daily at Disney's Animal Kingdom park, is a VIP safari adventure for groups of 12 or less. It includes hiking through a jungle, near the edge of a cliff, and over the savanna—plus many up-close encounters of the animal kind.

Available to guests age 8 and above, the rain-or-shine trek costs vary, depending on the season, and includes snacks (you can't bring your own) and an access code to view and download digital photos. Park admission is required but not included. This is an active experience—be sure to wear comfortable shoes and attire. Note that there are no "chicken exits" here. For pricing and information, visit *www.disneyworld.com*. To make a reservation, call 407-939-8687.

Guests who wish to participate in a less physical journey or a wheelchair-accessible trek may call 407-938-1373 to request an alternative offering.

admission). Guests should arrive 15 minutes early and wear their most comfortable walking shoes (expect to cover a lot of ground). It's available to guests age 12 and up.

WANYAMA SAFARI (daily; 3:30 P.M.): A 3-hour experience that includes a private tour of the animal savannas surrounding Disney's Animal Kingdom Lodge. Following the tour, guests have dinner at Jiko—The Cooking Place. (It's a family-style meal.) Guests must be at least 8 years old and staying at Animal Kingdom Lodge. Cost is about $191 per person. (Price includes tax and gratuity.) The Wanyama Safari

may be booked up to 180 days in advance. Call 407-938-4755 for details or to make a reservation.

WILDERNESS BACK TRAIL ADVENTURE (Tuesday through Saturday): A 2-hour experience, this adventure lets guests explore the Fort Wilderness area while aboard a Segway personal transporter. (It's a special model with off-road-type tires.) The first hour is devoted to training (it's not as easy as it looks!), with the second spent exploring with an experienced storytelling guide. Guests must be at least 16 and in good health. (You'll be on your feet the whole time, and operating the Segway requires more muscle than one might expect.) The cost is approximately $95 per person.

WORLD SHOWCASE: DESTINATIONS DISCOVERED (daily; 8:15 A.M.): A 4½- to 5-hour walking tour of World Showcase, DestiNations Discovered covers the culture, architecture, and design details of several of the park's international pavilions. Lunch is included at the Rose & Crown dining room in the U.K. pavilion. Cost is about $109 per person. Theme park admission is required, but not included. For pricing, schedules, and additional details call 407-939-8687, or visit *www.disneyworld.com*.

YULETIDE FANTASY (seasonal): A festive 3½-hour experience, this program showcases the way Disney weaves stories and folklore into decorations found in the theme parks and resorts. It offers a unique perspective on how colors, textures, architecture, and illusions help all of Walt Disney World deck the halls for the holidays.

The cost is about $99 per person. Theme park admission is not included or required for this experience. Guests must be at least 16 years old to participate in Yuletide Fantasy. All guests must present a photo ID.

Sports

SPORTS

First-time visitors don't always realize that Disney provides a plethora of sporting opportunities. Within WDW's 40 or so square miles, there are more tennis courts than at most tennis resorts and more holes of championship-caliber golf than at most golf centers, plus so many other diversions—from fishing and biking to boating, parasailing, and horseback riding—that the quantity and variety are matched by few other vacation destinations.

So while the family golfers are pursuing a perfect swing on one of several first-rate, 18-hole courses, tennis buffs can be wearing themselves out on the courts, parasailers can soar up to 600 feet above the area near the Magic Kingdom, and anglers can be casting away in hopes of hooking a big bass. Those who prefer to spectate rather than participate can visit a virtual sports mecca at the ESPN Wide World of Sports Complex, an enormous, state-of-the-art facility that hosts an array of sporting events, both amateur and professional. And those who prefer the sedate can treat themselves to a soothing spa treatment.

Instruction, as well as guides, drivers, and assorted supervisors, makes every sport as much fun for beginners as for hard-core aficionados. Moreover, the ready accessibility of WDW sporting activities—via an extensive system of public transportation (see *Transportation & Accommodations*)—means that no family member need curtail playtime to chauffeur others around.

WDW Golf

Most people don't immediately think of Disney World for a golf outing. Yet there are superb 18-hole courses here: The Magnolia and the Palm are across from the Polynesian Village resort. Nearby is the Lake Buena Vista course. Its fairways are framed by Saratoga Springs and Old Key West resorts. And the Four Seasons resort boasts a stellar course, too. While the WDW courses won't set anyone's knees to knocking, they're demanding enough to have merited the status of a stop on the PGA Tour tournament trail.

PALM & MAGNOLIA: The wide-open, tree-dotted Magnolia measures 5,127 yards from the front tees, 6,558 from the middle, and 7,516 from the back. The Palm (which was recently redesigned by Arnold Palmer Course Design) is tighter, with more wooded fairways and nine water hazards; it measures 5,213 yards from the front, 6,339 from the middle, and 7,010 from the back. Both courses have received a four-star ("outstanding") rating from *Golf Digest* magazine. The Magnolia and Palm share two driving ranges and putting greens.

HOT TIP!

Single-rider, adaptive golf carts and clubhouse accommodations are available for guests with disabilities at all Walt Disney World resort golf courses. Visit www.golfwdw.com, or call 407-WDW-GOLF (939-4653) for information.

Oak Trail: This walking nine-hole, 2,913-yard layout, a walking course tucked into a corner within the Magnolia, was designed for beginners and junior golfers, but it has some tough holes, including two par 5s. Many moderate and accomplished golfers enjoy the opportunity to tune up or play a quick 9.

LAKE BUENA VISTA COURSE: Joe Lee's design measures 5,194 yards from the front tees, 6,264 from the middle, and 6,749 from the rearmost markers. Among the shortest of the 18-hole, par-72 courses, it has a fair amount of water, and its tree-lined fairways are Walt Disney World's narrowest. The course is well suited for beginners but challenges experienced players. A driving range and putting green are also available.

Essentials

WHEN TO GO: January through April is peak golfing season. To beat the crowds, play on a Monday or Tuesday, and tee off in the late afternoons (mornings are very busy when the mercury rises). Summer discounts may apply. From June through late September, guests pay as little as $62 after 10 A.M. After 3 P.M., the price drops to $49. Florida resident, Theme Park Annual Passholder, Military, and Disney Vacation Club member specials may be offered. Annual golf memberships are also a possibility. Call 407-939-4653 for details.

SPORTS

RESERVATIONS: Call 407-WDW-GOLF (939-4653), or visit *www.golfwdw.com* to confirm rates and to secure tee times. From January through April, morning and early afternoon tee times should be reserved well in advance; starting times after 3 P.M. are often available at the last minute. Reservations must be made with a major credit card. Cancellations must be made at least 24 hours ahead to avoid penalties.

FEES: At the 18-hole courses, greens fees (including a required cart) vary with the course and season. Rates range from about $85 to $125 for day visitors (not staying at a Walt Disney World resort). Rates are usually discounted for guests staying at any resort on WDW property (including Swan, Dolphin, and the resorts on Hotel Plaza Boulevard).

Mid-afternoon rates, known as "twilight rates," may yield discounts. Available throughout the year, twilight rates run about $39 to $69.

Cost for adults to play Oak Trail is $40 for 9 holes; juniors (17 and under) pay $22 for 9 holes. Prices don't include tax and are subject to change.

INSTRUCTION: At the WDW Golf Studio at the Palm and Magnolia courses, private 45-minute lessons cost $75 for adults and $50 for juniors (up to age 17). Lessons are customized to all levels of experience. Video analysis may be used. Prices are subject to change. Walt Disney World resort guests may make reservations up to 120 days in advance; call 407-WDW-GOLF (939-4653).

DRESS: Proper golf attire is required. Collared shirts or golf-style collarless shirts are necessary, and any shorts must be Bermuda length.

EQUIPMENT RENTAL: Equipment can be rented at all courses; club rentals start at about $50, plus tax. Photo ID is required for rentals. Range balls (about $7 per basket) are among

available items. Guests staying at most Walt Disney World resorts receive $20 club rental when they purchase a non-discounted round of golf at Disney's Palm, Magnolia, or Lake Buena Vista courses. Also included is transportation to and from the Walt Disney World resort via taxi (paid with vouchers). Swan, Dolphin, Four Seasons, and resorts on Hotel Plaza Boulevard are not included in transportation.

Tennis

Saratoga Springs Resort & Spa has two clay courts. All other Walt Disney World tennis is played on hard courts. Yacht and Beach Club share one court; Fort Wilderness, Saratoga Springs, Contemporary's Bay Lake Tower, Animal Kingdom's Kidani Village, and BoardWalk each have two; Old Key West has three; and the Swan and Dolphin share a four-court facility. Courts are free to guests staying at a WDW resort. For details or to make lesson reservations, call 321-228-1146.

Essentials

WHEN TO GO: Courts are often open from about 8 A.M. to 7 P.M. daily; courts at the Swan and Dolphin are open 24 hours a day (lighted courts are available). Weather-wise, January, October, and November are prime months for playing tennis. All courts are available on a first-come, first-served basis. During very busy periods, the length of time a single group of players can occupy a court is restricted to two hours on any morning, afternoon, or evening.

Equipment rental is limited at Walt Disney World (Swan and Dolphin only). Guests should bring their own tennis racquets and balls.

DRESS: Tennis whites are appropriate, but not required, for play on Disney's courts. Tennis shoes are a must.

Waters of the World

Boating

Disney World is the home of the country's largest fleet of pleasure boats. Cruising on Bay Lake and the Seven Seas Lagoon can be excellent sport, and a variety of boats are available for rent at WDW resort marinas. Bay Lake excursions originate from the Contemporary, Wilderness Lodge, and Fort Wilderness. The Polynesian Village and Grand Floridian send boaters out from their marinas on the shore of Seven Seas Lagoon. The Yacht and Beach Club, BoardWalk, Swan, and Dolphin share a boating haven in 25-acre Crescent Lake.

To rent, guests must show a valid driver's license or passport. Rental of certain craft may carry other requirements. No privately owned boats are permitted on WDW waters. All prices and times are subject to change.

AMPHICARS: It's a car! It's a boat! It's a blast from America's motoring past (the 1960s to be precise). Yep, the amphibious Amphicar is back. Disney has brought nine of these classic vehicles out of retirement and put them back to work at Disney Springs. Doing double duty as artwork/water taxi, Amphicars are next to The Boathouse eatery. Up to three guests may enjoy a 20-minute tour of Disney Springs waterways for about $125 (captain included). Tours are offered from 10 A.M. until 10 P.M. daily, weather permitting.

BOSTON WHALER® MONTAUK BOATS: These 17-foot motorboats are a good choice for relaxing cruises. They accommodate up to six passengers, and may be rented for about $45 per half hour at the Polynesian Village, Contemporary, Grand Floridian, Wilderness Lodge, Yacht and Beach Club, and Fort Wilderness marinas.

CANOEING: A long paddle down the Fort Wilderness canals is such a tranquil way to pass a misty morning that it's hard to remember that the bustle of the Magic Kingdom is not far away. Canoes may be rented at the Bike Barn at Fort Wilderness (about $8 per half hour, $13 per hour). Ocean kayaks (open-top kayaks) may be rented here, too (expect to pay about $7 per half hour, $11 per hour). Note that these watercraft are for use on Fort Wilderness canals only, not for Bay Lake or the Seven Seas Lagoon.

MOTORBOATING: It seems there are always dozens of boats zipping back and forth across Bay Lake, Seven Seas Lagoon, and Crescent Lake. These are called Sea Raycers, and they're just as much fun as they look. The boats are quick enough so that a lot of watery terrain can be covered in a half hour (for about $35), though it's quite tempting to splurge on a full hour.

Sea Raycers can be rented year-round at the Grand Floridian, Polynesian Village, Wilderness Lodge, Contemporary, Yacht & Beach Club, and Fort Wilderness marinas. Guests must be at least 12 years old and 5 feet tall to rent Sea Raycer boats. Kids under the minimum age and height may ride as passengers, but they're not allowed to drive. We suggest that drivers wear a waterproof watch—it's amazing how the time flies!

PARASAILING: Excursions are offered at the Contemporary resort marina. Each 8- to 10-minute flight costs about $95 for one person to soar to 450 feet and $130 to rise to 600 feet, $170 for two to ride tandem at 450 feet and $195 for two to hit a height of 600 feet. Flights are offered 7 days a week, weather-permitting. (They will be canceled due to lightning, high wind, or other inclement weather—in which case a full refund will be issued.) Reservations must be made at least 24 hours in advance (and may be made up to a year ahead); call 407-939-0754, or visit *www.sammyduvall.com*. Walk-ups are accepted on a first-come, first-served basis. Wear loose-fitting clothing, but don't bother with a swimsuit—guests take off from and land on the back of the boat without getting wet.

The minimum age to parasail is 6. Guests younger than 18 must have an adult present. The minimum weight requirement is 130 pounds (guests under 130 pounds may fly tandem with another guest in order to reach the minimum weight allowance). The maximum weight per parasailing flight is 330 pounds.

PEDAL BOATS: These Swan-shaped watercraft rent for about $7 per half hour or $11 per hour at the Swan and Dolphin marina.

PERSONAL WATERCRAFT AND GUIDED EXCURSIONS: Three-seat personal Jet Ski–style watercraft are available for rent at Sammy Duvall's Watersports Centre at the Contemporary resort. Hours to rent are usually 9 A.M. to 5 P.M. (They open at 10 A.M. during the winter.) The cost is about $135 (plus tax) for an hour for up to three passengers (of any age). The maximum weight per vehicle is 400 pounds. Participants must be at least 16 years old to drive. Guests under age 18 must have an adult sign a waiver prior to the trip.

It's also possible to start the day with a guided excursion aboard a 3-seat personal watercraft. Starting daily at 9 A.M. from the Contemporary resort marina (departures start at 10 A.M. in the winter), a guide calls attention to points of interest on and around Bay Lake and the Seven Seas Lagoon. After the tour, guests have time to ride on their own, under the guide's supervision. A maximum of 4 rental units operate during each excursion. Cost is about $135 (plus tax) for up to 3 people. For information or to make reservations, visit *www.sammyduvall.com*; 407-939-0754.

PONTOON BOATS: Motorized, canopied platforms on pontoons are perfect for families, inexperienced boaters, and visitors more interested in serenity than in thrills. Available at select resort marinas, the 21-foot craft hold up to ten passengers and cost about $45, plus tax, per half hour. Guests must be at least 18 years old (with a valid driver's license) to drive a pontoon boat.

WATERSKIING, WAKEBOARDING, AND TUBING: Ski boats with Sammy Duvall instructors and equipment are available at the Contemporary resort marina. Watercraft may be reserved here, too. Reservations must be made at least 24 hours in advance and may be made up to a year ahead. Same-day walk-ups are accepted on a first-come, first-served basis; call 407-939-0754, or visit *www.sammyduvall.com* for pricing and to make reservations. Minors under 18 must have a legal guardian sign a waiver prior to departure. Note that activities may be canceled due to inclement weather (such as lightning, wind, etc.). Sammy Duvall's Watersports Centre operates seasonally: 9 A.M. to 5 P.M. in summer; 10 A.M. to 5 P.M. in winter.

Fishing

The 70,000 bass with which Bay Lake was stocked in the mid-1960s have grown and multiplied as a result of WDW's restrictive fishing policy. (It's strictly catch-and-release.) No angling is permitted on Bay Lake or the Seven Seas Lagoon, except on the guided fishing expeditions. Largemouth bass weighing two to eight pounds are the most common catch.

Fishing excursions are presented by BASS, the world's largest fishing organization. Guests who participate in a Walt Disney World excursion receive a one-year BASS membership, which includes 11 issues of *Bassmaster* magazine, a membership pack, decal, handbook, eligibility to compete in national events, discounts, and other benefits.

Bay Lake excursions depart daily (call 407-939-2277 for details). Trips last two or four hours and includes guide, gear, and refreshments (soft drinks). Guides will pick up guests at the Contemporary, Grand Floridian, Polynesian Village, Fort Wilderness, and Wilderness Lodge. Guides will pick up guests at Old Key West, Saratoga Springs, and Port Orleans Riverside and French Quarter, too. Two- and four-hour excursions accommodate up to five anglers and include guide, gear, and drinks. Kids under 16 must be accompanied by an adult.

Anglers might also consider two-hour tours that depart from the Yacht and Beach Club at 7 A.M., 10 A.M., and 1:30 P.M. All trips accommodate up to five people. A guide, gear, and soft drinks are included.

The Magic Kingdom resorts and Coronado Springs resorts also offer two-hour excursions on pontoon boats that accommodate one or two guests. They depart from the resort marinas at 7 A.M., 10 A.M., and 1:30 P.M. daily. The $235 to $455 price includes equipment and a guide.

Reservations must be made at least 24 hours in advance and may be made up to 180 days ahead; call 407-WDW-BASS (939-2277). Note that excursions may be canceled or cut short if the weather is stormy or there is lightning in the WDW vicinity.

Fishing on your own—again, strictly catch-and-release—is permitted in the canals at Fort Wilderness. Fort Wilderness guests may toss in lines from any campground canal shore. Fishing licenses are not required. Rods and reels and cane poles are available for rent at the Fort Wilderness Bike Barn. Bait may be purchased (worms and night crawlers are both about $4).

ESPN Wide World of Sports Complex

Variety is the name of the game at the ESPN Wide World of Sports Complex. The multi-million-dollar complex invites athletes and spectators alike to dive into more than 70 types of sporting experiences. It's a grand slam for die-hard sports fans.

The 220-acre facility—which is teamed up with ESPN—hosts events in everything from jump rope to wrestling. The home of the Pop Warner Super Bowl and National Cheer & Dance championships is also the spring training site for Major League Baseball's Atlanta Braves. (At press time, it was possible that the team would move elsewhere after the 2018 season. For updates, visit *www. atlanabraves.mlb.com*.)

Designed as a modern vision of old-time Floridian building styles, the architecture harks back to days when sports facilities were extensions of their neighborhoods; there is even a town commons (which serves as a welcome center).

The complex includes a baseball stadium; a field house that accommodates basketball, wrestling, and volleyball; a track-and-field complex; tennis courts; and multipurpose fields fit for football, soccer, and more.

A general-admission ticket costs about $18 for adults and $13 for kids ages 3 through 9. Tickets may be purchased at the front gate and allow guests to watch all "nonpremium" events. Guests are only admitted on days when events are scheduled. Tickets to premium events may be purchased through Ticketmaster (800-745-3000; or *www.ticketmaster.com*) and include general admission to the complex.

Premium-event tickets may also be purchased at the Wide World of Sports complex box office on the day of an event, depending on availability. Prices vary from event to event. Note that in addition to traditional seats, the baseball stadium has lawn seating. If you purchase lawn tickets, bring something to sit on and get there as early as possible. Prime locations go fast!

Essentials

HOW TO GET THERE: Direct bus transportation is available at All-Star, Pop Century, and Caribbean Beach resorts (based on the events scheduled). Other WDW resort guests must take a bus (plan to transfer at a park or Disney Springs) to one of these resorts. Allow at least an hour for the commute (more if you're attending a premium event). Buses run Thursday through Monday from 5 P.M. until about 11 P.M. Disney resort buses also run when events are taking place, starting one hour prior to complex opening time, until 11 P.M. or the time the complex closes (whichever is later).

If you are driving, take Exit 65 off I-4 to Victory Way. The complex is between U.S. 192 and Osceola Parkway. Parking is free but limited. If you plan to attend a premium event, arrive as early as possible—or risk scrambling for a spot in an unpaved, auxiliary lot.

WHERE TO EAT: The big-ticket eatery here is ESPN Wide World of Sports Grill. (This venue operates on event days only.)

There are more than 30 concessions for those seeking a somewhat lighter bite. They offer hot dogs, popcorn, soft drinks, and beer, as well as a few more substantial, yet just as portable, snacks.

It is also possible to pre-order boxed meals, pizza, and beverages meals via *www.espnwwos.com*. There is a minimum of $50 and all orders must be placed at least two days prior to the event. For hot buffet options, call 407-566-6698.

Touch Base

Get the scoop on all the scheduled action at the ESPN Wide World of Sports Complex by calling 407-541-5600 or visiting the website *www.espnwwos.com*.

More Sporting Fun

ARCHERY: Channel your inner Robin Hood at a Fort Wilderness program known as the Archery Experience. The 90-minute experience includes a quick but thorough lesson and lots of shooting time. It takes place every Thursday through Saturday at 2:45 P.M. Available to guests age 7 and older, the Archery Experience costs about $45 per person (plus tax). Book it up to 180 days in advance by calling 407-939-7529.

BIKING: Pedaling along the rustic pathways and lightly trafficked roads at Fort Wilderness can be a pleasant way to spend a couple of hours. Both areas are spread out, so bicycles are a practical way to get around. Bikes are also available for rent year-round at Old Key West, Wilderness Lodge, Port Orleans, Caribbean Beach, BoardWalk, Yacht and Beach Club, and Saratoga Springs. The cost is about $10 an hour or $20 per day. Bikes with training wheels or baby seats are available. Helmets are mandatory for guests up to the age of 16 and may be borrowed for free.

RUNNING: Except from late fall to early spring, the weather is usually much too steamy in Central Florida for jogging. If you run very early in the morning in warm seasons, the heat is somewhat less daunting. The 1.2-mile promenade around the lake at the Caribbean Beach resort is ideal for running, as is the three-quarter-mile promenade that surrounds Crescent Lake (a waterway that's bordered by the Swan and Dolphin, Yacht and Beach Club, and BoardWalk resorts), and the nearly mile-long path circling Coronado Springs' Lago Dorado. Fort Wilderness and the Wilderness Lodge are connected by a jogging trail that is about 2.5 miles long and features exercise stations. Old Key West also has scenic routes, averaging about a mile in length. There are also trails at All-Stars, Grand Floridian, Contemporary, Art of Animation, Port Orleans, and Pop Century.

MINIATURE GOLF: The Fantasia Gardens Miniature Golf complex, located near the Swan, Dolphin, and BoardWalk resorts, offers players two 18-hole courses themed to the Disney film *Fantasia*. The Fantasia Fairways course offers a difficult layout sure to tantalize serious golfers. It features traditional golf obstacles, such as water hazards, doglegs, and roughs. Don't be fooled by the small size of the Fantasia Fairways course— the challenges are big. (The record for the par-72 course is 47.)

Fantasia Gardens, on the other hand, is all in fun, with clever things (a dancing hippo, xylophone stairs, brooms dumping buckets of water) at every hole. The degree of difficulty varies from hole to hole, but this is an easy course to conquer. There are some challenges out there, however. Hole 15, for example, is one of the trickier ones. Here, golfers aim through mini-geysers that randomly squirt water into the air.

Disney's Winter Summerland miniature golf course is a mere stone's throw from the Blizzard Beach water park (they share a bus stop). Designed as a vacation retreat for Santa and his elves, the two 18-hole courses boast a festive atmosphere, complete with Christmas carol soundtracks. The sandy-surface course is a bit more challenging than its snowy-surface counterpart.

A round on any course costs about $14 for adults, $12 for kids ages 3 through 9. The second round is 25 percent off. Typical playing time is about an hour. Hours are generally 10 A.M. to 11 P.M., but vary seasonally. For information, call 407-WDW-PLAY (939-7529).

SPAS AND HEALTH CLUBS: Health clubs include the Contemporary's Olympiad Fitness Center, Sturdy Branches at Wilderness Lodge, Zahanati at Animal Kingdom Lodge, La Vida at Coronado Springs, Health Club at Saratoga Springs, Muscles and Bustles at BoardWalk, Health Club at the Grand Floridian, Resort Fitness Center at Old Key West, Ship Shape at the Yacht and Beach Club, and the fitness center at the Swan. Registered guests may use their respective resort's facility for free. Guests not registered in a resort with a health club can use the facilities for a fee.

In addition to fitness centers, full-service spas are located at the Grand Floridian, Saratoga Springs, the Dolphin, and Buena Vista Palace. There are special spa packages available at each of these resorts. (See pages 228–229 for details on WDW resort spas.)

SWIMMING: Although the beachfronts are strictly for strolling, sunbathing, and sand castle construction, swimmers may splash in one of the many elaborately themed pools that come in every shape and size imaginable. Typhoon Lagoon and Blizzard Beach water parks only add to the fun (see *Everything Else in the World* for water park specifics).

> ## HOT TIP!
> As signs posted along the beaches indicate, swimming and wading are not permitted in any of Walt Disney World's lakes. The rule is meant to protect guests from unguarded water and from exposure to naturally occurring bacteria and dangerous wildlife, such as snakes and alligators, common to Florida lakes.

POOLS: Walt Disney World resorts have at least one pool apiece. With the exception of sister resorts (Yacht and Beach Club; Port Orleans French Quarter and Riverside; All-Star Movies, All-Star Music, and All-Star Sports; and Swan and Dolphin), which share some of their recreational facilities, WDW hotel pools are open to guests staying at the respective resort. This policy was initiated to prevent overcrowding. All pools are heated in winter. Resort guests may borrow life jackets at no cost. Guests who cannot swim should wear life jackets at all times while in or near a pool.

Featuring one pool each are Animal Kingdom Lodge and Port Orleans French Quarter. The Grand Floridian, Contemporary, Polynesian, Fort Wilderness, the Wilderness Lodge, and All-Stars have two pools each. BoardWalk, Pop Century, and Art of Animation have three pools; Coronado Springs, Old Key West, and Saratoga Springs all feature four swimming holes; Port Orleans Riverside has six, and Caribbean Beach has seven. The Yacht and Beach Club resorts share three unguarded pools, plus a small water park known as Stormalong Bay. It features slides, a sand-bottomed wading area, and a lazy river. Saratoga Springs resort has four pools. The Swan and Dolphin share a lovely, themed grotto pool with a slide, one lap pool, and a third smaller pool. In addition, each of the resorts on Hotel Plaza Boulevard has its own pool.

There are no diving boards; swimmers in search of a big splash should head to Blizzard Beach or Typhoon Lagoon. Each park features a ginormous wave pool. Lifeguards are on duty during most daylight hours at each WDW resort's main pool.

TRAIL RIDES: Guided horseback rides into pine woods and palmetto country set off from the front of Fort Wilderness four times daily. This trip is not meant for seasoned gallopers— you can't wander off on your own. The horses have been culled for gentleness, so trips are suitable for novices. Cost is about $46 per person for a 45-minute tour. Kids under the age of 9 are not allowed to ride, and there's a weight limit of 250 pounds. (Younger kids can saddle up on ponies at the TriCircle D Pony Farm for about $8.) Reservations are necessary and may be made up to 180 days in advance by calling 407-WDW-PLAY (939-7529).

VOLLEYBALL & BASKETBALL: Resort volleyball courts are reserved for Walt Disney World resort guests. Caribbean Beach Resort, the Grand Floridian, Yacht and Beach Club, Fort Wilderness, Swan and Dolphin, Coronado Springs, and Old Key West have volleyball courts. Fort Wilderness, Saratoga Springs, Animal Kingdom Lodge (Kidani Village), and Old Key West have basketball hoops.

Good Meals, Great Times

GOOD MEALS, GREAT TIMES

Although fast food is in great supply, it is hardly the entire Walt Disney World dining story. Epcot adds international flavors to the WDW menu. Tempting options at the other theme parks, BoardWalk, and Disney Springs—not to mention new dining frontiers in the ever-growing brood of WDW resorts—make deciding where to eat a mouth-watering dilemma. Disney's ongoing effort to expand its culinary horizons has certainly been successful, producing prominent palate-pleasers such as Le Cellier Steakhouse, The Boathouse, Sanaa, California Grill, and Flying Fish, plus family favorites such as The Crystal Palace and 50's Prime Time Cafe.

Because there's such a large number and variety of eateries around the World, this chapter presents dining information in two formats. First, we've included an area-by-area rundown—a comprehensive section with descriptions of food purveyors, including sample menu options, that will prove most helpful when you get hungry in a particular part of the World. Second, we've compiled a collection of what we consider to be the best restaurants in a particular category. To select these standouts, we looked at the menu, theme, and overall enjoyability of each restaurant. And, of course, we sampled the food.

Finally, in the chapter's last section, we offer a guide to the varied lounges of the World, along with a briefing on Disney's reservations system and dinner show options—and assurance that great times are destined to follow.

The Restaurants of WDW In the Magic Kingdom

A lot has changed since Walt Disney World's original theme park opened in 1971. Back then, when it came to quelling hunger pangs, it was pretty much burger or bust. Nowadays, the options are a lot more diverse—with everything from egg rolls to cinnamon rolls, smoked turkey legs to lamb stew, and meatloaf to Marseilles-style mussels. And yes, you can still sink your teeth into a burger— beef or falafel! Regardless of your tastes or budget, the six "lands" in the Magic Kingdom boast a bounty of palate-pleasers for the whole family.

First Things First

The letters at the end of each entry refer to the meals served there: breakfast (B), lunch (L), dinner (D), or snacks (S).
- When you see a not-so-hidden Mickey (🐭) at the end of an entry, it means that eatery was a Disney Dining Plan* participant at press time (see page 20).
- Eateries in this chapter have been designated inexpensive (under $15), moderate ($15 to $36), expensive ($36 to $60), and very expensive ($60 and up). Prices are based on an adult-sized meal consisting of a beverage, an entrée, and either one appetizer, side order, or dessert (not including tax and tip). These classifications are reflected by dollar symbols at the end of each entry (all symbols are defined by the key at the bottom of each page). Note that breakfast and lunch generally cost less.
- All Walt Disney World restaurants and fast-food spots (except some with outside seating or at the Swan and Dolphin resorts) are nonsmoking only. Some restaurants at BoardWalk and Disney Springs may set aside outdoor sections for smokers.
- Reservations for table-service restaurants (and dinner shows) should be made 180 days in advance; call 407-WDW-DINE (939-3463), or visit *www.disneyworld.com/dining/*.
  We recommend calling 407-WDW-DINE to confirm all WDW restaurant information.
  *Disney Dining Plan locations are subject to change without notice.

Adventureland
TABLE SERVICE

JUNGLE NAVIGATION CO. LTD. SKIPPER CANTEEN: Known to many as "The Jungle Cruise Restaurant," this jovial joint is run by off-duty Jungle Cruise skippers—and the spirit of the ride permeates the place in a most amusing manner. The menu, infused with Asian, African, and South American influences, has starters such as Ginger's "Croc" of hot and sour soup, Falls Family Falafel, and shumai. Entrées at the Skipper Canteen include sustainable fish, curried vegetable stew, rice noodle bowls, and Trader Sam's Head-on shrimp. Beer, wine, and soft drinks are served. The eatery opens daily at 11 A.M. LD·$$–$$$·🐭

FAST FOOD & SNACKS

ALOHA ISLE: After you sing with the birdies in the Enchanted Tiki Room, stop here for all things pineapple—juice, spears, floats, and the ever-popular Dole Whip frozen pineapple soft-serve dessert. This spot has been around forever—they are definitely doing something right. Note that Aloha Isle and Sunshine Tree Terrace have swapped locations. S·$·🐭

SUNSHINE TREE TERRACE: This snack stand, across from the Swiss Family Treehouse, lets you take a break with a refreshing Citrus Swirl (vanilla soft-serve swirled with orange slush, served in a cup). It's possible to get a cup of vanilla soft-serve ice cream, plus lemonade, hot chocolate, iced coffee, and other soft drinks. Sunshine Tree has been dishing out treats for as long as we can remember. S·$·🐭

TORTUGA TAVERN: The shady spot across from the Pirates of the Caribbean offers jumbo turkey legs, hot dogs served with chips, chocolate almond cake, and chocolate chip cookies. Soft drinks and fruit punch slushies are available, too—in a regular cup or in a souvenir light-up skull mug. LS·$–$$·🐭

Fantasyland
TABLE SERVICE

BE OUR GUEST: Nestled under Beast's Castle, this eatery transports guests into the realm of Disney's *Beauty and the Beast*. Guests sit in one of three dining rooms—the cavernous Ballroom, West Wing, or Rose Gallery—and enjoy a quick-service breakfast or lunch or a table-service dinner. (Reservations are required for all meals.)

Breakfast and lunch guests enter the Beast's parlor to place their orders at touch terminals. Quick-service meals are delivered via a clever bit of technology involving an "enchanted" rose. Breakfast selections include vegetable quiche, open-faced bacon and egg sandwiches, scrambled egg whites, and more. The lunch menu includes items such as *croque monsieur* (ham and Gruyère cheese sandwich), carved roast beef on a baguette, tuna niçoise salad, and vegetable quiche. The portions here are a bit smaller and the prices a bit steeper here than at other M.K. quick-service eateries. The kids' lunch menu includes whole-grain macaroni, carved-turkey sandwiches, and Mickey meatloaf. While many lunch guests gravitate toward the stately Ballroom, we head right for the West Wing—don't tell the Beast!

Dinner is a more upscale affair, with starters such as Marseilles-style mussels, French onion soup, and salad with a champagne vinaigrette. Entrées pay homage to a castle feast from the 1400s with braised beef, pan-seared chicken breast, lamb chop, pork chop, and seasonal sustainable catch with vegetables. Cupcakes and mousse-filled cream puffs are served tableside. Beer and wine are offered with the evening meal. Book as early as possible. BLD·$$–$$$·❤

CINDERELLA'S ROYAL TABLE: You don't have to be a royal to eat like one. At least, not in the Magic Kingdom. This regal eatery, tucked inside Cinderella Castle, is a high-ceilinged, majestic mead hall. It's tiny as Disney spots go, but there's no feeling cramped—thanks to a small number of tables and towering windows. Hosts and hostesses wear Renaissance-inspired garb and address guests as "my lady," or "my lord." Cinderella welcomes "Fairytale Dining" guests into her home all day and greets them in the Castle lobby, while her princess friends mingle in the dining room. Breakfast favorites include shrimp and grits, baked quiche, and caramel apple-stuffed French toast, along with traditional fare. Lunch and dinner showcase seasonal ingredients, with items such as beef tenderloin with shrimp, pork two ways (loin and belly), chicken, and fish. Sparkling wines and Champagne are available, but not included in the price of the meal.

The all-inclusive cost for breakfast ranges from about $54–$67 for adults and $33–$43 for kids (ages 3–9); lunch and dinner range from about $65–$85 for adults, $39–$65 for kids. Prices include tax and gratuity and may be higher during peak times of the year. Alcoholic beverages are not included. (A photo package is no longer included. Guests may pose with Cinderella and purchase a PhotoPass photo for $15 or use their

One Tough Ticket

Cinderella's Royal Table is consistently one of the most difficult restaurant reservations to secure at Walt Disney World. Why? For starters, Cinderella is one popular princess. And there's the allure of dining in the castle—the most famous landmark in the world's most popular theme park.

Potential guests may make a reservation by visiting *disneyworld.com/dining* or by calling 407-WDW-DINE (939-3463) at *exactly* 7 A.M. Eastern Standard Time, 180 days in advance. (It can't hurt to start dialing a few seconds early.) The meal must be paid for when the reservation is made. There's no charge for infants, but they must be included in the reservation.

Expect your credit card to be charged immediately upon making the reservation. Cancellations or changes to the reservation must be made at least 24 hours ahead to receive a full refund. The only one who can change or cancel a reservation is the one whose name is on the credit card. Reservations cannot be transferred. Guests using the Disney Dining Plan must also book the table with a credit card, but it will not be charged. However, two table-service credits are required for all meals here, as it is a "Signature" restaurant.

Whew! That's a lot of work for one dining experience. Is it worth it? Judging by the smiles we see day in and day out, we have to say yes.

own cameras free of charge.) Reservations are an absolute must. **A 180-day advance booking is necessary for all meals. Full payment is required at time of booking.** Guests staying at a Disney–owned-and-operated resort should note our Hot Tip on page 248.

Cancellations must be made at least 24 hours in advance to avoid paying full price. Cinderella recommends that you arrive a few minutes early. This is an extremely difficult table to reserve (see page 245)—so don't get little ones' hopes up until you actually book it. B L D • $ $ $ – $ $ $ $ • 🐭

FAST FOOD & SNACKS

BIG TOP TREATS: Inside the Big Top Souvenirs tent, this confectionery-counter serves character apples, caramel apples, cake pops, caramel corn, brownies, cookies, and Goofy's Glaciers (sweet, frosty slush treats). S • $ • 🐭

CHESHIRE CAFE: This small stand is a good spot to cool off with raspberry or lemonade slushies (which come with a souvenir Mickey straw), orange juice, cold brew coffee, hot tea, and bottled water. The cafe also serves pastries. The cold brew coffee makes us smile like the Cheshire Cat. S • $ • 🐭

THE FRIAR'S NOOK: A window by Storybook Treats, this nook sells hot dogs with chips, (very) plain and BBQ chicken mac and cheese, lemonade slushies, and soft drinks. Menu items are subject to change. The Friar's Nook operates on a seasonal basis. L S • $ – $ $ • 🐭

GASTON'S TAVERN: A cozy little lodge nestled in Fantasyland's Enchanted Forest, Gaston's serves ham-and-cheese-stuffed pretzels, macarons, chocolate croissants, warm cinnamon rolls, and soft drinks. The specialty of this teetotaling tavern? LeFou's Brew—a not-too-sweet concoction made from frozen apple juice with a hint of toasted marshmallow and topped with all-natural passion fruit-mango foam. It tends to please palates of all ages. And, yes, Gaston really does use antlers in all of his decorating. L D S • $ • 🐭

PINOCCHIO VILLAGE HAUS: One of the better spots to target with kids in tow, Pinocchio Village Haus is also a good place to take picky adult eaters. It may seem small from the outside, but there are many dining rooms through that door. One room boasts picture windows that overlook the It's a Small World loading area. It's fun to watch the boats bob by as you munch on lunch. Pinocchio offers pizza (aka flatbread), chicken parmesan sandwiches and pasta, tomato basil soup, chicken nuggets, Caesar salads, fries, bread sticks (served with marinara sauce), and soft drinks. For dessert there's chocolate cake and tiramasu gelato. Kids' picks include mac and cheese, PB&J, and pizza, all served with applesauce and yogurt. L D S • $ – $ $ • 🐭

PRINCE ERIC'S VILLAGE MARKET: Appropriately anchored across from The Little Mermaid attraction, this alfresco snack spot sells fresh fruit (grapes and pineapple), pickles, cookies, and ham and cheese pretzels. The prince also proffers all-natural lemonade, fountain beverages, and frozen lemonade. S • $ • 🐭

STORYBOOK TREATS: Ice cream fans enjoy this window next to the Many Adventures of Winnie the Pooh attraction. It offers soft-serve cones and cups (vanilla, chocolate, or swirl); hot fudge and strawberry sundaes; plus ice cream floats. Coffee, tea, hot cocoa, and soft drinks are also served. S • $ • 🐭

Frontierland
FAST FOOD & SNACKS

GOLDEN OAK OUTPOST: This little wagon offers chicken nuggets, waffle fries, chocolate chip cookies, and soft drinks. Fountain beverages can come in a Country Bear Jug (for about $10). The Outpost operates seasonally. L D S • $ – $ $ • 🐭

Healthier Options

Health-conscious folks need not abandon all restraint for want of suitable sustenance. Walt Disney World has phased out added trans fats and partially hydrogenated oils from food served in parks and resorts. Most restaurants offer low-fat, low-cholesterol, low-salt, low-carb, and vegetarian entrées. Even fast-food stands feature healthier fare such as salads, grilled chicken sandwiches, fresh fruit, and veggie burgers. The WDW trend toward healthier dining extends to kids' meals, too. They come with a beverage choice of low-fat milk, 100 percent fruit juice, or water, and a side dish such as unsweetened applesauce, baby carrots, or fresh fruit. These healthy selections are easy to find on menus throughout Walt Disney World—keep an eye out for the Mickey check symbol.

Liberty Square
TABLE SERVICE

LIBERTY TREE TAVERN: Step back in time at this Early American tavern where the detailed decor has a tendency to outdazzle the fare. Here, wallpaper looks as if it might have come from Colonial Williamsburg, the curtains hang from cloth loops, and the rooms are filled with mementos that might have been found in the homes of Thomas Jefferson, George Washington, and Ben Franklin. The restaurant is aptly located across from the Hall of Presidents attraction.

The à la carte lunch menu (available from 11 A.M. until 3 P.M. daily) includes crab, artichoke, and spinach dip for two, pot roast, turkey, fish & chips, pasta with shrimp, and New England clam chowder. Lunch offers a family-style option, too. The all-you-care-to-eat lunch and dinner feasts feature salad, carved pork, roast turkey, pot roast, mac and cheese, stuffing, and more—all served family style. The menu also features beer, wine, and hard cider. Dinner costs about $35 for adults and $19 for children ages 3 through 9. Some drinks—including those of the spirited variety—cost extra. Reservations are recommended (arrive about 20 minutes early). Disney characters do not visit here. **L D · $ $ – $ $ $ ·** 🐭

PECOS BILL TALL TALE INN & CAFE:
Pecos Bill has been feeding hungry cowpokes for more than 40 years. The look has changed over time, as have the offerings (the prices have gone up a bit, too). These days Pecos Bill is serving taco burgers, beef nachos, burritos, fajita platters, Southwest chicken, spicy beef salad, and Southwest burgers (topped with pepper jack cheese and served with tortilla chips). Churros, tres leches (sponge cake), and yogurt are available, too. Kids can choose mini corn dogs or mac and cheese. (Kids' meals come with applesauce and carrot sticks and low-fat milk or bottled water.) Pecos Bill has a variety of soft drinks—including raspberry lemonade slushies. Many fountain beverages can be served in a souvenir Country Bears jug. **L D S · $ $ ·** 🐭

WESTWARD HO!: Mosey on over to Westward Ho! for chips, chocolate chip cookies, frozen lemonade, and other soft drinks. Corn dogs are offered seasonally. It's across from Prairie Outpost & Supply. **S · $ ·** 🐭

Magic Kingdom Mealtime Tips

- The hours from 11 A.M. to 2 P.M., and again from about 5 P.M. to 7 P.M., are the mealtime rush hours in Magic Kingdom restaurants. Try to eat earlier or later whenever possible.

- When a fast-food restaurant has more than one station from which to order, don't just amble into the nearest queue. Instead, inspect them all, because those farthest from an entrance may have the shortest lines.

- Table-service restaurants offering full-scale meals may be less crowded at lunchtime than they are during traditional dinner hours.

- To avoid queues, eat at a restaurant that offers reservations—Tony's Town Square, Crystal Palace, or the Plaza Restaurant on Main Street; Adventureland's Jungle Navigation Co. Ltd. Skipper Canteen; Liberty Tree Tavern in Liberty Square; Fantasyland's Be Our Guest or Cinderella's Royal Table. Reservations may be made by calling 407-WDW-DINE (939-3463), via *www.disneyworld.com*, or by using the My Disney Experience app. Note that it is next to impossible to get same-day reservations.

- Consider taking the monorail to the Contemporary, Polynesian, or Grand Floridian to have lunch or dinner in a resort restaurant, and then return to the Magic Kingdom after you eat. (Remember to keep your ticket or MagicBand handy for re-entry to the park.)

🐭 Disney Dining Plan participant at press time

FAST FOOD & SNACKS

COLUMBIA HARBOUR HOUSE: This lively spot adds some interesting (and healthy!) options to the quick-service lineup, including broccoli peppercorn salad served with chicken, grilled salmon with couscous and steamed veggie, tuna on toasted multigrain bread (aka the Anchors Away sandwich), yogurt, and the Lighthouse sandwich (with hummus, tomato, and broccoli slaw). You may find lobster rolls, fried shrimp, chicken nuggets, shrimp mac and cheese, chicken pot pie, vegetarian chili, and clam chowder, too. For dessert, there's seasonal cobbler. Kids' selections include chicken nuggets, mac and cheese, salad with chicken, and tuna sandwiches.

Disney has done up this fast-food emporium with style—complete with antiques, model ships, harpoons, nautical instruments, and lace tieback curtains. In addition to the chowder, we savor the salmon and love the Lighthouse sandwich. The upstairs dining rooms are often less crowded than those on the first floor. **L D S · $ – $ $ · ❦**

SLEEPY HOLLOW: Often missed by guests rushing toward park hot spots, this window has a lot to offer. Breakfast (plain waffles and waffles with ham, egg, tomato, and cheese) is served until noon. After that, look for sweet and spicy chicken waffle sandwiches, corn dogs served with housemade chips, baked potatoes, waffles with heavenly toppings (fresh fruit, chocolate hazelnut spread, whipped cream, etc.), ice cream cookie sandwiches, and funnel cakes (dusted with powdered sugar or strawberries and cream). Drink choices include lemonade with wildberry foam, coffee, hot cocoa, milk, and orange juice. Sleepy Hollow is near the Liberty Square bridge. Eat on the patio and get a stunning view of Cinderella Castle at no extra charge. **B L D S · $ – $ $ · ❦**

Main Street
TABLE SERVICE

THE CRYSTAL PALACE: What's the big draw here? Winnie the Pooh and his pals host meals all day. One of the Magic Kingdom's cherished landmarks, this spot takes its architectural cues from a similar structure that once stood in New York and from San Francisco's Conservatory of Flowers, which still graces that city's Golden Gate Park. The place is spacious, with tables scattered amid a Victorian-style indoor garden complete with flowers and hanging greenery. Tables in the front look out on flower beds, while those at the east end have views of a courtyard. The restaurant is on a path at the end of Main Street, U.S.A.

The all-you-care-to-eat buffet features a variety of breakfast items every morning; for lunch and dinner there's spit-roasted carved meat, chicken, pastas, fish, sides, and desserts. The salad bar, with its peel-and-eat shrimp, pasta salads, greens, and grains, is most satisfying. The cost for breakfast starts at about $32 for adults and $19 for kids ages 3 through 9; lunch and dinner start at about $45 for adults and $27 for children. Expect visits from Pooh and friends from the Hundred Acre Wood during your meal. Reservations are a must. BLD·$$–$$$· ❤

PLAZA RESTAURANT: This windowed establishment next to Plaza Ice Cream Parlor is done up in mirrors with sinuous Art Nouveau frames. The menu has salads, burgers, meatloaf, and hot and cold sandwiches such as fried green tomato, grilled Reuben, cheese steak, Plaza club, and tuna salad—plus hand-dipped milk shakes, chocolate cake, and caramel apple pie à la mode. Reservations are recommended. LD·$$· ❤

TONY'S TOWN SQUARE: Tony's decor was inspired by Walt Disney's feature *Lady and the Tramp* (which can be viewed in the waiting area). The menu offers Italian specialties, including calamari, spaghetti, and pizza. Entrées include ravioli, chicken parmesan, shrimp scampi, baked rigatoni, grilled pork chop, strip steak, and sustainable fish of the day. If you require gluten-free pasta, just ask—Tony's happy to accommodate. Beer, wine, and sparkling fruit beverages are offered, too. Top it off with an Italian sweet (gelato, tiramisú, or chocolate cake with hazelnut filling) or foamy cappuccino. If you time it right, you can fold your napkin, pay the bill, and mosey out to Main Street to enjoy the fireworks from one of the best vantage points in the park. Reservations are highly recommended. LD·$$$· ❤

HOT TIP!

Tomorrowland Terrace's dessert party offers unlimited snacks and a viewing of Happily Ever After, the Magic Kingdom's fireworks show. Prices vary, but expect to pay up to $79 per adult and $47 per child. For details and reservations up to 180 days in advance, call 407-WDW-DINE (939-3463). The treats are served in the waterside dining area at Tomorrowland Terrace, while fireworks viewing is offered from the dessert party's reserved viewing area on Main Street, U.S.A.

Magic Kingdom Resorts

Is the Magic Kingdom open late when you plan to visit? If so, consider heading over to the Contemporary, Polynesian, Grand Floridian, or Wilderness Lodge to have an early dinner, and then return to finish the day at the park. Each of the aforementioned resorts is reachable by monorail and/or water taxi. Remember to keep sporting that MagicBand if you used it for admission or keep your ticket handy for re-entry into the Magic Kingdom. (You will have to pass through a security check to re-enter the park.) Transportation generally runs for one hour after the park's posted closing time for the day (this does not include Extra Magic Hours). Note that, as with most Walt Disney World eateries, reservations are necessary at resort restaurants. Don't forget to book that table!

FAST FOOD & SNACKS

CASEY'S CORNER: Casey's is a grand slam for baseball fans—and those who just happen to love the food associated with "America's pastime," hot dogs and Cracker Jack! This old-fashioned stop is on the west side of Main Street (near the Crystal Palace). Tables line the sidewalk, where a ragtime pianist often tickles the ivories. There's a back room with indoor seating. The fare retains the baseball game mood—hot dogs, chili cheese dogs, mac and cheese dogs, corn dog nuggets, fries, cotton candy, Cracker Jack, and soft drinks. Hot dogs come in regular and foot-long sizes. Note that it is possible to order items à la carte. For breakfast, choose from muffins, bagels, croissants, and doughnuts. Casey's is a Magic Kingdom classic. BLDS·$–$$· ❤

MAIN STREET BAKERY: This Main Street landmark resembles a turn-of-the-twentieth-century bakery and coffee shop. If the sight of this old-fashioned storefront doesn't lure you in, the aroma most certainly will. The Main Street Bakery is a nice choice for a light breakfast, salads, sandwiches, or coffee break. The vast array of tea and coffee concoctions comes courtesy of Starbucks. Assorted pastries, fresh-baked cookies, fruit and veggies, and other snacks are also served. BLDS·$–$$· ❤

PLAZA ICE CREAM PARLOR: Plaza boasts the Kingdom's largest variety of hand-scooped ice cream flavors. It's perfect for a before-the-parade or an on-the-way-out-of-the-park nosh.

They have light breakfast items, too. The early morning selections, which are served until 11 A.M., include Mickey waffles, doughnuts, muffins, fruit parfait, and cereal. Of course, the big draw here is the ice cream. Guests of all ages enjoy the Mickey Mouse kids' cone. To keep things moving, choose flavors and desired number of scoops before jumping in line. They have floats and sundaes—including those served in a waffle bowl and the Mickey's Kitchen Sink for two (which is actually a sink-like version of the Mouse's red trousers). B S · $ · 🐭

Tomorrowland
FAST FOOD & SNACKS

AUNTIE GRAVITY'S GALACTIC GOODIES: Ice cream may not seem futuristic, but chances are it'll be around at least another billion years, give or take. Auntie G's offers up chilly smoothies made from nonfat yogurt (strawberry-banana, orange, and raspberry), soft-serve ice cream (chocolate, vanilla, or swirl), sundaes, and floats. Soft drinks are available, too. There's virtually no atmosphere in this corner of the galaxy, but we still gravitate toward the goodies. S · $ · 🐭

COSMIC RAY'S STARLIGHT CAFE: Ray's seems to offer something for everyone. Head here for rotisserie chicken, pulled pork, BBQ pork sandwiches, grilled chicken club sandwiches, chicken breast nuggets, bacon cheeseburgers, chicken sandwiches, veggie burgers, falafel burgers, quarter-pound hot dogs, and Greek salads. Sides include fries and a veggie. A kosher selection is available. An Audio-Animatronics lounge lizard known as Sonny Eclipse entertains in the dining area. Note that Cosmic Ray's Starlight Cafe has ample indoor and outdoor seating. L D S · $ – $ $ · 🐭

LUNCHING PAD AT ROCKETTOWER PLAZA: If it's a snack or simple meal you're after, stop at the base of the Astro Orbiter located in the center of Tomorrowland's concrete plaza. This quick-service window dispenses hot dogs, ham-and-cheese-stuffed pretzels, cream-cheese pretzels, Mickey pretzels, chips, soda slushies, and soft drinks. L D S · $ – $ $ · 🐭

TOMORROWLAND TERRACE: This stark spot serves simple fare such as sandwiches, burgers, chicken strips, and salads. Some tables on the lower terrace afford views of Cinderella Castle. It operates seasonally. L S · $ $ · 🐭

Baby Needs

Babies. They're a needy lot. Fortunately, most of the requisite supplies can be found somewhere at Disney World—if you know where to look. Formula and jarred food can be purchased at the Baby Care Center in each of the theme parks and at every WDW resort. Most restaurants have kids' menus with toddler-friendly food (mac and cheese, chicken nuggets, and the like).

If your baby is partial to a specific formula or brand of food, consider shipping a box of it to your hotel before you leave home. Keep in mind that there are several grocery stores near Walt Disney World. If you have a car, it is worth the trip (a Guest Relations clerk can help with directions). The selections are more varied, as are the prices. Stash perishables in an in-room refrigerator—they are standard in all Disney–owned-and-operated resorts. Some other points of interest regarding baby diners at Walt Disney World:

- Most eateries have high chairs and booster seats. Request one when you make your restaurant reservation.

- Stroller use inside restaurants is discouraged due to fire codes. Park it outside.

- WDW restaurants are often chilly. Be sure to pack a sweater or blanket.

- Be it a fast-food or table-service restaurant, bring toys to keep little ones busy.

- The following resorts have 24-hour snack bars: Grand Floridian, Dolphin, Polynesian Village, Wyndham, and Hilton Buena Vista Palace (on Hotel Plaza Blvd.). The middle-of-the-night pickings may be slim, but milk and cereal are served around the clock.

- If you'd like a spot to nurse an infant, head to a Baby Care Center in any of the theme parks. They all have rooms with rocking chairs.

- If you're headed for a long day in a theme or water park, pack simple, healthy snacks for hungry toddlers. And look for the Mickey check symbol on menus (see page 246 for details).

- To make your dining experience less harried, consider feeding your baby before you get to the restaurant.

- If you prefer organic milk (and more) for your children, consider ordering from *gardengrocer.com* or swinging by a local grocery store (for details, see Baby Food on page 47).

GOOD MEALS, GREAT TIMES

In Epcot

The eclectic, international lineup of fare offered here threatens to overshadow the attractions themselves. With no fewer than 11 different countries permanently represented in the World Showcase section of the park, Epcot provides guests with the opportunity to eat their way around the world without leaving Central Florida. Less ambitious diners will likely have their taste needs met, too—there's a bountiful food court in Epcot's Future World, as well as a smattering of simple yet satiating snack spots and quick-service locations. Reservations are an important factor in the Epcot dining equation; call 407-WDW-DINE (939-3463) up to 180 days in advance.

DID YOU KNOW?

More than 30 tons of fruits and vegetables have been grown at The Land pavilion in Epcot and served to guests dining in Walt Disney World restaurants.

Future World

TABLE SERVICE

CORAL REEF (The Seas with Nemo and Friends): This water-themed restaurant is all about nibbling on creatively prepared fish under the watchful eyes of their brethren. The place is decorated in cool greens and blues to complement its surroundings, and every table has a panoramic view of a living coral reef; some are right up against the glass. (Don't worry: You are not actually eating Epcot residents—most of Disney's catches come fresh from fishing boats each day.) Menu items run the gamut from a bounty of fresh fish and shellfish, including shrimp, mahi mahi, and salmon—prepared in a number of ways—to grilled New York strip steak and oven-roasted chicken breast for those who are satisfied by simply spying on the fish. The menu tends to vary seasonally. Reservations are recommended. **L D · $ $ $ · 🐭**

GARDEN GRILL (The Land): Guests are often so distracted by the sights and the jovial hosts (Chip, Dale, and friends) that they don't realize the restaurant is actually moving. As the eatery revolves, and it does so quite slowly, it moves past scenery featured in the Living with the Land boat ride. The view was designed with diners in mind, and provides them with a peek into a farmhouse window that's out of viewing range of the waterborne passengers.

Breakfast includes sticky buns, fruits, scrambled eggs, bacon, ham, hash-brown-style potato barrels, and Mickey waffles. For lunch and dinner, the Grill serves salad, pot roast, turkey breast, sausage with peppers and onions, mac and cheese, buttermilk mashed potatoes, french fries, fresh veggies (some of which are grown in The Land Pavilion), and short cake. Cost for breakfast is about $32 for adults, $19 for kids; lunch and dinner run about $45 for adults, $27 for kids. (Prices are higher during peak times of year.) Soft drinks are included. Meals are served family style (communal platters for the table; there is no kids' menu). It's not the most kid-friendly presentation, as gravy is involved (at lunch and dinner) and food items touch and overlap. Reservations are recommended.

The restaurant moves in a circle. It's imperceptible to most, but if you are highly sensitive to motion, it may be best to dine in a more stationary environment. **B L D · $ $ – $ $ $ · 🐭**

FAST FOOD & SNACKS

ELECTRIC UMBRELLA (Innoventions Plaza): This large establishment is a good bet when the weather is temperate enough to allow dining at the tables just outside—or when bound for the World Showcase with finicky eaters in tow. (There are indoor tables, too.) Offerings include seasonal salad with chicken, 3-cheese pizza, chicken nuggets, French Dip burger, sausage and pepper sandwich, fries, and soft drinks. Dessert options include strawberry cheesecake, cupcakes, and no-sugar-added brownies. It's possible to get yogurt or apple slices instead of fries with some menu selections. **L D S · $ – $ $ · 🐭**

FOUNTAIN VIEW (Innoventions Plaza): Set beside that drama queen of a water fountain known as Fountain of Nations, this popular Epcot destination is actually a Starbucks coffee shop. As such, it is an ideal spot for a satisfying java jolt, a light meal, or a sweet snack. Sandwiches, pastries, cookies, and fresh fruit are available— as are teas, Frappuccino drinks, souvenir mugs, and more. B L D S · $ – $ $ · ❤

SUNSHINE SEASONS (The Land): It's the closest thing to a mall food court you'll find in a WDW park, but a bit more upscale. Located near the entrance to Soarin' Around the World on the pavilion's lower level, Sunshine Seasons is an ideal destination for parties who can't quite agree on any one type of fare—there's bound to be something for everyone. Tables are scattered in several seating areas, beneath colorful hot-air balloons. Snagging a table can be a challenge during peak mealtimes. (There can be a bit of pedestrian congestion, too, thanks to the enormous popularity of the Soarin' attraction.)

Sandwich Shop is home of the vegan flatbread with grilled vegetables, fish tacos, and more. The **Soup and Salad Shop**'s creative salads include Power Salad (with oak-fired chicken, quinoa, almonds, and honey vinagrette) and seared tuna with sesame rice wine dressing. Soups are made fresh daily. **Grill Shop** features rotisserie chicken and slow-roasted pork. Sustainable catch of the day is also offered. **Wok Shop** serves Mongolian beef with fried rice, sweet and sour chicken, and shrimp stir-fry. The **Bakery** offers freshly made desserts. In addition to the seasonally inspired rotating desserts—expect to find brownies, ice

cream bars, and other sweet treats. There is a grab-and-go area with items such as hummus and pita, fruit and cheese plates, fresh vegetables, hard-cooked eggs, salads, and cookies.

A word of advice: It's a good idea to split up your party and stand in several lines at the same time. That'll increase your chances of actually eating together. Before doing so, select a table. That way, everyone in the group will know where to meet after they forage for their meals. It's also a nice spot to take a load off your feet while waiting for your Soarin' Fastpass+ window to kick in. B L D S · $ – $ $ · ❤

World Showcase
TABLE SERVICE

AKERSHUS ROYAL BANQUET HALL (Norway): The Norwegian castle of Akershus dominates Oslo's harbor and is considered the most impressive of all Norway's medieval fortresses. It is actually half fortress and half palace, and many of its grand halls continue to be used for elaborate state banquets. At Epcot's castle-like Akershus, guests are treated to authentic royal Norwegian cuisine. They also get to dine with royalty—as Disney princesses interact with guests during all meals.

An all-inclusive price entitles hungry Epcot guests to enjoy dishes that don't often leave Scandinavia. Included in the family-style sampling of the Norwegian *koldbord* are smoked salmon and seafood, Norwegian cheese, and chilled salads. Norwegian-inspired entrées

PHOTO BY JILL SAFRO

GOOD MEALS, GREAT TIMES

Let 'em Eat Cake!

What could possibly make celebrating a special occasion at Walt Disney World even more special? How about a custom-made, personalized cake? You can have one delivered to just about any table-service eatery on Disney property. Simply call the Cake Hotline (407-827-2253) at least 72 hours in advance to place an order.

If you miss the ordering deadline, don't despair—no one has to go cake-less at Disney World (perish the thought!). Spontaneous cake delivery is possible, provided you request one at the podium when you check in at a restaurant. At meal's end, you will receive a 6-inch non-personalized cake. It will add about $23, plus tax (and a few more calories), to the total.

include seafood, beef, and poultry selections. A kids' menu is available. Dessert and soft drinks are included.

For breakfast, guests enjoy the all-you-care-to-eat fare (bacon, eggs, potatoes, and sausage are brought to your table) as Disney characters mingle with diners. Belle, Ariel, Jasmine, Snow White, Sleeping Beauty, and Mary Poppins have made appearances. The character appearance schedule varies. Reservations are necessary. Cancellations must be made at least 24 hours in advance to avoid paying the $10-per-person penalty. Breakfast costs about $47 for adults (age 10 and up) and $29 for kids (ages 3–9); lunch and dinner run about $57 (adults) and $34 (kids). Prices may be higher during peak seasons. BLD·$$$·❤

BIERGARTEN (Germany): Located in the back of the St. Georgsplatz in the Germany pavilion, this tiered eatery is a jolly stop on the Epcot world tour. This is partly because of the long tables that encourage togetherness among guests. But equal credit for the *gemütlich* (pleasant) atmosphere goes to the spot's lively entertainment.

There are scheduled appearances by Bavarian musicians—each clad in lederhosen or dirndl—who play accordions, cowbells, a musical saw, and a harp-like stringed instrument known as the "wooden laughter." The entertaining shows take place at scheduled times in the dining room. The schedule is usually posted at the door. Diners are usually invited to join the fun on the dance floor.

The food is hearty and presented as an all-you-care-to-eat buffet, featuring bratwurst,

frankfurters, rotisserie chicken, spaetzle, German meatloaf, pork schnitzel, assorted cold dishes, potato salad, cucumber salad, pretzel rolls, and many more German specialties. Entertainment is intermittent and there's plenty of time to enjoy the pleasant setting. Reservations are recommended, particularly during peak seasons (book as early as possible). LD·$$–$$$·❤

CHEFS DE FRANCE (France): "Bright lights, big dining room" describes this airy Parisian brasserie. With some of France's best chefs responsible for this kitchen, the results are usually rewarding. The menu features fresh ingredients readily available from Florida purveyors, though the restaurant imports as many key ingredients from France as possible.

The offerings are in the nouvelle French cuisine style, which involves lighter sauces using less cream and butter than in classic French cooking. Menu items include broiled salmon, beef short ribs, and roasted chicken. Soups and appetizers such as onion soup, lobster bisque, and escargot are all-day staples. Chocolate tarts and crème brûlée are dessert specialties of note.

Chefs de France is one of the most popular (and pricey) World Showcase eateries, year in and year out. It is a Disney Dining Plan Signature restaurant. Reservations are recommended (book as far in advance as possible). LD·$$$–$$$$·❤

LE CELLIER STEAKHOUSE (Canada): This wine-cellar-like spot is a favorite place for a memorable meal. The atmospheric eatery has low ceilings, stone walls, and candlelight.

There's a full menu of tempting items, starting with a (complimentary) bread basket that includes fresh-baked pretzel roll, plus sourdough and whole-grain creations. Considered a Signature restaurant for both lunch and dinner (translation: It costs more to eat here than at most other WDW places and requires two Dining Plan credits per meal), the steakhouse specializes in high-quality beef. The filet mignon with white truffle-butter sauce is a real crowd-pleaser. Many choose to start with a longtime favorite, cheddar cheese soup made with Moosehead beer, but the *poutine* (fries with cheddar, truffle salt, and a red wine reduction) are a popular starter, too. Canadian beers and wines make for memorable pairings. A three-course, fixed-price menu is offered (for about $49) during the first hour or two of the restaurant's lunch service. Reservations are a must—this is an extremely popular and relatively tiny restaurant. LD·$$$–$$$$·❤

GOOD MEALS, GREAT TIMES

LA HACIENDA DE SAN ANGEL (Mexico): Open for dinner (starting at 4 P.M.), this festive facility fits nicely on the shore of World Showcase Lagoon. The menu features starters such as *queso fundido* (warm cheese with poblano pepper and chorizo); *agua chile de camaron* (shrimp ceviche), and *crema de elote* (creamy corn soup). Entrées include a mixed grill for two, short ribs with salsa de chile, and grilled tilapia. We are particularly fond of the *parrillada del mar* (seafood platter for two). For dessert, there's chocolate mousse, corn ice cream, and fruit empanadas.

If you book a table for about 8:30 P.M., you may be treated to prime seats for IllumiNations (Epcot's nightly pyrotechnic extravaganza). While windowside tables cannot be guaranteed, there's always standing room. As an added bonus, the show's soundtrack is pumped into the eatery. It's quite impressive. **D · $$$ · 🐭**

MONSIEUR PAUL (France): One flight above Chefs de France, this eatery is filled with mementos of Chef Paul Bocuse's extraordinary culinary honors. It is an elegant bistro, but a bit less formal than its predecessor, Bistro de Paris.

The menu was crafted by Chef Francesco Santin, who worked with Chef Bocuse in his restaurant in Lyon, France, for 15 years. It features starters such as wild-caught frog legs, lobster salad, and *vichyssoise classique*. Main course selections include grilled beef tenderloin with mushroom crust, roasted free-range chicken, and seared scallops with vegetables. The wine list is *très* French. You might want to stroll around the World Showcase promenade to walk off your meal—and your warm chocolate almond cake (with raspberry coulis in the center) and hazelnut ice cream. Note that this is a Disney Dining Plan Signature eatery (requiring two full-service meal redemptions). The dress code is "resort casual"—no tank tops or tattered clothing, please. Reservations are recommended. **D · $$$$ · 🐭**

NINE DRAGONS (China): This stop on Epcot's international restaurant tour transports guests to modern China when seated in the palatial dining room. À la carte selections allow guests to sample provincial cuisines. The menu includes starters such as General Tso's chicken buns, dumplings in chili sauce, and pot stickers. Entrée selections range from sweet-and-sour pork to Kung Pao chicken, veggie stir-fry, five-spiced fish, and Chinese barbecue. (No MSG is used in any dish.)

A selection of Chinese teas, beers, and wines is available. Desserts include banana cheesecake egg roll, strawberry red bean ice cream, caramel-ginger ice cream, and ginger cake. Reservations are recommended. **LD · $$–$$$ · 🐭**

RESTAURANT MARRAKESH (Morocco): It's not every day that you can slip into an exquisitely tiled Moroccan palace and be entertained by belly dancers and musicians as you polish off a plate of Moroccan cuisine. Want to know how authentic this place is? The king of Morocco sent craftspeople to Epcot to make sure they were creating a real Moroccan atmosphere. (Unfortunately, he didn't send his chef—the fare isn't apt to dazzle aficionados of Moroccan cuisine.) The menu includes roast lamb, chicken brochette, beef shish kebab, and couscous. Sampler platters are available. Reservations are recommended, but it is often possible to get in without too much of a wait. **LD · $$$ · 🐭**

ROSE & CROWN PUB AND DINING ROOM (United Kingdom): Don't let the word "pub" throw you. While this place serves up some excellent brews, its Dining Room is also known for such crowd-pleasing dishes as traditional fish and chips, steak, fish, shepherd's pie, and bangers and mash (sausages with mashed potatoes). Appetizer-wise, we recommend the Rose & Crown cheese plate. One of the side dishes that makes us happy? Mushy peas! (Sort of a lumpy-but-flavorful pea porridge.) For dessert, there are Jaffa tarts, sticky toffee pudding, and Banoffee tarts. Bass ale from England, Harp lager and Guinness stout from Ireland, and more are on tap. (They're served cold, not at room temperature, as some British guests may prefer.)

Special Requests

All WDW table-service eateries that accept reservations strive to accommodate food allergies and intolerances such as gluten, salt, wheat, shellfish, lactose, peanuts, etc., if requested at least 72 hours in advance. Kosher meals may be pre-ordered up to a day ahead at many table-service eateries. Note that 48 hours' notice is needed for eateries at the Swan and Dolphin, Yak & Yeti restaurant, and Rainforest Cafe. (Kosher meals are not available at Garden View Afternoon Tea [Grand Floridian] and Epcot's Teppan Edo and Tokyo Dining.) Make your request when booking your table by calling 407-WDW-DINE (939-3463). Note that kosher requests require a credit card guarantee and must be canceled within 24 hours of the reservation to avoid a penalty.

The decor is pretty—mainly polished woods, etched glass, and brass accents. In fine weather, it's nice to lunch under a canopy on the terrace outside and watch the FriendShip water taxis cruising across World Showcase Lagoon.

As for the pub's architecture, it incorporates three distinct styles. The wall facing the World Showcase promenade is reminiscent of urban establishments popular in Britain since the 1890s, while that on the south side evokes London's seventeenth-century Ye Olde Cheshire Cheese pub, with its brick-walled flagstone terrace, slate roof, and half-timbered exterior. The canal facade, with its stone wall and clay-tile roof, reminds visitors of the charming pubs so common in the English countryside.

The pub section of the Rose & Crown serves such snacks as fish and chips—along with all the brews noted earlier and traditional British mixed

Food & Wine Festival

Every year, Epcot's hopping dining scene expands exponentially in what's known as the International Food & Wine Festival. The event, which usually runs from September through early November, is a celebration of the flavors of dozens of nations. Those countries without permanent stations at World Showcase set up temporary displays from which authentic samples of food, wine, and other spirits are sold. The samples range in price from about $3 to $10. It's possible to eat and drink your way around the world for about the same price as some table-service restaurants.

The festival also features demonstrations from top chefs, as well as wine and cooking seminars. For details, call 407-824-4321, or visit *www.disneyworld.com*. Make reservations as early as you can—this is one popular festival.

drinks such as shandies (Bass ale and Sprite) and black and tans (Bass Ale and Guinness stout). The pub is quite popular, so it's often necessary to queue up at the door. Note that the pub section also spills out onto the World Showcase promenade—where the first-come, first-served waterside tables make for a nice spot to sip a drink and, possibly, enjoy some fish and chips from a nearby snack stand. Reservations are not available in the pub areas, but recommended for the adjacent dining room.

If you're lucky, you'll catch a performance by the pub's artist-in-residence. Feel free to sing along as she bangs out familiar tunes on her modest upright piano. She is quite a crowd-pleaser, so expect lots of company at the bar as you sip your pint. **LDS·$$$·♥**

SAN ANGEL INN (Mexico): The food at this establishment located to the rear of the plaza inside the Mexico pyramid (a corporate cousin of the famous Mexico City restaurant of the same name) may come as a surprise to most visitors. Although the tacos and tortillas and other specialties that usually fall under the broad umbrella of Mexican food are available, the menu also offers a wide variety of more subtly flavored fish, poultry, and meat dishes.

To start, there's *tostadas de tinga* (pulled chicken on fried corn tortillas with black refried beans, green tomatillo sauce, queso fresco, and sour cream) and beef tacos, plus much more. Entrées include *carne asada* (New York strip steak served with cheese enchilada), *peto an salsa poblana* (grilled wahoo fish served over roasted potatoes with vegetables and poblano sauce), and grilled fish tacos. The dinner menu is a bit more elaborate than at lunch. Mexican desserts are largely unfamiliar to many diners, with the possible exception of the *mousse de chocolate*, but are well worth trying. *Bebidas* (drinks) such as Dos Equis, Sol, and Tecate beer, and margaritas

make good accompaniments. Note that some of the dishes here have a bit of a kick. As of our last visit, this eatery does not offer hot sauce as a condiment. (Though they can whip you up a batch, should you have a hankerin' for heat.) Reservations are recommended. L D · $ $ $ · 🐭

SPICE ROAD TABLE (Morocco): Built on the shores of World Showcase Lagoon, this restaurant's style was inspired by outdoor cafés along the shores of the Mediterranean. Popular for its stunning views of IllumiNations and its freshly prepared, palate-pleasing fare, Spice Road Table has made its way onto Epcot diners' must-do list. The eatery's whitewashed facade is accented in icy shades of blue from the famous "Blue City of Chefchaouen" in Morocco's Rif Mountains.

The menu features Mediterranean small plates: zesty harissa chicken rolls; lamb sliders; salted cod croquettes; mussels with preserved lemons and tomato sauce baked in an earthenware tagine pot; Moroccan merguez sausage with a fresh tomato salad; garlicky jumbo shrimp in a spicy chile pepper sauce; fried calamari, and more. Mediterranean specialty entrées include coriander-crusted rack of lamb and the mixed grill skewers. Dessert selections include a chocolate pyramid with almond ice cream, saffron and lemon custard, and almond and rosewater cake. Soft drinks, beer, wine, and organic sangria are served. Reservations are recommended. L D S · $ $ – $ $ $ · 🐭

> ## HOT TIP!
> Thanks in part to the Disney Dining Plan and "Epcot After 4" (an admission pass for locals), World Showcase tends to be exceptionally busy in the evening hours year-round. Reservations for table-service eateries are an absolute must.

TEPPAN EDO (Japan): Tokyo Dining's lively neighbor, Teppan Edo offers a dinner-as-show experience. Guests sit around a large teppan grill and watch as a nimble chef demonstrates just how quickly enough chicken, beef, seafood, and vegetables can be chopped, seasoned, and stir-fried. Teppan Edo entrées are sizzling and satisfying. Soups, salads, sushi, desserts, and cocktails (including Japanese beer and sake) are also on the menu. Don't wear your finest attire: There's always the potential for a little splattering. Reservations are recommended. L D · $ $ – $ $ $ · 🐭

TOKYO DINING (Japan): A nice escape for lunch or dinner, this restaurant features freshly prepared sushi, sashimi, edamame, tempura, grilled items, bento boxes, and prix-fixe lunch specials. Other choices: garden salad, ika salad, miso soup, grilled chicken, grilled salmon, and grilled steak/shrimp tempura combo. Finish with chocolate ginger cake, green tea cheesecake, or soft-serve ice cream. Beer, wine, sake, and specialty cocktails are available. There are a few windowside tables that offer a great view of IllumiNations—Reflections of Earth. Reservations are recommended. L D · $ $ – $ $ $ · 🐭

TUTTO GUSTO (Italy): A welcome retreat for grown-ups, Tutto Gusto is a wine bar that transports guests to an ancient Italian wine cellar. Tutto Italia's next-door neighbor offers more than 200 wines, including grappa; Italian beers and specialty drinks; coffee concoctions; and a marvelous small-plate menu. Nibble on imported Italian cheeses, Sicilian eggplant salad, marinated olives, seafood salad, white asparagus, cured sliced meats, paninis (pressed sandwiches on ciabatta baguette), pastas, and more. For dessert, consider strawberries with mascarpone cream, cannoli, or mocha tiramisu. Reservations are not accepted—come in the afternoon for the smallest crowds. *Salute!* L D S · $ $ – $ $ $

TUTTO ITALIA (Italy): There's an impressive menu at one of the most popular (and expensive) World Showcase destinations, and its outdoor tables make it one of the more appealing spots for an Epcot meal. Traditional starters such as fried calamari, fresh mozzarella with tomatoes and basil, and Caesar salad can actually make a meal in and of themselves. Entrées extend toward

> ## Frozen Ever After Sparkling Dessert Party
>
> A sweet way to end an Epcot day, this soirée features VIP viewing of Illuminations, a steady stream of sweet and savory treats, and an after-hours boat ride at Norway's Frozen Ever After attraction. Snack selections include ice cream, cupcakes, fresh fruit, and cheese fondue. Beer, wine, cocktails, and soft drinks (melted snow!) are included. The one-hour party takes place on select evenings. It costs about $79 for adults and $47 for kids (including tax and gratuity). To make a reservation call 407-939-3463, or visit *mydisneyexperience.com*.

One-Stop Sweet Shop

A yummy destination on the World Showcase landscape, the Germany pavilion's Karamell-Küche is sure to satisfy your sweet tooth—provided that you're a fan of fresh, gooey caramel draped or drizzled over chocolate, cookies, crunchy apples, and much more. The line is often long, but it's worth the wait.

fresh pastas—spaghetti, ravioli, fettuccine, and lasagna. The menu includes fish, steak, and chicken. Paninis are offered at lunch. For dessert, choose from gelato, sorbet, cannoli, tiramisu, and cheesecake. Wine, beer, teas, coffees, and cocktails are served. Reservations are recommended. **L D · $$$ – $$$$ · ❤**

VIA NAPOLI (Italy): It was a long time coming (roughly 30 years!), but Epcot's Italy finally has a pizza place. Tucked into the back of the pavilion, this welcome addition has a casual atmosphere and seating for 300. How serious are they about the pizza? They import the flour from Italy and select water so the crust tastes as authentically Neapolitan as possible. In addition to pizza, specialties include pastas, salads, sandwiches, soft drinks, and Italian wine. The Aqua Fresca is quite refreshing (signature seasonal fruit cooler). Dessert offerings include *zeppole di catarina* (ricotta cheese fritters), gelato, sorbet, and tiramasu. Reservations are recommended. **L D · $$ – $$$ · ❤**

FAST FOOD & SNACKS

BLOCK & HANS (American Adventure): Mickey-shaped pretzels, anyone? You can get them here, along with cheese-y dipping sauce. Wash them down with a seasonal craft beer, black cherry hard cider, or bottled water. **S · $ · ❤**

LES HALLES BOULANGERIE PATISSERIE (France): The pastry shop in the France pavilion is not difficult to find: Just follow the wonderful aroma, then watch the crowds lining up to enjoy the fresh baguettes (standard and mini), croissants, quiches, cheese plates, ham and cheese or turkey sandwiches, cheese tartines, soups, salads, éclairs, fruit tarts, chocolate mousse, and more. Beer, wine, lemonade, smoothies, coffee, and other beverages are served. The patisserie is located toward the back of the France pavilion and is a favorite snack spot among Epcot veterans. There's always a line to order the treats, but it moves quickly. **L D S · $ – $$ · ❤**

LA CANTINA DE SAN ANGEL (Mexico): Located just outside the entrance to Mexico's pyramid, this eatery serves grilled chicken with cascabel sauce over rice; beef tacos (on fresh corn tortillas); Mexican salads; nachos topped with cheese, ground beef, black beans, jalapeños, tomatoes, and sour cream; cheese empanadas; fresh, housemade guacamole with corn tortilla chips; and *churros con cajeta* (churros with caramel) and *paletas* (fruit ice pops). Beer, margaritas (frozen and on the rocks), and soft drinks (including Mexican apple soda) are available. Kids' picks include cheese empanadas and chicken tenders, both served with tortilla chips and fruit. **L D S · $ – $$ · ❤**

LA CAVA DEL TEQUILA (Mexico): Mexico's national drink is the star of this show—there are more than 200 varieties to choose from. Also served: sangria, mezcal, beer, wine, and specialty drinks (the avocado margaritas are quite refreshing). Snack on *queso blanco* (warm, white nacho cheese with pico de gallo sauce and tortilla chips), or chips with guacamole or salsa—or go chip crazy and order them with all three. Doors open at noon. It's tiny, so expect a wait to get in. **S · $ – $$**

Check, Please!

Paying for a meal at Disney World is a piece of cake—especially if you have a MagicBand or Disney resort ID (and load it with your Disney Dining Plan or back it up with a credit card). Both are accepted by most restaurants on Walt Disney World property. Notable exceptions: eateries at the Swan and Dolphin resorts, Four Seasons, and the resorts on Hotel Plaza Boulevard, and some snack carts. Simply scan your MagicBand or resort ID when the bill arrives (don't forget to add a tip where appropriate), and the charge will appear on your hotel statement when you check out. (If you are not staying at a WDW–owned-and-operated resort, visit *www.disneyworld.com* for details on how you can get the most from the MagicBand service.)

Of course, there are many alternative ways to pay the piper. In addition to United States currency, traveler's checks and most major credit cards are accepted in most locations. Foreign currency is a no-no. Disney currency (aka Disney Dollars), though no longer sold, works like cash in all Disney-owned-and-operated venues. Disney Gift Cards are accepted at most of the aforementioned locations, too. (If you plan to pay with a gift card, tell your server when you place your order.)

REFRESHMENT COOL POST (between China and Germany): This is a nice spot for a snack and cold drink (soft drinks, beer, and other spirits are served). Snacks include hot dogs with chips, soft-serve ice cream, and non-alcoholic slushies. Beer, hard pineapple cider, and frozen cocktail selections round out the menu. L D S · $ – $ $ · 🐭

FIFE & DRUM TAVERN (The American Adventure): Located in front of the Liberty Inn, this small brick edifice proffers American favorites. Among the options: turkey legs, popcorn, soft-serve ice cream, slushies, soft drinks, wine, beer, and hard root beer. Souvenir popcorn buckets cost $10 and may be refilled for $1.50 a pop for the length of your stay. L D S · $ – $ $ · 🐭

KABUKI CAFE (Japan): Step up to cool down at this quick-service kiosk, where the specialty of the house is Kakigori, aka shaved ice. Flavors include cherry, tangerine, sweet strawberry, and more. Other chilly treats include green tea or ginger ice cream and strawberry smoothies (be sure to ask about the smoothie flavor of the day). Kabuki also offers edamame, sushi (California rolls and "box-style" salmon, shrimp, and tuna), Japanese beer (including frozen Kirin), plum wine, sake (hot and cold), and soft drinks. L D S · $ – $ $ · 🐭

KATSURA GRILL (Japan): Located to the left of the plaza, the exterior of the restaurant was inspired by the historic sixteenth-century Katsura Imperial Villa near Kyoto, Japan.

Among the fare here is Japanese chicken cutlet curry (a peppery sauce over rice with a panko-breaded chicken breast). That, along with teriyaki chicken, shrimp and beef (basted with soy sauce and sesame oil as it broils), sushi, miso soup, udon noodles (beef or shrimp tempura), and edamame typify the offerings. Drink choices include hot and cold sake, plum wine, green tea, beer, and soft drinks. The garden serves as a respite for those who want a break from the hustle and bustle of a busy Epcot day. Kids dig the koi pond—the fish are enormous. L D S · $ – $ $ · 🐭

KRINGLA BAKERI OG KAFE (Norway): Tucked between the Norway pavilion's wooden church and a cluster of shops, this popular eating spot serves kringlas, sweet pretzels reserved for special occasions in Norway; Troll horns (flaky pastry filled with cream and tart cloudberries); smørbrøds, sandwiches such as open-faced smoked salmon and eggs, ham and apple, Norwegian club, or roast beef; traditional Kjøttke (Norwegian meatballs), lefse (potato flatbread rolled with sweet cinnamon butter), and vegetable tortes. There are salads, berry cream puffs, Norwegian school bread, fruit cups, sweet pretzels with chocolate, rice pudding, and no-sugar-added trifle. Soft drinks, wine, beer, and coffee cocktails are served. Breakfast items are offered, too—convenient for early visits to Frozen Ever After. B L D S · $ – $ $ · 🐭

L'ARTISAN DES GLACES (France): An artisanal ice cream and sorbet shop, this spot fills cones and cups with ice cream and sorbets—all crafted in-house. The ingredients are simple and fresh: milk, sugar, cream, eggs, and fruit. There are usually more than a dozen flavors from which to choose. Specials include macaron ice cream sandwiches, iced cappuccino with ice cream, and sundaes in homemade waffle bowls. Adults over age 21 may indulge in an "ice cream martini"—two scoops with a shot of Grand Marnier, whipped cream vodka, or rum. S · $ · 🐭

LIBERTY INN (The American Adventure): To many visitors from other countries, American food means hot dogs, burgers, chicken nuggets, and fries—and these are the staples at the Liberty Inn, located on the left of The American Adventure pavilion. Also available at Liberty Inn: New York strip steak with fried shrimp, fries, and steamed broccoli; red, white, and blue chicken salad; grilled chicken sandwich (with bacon and avocado); and BBQ pork sandwich. Cobbler, rocky road mousse cake, and fruit cups round out the menu. For those in search of a meat-free meal, the vegetarian plate will do. L D S · $ – $ $ · 🐭

LOTUS BLOSSOM CAFE (China): The counter-service cafe is adjacent to the House of Good Fortune shopping gallery in the China pavilion. It offers orange chicken with steamed rice, beef noodle soup, Hong Kong–style vegetable curry (with or without chicken), shrimp fried rice, and sesame chicken salad, plus pot stickers, pork and vegetable rolls, and kid-friendly selections. Unlike most traditional Chinese cooking, the food here is prepared on a flat grill, as opposed to stir-fried. There is a small, covered seating area. L D S · $ – $ $ · ❤

REFRESHMENT PORT (Canada): A good spot for a thirst quencher or a quick snack—soft-serve ice cream in waffle cones, croissant doughnuts, chicken nuggets, and drinks. You will find the Refreshment Port on the World Showcase promenade, near Canada. S · $ – $ $ · ❤

SOMMERFEST (Germany): Bratwurst or frankfurter served on a roll with sauerkraut and housemade paprika chips, nudel gratin (baked macaroni with cheese custard—a fan favorite), traditional cold potato salad (with eggs), jumbo pretzels, Black Forest cake, apple strudel with vanilla sauce, soft drinks, shots of Jägermeister, steins of seasonal German beers, and Riesling wine are offered at this spot near the entrance to the Biergarten restaurant. There is outdoor seating nearby. L D S · $ – $ $ · ❤

TANGIERINE CAFE (Morocco): Named for the Moroccan city of Tangier, this casual spot serves lentil salad, tangierine couscous salad, marinated olives, tabbouleh, saffron rotisserie chicken, kefta (beef), and lamb combo platters, and veggie platters. Pastries, specialty coffees, frozen drinks, and beer are available, too. Kids can order hamburgers and chicken nuggets. L D S · $ – $ $ · ❤

YORKSHIRE COUNTY FISH SHOP (United Kingdom): A perfect choice for a simple meal, this stand offers classic fish and chips. (Don't forget the malt vinegar.) Soda, iced tea, light lemonade, Bass ale, and Harp lager are also available on draft. For dessert, there's Victoria sponge cake filled with jam and buttercream, and whole, seasonal fruit. L D S · $ – $ $ · ❤

Epcot Mealtime Tips

- The international restaurants of World Showcase offer some of the best dining on the property. Since many of them are very popular, it's a good idea to arrange advance reservations for all table-service restaurants by calling 407-WDW-DINE (939-3463) long before arriving. However, it's important to note that some tables may be available for same-day seating. To make arrangements, head to Guest Relations first thing in the morning, visit *mydisneyexperience.com*, or call the aforementioned number. Meals *may* be booked at some individual restaurants, but don't count on it.

- Don't dismiss the idea of an early seating if you can get it: A 5 P.M. dinner may not only be welcome, but may provide an opportunity to spend time enjoying the pleasant, more temperate evening hours at Epcot's World Showcase.

- Lunch provides guests with another chance to enjoy the most popular Epcot restaurants. It also has an additional appeal: With reservations for 1 P.M., it's possible to spend some of the busiest hours in the park consuming a pleasant meal while other visitors wait in some of the longest lines of the day. Note that Le Cellier (in Canada) offers a $49 prix-fixe lunch for the first hour or two of its lunch service. It's a great value (in our humble opinion).

- If you aren't able to secure reservations for a meal, don't despair. There are satisfying alternatives to a traditional sit-down restaurant. Tutto Gusto (Italian wine bar) and Spice Road Table (in Morocco) both offer small plates and full service. Japan has Katsura Grill, good for sushi and chicken curry. Sample Mexican lunch specialties at La Cantina. Try the smoked salmon sandwiches at Kringla Bakeri og Kafe in Norway, the fish and chips in the United Kingdom, or Germany's bratwurst sandwiches.

- Cravings for conventional fast foods will be satisfied at the Electric Umbrella in Innoventions and at the Liberty Inn in The American Adventure. Sunshine Seasons, in The Land pavilion, offers a bit of everything. However, it can get extremely congested at mealtime rush hours.

- The most unadventurous eaters can still find something pleasing—even in the more exotic restaurants of World Showcase. If you're undecided, ask at Guest Relations to see a booklet describing the menus. Keep in mind that most restaurants have menus for kids.

In Disney's Hollywood Studios

Lights, camera, lunch! This theme park, which was designed to resemble a working Hollywood backlot circa the 1940s, tackles the role of feeding guests with style and whimsy. Here you can sit in a classic car and enjoy a meal at a drive-in, rub elbows with the beautiful people at a reproduction of the Hollywood Brown Derby, and play the part of a sitcom kid as you're served by "Mom" or "Dad" at the 50's Prime Time Cafe (no elbows on the table, please!). While the attention to theming is obvious, it doesn't upstage the fare. The eateries at Disney's Hollywood Studios are a breed apart. Some feature decor that returns guests to a bygone era; others recapture memorable moments from the big or small screen. All reprise a beloved part of Hollywood's star-studded heritage. The Studios has five full-service restaurants, whose atmospheres and menus are so distinct, they satisfy altogether different moods and whims. Reservations are necessary; call 407-WDW-DINE (939-3463). Now grab a napkin, and get ready for your close-up.

TABLE SERVICE

50'S PRIME TIME CAFE: This retreat is an amusing amalgam of comfort food, kitschy 1950s-style kitchen nooks, and attentive servers of the "No talking with your mouth full" ilk. Nostalgia abounds, meant to bring guests back to the childhood of yesteryear; and TVs broadcast black-and-white clips from favorite fifties comedies (all related to food). Guests are waited on by "Mom" (and other family members) with considerable enthusiasm: They encourage everyone to keep their elbows off the table, eat their vegetables, and clean their plates (or no dessert!). Misbehave and you may have to stand in the corner (the 1950s version of the "time-out").

Adding to the appeal is the menu, which is packed with comfort foods. For openers, there is a choice of housemade chicken noodle soup or onion rings. Specialties of the house include meatloaf served with mashed potatoes and vegetables; fried chicken; and old-fashioned pot roast. There are wedge salads and chicken pot pies, too. Milk shakes, ice cream sodas, and root beer floats are filling accompaniments. And when you've finished everything on your plate, you may order dessert. Standouts include s'mores—graham crackers topped with chocolate and toasted marshmallows—sundaes, apple crisp, and no-sugar-added cheesecake topped with whipped cream and strawberry sauce. A full bar is available. Guests of all ages love this place. Reservations are highly recommended. L D · $$–$$$ · ❤

HOLLYWOOD & VINE: The distinctive Art Deco facade ushers guests into a contemporary version of a 1950s diner—all stainless steel with pink accents. An elaborate 42-by-8-foot wall mural depicts notable Hollywood landmarks, including the Disney Studios, Columbia Ranch, and Warner Bros. (back when they were the only film studios in the San Fernando Valley). At the center of the mural is the Carthay Circle Theatre, where *Snow White and the Seven Dwarfs* premiered in 1937.

The buffet breakfast and lunch, known as Disney Junior Play 'N Dine, are character affairs featuring Sofia the First, Doc McStuffins, Jake the Never Land pirate, and Handy Manny (characters are subject to change). The morning meal includes Mickey waffles, frittatas, fruit, pastries, and a create-your-own omelet station. Lunch may offer items such as sustainable fish of the day, salads, and lobster mac and cheese.

Minnie Mouse hosts the evening meal, along with Mickey, Daisy, Donald, and Goofy. The new "Minnie's Seasonal Dine" buffet offers carved meats, pasta dishes, strip steak, chicken parmesan, and seafood offerings such as cioppino, peel-and-eat shrimp, and mussels. The impressive dessert section boasts a chocolate fountain (among other treats). Soft drinks are included. Beer and wine are served at an extra cost.

Dinner starts at about $50 for adults and $30 for kids; lunch runs about $40 (adults) and $24 (kids); breakfast is about $32 for adults and $19 for kids. Prices are higher during peak times. Reservations are necessary. B L D · $ $ – $ $ $ · 💙

HOLLYWOOD BROWN DERBY: The home of the famous Cobb salad is alive and well. This re-creation of the former Vine Street mainstay is quite faithful, right down to the caricatures (reproduced from the original Derby collection) that cover the walls. Gossip queen rivals Louella Parsons and Hedda Hopper (portrayed by actresses) may still be spotted dining here, just as they did in the heyday of the real Brown Derby. The place is decorated predominantly in teak and mahogany, and the elegant chandeliers and perimeter lamps (shaped like miniature derbies) are reminiscent of those in the original eatery.

The menu features the famed Cobb salad, created by owner Bob Cobb in the 1930s. It's a mixture of ever-so-finely chopped fresh salad greens, tomato, bacon, turkey, egg, blue cheese, and avocado, served with French dressing.

Desserts are tempting—particularly double vanilla crème brûlée and the legendary grapefruit cake, a Brown Derby institution. Some of the selections are a bit highbrow (and high-priced) for the theme park crowd, but if you're up for a splurge, this spot will likely rise to the occasion. We recommend the seafood cioppino; the filet mignon gets good marks, too.

The slightly formal atmosphere is not likely to enchant most children, but youngster-friendly fare is available. The New World wine list is excellent. Reservations are recommended. Should you find yourself without reservations, consider dining at the Hollywood Brown Derby Lounge (see above, right). L D · $ $ $ · 💙

HOLLYWOOD BROWN DERBY LOUNGE: An alfresco oasis, the Brown Derby Lounge serves cocktails, wines by the glass, and tapas-style plates. Signature drinks are named for the park's very own Citizens of Hollywood performers Shelby Mayer, Honey Darling, Jack Diamond, etc. Small plates can come filled with savory treats: Derby sliders, andouille crusted shrimp, artisanal cheeses and charcuterie, Cobb salad, Florida tomato soup, and more. There is a tempting lineup of sweets, too—including warm blueberry cobbler, banana toffee cake on cocoa crunch and strawberry-banana pearls, Brown Derby original mini grapefruit cake, and dessert trios. Seating is limited and reservations are not accepted, so there may be a wait for a table. Drinks may be made to go. The Hollywood Brown Derby Lounge usually opens at about noon and closes an hour or so before the rest of the park does. L D S · $ $

MAMA MELROSE'S RISTORANTE ITALIANO: This pleasant Italian restaurant (with a California twist) is located in a warehouse that has been converted into a large dining room. Flatbreads are prepared in a wood-burning oven. The menu also features housemade pasta, grilled fish, and vegetarian options. Favorite dishes have included seafood arrabbiata, charred strip steak, and oven-baked chicken parmesan. They have penne alla vodka, too (served plain or with shrimp or chicken). Reservations are recommended. L D · $ $ – $ $ $ · 💙

SCI-FI DINE-IN THEATER: A convincing re-creation of a drive-in theater, the atmosphere here is completely absorbing. The tables are actually flashy, 1950s-era cars, complete with fins and whitewalls. Stars twinkle overhead in the "night sky," and drive-in theater speakers are mounted beside each car. Most seats are within cars, with most featuring front- and backseat counters facing front. Not terribly conducive to

Water Park Dining

Disney's duo of water parks, Typhoon Lagoon and Blizzard Beach, provides plenty of chances to defy Mom's plea to wait an hour to splash after you nosh. The fare is limited to the quick-service kind (who wants a sit-down meal in a soggy swimsuit?), and the quality of the offerings has been stepped up a bit of late. Typhoon Lagoon offers island burgers, tropical salads, and more.

At Blizzard Beach, you can order flatbreads, rice bowls, and specialty hot dogs. Snacks are sold at spots with names like Typhoon Tilly's (🐭), Leaning Palms (🐭), and Avalunch (🐭). Frozen drink specialties flow at Let's Go Slurpin' (Typhoon Lagoon) and at Blizzard Beach's Polar Bear Pool Bar.

Some folks prefer to pack a picnic lunch. Coolers may be brought into both of Disney's water parks, but alcoholic beverages and glass containers may not.

meaningful table talk, but ideal for viewing the large movie screen, where a 45-minute compilation of the best (and worst) science-fiction trailers and cartoons plays in a continuous loop. There are a couple of traditional tables within oversize cars—if this is your preference, make that known when you book the table and expect to wait a bit when you arrive.

HOT TIP!

While the Sci-Fi Dine-In Theater has tables that can accommodate guests who use wheelchairs, there aren't many. Be sure to request such a table when you make your reservations—and confirm it before you go: 407-WDW-DINE (939-3463).

Selections include Reuben sandwiches, pork ribs, burgers, and shrimp pasta. Kids enjoy the mac and cheese. Desserts include cheesecake, milk shakes, and ice cream sundaes. Reservations are recommended. Warning: Some of the movie trailers feature monsters and may frighten your little ones. L D • $ $ – $ $ $ • 🐭

FAST FOOD & SNACKS

ABC COMMISSARY: Located near the Chinese Theatre, this spot has featured jalapeño poppers, chicken nuggets, chicken club sandwiches, BBQ chicken and ribs, Mediterranean salads, hummus with pita chips, and cheeseburgers. Desserts include no-sugar-added strawberry parfait, Olaf cupcakes, and chocolate mousse. Beer, wine, and soft drinks are served. The dining area is huge and does indeed resemble an actual studio commissary. We could do without the ads for ABC shows, which play on a continuous loop from TVs scattered throughout the dining area. L D S • $ – $ $ • 🐭

BACKLOT EXPRESS: Resembling a crafts shop on an old studio backlot, this eatery is near the Star Tours—The Adventures Continue attraction. The indoor seating areas carry out the prop-shop theme, with paint-speckled floors, car engines, and various other spare prop parts. Typical menu offerings include cheeseburgers, chicken and waffles, hot dogs, sandwiches, salads, and chicken nuggets. For dessert there's cupcakes and slushes. Soft drinks, beer, and wine are served. L D S • $ – $ $ • 🐭

DINOSAUR GERTIE'S ICE CREAM OF EXTINCTION: Soft-serve ice cream is Gertie's go-to treat—vanilla, chocolate, or swirl, in a cup or cone. Mickey-shaped ice cream bars, cookies and cream sandwiches, trail mixes, and fruit are served, too. Gertie's operates seasonally and may not be open during your visit to the park. S • $ • 🐭

HOLLYWOOD HILLS AMPHITHEATER: If your stomach starts growling while waiting for Fantasmic! to begin, you can keep it quiet with a visit to this snack shack. Savory items include nachos with cheese, hot dogs, popcorn, and more.

Studios Mealtime Tips

- To avoid traffic jams at fast-food spots, consider eating at one of the restaurants that offer advance reservations—Hollywood Brown Derby, 50's Prime Time Cafe, Sci-Fi Dine-In Theater, Hollywood & Vine, or Mama Melrose's Ristorante Italiano.

- To arrange for reservations in advance, call 407-WDW-DINE (939-3463). Same-day seating is impossible for table-service restaurants at Disney's Hollywood Studios.

- The many indoor and outdoor nooks within the Backlot Express seating area are nicely removed from the beaten path; relative quiet can frequently be enjoyed there.

- The Fantasmic! "dinner and a show" package offers diners guaranteed seating for the nighttime spectacular. For details, see the Hot Tip at right.

Sweet treats such as ice cream bars, frozen bananas, fresh fruit, caramel corn, churros, and glazed almonds are also sold. Wash it all down with a soft drink, beer, or wine. S·$·$$·❤

ICE COLD: Need to cool off on a hot day? Swing by this stand near the park entrance. It sells ice cream bars, slushies, iced coffee, cool juices, and fizzy drinks. Other snack items include whole fruit, cookies, and chips. S·$·❤

PHOTO BY JILL SAFRO

MIN AND BILL'S DOCKSIDE DINER: This waterside window offers foot-long chili cheese dogs, pork sliders, loaded chili/cheese nachos, chips, milk shakes (with or without alcohol), frozen lemonade, soft drinks, and beer. Note that Min and Bill's may not be operating during all of 2018. S·$·$$·❤

OASIS CANTEEN: A tiny tin shack that sits beside the Indiana Jones Epic Stunt Spectacular, the Oasis Canteen dispenses funnel cakes topped

HOT TIP!

Hollywood Brown Derby, Mama Melrose's Ristorante Italiano, and Hollywood & Vine offer a "dinner and a show" combo (lunch is offered seasonally). Seating for Fantasmic!, the park's nighttime spectacular, is included at no extra cost (though tax, gratuities, and alcoholic beverages carry an extra charge). For pricing information or to make arrangements, call 407-939-3463 and request the Fantasmic! dinner package. Note that this dinner package was recently tweaked and once again offers guaranteed seating for the Fantasmic! show. Guests are advised to arrive at the theater 30 to 45 minutes before showtime to claim their seats.

HOT TIP!

That gift card burning a hole in your pocket? Disney gift cards may be redeemed at all Disney–owned-and-operated dining, shopping, and recreation locations where credit cards are accepted. They may be used to pay for all (or part) of the bill at a Disney resort, too. If you lose track of what's left on your card, call the number on the back to find out.

with strawberries, vanilla ice cream, powdered sugar, or cinnamon; vanilla soft-serve ice cream in waffle cones, cups, and cola or root beer floats; bottled water; assorted fountain beverages; and domestic draft beer. Spirited ice cream floats (Dreamsicle and Root Beer floats with vanilla vodka) are available for guests over age 21, too. S·$·❤

PIZZERIZZO: Occupying the space once filled by Toy Story Pizza Planet, this new Muppet-themed eatery continues the kid-friendly pizza tradition, plus meatball subs, antipasto salad, cannoli, and tiramasu. You'll find it directly across the courtyard from the Muppet★Vision 3-D attraction. L D S·$·$$·❤

SUNSET RANCH MARKET: A salute to California's outdoor lifestyle, this cluster of snack stands has something for just about everyone. Rosie's All-American Cafe serves cheeseburgers, chicken nuggets, fried green tomato sandwiches, and strawberry shortcake. Catalina Eddie's offers plain and pepperoni pizzas, chicken Caesar salads, and desserts. Fruit and vegetables, juice, and soft drinks are sold at Anaheim Produce. Hollywood Scoops sells creamy treats (including one of the no-sugar-added variety). And look no further than Fairfax Fare for empanadas, pulled pork sandwiches, fajitas, baked potatoes, and chili-cheese foot-long dogs, plus salads and desserts. Kids' selections are offered, too. Soft drinks are available, as is beer (with proper ID). L D S·$·$$·❤

THE TROLLEY CAR CAFE: Step into this trolley station/Starbucks for coffee-based beverages, sweet treats, savory snacks, and more. The cheery red building is at the corner of Hollywood and Sunset boulevards. Umbrellas dot the landscape. In addition to the fare, guests may purchase coffee cups with designs unique to the park. B L D S·$·$$·❤

In Animal Kingdom

Whether you eat like a horse or more like a bird, you'll have no trouble finding something to sink your teeth into at one of A.K.'s eateries. Disney's nature-oriented park has four table-service spots and takes "quick service" seriously—there are plenty of places to keep stomachs from growling like the beasts at the Kilimanjaro Safaris attraction.

TABLE SERVICE

RAINFOREST CAFE: Like the Oasis, the region it borders, this cafe is a lush, soothing jungle. Unlike the Oasis, a quiet moment here is merely a calm before the storm—as brief thunderstorms happen frequently. Waterfalls, twisting tree trunks, and colorful fish add to the ambience. The environmentally conscious cuisine includes Planet Earth Pasta and the portobello mushroom wrap. There is no net-caught fish, nor beef from countries that destroy rainforest land to raise cattle. Reservations are recommended. **BLDS·$$–$$$**

TIFFINS: Tiffins' exotic menu features cuisine from the many areas that inspired the creation of Disney's Animal Kingdom. Guests may dine indoors or in outdoor areas with waterfront views. The menu has included black-eyed pea fritters, fried mussels, apple walnut salad, Wagyu strip loin, braised short rib, pan-seared duck breast, chermoula-rubbed chicken, hoisin-glazed halibut, and whole-fried sustainable fish. For dessert there's lime cheesecake, chocolate ganache with carmelized banana, and a sorbet tasting. This is a Disney Dining Plan Signature restaurant. Reservations are recommended. **LD·$$$$·✸**

TUSKER HOUSE: Harambe village sets the stage for a dining adventure at this buffet restaurant. The all-you-care-to-eat selection is bountiful and satisfying to most palates. All meals are hosted by favorite Disney characters. At press time, the characters scheduled to attend were Donald, Daisy, Mickey, and Goofy (the latter three are subject to change). Reservations are recommended for all meals. Book as far in advance as possible. Tusker House opens at 8 A.M. **BLD·$$–$$$·✸**

YAK & YETI: Found in the Asia section of the park, Yak & Yeti opens for lunch at 11 A.M. It specializes in Asian fusion cuisine. Menu items include chicken tikka masala, crispy mahi mahi, baby back ribs, lo mein, and seared miso salmon.

Among the dessert options are fried (sweet) wontons and mango pie. African beers and cocktails are served, too. **LDS·$$–$$$·✸**

FAST FOOD & SNACKS

ANANDAPUR ICE CREAM TRUCK: Cool off with soft-serve (chocolate, vanilla, and swirl) from Asia's local ice cream truck. The snack is served in a waffle cone, cup, or soda float. Water and a variety of soft drinks (including root beer and light lemonade) are also offered. **S·$·✸**

CREATURE COMFORTS: A shop known as Creature Comforts has been converted into a home fit for a mermaid. Yep, the sippers' sanctum known as Starbucks is open for business on Discovery Island. It currently comforts creatures with all manner of coffee concoctions, pastries, and snacks. **BLDS·$–$$·✸**

DINO-BITE SNACKS: Restaurantosaurus's neighbor, this snack shack proffers plenty of sweet treats. Order items such as hand-scooped ice cream, floats, ice-cream cookie sandwiches, churros with chocolate sauce, fresh-baked cookies, plus Mickey pretzels, and chips. **S·$·✸**

FLAME TREE BARBECUE: To find this eatery, just follow your nose. It serves a fragrant selection of BBQ sandwiches and platters, all wood roasted. Sample the mild, tomato-based Carolina-style sauce with your chicken, pulled pork, or hickory-smoked St. Louis ribs. Smoked turkey breast sandwiches, watermelon salad, mixed green salad with chicken, fries (with or without pulled pork and cheese), onion rings, and lime mousse are also options. Platters come with beans, cole slaw, and cornbread. Beer, wine, and soft drinks are served. There's indoor seating along the river. Please don't feed the wildlife. It's on Discovery Island, near DinoLand, U.S.A. **LDS·$–$$·✸**

HARAMBE FRUIT MARKET: Sometimes a crunchy apple is just what the doctor—or hungry theme park guest—ordered. Apples (and other fruits) are available at this stand by the entrance to Kilimanjaro Safaris. Stop here for veggies, soft pretzels, chips, and beverages, too. **S·$·✸**

HARAMBE MARKET: Enshrined in an old train station, the Harambe Market features four proprietors offering African takes on American favorites: spice-rubbed ribs, sausages, grilled chicken skewers, beef gyro flatbreads, and more. Diners may enjoy the Harambe-style street fare in the open-air courtyard near the Mombasa Marketplace shop. L D S · $ – $ $ · 🐾

KUSAFIRI COFFEE SHOP & BAKERY:
The bakery at Tusker House sells breakfast sandwiches, fruit, cookies, croissants, and other desserts, plus cereal, yogurt, soft drinks, low-fat milk, and specialty coffees. Lunch and dinner sandwich options include smoked turkey, tomato and mozzarella, ham and cheddar, and roast beef and cheddar (the last two are paninis). There are tables at the nearby Dawa Bar. B L D S · $ · 🐾

PIZZAFARI: This spacious dining area offers a variety of flatbreads: cheese, shrimp, cheese-burger, Mediterranean, and pepperoni. Also served: salad with chicken or shrimp, garlic knots with marinara sauce, and tomato basil soup. Kids enjoy the Mickey pasta with turkey marinara. Vibrant animal murals decorate the walls of this Discovery Island eatery. B L D S · $ – $ $ · 🐾

RESTAURANTOSAURUS: This DinoLand spot is a fishing lodge turned commissary for student paleontologists. It offers bacon cheeseburgers, chili cheese hot dogs, grilled chicken BLT sandwiches, chicken nuggets, black bean burgers, mixed green salad with chicken—plus chili cheese fries, clam chowder, warm chocolate brownies and cheesecake topped with strawberries. The place is filled with fossils, dinosaur bones, and such; class notes line the walls. L D S · $ – $ $ · 🐾

ROYAL ANANDAPUR TEA COMPANY:
After hiking through Africa to get to Asia, park guests can build up quite a thirst. That's where this tea stand comes in handy. Near the Yak & Yeti in the village of Serka Zong, the hut sells iced and hot teas, specialty coffees, and treats. S · $ · 🐾

SATU'LI CANTEEN: Look for familiar dishes with a twist at this elegant canteen, featuring 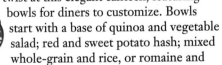 bowls for diners to customize. Bowls start with a base of quinoa and vegetable salad; red and sweet potato hash; mixed whole-grain and rice, or romaine and kale salad. They are finished by adding chicken, beef, fish, or fried tofu, and dressing. Steamed bao buns (stuffed with either vegetable curry or cheeseburger) are served, too. Kid-friendly items round out the menu at this Pandora— The World of Avatar locale. L D S · $ $ · 🐾

TAMU TAMU REFRESHMENTS: Stop by this spot in Africa's Harambe for a sweet treat. You can choose a double chocolate chip cookie ice cream sandwich, a chocolate waffle with ice cream, or the frozen pineapple treat known as a Dole Whip (with or without rum). This spot usually opens around 10:30 A.M. L D S · $ · 🐾

TERRA TREATS: Just across the river from Harambe, this kiosk serves Buffalo chicken wings, hummus with vegetables, fresh fruit cups, and other snack items. Bottled water, beer, and hard cider are also served. S · $ · 🐾

TRILO-BITES: In DinoLand U.S.A., just inside the land's entrance (not far from the dinosaur skeleton bridge), this kiosk dispenses Buffalo chicken chips, soft-serve waffle cones, floats, soft-serve ice cream with gummy worms and chocolate crumbles (aka The Boneyard Bounty), plus beer and soft drinks. L D S · $ · 🐾

YAK & YETI LOCAL FOOD CAFES: Next to Yak & Yeti, the quick-service cafes specialize in items with pan-Asian influences. Entrées include Korean-style stir-fry BBQ chicken, teriyaki beef bowl, roasted veggie couscous wrap, chicken fried rice, and ginger chicken salad. Egg rolls are also served. There is ample outdoor seating nearby. L D S · $ – $ $ · 🐾

Animal Kingdom Mealtime Tips

- Satu'li Canteen, Pizzafari, and Flame Tree Barbecue accept advance orders via the My Disney Experience app. Payments with Mobile Order must be made with a credit card.

- Tusker House and Rainforest Cafe are table-service places offering breakfast; a few spots, including Creature Comforts and Kusafiri Coffee Shop & Bakery, have light breakfast options.

- Restaurants that accept reservations for all meals are Tusker House and Rainforest Cafe. Yak & Yeti and Tiffins may be pre-booked for lunch and dinner. Reservations, which are recommended, can be made up to 180 days ahead via 407-939-3463 and the My Disney Experience website or app. For same-day seating, go to the restaurant (with your fingers crossed). Rainforest Cafe may keep longer hours than the Animal Kingdom park—plan exit transportation accordingly.

- A great place to meet Donald and pals such as Mickey, Daisy, and Goofy is at Tusker House at the daily character meals (three meals a day).

In Disney Springs

Disney Springs encompasses the Marketplace, West Side, Town Center, and The Landing. Restaurants operate from about 11 A.M. to midnight; most snack spots are open from 11 A.M. to late into the night. For the details, call 407-939-4636.

AMC DINE-IN THEATRES (West Side): Popcorn and soda are upstaged by selections such as chicken Alfredo and mango margaritas in this in-theater dining experience known as Fork and Screen. Seat-side, tabletop service (with a personal call button for the server) allows moviegoers to enjoy dinner before a screening. The menu includes appetizers, entrées, desserts, cocktails, and soft drinks—plus classic movie munchies. Seating is reserved (and assigned when you purchase your movie ticket). Guests under age 18 must be accompanied by an adult (over the age of 18). LDS·$-$$·❤

BLAZE FAST FIRE'D PIZZA (Town Square): If you fancy a freshly custom-made pizza, make a beeline for Blaze. The 5,000-square-foot eatery fires made-to-order pizzas in just three minutes with the help of super-hot pizza ovens. Guests may customize their 11-inch pies with a vast array of toppings (included in the price), as well as pick their own cheese and sauce. Gluten-free crusts are an option. The menu includes nearly a dozen signature pizzas, plus salads and desserts. LDS·$-$$·❤

THE BOATHOUSE (The Landing): An upscale waterfront destination, The Boathouse serves delicacies from land and sea for lunch and dinner. Raw bar highlights include oysters on the half shell, caviar corn blinis, and crab cakes (large enough to share, though you won't want to). Entrée selections have included coriander-seared tuna, Beach and Sea Lobster Bake for Two, and baked crab-stuffed lobster. Chicken, pasta, and a large lineup of steak dishes tempt, too. A kids' menu is available. Guests may enjoy

drinks and a full menu at any of the three bars. Doors close at 2 A.M. Reservations are highly recommended for tables, but bar stools are designated for walk-ins. LDS·$$$-$$$$

BONGOS CUBAN CAFE (West Side): Bongos' slate of traditional and nouvelle Cuban dishes includes plantains, steak topped with onions, and flan. Indoors, the elaborate mosaic mural and palm-leaf railings set the scene; the patio for outdoor seating wraps around a two-story pineapple. Diners are often treated to live music. Reservations are recommended for this Disney Dining Plan Signature restaurant. Details are subject to change. LDS·$$-$$$ ❤

COOKES OF DUBLIN (The Landing): Raglan Road's quick-service neighbor, this is the place to go for some of the best fish and chips in the World. And don't ask for the recipe—it's a Cooke family secret! Other choices include battered sausages, salads, beef and lamb pie, chicken and mushroom pie, and hog in a box (slow-roasted pork shoulder with roasted potatoes). Save room for a "lovely" dessert. LDS·$-$$ ❤

D-LUXE BURGER: D-Luxe Burger is a sweet spot for a quick bite. The burgers (big enough to share) are served on fresh-baked buns. The freshly cut fries (which come with dipping sauces) and (scrumptious) artisanal gelato shakes are sure to please. Place your order at the counter and grab a seat while your meal is prepared—they will deliver it to your table. There's indoor and outdoor seating. LDS·$$ ❤

EARL OF SANDWICH (Marketplace): This counter-service spot is brimming with possibilities. Among the fare are hot and cold sandwiches (on warm bread), wraps, salads, and desserts. Other selections such as Hawaiian BBQ (ham with fresh pineapple and Swiss cheese), The Original 1762 (warm roast beef sandwich with horseradish sauce and cheddar cheese), and Caribbean Jerk Chicken are served, too. The Veggie sandwich is an option. Breakfast includes warm sandwiches and baked goods. There are grab-and-go selections, too. Beer, wine, and Kona coffee are offered. Seating is available inside and out. The Earl welcomes visitors daily from 8:30 A.M. until 11 P.M. To save some cash, use the coupon at the back of this book. BLDS·$-$$·❤

FOOD TRUCKS (West Side): The Fantasy Fare food truck serves favorites from Magic Kingdoms around the world. Look for sticky chicken and waffles, corn dogs with waffle fries, shrimp & lobster mac and cheese, and chicken strips. World Showcase of Flavors features favorites from Epcot's International Food & Wine Festival. Possibilities include Chilean steak sandwiches, meatball sandwiches, pork belly sandwiches, and chicken cemita sandwiches. Springs Street Tacos offers a variety of tacos: grilled steak, pork belly, grilled fish, adobe chicken, and rice and bean. Menus and location are subject to change. The trucks usually open between 4 P.M. and 5 P.M. DS·$·$$·🐭

GHIRARDELLI ICE CREAM & CHOCOLATE SHOP (Marketplace): What is it about an old-fashioned ice cream parlor that makes just about everybody giddy? Oh, yes, the ice cream. This spot does it one better and throws in its world-famous chocolate to boot. Stop in for a chocolaty treat, root beer float, or a malt. And there is always a possibility of a free candy sample. How sweet is that?! S·$·$$

CHEF ART SMITH'S HOMECOMIN' (Town Center): "Florida heritage meets New Southern cuisine" at this gustatory homage to the Sunshine State. Created by Chef Art Smith, the menu focuses on Southern favorites such as homemade pimento cheese, Church Lady deviled eggs, fried chicken, Low Country shrimp and grits, and pork barbecue plate. Specialty desserts such as Mockingbird Cake and fresh doughnuts make for a sweet finish.

The family-friendly destination has a design inspired by Florida architecture of the late 1800s, and it supports the "Fresh from Florida" campaign, with many of the ingredients coming from local farms, ranches, and fisheries. Reservations are recommended. LDS·$$$ 🐭

FRONTERA COCINA (Town Center): The brainchild of six-time James Beard Foundation winner Chef Rick Bayless, this spot showcases his gourmet Mexican cuisine. Select from items such as hand-crafted tortas, tacos, salads, fresh-made guacamole, and braised meats— all prepared with locally sourced ingredients. Pair your Mexican meal with a marvelous margarita (the selection is impressively vast). Beer, wine, cocktails, and soft drinks are also served. Reservations are recommended. There's a walk-up window from which to order take-away items, too. LDS·$$$ 🐭

HOUSE OF BLUES (West Side): Thanks to the combination of its menu and rustic, folk-art-studded design, House of Blues doesn't disappoint. Menu favorites include flatbreads (grilled, then finished in the pizza oven), lobster mac and cheese, tacos, cornbread, and jambalaya. House of Blues is a good choice for a meal or a late-night bite. Live music is presented in the eatery and on the front porch on select days. There is a gospel brunch every Sunday. Reservations are recommended. To reserve a table at the House of Blues, call 407-934-BLUE (934-2583). LDS·$$–$$$ 🐭

HOUSE OF BLUES SMOKEHOUSE (West Side): This window at H.O.B. offers a variety of BBQ selections (pulled pork or chicken sandwiches, nachos, smoked turkey legs, ribs, etc.), soft drinks, spirits, and more. LDS·$–$$ 🐭

MORIMOTO ASIA (The Landing): Brought to you by Chef Masaharu Morimoto, TV's original Iron Chef, this eatery features dishes from across Asia. The two-story venue offers Pan-Asian cuisine prepared in show kitchens: dim sum, sushi and other seafood, and more. For menu specifics, visit *www.disneyworld.com*. Reservations are recommended. This is a Disney Dining Plan Signature restaurant for dinner. LDS· $$$$ 🐭

MORIMOTO ASIA—STREET FOOD (The Landing): This quick-service window, located on Morimoto Asia's patio, serves sushi, rice bowls, bao (flatbread) tacos, sticky ribs, pork egg rolls, beer, and soft drinks. LDS·$–$$

PADDLEFISH (The Landing): Originally known as the Empress Lilly (after Walt Disney's wife, Lillian), and recently known as Fulton's, this restaurant has been re-invented and given a new identity. Though Paddlefish looks as if it might set sail at any moment, the sleek replica of a boat that houses the seafood-centric eatery is permanently docked at the edge of Lake Buena Vista. The classic WDW space features a modern interior, rooftop lounge, and two interior bars.

Paddlefish boasts an elaborate selection of appetizers and entrées featuring the day's arrivals. Look for offerings such as lobster risotto, redfish, Alaskan king crab, and (heavenly) lobster corn dogs to appear on the menu. There's plenty for landlubbers, too. Reservations are recommended. Paddlefish is a Disney Dining Plan Signature restaurant and requires two table-service credits. LD·$$$–$$$$ 🐭

PARADISO 37 (The Landing): A lively, waterfront restaurant and bar (with indoor and outdoor seating, plus a live-performance stage), Paradiso 37 specializes in "swirl margaritas," stocks more than 100 different kinds of tequila, and offers the "coldest beer in the world." They serve food, too!

The menu focuses on "the taste" of the Americas. Starters include fire-roasted corn on the cob with a mild pepper sauce and cheese, salmon cakes, and P37 nachos. Entrées range from Argentinian skirt steak with chimichurri sauce to Chilean-style salmon. L D S · $$ – $$$

PLANET HOLLYWOOD OBSERVATORY (The Landing): Planet Hollywood does double duty as a restaurant and a 1900s-style observatory. This eatery has indoor and outdoor seating and a bar called Stargazers, featuring live entertainment. The menu has salads, sandwiches, pasta, burgers, and desserts. Reservations are recommended. L D S · $$ – $$$ · 🐭

THE POLITE PIG (Town Center): Created by award-winning Orlando chefs Julie and James Petrakis, this casual quick-service destination features "modern barbecue" and Southern sides. The menu includes sandwich selections such as brisket melt, salmon BLT, and smoked chicken salad. Items from the smoker include pork shoulder, half chicken, brisket, wild salmon, and St. Louis ribs. There are plenty of salads and sides to mix and match, too (chopped salads, crispy Brussels sprouts, BBQ cauliflower, peel-and-eat shrimp, and much more). For dessert, choose from orange blossom honey cake or Key lime pie. Beer, wine, and cocktails are served—and there's a mighty extensive bourbon menu, too. There is indoor and outdoor seating and a full bar. L D · $$ – $$$

RAGLAN ROAD (The Landing): As authentically Irish as you can get on this side of the Atlantic, this warm and lively establishment blends fresh ingredients to create traditional Irish fare with a modern flair. The menu comes courtesy of Kevin Dundon, one of Ireland's best-known chefs. His selections are complemented by the welcoming atmosphere, complete with antiques and bric-a-brac, spirits, and live entertainment (starting at 4 P.M. on most days). Reservations are accepted. The shop stocks Raglan Road–branded items, Irish shirts, CDs, jewelry, cookbooks, family crests, and more. Brunch (with entertainment) is served on Saturday and Sunday. Brunch L D S · $$ – $$$ · 🐭

RAINFOREST CAFE (Marketplace): The Amazon-emulating eatery transports diners to a makeshift rainforest, complete with banyan trees, tropical fish, waterfalls, and parrots.

Special effects envelop guests in tropical storms with lightning and thunder. Menu items include Planet Earth Pasta, Mojo Bones, and Rumble in the Jungle Turkey Wrap. A shop stocks logo clothing and souvenirs. Reservations may be made by calling 407-827-8500. Without them, expect quite a wait. L D S · $$ – $$$ 🐭

SPLITSVILLE (West Side): Some go expecting just to bowl, not realizing that Splitsville's two kitchens turn out impressive casual fare such as freshly rolled sushi, three-pepper calamari, seared ahi tuna, and sliders. They've also got pizzas, cheeseburgers, sandwiches, and salads. Many menu items are gluten free. Huge desserts include sundaes, brownie à la mode, and chocolate cake. There is a full bar and a mix-your-own Coca-Cola machine. Food is served lane-side or at "non-bowling" tables. Visit *www.splitsvillelanes.com* for additional details. L D S · $$ – $$$ 🐭

STARBUCKS (West Side and Marketplace): The Disney Springs links of the famous coffee chain serve up all the usual Starbucks specialties: fresh-brewed coffee (hot or iced), Frappuccino blended drinks, teas, and kids' drinks, plus sweet and savory snack items. B L D S · $ – $$ · 🐭

STK ORLANDO (The Landing): Steak is the obvious star here, but this modern restaurant has a lot more to offer. Specializing in American cuisine, most palates can be pleased here. This modern steakhouse-meets-sleek-lounge features a tempting raw bar, salads, appetizers (crispy rock shrimp, tuna tartare, mini burgers), and entrées such as burgers, fish, chicken, and all manner of steak. Enjoy your beefy dinner with sides such as jalapeño and cheddar grits, Brussels sprouts and bacon, wild mushrooms, or parmesan truffle fries. Kid-friendly selections are offered, too. Finish with a mini ice cream cone sampler,

---

HOT TIP!

Portobello Italian Country Trattoria has undergone a multi-million-dollar renovation. The new iteration of the eatery—Terralina Crafted Italian—was masterminded by "Top Chef Master" Tony Mantuano and features dishes inspired by his culinary adventures across Italy. For menu details and reservations, call 404-939-3463, or visit *www.disneyworld.com*.

B breakfast   L lunch   D dinner   S snacks   / $ under $15 $$ $15–$36 $$$ $36–$60 $$$$ $60 and up

The Edison

A lavish "Industrial Gothic"–style venue in The Landing, The Edison (modeled after the original Los Angeles version) is a 1920s-themed restaurant, bar, and nighttime destination. Designed to resemble a power plant, it recalls a robust era of invention and imagination. The menu features classic American cuisine, craft cocktails, and live entertainment. Reservations are recommended for this new hotspot. **D·$$$–$$$$**

orange cheesecake, or warm berry parfait. There's a full bar and a well-rounded wine list. Guests may dine on the rooftop or in the modern main dining area. Note that the volume of the "background" music is on the high side. Reservations are recommended. **LDS·$$$–$$$$**

TEA TRADERS CAFE (The Landing): The counter-service spot (with 6 stools) serves tea in many ways: loose-leaf, iced, frozen, etc. Scones, cookies, and ginormous doughnuts are also at the ready. The shop sells cast-iron teapots, tea sets, and more tea-based paraphernalia. There are outdoor tables nearby. **S·$–$$**

PHOTO BY JILL SAFRO

T-REX CAFE: A PREHISTORIC FAMILY ADVENTURE (Marketplace): Dinosaurs throw one heck of a dinner party. See for yourself at this dino-themed feasting facility. When you enter, take note of hosts we were all led to believe were extinct. Okay, they're *mechanical* dinosaurs, but they're still pretty cool. As are the waterfalls, bubbling geysers, and fossil dig site. Appease hunger pangs with anything from Jurassic Salad to Mammoth Mushroom Ravioli. With soup, sandwiches, pasta, seafood, and steaks, this place aims to please. Reservations are recommended. Doors open at 11 A.M. daily and close at 11 P.M. Sunday through Thursday and at midnight on Friday and Saturday. **LD·$$–$$$·🐭**

VIVOLI IL GELATO (The Landing): A family-run establishment, Vivoli il Gelato comes to you from Florence, Italy. Creamy gelato is offered in 24 flavors. That could include hazelnut, coffee, banana, peanut butter, brandied cherry, salted caramel, and more. Baked treats are available, too. There are outdoor tables at this sweet spot across from The Boathouse. **LDS·$–$$**

WINE BAR GEORGE (The Landing): The masterpiece of Master Sommelier George Miliotes, this 210-seat lounge resembles a winemaker's estate. It's a cozy yet elegant environment in which to savor sips from acclaimed wineries and promising up-and-comers. There are more than 100 selections on the list, available by the glass or bottle. They pair beautifully with small plate offerings.

FYI: George Miliotes is one of just 230 Master Sommeliers in the world. Impressive! **LDS·$$–$$$**

WOLFGANG PUCK BAR & GRILL (Town Center): "Elegant farmhouse" is the theme behind Chef Puck's latest contribution to the Disney dining scene. Capturing the essense of laid-back California, the new eatery features fresh takes on comfort classics, signature dishes with Mediterranean influences, and hand-crafted specialty drinks. Reservations are recommended. **LDS·$$–$$$$·🐭**

WOLFGANG PUCK EXPRESS (Marketplace): This quick-service spot by Disney Days of Christmas shop offers pizzas, pasta, salmon, chicken, meatloaf, mac and cheese, sandwiches, soups, salads, and more. **LDS·$–$$·🐭**

JALEO BY JOSÉ ANDRÉS (West Side): The flavors of Spain have found a home in Disney Springs, thanks to world-renowned Chef José Andrés. The extensive tapas (small plates) menu features a combination of classic and contemporary España. Savory selections include hand-carved Jamon Iberico de Bellota, wood-grilled Iberico pork, and paella cooked over a wood fire. Reservations are recommended. The multilevel eatery features a grab-and-go area, too. It offers a variety of Spanish-style sandwiches, snack items, and beverages. At press time, Jaleo by José Andrés was on course to open in 2018. For updates, visit *www.disneyworld.com*. **LDS·$$–$$$**

Each of the nearly 30 resorts at Walt Disney World offers its own set of specially themed eateries. There are clambakes at the Beach Club, luaus at the Polynesian Village, wild game at the Wilderness Lodge, and beignets at Port Orleans French Quarter. Meals may be served buffet, family, or traditional table-service or fast-food style. Disney characters are often on hand, especially for breakfast, and some snack spots stay open 'round the clock. In fact, the resort dining scene has expanded and been upgraded so much of late that the (occasionally arduous) task of resort-hopping is a more worthwhile experience than ever before.

Reservations are a key part of the Disney dining circuit (call 407-WDW-DINE [939-3463]).

All-Star Resorts

Each of these resorts features a colorful, themed central food court. All-Star Sports has the End Zone food court in Stadium Hall. The Intermission food court is in Melody Hall at the All-Star Music resort. And All-Star Movies has the World Premiere food court in Cinema Hall. The food courts offer similar food stands, with Music and Sports having undergone recent refurbishments. The selections include pasta, pizza, burgers, hot dogs, sandwiches, salads, ice cream, a variety of breakfast and baked goods, plus grab-and-go selections. Expect to find kid-pleasers, such as chicken nuggets and mac and cheese, too. **BLDS·$–$$·**

Animal Kingdom Lodge

BOMA—FLAVORS OF AFRICA: Resembling an African marketplace, Boma offers an impressively diverse selection—the fare served represents the continent of Africa. It's one big buffet with multiple stations, and the food is as good as what you'd expect in a fine dining place.

The all-you-care-to-eat affair provides an excellent bang for your Disney dining buck. Breakfast features Kenyan coffee, Jungle Juice, omelets, cereals, fresh fruit, sausage, biscuits, ham, corned beef, and more. At dinner, expect to fill your plate with items such as salads (including watermelon rind salad and Tunisian couscous salad); an assortment of breads, soups, and stews; grilled seafood; roasted meats; and a nice array of vegetarian selections. For dessert, do sample the decadent zebra domes—you'll regret it if you

Fill 'er Up—Rapid Fill Mugs

Buy one cup and get unlimited refills for your entire Walt Disney World vacation? It sounds too good to be true. Yet, any guest staying at a WDW–owned-and-operated resort may purchase a plastic mug—for about $18, plus tax—and refill it with coffee, tea, lemonade, and other soft drinks for the length of their stay.* At press time, the following resorts offered the popular "Rapid Fill" refillable mug program (filling stations can be found at the spots noted in parentheses):

All-Star resorts (food courts); Animal Kingdom Lodge (The Mara, Johari Treasures, and Maji pool bar); BoardWalk (Belle Vue Lounge [morning coffee only], Leaping Horse Libations, and BoardWalk Bakery); Caribbean Beach (Island Markets); Contemporary (Contempo Cafe and Cove Bar); Coronado Springs (Pepper Market and Siesta pool bar); Fort Wilderness (Trail's End and by the Meadow pool); Grand Floridian (Gasparilla Island Grill and Beaches Pool Bar); Old Key West (Good's Food To Go and Turtle Shack); Polynesian (Capt. Cook's); Pop Century (food court); Port Orleans (food courts); Saratoga Springs (Artist's Palette and On the Rocks pool bar); Wilderness Lodge (Roaring Fork snack bar); Art of Animation (Landscape of Flavors); and Yacht and Beach Club (Beaches & Cream, Beach Club Marketplace, Hurricane Hanna's Grill, and Market at Ale & Compass).

* Refills may be made at any Disney–owned-and-operated resort, but not at any park.

don't. It's tempting to overeat at a bounteous feast such as this, so consider taking tiny portions of everything. You can go back for seconds of your favorites. Note that the menu does change throughout the year. The wine list includes selections from various African vineyards. Even if you're not staying at the lodge, it's worth the trip. Reservations are required. **BD·$$–$$$·**

JIKO—THE COOKING PLACE: Jiko offers one of the more unusual Walt Disney World dining experiences. Its cuisine is inspired by the tastes of Africa, with influences from around the globe. Start with one of the paper-thin flatbreads (like roasted chicken with lime chakalaka, lamb chopper cheese, and pickled sweet bell peppers), grilled wild boar tenderloin, artisanal cheeses, or seasonal salads. You may find curry-rubbed lamb

GOOD MEALS, GREAT TIMES

loin, braised beef short ribs, maize-crusted grouper, vegetable and tofu sambusas, and oak-grilled filet mignon on the menu, too. End your meal with a fabulous cheese course and/or sweets such as avocado custard cake, no-sugar-added pistachio and cherry trifle, or seasonal crème brûlée. The wine list is exclusively South African, one of the most extensive collections in the U.S. It's a nice spot for a grown-up splurge. Though it's hardly a kid favorite—the sometimes exotic cuisine may not appeal to timid palates—there are child-friendly offerings. Reservations are recommended. The small lounge area offers the full menu, too. Incidentally, the word *jiko* is Swahili for "the cooking place." D·$$$–$$$$·❤

THE MARA: An impressive quick-service restaurant that has something for everyone—including a small grab-and-go section for those in a hurry. There are a couple of stations at which (excellent) hot entreés are freshly prepared. Among the prepackaged options are sandwiches, salads, fruit, yogurt, and baked goods. FYI: The eatery is named for a river that flows through Kenya and Tanzania. B L D S·$–$$·❤

SANAA: Pronounced *sa-NAH*, the name of this eatery means "artwork" in Swahili. The Kidani Village spot has a family-friendly menu featuring Disney's take on African-Indian cuisine. The Indian-style bread service, good for sharing and served with a choice of three accompaniments, is a nice way to start the meal. Signature dishes include chicken or shrimp curry and slow-cooked beef short ribs. For lunch, try the salad sampler. Even the burgers have an Indian touch, served on soft, warm naan bread. Desserts introduce many tastes, from mango berry tapioca pudding to Tanzanian chocolate mousse. The quality of the fare here is nothing short of outstanding. Reservations are recommended. L D·$$–$$$·❤

PHOTO BY MIKE CARROLL

Art of Animation

LANDSCAPE OF FLAVORS: "Better for you" options is the theme of this vividly adorned food court, where everything is made fresh once it is ordered. Breakfast offerings include egg white frittata, challah French toast, and vegetarian breakfast sandwiches on naan bread, as well as more traditional selections. Four mini shops offer soups, salads, pizza, sandwiches, burgers, pasta, shrimp, chicken, braised short ribs, grilled fish, and lo mein. There is a small selection of grab-and-go items, too. Made-to-order beverage options include smoothies and specialty coffees. Also available are organic teas, beers (including a gluten-free selection), wine, coffee, and juices. There is a gelato station, too. B L D S·$–$$·❤

BoardWalk

AMPLE HILLS CREAMERY: The hand-crafted ice cream—lovingly made with hormone-free milk from grass-fed cows and organic cane sugar—is a bona fide crowd-pleaser. Flavor offerings may differ a bit from day to day, providing a great reason to come back. You'll find it next to ESPN Club. S·$·❤

BELLE VUE LOUNGE: This cozy cocktail spot, located on the resort's second floor, offers continental breakfast each morning. Expect to find items such as bagels, cereal, yogurt, whole fruit, muffins, and croissants, plus juice, milk, coffee, and tea (the latter two can go straight into a Rapid Fill mug). B·$·❤

BIG RIVER GRILLE & BREWING WORKS: Guests may observe (and sample) as the brew-master creates flagship ales and two seasonal brews at this working brew pub. The straightfor-ward-but-satisfying menu generally includes burgers, steaks, and salads. Sandwiches are a cut above. Other menu favorites: flame-grilled meatloaf and Atlantic salmon. The interior has a nice, pubby feel—but we prefer to sit at outdoor tables on the boardwalk (especially in the cooler evening hours). Seating is available on a first-come, first-served basis. L D S·$$–$$$·❤

BOARDWALK BAKERY: Trattoria al Forno's next-door neighbor offers baked goods, sandwiches, soups, salads, and beverages. Sandwiches include roast beef with horseradish mayo and provolone, and smoked turkey on seven-grain bread. Sweet treats (the specialty of this house) run from eclairs and crumb cake to apple tarts and cupcakes. This is also the place to buy and fill refillable resort mugs. **B L D S · $ – $ $ · ♥**

BOARDWALK PIZZA WINDOW: Nestled into Trattoria al Forno is an opportunity to enjoy freshly prepared plain and pepperoni pizza, served by the pie or the slice (cheese, pepperoni, kale and chicken, and "signature combo" topped with sausage, onions, peppers, and a balsamic glaze). Salads, chips, cookies, beer, wine, and soft drinks are dispensed here, too. The quick-service window is usually open from noon until about midnight. **L D S · $ – $ $ · ♥**

ESPN CLUB: For sports fans, this joint is pure heaven. The friendly, occasionally frenzied bar/family restaurant is a hard-core sports club. If there's a game being played, chances are it's on one of the million (okay, hundred) TVs.

The standard, reliable fare includes wings, burgers, sandwiches, grilled fish, and salads. Both the dining room and the bar area serve cocktails and the full menu. We make an effort to get there at least an hour ahead to get a table or a spot at the bar on days when big games are

PHOTO BY JILL SAFRO

scheduled. ESPN Club accepts weekday lunch reservations (11:30 A.M. to 4 P.M.), but it's a first-come, first-served establishment at most other times. Get there early. Note that the Club may offer premium seating for select "Big Games." Call 407-566-5656 for reservations and additional information. On very busy days, ESPN Club provides bar service out on the boardwalk. **L D S · $ $ – $ $ $ · ♥**

FLYING FISH: The decor elevates the appeal of this upscale dining destination, which recently underwent a thorough and dramatic refurbishment. Be sure to look up—the flying fish chandelier is quite a sight to behold. As always, this restaurant gives most fine, big-city spots a run for their money. (The tab rivals said hotspots, too.)

The menu changes often, but the stars of the show are Chef Tim Majoras' creatively prepared sustainable seafood dishes. You'll always find the signature potato-wrapped snapper with a rich leek fondue and red wine and butter sauce, the crisp crab cakes, plus a char-crusted New York strip steak. We are routinely impressed by the service and find the menu worthy of the price tag. Reservations are recommended. As far as the Disney Dining Plan goes, Flying Fish is designated as a Signature restaurant. **D · $ $ $ $ · ♥**

TRATTORIA AL FORNO: Taste buds take a tour of Italy with Trattoria's tempting array of regional specialties and crowd-pleasing classics. Signature standouts include wood-fired pizzas and pastas prepared *al forno* (baked in an oven). The family-friendly eatery celebrates the diversity of Italian cuisine with housemade mozzarella atop Neapolitan-style pizzas, hand-rolled pastas, seasonal seafood, and vegetables. The exclusively Italian wine list features more than 60 offerings by the bottle and 25 by the glass. Draft and bottle beers, grapa, cocktails, and soft drinks round out the drink menu. For dessert, consider

Dinner at Sea

For Disney's ultimate dinner-and-a-show splurge, consider reserving the elegant *Grand 1* yacht. You and up to 17 lucky invitees can enjoy a private tour of the lakes near the Magic Kingdom capped off with a viewing of Happily Ever After, the park's fireworks show—all the while devouring delicacies prepared by chefs at the Grand Floridian resort. The possibilities range from an intimate cruise for two, complete with dinner and champagne, to a swinging cocktail party for up to 18, with a boatload of shrimp, chips, wings, beer, wine, and soft drinks.

Cost starts at about $400 (plus tax) per hour to rent the 5-room floating fantasyland. Driver and deckhand are included; refreshments are not. Prices vary depending on the time of day. To book, call 407-WDW-PLAY at least 24 hours and up to 90 days ahead. The *Grand 1* docks at the Grand Floridian but can pick up passengers at the Contemporary, Polynesian Village, and Wilderness Lodge.

B breakfast   **L** lunch   **D** dinner   **S** snacks   /   **$** under $15   **$$** $15–$36   **$$$** $36–$60   **$$$$** $60 and up

tiramisu, zeppoli (sugar-coated fried dough), or assorted flavors of gelato. The morning meal comes with a side of Disney characters. Expect to see favorite friends from films such as *Tangled* and *The Little Mermaid* at the new Bon Voyage Breakfast. The menu has selections such as frittatas, steel-cut oatmeal, and waffles with espresso-mascarpone cream. B D · $$–$$$ · 🦇

Caribbean Beach

Caribbean Beach resort is undergoing an extensive refurbishment. Its usual dining destinations, Old Port Royale food court, Shutters restaurant at Old Port Royale, Calypso Trading Post, and Banana Cabana pool bar are expected to remain closed during most of 2018. Here are some dining choices for Caribbean Beach Resort guests to enjoy until all of the pixie dust settles:

CENTERTOWN: A bountiful, all-you-care-to-eat buffet is offered for lunch and dinner. Expect family-friendly selections at both meals. Soft drinks and cocktails are served. B D · $$–$$$ · 🦇

IN-ROOM DINING: Guests may have pizza, sandwiches, and pasta delivered to their rooms from 4 P.M. until midnight. To place an order, press Pizza Delivery on your in-room phone. Beer and wine are also available. (Please have your government-issued photo ID handy to prove you are at least 21 years old.) Note that an 18 percent gratuity and a $3 delivery charge apply to in-room delivery orders. D · $$ · 🦇

ISLAND MARKETS: There are three grab-and-go locations where guests can pick up food for breakfast, lunch, and dinner. You'll find them near the Martinique pool and in the Aruba and Jamaica regions of the resort. B L D S · $$ · 🦇

HOT TIP!

Would you like to watch Happily Ever After, the Magic Kingdom's fireworks display, from the private perch at California Grill? You'll need to dine at the Grill—but it doesn't have to be during the show. If you finish your meal pre-fireworks, return to the second-floor check-in desk later that day, present your receipt, and you'll be escorted to the eatery via private elevator.

Contemporary

CALIFORNIA GRILL: Delighting diners for decades, the World-famous California Grill still graces most guests' must-do lists. The West Coast theme shines through in dishes prepared with the freshest seasonal and local produce available. "Brunch at the Top" features blueberry pancakes, poached lobster Benedict, shrimp and grits, Chef's frittata, and other creatively prepared dishes. The fixed-price brunch costs about $80 for adults, $48 for kids (ages 3 to 11).

Dinner standouts include grilled pork tenderloin with goat cheese polenta, mushrooms, and applesauce; oak-fired filet of beef; ostrich filet with crispy potato croquettes, grilled royal trumpet mushrooms, and Brussels sprouts leaves; and wild-caught Alaskan halibut. Sushi classics include dragon roll with spicy tataki tuna, shrimp tempura, bell pepper, avocado, and chili-soy glaze; and spicy kazan roll (crab, shrimps, and scallops in a spicy fireball sauce).

The wine list—which includes 250 selections, 80 of which are available by the glass—is a nice mix of greatest hits and good finds. There are ten varieties of saki and a selection of (predominantly Californian) craft beers. Housemade desserts provide the finishing touches, and there are sweeping views of the Magic Kingdom and the Seven Seas Lagoon (from select seats).

California Grill is always busy and the fare is first-rate. Reservations are a must. Changes or cancellations must be made at least 24 hours ahead to avoid the $10-per-person fee. This is a Disney Dining Plan Signature restaurant (so it requires two table-service credits per diner).

An outdoor perch (exclusively available to California Grill patrons) affords bird's-eye views of the Magic Kingdom and its fireworks presentations (complete with the show's music). Guests (including those planning to visit the lounge) check in on the hotel's second floor and are escorted to the restaurant's express elevator. Dinner starts at 5 P.M. Brunch D · $$$$ · 🦇

CHEF MICKEY'S: Chef Mickey and his pals host this buffet-style meal, with dramatic views of the monorail passing above. The eatery serves family-friendly buffet breakfast, brunch, and dinner. The changing menu takes advantage of seasonal offerings; a sundae bar provides a sweet finish. At some point during the meal, Chef Mickey will stop by your table, as will several of his friends. Be prepared to drop your fork and twirl your napkin at a moment's notice. This is a very popular eatery with a loyal following. Kids

PHOTO BY MIKE CARROLL

simply adore the experience. It's a fun place to celebrate a child's birthday, too. Reservations are an absolute must. B·Brunch·D·$$$·🐭

CONTEMPO CAFE: The Contemporary resort snack bar can be found on the fourth floor, beside Chef Mickey's. This spot serves impressive made-to-order fare. The grab-and-go section offers drinks (including beer and wine), wraps, yogurt, fresh fruit, sushi, desserts, and more. BLDS·$–$$·🐭

THE WAVE . . . OF AMERICAN FLAVORS: A stellar full-service eatery, this establishment features creative American fusion cuisine. Think "bold cooking inspired by locally sourced ingredients." Starters of note: jumbo lump crab cake, bacon and egg with smoked cheddar grits, and artisanal cheeses. Main courses have included grilled beef tenderloin, cioppino, roasted chicken breast, and Tamarin noodle bowl. The dessert menu tempts with bananas Foster, apple cobbler with caramel ice cream (yum!), and chocolate peanut butter cake. It's possible to sip selections from the New World wine list via flight samplers. The Wave is on the resort's first floor.

We would eat breakfast, lunch, or dinner here without a moment's hesitation. The adjacent lounge is a perfect place for an aperitif, an after-dinner drink, a light snack, or a meal (the full menu is available to lounge guests). Reservations are recommended. BLD·$$–$$$·🐭

Coronado Springs

CAFE RIX: Stop here for bagels and croissants, salads (Cobb, Greek, and house), chicken Caesar wraps, pastries, gelato, sorbet, beer, wine, soft drinks, and specialty coffee drinks. Additional snacks include fruit cups, veggies and hummus, side salads, yogurt parfait, and chocolate or Key lime mousse. BLDS·$–$$·🐭

LAS VENTANAS: An unpretentious locale, Las Ventanas serves simple yet satisfying American fare. Breakfast runs from "ancient grain" pancakes to steak and eggs. Burgers, herb-marinated chicken breast sandwiches, and blackened mahi mahi are lunch and dinnertime possibilities. Cap off the meal with sorbet, Key lime pie, or Chambord mascarpone. There are kid-friendly choices (grilled cheese and chicken sandwiches), but the atmosphere is unlikely to enchant wee ones. Reservations are recommended. BLDS·$$–$$$·🐭

MAYA GRILL: Guests here dine inside a Mayan pyramid, beside a volcano (dormant, of course). The menu has a bit of everything: seafood, meat, and poultry, with a touch of Latino spices added to some of the creations. Entrées range from sirloin fajitas to Veracruz-style snapper or Yucatán roasted pork. Desserts include coconut flan and panna cotta. Dinner is served from 5 P.M. to 10 P.M. Reservations are recommended. BD·$$$·🐭

PEPPER MARKET: This busy, casual food court has a large seating area and a variety of food stations. Choose from barbecue ribs, Yucatán chicken, tacos, paninis, pizza, pasta, salads, empanadas, and other Mexican fare—all freshly prepared. For breakfast, there are eggs, Mickey waffles, breakfast bowls, Southwestern omelets, and more. Anything may be ordered to go. Given this resort's popularity with the convention set, expect a proliferation of hungry humans during traditional weekday breakfast and lunch times. BLDS·$–$$·🐭

Tables in Wonderland

Annual Passholders and Florida residents are eligible for the Tables in Wonderland (T.I.W.) discount dining program. It affords members up to 20 percent savings off food and beverages at many WDW table-service eateries. The discount is good for you and up to 9 members of your party. Present a valid photo ID and your T.I.W. card when you place an order with a server. To net the discount for the rest of the party, the check must be paid by the T.I.W. member. Membership is valid for one year and costs $150 for Annual Passholders and $175 for Florida residents (note that the price went up substantially last year). For details, call 407-566-5858. For a list of participating locations, go to: *http://disneyworld.disney .go.com/passholderprogram/dining-discounts/.*

Disney's Old Key West

GOOD'S FOOD TO GO: A walk-up window with a simple-yet-satisfying menu: Hamburgers, cheeseburgers, deli sandwiches, salads, ice cream, snacks, and breakfast items are among the offerings at Good's. BLDS·$–$$·❤

GURGLING SUITCASE: This pocket-sized lounge packs a real punch! In addition to a full bar, the Suitcase features nibbles such as burgers, pulled pork nachos, conch fritters, grouper bites, and onion rings. It's possible to order from the Olivia's Cafe menu, too. Many items can be ordered to go. LDS·$–$$$·❤

OLIVIA'S CAFE: We thoroughly enjoy the Key West manner with which Olivia's approaches its theme. The laid-back setting and menu convey the spirit of the leisure-centric locale. Breakfast includes standards, but also interesting combos like poached eggs served over sweet potato hash, topped with Key West hollandaise. The lunch/dinner menu offers salads, conch chowder, crab cakes, seared scallops, burgers, and sandwiches. End with a Key lime tart, chocolate cake, or a banana bread pudding sundae. The menu changes seasonally. Wine, beer, and specialty cocktails are served. Reservations are recommended for all meals. BLD·$$–$$$·❤

Fort Wilderness

Many people choose to cook their own meals here. Some supplies are available at the Meadow and Settlement Trading Posts (open from 8 A.M. to 10 P.M. in winter; to 11 P.M. in summer), others may be delivered by a nearby grocery store (see page 227 for details). Trail's End is the only eat-in restaurant, but it has a corner dedicated to takeout: P & J's Southern Takeout offers breakfast, lunch, and dinner selections to bring back to a campsite or enjoy at a nearby table.

TRAIL'S END RESTAURANT: True, it's a bit out of the way for anyone but Fort Wilderness guests (and even for some of them!), but for many, this rustic spot is well worth the trip.

The informal log-walled restaurant offers a hearty buffet breakfast. The fare is basic but bountiful. Breakfast selections include grits, biscuits and gravy, and breakfast pizza. Brunch is offered on weekends (about $23 for adults; $13 for kids). Lunch is served à la carte and features fried chicken and waffles, sandwiches, salads; sautéed catfish, and fried green tomatoes. For dinner,

expect the buffet to have smoked pork ribs, peel-and-eat shrimp, fried chicken, carved meats, a salad bar, plus a variety of side dishes and desserts. Pizza is served daily from 4 P.M. until 10 P.M. Beer and wine are served by the glass (or mason jar). Reservations are recommended. Breakfast costs about $19 for adults, $11 for kids; lunch is à la carte; dinner is about $28 for adults, $16 for kids. After the meal, you can relax in a rocking chair on the front porch. (Allow extra travel time to get here, just in case.) B Brunch LDS·$–$$·❤

Grand Floridian

CÍTRICOS: From the aromas wafting from the open kitchen, it's clear that the chef has vowed to wow you with cuisine from the Americas and the Mediterranean, herb by fragrant herb. The fare varies seasonally but may include such items as crispy risotto with mascarpone or beef short rib. Adventurous palates are most at home here. The menu is not extensive, but the wine list sure is. Restaurant sommeliers are on hand to recommend wine pairings.

A private dining room is available for parties of up to 12. The lounge is ideal for solo diners or those without a reservation. Reservations are necessary for the restaurant. D·$$$–$$$$·❤

GASPARILLA ISLAND GRILL: Breakfast items along the lines of scrambled eggs, waffles, bagels, and cereal are served until 11 A.M. After that, made-to-order selections such as sandwiches, burgers, pizza, and freshly tossed salads are available. Grab-and-go options such as sushi, yogurt, fresh fruit, and snacks are on hand 24/7 in this quick-service spot near the marina (overnight pickin's may be slim). There is indoor and outdoor seating. If you purchased a refillable mug, this is the place to fill it up. BLDS·$–$$·❤

GRAND FLORIDIAN CAFE: A pleasant spot, the cafe is a relatively reasonably priced, low-key way to check out one of Walt Disney World's poshest resorts.

Breakfast extends a wee bit beyond the usual fare. Lunch and dinner menus vary seasonally but have traditional American dishes: onion soup, burgers, and the signature Grand Floridian sandwich. The wine selection is excellent. Reservations are recommended, but it may be possible to get a table without one if you're willing to wait. **BLD · $$$ · ✿**

NARCOOSSEE'S: Named for a nearby Central Florida town, Narcoossee's specializes in fresh sustainable seafood—with the occasional land-based entrée making surf-and-turf combinations a decadent possibility. Narcoossee's has upscale selections (and prices), but the atmosphere is rather relaxed. The display kitchen presents dinner dishes such as steamed mussels, grilled steak, and Maine lobster. The international wine selection is quite good—you might even enjoy a pre-dinner glass on the veranda. The view of the Seven Seas Lagoon and Cinderella Castle (in the distance) completes the experience. Brunch offers housemade pastries, shrimp and grits, brioche French toast, lobster eggs Benedict, chicken and waffles, steak and eggs, and pan-fried salmon. Reservations are recommended. The lounge here offers a full menu (and does not require a reservation) as well as a full bar and an abundance of wines offered by the bottle or the glass. The dress code is business casual. The prix-fixe brunch costs about $69 for adults, $41 for kids (ages 3 to 11). **Brunch D · $$$–$$$$ · ✿**

1900 PARK FARE: The atmosphere is reminiscent of an old-time amusement park, but the sophisticated buffet menu and subtle decor make this one of the most elegant character restaurants on the property. Mary Poppins and her friends mingle with guests during the bountiful daily breakfast. Cinderella and members of her royal family visit the dining room during the dinner hours. Keep in mind that the lineup of characters does change from time to time.

Dinner features seafood, salads, pastas, veggies, breads, carved meats, and housemade desserts. The offerings change seasonally. A salad bar and dessert bar stand nearby. There's a kids' buffet, too. It offers pizza, pasta, and vegetables. The restaurant's focal point is Big Bertha, a band organ built in Paris nearly a century ago. She sits in a proscenium and rises 15 feet above the floor. Reservations are recommended. Brunch may be offered seasonally. **B Brunch D · $$$ · ✿**

VICTORIA & ALBERT'S: The dining room in the only AAA 5-Diamond restaurant in Central Florida seats just 54 guests (all of whom must have already celebrated their 10th birthday). It is indulgent without being too haute to handle (although the steep prices may curb some folks' enthusiasm) and is considered by many to be the grand dame of the Disney dining scene.

The 7-course "Chef's Tasting Menu" changes frequently, always offering a selection of farm-fresh fish, poultry, and beef as main courses. But the beauty of this high-end experience is all the little tastes as you make your way through the $185-per-person (plus tax and gratuity) adventure. You might start with lobster or quail, then move on to seared wild turbot or pork tenderloin. The cheese course is worth every calorie. And, even with seven courses, you must reserve room for the indulgent desserts: a flurry of soufflés, chocolate, and more. Perfect portions keep it all surprisingly manageable. The strains of a harp or violin provide a romantic backdrop. The wine list is encyclopedic. Wine pairings are available for an additional $65 per person (do let your server know about any personal wine preferences).

The main dining room also serves a 10-course "Chef's Degustation Menu"—a series of small courses inspired by Chef Scott Hunnel's travels to Asia, Spain, Italy, and France. The cost is $235 per person ($340 with wine pairing).

For an extra-special (and extra-splurgy) experience, book the Chef's Table (for up to 10 guests; $250 per person, plus tax and gratuity) or the Queen Victoria Room ($225 per diner, plus tax and tip). With just four tables, the latter provides the restaurant's most exclusive, luxurious setting.

At the end of the meal, all guests are given a souvenir menu to commemorate the occasion.

In sum, though the experience is an extremely expensive one, for many it is also quite special. Jackets are required for men. Guests must be at least 10 years old to dine here. Reservations are an absolute must; call 407-939-3862. Restaurant information and sample menus are available at *www.victoria-alberts.com*. D·$$$$

Polynesian Village

CAPT. COOK'S: The captain dispenses snacks and light fare 24 hours a day. It's a good spot for made-to-order breakfast items such as eggs, Mickey waffles, or the ever-popular fried, banana-stuffed Tonga toast. Lunch and dinner bring burgers, curried seafood stew, pulled pork nachos, Thai coconut meatballs, hot dogs, flatbreads (plain, pepperoni, and Hawaiian [marinara, pineapple, onions, ham, mozzarella, and parmesan]), Caesar salad with chicken, sandwiches, and grab-and-go items such as noodle salad, yogurt, fruit, pastries, and snacks. Milk, beer, wine, and soft drinks are available here, too. Come here to buy and fill the Poly's refillable mug (aka Rapid Fill) with soft drinks. B L D S·$–$$·❤

KONA CAFE: Warm colors and South Seas decor render the crisp, fluid design of this open dining space cozy and casual. The menu tends a tad toward the exotic side, but there's a nice variety of choices. Lunch and dinner menus feature Asian-influenced entrées. Possibilities include pot stickers, pan-Asian noodles, Kona-coffee-rubbed pork tenderloin, sushi, and market-fresh sustainable fish. The morning meal offers Tonga toast (banana-stuffed, fried sourdough bread coated with cinnamon sugar), plus traditional breakfast items. There is a solid wine list, and islands-inspired cocktails are served. The pressed-pot coffee is a fan favorite. You'll find Kona Cafe on the second floor of the Great Ceremonial House, just around the corner from 'Ohana. Reservations are recommended for all meals. B L D S·$$–$$$·❤

KONA ISLAND: A coffee bar by day, this is a super spot for a quick sip on your way to the monorail. Light breakfast items such as fruit, bagels, and pastries are offered, too.

Later in the day this area becomes something of a Kona Cafe annex/sushi bar. Guests may sit at the Kona Island counter and order from the Cafe menu. A member of the Kona Cafe waitstaff will take your order. Seating is limited, but many selections may be ordered to go. Beer, wine, sake, and cocktails are served. B L D S·$–$$$·❤

'OHANA: On the second floor of the Great Ceremonial House, this restaurant is a meticulously themed, family-friendly eatery, complete with entertainment. An interesting twist of note: 'Ohana's family-style dinner experience—a South Pacific feast prepared in the restaurant's open-fire cooking pit—does not come with a menu, so no decisions have to be made. The oak-grilled skewers of chicken, steak, and spicy shrimp just keep coming. Honey coriander chicken wings, pot stickers, green salad, coconut bread, pan-Asian noodles tossed in teriyaki sauce, and stir-fried veggies are among the accompaniments, and dessert is bread pudding served à la mode with warm caramel sauce. Soft drinks are included. Beer, wine, and cocktails are extra.

'Ohana's setting, which features wood carvings under a vast thatched roof, is rather festive. So much so that there are periodic boisterous hula dances, limbo, and coconut-rolling contests for the little ones. A Polynesian singer croons from time to time.

Breakfast is also a family affair—make that extended family, as Lilo, Stitch, and their good friends Mickey and Pluto host the morning meal. Breakfast fare is basic and presented family style. Keep in mind that the character lineup does change from time to time. Reservations are strongly recommended. B D·$$$–$$$$·❤

OASIS GRILL: The laid-back Oasis Grill is situated next to the Polynesian's Oasis pool. It serves up items such as cheeseburgers, fish tacos, chicken avocado wraps, and more. The O.G. is adjacent to the Oasis Bar. L D S·$–$$·❤

PINEAPPLE LANAI: This sweet stop offers WDW's classic Dole Whip frozen pineapple dessert—served plain, twisted with vanilla soft-serve, or as a float with pineapple juice. It's located on the ground level. S·$·❤

GOOD MEALS, GREAT TIMES

TRADER SAM'S GROG GROTTO: It's hard to be grouchy at this spot—Trader Sam will see to that. With a theme inspired by the Jungle Cruise and Enchanted Tiki Room attractions, Trader Sam's features drinks (tropical and otherwise) and small plates such as pan-fried dumplings, chicken lettuce wraps, and sushi rolls. Patio seating is relatively easy to snag, but securing indoor seats often requires time, patience, and a pager. Doors open at 4 P.M. and close promptly at midnight. Note that folks start lining up for the inside seats at about 3:30 P.M. S·$–$$

Pop Century

EVERYTHING POP!: The selection at this colorful food court in Classic Hall has included burgers, flatbreads, omelets, pizza, rotisserie chicken, roast turkey, nachos, Asian dishes, made-to-order salads, seafood, salads, hot dogs, sandwiches (tuna, meatball, turkey, or veggie), breakfast items, and baked goods (tie-dyed cheesecake!). Feel free to join the jolly cast members as they dance the Twist at 8 A.M. and the Hustle at 6 P.M. BLDS·$–$$·❤

Port Orleans French Quarter

SASSAGOULA FLOATWORKS & FOOD FACTORY: A food court with a Mardi Gras theme, this spot offers pizza, pasta, burgers, sandwiches, soups, salads, fried chicken, BBQ ribs, gelato, and bakery products. The Big Easy is well represented here: New Orleans–inspired menu items include classic gumbo, po' boys, muffalettas, jambalaya, and made-to-order beignets (with dipping sauces). BLDS·$–$$·❤

HOT TIP!

Guests staying at Port Orleans French Quarter and Riverside may have pizza delivered to their rooms between 4 P.M. and midnight. Call Sassagoula Pizza Express from your resort room telephone to order whole pies, drinks, and sweet snacks. There is a $15 minimum per order and the Disney Dining Plan is accepted. Guests using the Disney Dining Plan should note that pizza delivery requires two entitlements per order. Each order provides enough to satisfy two grown-up appetites (in most cases).

Port Orleans Riverside

BOATWRIGHT'S DINING HALL: Southern specialties and American comfort food is the big draw here—think prime rib and jambalaya. Beer, wine, and cocktails are available, as are soft drinks. The restaurant is quite popular, as it's the resort's only table-service eatery. Reservations are recommended. Walk-up requests are typically admitted when the restaurant opens at 5 P.M. D·$$–$$$·❤

RIVERSIDE MILL: This high-ceilinged food court styled in the image of a cotton mill (complete with working waterwheel) offers a half dozen food counters. Collectively, the stands serve pizza; pasta; fried, grilled, and roast chicken; cheeseburgers; salads; sandwiches (including New Orleans–style muffalettas); ice cream; and fresh-baked goods. They're big on "create your own" here, too. (You can customize an omelet, salad, and/or pasta dish.) There's ample seating, so it's usually possible to get a table. All items may be packaged to go. BLDS·$–$$·❤

Saratoga Springs

THE ARTIST'S PALETTE: Set in a converted artist's loft within Walt Disney World's sprawling resort, this spot offers breakfast, lunch, and dinner. Among the selections are fresh tossed salads, made-to-order sandwiches, pizza, baked goods, and more. There are some grocery items, as well as a variety of grab-and-go selections. BLDS·$–$$·❤

THE PADDOCK GRILL: Head to this quick-service window for freshly prepared sandwiches (grilled chicken, spice-crusted fish, roasted veggie, etc.), chicken chopped salad, bacon cheeseburgers, and housemade potato chips (which were actually invented in Saratoga). BLDS·$–$$·❤

THE TURF CLUB BAR & GRILL: A restaurant with an old-fashioned horse racing theme, this table-service eatery serves soup, prime rib, pan-seared scallops, sustainable fish of the day, pasta, salads, New York strip steak, roasted lamb, fried chicken breast, spice-rubbed pork tenderloin, and more. D·$$$·❤

Swan & Dolphin

CABANA BAR & BEACH CLUB: An elegant poolside eatery, the Dolphin's Cabana serves a sophisticated selection of starters, salads, and entrées. Appetizer options include fish tacos and chicken wings. The main bites menu offers flatbreads, lobster rolls, cheesesteaks, grilled chicken BLT, buttermilk-battered chicken crisps, and burgers made from farm-raised, grass-fed, organic beef. Among the many signature cocktails are the Dolphin Mai Tai, Montego Punch, and the Dark and Stormy. For kids, Cabana serves pizza, burgers, hot dogs, chicken fingers, and more. L D S · $ – $ $

THE FOUNTAIN: A soda fountain with some grown-up appeal, this is an ideal spot for a sweet snack or a satisfying meal. Homemade soft-serve ice cream is the house specialty. Be it served in a simple cone or in an elaborate sundae (the caramel apple sundae is a standout), the chilly treat is sure to please. Among the entrées from which to choose are cheeseburgers, Southern pulled pork sandwiches, and Chicago-style hot dogs. Soups and salads can augment the meal, as can fries, onion rings, and soft pretzels. Save room for the impressively inventive shakes (including the PB&J, coco loco, and peppermint concoctions), plus beer and wine. The Fountain is located at the Dolphin. An adjacent walk-up window, known as Sweet Treats, offers ice cream and heavenly milk shakes for hungry folks on the go. L D S · $ – $ $

FRESH MEDITERRANEAN MARKET: The Dolphin's airy eatery offers salads, sandwiches, and soups. The morning menu includes pastries, yogurt, fresh granola, hot cereals, eggs, pancakes, and more. It's also possible to have a light lunch here, provided that you are a salad fan. Fresh offers many wines by the glass, plus sangria, Bloody Marys, beer, and soft drinks. Reservations are recommended. B L · $ $ – $ $ $

GARDEN GROVE: This Swan eatery means to transport guests to the peaceful gardens of New York's Central Park—and the 25-foot oak tree is a most realistic touch. The restaurant offers a full breakfast menu (with Disney characters in the house on Saturday and Sunday mornings), and salads, sandwiches, and more for lunch. What's the dinner "special"? It comes with a side of Disney characters. Different nights also bring different fare. At press time, Sunday through Thursday featured a traditional menu of salads, soups, and entrées; Friday and Saturday offered a seafood buffet. Disney characters are on hand for dinner every night and for breakfast on Saturday and Sunday. Reservations are recommended. Visit *www.swandolphin.com* for more information. B L D · $ $ – $ $ $

IL MULINO NEW YORK TRATTORIA: A swank Swan destination, Il Mulino offers upscale Italian cuisine in a vibrant trattoria-like setting. Specializing in *Piatti per il Tavolo*, or family-style dining, the spot is ideal for groups. The seasonal menu is characterized by blends of fresh ingredients drawn from the Abruzzi region of Italy. Signature items include *gamberi al Mulino* (jumbo shrimp with spicy cocktail sauce), *gnocchi bolognese* (potato dumplings with meat sauce), *pollo fra diavolo* (chicken in a spicy red sauce with sausage), and *salmone* (sautéed salmon in garlic and olive oil with wild mushrooms and broccoli rabe). *Mangia!*

Dinners begin with an antipasti tasting, on the house (quite the treat!). Enjoy it while perusing the wine list's 250 or so varietals. The children's menu offers pizza, pasta, and chicken parmigiana. To make reservations, call 407-934-1199, or visit *swandolphin.com*. D · $ $ $ – $ $ $ $

KIMONOS: In the mood for sushi with a side of karaoke? You've come to the right place! This Swan lounge is an honest-to-goodness karaoke bar (the only one at Walt Disney World). Some guests come to sing, while others are drawn to the sushi, sashimi, and tempura. It's also possible to order miso soup, salad, edamame, tempura udon, gyoza, and Wagyu beef satay, among other selections. There's a full bar featuring such specialty cocktails as the Sake Sangria and the Mt. Fuji Rain. This spot opens around dinnertime, serving Japanese food and drinks. The singing gets started at about 9 P.M. A good time (and meal) is generally had by all. If you'd like to get some sustenance to go, place your order with the bartender. D S · $ – $ $

PICABU: This Dolphin cafeteria is a bit above the norm. (The folks who work here are pretty amazing, too.) Much of the food is freshly prepared —with sandwiches and salads, plus a customize-your-own taco and burrito station. The house coffee is Starbucks (free refills during your meal). The shop offers snacks and sundries. Picabu is a tad pricier than the average WDW quick-service eatery, but the quality is appreciated by most. And some of the portions are big enough to share. The cafeteria (and convenience store) is open 24/7. B L D S · $ – $ $

SHULA'S: This Dolphin spot specializes in generous portions of certified Angus beef, plus soups, salads, chicken and fish dishes. For dessert, there's apple crisp, vanilla cheesecake, molten chocolate lava cake, and more. The upscale eatery pays tribute to the 1972 Miami Dolphins—

PHOTO BY JILL SAFRO

Resort to Resort

If you're staying in one resort and dining in another, you need to plan ahead—even if the resorts are linked by monorail or water taxi. Why? The transportation may be operating before dinner, but if you're out late enough you'll have to get yourself home another way.

The good news is you will never be stranded. Bus transportation runs until about 1 A.M.—but it's not direct. If the theme parks are closed, you'll have to take a bus to Disney Springs and transfer to a bus to your hotel. If the theme parks are open, you can take a bus to any park and transfer to one that's headed to your resort. Keep in mind that the trip can take up to 90 minutes in either direction. If that thought is unpleasant, do what we sometimes do: splurge on an Uber or a Lyft ride, or a trip in a taxi cab. Taxis should run between $15 and $35 (before tip), depending on the destination and traffic. Ride-sharing rates may be lower (but surge pricing is always a possibility). All resort bell services desks can arrange for a taxi pickup.

the year coach Don Shula led his team to a perfect NFL season. Though the interior celebrates the game of football, this is not a casual sports bar. The dress code is business or resort casual. Reservations are recommended. There is a kids' menu, too. **D·$$$$**

SPLASH TERRACE: Just steps from the Swan lap pool and offering lake views, Splash serves contemporary lunch fare. The menu includes Maine lobster rolls, fish tacos, cheeseburgers, meatball hoagies, Caesar salad, and fried chicken salad. Soft drinks, beer, wine, and specialty drinks (including blood orange mimosas and frozen margaritas) are served. **LS·$$**

TODD ENGLISH'S BLUEZOO: A sophisticated member of the Disney dining scene, the menu at this Dolphin spot features coastal cuisine, incorporating an innovative selection of fresh

seafood with international and New American culinary influences. The raw bar's stocked with oysters and clams. If you prefer your seafood cooked, try the chilled poached jumbo shrimp or chilled Maine lobster tail. A popular starter is the clam chowder with salt-cured bacon and oyster crackers. All of the entrées are tempting: from miso-glazed mero to bluezoo's signature dancing fish (whole fish roasted on a rotating spit).

Landlubbers should consider cast-iron filet mignon or Colorado rack of lamb. The dessert menu tempts with treats such as warm chocolate cake with a liquid ganache center. Reservations are recommended. It's possible to get food at the bar, a plus for small groups or solo diners. Closing time at the bar tends to vary nightly (depending on how crowded the place is). **DS·$$$–$$$$**

Wilderness Lodge

ARTIST POINT: The Pacific Northwest theme of this eatery is announced in landscape murals, while tall red-framed windows look out to Bay Lake. The cavernous dining room is by no means intimate, but it's not without charm.

Artist Point's hallmark is its knack for translating fresh, seasonal ingredients from the Pacific Northwest into flavorful creations. One house specialty is the ever-popular cedar plank Chinook salmon. The menu also features beef, buffalo, chicken, and seafood selections. The award-winning wine list includes more than 130 selections from the Pacific Northwest.

For dessert, loyal visitors swear by the berry cobbler, which is made with seasonal berries and is far from ordinary. And the warm housemade doughnuts are a decadent delight. Reservations are recommended. The dress code is resort casual. Artist Point is a Disney Dining Plan Signature eatery. **D·$$$–$$$$·🐭**

GEYSER POINT BAR & GRILL: A rustic yet modern, open-air oasis, Geyser Point is nestled in the heart of the Wilderness Lodge resort near the shores of Bay Lake. A combination table-service/quick-service location, Geyser Point serves all three meals. For breakfast, the menu includes items such as crab cake eggs Benedict, smoked salmon bialy, scrambled eggs, and yogurt parfait. Lunch and dinner feature crab cake sandwiches, bison cheeseburgers, grilled salmon BLT, salads (grilled portobello, salmon, or chicken), chocolate brownie mousse, and seasonal pies. A full bar stands at the ready. **BLDS·$–$$·🐭**

ROARING FORK: Set in a stone-walled area (a bit dungeon-like, but in a cool way), this snack bar serves salads, burgers, fries, pizza, sandwiches, chili, and snacks. Breakfast items such as cereal, yogurt, oatmeal, eggs, and waffles are available. Soft drinks, beer, and wine are also offered. This is the spot to top off refillable resort mugs. (See page 270 for details.) B L D S · $ · 🐭

WHISPERING CANYON CAFE: The name is ironic, as there is nothing quiet about this place. A family favorite, Whispering Canyon is one of the most boisterous Disney restaurants. All meals are offered à la carte and "all you can eat" style. The latter means heaping plates keep coming to the table until you say "when."

In the morning, the air is filled with aromas of bacon and potatoes and other breakfast fare (omelets, waffles, etc.). Lunch offers pulled pork sandwiches, bison burgers, salads, and more. For supper, expect such items as baked chicken and smoked pork ribs. The smoothies, milk shakes, and homemade desserts are quite popular. Reservations are recommended. B L D · $ $ $ · 🐭

Yacht & Beach Club

BEACH CLUB MARKETPLACE: The beachy setting extends to this snack bar/convenience store. There are baked goods, grocery items, made-to-order sandwiches, and packaged grab-and-go items. There is limited seating. If you purchase a refillable resort mug, head here to fill 'er up. B L D S · $ – $ $ · 🐭

BEACHES & CREAM SODA SHOP: This classic soda fountain is poolside at Beach Club. It offers sundaes, cones, floats, shakes, and sodas. Cheeseburgers, chicken sandwiches, hot dogs, and fries are served, too. Reservations are highly recommended. B L D S · $ – $ $ · 🐭

CAPE MAY CAFE: Minnie and her friends greet visitors each morning at this whimsical dining area. The breakfast buffet includes all the standards, plus a few specialties. Breakfast fare doesn't disappoint, but dinner is the big event here. Dinner is an all-you-can-eat New England–style clambake buffet, and it's one of WDW's most popular meals and better values (unlike breakfast, the evening meal does not include character appearances). The lineup includes crab legs, mussels, steamed clams, carved meat, salads, pastas, corn on the cob, potatoes, and desserts. Soft drinks are included, but cocktails are not. Reservations are recommended. B D · $ $ $ · 🐭

ALE & COMPASS RESTAURANT: Capturing the essence of an off-shore lighthouse, this newly re-imgined Yacht Club spot serves New England comfort food for breakfast, lunch, and dinner. Guests can watch as chefs prepare flatbreads and other items in the onstage open-hearth oven, the focal point of the nautically-themed dining area. For menu specifics, visit *www.disneyworld.com*, or the My Disney Experience mobile app or website. B L D · $ $ – $ $ $ · 🐭

CRESCENT SOLARIUM: The afternoon tea service offers artisanal cheeses and seasonal accompaniments, tiny sandwiches and canapés on homemade bread, and scones served with clotted cream, lemon curd, and jam; plus pastries, cookies, and, of course, loose-leaf teas. The kids' option features Mickey-shaped sandwiches, a scone, cookies, and chocolate milk. Reservations are recommended. L S · $ $ – $ $ $ · 🐭

HURRICANE HANNA'S WATERSIDE BAR & GRILL: Hanna's serves burgers, seafood rolls, field green salad, grilled chicken sandwiches, and vegetarian offerings—plus cocktails and frozen concoctions. Kids' meals come in a small sand bucket, complete with a shovel. This is also a refillable WDW resort mug station. L S · $ · 🐭

MARKETPLACE AT ALE & COMPASS: A welcome addition to the Yacht Club, this upscale quick-service spot serves specialty coffees and breakfast selections such as turkey, egg, and cheese rolls; egg white wraps; and sticky buns. The rest of the day brings paninis; veggie sandwiches; spinach and feta pastries; and more. There is a nice selection of grab-and-go items, too. Got a refillable mug? Here's where to make it happy. B L D S · $ – $ $ · 🐭

YACHTSMAN STEAKHOUSE: You know you're in for a serious steak experience the moment you walk through the door. There's an actual butcher shop here! Meals begin with fresh-baked onion rolls and may continue with an appetizer such as lobster bisque. There's no skimping on the expertly prepared entrées, so good luck finding room for crème brûlée. In addition to beef, the menu includes lamb, chicken, and seafood entrées. One could feast on side dishes alone, with sautéed mushrooms, creamed spinach, and truffle mac and cheese all vying for attention. Reservations are recommended. D · $ $ $ – $ $ $ $ · 🐭

WALT DISNEY WORLD

Name & Location	Meals	Style*	Price**	Characters	Theme
Akershus Norway Pavilion, Epcot (page 252)	Breakfast Lunch Dinner	Family style	B: $47/28 L/D: $57/34	Belle, Jasmine, Snow White, and Aurora	Fourteenth-century Norwegian castle
Cape May Cafe Beach Club resort (page 281)	Breakfast	Buffet	B: $35/20	Goofy, Minnie, and Donald Duck	Seaside picnic
Chef Mickey's Contemporary resort (page 273)	Breakfast Brunch Dinner	Buffet	Breakfast: $40/25 Brunch: $40/21 Dinner: $50/30	Mickey, Minnie, Donald, Goofy, and Pluto	A family celebration
Cinderella's Royal Table Magic Kingdom (page 245)	Breakfast Lunch Dinner	B/L: Family style D: À la carte	B: $54/33 L/D: $65/39	B, L, D: Princesses B, L, D: Cinderella greets guests in the Castle lobby	Medieval banquet
The Crystal Palace Magic Kingdom (page 248)	Breakfast Lunch Dinner	Buffet	B: $32/19 L/D: $45/27	Pooh, Eeyore, Tigger, and Piglet	Sunlit conservatory
Garden Grill Epcot (page 251)	Breakfast Lunch Dinner	Family style	B: $32/19 L/D: $45/27	Mickey, Pluto, Chip, and Dale	Home-style country cooking

* Family-style and buffet meals are all-you-can-eat dining experiences. Family-style features a set menu and table service; buffet-style meals usually present more dining options and are self-serve.

** Adult prices are followed by children's prices (diners ages 3 through 9). Prices may be higher during select "peak" times of year.

CHARACTER DINING

Featured Items	For Dessert	Tip	Wins for ...
B: Scrambled eggs, potato casserole, dill salmon gravlax, bacon, sausage, cheese, fruit L/D: Norwegian fare and kid-friendly selections	Chocolate mousse cake, traditional rice cream topped with strawberry sauce	The eatery is about a half-mile from Epcot's front entrance—plan your travel time accordingly.	It's not Cinderella's Castle, but it's still pretty cool. (It's much easier to score reservations here, too.)
Eggs, breakfast pizza, Mickey waffles, sausage, fruit, cereal, grits	Doughnuts, muffins, Danish, fresh fruit	For guests staying in the Epcot area, Cape May is one of the best breakfast options.	Best Chance of Getting a Table Without Reservations (But make the arrangements, anyway—there's usually a wait to get in.)
B: Eggs, fruit, pancakes, Mickey waffles, cereal Brunch: BBQ ribs, salmon, mac and cheese, and more D: Carved meats, pasta, seafood, veggies, pizza, salads	Make-your-own sundaes, cheesecake, cookies, and other fresh housemade desserts	A celebration happens every 45 minutes. Be sure to stick around for at least one little napkin-swinging party.	Best All-Around Character Meal (It has a fun and festive setting and a kid-pleasing menu.)
B: Frittata, lobster and crab crepes, eggs, French toast, bacon, pastries L/D: Catch of the day, pork shank, beef short ribs, and beef tenderloin	Seasonal cheesecake, flourless chocolate cake, and dessert trio	Payment in full is required at time of booking for all meals.	Best Setting (The restaurant is inside Cinderella Castle!)
B: French toast, eggs, cereal, frittatas, fruit L/D: Shrimp, carved meats, pasta, veggies, pizza, salad	B: Sticky buns L/D: Cakes, pies, make-your-own sundaes, cookies	Don't be put off by this restaurant's size—the characters make the rounds surprisingly quickly.	Best Theme Park Buffet (Scores points for its lovely setting, convenient location, and appetizing menu.)
B: Sticky buns, scrambled eggs, fruit, waffles L/D: Pot roast, turkey, veggies, potatoes (mac and cheese for kids)	Freshly made desserts	The room rotates very slowly throughout the meal. It's hardly noticeable to most, but may be disorienting to those highly sensitive to motion.	Best for Vegetarians (Be sure to ask for the vegetarian meal—it's usually a tasty seasonal selection.)

All characters, menu items, and prices are subject to change. Prices are rounded to the nearest dollar. Call 407-WDW-DINE (939-3463) for details or to make reservations. This listing is not comprehensive. Character meals are also presented at the Hilton Lake Buena Vista (Sunday breakfast at Covington Mill) and Buena Vista Palace (Sunday breakfast at Letterpress). See pages 108 and 110 for details.

Name & Location	Meals	Style*	Price**	Characters	Theme
Garden Grove Swan resort (page 279)	Breakfast (weekends) Dinner (daily)	Breakfast: Buffet Dinner: À la carte	B: $21/13 D: $30/18 (plated)	B: Goofy & Pluto (Sat.); Goofy, Pluto, Chip, & Dale (Sun.) D: Goofy & Pluto (Sat.–Thurs.); Goofy, Pluto, Chip, & Dale (Fri.)	Picnic in the park
Hollywood & Vine Disney's Hollywood Studios (page 260)	Breakfast Lunch Dinner (seasonal)	Family style	B: $32/19 L: $40/24 D: $50/30	Breakfast and Lunch: Doc McStuffins, Sofia the First, Handy Manny, and Jake Dinner: Minnie and friends (Visit *www.disneyworld.com* for details.)	A salute to Playhouse Disney or a seasonal celebration
Trattoria al Forno Bon Voyage Breakfast at BoardWalk resort (page 272)	Breakfast	Prix-fixe menu	$34/20	Rapunzel, Flynn Rider (aka Eugene Fitzherbert), Ariel, and Prince Eric	Pre-adventure party
Mickey's Backyard Barbecue Dinner show at Fort Wilderness (page 300)	Dinner	Buffet	$62/37	Mickey and friends such as Goofy, Minnie, Chip, and Dale	Backyard barbecue/ hoedown
'Ohana Polynesian Village resort (page 277)	Breakfast	Family style	$32/19	Lilo, Stitch, and others, such as Pluto and Mickey	Polynesian family feast
1900 Park Fare Grand Floridian resort (page 276)	Breakfast Brunch (seasonal) Dinner	Buffet	B: $34/20 D: $47/29	B: Stars like Mary Poppins and Alice D: Cinderella and friends	Turn-of-the-century circus
Tusker House Donald's Dining Safari at Animal Kingdom (page 264)	Breakfast Lunch Dinner	Buffet	B: $32/19 L: $40/25 D: $45/27	Donald, Daisy, Goofy, and Mickey	Safari feast

* Family-style and buffet meals are all-you-can-eat dining experiences. Family-style features a set menu and table service; buffet-style meals usually present more dining options and are self-serve.

** Adult prices are followed by children's prices (diners ages 3 through 9). Prices will be higher during select "peak" times of year.

Featured Items	For Dessert	Tip	Wins for ...
B: Omelets, eggs, bacon, fruit D: Prime rib, roast chicken, cedar plank salmon	Fresh pastries	Dinner, Sunday–Monday offers a choice of entrée with unlimited soup, salad, and dessert buffet; Friday and Saturday features Seafood Sensations Buffet ($36 for adults; $17 for kids).	**Best-kept Secret** (Garden Grove allows for a classic Disney character dining experience without major pre-planning. A true bonus at WDW!)
B: Mickey waffles, scrambled eggs, yogurt L: Salads, pasta dishes, fish, and chicken D: Offerings vary seasonally	Pineapple upside-down cake, Key lime tart	Request Play 'N Dine when you reserve lunch and Minnie's Seasonal Dine when booking dinner.	**Tot-Pleasing** (Little ones love to dine along with Doc McStuffins, who appears at breakfast and lunch.)
Scrambled eggs, frittatas, pancakes, egg-white omelet with smoked salmon, oak-grilled steak, cheesy egg torte, calzone	Cherry turnovers, clam shells, vanilla and blueberry muffins, fruit	Expect lots of photo ops, but no PhotoPass photographers. Be sure to bring your camera or smartphone to capture magical moments.	**Best Place to Meet Flynn Rider and Prince Eric** (It's also the only place to meet these gents.)
Chicken, ribs, hot dogs, corn on the cob, baked beans	Watermelon, marble cake, and warm fruit cobbler	The dinner show is presented on Tuesday and Thursday evenings from March through December.	**Country Music Fans** (There is a live country band and line dancing.)
Mickey waffles, eggs, biscuits, fruit, bacon	Sweet baked goods	Don't forget your autograph book and camera. The characters spend a good amount of quality time at each table.	**Speediest Service** (Servers keep those family-style platters coming fast and frequently.)
B: Pancakes, eggs, waffles D: Prime rib, pasta, seafood	B: Sticky buns, muffins, Danish D: Key lime pie, cheesecake, bread pudding	Breakfast here is a nice way to start a Magic Kingdom day. The park is just one monorail stop away.	**Fanciest Foods** (The quality is superior to many buffets, and there's plenty to please the kids.)
B: Mickey waffles, quiche, eggs, fruit L/D: Spit-roasted chicken and beef, roasted pork loin, vegetarian offerings, salmon, salads, bread	B: Danish, muffins L and D: Warm cinnamon bread pudding with vanilla sauce, chocolate cake	This spot is just steps from Kilimanjaro Safaris, making it an ideal location for a pre-safari breakfast or post-safari lunch.	**Best Place to Dine with Donald Duck** (The Duck and his pals greet guests at breakfast, lunch, and dinner.)

All characters, menu items, and prices are subject to change. Prices are rounded to the nearest dollar. Call 407-WDW-DINE (939-3463), or visit *www.disneyworld.com/dining/* for updates or to make reservations. This listing is not comprehensive.

RESTAURANT ROUNDUP

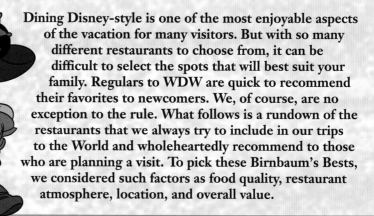

Dining Disney-style is one of the most enjoyable aspects of the vacation for many visitors. But with so many different restaurants to choose from, it can be difficult to select the spots that will best suit your family. Regulars to WDW are quick to recommend their favorites to newcomers. We, of course, are no exception to the rule. What follows is a rundown of the restaurants that we always try to include in our trips to the World and wholeheartedly recommend to those who are planning a visit. To pick these Birnbaum's Bests, we considered such factors as food quality, restaurant atmosphere, location, and overall value.

TOP WDW RESTAURANTS FOR FAMILIES WITH KIDS

TABLE SERVICE

Boma—Flavors of Africa .... Animal Kingdom Lodge resort (p. 270)
Cape May Cafe .... Beach Club resort (p. 281)
Chef Mickey's .... Contemporary resort (p. 273)
Cinderella's Royal Table .... Magic Kingdom (p. 245)
The Crystal Palace .... Magic Kingdom (p. 248)
50's Prime Time Cafe................................... Disney's Hollywood Studios (p. 260)
Garden Grill .... Epcot (p. 251)
1900 Park Fare .... Grand Floridian resort (p. 276)
Rainforest Cafe .... Animal Kingdom and Disney Springs (pp. 264, 268)
Sci-Fi Dine-In Theater .... Disney's Hollywood Studios (p. 261)
T-Rex Cafe .... Disney Springs (p. 269)
Tusker House .... Animal Kingdom (p. 264)
Via Napoli .... Epcot (p. 257)
The Wave . . . of American Flavors .... Contemporary resort (p. 274)

QUICK SERVICE

Columbia Harbour House .... Magic Kingdom (p. 248)
Cookes of Dublin .... Disney Springs (p. 266)
Earl of Sandwich .... Disney Springs (p. 266)
Everything Pop! .... Pop Century resort (p. 278)
Flame Tree Barbecue .... Animal Kingdom (p. 264)
Liberty Inn .... Epcot (p. 258)
The Mara... Disney's Animal Kingdom Lodge (p. 271)
Pinocchio Village Haus .... Magic Kingdom (p. 246)
Sunset Ranch Market .... Disney's Hollywood Studios (p. 263)
Sunshine Seasons .... Epcot (p. 252)

BEST PLACE TO CELEBRATE A CHILD'S BIRTHDAY

Chef Mickey's ....Contemporary resort (p. 273)

RUNNER-UP

Mickey's Backyard Barbecue .... Fort Wilderness (p. 300)

BEST VEGETARIAN MEALS

Boma
Animal Kingdom Lodge resort (p. 270)

Tusker House
Animal Kingdom (p. 264)

Via Napoli
Epcot (p. 257)

BEST FIREWORKS VIEWS

California Grill ....Contemporary resort (p. 273)
La Hacienda de San Angel.............Epcot (p. 254)

BEST SPLURGE FOR GROWN-UPS

Victoria & Albert's .... Grand Floridian resort (p. 276)

RUNNERS-UP

The Boathouse .... Disney Springs (p. 266)
California Grill .... Contemporary resort (p. 273)
Cítricos .... Grand Floridian resort (p. 275)
Flying Fish .... BoardWalk resort (p. 272)
Jiko—The Cooking Place .... Animal Kingdom Lodge resort (p. 270)
Monsieur Paul.. Epcot (p. 254)
Paddlefish.. Disney Springs (p. 267)
Yachtsman Steakhouse .... Yacht Club resort (p. 281)

BEST DINNER SHOW

Hoop-Dee-Doo Musical Revue: This crowd-pleasing saloon hall show has been going like gangbusters since 1974. Enjoy the music and silly humor while feasting on buckets of ribs, fried chicken, mashed potatoes, corn, and strawberry shortcake. Presented at Fort Wilderness (p. 300).

RUNNER-UP

Mickey's Backyard Barbecue: It's more of a big, informal party than a show, complete with a kickin' country band, games for the kids, and line dancing with Disney characters. The self-serve, all-you-can-eat barbecue fare is plentiful, if basic. Presented at Fort Wilderness (p. 300).

BEST PIZZA FOR GROWN-UPS

Blaze Fast Fire'd Pizza................................... Disney Springs (p. 266)
Via Napoli .... Epcot (p. 257)

BEST PIZZA FOR KIDS

California Grill .... Contemporary resort (p. 273)
Pinocchio Village Haus..Magic Kingdom (p. 246)
Pizzafari .... Animal Kingdom (p. 265)

BEST FIXIN'S BAR

Cosmic Ray's Starlight Cafe
Magic Kingdom (p. 250)

BEST ROOM SERVICE

Swan and Dolphin resorts
(pages 89 and 278–280)

BEST BUYS

Trail's End Restaurant .... Pioneer Hall, Fort Wilderness (p. 275)
Boma—Flavors of Africa .... Animal Kingdom Lodge (p. 270)

BEST ITALIAN FARE

Via Napoli .... Epcot (p. 257)

RUNNERS-UP

Il Mulino New York Trattoria .... Swan resort (p. 279)
Tutto Italia .... Epcot (p. 256)
Trattoria al Forno... BoardWalk resort (p. 272)

BEST THEME

50's Prime Time Cafe ....Disney's Hollywood Studios (p. 260)

RUNNERS-UP

Sci-Fi Dine-In Theater .... Disney's Hollywood Studios (p. 261)
T-Rex Cafe... Disney Springs (p. 269)

BEST OUTDOOR DINING

The Boathouse ....Disney Springs (p. 266)

RUNNER-UP

STK Orlando .... Disney Springs (p. 268)

GOOD MEALS, GREAT TIMES

BEST SEAFOOD

The Boathouse .... Disney Springs (p. 266)
Paddlefish .... Disney Springs (p. 267)

RUNNERS-UP

Flying Fish .... BoardWalk resort (p. 272)
Narcoossee's .... Grand Floridian resort (p. 276)

BEST CRAB CAKES

Paddlefish .... Disney Springs (p. 267)

RUNNERS-UP

The Boathouse .... Disney Springs (p. 266)
The Wave . . . of American Flavors .... Contemporary resort (p. 274)

BEST PIÑA COLADA

Tambu Lounge .... Polynesian Village resort (p. 307)

BEST ALL-AROUND WDW RESTAURANT

he Wave . . . of American Flavors .... Contemporary resort (p. 274)

BEST STEAK

Yachtsman Steakhouse ....Yacht Club resort (p. 281)

RUNNERS-UP

Le Cellier Steakhouse .... Epcot (p. 253)
Shula's .... Dolphin resort (p. 279)

BEST SUSHI

Kimonos .... Swan resort (p. 279)

RUNNERS-UP

California Grill .... Contemporary resort (p. 273)
Kona Cafe.................................. Polynesian Village resort (p. 277)

BEST ICE CREAM

Ample Hills Creamery .... BoardWalk resort (p. 271)
Beaches & Cream Soda Shop .... Beach Club resort (p. 281)
L'Artisan des Glaces .... Epcot (p. 258)

BEST SPORTS BAR

ESPN Club
BoardWalk resort (p. 272)

BEST COFFEE

California Grill .... Contemporary resort (p. 273)

RUNNERS-UP

Kona Cafe .... Polynesian Village resort (p. 277)
Boma—Flavors of Africa .... Animal Kingdom Lodge resort (p. 270)
Starbucks... (multiple locations; see Index)
Ghirardelli Ice Cream & Chocolate Shop .... Disney Springs (p. 267)

BEST MILK SHAKE

Ample Hills Creamery .... BoardWalk resort (p. 271)

RUNNERS-UP

Sweet Treats .... Dolphin resort (p. 279)
Beaches & Cream Soda Shop............................... Beach Club resort (p. 281)

BEST CHARACTER MEAL

Cinderella's Royal Table ....Magic Kingdom (p. 245)
Hollywood & Vine (dinner) .... Disney's Hollywood Studios (p. 260)

RUNNERS-UP

Akershus Royal Banquet Hall ....Epcot (p. 252)
Tusker House ....Disney's Animal Kingdom (p. 264)
Garden Grill ....Epcot (p. 251)
1900 Park Fare .... Grand Floridian resort (p. 276)

BEST RESORT SNACK BAR

Picabu .... Dolphin resort (p. 279)

RUNNERS-UP

Capt. Cook's .... Polynesian Village resort (p. 277)
Contempo Cafe............................. Contemporary resort (p. 274)

GOOD MEALS, GREAT TIMES

Where to Find ...

From french fries to filet mignon, fried chicken to seared scallops with black truffle spaghettini, Disney dishes truly run the gamut. To help you zero in on the eateries that best fit your needs, we've created a handy index of specialized lists:

PHOTO BY JILL SAFRO

BAKERIES/PASTRY SHOPS
Beach Club Marketplace (Beach Club resort)
BoardWalk Bakery (BoardWalk resort)
Goofy's Candy Co. (Disney Springs, Marketplace)
Kringla Bakeri og Kafe (Epcot, World Showcase)
Kusafiri Coffee Shop & Bakery (Animal Kingdom, Harambe)
Les Halles Boulangerie Patisserie (Epcot, World Showcase)
Main Street Bakery (Magic Kingdom, Main Street, U.S.A.)
Sunshine Seasons (Epcot, The Land)
Trolley Car Café (Disney's Hollywood Studios)

BARBECUE
Flame Tree Barbecue (Animal Kingdom, Discovery Island)
House of Blues Smokehouse (Disney Springs, West Side)
Mickey's Backyard Barbecue (see Dinner Shows, page 300)

BEST BANG FOR THE BUFFET BUCK
(all-you-can-eat)
Biergarten (Epcot, World Showcase)
Boma—Flavors of Africa (Animal Kingdom Lodge)
Cape May Cafe (Beach Club resort)
Chef Mickey's (Contemporary resort)
Hollywood & Vine (Disney's Hollywood Studios)

1900 Park Fare (Grand Floridian resort)
Trail's End Restaurant (Fort Wilderness resort)
Tusker House (Animal Kingdom, Harambe)

BEST WITH BABIES (table service)
Akershus Royal Banquet Hall (Epcot, World Showcase)
Biergarten (Epcot, World Showcase)
Chef Mickey's (Contemporary resort)
Crystal Palace, The (Magic Kingdom, Main Street, U.S.A.)
Donald's Safari Breakfast at Tusker House (Animal Kingdom, Harambe)
Garden Grill (Epcot, Future World)
Hollywood & Vine (Disney's Hollywood Studios)
'Ohana (Polynesian Village resort)
Olivia's Cafe (Disney's Old Key West resort)
Rainforest Cafe (Animal Kingdom and Disney Springs)
Tony's Town Square (Magic Kingdom, Main Street, U.S.A.)
Trail's End Restaurant (Fort Wilderness resort)

BRUNCH
California Grill (Contemporary resort)
Chef Mickey's (Contemporary resort)
House of Blues (Disney Springs, West Side)
Narcoossee's (Grand Floridian resort)
Raglan Road (Disney Springs, The Landing)
Trail's End (Fort Wilderness; select days)

BUFFET (all-you-care-to-eat)
Akershus Royal Banquet Hall (Epcot, World Showcase—*appetizers only*)
Biergarten (Epcot, World Showcase)
Boma—Flavors of Africa (Animal Kingdom Lodge)
Cape May Cafe (Beach Club resort)
Chef Mickey's (Contemporary resort)
Crystal Palace, The (Magic Kingdom, Main Street, U.S.A.)
Garden Grove (Swan resort)
Hollywood & Vine (Disney's Hollywood Studios)

1900 Park Fare (Grand Floridian resort)
Trail's End Restaurant (breakfast and dinner; Fort Wilderness)
Tusker House (Animal Kingdom, Harambe)
Wave ... of American Flavors, The (Contemporary resort, breakfast only)

BURGERS
Backlot Express (Disney's Hollywood Studios)
Cabana Bar & Beach Club (Dolphin resort)
Capt. Cook's (Polynesian Village resort)
Cosmic Ray's Starlight Cafe (Magic Kingdom, Tomorrowland)

PHOTO BY JILL SAFRO

D-Luxe Burger (Disney Springs, Town Center)
Electric Umbrella (Epcot, Future World)
ESPN Club (BoardWalk resort)
Everything Pop! (Pop Century resort)
Food Courts (All-Star resorts)
Fountain, The (Dolphin resort)
Liberty Inn (Epcot, World Showcase)
Restaurantosaurus (Animal Kingdom, DinoLand)
Riverside Mill (Port Orleans Riverside resort)
Sassagoula Floatworks & Food Factory (Port Orleans French Quarter resort)
Sunset Ranch Market (Disney's Hollywood Studios)
Tortuga Tavern (Magic Kingdom, Frontierland)

CHEAP EATS—FAST FOOD
Backlot Express (Disney's Hollywood Studios)
Columbia Harbour House (Magic Kingdom, Liberty Square)
D-Luxe Burger (Disney Springs, Town Center)
Everything Pop! (Pop Century resort)
Flame Tree Barbecue (Animal Kingdom, Discovery Island)
Harambe Market (Animal Kingdom, Harambe)
Katsura Grill (Epcot, World Showcase)
Landscape of Flavors (Disney's Art of Animation resort)

Pinocchio Village Haus (Magic Kingdom, Fantasyland)
Pizzafari (Animal Kingdom, Discovery Island)
Restaurantosaurus (Animal Kingdom, DinoLand)
Satu'li Canteen (Animal Kingdom, Pandora— World of Avatar)
Sommerfest (Epcot, World Showcase)
Sunshine Seasons (Epcot, Future World)
Wolfgang Puck Express (Disney Springs, Marketplace)
Yorkshire County Fish Shop (Epcot, World Showcase)

CHEAP EATS (relatively speaking)
Table Service
Beaches & Cream Soda Shop (Beach Club resort)
Cape May Cafe (Beach Club resort)
ESPN Club (BoardWalk resort)
Geyser Point Bar & Grill (Wilderness Lodge Resort)
Kimonos (Swan resort)
Olivia's Cafe (Disney's Old Key West resort)
Planet Hollywood (Disney Springs, West Side)
Plaza Restaurant (Magic Kingdom, Main Street, U.S.A.)
Rainforest Cafe (Animal Kingdom and Disney Springs, Marketplace)
Spice Road Table (Epcot, World Showcase)
Trail's End Restaurant (Fort Wilderness resort)
T-Rex Cafe: A Prehistoric Family Adventure (Disney Springs, Marketplace)
Tusker House (Animal Kingdom, Harambe)
Via Napoli (Epcot, World Showcase)

DISNEY CHARACTERS (dining with)
(see pages 282–285)

ETHNIC EATERIES
African
Boma—Flavors of Africa (Animal Kingdom Lodge)
Harambe Market (Animal Kingdom, Harambe)
Jiko—The Cooking Place (Animal Kingdom Lodge)
Restaurant Marrakesh (Epcot, World Showcase)
Sanaa (Animal Kingdom Lodge, Kidani Village)
Spice Road Table (Epcot, World Showcase)
Tangierine Cafe (Epcot, World Showcase)
Tiffins (also serves Indian cuisine; Animal Kingdom, Discovery Island)
Tusker House (Animal Kingdom, Harambe)

American

Artist Point (Wilderness Lodge)
Big River Grille & Brewing Works (BoardWalk resort)
Boathouse, The (Disney Springs, The Landing)
Boatwright's Dining Hall (Port Orleans Riverside resort)
California Grill (Contemporary resort)
ESPN Club (BoardWalk resort)
50's Prime Time Cafe (Disney's Hollywood Studios)
Flying Fish (BoardWalk resort)
Garden Grill (Epcot, Future World)
Grand Floridian Cafe (Grand Floridian resort)
Hollywood Brown Derby (Disney's Hollywood Studios)
House of Blues (Disney Springs, West Side)
Liberty Inn (Epcot, World Showcase)
Liberty Tree Tavern (Magic Kingdom, Liberty Square)
Narcoossee's (Grand Floridian resort)

PHOTO BY JILL SAFRO

1900 Park Fare (Grand Floridian resort)
Olivia's Cafe (Old Key West resort)
Sci-Fi Dine-In Theater (Disney's Hollywood Studios)
Trail's End Restaurant (Fort Wilderness resort)
Wave . . . of American Flavors, The (Contemporary resort)

British

Earl of Sandwich (Disney Springs, Marketplace)
Rose & Crown Pub & Dining Room (Epcot, World Showcase)
Yorkshire County Fish Shop (Epcot, World Showcase)

Canadian

Le Cellier Steakhouse (Epcot, World Showcase)

Chinese and Southeast Asian

Jungle Navigation Co. Ltd. Skipper Canteen (Magic Kingdom, Adventureland)
Lotus Blossom Cafe (Epcot, World Showcase)
Nine Dragons (Epcot, World Showcase)
Yak & Yeti (Animal Kingdom, Asia)

French

Be Our Guest Restaurant (Magic Kingdom, Fantasyland)
Chefs de France (Epcot, World Showcase)
Les Halles Boulangerie Patisserie (Epcot, World Showcase)
Monsieur Paul (Epcot, World Showcase)

German

Biergarten (Epcot, World Showcase)
Sommerfest (Epcot, World Showcase)

Italian/Mediterranean

Blaze Fast Fire'd Pizza (Disney Springs)
Il Mulino New York Trattoria (Swan resort)
Mama Melrose's Ristorante Italiano (Disney's Hollywood Studios)
Spice Road Table (Epcot, World Showcase)
Tony's Town Square (Magic Kingdom, Main Street, U.S.A.)
Trattoria al Forno (Disney's BoardWalk)
Tutto Gusto (Epcot, World Showcase)
Tutto Italia (Epcot, World Showcase)
Via Napoli (Epcot, World Showcase)

Japanese

Kabuki Cafe (Epcot, World Showcase)
Katsura Grill (Epcot, World Showcase)
Kimonos (Swan resort)
Morimoto Asia (Disney Springs, The Landing)
Teppan Edo (Epcot, World Showcase)
Tokyo Dining (Epcot, World Showcase)

Mexican/Latin American

Frontera Cocina (Disney Springs, Town Center)
La Cantina de San Angel (Epcot, World Showcase)
La Hacienda de San Angel (Epcot, World Showcase)
Maya Grill (Coronado Springs resort)
Paradiso 37 (Disney Springs, The Landing)
Pecos Bill Tall Tale Inn (Magic Kingdom, Frontierland)
San Angel Inn (Epcot, World Showcase)

Norwegian

Akershus Royal Banquet Hall (Epcot, World Showcase)

Kringla Bakeri og Kafe (Epcot, World Showcase)

FAMILY-STYLE (all-you-can-eat)

Akershus Royal Banquet Hall (Epcot, World Showcase)

Cape May Cafe (Beach Club resort)

Garden Grill (Epcot, Future World)

Garden Grove (Swan resort)

Hoop-Dee-Doo Musical Revue (see page 300)

Liberty Tree Tavern (Magic Kingdom, Liberty Square)

Mickey's Backyard Barbecue (see page 300)

'Ohana (Polynesian Village resort)

Spirit of Aloha (see page 300)

Whispering Canyon Cafe (Wilderness Lodge)

FRUIT

Aloha Isle (Magic Kingdom, Adventureland)

Harambe Fruit Market (Animal Kingdom, Harambe)

Liberty Square Market (Magic Kingdom, Liberty Square)

Prince Eric's Village Market (Magic Kingdom, Fantasyland)

Sunset Ranch Market (Disney's Hollywood Studios)

Sunshine Seasons (Epcot, Future World)

GOOD FOR GROUPS

Boathouse, The (Disney Springs, The Landing)

Boma—Flavors of Africa (Animal Kingdom Lodge)

California Grill (Contemporary resort)

Cape May Cafe (Beach Club resort)

Crystal Palace, The (Magic Kingdom, Main Street, U.S.A.)

Flame Tree Barbecue (Animal Kingdom, Discovery Island)

Flying Fish (BoardWalk resort)

Hollywood & Vine (Disney's Hollywood Studios)

House of Blues (Disney Springs, West Side)

Mickey's Backyard Barbecue (see page 300)

'Ohana (Polynesian Village resort)

Paddlefish (Disney Springs, The Landing)

Raglan Road (Disney Springs, The Landing)

Sunshine Seasons (Epcot, Future World)

Teppan Edo (Epcot, World Showcase)

Todd English's bluezoo (Dolphin resort)

Trail's End (Fort Wilderness)

Tusker House (Animal Kingdom, Harambe)

Via Napoli (Epcot, World Showcase)

Wave . . . of American Flavors, The (Contemporary resort)

HOT DOGS

Backlot Express (Disney's Hollywood Studios)

Casey's Corner (Magic Kingdom, Main Street, U.S.A.)

Liberty Inn (Epcot, World Showcase)

Lunching Pad, The (Magic Kingdom, Tomorrowland)

Min and Bill's Dockside Diner (Disney's Hollywood Studios)

Restaurantosaurus (Animal Kingdom, Dinoland)

Sunset Ranch Market (Disney's Hollywood Studios)

Wetzel's Pretzels (Disney Springs, Marketplace)

ICE CREAM AND FROZEN TREATS

Aloha Isle (Magic Kingdom, Adventureland)

Ample Hills Creamery (BoardWalk resort)

Anandapur Ice Cream Truck (Animal Kingdom, Asia)

Beaches & Cream Soda Shop (Beach Club resort)

Cheshire Cafe (Magic Kingdom, Fantasyland)

Cool Post (Epcot, World Showcase)

Dino-Bite Snacks (Animal Kingdom, DinoLand)

The Fountain (Dolphin resort)

Fountain View (Epcot, Future World)

PHOTO BY JILL SAFRO

Gaston's Tavern (Magic Kingdom, Fantasyland)

Ghirardelli Ice Cream & Chocolate Shop (Disney Springs, Marketplace)

Hollywood Scoops (Disney's Hollywood Studios)

Plaza Ice Cream Parlor (Magic Kingdom, Main Street, U.S.A.)

Plaza Restaurant (Magic Kingdom, Main Street, U.S.A.)

Storybook Treats (Magic Kingdom, Fantasyland)

Sunshine Tree Terrace (Magic Kingdom, Adventureland)

Tamu Tamu Refreshments (Animal Kingdom, Harambe)

KIDS' FAVORITES

Akershus Royal Banquet Hall (Epcot, World Showcase)

Cape May Cafe breakfast (Beach Club resort)

Casey's Corner (Magic Kingdom, Main Street)

Chef Mickey's (Contemporary resort)

Cinderella's Royal Table (Magic Kingdom, Fantasyland)

Cosmic Ray's Starlight Cafe (Magic Kingdom, Tomorrowland)

Crystal Palace, The (Magic Kingdom, Main Street)

50's Prime Time Cafe (Disney's Hollywood Studios)

Hollywood & Vine (Disney's Hollywood Studios)

Hoop-Dee-Doo Musical Revue (see page 300)

Liberty Inn (Epcot, World Showcase)

1900 Park Fare (Grand Floridian resort)

'Ohana (Polynesian Village resort)

Pinocchio Village Haus (Magic Kingdom, Fantasyland)

Pizzafari (Animal Kingdom, Discovery Island)

PizzeRizzo (Disney's Hollywood Studios)

Rainforest Cafe (Animal Kingdom and Disney Springs, Marketplace)

Sunset Ranch Market (Disney's Hollywood Studios)

Sunshine Seasons (Epcot, Future World)

T-Rex Cafe: A Prehistoric Family Adventure (Disney Springs, Marketplace)

Tusker House (Animal Kingdom, Harambe)

Whispering Canyon Cafe (Wilderness Lodge)

KNOCKOUT VIEWS

Big River Grille & Brewing Works (outdoor seating; BoardWalk)

Boathouse, The (Disney Springs, The Landing)

California Grill (Contemporary resort)

Coral Reef (Epcot, Future World)

Jock Lindsey's Hangar Bar (Disney Springs, The Landing)

La Hacienda de San Angel (Epcot, World Showcase)

Paddlefish (Disney Springs, The Landing)

Sanaa (Animal Kingdom Lodge)

KOSHER (fast-food selections)

ABC Commissary (Disney's Hollywood Studios)

Artist's Palette, The (Saratoga Springs resort)

Cosmic Ray's Starlight Cafe (Magic Kingdom, Tomorrowland)

Electric Umbrella (Epcot, Future World)

Everything Pop! (Pop Century resort)

Food Courts (All-Star and Port Orleans Riverside resorts)

Gasparilla Island Grill (Grand Floridian resort)

Landscape of Flavors (Art of Animation resort)

Liberty Inn (Epcot, World Showcase)

Mara, The (Animal Kingdom Lodge)

Pizzafari (Animal Kingdom, Discovery Island)

Roaring Fork (Wilderness Lodge)

LOUNGES AND BARS (with food)

Big River Grille & Brewing Works (BoardWalk resort)

Boathouse, The (Disney Springs, The Landing)

Cabana Bar & Beach Club (Dolphin resort)

California Grill Lounge (Contemporary resort)

Cítricos Lounge (Grand Floridian resort)

PHOTO BY JILL SAFRO

Crew's Cup (Yacht Club resort)

Crockett's Tavern (Fort Wilderness resort)

The Edison (Disney Springs, The Landing)

ESPN Club (BoardWalk resort)

Gurgling Suitcase (Old Key West resort)

Hurricane Hanna's (Yacht & Beach Club resorts)

Il Mulino New York Trattoria Lounge (Swan resort)

Jock Lindsey's Hangar Bar (Disney Springs, The Landing)

Kimonos (Swan resort)

La Cava del Tequila (Epcot, World Showcase)

Leaping Horse Libations (BoardWalk resort)
Mardi Grogs (Port Orleans French Quarter resort)
Martha's Vineyard (Beach Club resort)
Mizner's (Grand Floridian resort)
Muddy Rivers (Port Orleans Riverside resort)
Narcoossee's (Grand Floridian resort)
Nomad Lounge (Animal Kingdom, Discovery Island)
Outer Rim (Contemporary resort)
Paddlefish (Disney Springs, The Landing)
Paradiso 37 (Disney Springs, The Landing)
Raglan Road (Disney Springs, The Landing)
Rainforest Cafe (Magic Mushroom bar; Animal Kingdom and Disney Springs, Marketplace)
River Roost (Port Orleans Riverside resort)
Rix Lounge (Coronado Springs resort)
Rose & Crown Pub (Epcot, World Showcase)
Sanaa Lounge (Animal Kingdom Lodge)
Sand Bar (Contemporary resort)
Shark Bar at T-Rex Cafe (Disney Springs, Marketplace)

Siestas Cantina (Coronado Springs resort)
Sommerfest (inside Germany; Epcot, World Showcase)
Splash Terrace (Swan resort)
Tambu Lounge (Polynesian Village resort)
Territory Lounge (Wilderness Lodge)
Trader Sam's Grog Grotto (Polynesian resort)
Tune-In Lounge (Disney's Hollywood Studios)
Turf Club Bar & Grill, The (Saratoga Springs Resort & Spa)
Turtle Shack (Disney's Old Key West resort)
Tutto Gusto (Epcot, World Showcase)
Uzima Springs (Animal Kingdom Lodge)
Wine Bar George (Disney Springs, The Landing)
Yak & Yeti Lounge (Animal Kingdom, Asia)

OPEN 24 HOURS

Capt. Cook's (Polynesian Village resort)
Gasparilla Island Grill (Grand Floridian resort)
Picabu (Dolphin resort)
Sundial Cafe 24-7 (Wyndham hotel)

PIZZA

Blaze Fast Fire'd Pizza (Disney Springs, Town Center)
Capt. Cook's (Polynesian Village resort)
Everything Pop! (Pop Century resort)
Food Courts (All-Star resorts)
Gasparilla Island Grill (Grand Floridian resort)
Mama Melrose's Ristorante Italiano (Disney's Hollywood Studios)
Pinocchio Village Haus (Magic Kingdom, Fantasyland)
Pizzafari (Animal Kingdom, Discovery Island)
PizzeRizzo (Disney's Hollywood Studios)
Riverside Mill (Port Orleans Riverside resort)
Roaring Fork (Wilderness Lodge)
Sassagoula Floatworks & Food Factory (Port Orleans French Quarter resort)
Sunset Ranch Market (Disney's Hollywood Studios)
Trail's End Restaurant (Fort Wilderness resort)
Via Napoli (Epcot, World Showcase)
Wolfgang Puck Bar & Grill (Disney Springs, Town Center)
Wolfgang Puck Express (Disney Springs, Marketplace)

SALADS

Artist's Palette, The (Saratoga Springs resort)
Big River Grille & Brewing Works (BoardWalk)
Boathouse, The (Disney Springs, The Landing)
Boma—Flavors of Africa (Animal Kingdom Lodge)
Cape May Cafe (Beach Club resort)
Columbia Harbour House (Magic Kingdom, Liberty Square)
Earl of Sandwich (Disney Springs, Marketplace)
Flame Tree Barbecue (Animal Kingdom, Discovery Island)
Gasparilla Island Grill (Grand Floridian resort)
Hollywood Brown Derby (Disney's Hollywood Studios)
Il Mulino New York Trattoria (Swan resort)
Pecos Bill Tall Tale Inn & Cafe (Magic Kingdom, Frontierland)
Pepper Market (Coronado Springs resort)
Picabu (Dolphin resort)
Pinocchio Village Haus (Magic Kingdom, Fantasyland)

Plaza Restaurant (Magic Kingdom, Main Street, U.S.A.)

Rainforest Cafe (Animal Kingdom and Disney Springs, Marketplace)

Sunshine Seasons (Epcot, Future World)

Wave . . . of American Flavors, The (Contemporary resort)

Wolfgang Puck Bar & Grill (Disney Springs, Town Center)

SEAFOOD

Artist Point (Wilderness Lodge)

Boathouse, The (Disney Springs, The Landing)

California Grill (Contemporary resort)

Cape May Cafe (Beach Club resort)

Columbia Harbour House (Magic Kingdom, Liberty Square)

Coral Reef (Epcot, Future World)

Flying Fish (BoardWalk resort)

Kimonos (Swan resort)

Kona Cafe (Polynesian Village resort)

Narcoossee's (Grand Floridian resort)

Paddlefish (Disney Springs, The Landing)

Todd English's bluezoo (Dolphin resort)

Wave . . . of American Flavors, The (Contemporary resort)

SNACK BARS (at the resorts)

Beach Club Marketplace (Beach Club resort)

Cabana Bar & Beach Club (Dolphin resort)

PHOTO BY JILL SAFRO

Capt. Cook's (Polynesian Village resort)

Contempo Café (Contemporary resort)

Gasparilla Island Grill (Grand Floridian resort)

Mara, The (Animal Kingdom Lodge)

Picabu (Dolphin resort)

Roaring Fork (Wilderness Lodge)

SOLO DINERS

Boathouse, The (Disney Springs, The Landing)

California Grill (Contemporary resort)

Cítricos lounge (Grand Floridian resort)

Crew's Cup (lounge, Yacht Club resort)

ESPN Club (BoardWalk resort)

Flying Fish (BoardWalk resort)

Il Mulino New York Trattoria (Swan resort)

Jiko—The Cooking Place Lounge (Animal Kingdom Lodge)

Narcoossee's Lounge (Grand Floridian resort)

Paddlefish (Disney Springs, The Landing)

Tune-In Lounge (Disney's Hollywood Studios)

Wave . . . of American Flavors Lounge (Contemporary resort)

Wine Bar George (Disney Springs, The Landing)

STEAK

Be Our Guest Restaurant (Magic Kingdom, Fantasyland)

Flying Fish (BoardWalk resort)

La Hacienda de San Angel (Epcot, World Showcase)

Le Cellier Steakhouse (Epcot, World Showcase)

Paddlefish (Disney Springs, The Landing)

Shula's Steak House (Dolphin resort)

STK Orlando (Disney Springs, The Landing)

Wave . . . of American Flavors, The (Contemporary resort)

Yachtsman Steakhouse (Yacht Club resort)

SUPER SPLURGES (for grown-ups)

Artist Point (Wilderness Lodge)

Boathouse, The (Disney Springs, The Landing)

California Grill (Contemporary resort)

Chefs de France (Epcot, World Showcase)

Flying Fish (BoardWalk resort)

Hollywood Brown Derby (Disney's Hollywood Studios)

Il Mulino (Swan resort)

Jiko—The Cooking Place (Animal Kingdom Lodge)

Le Cellier Steakhouse (Epcot, World Showcase)

Monsieur Paul (Epcot, World Showcase)

Morimoto Asia (Disney Springs, The Landing)

Narcoossee's (Grand Floridian resort)

Paddlefish (Disney Springs, The Landing)

Sanaa (Animal Kingdom Lodge)

Tiffins (Animal Kingdom, Discovery Island)

Victoria & Albert's (Grand Floridian resort)

Yachtsman Steakhouse (Yacht Club resort)

SUSHI

California Grill (Contemporary resort)

Kabuki Cafe (Epcot, World Showcase)

Katsura Grill (Epcot, World Showcase)

Kimonos (lounge; Swan resort)

Kona Cafe (Polynesian Village resort)

Kona Island (after 5 P.M.; Polynesian Village resort)

Morimoto Asia (Disney Springs, The Landing)

Splitsville (Disney Springs, West Side)
Tokyo Dining (Epcot, World Showcase)

TERRIFIC THEMING
Akershus Royal Banquet Hall (Epcot, World Showcase)
Be Our Guest Restaurant (Magic Kingdom, Fantasyland)
Biergarten (Epcot, World Showcase)

PHOTO BY MIKE CARROLL

Boathouse, The (Disney Springs, The Landing)
Cinderella's Royal Table (Magic Kingdom, Fantasyland)
50's Prime Time Cafe (Disney's Hollywood Studios)
Jungle Navigation Co. Ltd. Skipper Canteen (Magic Kingdom, Adventureland)
Liberty Tree Tavern (Magic Kingdom, Liberty Square)
'Ohana (Polynesian Village resort)
Rainforest Cafe (Animal Kingdom and Disney Springs, Marketplace)
Sanaa (Animal Kingdom Lodge)
Sci-Fi Dine-In Theater (Disney's Hollywood Studios)
T-Rex Cafe: A Prehistoric Family Adventure (Disney Springs, Marketplace)
Tusker House (Animal Kingdom, Harambe)

VEGETARIAN SELECTIONS
Boma—Flavors of Africa (Animal Kingdom Lodge)
Columbia Harbour House (Magic Kingdom, Liberty Square)
Cosmic Ray's Starlight Cafe (Magic Kingdom, Tomorrowland)
Everything Pop! (Pop Century resort)
Food Courts (All-Star resorts)
Jiko—The Cooking Place (Animal Kingdom Lodge)
Mama Melrose's Ristorante Italiano (Disney's Hollywood Studios)
Pinocchio Village Haus (Magic Kingdom, Fantasyland)
Pizzafari (Animal Kingdom, Discovery Island)
PizzeRizzo (Disney's Hollywood Studios)

Rainforest Cafe (Animal Kingdom and Disney Springs, Marketplace)
Sanaa (Animal Kingdom Lodge)
Sunset Ranch Market (Disney's Hollywood Studios)
Sunshine Seasons (Epcot, Future World)
Tony's Town Square (Magic Kingdom, Main Street, U.S.A.)
Tusker House (Animal Kingdom, Harambe)
Via Napoli (Epcot, World Showcase)

PHOTO BY JILL SAFRO

Wolfgang Puck Express (Disney Springs, Marketplace)

WINE AND DINE (great wine lists)
Artist Point (Wilderness Lodge)
Be Our Guest Restaurant ([dinner] Magic Kingdom, Fantasyland)
Boathouse, The (Disney Springs, The Landing)
Boma—Flavors of Africa (Animal Kingdom Lodge)
California Grill (Contemporary resort)
Chefs de France (Epcot, World Showcase)
Cítricos (Grand Floridian resort)
Flying Fish (BoardWalk resort)
Hollywood Brown Derby (Disney's Hollywood Studios)
Il Mulino New York Trattoria (Swan resort)
Jiko—The Cooking Place (Animal Kingdom Lodge)
Monsieur Paul (Epcot, World Showcase)
Morimoto Asia (Disney Springs, The Landing)
Narcoossee's (Grand Floridian resort)
Paddlefish (Disney Springs, The Landing)
Sanaa (Animal Kingdom Lodge)
Shula's Steak House (Dolphin resort)
STK Orlando (Disney Springs, The Landing)
Tiffins (Animal Kingdom, Discovery Island)
Victoria & Albert's (Grand Floridian resort)
Wave . . . of American Flavors, The (Contemporary resort)
Wine Bar George (Disney Springs, The Landing)
Yachtsman Steakhouse (Yacht Club resort)

Reservations Explained

Disney's reservation system, formerly known as "priority seating," covers most full-service restaurants on WDW property. The name may have changed, but the procedure is the same. It was designed to provide the assurance of a reservation without delays caused by no-shows and latecomers. Here's how it works: You call ahead to request a seating time; you arrive five minutes before the assigned time and check in at the podium; you receive the next available table that can accommodate your party.

It is virtually impossible to walk into a table service eatery without a reservation—secure yours as far in advance as possible. Seating times can be reserved up to 180 days ahead (see box below) for most Walt Disney World eateries by calling 407-WDW-DINE (939-3463), by visiting *www.disneyworld.com/dine*, or via the My Disney Experience app or website. The phone hotline is open daily from 7 A.M. to 10 P.M. The number of tables available in advance varies. If you are unable to book in advance, try to make same-day arrangements. *Note that a fee of $10 per person will be charged to guests who do not show up or cancel a reservation less than one day in advance.*

Most Disney resorts have a phone in the main lobby that provides direct contact with the Dine Line. Simply touch 55—the call is free. From other locations, dial 407-WDW-DINE (939-3463). Once at the theme parks, reservations can be made at the eatery itself; at City Hall in the Magic Kingdom; in Epcot at Guest Relations by Spaceship Earth; by Hollywood Junction in Disney's Hollywood Studios; and at Guest Relations in Animal Kingdom. Bookings can also

Advance Planning

While some WDW restaurants always seem to have an open table (like Marrakesh in Epcot's World Showcase), most are booked far in advance. The restaurants for which careful planning is essential include Be Our Guest and Cinderella's Royal Table in the Magic Kingdom (call 180 days ahead and keep your fingers crossed!), Le Cellier Steakhouse and Via Napoli in Epcot, Tusker House breakfast and lunch in Disney's Animal Kingdom, and California Grill in the Contemporary resort.

be made at Guest Relations at the Welcome Center in Town Center.

While the Walt Disney World reservation system is often successful, there are times when the wait for a table can be unexpectedly long. This is most likely to occur during peak mealtimes at restaurants that offer buffets or family-style meals, where patrons will often opt for seconds (or thirds). For this reason, be sure to check in at the restaurant particularly early for all character-hosted meals.

HOT TIP!

At most WDW restaurants, reservations are scheduled in five- or ten-minute intervals. If they don't have a 6 P.M. availability, ask about a 6:05 P.M.

Reservations are necessary for all dinner shows—the Hoop-Dee-Doo Musical Revue, Mickey's Backyard BBQ, and the Polynesian Village resort's Spirit of Aloha; they can be made by calling 407-WDW-DINE (939-3463). Reservations can be booked up to 180 days in advance. If you can't get a table for an early performance, consider a later one (they are usually less heavily booked).

Keep in mind that, with the exception of dinner shows, a WDW seating time does vary from a traditional reservation—you may have to wait a bit when you arrive at your assigned time. Your party will be given the first table that opens up.

Note: Because the dining scene at Walt Disney World is ever-evolving, we advise calling 407-WDW-DINE (939-3463) to confirm current reservation policies.

For Disney Resort Guests Only

Do you have a confirmed reservation at a Disney–owned-and-operated resort? If so, you are entitled to a special perk: Call 180 days prior to the first day of your hotel reservation and you can make dining reservations for up to 10 days of your stay. That's like getting a 1- to 10-day jump on everyone else! (Stays longer than 10 days will require a second call. Inquire when you make your first set of dining reservations.) Have your confirmation number handy when you call 407-WDW-DINE.

Dinner Shows

The fact that Disney is expert in family entertainment is nowhere more readily apparent than amid the whooping and hollering troupe of singers and dancers who race toward the stage at Fort Wilderness resort's Pioneer Hall. As guests plow through filling barbecue fare (ribs, fried chicken, strawberry shortcake, beer, wine, and soft drinks), these enthusiastic performers sing, dance, and joke up a storm.

The gags are groaners, but the audience eats 'em up. It's all in the course of an evening at the *Hoop-Dee-Doo Musical Revue*, presented nightly at 4 P.M., 6:15 P.M., and 8:30 P.M. Cost is about $64 per adult and $38 for children (ages 3 through 9) for Category 3 seating; about $67 for adults, $39 for kids in Category 2; and about $72 and $43 for Category 1. (The best views are in Category 1—seating is on the main floor.)

Note that the dining room in Pioneer Hall can be chilly year-round. Bring a sweater to combat the sometimes intense air-conditioning.

HOT TIP!

The Hoop-Dee-Doo Musical Revue is a very popular show. Make your reservations as far in advance as possible.

Also presented at Fort Wilderness is *Mickey's Backyard BBQ*. A country band gets guests out on the floor to kick up their heels, and Disney characters join in the fun.

Dinner consists of plenty of basic picnic favorites: barbecued ribs and chicken, corn on the cob, and baked beans. The seasonal dinner show costs about $62 per adult and $37 for kids. Tickets are required, so book ahead.

Disney's Polynesian luau show is called *Spirit of Aloha*. Set in the beachfront backyard of a Hawaiian house (at the Polynesian Village resort), the show invites guests to join in a musical celebration.

The luau experience combines traditional music as well as more contemporary ditties. The performers' dancing is some of the most authentic this side of Hawaii. The Spirit of Aloha is presented in an open-air dining theater in Luau Cove, adjacent to the Seven Seas Lagoon.

The all-you-can-eat feast is influenced by the flavors of Polynesia and includes draft beer, wine,

soft drinks, and dessert. Menu items include roasted chicken, barbecued pork ribs, fresh pineapple, Polynesian-style rice, and vegetables. The kids' menu features PB&J sandwiches, mac and cheese, chicken nuggets, and hot dogs. The cost is about $66 for adults and $39 for kids in Category 3; about $74 and $44 for Category 2; and about $78 and $46 for Category 1 (the best views are from Category 1 seats).

Plan to arrive at least 30 minutes before showtime, and allow extra time for transportation and parking. (Note that all prices are subject to change.) The show may be canceled due to inclement weather (though tables are sheltered).

Reservations: Arrangements for dinner shows may be made up to 180 days in advance by calling 407-WDW-DINE (939-3463). Groups of eight or more should call 407-939-7707. *Prices include tax and gratuity and may be higher during peak seasons.*

A credit card number is required for all dinner show reservations. Full payment is required upon booking. It's also possible to redeem Disney Dining Plan credits for dinner shows. At press time, all Disney dinner shows were participating in the dining plan. They are considered Signature meals and cost two table-service meals per person. *Note that cancellations for dinner shows must be made at least 48 hours prior to showtime to avoid paying full price.*

Bars & Lounges of WDW

What distinguishes Walt Disney World pubs and lounges from many bars in the real world? Well, in addition to over-the-top theming, you can almost always get a savory nibble to accompany that cocktail. Most Disney lounges serve food, be it from their own menu or from that of a neighboring restaurant.

Hours vary, but theme park watering holes (at Epcot, Disney's Hollywood Studios, and Animal Kingdom) shut their doors at park closing time. Pool bars at the resorts keep daytime pool hours. Last call at resort lounges can be anywhere from about 10 P.M. to midnight. Disney Springs Marketplace spots stay open till the shops close, usually 11 P.M. Other lounges may keep things going until about 1 A.M.

All-Star Movies, All-Star Music & All-Star Sports

POOL BARS: There are small poolside oases in All-Star Movies, All-Star Music, and All-Star Sports: Silver Screen Spirits, Singing Spirits, and Grandstand Spirits, respectively. Each serves a selection of beer, wine, traditional cocktails, and specialty drinks.

Animal Kingdom

DAWA BAR: A shady spot in a busy neighborhood, Dawa is a pleasant place to take a load off weary feet and sip Safari Amber beer and other cocktails. It's next to Tusker House, on Kivulini Terrace. There is occasional live music, too.

NOMAD LOUNGE: Adventurers can take a load off and relish in a savory snack and/or frosty beverage at this exotic Animal Kingdom destination. The lounge proffers libations from the world over. The freshly prepared cuisine at Nomad includes vegetarian summer rolls, Indian butter chicken wings, seared Wagyu beef skewers, and honey-glazed, coriander-spiced pork ribs. Festive banners post questions about world travel and the thrill of discovery. Jot your answers on a decorative (and free) tag and cast members will post them to a chandelier for all the world to see. This lounge earned a spot on our favorites list the day it opened (in 2016).

THIRSTY RIVER BAR & TREK SNACKS: In the shadows of Expedition Everest, this casual outdoor oasis offers many spirited selections, including specialty drinks known as the Himalayan Ghost, Durbar Margarita, and Khumbu Icefall. Savory snacks are available too. The menu has featured crudité and hummus, edamame, Asian noodle salads, smoked turkey sandwiches, Bahn Mi (roasted pork topped with pickled vegetables, cilantro, and sriracha dressing), Som Tam (Thai shrimp, green papaya salad, crushed peanuts, and chilis), and sushi.

RAINFOREST CAFE: The Magic Mushroom bar serves, among other things, fruit blends and specialty drinks. Bar stools resemble animal legs (hooves and all). Guests may order from the restaurant's menu, too. The bar is inside the Rainforest Cafe. Admission to Animal Kingdom is not necessary to enter. Note that Rainforest Cafe may keep longer hours than the park.

YAK & YETI LOUNGE: A small but escapist space inside one of the restaurant's themed dining areas, the Yak & Yeti lounge has a fully stocked bar and seating for six. (There's standing room, too.) House specialties include the Yak Attack, Bonsai Blast, Big Bamboo, and Everest Avalanche. Beer, wine, and sake are also served.

Animal Kingdom Lodge

CAPE TOWN LOUNGE AND WINE BAR: Sip African wines at this intimate spot adjacent to Jiko—The Cooking Place. In addition to a full menu, it has the largest selection of African wines in the United States.

MAJI: A poolside bar (*maji* means "water" in Swahili) serves beverages when the Samawati Springs pool is open (in Kidani Village).

SANAA: Located in the resort's Kidani Village, this lounge is within the restaurant of the same name. South African beers and wines are served.

UZIMA SPRINGS: The bar near the main pool serves beer, wine, and specialty drinks during pool hours. The (liquor-free) Lava smoothie is a nice way to counter the Florida heat.

VICTORIA FALLS: On the mezzanine level overlooking Boma—Flavors of Africa, this lounge offers coffee and spirits, plus the soothing sounds of the falls. (The actual Victoria Falls are located in Africa, between Zambia and Zimbabwe, and are nearly a mile wide.)

Art of Animation

DROP OFF BAR: Open from noon until midnight, this poolside location offers a variety of cocktails (with and without alcohol), soft drinks, and smoothies—plus sandwiches, fruit, and other snack items.

BoardWalk

ABRACADABAR: A "curious cocktail lounge," adjoining Flying Fish, AbracadaBAR merges the Golden Age of Magic with the magic of the Mouse. The sophisticated social club, once frequented by famous magicians and boardwalk illusionists, is back in the spotlight and open to all. Concoctions of note: The Magic Hattan, The Conjurita, and Pepper's Ghost. Curious Cocktails include alcohol-free options. ❤

ATLANTIC DANCE: This club has music, videos, and a deejay. The design is Art Deco, but the tunes are more current. It's open Tuesday–Saturday nights, and guests must be at least 21 (with government-issued photo ID) to enter.

Got I.D.?

The legal drinking age in the state of Florida is 21. However, just being 21 isn't enough to get served—you have to prove it. To do so, present a government-issued photo ID. If your driver's license doesn't have a photo, bring it and an official photo ID (a passport is ideal). Otherwise, you'll have to stick to soft drinks.

BELLE VUE LOUNGE: A full bar accompanies old-time tunes from antique radios in this casual space. Continental breakfast is offered (from 6 A.M. until 11 A.M.). Board games are usually available for on-site use (free of charge). There's limited seating at the bar, but there are plenty of tables and comfy couches to lounge on. The lounge starts serving cocktails at about 5 P.M. ❤

BIG RIVER GRILLE & BREWING WORKS: Big River patrons may order appetizers at the bar and sample the brewmaster's flagship ales and specialty beers. They may even get to watch as a new batch is brewed. In addition to the fresh-brewed beer, beverage selections include fresh-squeezed lemonade, strawberry lemonade, pomegranate lemonade, and more. Note that Big River does not accept reservations, so the bar can get crowded during mealtimes (and right after Epcot closes for the night). ❤

ESPN CLUB: The sports bar provides live radio and TV broadcasts along with a full menu. With nearly 100 screens, chances are you'll find the game you seek. The place fills up quickly on big game days—arrive at least an hour early on such occasions. Note that on NFL Sundays, the match-ups scheduled for screening are often noted right on the TVs. If not, ask the bartender or inquire at the podium near the front entrance. ❤

JELLYROLLS: Dueling pianos and lively sing-alongs are the draw at this club, serving beer, wine, and other drinks. There is a cover charge in the neighborhood of $12, and guests must be at least 21 years old to enter. (Government-issued photo ID is required.) Requests are encouraged. And don't forget to tip the piano players before you leave. Note that it can be exceptionally cool here: Bring a sweater.

PHOTO BY JILL SAFRO

LEAPING HORSE LIBATIONS: The pool bar—designed to resemble a carousel (hence, the leaping horses)—offers cocktails, sandwiches, soft drinks, and simple snacks during pool hours.

Caribbean Beach

CENTERTOWN: Caribbean Beach resort is currently undergoing a massive refurbishment. During this time there is no dedicated lounge, but cocktails are served at Centertown (the resort's temporary dining location).

Contemporary

CALIFORNIA GRILL LOUNGE: Perched atop the Contemporary resort, this revitalized space tops many a "must-visit" list. Tucked within the acclaimed restaurant, the lounge offers the full menu and shares access to California Grill's exquisite wine list that boasts about 250 vintages (about 80 offered by the glass), featuring California's finest. If you need help navigating the wine list, fear not: One of the Grill's 20 sommeliers will be happy to help you make a selection.

In addition to wine, the lounge features sake, craft beers and ciders, mixed drinks, alcohol-free signature drinks, and more. Guests of the lounge may order anything off the restaurant menu (including the spectacular sushi). Just as with the restaurant itself, all guests hoping to visit the California Grill Lounge must check in at the desk on the Contemporary's second floor. From there they are escorted to an express elevator. The lounge does not accept reservations. 🐭

COVE BAR: Set beside the pool in the resort's Bay Lake Tower, Cove Bar serves sweets (apple slices with caramel dipping sauce, fruit, and frozen desserts) and lunch items (shrimp cocktail, turkey BLT wrap, nachos with cheese, veggie wrap, hot dog, and sushi). Wash it all down with one of their specialty drinks, such as the Banana Cabana or Poolside Plunge. 🐭

OUTER RIM: Located on the resort's fourth floor across from Contempo Cafe, this modern lounge has about seven bar stools and an abundance of tables with cocktail service. The main draw here is not the view of the large-screen TV, but rather the sweeping views of Bay Lake and the natural wonder of Fort Wilderness

HOT TIP!

At some Walt Disney World lounges, you may order food from a neighboring or nearby restaurant's menu. Just ask.

(on the lake's far shore). Parts of this lounge may host guests waiting for a table at the popular Chef Mickey's restaurant, so it can be a tad congested here at mealtimes. Beer, wine, sangria, specialty drinks, and alcohol-free kiddie cocktails are served from about 11:30 A.M. till 10 P.M.

SAND BAR: A full bar is offered poolside, weather permitting. Quick-service food, salads, and sandwiches are available at the adjacent counter area. 🐭

THE WAVE . . . OF AMERICAN FLAVORS LOUNGE: On the first floor of the resort, this spacious bar boasts a wine list that is mostly screw cap (yes, that's a good thing)—a quaffable selection of quality vintages. About 50 are available by the glass; tasting flights are a great choice for those who wish to sample several selections. Also poured: organic beers, ports, and specialty drinks. Guests may order from The Wave's outstanding menu, too. Our humble opinion? The Wave is one of the best Disney World lounges. It's also an excellent place for groups to gather.

Coronado Springs

RIX LOUNGE: Located in the resort's main building, this upscale, eye- and palate-pleasing lounge serves specialty drinks, beer, wine, soft drinks, and tapas-style appetizers. Cappuccino is an option. The 300-seat venue features house music and a Mediterranean-inspired atmosphere.

SIESTAS CANTINA: Swimmers can take time out for burgers, sandwiches, tacos, and cocktails at this spot near the pool in the Dig Site area. 🐭

HOT TIP!
Wide World of Sports Cafe is only open during select events at the Sports Complex. Call 407-WDW-DINE to see if it will be open during your visit. It is a Disney Dining Plan participant.

Disney's Hollywood Studios

THE HOLLYWOOD BROWN DERBY LOUNGE: An inviting alfresco enclave, the Derby Lounge serves as an extension of the elegant eatery to which it is attached. The all-day menu touts specialty cocktails (including the Grapefruit Cake Martini) and small plates. Choose from items such as andouille-crusted shrimp, Wagyu beef sliders, and Florida tomato soup. For a sweet treat, consider the warm blueberry cobbler or banana toffee cake.

TUNE-IN LOUNGE: A sitcom living-room setting with comfy stools and couches characterizes this lounge next to the 50's Prime Time Cafe. Old TV sets play scenes from beloved sitcoms (all of which feature food). Appetizers, cocktails, beer, wine, and soft drinks are served.

Disney's Old Key West

GURGLING SUITCASE: This friendly, pocket-size lounge on the Turtle Krawl boardwalk serves an assortment of Key West specialties, along with traditional cocktails, beer, and wine.

TURTLE SHACK: Refreshments at this poolside counter include cocktails and a small selection of fast-food items.

Disney Springs

BONGOS: Mojitos are the specialty of the house, but martinis and other mixed drinks, wine, sangria, and beer are also served. Bongos' two-story pineapple bar has indoor and outdoor seating and offers a full bar, plus appetizers. This is one of the more atmospheric spots at Disney Springs, West Side. Note that Bongos may not be open in all of 2018.

DOCKSIDE MARGARITAS: Get "a taste of the Sunshine State" at this new waterside bar at the Marketplace. In addition to creatively

blended margaritas, this breezy spot serves rum runners, mojitos, locally brewed craft beers, and tropical Florida wines such as Key Limen and Mango Mama. Live entertainment is provided most evenings.

HOLE IN THE WALL: Blink and you miss it. This tiny establishment is bookended (and dwarfed) by Raglan Road on the left and Cookes of Dublin on the right. A full bar is available, but the Irish stout stands out. In addition to the outstanding nibbles (whipped up over at Raglan Road), this diminutive spot boasts something that is beyond rare at Walt Disney World: Happy Hour specials (from 3 to 6 or 7 P.M.).

PHOTO BY MIKE CARROLL

HOUSE OF BLUES: Set in the back of the eatery section of H.O.B., this bar serves drinks that are as cool as the atmosphere. It's also possible to have drinks in the enclosed Voodoo Garden (table-service only). Guests may order from the restaurant menu.

JOCK LINDSEY'S HANGAR BAR: An aviation-themed, waterside lounge, Jock Lindsey's seats 150 adventurous guests at a time. Visitors may sip cocktails or specialty drinks and nibble on small-plate treats such as Rolling Boulder Sliders, Brody's Brats (grilled bratwurst with mustard and pickled cabbage), and Air Pirates Pretzels (with housemade mustard and beer cheese fondue). There's indoor and outdoor seating. The lounge is situated on The Landing, between Paradiso 37 and The Boathouse. FYI: Jock Lindsey is Indiana Jones' frequent pilot and the proud owner of a pet snake named Reggie.

MAGIC MUSHROOM BAR: When the Rainforest Cafe restaurant is mobbed, we recommend taking in the thunderstorms and waterfalls from this central, mushroom-capped bar. Simply saddle a stool (all of which are shaped like animal legs) and enjoy the festive "natural" ambience. You can sip a cocktail and order a snack from the restaurant's menu. There is another Magic Mushroom Bar inside the Rainforest Cafe at Disney's Animal Kingdom. (See page 264.)

PARADISO 37: The bar at Paradiso 37 features an international wine list, an extensive selection of tequilas, frozen margaritas, and the "coldest beer in the world." This spot offers indoor and outdoor seating. It is possible to order items from the restaurant's menu, too.

PLANET HOLLYWOOD OBSERVATORY: The redesigned Planet Hollywood lounge space includes an inviting outdoor terrace—perfect for sipping cocktails under the stars.

RAGLAN ROAD: Top o' the evening to you! This jovial joint is an authentic Irish pub and simply oozes Irish charm. The polished interior is a meticulously decorated Emerald Isle oasis—complete with freshly prepared Irish cuisine and live entertainment (the latter starting at about 4 P.M. on weekdays, noon on weekends). Oh, and of course, pints of stout and other spirited beverages. This place is popular and can get quite crowded on weekend evenings—get there early if you can.

SHARK BAR: This space, inside the T-Rex Cafe, puts the water in watering hole. Anchored under the belly of a Technicolor squid, the aqueous area serves all kinds of cocktails, plus

HOT TIP!

The spirits are forever flowing at Disney Springs. In addition to the dynamic destinations detailed on these pages, these Disney Springs venues also boast ever-so-lovely lounges: Paddlefish, The Boathouse, Chef Art Howe's Homecomin', The Polite Pig, The Edison, Morimoto Asia, and STK Orlando. Cheers!

items from the restaurant's menu. (One of our favorite things to order here is the tomato soup.) Guests must be at least 21 to sit at the bar.

WINE BAR GEORGE: The brainchild of Master Sommelier George Miliotes, this 210-seat establishment resembles a winemaker's estate. It's a cozy yet elegant environment in which to savor sips from acclaimed wineries and promising up-and-comers. They pair perfectly with small plate offerings here. FYI: George Miliotes is one of just 230 Master Sommeliers in the world. Impressive!

Epcot

All eateries, including some fast-food spots, serve alcoholic beverages. A few other Epcot locales specialize in liquid refreshments.

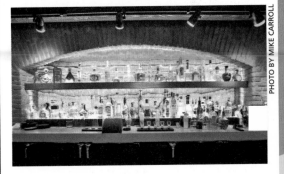

LA CAVA DEL TEQUILA: A warm glow envelopes guests who visit this little lounge in the big pyramid at the Mexico pavilion—and that's before they sample any of the 70-plus tequilas on the menu. In addition to blended margaritas (many made with fresh fruit and spices), guests may sip Mexican beer, wine, cocktails, and soft drinks. Snack selections include fresh guacamole and chips and salsa. This 30-seat escape is open from about noon until Epcot closing time.

ROSE & CROWN PUB: This classic pub—a veritable symphony of polished woods, brass, and etched glass—adjoins the Rose & Crown Dining Room in the United Kingdom pavilion. English, Scottish, and Irish beers are available, along with a score of specialty drinks and appetizing snacks imported from the other side of the Atlantic. If you're lucky, there will be live (and lively) piano music during your visit. Feel free to sing along. (Showtimes are listed in the park's Times Guide.) Seating indoors and out is limited and available on a first-come, first-served basis. ❦

SOMMERFEST: Just outside the Biergarten in Germany, there's a window serving soft pretzels, bratwurst, frankfurters, apple strudel, and other treats. Wash 'em down with a stein of cold German beer. They also serve German Riesling, Jägermeister, bottled water, and fountain drinks. There are tables nearby. ❦

TUTTO GUSTO: A happy addition to the Italy pavilion, Tutto Gusto offers 200 different wines (including grappa), beers imported from Italy, Italian specialty drinks, coffee drinks, and a small-plate menu. The best time to visit is in the afternoon (that's when crowds are usually lightest). Reservations are not available.

Fort Wilderness

CROCKETT'S TAVERN: You needn't brandish a coonskin cap to belly up to the bar in this rustic saloon, merely a government-issued photo ID to prove you're not a young'un (all guests must be at least 21 years of age to drink spirits of any kind). Tucked into a corner of the Trail's End restaurant, this spot is small but cozy, and the barkeeps are as amiable as they come. Last we visited, there were a couple of domestic beers on tap, plus a full bar. Pizza, chicken wings, and nachos are served, too. The TV is usually tuned to the big game of the moment. ❦

Grand Floridian

CÍTRICOS LOUNGE: As inviting as any lounge on Disney property, this place has one stellar wine list. Old World, New World, red, white, sparkling . . . you name it, they got it. Also on tap are beer, port, sherry, specialty coffees, and creative cocktails (think along the lines of a Citropolitan or Pomegranate Splash).

Cocktails and appetizers may be ordered until about 10 P.M. (If it's busy, the bar may continue to serve drinks until the crowd dwindles.) Menu

selections have included sautéed shrimp, crab salad, heirloom beet salad, slow-roasted pork belly, seasonal flatbread, artisanal cheese board, charcuterie, and the exquisitely crispy arancini risotto (fried balls of rice with cremini mushrooms, Asiago cheese, and white truffle aioli). There are a handful of seats at the bar and roughly ten tables in the lounge. If you sit at a table, be sure to place your order with the bartender before grabbing a seat.

MIZNER'S: Named after the eccentric architect who defined much of the flavor of Florida's Gold Coast, this handsome retreat serves beer, wine, cocktails, ports, brandies, and appetizers. Cigars may be purchased here, too (although they must be puffed elsewhere, as this, like most WDW bars, is a nonsmoking venue).

If you're in the mood for a nibble, consider the barbecue shrimp and grits, cider-braised mussels and cream, artisanal cheese plate, or crispy Rhode Island calamari. Sweet temptations include lemon custard, strawberry shortcake, and almond-crusted cheesecake. Food is usually served from about 5:30 P.M. until about 10 P.M., while the spirits usually flow until about midnight.

NARCOOSSEE'S LOUNGE: This upscale bar-within-a-restaurant offers a little bit of everything: appetizers, entrées, desserts, and cocktails (including dessert drinks). There is an extensive list of international wines, 40 of which are available by the glass. How serious are they about wine here? Our last bartender was a certified sommelier. A large selection of bottled craft beers is available, too. Note that the dress code for this lounge is "business casual." ❦

POOL BARS: The Courtyard Pool Bar (near the big pool) and Beaches Pool Bar & Grill (by the zero-depth-entry pool) stand by with beer, wine, frozen specialty drinks, soft drinks, and snacks. Courtyard has table tennis, too.

HOT TIP!

Grand Floridian visitors take note: The resort's grand lobby is a divine setting in which to savor a fine wine or a frosty brew. While there's no in-lobby service, guests may buy a drink at Mizner's (see above) and sip it while relaxing on an overstuffed lobby chair or comfy couch. If you time it right, you'll be serenaded by the lobby pianist or a live band.

Polynesian Village

BAREFOOT BAR: Adjacent to the Lava pool, this unassuming bar serves beer, wine, frozen tropical drinks (with and without alcohol), and soft drinks. Items of note: frozen strawberry daiquiri and piña colada. (We like them mixed together, aka The Lava Flow.)

OASIS BAR: Set beside the resort's "quiet" pool, Oasis offers a full bar and a number of specialty cocktails. It is available exclusively to guests staying at Disney's Polynesian Village and may be accessed with a valid MagicBand.

TAMBU: Adjoining 'Ohana, this small tiki bar offers cocktails and specialty drinks in a tropical setting. There is seating at the bar and at tables. Note that the table section serves as the waiting area for guests dining at 'Ohana, so it tends to get very busy at mealtimes. Libation of note: the Lapu Lapu. It's a mixture of rum and fruit juices served in a fresh pineapple.

TRADER SAM'S GROG GROTTO: There's so much to see in this festive first-floor lounge that guests may not notice there is a world beyond Sam's walls. Guests may enjoy tropical drinks and small plates in the richly themed locale (Jungle Cruise meets the Enchanted Tiki Room). Drink favorites include the Krakatoa Punch, the Nautilus, and Dark and Stormy. Sam's doors open at 4 P.M. Guests under 21 are not admitted after 8 P.M. Seats on the patio, aka Sam's Tiki Terrace, are much easier to come by than those inside. If you simply must infiltrate the grotto, arrive at about 3:30 P.M. and wait for the doors to open. (Don't be surprised if there is already a line when you arrive.) You can also put your name on a list and be reached via pager when a spot opens up. This boisterous grotto is a real crowd-pleaser.

Pop Century

PETALS: This poolside watering hole serves beer, wine, and cocktails.

Port Orleans French Quarter

MARDI GROGS: Beer, specialty drinks, and snacks are among the offerings at this pool spot.

SCAT CAT'S CLUB: Next to the Sassagoula Floatworks & Food Factory, this large, informal lounge pays tribute to the uniquely American

music that is jazz. In fact, live jazz music is presented four nights a week (Wednesday through Saturday, from 8 P.M. till about 12 A.M.). In addition to the usual brews and blends, this spot specializes in Southern drinks—including Hurricanes. There is an appetizer menu, too.

Port Orleans Riverside

MUDDY RIVERS: The poolside bar serves beer, specialty concoctions, and snack items.

RIVER ROOST: Situated in a room designed as a cotton exchange, this spacious lounge features specialty drinks, as well as light hors d'oeuvres. Sink into a comfy chair, beside the glow of the fireplace, and sip cocktails with a Southern flair. There are stools at the bar and tables, too. Live entertainment is presented on select evenings (usually Wednesday through Saturday, from 8 P.M. until about midnight).

Saratoga Springs

THE TURF CLUB: This casual, frill-free corner of the resort serves all manner of spirits (from a walk-up window). There's a pool table, too.

Swan & Dolphin

CABANA BAR & BEACH CLUB: Come for the food, stay for drinks. This Dolphin spot's sophisticated air and edgy design is a definite draw for the grown-up set, yet the place doesn't take itself so seriously that it fails to please little ones (think pizza, fruit bars, and lemonade). Grown-up pleasers include the lobster roll and the grilled chicken BLT.

Classic cocktails such as the Mai Tai, Rum Runner, and Caipirinha share the stage with creative, original concoctions. Frozen libations abound, as do beer (micro- and macrobrews), rum, and tequila. Wine, scotch, cognac, cigars and soft drinks are offered, too.

IL MULINO NEW YORK TRATTORIA

LOUNGE: A lovely spot (at the Swan) to sip wines and cocktails and/or enjoy the bar menu, this lounge features live music on Friday and Saturday evenings. There are lots of seats at the bar, plus tables and comfy couches. It's usually open for business starting in the late afternoon.

KIMONOS: This Swan lounge, attractively decorated in Japanese style, has a full bar, as well as sushi and other culinary treats. It opens in late afternoon/early evening, and last call is usually between 10:30 P.M. and 1 A.M. The karaoke starts cranking at about 9:30 P.M.

LOBBY LOUNGE: The Dolphin lobby bar serves beer, wine, cocktails, and soft drinks, sometimes accompanied by live piano music. Lobby Lounge hours are generally 3 P.M. until about 11 P.M.

SHULA'S LOUNGE: This small, austere Dolphin saloon within Shula's Steak House features rich wood tones and plush seating— the perfect place to sip a cocktail while playing armchair quarterback.

SPLASH TERRACE: A poolside oasis near the Swan, Splash offers custom-made sandwiches, pizza, ice cream, snacks, soft drinks, beer, wine, cocktails, and specialty drinks. Open seasonally.

PHOTO BY MIKE CARROLL

TODD ENGLISH'S BLUEZOO BAR:

The underwater mojo of Todd's bluezoo restaurant extends to the sizable bar/lounge area (booths and tables augment the bar seating, easily accommodating large parties). In addition to the liquid refreshments, this is a genuine raw bar—many guests order a cocktail with a side of something fishy.

Last call varies, depending on how crowded the place is at any given moment. Figure on getting the boot between 9 P.M. and 11 P.M.

Wilderness Lodge

TERRITORY LOUNGE: Located between Artist Point and Whispering Canyon Cafe, this rustic homage to the explorers of the Great West is a nice spot for a pre-dinner treat. Appetizers, soft drinks, beer, wine, and cocktails are served. The Pomegranate Sparkler is a no-alcohol treat.

TROUT PASS: This poolside bar serves beer, wine, and frozen drinks.

Yacht & Beach Club

ALE & COMPASS LOUNGE: The newly expanded, nautically themed Yacht Club lobby lounge offers a full drink menu with premium spirits and appetizers. Ale & Compass Lounge is usually open until about midnight. ♥

PHOTO BY MIKE CARROLL

CREW'S CUP: Styled after a traditional New England waterfront pub, this casual lounge has a seafaring feel to it. It's next door to the Yachtsman Steakhouse and has well over 25 beers. There is also a tempting menu. This is one of our favorite places to relax after a long day in the parks. Nibbles are generally served from about noon until midnight.

HURRICANE HANNA'S WATERSIDE BAR & GRILL: This poolside oasis is a sophisticated yet casual place to sip a beverage and enjoy a savory snack. The menu includes items such as sea salt fries, pulled pork sandwiches, Buffalo chicken wraps, seafood rolls, and more. Kids' meals come in a small sand bucket, complete with attached shovel. ♥

MARTHA'S VINEYARD: While a full bar is available, a small but satisfying selection of wines from Martha's Vineyard (and other areas) is this Beach Club bar's specialty. Light appetizers are served, too.

Disney Cruise Line

W alt Disney World, which boasts one of the largest fleets of pleasure craft on the planet, has an inimitable nautical neighbor: Disney Cruise Line. And three of its majestic ocean liners—the award-winning *Wonder*, *Dream*, and *Fantasy*—set sail from Central Florida's Port Canaveral. That's a mere 50 miles from Walt Disney World, making the prospect of pairing a visit to WDW with a Disney Cruise a convenient temptation for many a World traveler.

A voyage with Disney Cruise Line, however, is atypical in a number of ways. First, there's the simultaneous catering to families with kids and grown-ups *sans* offspring. In fact, each ship has programming designed to draw young and old, and those in between, to entirely different recreational areas. Then there's the innovative "rotational dining system," a lineup of lavish musical productions, deck-shaking dance parties, and, of course, the possibility of a unique grand finale: a full day at Castaway Cay—Disney's private, tropical island.

Like swaying in a hammock in the aforementioned paradise, the process of selecting a cruise package and combining it with a stay at Walt Disney World should be as carefree as possible. Within this Birnbaum bonus chapter, you'll find detailed information meant to ensure that planning a "land and sea" holiday is smooth sailing. Bon voyage!

Land & Sea Vacations
Pairing a Disney Cruise with a Walt Disney World Vacation

It's the ultimate surf-and-turf experience for Disney fans—a Walt Disney World vacation that's paired with a Disney cruise. (What better way to chase the Pirates of the Caribbean attraction than by visiting the Caribbean?! Minus real pirates, of course.) And with three Disney ships sailing out of Port Canaveral, Florida, this year, "land and sea" opportunities abound. The pages that follow describe how Land and Sea vacations work and give a brief overview of the Disney Cruise Line fleet.

If you've been to Disney's world before (or read the first 300 or so pages of this book), you know that it is not a small one. In fact, it covers 40 square miles—and with about as many attractions, restaurants, and places to stay as one might expect from an area that size. There are four theme parks, two water parks, two dozen hotels, a dining, shopping, and entertainment district, championship golf courses, boating, fishing, tennis, and more. Add a cruise to the mix, and even seasoned Disney veterans run the risk of becoming overwhelmed.

The good news is that a customized vacation package can include just about everything you'd ever want. That frees you up to focus on a very important goal: having fun.

HOT TIP!
Disney Cruise Vacations offers a day-before option at a non-Disney resort with some packages. For information, contact a travel agent or call 800-951-3532.

Surf & Turf

Folks dreaming of a "land and sea" escape can customize that dream vacation with (or without) a little help from Disney Cruise Line or a travel agent). In addition to settling on a budget, there are decisions to be made: 1. Do you want to cruise before or after you visit WDW? 2. How long do you wish to play on land and on sea? 3. Where do you want to stay on Land? 4. Which sailing itinerary is best for you? (See page 312 for a selection of popular itineraries that depart from Central Florida's Port Canaveral. Note that the *Disney Magic* sails out of Miami in 2018.)

Disney Cruise Line Air Program

If you plan to fly to the port, consider allowing the Disney Cruise Vacations Air Program to help you make the arrangements. In addition to lining up round-trip airfare for your whole party, they will secure motor coach ground transportation and baggage transfers.
The service is available in more than 150 cities in the United States, United Kingdom, and Canada. At press time, this service was not included in the price of any Disney Cruise Line vacation packages. For details and pricing, call 877-566-0967.

To pair a visit to Walt Disney World with a Disney cruise, contact a travel agent or call 800-951-3532. (That's the number to call if you'd like help finding a hotel near Disney Cruise Line's other home ports, too.)

PHOTO BY JILL SAFRO

Combination Vacation

Walt Disney World/Disney Cruise Line combination vacations can include accommodations on land (at a WDW resort) and a stateroom on a Disney ship. In addition to accommodations, shipboard meals, snacks, soft drinks, and entertainment are included with all Disney Cruise Line packages.

What's not included in a "Land and Sea" combination vacation? Meals and beverages at Walt Disney World (unless the WDW Dining Plan is purchased in advance), transfers to Port Canaveral (these may also be purchased in advance), airfare, excursions, meals ashore in ports of call—with the exception of Castaway Cay, where food and soft drinks are included (see page 343)—extra gratuities, laundry or valet services, parking at the port, or any other items not specifically included.

What can be added? Just about everything. Options include tickets to Disney World theme and water parks, dinner shows, and more. For details, visit *www.disneycruise.com*, or call 800-951-3532.

DISNEY CRUISE LINE

Walt Disney World Resort Options

The following is a comprehensive list of Walt Disney World–owned-and-operated resort hotels. For details on these resorts, turn to our *Transportation & Accommodations* chapter. The information was correct at press time but is subject to change. In addition to Walt Disney World, it's possible to book vacations that pair a cruise with a hotel stay in Miami and other port cities. For additional information, visit *www.disneycruise.com*, or call 800-951-3532.

DELUXE:

Animal Kingdom Lodge (see page 99)

BoardWalk (see page 91)

Contemporary Resort (see page 76)

Dolphin (see page 89)

Grand Floridian Resort & Spa (see page 80)

Old Key West Resort (see page 97)

Polynesian Village Resort (see page 78)

Saratoga Springs Resort & Spa (see page 96)

Swan (see page 89)

Wilderness Lodge (see page 82)

Yacht & Beach Club (see page 86)

MODERATE:

Cabins at Fort Wilderness resort (see page 84)

Caribbean Beach Resort (see page 85)

Coronado Springs Resort (see page 101)

Port Orleans French Quarter (see page 94)

Port Orleans Riverside (see page 95)

VALUE:

All-Star Movies (see page 98)

All-Star Music (see page 98)

All-Star Sports (see page 98)

Art of Animation (see page 103)

Campsites at Fort Wilderness
 resort (see page 83)

Pop Century (see page 102)

Sample Itineraries

Three Disney ships—the *Wonder*, *Dream*, and *Fantasy*—are scheduled to cruise out of Port Canaveral, Florida, in 2018. The *Magic* will sail from Miami, Florida. (Though some visit other home ports, there's usually at least two ships to choose from at all times.) What follows is a sampling of the itineraries offered from Port Canaveral, the port closest to Walt Disney World—and most logically paired with a WDW vacation. Note that most include a stop at Disney's private island, Castaway Cay (see page 343). For a complete list of ports and itineraries, visit *www.disneycruise.com*.

3-Night Bahamian Cruise — *Disney Dream*

DAY	ITINERARY
DAY 1	Check in at Port Canaveral Terminal. Aboard by 3:45 P.M.
DAY 2	Ashore at Nassau at 9:30 A.M. Aboard by 5:15 P.M.
DAY 3	Ashore at Disney Castaway Cay at 8:30 A.M. Aboard by 4:45 P.M.
DAY 4	Ship at Port Canaveral beginning at 7:30 A.M.

4-Night Bahamian Cruise — *Disney Wonder*

DAY	ITINERARY
DAY 1	Check in at Port Canaveral Terminal. Aboard by 4 P.M.
DAY 2	Ashore at Nassau at 9:30 A.M. Aboard by 5:15 P.M.
DAY 3	Ashore at Disney Castaway Cay at 8:30 A.M. Aboard by 4:45 P.M.
DAY 4	Full day at sea.
DAY 5	Ship at Port Canaveral beginning at 7:30 A.M.

4-Night Bahamian Cruise — *Disney Dream*
(with two stops at Castaway Cay)

DAY	ITINERARY
DAY 1	Check in at Port Canaveral Terminal. Aboard by 3:45 P.M.
DAY 2	Ashore at Castaway Cay at 8:30 A.M. Aboard by 4:45 P.M.
DAY 3	Ashore at Nassau at 8:15 A.M. Aboard by 5:15 P.M.
DAY 4	Ashore at Castaway Cay at 8:30 A.M. Aboard by 4:45 P.M.
DAY 5	Ship at Port Canaveral beginning at 7:30 A.M.

7-Night Eastern Caribbean Cruise — *Disney Wonder*

DAY	ITINERARY
DAY 1	Check in at Port Canaveral Terminal. Aboard by 4 P.M.
DAY 2	Full day at sea.
DAY 3	Full day at sea.
DAY 4	Ashore at St. Maarten at 9 A.M. Aboard by 5:45 P.M.
DAY 5	Ashore at San Juan, Puerto Rico, at 8 A.M. Aboard by 4:45 P.M.
DAY 6	Full day at sea.
DAY 7	Ashore at Disney Castaway Cay at 8:30 A.M. Aboard by 4:45 P.M.
DAY 8	Ship at Port Canaveral beginning at 7:30 A.M.

7-Night Western Caribbean Cruise — *Disney Fantasy*

DAY	ITINERARY
DAY 1	Check in at Port Canaveral Terminal. Aboard by 3:45 P.M.
DAY 2	Full day at sea.
DAY 3	Ashore at Cozumel, Mexico, at 8:30 A.M. Aboard by 4:45 P.M.
DAY 4	Ashore at Grand Cayman, Cayman Islands, at 10:30 A.M. Aboard by 5:30 P.M. (This port requires tendering.)
DAY 5	Ashore at Falmouth, Jamaica, at 7:30 A.M. Aboard by 4:45 P.M.
DAY 6	Full day at sea.
DAY 7	Ashore at Castaway Cay at 8:30 A.M. Aboard by 4:45 P.M.
DAY 8	Ship at Port Canaveral beginning at 7:30 A.M.

Before You Sail

What to do, what to do. There are many factors to consider when pairing a cruise package with a stay at Walt Disney World. Among the most important are destination, budget, time available, stateroom needs, and preferred itinerary.

If you want to take the most inexpensive cruise possible, then a shorter cruise in a standard inside stateroom is probably a good choice. If money is no object, consider a 7-night adventure in the super-deluxe Walter E. Disney suite. Of course, there are plenty of things in between.

Check Your Calendar

Determining the length of your cruise depends on several things—the first, how much time do you have in your busy schedule to devote to leisure? If your answer is only four days, don't despair: Disney has short cruises to the Bahamas (most of which include a stop at Disney's own private island, Castaway Cay). If you have at least a week to sail, you may choose a 7-night-or-longer cruise to the Caribbean. For details, call 800-910-3659, or visit *www.disneycruise.com*.

www.disneycruise.com

We've done our best to provide accurate, current information regarding all things Disney Cruise Line. That said, rates, itineraries, excursions, and other specifics are subject to change. For additional information or to book a cruise, shore excursion, and more, visit the interactive website: *www.disneycruise.com*. It's one of the most user-friendly websites we have ever seen.

Check Your Checkbook

The cost of your cruise is the next issue on the planning board. Budget constraints can be eased in several ways: by taking one of the shorter cruises, choosing a less-expensive stateroom class, and by limiting the number of land tours and excursions you take at the various ports of call. (We often forgo pricey excursions because the ships themselves have so much to offer.) Plan to eat aboard the ship, too—meals and snacks are included in the vacation package, as are many extras, including stage shows, movies, tours, lectures, games, bands, deck parties with Disney characters, and more.

Selecting a Stateroom

Sure, you'd like the largest suite on the ship. No question, you want the biggest verandah. And, of course, you absolutely must have a great view. But if these don't fit your budget, there are other appealing options. Consider this: Every stateroom boasts nautical decor, has ample closet space, a television, and a small safe. Inside staterooms can be a bit less expensive and not much smaller than their outside counterparts; on the *Dream* and the *Fantasy* they have virtual portholes (aka "magical" portholes, these high-tech wonders have HD digital screens). On the other hand, should you decide to splurge, know that there are concierge rooms and larger suites with private verandahs where you can savor a refreshing beverage and read the newest page-turner, periodically taking a moment to gaze out at the sea.

Of course, there are other factors to think about when selecting a stateroom. How many people are in your party? Are you traveling with young children? Perhaps a Deluxe Stateroom would suit your family's needs. These accommodations have queen-size beds, bunk beds for the kids, and a split bath (one room with a sink and a toilet and another with a sink and a shower/tub). A curtained divider provides a bit of privacy.

Of course, there's always the Walter E. Disney Suite and the Roy O. Disney Suite—so if money is no object, treat your crew to one of these thousand-plus-square-foot homes away from home. No matter what your requirements, chances are good that Disney Cruise Line can meet them.

What's Not Included with a Cruise?

Rest assured that all of your basic vacation needs are covered by the "all-inclusive" price of the cruise. However, there are always "extras" for which you may want to ante up a little cash. Here's a list of items and services that carry an extra charge while aboard Disney ships:

- Child care for tots ages 6 months to 3 years (see pages 319 and 340)
- Port Adventures (aka shore excursions)
- Expenses incurred while on land in ports of call (with the exception of food and most soft drinks at Castaway Cay)
- Alcoholic beverages and Royal Court Tea
- Palo and Remy (These optional, reservations-necessary, adults-only restaurants carry an extra charge: about $30 per person for dinner and brunch at Palo; about $60 per person for champagne brunch and $95 for dinner at Remy.)
- Vanellope's Sweets & Treats (on the *Dream*)

- Refreshments at Cove Cafe, Vista Cafe, and any bar
- Spa and Bibbidi Bobbidi Boutique services
- Merchandise purchased onboard
- Arcade games and sports simulators
- Photos snapped by the ship's photographers
- Internet usage (see page 321)
- Cell phone usage (see page 322)
- Ship-to-shore telephone calls (There is a sizable fee for all calls, incoming and outgoing. Calls within the ship are free.)

With the exception of non-Disney ports of call, all "incidental" charges will be billed to your stateroom, provided that you leave a credit card number upon check-in. It's a good idea to have some cash on hand (we bring about $300, just in case), but there are few chances to use it. Except for tips, cash isn't accepted on the ships. Same goes for Castaway Cay, with the exception of the post office—stamps must be purchased with cash. Most of the non-Disney port shops accept major credit cards, and most accept U.S. currency.

How to Book a Cruise

In addition to using *www.disneycruise.com* or calling Disney Cruise Line (800-910-3659), many guests book through travel agents.

PAYMENT METHODS: Cruise packages, as well as incidentals, gratuities, hotel bills, and deposits, may be paid by major credit card (Visa, MasterCard, JCB Card, American Express, Diners Club, etc.), Disney gift cards, Disney Rewards Redemption cards, traveler's check, cashier's check, money order, or personal check. Personal checks must bear the guest's name and address, be drawn on a U.S. bank, and be accompanied by proper identification (a valid driver's license with photo or government-issued photo ID). The reservation number must be written on the face of the check. Checks will not be accepted within 21 days prior to vacation commencement date. The final payment for a cruise package must be made between 75 and 150 days prior to the cruise, depending on the itinerary and category. Final payment due date varies for special itineraries.

Payments sent via mail should be addressed to: Disney Cruise Line, P.O. Box 277763, Atlanta, GA 30384-7763.

Payments sent via courier service (e.g., FedEx or UPS) should be sent to: Disney Cruise Line, Bank of America, Lockbox Services, Lockbox 277763, 6000 Feldwood Road, College Park, GA 30349 (407-566-3500).

DEPOSIT REQUIREMENTS: When you book a cruise, you'll get a "due date" for a deposit. The deposit is 20 percent of the total fare. Reservations will be canceled if a deposit is not received by the deadline. (Packages that are booked within the final payment due date or in categories IGT, OGT, and VGT get special instructions.)

CANCELLATION POLICY: Cancellations may be made by phone or mail (we prefer the phone). To avoid the sad fate of paying for a canceled cruise, we recommend insuring your trip.

Fees paid for canceling depend on when that call is made. For cruises of less than 10 days

Ground Transfers

Disney Cruise Line provides reliable, friendly service aboard its motor coaches (aka: buses). Getting to the buses is easy. Upon arrival at Orlando International Airport, take a shuttle to the Main Terminal. Once there, proceed to Disney's Magical Express Welcome Center. It's on Level One, Side B. The real bonus here is the baggage handling: For flights before 10 P.M., Disney reps will pull your tagged luggage and make sure it gets delivered to your room. (Guests arriving after 10 P.M. may collect their luggage and proceed to the Magical Express Welcome Center.) From the airport, a bus will take you to Port Canaveral or a WDW hotel. (For guests with transfers included in their package, your bus departure location and information is included in your cruise documentation.) What if you're staying at a resort that's not designated as a departure location or at an off-property hotel? You'll have to get yourself to one of the WDW departure spots to catch a bus to the ship. Here's the pricing for Orlando ground transfers:

TRANSFER TRIP	PRICE*
Airport to select WDW resort (one-way)	Free**
Select WDW resort to Port Canaveral	$35
Round-trip from Orlando International Airport (MCO) to Port Canaveral	$70
Land and Sea vacation (Orlando airport to select WDW resort; WDW resort to Port Canaveral; Port Canaveral to airport)	$70

*Prices are per person, were correct at press time, and are subject to change.
**Disney's Magical Express transportation is a free service for WDW resort guests. For pricing details about transfers to and from other locations, call 800-951-3532.

where embark or debark is a U.S. port, cancellation fees are as follows:
- For all suites and concierge rooms, the deposit is nonrefundable regardless of when the reservation is canceled.
- For each non-suite/concierge stateroom guest, canceling 74 to 45 days before sailing costs the whole deposit.
- For all rooms, a cancellation within 44 to 30 days costs 50 percent of the vacation price.
- For all staterooms, a cancellation within 29 to 15 days costs 75 percent per guest.
- Should a cruise be canceled less than 14 days ahead, you'll pay for the whole package.

For cruises 10 days or more or less than 10 days where embark and debark is a non-U.S. port, the fees are as follows (this does not apply to cruises out of Port Canaveral, Florida):

- For all suites and concierge rooms, the deposit is non-refundable regardless of when the reservation was canceled.
- For all non-suite/concierge staterooms, canceling within 119 to 56 days before the sailing costs the deposit per guest.
- Canceling within 55 to 30 days costs 50 percent of the vacation cost per guest.
- Canceling within 29 to 15 days costs 75 percent of the vacation package per guest.
- Canceling less than 14 days ahead means you will pay for the whole package.

What to Pack

"Cruise Casual" is the operative phrase with Disney. Shorts, T-shirts, sundresses, and the like are fine daytime wear. At dinnertime, casual takes on a more formal meaning: Set aside flip-flops and plan on nice slacks (jeans are okay, as long as they're in good condition) and a collared shirt for men, with real shoes, as opposed to the tennis kind. The same goes for women, while dresses are fine, too. There is an optional dress-up night, too.

HOT TIP!

Guests who plan to arrive at Port Canaveral the night before setting sail might consider staying at one of these resorts on nearby Astronaut Boulevard:

Country Inns & Suites by Carlson. Rates range from about $89–$129, and there is a shuttle to the cruise terminal; 321-784-8500 or 888-201-1746.

Residence Inn by Marriott. Rates range from about $169–$220; 321-323-1100 or 800-331-3131.

Identification Papers

Unlike a visit to Disney's Epcot, where it only feels as if you're leaving the country, in the case of a Disney Cruise Line vacation, you usually do. Given that, you'll need a passport to provide proper proof of citizenship when passing through Customs for most cruises. (There are some itineraries for which U.S. citizens may use other forms of proof of citizenship such as a state-issued birth certificate.) U.S. government regulations related to passport requirements are subject to change. Therefore, all guests are advised to have a valid passport for all cruises. Visit *http://travel.state.gov*, or call 877-487-2778 for current requirements. Non-U.S. citizens are required to travel with valid government-issued passports at all times.

On 7-night-or-longer cruises, there is a semi-formal and a formal night. While some folks don black tie and sequins, it's fine to sport a less formal look. The *Personal Navigator* (see page 330) will tip you off as to the appropriate attire. Many guests pack pirate garb, too, in anticipation of "Pirates IN the Caribbean" party night—don't forget to pack your puffy shirt and eye patch. (The Pirate party takes place on most sailings.)

Bathing suits are a must, as are beach shoes, wraps, sunscreen, sunglasses, and hats. Some sundries, such as shampoo and body lotion, are provided. Others are available for purchase, but the prices are steep, and the shops aren't always open (U.S. Customs limits the operating hours).

PACK A DAY BAG: Guests may check in at the port and board the ship as early as 1 P.M., but your checked luggage may not arrive until 6 P.M. (though usually earlier). Keep in mind that you will have access to your stateroom beginning at 1:30 P.M., along with most shipboard amenities, including all pools, so pack your swimsuit in a day bag. This should serve as, or fit in, a carry-on, as checked bags will be out of your hands once you surrender them. (Day bags can't be larger than 9

HOT TIP!

You must show your "Key to the World" card (Disney-issued stateroom key and ID) when disembarking or boarding the ship. Adults also need a government-issued photo ID (a passport is ideal). Note that your WDW MagicBand or hotel key won't work on the ship.

What's in a Name?

A whole lot, when it comes to Disney Cruise Line accommodations. Here's a listing of the types of rooms available on each of the ships. Note that it is possible to request side-by-side staterooms, but it can't be guaranteed. For specifics on staterooms, see page 328.

- Standard Inside Stateroom
- Deluxe Inside Stateroom
- Deluxe Ocean-view Stateroom
- Deluxe Family Ocean-view Stateroom (*Dream* and *Fantasy*)
- Deluxe Ocean-view Stateroom with Navigator's Verandah (*Magic* and *Wonder*)
- Deluxe Ocean-view Stateroom with Verandah
- Deluxe Family Ocean-view Stateroom with Verandah
- Concierge Family Ocean-view Stateroom with Verandah
- Concierge 1-Bedroom Suite with Verandah
- Concierge 2-Bedroom Suite with Verandah (*Magic* and *Wonder*)
- Concierge Royal Suite with Verandah

inches by 14 inches by 22 inches and do not count as part of the two-bags-per-passenger quota.) The bag should also include your passports, valuables, breakable items, and anything else you might need during those first hours on board. Note that most airlines require that carried-on liquids be in 3.4-ounce-or-smaller containers and fit into one quart-size, clear, plastic zip-top bag.

Booking Shore Excursions

Shore Excursions, aka Port Adventures, book early. To reserve yours, visit *www.disneycruise.com*. To make last-minute arrangements, visit your ship's Port Adventures desk. Note that Port Adventures are not operated by the Walt Disney Company—not even those on Castaway Cay (see page 343).

For descriptions of all excursions offered in more than 70 worldwide destinations, including Castaway Cay, visit *www.disneycruise.com*. (We considered including all of them here, but that would have added about 600 pages to this book!)

Cancellations or changes to reservations must be made up to 3 days before a cruise starts to get a refund. After that, you pay whether you play or not.

How to Get to Port Canaveral

BY PLANE: Fly to Orlando International Airport. We prefer to arrive the night before or take a flight that is scheduled to arrive in the early morning hours. (That helps avoid potential travel delays.) If you get there on the early side, you can make a day of it. And, if your flight is delayed, you'll still have a shot at making it to the port before the ship sails. (When you book your cruise, ask about the check-in cutoff time. Don't be late!)

FROM THE AIRPORT: As you get off the shuttle and enter the main terminal, proceed directly to the Disney Magical Express Welcome Center. It's on Level 1, Side B of the terminal. After your party has checked in, a Disney rep will direct you toward a motor coach. Don't worry about checked luggage. For guests with transfers, all bags bearing appropriate tags will be claimed by Disney and delivered to your stateroom. (If you are driving to the ship, see information to the right.)

The following details apply specifically to cruises departing from Port Canaveral, Florida. For details for other departure ports (such as Miami, Vancouver, or Barcelona), call 800-910-3659, or visit *www.disneycruise.com*.

DISNEY MOTOR COACH: The bus trip from Orlando International Airport or a Disney World resort to Port Canaveral takes about 90 minutes (without traffic). While on board, you can fill out paperwork (though it is best to do this ahead of time). There's a restroom onboard. Motor coach transportation may be purchased with a cruise package.

CAR SERVICE: Noris Limousine and Florida Towncar offer friendly, reliable service between Orlando International Airport (MCO) and Port Canaveral. For rates, information, or to make a reservation with Noris Limousine, call 407-240-4533, or visit *www.norislimousine.com*. For Florida Towncar, go to *www.floridatowncar.com*, or call 800-525-7246 or 407-277-5466. Reservations are necessary, and cancellations must be made at least 24 to 48 hours in advance. Disney Cruise Line's reservations department can take your car service request, too.

AUTOMOBILE: Disney Cruise Line's Port Canaveral Terminal is located at Cruise Terminal 8 (CT8); 9155 Charles M. Rowland Drive, Port Canaveral, Florida 32920. It's about a 90-minute drive from Orlando International Airport and from Disney World. The parking facility, which is operated by the Canaveral Port Authority, accepts cash (U.S. currency), Visa, MasterCard, and traveler's checks only. Personal checks are not accepted. Parking costs about $16 per day. Rates are subject to change. Guests may also make a reservation for a parking space prior to arrival. To do so, have a credit card handy and visit *http://portcanaveral.com/cruising/parking.php*.

From Orlando International Airport, take State Road (S.R.) 528 East (Beachline Expressway). Continue over the Indian River and the Banana

River. Turn right onto S.R. 401, which will loop and head north over the channel locks. Stay in the right-hand lane and follow signs to the "A" Cruise Terminals. S.R. 528 is a toll road.

If you are driving from Walt Disney World, take State Road 536 East to 417 (the GreeneWay). Follow 417 to S.R. 528 East (Beachline Expressway). At the fork in the road, veer right to stay on S.R. 528. Continue over the Indian and Banana rivers. Turn right onto S.R. 401. Stay in the right lane and follow signs leading to the "A" Cruise Terminals. Note that 417 and 528 are toll roads.

Guests who are driving from North Florida should take I-95 South exit #205 for S.R. 528 East (Beachline Expressway). Continue over the Indian and Banana rivers. Turn right onto S.R. 401. Stay in the right lane and follow signs to "A" Cruise Terminals.

Drivers originating in South Florida should take I-95 North. Exit at #205 for S.R. 528 East (the Beachline). Take S.R. 528 to S.R. 401. Keep to the right and follow the signs to "A" Cruise Terminals.

GETTING TO PORT CANAVERAL FROM WALT DISNEY WORLD WITHOUT A CAR: Disney Cruise Line has buses to take guests directly from many WDW resorts. One-way transfers cost $35 per person, while $70 will cover the round-trip. Guests with transfers will get a letter in their resort room with departure details. Bell services will automatically pick up luggage when transfers have been prearranged. (Car services make the trip to and from Port Canaveral, too. See page 318 for details.)

Customized Travel Tips

TRAVELING WITH BABIES:

Cribs: If you are traveling with a baby, it is possible to have a playpen-like, foldaway crib sent to your stateroom. (The cribs are 39.8 inches long, 28.25 inches wide, and 31.25 inches high.) Request one when you make a reservation, and confirm it before leaving home. Supplies are limited. Bring a blanket, as the cribs come with fitted sheets only.

Diaper Service: It is possible to have a disposable diaper system sent to your stateroom. You can request it when you make a reservation, or speak with your Stateroom Host or Hostess upon arrival.

Food: Staterooms on all Disney ships have small refrigerators, perfectly safe for storing formula and food. Note that homemade baby food is not permitted on board any Disney ship.

Tag Your Bags

Flying to Orlando International Airport for a cruise out of Port Canaveral? After you book your cruise and purchase ground transfers, you'll get a personalized info packet in the mail. Included in this valuable envelope will be colorful luggage tags. We cannot overemphasize the importance of affixing these tags to all checked luggage. Why? Once you say good-bye to your bags at the airport, you won't see them again until they arrive at your stateroom. Disney reps collect bags and deliver them to your stateroom typically by 6 P.M.

If you arrive by car or bus, drop your bags with porters at the terminal. They will be delivered to your stateroom for you. Guests who arrive from Walt Disney World via Disney motor coach need to tag their bags, too. (Tags come with cruise documents.) The driver will see to it that tagged bags are removed from the bus and loaded on the ship.

If you'd rather not haul your bags off the ship, expect to use a similar color-coding/character method at the end of your cruise (this applies to all cruises). A set of tags will be left in your stateroom. Slap them on your bags, make a note of the color/character and place them in the hall on the last night of the cruise. (Be sure to keep items such as pajamas, sundries, and clothes for the morning in a day bag.) Look for them in the designated section of the terminal once you debark. Guests participating in onboard airline check-in don't have to claim their bags until their plane lands at their home airport. Restrictions apply. Note that it is not mandatory that guests surrender their bags on the last night of a cruise—but guests are responsible for removing all of their luggage from the ship in the morning.

At least one shop on board sells diapers, formula, and a limited selection of baby food. (The shop isn't always open, as U.S. Customs limits its hours.) If you'd like to save money, pack as many baby rations as possible.

Babysitting: Onboard babysitting is available for tots ages 6 months to 3 years (for most cruises). The cost is $9 an hour for the first child, with a one-hour minimum stay. Each additional child (who must be the first child's sibling) is $8 per hour. The service is offered in the ship's It's a Small World nursery. Reservations for the nursery can be made at *www.disneycruise.com* or on board (based on availability). In-room babysitting is not offered on any ship.

Cold and Flu Advisory

Disney Cruise Line follows extraordinary sanitation efforts to ensure the safety and comfort of guests. Even so, people can get sick. If you or a member of your party experiences any symptom of illness (cold, flu, etc.) within 72 hours of sailing, you may be evaluated by a medical team. (If necessary, Cruise Line representatives will direct you to someone to help your party make alternate plans.) Fees apply at the Health Center.

Once on board, all guests are asked to wash their hands frequently and thoroughly, as this is a highly effective barrier to spreading germs. If you or someone in your party does become ill during your trip, please contact the Health Center. You'll be taken care of there, and immediate treatment will help limit the potential impact to others.

HOT TIP!

If you will be using an ECV (Electronic Conveyance Vehicle) during your cruise, be sure to book an accessible stateroom (other rooms can't accommodate ECVs). No ECV parking is allowed in stateroom corridors or on elevator landings. There are ECV charging stations on Deck 6 midship on the *Magic* and *Wonder*, and on Deck 2 midship, outside Enchanted Garden, on the *Dream* and *Fantasy*.

handheld showerheads, and lowered towel and closet bars. Captioning is available for stateroom televisions, and for some onboard video monitors and movies. Stateroom communication kits may be reserved upon request. They include door-knock and phone alerts, bed shaker notification, and a strobe light smoke detector; a text type-writer (aka TTY) may also be requested. There is no charge for the kit, but supplies are limited. Make your needs known when you make your reservation and confirm them prior to sailing. Wheelchair-accessible restrooms are available in several common areas on board. There are pool lifts on the *Magic*, *Wonder*, *Dream*, and *Fantasy*. A small number of sand wheelchairs are available on Castaway Cay. American Sign Language interpretation is available for live performances on various cruise dates. (The service is not available on every cruise, so be sure to start planning your trip as far in advance as possible.) For additional information or to make special requests, ask your reservationist. For more information via TTY (text typewriter), please call 407-566-7455.

Other Supplies: Diapers, pacifiers, pool toys, and more can be purchased on board. The ships' shops aren't always open, so take inventory and plan ahead to avoid being caught short. If it's an emergency, inquire at Guest Services. They can help with just about any onboard crisis.

Bottle sterilizers and warmers are available at the Guest Services desk.

TRAVELERS WITH DISABILITIES:
Measures have been taken to make your stay as comfortable and effortless as possible. Disney Cruise Line offers special equipment and facilities for guests with disabilities. Each ship has staterooms that are equipped for guests using wheelchairs. They have ramped bathroom thresholds, open bed frames, bathroom and shower grab bars, fold-down shower seats,

TRAVELERS WITHOUT CHILDREN: This being a Disney cruise, one could argue that you—the footloose, fancy-free folks—are on their turf. And, as such, you might expect to have youngsters underfoot at all times. This is simply not the case. The Disney ships were designed with three specific types of vacationers in mind: families, kids, and grown-ups without kids. On board, there is an adults-only deck area, complete with its own pool (not to mention music and games). There's a gourmet restaurant (two on the *Dream* and *Fantasy*) and a cozy coffee bar. It goes without saying that those spots, as well as several lounges, are strictly for the grown-up set (as in adults with legal proof of age). Plus, there are countless other ways to enjoy a grown-up getaway in the various ports of call. With that in

DISNEY CRUISE LINE

mind, Castaway Cay (Disney's private island) guarantees you and your ilk a piece of prime beachfront real estate where you can bask in the sun or read a novel in the shade without the fear of sand being kicked in your face. You can even have a massage in a cabana overlooking the ocean. Can you manage to spend days on end without encountering the wee ones of our species? No way. But who'd want to?

MEDICAL MATTERS: The Health Center, located forward on Deck 1, is open daily to provide non-emergency medical care throughout each cruise. All Disney Cruise Line ships have a physician and nurse on call 24 hours a day (even while in port) for conditions that require immediate attention. Health services are provided by a company independent of Disney Cruise Line, and standard prevailing fees will be charged for all medical services. Fees will be charged to your stateroom account.

In extreme cases, Disney Cruise Line will arrange to have a passenger taken to the nearest port to receive medical care. The cost of this varies with the location of the ship and the nearest port. Because all health care provided qualifies as "care outside the United States,"

New Ships on the Horizon!

Ahoy! Disney Cruise Line's family is growing—three new ships, currently being constructed, are expected to join the D.C.L. fleet in the not-too-distant-future. The new vessels will be slightly larger than the *Disney Dream* and *Disney Fantasy*, each weighing approximately 135,000 gross tons and housing about 1,250 staterooms. At press time, the ships had not been named. What do *you* think they'll be called? It's fun to speculate.

you will be responsible for paying any charges that are incurred while on board prior to debarkation and submitting the request for coverage to your insurance carrier (all paperwork will be provided).

If you get sick while on shore, your guide should direct you to your ship's tour director at the dock, who will help you get back to the ship.

Regarding younger passengers, know that any child exhibiting symptoms of illness will not be allowed to participate in the youth activities or be cared for in the ship's nursery. No exceptions.

Fingertip Reference Guide

BUSINESS SERVICES: Wait a minute, aren't you here to relax? For those of you who must get a little work done while at sea, there are some business services available for an additional charge. Among them are fax transmission, copies, and AV equipment. Wireless Internet service is available throughout the ships (including staterooms) for a fee. Guests access the Web via cell phone and various personal computing devices. Computer devices are available for rental (at the ships' Connect@Sea desk). Note that the Wi-Fi service at sea can best be described as "low speed." As you sail, you may experience buffering and dropped connections. Internet connectivity can be intermittent based on satellite connectivity. All staterooms have phones (ship-to-shore rates apply), and electrical outlets are laptop friendly. Note that the ships' computers don't accept uploads and do not run any Microsoft Office applications (so any attachments from associated e-mail accounts cannot be opened). There is, however, a handy printer at the ready. Are you planning on holding meetings during your cruise? For details on business services, visit *www.disneymeetings.com.*

CAMERA NEEDS: By all means, bring a camera. Memory cards and accessories are sold on board. There are also roving photographers capturing moments throughout the day. You'll find shots taken at "static locations" (e.g., character sets in the lobby) are available for viewing at photo kiosks at Shutters (the photo store on all Disney ships). These photos may be viewed and purchased during the cruise. (Some photo packages may be purchased in advance, with special promotions.) Pictures taken by roaming

Getting Around It

Travelers with disabilities already know that travel requires a lot of advance planning. Disney has equipped all of its ships with a variety of amenities geared toward those guests with special needs.

Wheelchair-accessible staterooms are equipped with ramp entrances to bathrooms, fold-down shower seats, handheld shower-heads, lowered towel and closet racks, and emergency call buttons.

There is a limited number of sand wheelchairs available on Disney's private island, Castaway Cay (first come, first served). **Note:** If you will need a wheelchair throughout the cruise, you are encouraged to bring your own.

Throughout the ship, there are wheelchair-accessible restrooms.

Pool lifts are available on the *Magic*, *Wonder*, *Dream*, and *Fantasy*.

Guests with hearing disabilities need not miss any of the fun on board. In-stateroom TVs can be equipped with captioning, and assistive-listening devices may be rented from Guest Services and may be used at most theaters and show rooms. Also available are communication kits equipped with alarm clock, door-knock, and telephone alerts with bed shaker notification. Make your needs known when you book your cruise.

photographers (e.g., in the dining rooms, by the pool, on Castaway Cay, etc.) may be viewed, printed, and purchased at Shutters on all four ships. Photos can be purchased on a single media USB storage device—one-stop shopping. The photographs are very high in quality (which is reflected in the price).

DRINKING LAWS: The drinking age on Disney's ships is 21 and is strictly enforced. Valid government-issued photo ID is required. Disney Cruise Line reserves the right to refuse alcohol sales to anyone. On cruises departing from European countries where the legal age is lower than 21, a legal guardian who is sailing with a passenger between the ages of 18 and 20 may sign a waiver allowing their charge to imbibe.

MAIL: Letters and postcards may be mailed from the post office at Disney's private tropical island, Castaway Cay. Stamps are the only things available for purchase here (cash only). It is also possible to mail items from other ports—it's just

less convenient. If you plan to buy stamps from the Castaway Cay post office, do so early. The office is operated by Bahamian authorities and may not be open late in the day. Even if it's closed, you can still mail letters from the post office, and items will be delivered with a Castaway Cay postmark. Note that postcards and stamps may be purchased on the ship.

MONEY MATTERS: There is no need for cash on the ship. You will apply a credit card to your account during check-in. (Most major credit cards, including MasterCard, JCB, Visa, and American Express, are accepted.) From then on, all you'll need to do is sign for extras you want (including excursions booked on the ship), and these amounts will be charged to that card.

Cash or credit cards will be necessary for meals, taxis, and other purchases made in ports and during some shore excursions. Purchases made at Castaway Cay, however, are covered with a stateroom key (except for stamps, which must be bought with cash). A few hundred dollars should suffice. Standard gratuities are automatically attached to your cruise folio. Extra gratuities may be charged to a stateroom or paid in cash. Special envelopes will be delivered to your stateroom. They may be used to present extra gratuities and/or receipts for prepaid tips.

Automated teller machines may be available in ports of call, but there are none on the ship. Be sure the machine dispenses U.S. currency before you use it. It's a good idea to alert your bank and credit card company to the fact that you'll be using cards while travelling.

HOT TIP!

If you plan to use your cell phone during your cruise, be sure to check with your wireless provider before leaving home. Ask if you will be able to get service through them while on board and how much voice, data, and text service costs—including roaming rates.

SMOKING: All Disney ships are, for the most part, smoke-free zones. Smoking (including e-cigarettes) is prohibited in all staterooms and verandahs. (Guests who violate this policy are subject to a $250 deep-cleaning fee.) There are designated smoking areas on each ship.

TELEPHONE CALLS: All staterooms have phones with ship-to-shore capability. Rates range from about $7 to $9.50 per minute (rates are subject to change). Toll-free and collect calls can't be placed from ship phones. Wireless service is available on the ship (fees apply). Be sure to check with your mobile carrier (before you leave home) for talk and text rates and roaming fees. Note that text rates are usually lower than talk rates. Some ports have pay phones (you will need an international calling card to use them).

TIPPING: Some servers, such as bartenders, get an automatic 15 percent gratuity each time you call upon their services, while spa services have an automatic 18 percent tip. That said, folks such as your dining room servers and stateroom host or hostess rely on guests to tip them appropriately. Suggested gratuity amounts will be posted to your account during the cruise (it's okay to leave more if you deem the service to be outstanding). If you prefer to pay in cash, inform Guest Services at the beginning of the cruise. For those guests dining at Palo and Remy, the gratuity amount is at your discretion.

WEDDINGS: Whether you are saying your "I do's" for the first time, committing yourselves to each other, or renewing your vows, Disney Cruise Line has the means to make the occasion exceptionally memorable. Ceremonies may be performed on the ship or at Castaway Cay. Some happy couples invite family members along for the trip, while others prefer to have this time to themselves. For details, call 800-951-3532, or contact your travel agent. Call as far in advance as possible and before you book your cruise.

All Good Things

How time flies when you're having fun. You blink and it's time to go home! Here are a few tips about the debarkation process.

The day before your return to the debarkation terminal, you'll receive an information packet that includes a set of character luggage tags. The character coding designates the area of the terminal in which you can pick them up. Be sure to remove the original tags from the inbound trip before you put new tags on all bags. (Guest Services has extra tags.) You'll also get a U.S. Customs form when applicable. Hand this form in as you leave the terminal (one form per household).

On the night before debarkation, you'll place luggage outside your stateroom. (Bags will be collected and delivered to a color/character-coded area in the terminal.) Keep valuables, clothing for debarkation, medications, tickets, passports, and other key documents with you. (You have the option of "express walk off" if you're able to take your own bags off the ship in the morning.) Your waitstaff will tell you about last-morning breakfast options. After breakfast, it's time to leave the ship, taking all your happy memories and, quite possibly, the promise to return again soon. Of course, guests participating in onboard airline check-in don't have to claim bags until their plane lands at their home airport. Certain restrictions apply.

About to begin the "land" part of your vacation? Fetch your bags in the terminal and make a beeline for the bus depot. Flash your Key to the World card (to show you purchased the transfer) and climb aboard. You're going to Disney World!

All Aboard!

The moment you cross the gangway, you'll realize this vessel is no ordinary home away from home. Step into the grand, multi-story atrium, and, amidst the happy hubbub, your presence is made known in dramatic fashion—with a heart-felt announcement for all to hear. And so begins your high-seas adventure.

The *Disney Magic, Wonder, Dream*, and *Fantasy* rank among the world's finest ocean-going vessels. The ships are casually elegant and designed to capture the majesty of early ocean liners. They're equipped to satisfy most cruisers, with a mix of traditional seafaring diversions and classic Disney touches. Though some theming and entertainment vary from ship to ship, the accommodations and amenities are similar. As is the service, which is expertly provided by a cast of thousands (representing dozens of countries). All staterooms aboard the quartet of ships are a cut above normal cruising quarters—with an average of 25 percent more space than industry standard. The ships were designed to lure families and grown-ups without offspring to entirely different recreational areas. So, cast aside any preconceived notions you may have about cruising, and expect the unexpected.

Checking In

No matter where it is they call home—be it Bangkok or Boca—all Disney Cruise Line guests begin their respective journeys by checking in at a port terminal. Most Bahamas- and Caribbean-bound guests leaving from Port Canaveral check in at Cruise Terminal 8 (CT8). Guests may

choose from several different queues at check-in: Concierge, Castaway Club (for repeat guests), and general check-in. For details on other ports the ships may visit throughout 2018, call 800-910-3659, or go to *www.disneycruise.com*.

Though no one may board the ship until 1 P.M., guests are welcome to arrive earlier—and guests who check in online choose assigned times in advance. (All guests must board the ship by 3:45 P.M.) The terminal has restrooms and ample seating to relax in while waiting to board. (At Port Canaveral, Florida, there's also a nifty model of the ship to give you a preview of the real thing.) And, if little ones get antsy, there's lots of room for them to roam around, plus a TV that runs a loop of Disney cartoons. Mickey Mouse and his friends occasionally greet guests in the terminal, too.

Okay, we may have gotten ahead of ourselves. Before you can enter the main part of the terminal, all members of your party must go through a security checkpoint. It's a lot like airport security, so save the holey socks for the second day of your trip (you may be asked to remove your shoes, along with jackets, glasses, belts, etc.). Since kids must go through the security check, too, we recommend having snacks and games to entertain them while you wait (in case the line is more than a few minutes long). Once you've cleared security, your whole party needs to go to the check-in counter so ID photos may be taken.

At the counter, you will be asked to present a valid passport for yourself and each member of your party (see page 317). This is also where you'll be asked for all of your completed cruise paperwork (which can also be completed via the Internet at *www.disneycruise.com* under the "My Online Check-in" section; be sure to select your port arrival time, print the forms, and remember to bring them with you) and a major credit card. This card will be the one to which all of your extra cruise expenses are charged. If you'd like to split expenses with another guest staying in your room, it is possible to register two credit cards. Once the cruise begins, you'll use your stateroom key—aka Key to the World card—to make purchases and to open your stateroom door. The card also serves as ID for debarking and reboarding purposes (though all ports of call also require a photo ID such as a driver's license for guests over age 18). If you'd prefer that any member of your party not have charging privileges, advise a representative at check-in (or indicate your preference when you check in online).

Once the check-in process is complete, take a peek at your watch. Is it before 1 P.M.? If so, sit back, relax, and wait for the boarding process to begin. If it's after 1 P.M., wait for your boarding number to be called (every party receives one when they check in). When your number's called, grab the kids and your day bags and head for the gangway. All aboard!

The Boarding Experience

After you slip through the entry portal, you'll enter a subdued hallway. This is where you may have your "pre-cruise" photo taken by a Cruise Line photographer. Try to look as stressed out as possible. That'll make the post-boarding shots that much more enjoyable. (You can view/buy the photo on the ship later that day or soon after. Just stop by Shutters, the ship's photo shop.)

Beyond the photo-op area, there's a door leading to a gangway. Cross it and you'll be deposited in the ship's grand lobby—a dramatic backdrop for a dramatic entrance.

Depending on the time (staterooms are usually ready at about 1:30 P.M.) and your level of starvation, you may want to make a quick stop, change, and head out for lunch or a snack. Ships' pools are usually open all afternoon. After that, it's safety drill time! The mandatory safety drill takes place at 4 P.M. on all Disney ships for most itineraries. Once the safety drill is complete, you may head back to your room to prepare for the sailaway deck celebration known as Adventures Away

HOT TIP!
Disney Cruise Line has called Port Canaveral home since 1998 and will do so for the foreseeable future. For details on how to sail from ports such as New York, Miami, Vancouver, Barcelona, and more, visit **www.disneycruise.com**.

(*Magic* and *Wonder*) and Sailing Away (*Dream* and *Fantasy*). If you've got an early dinner seating, this is the ideal time to change into your evening attire.

Finally, we simply cannot overemphasize the importance of making reservations for spa treatments and for Palo and Remy (adults-only eateries) as early as possible. (It's best to book before the trip begins, via *www.disneycruise.com*.) Make last-minute spa appointments at the spa itself. For Palo, which begins accepting reservations at about 1 P.M. on day one of the cruise, head for Fathoms (*Magic*), Azure (*Wonder*), or D Lounge (*Dream* and *Fantasy*). Reservations for Remy (upscale dining for grown-ups on the *Dream* and *Fantasy*) may be made here, too. Plan to register children for youth activities in the terminal or soon after boarding.

The Disney Ships

The Disney ships are equipped to satisfy even the most savvy of cruisers, with a mix of traditional seafaring diversions and Disney touches. The ships' classic exteriors recall the majesty of early ocean liners. Guests enter a three-story atrium, where traditional definitions of elegance expand to include bronze character statues and subtle cutout character silhouettes along a grand staircase. Recreation areas are designed to draw families and kid-free adults to different parts of the ship. By day, fun in the sun alternates with touring, lunch, indoor distractions, and perhaps even a little bingo action. Evenings give way to sunset sail-away celebrations, themed dining experiences, and theatrical extravaganzas.

Decked Out

What follows is a deck-by-deck rundown, from top to bottom (the first section of this deck-specific data refers to the *Magic* and *Wonder*; the section that follows covers the *Dream* and *Fantasy*). Note that the *Wonder* was recently refurbished.

MAGIC AND WONDER

DECK 11: On the *Wonder*, you'll find the teen club Vibe (though access to the club is on Deck 10). This venue is exclusively for teenage guests.

DECK 10: Known as the Wide World of Sports Deck (*Magic* and *Wonder*), we find it a perfect late-night place to watch the moon and stars. There's also the Wide World of Sports fun zone. And this is one of the best places to be during the sail-away party. Palo is here, too (see page 333). For adults only, this dining spot offers fine cuisine and panoramic views. The *Disney Wonder* has the Twist and Spout splash zone, too. The ships' concierge lounge and entrances to Vibe and the Bibbidi Bobbidi Boutique can be found on Deck 10.

DECK 9: Pampering, Disney style, can be enjoyed in the Senses Spa & Salon. At the soothing spa, guests may experience treatments in the villas, as well as a little Rest & Relaxation on the outdoor verandah. Fitness-minded folk can get a one-on-one fitness consultation. There's lots of exercise equipment, saunas, a steam room, and spa treatments. Personal training is offered too. (For details, see page 343.)

Deck 9 is where you'll find the ships' pools: Quiet Cove pool (for adults) and Goofy's family pool, plus a slide and a splash zone for little ones. (Life jackets may be borrowed for free.) Both ships have the Aqua Lab splash area on Deck 9. The *Magic* also has the AquaDunk water slide. Sunscreen, towels, toys, sundries, and more may be bought at Quacks on Deck 9 (both ships).

HOT TIP!
If you or a member of your party misplaces a Key to the World card while on board, head to the Guest Services desk on Deck 3. They can issue a new one (free of charge).

This deck is also home to Cove Cafe (coffee bar/lounge for guests over age 18), Pinocchio's Pizzeria, Cabanas, Daisy's De-Lites, Pete's Boiler Bites, plus Frozone Treats (*Magic* only), and Eye Scream. The *Wonder* has Sully's Sips. This is also the location of Edge, the tween-only hangout for 11- to 14-year-olds. The interactive area has a lab with child-friendly computers, video game consoles, arts and crafts tables, TVs, and comfy couches. Kids sing karaoke, do scavenger hunts, and more.

DECK 5: Kids have the run of more than half of this deck. The Oceaneer Lab and Oceaneer Club combine to form one of the largest dedicated areas of children's space afloat, with comprehensive, interest-specific activities.

The Buena Vista Theatre and It's A Small World Nursery are also located here.

DECK 4: Here you'll find the Walt Disney Theatre, Shutters (photo shop), and Animator's Palate (restaurant). D Lounge (family games and entertainment) can be found on both ships. This is also a lovely deck on which to enjoy shuffleboard, a leisurely stroll, a jog, or a nice nap.

The Walt Disney Theatre is a grand venue that features one of the most sophisticated show settings at sea or on land. The formal theater boasts extraordinary lighting and technical facilities and showcases up to three distinct Broadway-style musical productions (each with a decidedly Disney touch) during each cruise.

Animator's Palate is a cheerful restaurant that serves cuisine in a room that features a colorful masterpiece of synchronized light and sound. Deck 4 on the *Magic* and *Wonder* is also the place where you can find Vista art gallery and shops selling Disney Cruise Line–themed clothing for the family, character merchandise, collectibles, specialty items, jewelry, and sundries (see page 341 for more details).

DECK 3: This is the place for dining and dancing on the *Magic* and *Wonder*; After Hours is an adult-oriented evening entertainment district that offers themed clubs. Both ships feature

DISNEY CRUISE LINE

nightclubs that often have themed parties—and don't forget one of the ship's biggest attractions . . . bingo! There is a sports bar on the *Magic* (O'Gills Pub) and an English Pub (Crown & Fin) on the *Wonder*; Sea Treasures shop; Keys (on the *Magic*) and Cadillac Lounge (on the *Wonder*) are casual yet sophisticated places to relax and listen to live piano music; and Promenade Lounge is a place to enjoy a drink and hear music (on the *Magic* and *Wonder*). Also here are Tiana's Place (*Wonder*), a restaurant inspired by Disney's animated feature *The Princess and the Frog*; Carioca's (*Magic*), an eatery inspired by Rio de Janeiro; and Lumière's, serving continental cuisine (on the *Magic*). Lumière's has a French flair and a beautiful mural of Disney's *Beauty and the Beast*. Its counterpart on the *Wonder*, Triton's, has an underwater-like setting of blues, greens, and purples. Guest Services is also on this deck and is open 24 hours a day. The Port Adventures (aka shore excursions) Desk is nearby.

DECK 2: All four Disney ships have staterooms on this deck.

DECK 1: This is where you will find the ship's Health Center. There are some staterooms located here, too.

DECKS 1, 2, 5, 6, 7, AND 8: Shipboard accommodations are spread over these decks.

DREAM AND FANTASY

DECK 14: The pinnacle of these sister ships, Deck 14 is the site of Outlook, a lounge that offers sweeping ocean vistas in addition to a variety of adult beverages.

DECK 13: Here you'll find Edge (tweens hangout), Currents (open-air bar), and Goofy's Sports Deck. This is also where concierge guests may enjoy a private sundeck. Deck 13 is the site of Satellite Falls—a waterfall-endowed wading pool for guests age 18 and older, and mini-golf.

DECK 12: This is the home of Meridian (lounge), Palo, and Remy (both are upscale eateries for grown-ups; Remy is très indulgent). Grown-up guests may sip spirits and soft drinks at Waves Bar (*Dream*). Deck 12 is also the site of AquaLab (*Fantasy*) and the AquaDuck water coaster (*Dream* and *Fantasy*).

DECK 11: On the *Dream* and *Fantasy*, this a destination deck for hungry guests: Cove Cafe (coffee bar for adults); Cabanas (buffet); and Flo's Cafe, a quick-service eatery with three stations (Luigi's Pizza, Tow Mater's Grill, and Fillmore's Favorites). Also on this deck are Eye Scream, Frozone Treats, and Vanellope's Sweets and Treats (*Dream*). Deck 11 is home to Mickey's Pool, Quiet Cove Pool, Donald's Pool, Nemo's Reef (splash zone), Arr-cade (*Fantasy*), and the Senses Spa & Salon (which extends to Deck 12).

DECKS 10, 9, 8, 7, 6, AND 2: These decks are devoted primarily to staterooms.

DECK 5: Deck 5 is kid-central—and they wouldn't want it any other way! In addition to the It's a Small World Nursery (see page 340), this is the site of the kids' programming areas known as Disney's Oceaneer Club and Lab (page 340), as well as Vibe (teen club). It's also the site of the Buena Vista (movie) Theatre's balcony. Bibbidi Bobbidi Boutique and Pirate's League (princess and pirate makeovers) are here, too. This deck houses the Port Adventures Desk.

DECK 4: Here you'll find the Buena Vista Theatre (movies), Vista Gallery (art), Shutters (photo shop), Connect@Sea Internet area, and Port Shopping Desk. The Walt Disney Theatre is a grand venue that showcases Broadway-style productions (with a distinct Disney flair) during each cruise. This venue extends to Deck 3.

Also found on Deck 4 of the *Dream* and *Fantasy*: D Lounge (family lounge and nightclub) and the ships' respective adults-only entertainment zones. Among the offerings in The District on the *Dream*: Skyline (lounge with panoramic views of various city skylines), District Lounge, Evolution (dance club), a sports bar called Pub 687, and Pink: Wine and Champagne Bar. On the *Fantasy*, expect to find these spots in the Europa entertainment district: La Piazza (a lounge that celebrates Italian plazas), Skyline (bar with panoramic views of famous cities), O'Gills Pub (sports bar), Ooh La La (an elegant champagne bar inspired by a French boudoir), and The Tube (a dance club with a London Underground motif).

DECK 3: This deck is home to the ship's lobby, the Walt Disney Theatre (stage shows), a bar, shops, and restaurants. Bon Voyage lounge is on the port side of the grand lobby. Beyond this imbibing zone are the ship's shops: Mickey's Mainsail, White Caps, and Sea Treasures.

Animator's Palate is a cheerful restaurant that offers creatively prepared cuisine in an impeccably designed dining room (for additional information on the restaurant, see page 331).

Other Deck 3 dining options include Royal Palace (*Dream*) and Royal Court (*Fantasy*).

Guest Services, which is open around the clock, is also located on Deck 3.

DECK 2: The Enchanted Garden eatery is located here.

DECKS 2 AND 5–12: Shipboard accommodations are spread over these decks.

DECK 1: The Health Center is on Deck 1.

Staterooms

The accommodations on Disney's ships range from standard inside rooms to suites with verandahs. All staterooms are a cut above the standard cruising cabin. On average, Disney's staterooms offer more space; most have a split bath (one room with a sink and toilet and another with a sink and a shower/tub), and the majority of them are outside rooms with ocean vistas—many with verandahs.

Staterooms are decorated in a nautical theme with natural woods and imported tiles. Universal amenities include a TV, Wave phones that allow you to call or text another member of your party while on board (two phones are included per

stateroom—extras may be rented), telephone with voice mail (and ship-to-shore capability), a safe, a room service menu, and lots of drawer space. All staterooms also come equipped with small refrigerators. After that, different types of accommodations—which are labeled by category—offer different amenities (verandahs are included in the square footage):

MAGIC AND WONDER

CATEGORIES 11A–11C: Standard inside staterooms. They have a queen bed, a single convertible sofa, a privacy divider, and a bath. Some have an upper berth pull-down bed. Each room measures 184 square feet and sleeps up to 3 or 4. (11-C sleeps up to 3.)

CATEGORIES 10A–10C: Deluxe inside staterooms. These accommodations are similar to those found in categories 11A–11C but have 214 square feet of space and a split bath.

CATEGORIES 9A–9D: Deluxe ocean-view staterooms. These come with a queen bed, a single convertible sofa, a privacy divider, and split bath. Some have an upper berth pull-down bed. Rooms on Deck 1 have two small windows, while those on Deck 2 and above feature one large window. Each room is 214 square feet. It sleeps up to 3 or 4 guests.

CATEGORIES 5A–5C, 6A, AND 7A: Deluxe ocean-view staterooms with verandahs. Each has one queen bed, a single convertible sofa, a privacy divider, split bath, and a verandah. These rooms are 268 square feet (including the verandah) and sleep 3 or 4. Category 7A has an enclosed

Laundry Facilities

Laundry and dry cleaning services are available for a fee. Items will be picked up and delivered to your stateroom. If you'd rather go the self-service laundry route, you can do so in one of several Guest Laundry Rooms. Here you'll find washers, dryers, and ironing equipment. (Due to safety concerns, the laundry room is the only place in which iron use is permitted.) There is no fee to use an iron. Machines run about two bucks a load. Laundry detergent may be purchased here, too. At press time, a small box cost about $1. Simply wave your Key to the World card and charge it to your stateroom account.

Guest Services Desk

If you have any questions or concerns while on board, head to the Guest Services Desk (Deck 3, midship). This is also the spot to go to secure copies of the *Personal Navigator*, color-coded luggage tags (for use on the last day of the cruise), and postage stamps. Should you have any type of problem while on board, bring it to their attention. More often than not, they will resolve the issue in a matter of minutes.

"Navigator's Verandah" (a private balcony with nautical touches), and sleeps up to 3. Some have an upper berth pull-down bed. Verandahs in 5A–5C are open, while those in 6A feature a solid whitewall verandah. Accommodations are otherwise the same.

CATEGORIES 4A, 4B, AND 4E: Deluxe ocean-view family staterooms with verandah. This room type has a queen bed, a single convertible sofa, and a bed that pulls down from the wall. Some have an upper berth pull-down bed. There is a privacy divider, split bath, and open verandah (verandahs in the aft area are not open). It covers 304 square feet (including verandah) and sleeps up to 5.

CATEGORY 00T: Concierge one-bedroom suites with verandah. These have a queen bed, an area with a double convertible sofa, and a pull-down bed, two full baths, walk-in closet, wet bar, DVD player, open verandah (except for the aft-area staterooms), and concierge service. The suite is 614 square feet (including the verandah) and sleeps up to 4 or 5 guests.

CATEGORY 00S: Concierge two-bedroom suites with verandahs. These suites come with a queen bed, a sleeper-sofa, and a pull-down bed. There are 2.5 baths, a whirlpool tub, walk-in closets, a DVD player, unstocked wet bar, verandah, and concierge service. The suite measures 945 square feet (including the verandah) and sleeps up to 7 guests.

HOT TIP!

The midship elevators are the most crowded throughout the day—especially at mealtimes. Try to use the forward and aft elevators whenever possible.

CATEGORY 00R: Concierge royal suite with verandah. Comes with a queen bed in one bedroom, two twin beds in a second bedroom, and two ceiling pull-down upper berths. There are 2.5 baths, a whirlpool tub in the master bedroom, a living room, media library (with a pull-down bed), dining salon, pantry, unstocked wet bar, walk-in closets, DVD player, private verandah, and concierge service. The suite measures 1,029 square feet (including the verandah) and sleeps up to 7.

DREAM AND FANTASY

CATEGORIES 11A–11C: Standard inside staterooms. They have a queen, a single convertible sofa, upper berth pull-down bed (in some), and a bath with a tub and shower. Each room measures 169 square feet and sleeps up to 3 or 4 guests. They also have "magical portholes" (see Category 10A).

CATEGORY 10A: Deluxe inside staterooms. These accommodations are similar to those found in categories 11A–11C, but have 204 square feet and sleep up to 3 to 4 guests. They also have split baths, plus a bit of technological and artistic wizardry known as "magical portholes." These beauties have a real-time digital view that could be seen from a real porthole at any given time of day, and they feature visits from animated Disney characters. Most folks say they forget they are in an inside stateroom—the effect is that convincing.

CATEGORIES 9A–9D: Deluxe ocean-view staterooms. These come with a queen bed, a single convertible sofa, upper berth pull-down bed (in some), split bath, and porthole. Each room is 204 square feet and sleeps up to 3 or 4 guests.

CATEGORIES 8A–8D: Deluxe family ocean-view staterooms. These come with a queen bed, a single convertible sofa, wall pull-down bed (in most) or upper berth pull-down bed, and a split bath with a round tub (in most). Each stateroom features a large porthole window with built-in seating, measures 241 square feet, and sleeps up to 3 or 5. The 8A stateroom has two large porthole windows but does not have a split bath.

CATEGORIES 5A–5E, 6A–6B, 7A: Deluxe ocean-view staterooms with verandahs. Each has one queen bed, a single convertible sofa, pull-down bed if sleeping 4, a split bath, and a verandah. These rooms are 246 square feet

(including the verandah) and sleep up to 3 or 4. Verandah staterooms in 6A and 6B feature whitewall verandahs. 7A rooms either have a smaller verandah or an obstructed view. 5E staterooms have larger verandahs and are all aft. Accommodations are otherwise the same.

CATEGORIES 4A–4E: Deluxe ocean-view family staterooms with verandah. This room type has a queen bed, a single convertible sofa, upper berth pull-down bed (in most), a split bath with a round tub (in most) and a shower, and a verandah. Each stateroom is 299 square feet (including verandah) and sleeps up to 5. The verandahs in 4E rooms are twice the size of the verandahs in other Category 4 staterooms.

CATEGORY 00V: Concierge Deluxe family ocean-view staterooms with verandah. This room type has a queen bed, a double convertible sofa, upper berth pull-down bed, full bath (with a vanity, sink, round tub, and shower), half bath (vanity, sink, and toilet), a verandah, and concierge service. Each stateroom covers 306 square feet (including verandah) and sleeps up to 5.

CATEGORY 00T: Concierge one-bedroom suites with verandah. The suites have a bedroom with a queen bed, a living area with a double convertible sofa and a single pull-down bed, a walk-in closet, two full bathrooms (with a whirlpool in the master bath), verandah, and concierge service. The suite is 622 square feet (including verandah) and sleeps up to 5.

CATEGORY 00R: Concierge royal suite with verandah. Comes with a queen bed in the master bedroom, plus a wall pull-down double bed and a wall pull-down single bed in the living room. There are 2 full bathrooms, including a master bath with double sinks, rain shower, and whirlpool tub (there is also a whirlpool tub on the verandah), plus living room, media library, open dining salon, pantry, wet bar, walk-in closet, verandah, and concierge service. The suite measures 1,781 square feet and sleeps up to 5.

The Personal Navigator

An in-house publication called the *Personal Navigator* will help you make the most of every day. Updated daily and delivered to all staterooms (also available via the DCL Navigator App—which must be downloaded before the day one sailaway), the *Navigator* is a comprehensive listing of a day's onboard activities, events, and entertainment.

The *Personal Navigator* is an indispensable tool. When you get your hands on it (the first one should be given to you at the Terminal), read it cover to cover. In addition to listing the lineup of activities scheduled for the rest of the day, it will provide handy bits of information such as the suggested evening attire for that day. It changes from day to day, so be sure to take note. The *Personal Navigator* also gives the time and location of character appearances, any points of interest the ship may have scheduled, and a notification of any time zone changes, as well as any special offers or promotions for merchandise, events, or services aboard the ship.

Dining

A Disney cruise is not the place where you'll want to count calories—although most special dietary needs can be accommodated upon

Disney Cruise Line Gifts

Whether you'll be celebrating a special occasion or simply consider a cruise special occasion unto itself, you may want to have a gift delivered to your stateroom. Among the items that can be pre-ordered by calling 800-601-8455 or visiting disneycruise.com are floral arrangements, food and beverage packages, wine packages, cakes, and Disney Cruise Line merchandise. Specialty cakes must be ordered at least 7 days in advance. Other orders must be placed at least 72 business hours before sail date.

request. There's no shortage of rations on these ships. If your tastes are simple (say, a hot dog) or sublime (how does a juicy filet mignon, prepared at Palo, sound?), rest assured you'll never be hungry. Or understimulated, for that matter, as many of the restaurants are downright entertaining. And, thanks to a system called "rotational dining," you will get to experience three restaurants, all the while being made to feel like a VIP by your serving staff. That means you'll eat at a different one of the three main restaurants each evening, often with the same table guests, and enjoy the services of the same waitstaff. Your serving team gets to know you, as well as your likes and dislikes, very well. The system, which is unique to Disney Cruise Line, tends to get the thumbs-up from cruise veterans and newcomers alike. The only exceptions are Palo and Remy, the adults-only, reservations-necessary restaurants.

How do you know where to go on which night? Easy. A ticket with details will be placed in your stateroom. Check the *Personal Navigator* to note the style of attire for the evening.

TABLE SERVICE

ANIMATOR'S PALATE: The pièce de résistance—as far as Disney creativity goes—is without a doubt Animator's Palate, a place where diners not only have to decide what to eat, but also what to watch! Simple surprises abound at each stage of the evening meal. There is an Animator's Palate eatery on each of the four ships, but the dining experience varies depending on which ship you are sailing. The Animator's Palate experience on the *Magic* and *Wonder* is a culinary journey—from black-and-white to full color: Upon entering the monochromatic room, note the soft background music and the black-and-white sketches along the wall. While you're doing so, drinks and appetizers will be served. If you ignore this distraction and keep your gaze fixed on the walls, you may notice a bit of color

creeping into that sketch of Cinderella. By the time the entrées make their entrance, the room is ablaze in living color.

If you are sailing on the *Dream* or *Fantasy*, your Animator's Palate experience will be a bit different. Like its siblings on the *Magic* and *Wonder*, the decor was inspired by the magic of Disney and Pixar animation. It's teeming with everything you'd expect to find in an animator's studio: character sketches, paintbrushes, colored pencils, computer workstations, and other tools of the animation trade. Scenes and characters from Disney films adorn the walls, and that totally awesome, animated turtle called Crush actually interacts with diners on the *Dream* and *Fantasy*.

The *Magic*, *Wonder*, and *Fantasy* also feature a show called Animation Magic. The experience encourages guests to express themselves with a drawing—and over the course of dinner, they'll witness their drawings being brought to life through the magic of Disney animation. The show is a hit with artists of all ages.

Dining rooms details vary, but the menu is the same on all four ships. It has featured starters such as smoked salmon tartare, sliced serrano ham with Manchego cheese and olive bread, and black truffle pasta purseittes. Entrées have included grilled herb-crusted pork chop with wine sauce, lemon-thyme marinated all-natural chicken breast, black bean chipotle cakes, and ginger-teriyaki and dusted beef tenderloin. If they're available, we recommend starting with the butternut squash soup and ending with a slice of white chocolate fudge cheesecake or the crunchy walnut cake.

ENCHANTED GARDEN: This picturesque spot, which is located on the *Dream* and *Fantasy*, seems to be truly enchanted, as the immersive, outdoorsy environment transforms from day to night over the course of your dinner.

Breakfast, served buffet style, is offered on select days of each cruise. Ditto for lunch. The daily dinner is a four-course affair of seasonal selections. For an extra charge (plus gratuity), guests may enjoy bar drinks, bottled water, and specialty coffee. Soft drinks (coffee, soda, fruit juice, milk, and tea) carry no charge.

LUMIÈRE'S: Located on the *Magic* only, this elegant spot provides fine dining in a setting inspired by Disney's *Beauty and the Beast.* The sprawling dining room is elegant and softly lit, though a bit more raucous than its cosmopolitan contemporaries. Note that the later seating is usually a bit more sedate (fewer small kids).

Menu selections at dinner have included crispy roasted duck breast with braised napa cabbage, and aged Angus beef tenderloin. Vegetarians can opt for the mushroom-stuffed pasta in a vegetable broth. And vegetarians won't feel at all cheated by the grilled marinated tofu. For dessert, consider crème brûlée or a soufflé.

TRITON'S: Passengers aboard the *Wonder* may dine in the elegant Triton's, where the specialty of the house is seafood. The ocean theme is enhanced by subtly changing lighting with every course, the room getting more under-the-sea-like as the meal progresses. The menu has featured French onion soup; Conchiglie pasta with buttered lobster in a tomato, shrimp, and tarragon brandy sauce; oven-baked salmon royale crowned with king smoked salmon; and roasted rack of lamb. For dessert, there's chocolate mousse, Grand Marnier soufflé, sundaes, and more.

TIANA'S PLACE: A festive homage to New Orleans' dining and entertainment, Tiana's Place takes its inspiration from Disney's animated feature *The Princess and the Frog.* The *Wonder* exclusive transports guests to an era of southern charm, spirited jazz, and street party celebrations. The walls are lined with Princess Tiana's family photos and culinary awards. Chefs cook up all of her favorite recipes, drawing inspiration from the flavors of the Louisiana bayou. The cuisine is complemented with live music. Performed on the main stage, rhythmic notes of jazz, swing, and blues set the tone for a lively, Big Easy–style supper club.

CARIOCA'S: A vibrant restaurant (on the *Magic*), Carioca's is a tribute to the city of Rio de Janeiro (the second-largest city in Brazil). The name of the eatery, however, honors José Carioca—one of the stars of *The Three Caballeros.* The menu has offered items with Latin-infused flavors such as adobo-rubbed rack of lamb; lobster *croquetas* with banana and lentil salad; and chicken criollo salad (roasted cilantro-marinated chicken breast with papaya, mango, lettuce, and goat cheese). Finish the meal with cream cheese flan with caramel bananas.

ROYAL PALACE/ROYAL COURT: This regal restaurant (Royal Palace on the *Dream* and Royal Court on the *Fantasy*) got its inspiration from classic Disney animated features such as *Sleeping Beauty, Cinderella,* and *Beauty and the Beast.* You will find the eatery on Deck 3, midship.

French-inspired, continental cuisine is offered for breakfast, lunch, and dinner. Breakfast is offered on select mornings of each cruise, as is a full-service lunch. A four-course dinner takes place nightly. One of the favorite appetizers at dinner is the *escargots gratinés* (herb-marinated snails). Grilled beef tenderloin and shrimp is a featured entrée. Vegetarian selections such as mushroom-filled pasta are served, too. And do save room for an ice cream sundae, crème brûlée, peanut butter mousse, or other tempting treat. Yum!

Seating Times and Situations: There are normally two seating sessions for dinner; however, the times vary depending on what itinerary the ship is sailing at the time. The most common times are 5:45 P.M. and 8:15 P.M. If you have a preference, tell your travel agent or reservationist the moment you book your cruise. Requests for any seating cannot be guaranteed. If you get closed out of a preferred seating time, check with Guest Services after boarding. Seating times may open up after boarding. Most seating at table-service restaurants is communal, except at Palo and Remy. If you are traveling as a family with children, expect to be seated with similar travelers. Adults without children will be seated together if possible.

Parents of young children, listen up! There is a dining convenience designed especially for you. Dine and Play lets parents with late dinner seatings check their kids (ages 3 to 12) into the Youth Activities programs starting about 45 minutes after dinner seating has begun. In other words, after the youngsters have downed kid-friendly fare, they can go play while you finish your meal in a leisurely manner. Neat, huh? If you wish to partake of the complimentary Dine and Play service, simply inform your servers upon arrival in the dining room. They will make sure kids get their meals quickly, while serving the grown-ups at a more relaxed pace.

Youth activities counselors arrive in the restaurant 45 minutes after the seating begins and assign children to groups right there in the dining room. No need for parents to escort Junior to Deck 5. (Though they will eventually have to pick the kids up!) Remember, this service is for guests with late dinner seatings only.

PALO: For adults only (age 18 and up), Palo is an ideal spot for special celebrations or just a quiet, romantic evening. Offering brunch and dinner, Palo is worth the per-person surcharge (at press time, prices were $30 for brunch and dinner) to indulge in a five-star dining experience that includes an ocean view.

True to its roots (*palo* means "pole" in Italian), the restaurant has echoes of Venice, Italy—and the menu reflects some of the best continental fare you'll find on either side of the Atlantic. Dinner appetizers include *fritto di*

HOT TIP!

Palo and Remy reservations will not appear on your *Personal Navigator*. (It's not that personal.) Make sure you don't miss it—there's a per-person charge for all meals. Call 800-910-3659 for specifics.

calamari e gamba and soft potato gnocchi tossed in a piennolo tomato sauce. The entrée menu tempts with selections such as roasted rack of lamb with caponata and olive potatoes, and *parpadelle con aragosta*.

A warning: Save room for dessert, or you will never forgive yourself. The chocolate soufflé (with hot chocolate and vanilla sauces) is beyond amazing. (The sweet soufflé must be ordered in advance.) Of course, just about every one of Palo's homemade treats yield raves, too.

Brunch at Palo is a special event. (It's only offered on select cruises, making it even more special!) The buffet is so vast that it requires a guided tour. Expect fruit, salads, seafood, heavenly flatbreads, pastries, made-to-order omelets, fish, and chicken entrées, and more.

Palo is for diners ages 18 years and older. Make reservations at *www.disneycruise.com*; at Fathoms (*Magic*), Azure (*Wonder*), Royal Court (*Fantasy*), or Royal Palace (*Dream*); or at the restaurant itself starting at approximately 1 P.M. on the first day of the cruise.

REMY: For adults (guests age 18 and older) on the *Dream* and *Fantasy*, Remy is a ritzy, palate-pleasing delight. Considered the most upscale dining experience available on the ship, Remy serves fine French-inspired cuisine for dinner (on all cruises) and brunch (select cruises). The luxurious dining room has Art Nouveau touches and a rich color scheme. Tables are set with Frette linens, Riedel

A Tender Subject

Some ports require a process called "tendering." This means, rather than pulling right up to a dock, the ship will pull close to port and drop anchor. Ferries take guests back and forth to shore. It's an efficient system, but it could knock you for a loop if you're not expecting it—especially if you've got an early excursion booked. In this case, you may have to leave a bit earlier than you originally anticipated. That is accounted for in the "meet time" for all excursions.

glassware, Christofle silverware, and custom-created Bernardaud china.

Once the meal is booked and guests are aboard the ship, they can meet with a sommelier in Remy's wine room to pick out wines for their pending feast (for an additional price).

The evening meal begins with a champagne cocktail and continues with 8 to 9 small (and delectable) courses. There's nothing more thrilling than a tableside visit from the trolley of international cheeses—except, perhaps, for the wine decanting stations and after-dinner coffee service.

The private Chef's Table experience takes place in a special 8-seat dining room and features *Ratatouille*-inspired decor.

Oenophiles appreciate the lovely Wine Room, which accommodates up to 8 guests. Here, guests dine in a glass-walled room with marble flooring amid 900 bottles of wine.

Reservations are required to dine at Remy, and meals come with a $95-per-person surcharge for dinner (an additional $50 for the decadent Dessert Experience) and $60 per person for brunch. Reservations may be made online (75 days ahead for first-time cruisers, 90 for Silver Castaway Club members, 105 days ahead for Gold members, and 120 days in advance for concierge guests and Platinum members).

Like its neighbor, Palo, Remy also has a dress code. Dinner is more formal here than at Palo: jackets, dress pants, and dress shoes for men (ties are optional); dresses, suits, blouses, and dress pants for women. Leave the jeans, shorts, tank tops, yoga pants, sandals, flip-flops, and sneakers in your room. Jackets are optional for brunch.

What to Wear for Dinner: Generally speaking, "cruise casual" is the way to go in all spots except for Palo and Remy: collared shirts, blouses, cotton

pants, jeans (Palo only, and they must be in good condition, without holes), and sundresses are generally acceptable for evenings in all other restaurants—swimsuits, T-shirts, hats, flip-flops, tennis shoes, and tank tops are not. On select nights, there will be a theme: pirate attire, semi-formal, etc. On such days, the desired style of dress will be noted in the *Personal Navigator*. (While parents are the best judges of what attire is appropriate for their children, most guests over the age of 13 are usually comfortable wearing attire that is similar to what is recommended for all passengers.) Note that Palo and Remy, grown-ups-only destinations, are considered more formal and guests are asked to dress accordingly: long pants and shirt are required for men (jacket optional at Palo, required for Remy), and a dress or pants and shirt combo for women. No ripped jeans, shorts, flip-flops, or sneakers, please. Likewise, the indoor area of Meridian Bar, located between Palo and Remy, has the same formal dress code as Palo. However, the outdoor patio of Meridian Bar has a slightly more relaxed vibe (think business casual).

Wine and Dine: Most of the table-service restaurants offer many vintages by the glass or by the bottle. If you order a bottle and fail to finish it by meal's end, ask your server to store it for you. (You'll get it with the next evening's meal.) Disney offers two wine packages (premium and classic selections).

Special Dietary Needs: Certain special dietary needs may be met aboard Disney cruise ships. All requests should be made well in advance, preferably at the time of booking the cruise package. It's always a good idea to confirm the request prior to setting sail.

SELF-SERVE, FAST FOOD, AND SNACKS

VIBE: This teens-only spot—which can be found on all ships—serves up fruit smoothies and other soft drinks. There are lots of games and activities, and the refreshments are free of charge. This area is hopping all day—and often past midnight. FYI: The teen spots on the *Magic* and *Wonder* used to be known as Aloft and The Stack, respectively.

BEVERAGE STATION: There is a self-serve station on every ship. On the *Magic* and *Wonder*, you'll find it on Deck 9, aft (port side). On the *Dream* and *Fantasy*, look for the beverage station

on Deck 11, midship (there is a station on each side of the Mickey pool). Help yourself to water, juice, soda, iced tea, lemonade, coffee, hot chocolate, and hot tea. There is an ice machine, too. The station is open 24/7, though not all selections are available at all times. Soft drinks are free here and with meals, but not at bars or through room service.

CABANAS: Located on all four ships, this casual indoor eatery serves three meals a day. This spot recalls a breezy boardwalk along the coast, with a dash of Disney (e.g., colorful *Finding Nemo*–themed mosaics). Made-to-order breakfast and lunch selections are offered "on the board-walk" on most days (check your *Personal Navigator* for times and specifics). In other words, a variety of food stations proffer freshly prepared edibles. Dinner is a table-service affair. Cocktails may be ordered from the Clam Bar. Cabanas is located on Deck 11, aft on the *Dream* and *Fantasy*; Deck 9 aft on the *Magic* and *Wonder*.

COVE CAFE: A cozy, adults-only lounge, Cove Cafe can be found on all ships. It features espresso and specialty coffees and a full bar (fees apply). Complimentary snacks are available. Books and magazines are on hand for on-site perusing, as is a TV (often showing a big game or the news). Board games may be borrowed, too. Guests must be at least 18 years old to visit Cove Cafe, located near the Quiet Cove pool.

DAISY'S DE-LITES: *Magic* and *Wonder*: Visit Daisy's for bagels, fresh fruit, salads, wraps, sandwiches, cookies, and more. Hours are usually from 11 A.M. till 6 or 7 P.M. daily.

EYE SCREAM AND FROZONE TREATS: *Magic, Dream*, and *Fantasy*: Guests craving a chilly treat can find satisfaction at adjoining snack stations. Eye Scream (with theming inspired by famous eyeball Mike Wazowski) has self-serve ice cream. Mike's neighbor, a snack spot that pays tribute to Frozone from *The Incredibles*, serves made-to-order mixed fruit smoothies and cocktails (for a fee).

FLO'S CAFE: *Dream* and *Fantasy*: Flo's Cafe, located on Deck 11 near the Donald pool, is actually a trio of side-by-side walk-up windows, all themed to characters from the animated feature *Cars*. Here you'll find Luigi's Pizza, Tow Mater's Grill, and Fillmore's Favorites. Menu options at these filling stations include pizza (often featuring a special pizza of the day), chicken tenders, salads, sandwich wraps, fruit, burgers, and more. Luigi's tends to stay open the latest of the three.

PETE'S BOILER BITES: *Magic* and *Wonder*: Looking for a tasty treat without the formality of a table-service eatery? Or perhaps a nibble between meals? Head here! Pete proudly serves chicken tenders, burgers, hot dogs, veggie burgers, and gyros.

PINOCCHIO'S PIZZERIA: *Magic* and *Wonder*: This counter-service spot serves spirits and soft drinks (for a fee), and cheese and pepperoni pizzas (no charge for food). There is often a special pizza of the day. Be sure to ask.

ROOM SERVICE

Stateroom dining service delivers 24 hours a day (except on the final night of a cruise, when service stops promptly at 1:30 A.M.)—handy if you're traveling with kids or if you have a snack craving in between meals. Most menu items are included with your cruise package. At press time, selections included soups, salads, sandwiches, burgers, pizza, cookies, and selections for kids. There is a charge for some beverages and snack selections (such as candy, popcorn, wine, beer, soda, and bottled water). Note that a gratuity is not always included.

SPECIAL DINING EXPERIENCES

PIRATES IN THE CARIBBEAN PARTY: If there's one thing Disney really knows how to do right, it's throw a party. On one night during most cruises, guests enjoy a buccaneering soirée. If you own any pirate attire or regalia, wear it to the big event. (You may purchase some from a ship shop, too.) It takes place on the upper decks, where pirate villains set their sights on taking over the ship. An epic battle ensues as the good guys take on the villains. The greatest spectacle of all is the show's grand finale—fireworks (offered on most itineraries). A feast fit for a pirate king is served post pyrotechnics (usually served in Cabanas).

CHARACTER BREAKFAST: An up-close-and-personal morning starring favorite characters is a very Disney way to start the day.

The character breakfast is offered on select itineraries, usually the 7-night-or-longer cruises with at least two days at sea. To attend, you will need a ticket. Reserve tickets *before* your cruise begins by visiting My Cruise Line Activities at *disneycruise.com* within your advanced booking window. (For details, call 800-951-3532.)

Many of the character breakfast selections remain staples—eggs, bacon, cereal, fruit, yogurt, and French toast, for example.

CAPTAIN'S GALA DINNER: Even on this, one of the planet's most casual of cruises, there is a chance to don your finery and join the sparkle and glitter of this black-tie (optional) affair. If you'd rather not get completely decked out, go with a business casual look (but not too casual). The French-continental menu is offered in each of the main dining rooms on all ships. A menu favorite is the baked lobster tail served in the

shell with lemon pesto mash with asparagus. The Captain's Gala is offered on most cruises of 7 nights or longer.

FAREWELL DINNER: Presented on the final evening of cruises 7 nights or longer, this evening meal is a chance to enjoy favorite dishes, celebrate new friends, and perhaps start planning (or at least dreaming about) your next cruise.

Bars and Lounges

From elegant spots with live piano music to lively sports bars, Disney ships have a bounty of bars and lounge—many of them located in the ships' grown-up-only entertainment zones (Europa on the *Fantasy*, The District on the *Dream*, and After Hours on the *Magic* and *Wonder*).

AZURE: A celebration of the sights and sounds of the sea set the stage for a lively dance club. A deejay keeps the place grooving till the wee hours. All manner of drinks are available at this After Hours venue on the *Wonder*.

BON VOYAGE: A casual lounge located on Deck 3, midship (*Dream* and *Fantasy*). Beverages are available all day.

CADILLAC LOUNGE: Unique to the After Hours zone aboard the *Wonder*, this sophisticated spot celebrates classic cars with soothing music, wine, martinis, and other drinks.

COVE CAFE: This cozy adults-only lounge can be found aboard all Disney ships. It has specialty coffees and a full bar (charges apply). Snacks are available, too (no charge). Magazines and books are on hand for on-site perusing. Board games may be borrowed for on-site use.

CROWN & FIN: Unique to the After Hours zone aboard the *Disney Wonder*, this jolly spot resembles a classic British pub.

CURRENTS: A breezy spot with stellar ocean views, Currents is on Deck 13, forward (*Dream* and *Fantasy*).

DISTRICT LOUNGE: This intimate bar is located in the *Dream*'s grown-ups-only District entertainment zone.

HOT TIP!

If your mobile phone, laptop, or tablet is equipped for wireless Internet access, bring it along. Most areas on the Disney ships offer Wi-Fi service known as Connect@Sea. Rates may vary, but expect to pay 25 cents per megabyte (mb) of data or buy a package of 100 mb for $19, 300 minutes for $39, or 1,000 mb for $89. Prices are per stateroom, and packages may be shared. For additional information, visit *www.disneycruise.com*. Prices are subject to change.

DANCE CLUB: A butterfly-themed hot spot, Evolution celebrates all styles of music on the *Dream*. On the *Fantasy*, it's The Tube, a dance spot that pays tribute to the city of London. The venues feature various activities and dance parties. (Guests must be at least 18 years old to come here at night, 21 to imbibe.)

FATHOMS: This After Hours joint (*Magic*) fancies itself a celebration of the sea. It uses special effects, lighting, and sound to create different festive atmospheres. There's a dance floor, plus tables and bar seating. Themed parties are thrown on select evenings.

KEYS: The *Magic*'s version of an intimate piano bar, this lounge serves cocktails and wines by the glass. Keys provides a refined retreat.

LA PIAZZA: The *Fantasy*'s celebration of Italian cities features a festive carousel bar. Venetian masks and glasswork add to the fun.

MERIDIAN BAR: Found on the *Dream* and *Fantasy*, Meridian is located on Deck 12, aft, and has indoor and outdoor seating. The dress code for the indoor area: Dress pants and shirt are required for men and a dress or dress pants for women. On the outside deck, the dress code is cruise casual (jeans and shorts are okay, swimsuits and tank tops are not).

OOH LA LA: A *Fantasy* champagne bar, this space was inspired by a French boudoir.

PINK: WINE AND CHAMPAGNE BAR: An elegant nightspot designed to look like the inside of a champagne bottle, this lounge is in the *Dream*'s District entertainment zone. Pink definitely gets an A+ for atmosphere.

PROMENADE LOUNGE: This lounge serves cocktails and soft drinks on the *Magic* and *Wonder*. At night, it offers live music.

SIGNALS: On Deck 9 of the *Magic* and *Wonder*, this poolside spot serves cocktails and soft drinks.

SKYLINE: The *Dream*'s District area and the *Fantasy*'s Europa boast Skyline, a cosmopolitan bar with majestic views of famous cities from around the world. The cityscapes change over the course of the evening.

SPORTS BAR: A sports fan's dream, this lounge has a big screen (often featuring a big game), plus suds, wings, hot dogs, or other munchies. It's Pub 687 on the *Dream* and O'Gills Pub on the *Fantasy* and *Magic*.

THE TUBE: Housed in the *Fantasy*'s Europa district, The Tube is a metropolitan dance club themed to the London Underground (aka the tube).

VISTA CAFÉ: *Dream* and *Fantasy* guests in need of a java jolt can head to this cheery destination on Deck 4, midship. Snacks and cocktails are served, too.

WAVES: An open-air bar on the *Fantasy* and *Dream*, this spot serves beverages all day.

Entertainment

For some, a deck chair, a good book, and a steady stream of sunshine are all the entertainment required. Others may delight in an evening of dancing or a bingo-filled afternoon. And some are satisfied with nothing short of a Broadway-style stage show. Fortunately, Disney Cruise Line has it all, plus guest lecturers, tours, and more. Note that all shows are not presented every day or on every cruise. The lineup is tweaked from time to time, so details may differ during your cruise.

THE GOLDEN MICKEYS—A TIMELESS TRIBUTE: A dynamic production that pays tribute to the musical legacy of Walt Disney Studios. It's got all the glitz and glamour of a Hollywood celebration, paying homage to the comedy, romance, and heroes (plus a few key villains) of classic Disney animated films. This theatrical event is presented on the *Wonder* and *Dream*. It's a classic crowd-pleaser worthy of a Golden Mickey.

WELCOME ABOARD SHOW: This sweet presentation is a nice way to "meet" your ship's crew. The captain, cruise director, and many of their comrades introduce themselves and welcome guests aboard. Musical numbers and vaudeville-like variety acts round out the bill. This show is presented on most cruises of 7 nights and longer.

FROZEN, A MUSICAL SPECTACULAR: The *Disney Wonder* proudly presents a heart-warming, humorous retelling of the beloved film. The *Frozen*-inspired musical show transport guests to the icy, beautiful land of Arendelle and stars favorite characters from the animated feature: Anna, Elsa, Kristoff, Olaf, and Hans (okay, Hans may not be a favorite, but he *was* in the film!).

DISNEY'S ALADDIN—A MUSICAL SPECTACULAR: A comic musical, this production showcases a variety of classic (and new) tunes and characters from Disney's animated feature *Aladdin* and regales guests with theatrical treats. The action often spills out into the audience, such as when a magic carpet soars overhead or the evil Jafar turns into a gigantic snake (warn timid tots). Rest assured, it all ends happily! Disney's Aladdin—A Musical Spectacular is a *Fantasy* exclusive.

DISNEY'S BELIEVE: Who doesn't believe in the power of pixie dust? A little girl named Sophia certainly does. But her serious-minded father, Mr. Greenaway, is a much tougher sell. Follow his journey from skeptic to believer in this rousing musical stage show. In addition to classic Disney tunes, this crowd-pleaser features the lovely original song "What Makes a Garden Grow." It is presented on the *Dream* and *Fantasy*.

DISNEY DREAMS—AN ENCHANTED CLASSIC: This bedtime story features a galaxy of familiar Disney stars, including the Blue Fairy, Peter Pan, Belle, Beast, Aladdin, Cinderella, and Ariel. Together and through the power of song and dance, the characters teach a skeptical girl about the power of dreams. It takes place on the *Magic* and *Wonder*.

TWICE CHARMED—AN ORIGINAL TWIST ON THE CINDERELLA STORY: A Broadway-style extravaganza (presented on the *Magic* only), this musical production begins with the wedding of Cinderella and Prince Charming. Things take a sudden turn when the wicked Fairy Godfather makes his presence known and, after granting a wish to one evil stepmother, sends the family back in time, where—*gasp*—the glass slipper gets broken! Does this turn of events destroy Cinderella's chances of living happily ever after? You'll just have to catch the show to find out.

DISNEY'S WISHES: As high school kids face graduation day, they discover that the secret to becoming a grown-up is to stay connected to your inner child. And what's a wonderful way to do that? By making a wish and spending a fun-filled, musical—and magical—day at Disneyland. It's a *Fantasy* exclusive.

REMEMBER THE MAGIC—FAREWELL SHOW: This show wraps up the trip as performers celebrate a week of shipboard activities and island-hopping. (This production is presented on the *Magic* and *Wonder* on select cruises.) The *Fantasy* has a good-bye show known as An Unforgettable Journey.

TANGLED—THE MUSICAL: A Disney Cruise Line original, this show follows the story of Rapunzel, from her escape from the tower and the clutches of the evil Gothel to her unlikely friendship with the crown-stealing bandit, Flynn Rider. With a mix of familiar and new songs (all written by Alan Menken and Glen Slater), Tangled is fun for all ages. This one-hour show is presented exclusively on the *Magic*.

DECK PARTIES

When it comes to on-deck celebrations, the area by the family pool is party central. Starting with a Sailing Away Celebration and continuing with daily dance fests with Disney characters, live bands, and fireworks (on most itineraries), it seems like there is always a reason to party. Deck parties are offered on all sailings on the *Magic* and *Wonder*.

FAMILY ENTERTAINMENT

D LOUNGE: This family-friendly lounge and nightclub is on all ships (Deck 4, midship). Head here for dance parties, character greetings, games, and more. Mickey Mania lets you put your knowledge of Disney trivia to the test, while Karaoke Night encourages families to take the stage and sing together. Finally, the Family Dance Party gives everyone a chance to kick up their heels (or sneakers) and enjoy a party for guests of all ages. Keep in mind that the entertainment lineup, though always dynamic, is subject to change from time to time.

CHARACTER BREAKFAST: On most cruises that are 7 nights or longer, a bountiful breakfast is hosted by familiar Disney friends. Tickets (no cost) are required.

FOR GROWN-UPS ONLY

The 18-and-over set on the *Magic* and *Wonder* can attend demonstrations (e.g., Disney's Art of Entertaining), lectures and conversations with guest speakers, tours, and specially tailored nighttime events (such as Match Your Mate, a game show in which you and your mate will find out how much you know about each other), as well as theme nights, cabaret shows, and much more.

On the *Dream* and *Fantasy*, adults have the chance to participate in interactive cooking demonstrations as part of the Anyone Can Cook! series; learn the secrets of Disney animation in the Illusion of Life series; and attend a presentation about the making of the ship.

JUST FOR KIDS

The wildly popular kids' programs and activities tend to elicit raves from participants and parents alike. For starters, adults who leave their kids at supervised facilities can be assured that the watchword here is safety. There are plenty of counselors on hand, and the secured programming ensures that they know where every child is at any given time. Kids are checked in with Youth Activities when entering and signed out when exiting with an authorized guardian. Upon check-in, each child is given an electronic wristband, aka Oceaneer band. (It assists with the check-in and check-out process and adds an additional level of security to youth venues.) Records of a child's allergies or other particular needs are entered into their file.

Parents have Wave Phones (which can be found in all staterooms) and can be contacted with them (or via the Disney Cruise Line app) if their child has a problem or just wants to see them. (Though it has been our experience that youngsters rarely, if ever, want to leave the kids' programming areas.)

Cleanliness is a priority, too. In fact, kids entering the Oceaneer Club and Lab are promptly asked to wash their hands.

Kids' programs are concentrated on Deck 5, and kids registered into secured programming always remain in either the Lab or Club. The specially tailored programming is open to kids age 3 and older who are completely potty-trained, able to interact comfortably within the counselor-to-child ratio groups, and able to mix well with peers. (Non-potty-trained tykes, ages 6 months to 3 years, may go to a colorfully themed nursery. Fees apply.)

Kids between ages 3 and 12 can choose to play in the Oceaneer Club or Oceaneer Lab based on whatever interests them. Siblings and friends between the ages of 3 and 12 can play together regardless, as kids are not segregated by age group. And don't worry about little ones ever being dominated by bigger kids—participants are closely monitored at all times.

Kids who exhibit any symptoms of illness— even if it's just a runny nose—will not be allowed to participate. If a child becomes disruptive, he or she will be asked to play with a parent or guardian during open house hours.

Except for the nursery, there is no fee for youth activities on any Disney ship. The following descriptions of the youth activities were accurate at press time, but specifics are subject to change from time to time.

OCEANEER CLUB: A wonderfully detailed adventure zone, this club has several distinctly themed areas on every ship. In addition to computer games, costumes, and other games, there are many organized activities. It's open to all kids age 3 to 12 (potty-trained) on all ships (provided the kids show no sign of illness).

At the Oceaneer Club, kids find a combination of free play and structured activities featuring interactive, playful experiences with some of their favorite Disney characters. These may include reading a story with Belle and playing games with Mickey Mouse. Lunch and dinner are served (at no extra charge). It's usually open daily from 9 A.M. till midnight.

OCEANEER LAB: The Oceaneer Lab is open to (potty-trained) kids ages 3 to 12 on all Disney ships. It is located on Deck 5, midship. The entertaining space is filled with wacky inventions and opportunities for exploration. There are games, books, toys, child-friendly computers, video games, drawing materials, and more. As with the Oceaneer Club, there are also several imaginative organized activities. It is usually open daily from 9 A.M. till midnight.

Programs here allow young guests to be very hands-on while learning the skills of Disney animators, becoming a sleuth to solve mysteries with Disney characters, and joining a chef for a *Ratatouille*-inspired cooking experience. Check a *Personal Navigator* for specific dates and times for various activities while on board. Lunch and dinner are served daily (at no additional charge).

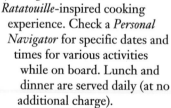

Reminder: Kids between the ages of 8 and 12 may check themselves in and out of the Oceaneer Lab and Oceaneer Club with their parents' permission.

EDGE: There are video games, arts and crafts, and movie screenings in this tween hangout. There are evening activities such as scavenger hunts and karaoke, too. Edge can be found on Deck 9 on the *Magic* and *Wonder*.

Also a tween space on the *Dream* and *Fantasy*, Edge is located on Deck 13 inside the forward funnel. Its high-tech features include an

illuminated dance floor, a video wall, and game-playing.

IT'S A SMALL WORLD NURSERY: Open to kids ages 6 months through 3 years, these colorful spaces are the ships' babysitting centers. For an hourly fee, the nursery offers activities and a quiet area, complete with cribs.

Food is available at the nursery, but if parents provide prepared bottles or jarred food that is clearly labeled with a child's name, staffers will happily feed their hungry tyke. Space is limited and gets booked early. In fact, advance reservations are accepted via *www.disneycruise.com* and on embarkation day on a first-come, first-served basis. Due to the high demand, multiple requests might not be honored —so don't count on securing several sessions, though it can't hurt to try. The fee for the babysitting service is $9 per hour for the first child, $8 per each additional child with a one-hour minimum (only siblings net the discount). Nurseries are generally open from 9 A.M. until 11 P.M. Stateroom babysitting is not available on any Disney ship.

TEENS ONLY

Teenaged guests may enjoy their own special hangout and activities while aboard all Disney ships. Vibe is their exclusive place to hang out. (If you are old enough to vote, KEEP OUT!) It's got popular music, games, dance parties, big-screen TVs, and more. Other programs may include karaoke, organized sports activities, a pool party (*Dream* and *Fantasy*), and a whole lot more. Specialty soft drinks, including smoothies, are available for a fee. Vibe is generally open from 11 A.M. till 2 A.M.

FUN AND GAMES

ARCADE: Exclusive to the *Fantasy*, the pirate-themed—and appropriately named—Arr-cade is on Deck 11. You will have to purchase credits to play in the ship's arcade.

BINGO: Perhaps it's something in the ocean air, but nothing brings out the bingo fanatic in you like a few days at sea. The closest thing to gambling that you'll find on a Disney vessel, the bingo sessions are extremely popular. You have to be at least 18 to play, but kids can watch over a grown-up's shoulder and cheer them on.

GAMES: Ping-pong, foosball, shuffleboard, basketball . . . they're all here. Equipment can usually be found by the tables or courts. (Don't monopolize it—it's for everyone to share.) Kooky competitions are sometimes held poolside. The *Dream* and *Fantasy* offer mini-golf and sports simulators (there is a charge to use the simulators). Refer to the ship's *Personal Navigator* for details.

MOVIES: The Buena Vista Theatre shows new film releases—some in 3-D (courtesy of Disney's patented technology). This is the perfect place to head when the weather is less than ideal. Get there early, as the seats fill up quickly.

If you prefer your flicks alfresco, make a beeline for the Goofy or Donald pool. A jumbo screen (on the forward funnel and known as Funnel Vision) broadcasts Disney features, sports, and more throughout the cruise.

Shopping

While on board Disney's cruise ships, you can enjoy tax-free (on all items) and duty-free (select items) shopping.

The shops have limited hours due to U.S. Customs regulations and can't operate during any time when the ship is in port. Use your stateroom key (Key to the World) to buy items in the ship's shops and on Castaway Cay. Purchases will be charged to your stateroom account. (Note that the Castaway Cay post office does not honor Key to the World cards. It accepts cash only.) Shops in all other ports of call generally accept major credit cards, and many accept cash.

ONBOARD SHOPS

PRELUDES (All ships): There is a snack bar/concessions window on either side of the Walt Disney Theatre. Among the items for sale are cookies, candies, nuts, and drinks (spirits and soft drinks are served for a fee, too).

MICKEY'S MAINSAIL (all ships): Mickey stocks Disney and Disney Cruise Line merchandise, including souvenirs, clothing, beach towels, mugs, costumes, postcards, frames, books, watches, snack items, and plush toys. The shop is located on Deck 3 (*Dream* and *Fantasy*) and Deck 4, forward (*Magic* and *Wonder*).

QUACKS (all ships): Quacks sells a selection of swimming essentials—including Disney Cruise Line bathing suits, T-shirts, towels, and the all-important sunscreen. It's on Deck 9, midship, on the *Magic* and *Wonder*, and Deck 11 on the *Dream* and *Fantasy*.

SEA TREASURES (all ships): Located on Deck 3, forward, the treasures here may include jewelry and limited-edition Disney collectibles. There may be a selection of clothing, including shirts, sweatshirts, purses, fragrances, hats, jackets, and other Disney Cruise Line logo items.

WHITE CAPS (all ships): This is the place for duty-free items such as perfume, watches, jewelry, liquor, and tobacco products. Note that any liquor purchased here may not be consumed while on board. It will be delivered to your room on the last evening of your cruise. It may be possible to pick up sundries, sunglasses, snacks, and sunscreen—plus Disney Cruise Line-themed souvenir bags and more.

WHOZITS & WHATZITS (*Dream* and *Fantasy*): A tiny shop located on Deck 11, midship, near the Donald pool, Whozits & Whatzits sells deckwear, sunscreen, towels, and other poolside necessities.

SPORTS AND RECREATION

FITNESS CENTER: The fitness center is located within the Senses Spa & Salon on all ships. There is no fee to use the equipment, which includes treadmills, bikes, stair-climbing machines, free weights, and more. (Some of the machines sport TVs—bring headphones or borrow a pair at the front desk.) Fitness consultations are offered. The fitness center is generally open from about 6 A.M. to 10 P.M., while spa hours run from 8 A.M. to 8 P.M.

WIDE WORLD OF SPORTS DECK (*Magic* and *Wonder*): Deck 10 is home to the Wide World of Sports deck. Though open to everyone, it's a huge kid and teen magnet. The basketball hoops are hopping day and night. Basketballs and other equipment are on-site (no charge). This deck is also popular with casual strollers, though jogging on the *Magic* and *Wonder* is relegated to Deck 4 (where one lap is about one-third of a mile). Deck 4 is where you'll find the shuffleboard court, too.

GOOFY'S SPORTS DECK (*Dream* and *Fantasy*): Located on Deck 13, aft, the always bustling Goofy's Sports Deck is an all-ages, open-air activity center. The basketball court can easily be converted to a volleyball court or a small soccer arena. The zone also has a sports simulator (soccer, golf, football, hockey, and basketball; fees apply) and an honest-to-goodness (or is that Goof-ness?) mini golf course.

SWIMMING (*Magic* and *Wonder*): There are three guest swimming areas on board, all located on Deck 9: Dory's Splash Zone (*Wonder*), Nephews' Splash Zone (*Magic*), Twist 'n' Spout water slide (*Magic* and *Wonder*), and AquaLab (*Magic* and *Wonder*) are located toward the back, or aft; Goofy's Family Pool is midship; and the Quiet Cove Adult Pool is on Deck 9, forward. Though the names are self-explanatory, we'll state the obvious: the splash zones are for the wee young'uns and their friends. The Quiet Cove pool is earmarked for splashers age 18 and up. Don't

let the name fool you; Quiet Cove may be for grown-ups, but it isn't always the picture of serenity. Organized games engage giddy adults from time to time. Finally, Goofy's Pool is for everyone, but kids under age 10 must be accompanied by an adult, and swimmers must be potty-trained. (Life jackets may be borrowed for free.) Goofy's Pool and Quiet Cove have two whirlpools each.

SWIMMING (*Dream* and *Fantasy*): Deck 11 is pool central on these ships. Donald's Pool is the family pool and can be found midship. Mickey's Pool is strictly for kids and their guardians, and the Quiet Cove pool is a grown-ups-only splash zone. Nemo's Reef is a spray zone for the toddler set (swim diapers are required at all times).

AQUADUCK (*Dream* and *Fantasy*): Tired of all that poolside relaxation? Head for Deck 12 and the ship's ultimate adrenaline inducer: the AquaDuck. This 765-foot-long "water coaster" propels guests through a clear tube on a journey that includes a trip over the ocean and through the forward funnel, and a 4-deck drop. Check a *Personal Navigator* for operating hours. Guests must be at least 42 inches tall to ride the AquaDuck and 54 inches tall to ride alone. Kids under age 7 must be accompanied by someone 14 years of age or older. It's a hoot—and not as scary as it looks.

AQUADUNK (*Magic*): Step into the 3-story, translucent tube, the trapdoor opens and . . . *kerplunk!* The ride is quick and splashy. Guests must be at least 48 inches tall to take the plunge. It is accessed via steps on Deck 10.

AQUALAB (*Magic, Wonder*, and *Fantasy*): Found on Deck 12, aft, on the *Fantasy* and Deck 9, aft, on the *Magic* and *Wonder*, Aqualab is a family splash zone. This interactive playground is open to guests age 3 and up. Families may frolic among pop jets, bubblers, and geysers, and slip along the "Twist 'n' Spout" waterslide. (Guests must be at least 38 inches tall to ride.)

DORY'S SPLASH ZONE (*Wonder*): Deck 9, aft, is home to the *Wonder*'s new watery fun zone. It's a great spot for tots to cool off.

NEPHEWS' SPLASH ZONE (*Magic*): Deck 9, aft, is home to the *Magic*'s "splashtacular" zone. Designed for guests age 3 and under, the 500-square-foot play area features geysers and bubble jets and a soft deck surface.

SATELLITE FALLS (*Dream* and *Fantasy*): A watery haven for grown-ups, this Deck 13, forward, spot has a circular splash pool with benches and a cascading curtain of water. The shaded Satellite Sundeck has comfy lounge chairs, available on a first-come, first-served basis.

SPA & SALON (All ships): Pampering, Disney style, can be enjoyed at the ships' ocean-view spas and salons—known as Senses on all Disney ships. Here, fitness-minded folk can work with a trainer, take a class, or work out solo. As for the pampering, well, that can come by way of any number of treatments.

Book appointments ahead of time by visiting *www.disneycruise.com*, or go to the spa when you board the ship. The spa and salon are open to guests age 18 and older.

The spa is open from 8 A.M. to 8 P.M. every day, except on days when the ship is docked at its home port. Prices are posted in the spa. If you miss a reserved treatment, your stateroom will be charged 50 percent of the treatment cost. Note that Cabana Massages (located at Serenity Bay on Castaway Cay) and the Senses Spa Villas (indoor-outdoor treatment villas for one or two at Senses Spa) may be booked here, too.

Spa amenities include sandals and robes for use during treatments, steam room, sauna, locker room, showers, and more. A selection of beauty products is available for purchase.

CHILL SPA (all ships): A spa within a spa, Chill is exclusively for teen guests. It offers a variety of spa services and treatments, including facials, massages, and manicures.

Reservations for Chill Spa may be made by phone or on-site any time after 1 P.M. on the first day of your cruise. Appointments book fast—book as soon as you board.

Castaway Cay

If you've ever dreamed of getting away to a private, tropical island, the folks at Disney Cruise Line have made it easy to fulfill that fantasy. Almost every Disney Cruise Line trip that departs from Port Canaveral or Miami, Florida, wraps up with a visit to Castaway Cay (pronounced *key*), a tiny island in the Abacos, one in the string of Bahamian isles. This little patch of paradise was secured for the sole use of passengers cruising on Disney ships. It's small—only 3.1 miles long by 2.2 miles wide—and most of it was intentionally left undeveloped so that nature lovers may enjoy the still-unspoiled terrain.

Here you can take a ride in a glass-bottom boat, go back to nature on a kayak adventure, try your wings at parasailing, or go snorkeling offshore—and then return to a barbecue feast. Of course if you'd prefer to loll about in a palm-tree-shaded, beach-side hammock, refreshing beverage in hand, well, that can be arranged.

Other island amenities include biking, beach games, organized activities for kids and teens; a shaded pavilion complete with billiards, ping-pong, basketball, shuffleboard, and more; Disney character greetings; plus a secluded grown-ups-only beach.

Returning guests (they always come back!) will be pleased to see that this happy place has gotten even happier—recent additions include an expansion of the family beach, two water play areas known as Pelican Plunge and Spring-a-Leak, and nearly two dozen furnished beach cabanas.

For details or to book Castaway Cay port adventures, visit *www.disneycruise.com*.

Index

Where in the World?
(photo locations)

Magic Kingdom:
1. Pete's Silly Sideshow, Fantasyland
2. Mad Tea Party, Fantasyland
3. Big Thunder Mountain Railroad, Frontierland
4. Walt Disney's Carousel of Progress, Tomorrowland
5. Casey Jr. Splash 'N' Soak Zone, Fantasyland (Storybook Circus)
6. Haunted Mansion, Liberty Square

Epcot:
1. Meet-and-Greet, Future World (across from Epcot Character Spot)
2. Mexico pavilion, World Showcase
3. Imagination! pavilion, Future World
4. The American Adventure show, World Showcase
5. Living with the Land, Future World's The Land pavilion
6. Test Track pre-show, Future World

Disney's Hollywood Studios:
1. Dinosaur Gertie, Echo Lake
2. Rock 'n' Roller Coaster (exterior)
3. Minnie at "Mickey and Minnie Starring in Red Carpet Dreams"
4. Tune-In Lounge, next to the 50's Prime Time Cafe
5. Sid Cahuenga's, Hollywood Blvd.
6. View from the path connecting The Studios with Epcot

Animal Kingdom:
1. Festival of the Lion King, Harambe
2. Rivers of Light, Asia
3. Expedition: Everest, Asia
4. Adventurer's Outpost, Discovery Island
5. Majarajah Jungle Trek, Asia
6. DINOSAUR, DinoLand U.S.A.

Coupons

10% OFF
ENTIRE PURCHASE
Offering authentic Disney collectibles,
exquisite crystal mementos,
and sparkling hand-blown glass gifts.

Subject to terms and conditions on reverse side.

FREE TRAIN OR CAROUSEL RIDE
with the purchase of one ride
Little ones and the young at heart can enjoy an
old-fashioned carousel or train ride on the Marketplace
Carousel or the Marketplace Train Express.

Subject to terms and conditions on reverse side.

10% OFF
a chocolate purchase
or $1 OFF
a specialty sundae

Subject to terms and conditions on reverse side.

FREE KIDS MEAL*

WOLFGANG PUCK EXPRESS

*with purchase of entree

Located at Disney
Springs Marketplace
behind Disney's
Days of Christmas

1780 E. Buena Vista Dr
Lake Buena Vista, FL 32830
407-828-0107

COFFEE & TEA COMPANY®

20% OFF
food and beverages
(Excludes alcohol)
Experience a world of magical flavors
at Joffrey's Coffee and Tea Co. kiosks
throughout *Walt Disney World®* Parks and Resorts.

Subject to terms and conditions on reverse side.

$25 OFF
Your purchase of $150 or more
Renowned for unique, beautiful, and exclusive
fashion jewelry and accessory collections.

Subject to terms and conditions on reverse side.

TERMS AND CONDITIONS

Located in the heart of Disney Springs™ Marketplace.

Guests of all ages may ride.

At carousel, guests under 42 inches tall must be accompanied by an adult (who does not have to pay) 18 years of age or older. At train, kids under 36 inches tall must be accompanied by a guest (who does not have to pay) 14 years of age or older.

Coupon must be surrendered at time of purchase.

Coupon cannot be combined with any other discount or offer.

Reproductions of coupon not accepted.

No cash value.

Offer subject to change without notice

Expires 12/31/18

TERMS AND CONDITIONS

Valid at the Arribas Brothers stores at the Magic Kingdom at Crystal Arts on Main Street, U.S.A., at Epcot® in the Germany and Mexico Pavilions (park admission is required), and Disney Springs® Marketplace.

Coupon excludes shipping charges and online purchases. Other restrictions apply.

Discount cannot be combined with any other offers or discounts.

No cash value.

Coupon must be presented at time of purchase to receive discount.

Reproductions not accepted.

Offer subject to change without notice.

For more information, visit *www.arribas.com*, or call (407) 828-4840.

Offer valid through 12/31/18

4 09915 01645 6   ABFLBIRN

TERMS AND CONDITIONS

Valid at Disney Springs™ Marketplace location only.

Cannot be combined with any other offers.

Cannot be redeemed for cash in whole or in part.

Reproduction of coupon not accepted.

Must present this card at time of purchase.

Alcohol, tax, and gratuity not included.

Offer subject to change without notice.

For more info, call (407) 828-0107.

www.wolfgangpuck.com

Expires 12/31/18

TERMS AND CONDITIONS

Valid at Disney Springs™ Marketplace location only.

Coupon cannot be combined with any other offers or discounts.
Must present original coupon at time of purchase.
Reproductions of coupon not accepted.
No cash value in whole or in part.
Offer subject to change without notice.

For more information, call 407-934-8855.

Expires 12/31/18

7 47599 10470 1

TERMS AND CONDITIONS

Valid only at the Disney Springs™ The Landing location.

Offer excludes 14Kt, BOGO, and all sale merchandise.

Coupon cannot be combined with any other offers or discounts.

Coupon not redeemable for cash in whole or part.

Coupon must be surrendered at time of purchase.

Reproductions of coupon not accepted.

Exchange within 14 days of purchase. No returns.

Offer subject to change without notice.

For more information, call (407) 560-9945.

www.erwinpearl.com

Expires 12/31/18

TERMS AND CONDITIONS

Birnbaum 2018

Valid at Joffrey's Coffee kiosk locations throughout the *Walt Disney World*® Parks & Resorts.

Coupon cannot be combined with any other offers or be redeemed for cash in whole or in part.

Must present coupon to receive offer.

Reproduction of coupon not accepted.

Offer subject to change without notice.

Excludes alcoholic beverages.

www.joffreys.com

Expires 12/31/18

Coupons

HOUSE OF BLUES
RESTAURANT & BAR

20% OFF LUNCH
or 10% OFF DINNER

for up to 8 guests in the HOB Restaurant
(discount on food and non-alcoholic beverages only)

Enjoy distinctive Southern-inspired cuisine in an enjoyable atmosphere filled with creative folk art. Opens daily at 11:30 A.M. For reservations, call 407-934-2623.

Subject to terms and conditions on reverse side.

RAGLAN ROAD
IRISH PUB AND RESTAURANT

20% OFF LUNCH

Subject to terms and conditions on reverse side.

SEPHORA

Free Mini-Makeover
&
Free Cosmetic Sample

Pop in for a FREE mini-makeover and receive a FREE cosmetic sample of your choice

Subject to terms and conditions on reverse side.

Paradiso 37
TASTE OF THE AMERICAS

10% OFF

food only at lunch and dinner

Subject to terms and conditions on reverse side.

kipling

15% OFF

one item of your choice

Featuring a colorful array of bags and lifestyle accessories designed to lighten your day.

Subject to terms and conditions on reverse side.

pop gallery
Orlando

10% OFF
ENTIRE PURCHASE

Experience Art that Pops! Embellish your life with unique art, gifts, toys, and jewelry.

Subject to terms and conditions on reverse side.

Coupons

China Pavilion

10% OFF

Nine Dragons Restaurant, Lotus Blossom Café, and merchandise

(offer good for lunch and dinner; excludes alcohol)

Subject to terms and conditions on reverse side.

SPICE ROAD TABLE

mediterranean small plates

10% OFF

Food, beverages, and merchandise

(offer good for lunch and dinner; excludes alcohol)

Subject to terms and conditions on reverse side.

Splitsville

LUXURY LANES™

10% OFF

ON BOWLING AND SHOE RENTAL

Subject to terms and conditions on reverse side.

RESTAURANT MARRAKESH

10% OFF

Food, beverages, and merchandise

(offer good for lunch and dinner; excludes alcohol)

Subject to terms and conditions on reverse side.

Disney's

HILTON HEAD ISLAND RESORT

A Disney Vacation Club Resort

Save on Accommodations on select dates in 2018

For offer details and to check availability, call 407-939-7652 and ask about the Birnbaum offer.

Subject to terms and conditions on reverse side.

Disney's

VERO BEACH RESORT

A Disney Vacation Club Resort

Save on Accommodations on select dates in 2018

For offer details and to check availability, call 407-939-7652 and ask about the Birnbaum offer.

Subject to terms and conditions on reverse side.

TERMS AND CONDITIONS

Located at Epcot®

Park admission is required.

Coupon cannot be combined with any other offers.

Coupon cannot be redeemed for cash
in whole or in part.

Reproduction of coupon not accepted.

Offer subject to change without notice.

Expires 12/31/18

TERMS AND CONDITIONS

Located at Epcot®

Park admission is required.

Coupon cannot be combined with any other offers.

Coupon cannot be redeemed for cash
in whole or in part.

Reproduction of coupon not accepted.

Offer subject to change without notice.

Expires 12/31/18

TERMS AND CONDITIONS

Located at Epcot®

Park admission is required.

Coupon cannot be combined with any other offer.

Reproductions of coupon not accepted
in whole or in part.

Offer subject to change without notice.

www.moroccopavilion.com

Expires 12/31/18

TERMS AND CONDITIONS

Offer good at Splitsville Luxury Lanes™.

Located at Disney Springs™ West Side.

Must present coupon to receive discount. Subject to availability and limited to groups of 10 or less. Cannot be applied to lane reservations or private events. Limit one coupon per transaction. Reproductions of coupon not accepted. Coupon may not be redeemed for cash In whole or in part. Coupon cannot be combined with any other offer or discount. Offer subject to change without notice.

Call 407-938-PINS (7467) for reservations.

Expires 12/31/18

TERMS AND CONDITIONS

The number of rooms allocated for this offer is very limited. Length of stay requirements may apply.

Receive 20% off the non-discounted rate most nights: (1/3–3/10/18); (4/6–5/10/18); (8/19–12/27/18); (1/1–1/31/19).

Receive 10% off the non-discounted rate most nights: (1/1-1/2/18); (3/11-4/5/18); (5/11-8/18/18); (12/28-12/31/18).

Excludes 3-bedroom Beach Cottages at Disney's Vero Beach Resort.

Cannot be combined with any other discount or promotion. Advance reservations required.

For information about Disney's Vero Beach Resort, visit https://beachresorts.disney.go.com

Offer expires 12/31/18   © Disney

TERMS AND CONDITIONS

The number of rooms allocated for this offer is very limited. Length-of-stay requirements may apply.

Receive 20% off non-discounted rates most nights: (1/1–3/29/18); (4/8–5/24/18); (8/26–12/20/18); (1/1–1/31/19).

Receive 10% off the non-discounted rate most nights: (3/30–4/7/18); (5/25–8/25/18); (12/21–12/31/18).

Excludes 3-bedroom Grand Villas at Disney's Hilton Head Island Resort.

Cannot be combined with any other discount or promotion. Advance reservations required.

For information about Disney's Hilton Head Island Resort, visit https://beachresorts.disney.go.com

Offer expires 12/31/18   © Disney

Coupons

10% OFF
ADMISSION
for up to 4 guests

Immerse yourself in a fascinating and educational dolphin encounter open to all guests ages 13 and up.

Call 407-WDW-PLAY (407-939-7529) for reservations.

Subject to terms and conditions on reverse side.

15% OFF
admission to the Behind the Seeds Tour at The Land for up to 10 guests

Bring the entire family backstage for a one-hour, interactive tour of the greenhouses and fish farm at The Land. For same-day reservations, present coupon at the Tour Desk next to the entrance of Soarin'. Or call ahead to 407-WDW-PLAY (407-939-7529) and mention the Birnbaum offer. Admission to Epcot® is required.

Subject to terms and conditions on reverse side.

10% OFF
Epcot® Dive Quest admission

Dive into a scuba diving adventure open to all certified scuba divers ages 10 and up.

Call 407-WDW-PLAY (407-939-7529) for reservations.

Subject to terms and conditions on reverse side.

10% OFF
ADMISSION

This amazing aqua adventure takes you on a tour of the aquarium and into the water to explore The Seas with Nemo & Friends marine environment using a Scuba Assisted Snorkel unit.

Call 407-WDW-PLAY (407-939-7529) for reservations.

Subject to terms and conditions on reverse side.

20% OFF
2-Hour WALT DISNEY WORLD® Guided Fishing Excursion for you and up to 4 guests.

To make your reservation, call 407-WDW-BASS (407-939-2277) and mention the coupon to be added in the Additional Comments section. This coupon must be presented upon arrival.

Subject to terms and conditions on reverse side.

FREE SAME-DAY REPLAY
WITH PURCHASE OF A TEE TIME

Subject to terms and conditions on reverse side

Book your tee time now by calling 407-WDW-GOLF or go online at www.golfwdw.com

Coupons

FREE UPGRADE

Book at *www.alamo.com*
or call 1-800-462-5266.

Reference Coupon Code **AU526WSD9**
at the time of reservation.

Subject to terms and conditions on reverse side.

15% OFF ALL SAMMY DUVALL'S WATERSPORTS CENTRE ACTIVITIES

- PARASAILING
- WATERSKIING, WAKEBOARDING, AND FAMILY TUBING
- PERSONAL WATERCRAFT
  RESERVATIONS ARE SUGGESTED.

Subject to terms and conditions on reverse side.

極度乾燥(しなさい)
Superdry.
$15 OFF
TOTAL PURCHASE

Unique Apparel & Accessories where
vintage Americana, Japanese–inspired graphics,
and British style come together.

Subject to terms and conditions on reverse side.

Complimentary Swarovski customization with any purchase (up to a $35 value)

The ultimate comfort in shoes, slippers, and boots

Subject to terms and conditions on reverse side.

$5 OFF
One single or double stroller rental

To make a reservation, go to
www.magicstrollers.com

Subject to terms and conditions on reverse side.

$75 SAVINGS
ONE-TIME MEMBERSHIP FEE WAIVED FOR BIRNBAUM READERS

To sign up for "the purple place to store your vacation
stuff," go to *www.ownerslocker.com/Birnbaum*

Subject to terms and conditions on reverse side.

Coupons

BASIN
15% OFF Merchandise

Subject to terms and conditions on reverse side.

FREE PRETZEL
When you purchase 2 pretzels
of equal or greater value

Subject to terms and conditions on reverse side.

Vera Bradley

RECEIVE $30 OFF
YOUR PURCHASE OF $125 OR MORE

Fashionable handbags, accessories,
luggage, and travel items.

Subject to terms and conditions on reverse side.

Located at DISNEY SPRINGS™ West Side

10% OFF
all Curl® merchandise

Orlando's Premier Surf and Fashion Store

Subject to terms and conditions on reverse side.

The Original. World's #1.™

20% OFF
ENTIRE PURCHASE

Famous yo-yos and skill toys, Est. 1929

Subject to terms and conditions on reverse side.

Sprinkles

FREE ICE CREAM TOPPING

with each ice cream purchase

"The Original Cupcake Bakery"

Subject to terms and conditions on reverse side.

Coupons

L'OCCITANE EN PROVENCE

10% OFF
SELECT MERCHANDISE

Plus enjoy a complimentary
hand massage and mini facial.

*Natural Beauty from the South of France
Skincare, Body care & Fragrance*

Subject to terms and conditions on reverse side.

15% OFF
LUNCH AND DINNER
UP TO 8 GUESTS
(Discount excludes alcohol)

*Experience authentic Cuban Cuisine
from the late 1940s and 1950s
with Live Music and Latin Dancers!*

Subject to terms and conditions on reverse side.

10% OFF
ANY PURCHASE

(Valid on food & beverage only)

Subject to terms and conditions on reverse side.

Edward Beiner™
PURVEYOR OF FINE EYEWEAR

15% OFF
PLUS FREE LENS CLEANER

with your eyewear purchase

Subject to terms and conditions on reverse side.

**A FREE SLICE OF SHINE CAKE
OR HUMMINGBIRD CAKE**

with purchase of a meal or appetizer

Southern Favorites and Comfort Food

Subject to terms and conditions on reverse side.

20% OFF
ENTIRE PURCHASE

Flip-flops and Sandals for Women, Men & Kids

Subject to terms and conditions on reverse side.

Coupons

HOUSE OF BLUES

15% OFF
**YOUR MERCHANDISE PURCHASE
OF $30 OR MORE**

Subject to terms and conditions on reverse side.

Levi's

20% OFF
ONE SINGLE ITEM IN-STORE

Subject to terms and conditions on reverse side.

melissa

10% OFF
ENTIRE PURCHASE
*Comfortable, stylish & eco-friendly
jelly footwear*

Subject to terms and conditions on reverse side.

PADDLEFISH

10% OFF
FOOD & BEVERAGES
(Discount excludes alcohol)

Subject to terms and conditions on reverse side.

planet hollywood™

15% OFF
Food & Beverages
(Valid from 11 A.M. to 4 P.M.; excludes alcohol)

Subject to terms and conditions on reverse side.

RAGLAN ROAD
IRISH PUB AND RESTAURANT

15% OFF
MERCHANDISE

Subject to terms and conditions on reverse side.

TERMS AND CONDITIONS

Offer valid 9/25/17–12/31/18 towards one item at Disney Springs™ Levi's® Store only.

Levi's® collaborations, Levi's® Commuter™, Levi's® Vintage Clothing, Levi's® Made and Crafted™, Tailor Shop services, and vintage product excluded. Non-transferable. No adjustments on previous purchases. May not be used in conjunction with any other coupon, in-store promotion, or for gift card purchases. LS&Co. employees not eligible for discount. This offer may be modified by LS&Co. in its sole discretion without notice at any time.

Promo code: SINGLE20

www.levi.com

TERMS AND CONDITIONS

Offer valid at House of Blues Orlando.

Not valid with any other offer.

Excludes CDs, sundries, artwork, and gift cards.

Not valid for online purchases.

Expires 12/31/18

TERMS AND CONDITIONS

Located at Disney Springs™, The Landing

Excludes alcohol and gift cards.

Reproductions of coupon not accepted. Coupon may not be redeemed for cash in whole or in part. Coupon cannot be combined with any other offer or discount. All minors must be accompanied by a paying adult.

Offer subject to change without notice.

For reservations, call 407-934-2628 or visit *www.paddlefishrestaurant.com.*

Expires 12/31/18

TERMS AND CONDITIONS

Exclusively at Melissa Disney Springs™.

Offer valid on full-price items only.

Not valid with any other offers or promotions.

Not valid on past purchases.

For more information, call 407-560-0779.

www.shop601.com

Expires 12/31/18

TERMS AND CONDITIONS

Valid at Disney Springs™, The Landing location.

Cannot be combined with any other offers.

Reproduction of coupon not accepted.

Must present coupon at time of purchase.

Coupon may not be redeemed for cash.

Offer subject to change without notice.

Expires 12/31/18

TERMS AND CONDITIONS

No minimum purchase required.
Not valid with any other offers or discounts.
One coupon per visit, per check.
Unauthorized distribution prohibited.
No cash value.
Excludes group menus, tax, alcohol, merchandise & purchase of gift cards.
Valid at Planet Hollywood Orlando only.
Valid 11 A.M. to 4 P.M. only.
Planethollywood.com
407-827-7827
Expires 12/31/18

53190-9030-7060